Office and Ordination in Luther and Melanchthon

Hellmut Lieberg

TRANSLATED BY
Matthew Carver

CONCORDIA PUBLISHING HOUSE · SAINT LOUIS

Special Notice:

This material is being released for use as a historical study and for discussion purposes and not as a source of doctrine, and the author is solely responsible for its contents. It has not been submitted to the process for doctrinal review stipulated in the Bylaws of The Lutheran Church—Missouri Synod and does not reflect the theology of the Lutheran Confessions or the doctrinal position of The Lutheran Church—Missouri Synod.

3558 S. Jefferson Ave., St. Louis, MO 63118-3968
1-800-325-3040 • cph.org

Unless otherwise indicated, Scripture quotations in this volume are translated from Luther's writings.

Manufactured in the United States of America

Library of Congress Cataloging-in-Publication Data

Names: Lieberg, Hellmut, author. | Carver, Matthew, translator.

Title: The office and ordination in Luther and Melanchthon / Hellmut Lieberg ; translated by Matthew Carver.

Other titles: Amt und Ordination bei Luther und Melanchthon. English

Description: St. Louis, MO : Concordia Publishing House, [2020] | "Original title: Hellmut Lieberg, Amt und Ordination bei Luther und Melanchthon, Göttingen, 1963." | Includes bibliographic references. | Summary: "This book is a study of the doctrine of the ministry as found in the writings of Luther, Melanchthon, and the Lutheran Confessions. The author specifically discusses the relationship between the spiritual office and the universal priesthood of believers as well as the question of ordination"—Provided by publisher.

Identifiers: LCCN 2020028719 (print) | LCCN 2020028720 (ebook) | ISBN 9780758669698 (hardback) | ISBN 9780758669704 (ebook)

Subjects: LCSH: Pastoral theology—History. | Luther, Martin, 1483–1546. | Melanchthon, Philipp, 1497–1560. | Clergy—Office.

Classification: LCC BV4006 .L513 2020 (print) | LCC BV4006 (ebook) | DDC 262/.1441—dc23

LC record available at https://lccn.loc.gov/2020028719

LC ebook record available at https://lccn.loc.gov/2020028720

---

5 6 7 8 9 10 11 12 32 31 30 29 28 27 26

Contents

Abbreviations

AC	Augsburg Confession
AE	*Luther's Works: American Edition*. Vols. 1–30: Edited by Jaroslav Pelikan. St. Louis: Concordia, 1955–76. Vols. 31–55: Edited by Helmut Lehmann. Philadelphia/Minneapolis: Muhlenberg/Fortress, 1957–86. Vols. 56–82: Edited by Christopher Boyd Brown and Benjamin T. G. Mayes. St. Louis: Concordia: 2009–.
Ap	Apology of the Augsburg Confession
Baseley	Joel R. Baseley, trans. *Festival Sermons of Martin Luther: The Church Postils*. Dearborn, MI: Mark V Publications, 2005.
BKS	*Die Bekenntnisschriften der evangelisch-lutherischen Kirche* (1930)
CR	*Corpus Reformatorum*. Vols. 1–28: *Philippi Melanthonis Opera quae supersunt omnia*. Edited by C. G. Bretschneider and H. E. Bindseil. Halle: C. A. Schwetschke, 1834–60.
EA	*Dr. Martin Luther's sämmtliche Werke*. 2nd ed. 26 vols. in 27. Frankfurt and Erlangen: Heyder & Zimmer, 1862–85.
End./Enders	Ernst Ludwig Enders, ed. *Dr. Martin Luthers Briefwechsel*. 19 vols. Frankfurt a/M, 1884–1932. Continued by Gustav Kawerau.
LC	Large Catechism
Lenker	John Nicholas Lenker, ed. *Sermons of Martin Luther: The Church Postils*. Grand Rapids: Baker Books, 1996 (8 vols. in 4). Reprint, vols. 1–4 of *The Complete Sermons of Martin Luther*. Grand Rapids: Baker Books, 2000. Originally published as vols. 7–14 of *The Precious and Sacred Writings of Martin Luther*. Minneapolis: Lutherans in All Lands/Luther Press, 1904–9).
SA	Smalcald Articles
Sehling	Emil Sehling et al., eds. *Die evangelischen Kirchenordnungen des XVI. Jahrhunderts*. Vols. 1–5: Leipzig: O. R. Reisland, 1902–13. Vols. 6–: Tübingen: Mohr (Paul Siebeck), 1957–.
Stud. Ausg.	Philip Melanchthon. *Werke in Auswahl*. 7 vols. General editor Robert Stupperich. Gütersloh: Bertelsmann (Gerd Mohn), 1951–.
Tr	Treatise on the Power and Primacy of the Pope
WA	*D. Martin Luthers Werke: Kritische Gesamtausgabe*. 73 vols. in 85. Weimar: H. Böhlau, 1883–.

WA Br	*D. Martin Luthers Werke: Briefwechsel.* 18 vols. Weimar: H. Böhlau, 1930–.
WA TR	*D. Martin Luthers Werke: Tischreden.* 6 vols. Weimar: H. Böhlau, 1912–21.
Walch	Johann G. Walch, ed *D. Martin Luthers sowol in Deutscher als Lateinischer Sprache verfertigte und aus der letztern in die erstere übersetzte Sämmtliche Schriften.* 24 vols. Halle: Gebauer, 1740–53.

PART I

THE OFFICE AND ORDINATION IN LUTHER

CHAPTER I

The Concept of the Office Founded on *Sola Gratia* and *Sola Fide*

1. The Internal Root of Luther's Concept of the Office: The Necessity of the Ministry of the Word from the Standpoint of Justification

The heart of Luther's theology is the article of the justification of the sinner by grace alone through faith alone on account of Christ alone.[1] "There can be no turning aside from or yielding this article, though heaven and earth or whatever is temporary should pass away."[2] Luther himself sees his whole work of reformation and his struggle against the papacy under this article of justification.[3] If there is not full assurance from Scripture in this article, ". . . it is all in vain, and the pope and devil and all our opponents claim the victory and right."[4]

The justification of the sinner for Christ's sake through faith rests entirely on the mediating *ministry of the Word*. The Gospel brings us the treasure of the justifying grace of God in Christ. For this reason, it is itself the true treasure of the Church.[5] From it comes the righteousness of faith. The Word as means of

---

[1] In 1520, at any rate, Luther finally reached full clarity on the doctrine of forensic justification as a synthetic judgment of God, as the imputation of Christ's righteousness through faith (*justitia Dei passiva* [passive righteousness of God]) and from that time represented this doctrine exclusively. Cf. T. Harnack, *Luthers Theologie*, vol. 2 (Munich, 1927), pp. 327ff.

[2] WA 50:199.22ff.

[3] WA 50:199.31ff.: "And on this article stands all that we teach and live, contrary to the pope, devil, and world."

[4] WA 50:200.2ff. Luther sees opposition to the papacy so greatly necessitated by justification that he can even say: "This being established—that God alone justifies by pure grace through Christ—we not only want the pope to carry it in his hands, but even to kiss its feet" (WA 40/1:181.11ff.).

[5] WA 1:236.22f.: "The true treasure of the Church is the most holy Gospel of the glory and grace of God" (Thesis 62 of the *Ninety-Five Theses*); WA 30/1:145.16f.: "For the Word of God is the relic above all relics—yea, the only one which we Christians know of and possess"; WA 30/1:145.20f.; cf. WA 50:629.2f.

grace is for Luther the basis on which justification is made possible. Neither the individual nor the Church can therefore be without the Word.[6] "Thus we must be certain that the soul can be stripped of all else save the Word of God, and without the Word of God it is not helped in any way."[7] God's salvific act in Christ is present in the Word, the Holy Spirit calls to faith in Christ "through the Gospel," and faith can take hold of Christ only in the Word.[8]

The Word as means of grace, however, is separated into the binary of Law and Gospel. "And it should be known that all Holy Scripture is divided into two different propositions, which are God's commandment or Law and His promise or pledge. The commandment . . . is designed only that a man might see therein his own inability toward good and learn to despair of himself. . . . Then the second proposition, the divine promise and pledge, comes and says, '. . . Believe in Christ, in whom I promise you all grace, righteousness, peace, and freedom. . . .' "[9] In the preaching of the Law "you hear your God tell you how all your life and works are nothing before God, and you must perish eternally along with all that is in you. . . ."[10] The Gospel, however, announces deliverance from this devastation: ". . . But in order that you may come out of yourself and away from yourself—that is, from your own devastation—He sets before you His beloved Son, Jesus Christ, and causes you to be told through His living, comforting Word: 'Commit yourself to Him with firm faith and trust actively in Him, and because of this faith all your sins will be forgiven and all your devastation overcome.' "[11]

The preaching of Law and Gospel is the divinely instituted means for the justification of the sinner. And since God's entire work of salvation in Christ hinges on justification, the function of the Word in Law and Gospel is itself God's salvific activity for man and belongs inseparably to the Church, whose very reason for existing is that sinners may receive justification before God. Thus for Luther *the Gospel is the chief mark of the true Church.* "Thus shall the Christian congregation be recognized with certainty: where the pure Gospel is preached."[12] For

[6] The necessity of the Gospel is for Luther above that of the Sacrament: WA 1:604.35f.: "It is better . . . to omit the Sacrament than not to proclaim the Gospel"; WA 38:253.12ff.: ". . . And in a case of necessity one could be saved without the Sacrament, but not without the Word, such as those who die before they receive the desired Baptism."

[7] WA 7:22.9ff.; cf. WA 7:22.3ff. and 15ff.

[8] WA 30/1:296.28; cf. WA 30/1:188.6ff.

[9] WA 7:23.29ff.

[10] WA 7:22.26ff.

[11] WA 7:22.31ff.

[12] WA 11:408.9f. and 11f.; cf. WA 8:491.35f.; 41:131.14ff.; 50:628.29f. It should be noted here that Luther has in view the *viva vox evangelii* [living voice of the Gospel] in oral preaching (WA 50:629.16ff.: "But we speak of the external Word preached orally by men as by you and me. For Christ left this behind as an external sign by which we might recognize His Church or His holy Christian people in the world"). That the Sacraments are not excluded from the Word, but rather included in it, is evident from WA 50:630ff., esp. 631.25ff.: "For as it was said above concerning the Word—that wherever the Word of God is, the Church must be—so also wherever Baptism and the Sacrament are, God's people must be, and vice versa."

Luther, it is based on the promise (Isa. 55:11) tied to the Word, that wherever the Gospel is, there must also be Christians, that is, those who believe in Christ and are justified by faith. "Therefore, we are sure that it is impossible for there to be no Christians wherever the Gospel is at work."[13] But it is no less impossible "for there to be Christians and not exclusively heathens where the Gospel does not go and the doctrines of men hold sway."[14] The Church is founded on the Word of reconciliation and cannot stand without it. The Word is the decisive, constitutive element of the Church.[15]

> Luther distinguishes between the "spiritual, internal Church" (WA 6:297.1), the "gathering of all believers on earth" (WA 6:292.38), which is a "gathering of hearts in one faith" (WA 6:293.4), and the "physical, external church" (WA 6:297.2), the outward gathering around Word and Sacrament. In the first analysis, the Church is invisible, an article of faith, not of sight (WA 6:300.32ff.; cf. WA 7:710.1ff., 722.4ff.); in the latter, it is visible. For Luther, however, the internal and external churches are not two independent quantities standing beside each other without connection, but they overlap each other and relate to each other like body and soul in a human being (WA 6:297.4f.). "They are held together by their identical center, which is the effective Word of God" (R. Seeberg, *Dogmengeschichte* IV, 1, *Die Lehre Luthers* [Leipzig, 1917], 3rd. ed., p. 292; cf. also pp. 96, 279ff.; and E. Seeberg, *Luthers Theologie,* vol. II [Stuttgart, 1937], p. 290). The visible church is gathered around the Word, and the invisible gathering of all believers on earth within her is created and sustained by the Word.[16] Membership in the visible gathering around Word and Sacrament is therefore prerequisite to membership in the invisible congregation of believers and saints. Apart from the Gospel there is no Church and therefore no membership in it.[17] In Luther, the concept of the Gospel—as K. Holl says—forms "the bridge from the invisible to the visible church" (op. cit., pp. 304f.). The Gospel is for Luther the Church's basis of existence and her point of unity.[18] Even in the classical formulation of the concept of church in the *Smalcald Articles* [III XII]: "God be praised, a child of seven years knows what the Church is: the holy believers and the lambs who hear their Shepherd's voice" (WA 50:250.1ff.), this link between the concept of church

---

[13] WA 11:408.16ff.; cf. WA 50:629.34f.: "For God's Word cannot be without God's people; and vice versa: God's people cannot be without God's Word"; also WA 2:208.25ff.; 3:258.38; 6:301.5f.

[14] WA 11:408.19f.; cf. WA 11:411.22f.; 30/1:189.1ff.: ". . . Where Christ is not preached, there is no Holy Spirit, who makes, calls, and gathers the Christian Church, apart from whom no one can come to the Lord Christ."

[15] K. Holl (*Gesammelte Aufsätze* I, *Luther*, 6th ed. [1932], pp. 288f.) distinguishes as an original concept of Luther's the intimate connection of his concept of the church with the teaching of justification through the Word.

[16] WA 6:560.33ff.; 8:491.34f.; 8:419.34ff.; 12:191.16ff.; cf. also WA 2:191.34f.; 2:205.27ff.; 7:721.12f.; 30/1:188.23ff.

[17] WA 30/1:189.1ff.; 30/1:190.8ff.: ". . . incorporated by the fact that I have heard, and still hear, the Word of God, which is the beginning of entering therein"; WA 30/1:190.32f., 192.10ff.

[18] WA 26:506.30ff., where the Church is depicted in the most intimate relation to the Gospel, esp. WA 26:506.39f.: "gathered spiritually in one Gospel and faith under one Head, which is Jesus Christ."

and the Gospel ("their Shepherd's voice") is plainly evident. To the extent that the Church as community is based in Luther on the institutional factor of the preaching of the Gospel, E. Seeberg is inclined to agree that the sociological concept of church in Luther depends "directly on the institutional" (*Luthers Theologie* II, p. 442). —

On Luther's concept of church, cf. J. Köstlin, *Luthers Lehre von der Kirche* (Stuttgart 1853); W. Walther, *Das Erbe der Reformation*, book IV, *Luthers Kirche* (Leipzig, 1917); R. Seeberg, *Dogmengeschichte* IV, I, *Die Lehre Luthers*, 3rd ed. (Leipzig, 1917), pp. 278ff.; F. Kattenbusch, *Die Doppelschichtigkeit in Luthers Kirchenbegriff*, Lutherana V (5. Lutherheft der Theol. Stud. u. Kritiken) (Gotha, 1928); W. Elert, *Morphologie des Luthertums*, vol. I (Munich, 1952), pp. 224ff., and the additional literature noted therein. —

If the salvation of the individual and the existence of the whole Church have been tied to the Word, there must needs be a ministry of the Word. Hence the concept of the *ministerium verbi* is furnished. The Word must be communicated if the saving counsel of God in Christ is to accomplish its purpose with the individual, if sinners are to obtain justification by faith.[19] The *sola gratia* no less than the *sola fide* of the doctrine of justification necessitates the ministry of the Word. *Sola gratia* stipulates that man cannot work salvation out of himself, but, to the contrary, it is given to him so that it can only be received freely as a gift. But to say so is also to say that it must be brought to him from outside without his participation, thus necessitating the *ministerium verbi*, the ministry of Word and Sacrament. Rooted in *sola gratia* is Luther's passionate dispute with Enthusiasm, which discounts the external Word as means of grace in the belief that grace and the Holy Spirit are under the power of the individual. "And in these points, regarding the spoken, external Word, we must hold firmly that God gives no one His Spirit or grace except by or with the external Word coming first, that we may defend ourselves against the Enthusiasts, that is, those spirits who claim to have the Spirit without and before the Word. . . ."[20] This Enthusiasm, which circumvents the external Word, is for Luther "the origin, power, and strength of all heresy. . . ."[21] *Sola gratia* is the fundamental basis on which Luther posits as a guiding principle "that God will not deal with us men except by His external Word and Sacrament. But if anything without Word and Sacrament is claimed to be from the Spirit, it is the devil."[22] The gracious will

[19] WA 30/1:190.21ff.; WA TR 5:431.8, no. 5998: "The faithful Church exists by the ministry of the Word."

[20] WA 50:245.1ff.; cf. WA 11:95.18f.; 37:136.9ff.; 45:312.1f.

[21] WA 50:246.23f.

[22] WA 50:246.25ff.; cf. WA 43:81.25ff.: "He could teach and enlighten hearts without the ministry of the Word, but He does not wish to. Thus He has ordained the external ministry and instituted the Sacraments"; WA 30/2:455.18ff. and 38ff.: ". . . Rest assured, God does not have, nor does He wish to have, any other way to forgive sins except by the spoken Word, which He has committed to us men. If you do not seek forgiveness in the Word where God deposited it, you will stare at the heavens in vain looking for grace"; WA 30/2:456.17ff., 497.25ff., 498.26ff.; WA TR 5:2.23ff., no. 5189. — On the "inverbation" of the Holy Spirit in Luther, cf. K. D. Schmidt, "Luthers Lehre vom Heiligen Geiste," in *Schrift und Bekenntnis, Festschrift for J. S. Schöffel* (Hamburg-Berlin, 1950), pp. 145ff.

of God that desires by the cross of Christ to redeem and deliver humans corrupted in sin is the same that desires to deal with us only by the external Word and Sacrament. *Sola gratia* means *non sine verbo*.[23] But this Word, which makes known to us the grace of God, is quite decidedly the very Word of promise that demands faith and can only be apprehended in faith.[24] Thus *sola fide* depends on *sola gratia. Sola gratia*, then, is not, as the Enthusiasts think, the release from all external means of salvation, but, on the contrary, it presupposes them, and in it they fulfill their purpose. Luther denounces the Enthusiasts, who are "so insane that they separate faith and the thing to which faith clings and is tied, although it is external."[25] "But their blind leaders refuse to see that faith has to have something to believe, that is, to which it may cling and on which it may stand and be based."[26] This applies to *sola fide* as well: "Indeed, it should and must be external so that it can be grasped and apprehended with the senses and so absorbed by the heart, even as the whole Gospel is an external, spoken proclamation. In short, what God does and works in us He wishes to work by this external ordinance."[27]

The necessity of Word and Sacrament for appropriating salvation is relentlessly stressed by Luther in terms of *sola fide* as well as of *sola gratia* and is founded on a *divine ordinance* that has the character of exclusivity and must therefore be respected if man is not to forfeit his salvation. But God's ordaining of the means of grace, of Word and Sacraments, includes the positive ordinance of the ministry of Word and Sacraments as it appears in Scripture in Christ's command to preach the Gospel and administer the Sacraments. The Gospel fulfills its purpose only as Gospel actually enacted, and the Sacraments only as Sacraments actually administered. Only when standing in living function are Word and Sacrament the *means* of grace by which justification is actually appropriated. Therefore, according to God's salvific order, Word and Sacrament are necessary to the *ministry* of Word and Sacrament (*ministerium verbi et sacramentorum*). In Luther's thinking, the ministerial office is most fundamentally rooted in this necessity, and thus from the outset his view of the office retains a functional character.

---

[23] In Luther, as mentioned already, the term "Word" implicitly includes the Sacraments, which only become Sacraments by the Word and do not exist without it. WA 38:231.8ff.: "For the Sacraments cannot exist without the Word . . ."; WA 38:253.30ff.: "And it all depends on the Word of God as on the highest office. . . . All sacraments must come into being by the Word, which is the chief component of all sacraments." WA 30/1:214.18ff. and 36f., 215:15f. The Sacraments, too, are conducive to faith and convey salvation (WA 52:570.18ff.). The absolute necessity of salvation is ascribed only to the Word (WA 12:171.21f. and 31ff.). — On the question "Sacrament and Word," cf. M. Doerne, *Luth. Pfarramt*, Theol. mil. 10 (Leipzig, 1937), p. 10; and E. Roth, *Sakrament nach Luther* (Berlin 1952).

[24] WA 30/1:216.24f.: "But God's works" (= the means of grace) "are saving and necessary for salvation and do not exclude faith but demand it, for without faith they could not be taken hold of."

[25] WA 30/1:215.32ff.

[26] WA 30/1:215.24ff.

[27] WA 30/1:215.34ff.; cf. WA 17/1:329.14ff.

In the preceding, we have indicated one component in the rationale of Luther's view of the office. Yet based on the interior groundwork just outlined here, a number of possibilities remain open for treating the doctrine of the office in detail. The form of the doctrine of the office actually present in Luther is essentially determined in part by the situation into which Luther was placed by his reformatory struggle, and especially by his confrontation with the papistic church, and which in many respects sketched out the paths in which Luther's thinking of the office was consummated practically.

2. The External Root of Luther's Concept of the Office: The Necessary Polemic against Rome's Distortion of the Office

The image promulgated by the [Roman] Church and its authorities was definitively shattered by Luther in connection to the Leipzig Debate (June–July 1519).[28] He was no longer able to support the divine right of the papacy, which he had already called into question in the time following the Diet of Augsburg (autumn 1518), nor the inerrancy of the councils. Thus the whole hierarchical organization of the Roman Church lost the mantle of divinity, and the way was opened to an impartial critique of what was presented to Luther as the "spiritual estate" in the papistic church. In the process, Luther—ever driven by the motivations of his doctrine of justification—was confronted by elements which stood in stark opposition to Scripture and so demanded his polemic. We name three of these distortions: the satisfactionary, the legalistic, and the hierarchical. The dispute against this threefold distortion of the Roman office is plainly present in the reformatory writings of the year 1520 and is lodged continually by Luther from that time on. Luther's view of the office, then, clearly evolved against the background of this Roman distortion of the office and in steady correlation to his necessary polemic against it.[29] Constantly reflected in Luther's positive statements concerning the office is the protest against the false form of the office standing before his eyes in the papistic church. This is not to assert that Luther's view of the office is a secondary product of a polemical situation. We have already shown how Luther's view of the office is founded objectively and substantively on his doctrine of justification. Neither can one overlook to what a great extent Luther's propositions concerning the office are conditioned strictly by the legitimate exegesis of those passages of Scripture dealing with the office. Yet the objective motivation of the doctrine of justification and the formal motivation of obedience to Scripture were joined instinctively by a further motivation—a combative stance toward the office as distorted by Rome.

[28] Cf. R. Seeberg, op. cit., pp. 281ff.

[29] Cf. the remarks by G. Hök, op. cit., p. 177, who also suggests that Luther's concept of the office was substantially the result of negating the sacrifice of the Mass and the power politics of the Curia. Also E. Sommerlath, "Amt und Allgemeines Priestertum," p. 49.

This third motivation should not be underestimated in its significance for the whole of Luther's doctrine of the office. We therefore identify it as the external root of Luther's view of the office. For the development of Luther's view of the office, the polemical situation against the Enthusiasts does not have the formative importance of that against Rome since the basic features of Luther's view of the office were already defined when the dispute with the Enthusiasts began, and this dispute itself effected only new nuances in Luther's thinking about the office, not a new groundwork or a restructuring of the concept of the office. We now turn to examine in detail the Roman form of the office to the extent that it is subject to Luther's critique.

A. The Satisfactionary Distortion

The Roman *ordo* bestowed the authority to offer the sacrifice of the Mass. This had a satisfactionary character. Thus the celebrating priest, who offered it and had been consecrated precisely for this work, occupied a mediating role between God and man. This obscured the cross of Christ, His sole mediatorship of salvation, and His only propitiating sacrifice once for all, and the whole character of the administration of the means of grace was perverted to the opposite of that properly intended in their institution. In the function of this satisfactionary priesthood, an orientation from man to God came decidedly to the fore and corrupted the whole *cultus*, which thus shifted to the perspective of man's meritorious work and lost its basis in the free gift of God.[30] The article of justification *sola gratia* and *sola fide* was thereby turned on its head. Luther, from the perspective of his doctrine of justification, had to regard the Roman sacrificial Mass with its satisfactory character as the "greatest and most terrible abomination," which "directly and vehemently contradicts this chief article."[31] The sacrifice of the Mass, then, was based on the *ordo*, which in turn received from the Mass its characteristic shape. The distorting and perverting of the Mass, the Holy Supper, by which it was turned from God's salutary gift to men to a meritorious, satisfactionary work of sacrifice which man offers to God, presupposed the distortion of the office to a sacrificial priesthood. Against this Luther defines the true character of the office as *ministerium verbi, nicht sacerdotium* [ministry of the Word, not a priesthood]. Let us demonstrate this with a few of Luther's fundamental writings.

In the treatise *The Babylonian Captivity of the Church* (1520), Luther opposes the sacramental character of the Roman consecration of priests and reaches the conclusion that "the sacrament of ordination was and is a very beautiful mechanism for confirming all the monstrosities that have been done

---

[30] V. Vajta showed that the concept of the office is inevitably tied to and dependent on the conception of the worship service. "Tied to the sacrificial Mass . . . is a priesthood that carries out a sacrificial service before God" (as in Rome). "The *ministerium verbi divini* [ministry of the divine Word] is integrally linked together with the idea of worship service as *beneficium*" (as in Luther) (*Theologie des Gottesdienstes*, p. 199).

[31] WA 50:200.9ff.; cf. WA 50:202.26ff.

in the church up till now and are still being done."[32] This evaluation is made in view of the fact that the Roman consecration of priests is not a call to preach and administer the sacraments but to celebrate the sacrificial Mass and recite the Hours.[33] In accordance with Mal. 2:7, Luther declines to recognize a true priestly character in any man who is not or has not been called to preach.[34] The true *sacerdotium* [priesthood] of the office is nothing other than the *ministerium verbi*, the ministry of the Word on behalf of the congregation.[35] Those who were ordained only to read the canonical Hours and to offer Masses might well be papistic priests, but they are no Christian priests, but rather "living idols [*idola quaedam viva*],"[36] "priestly monsters [*monstra sacerdotalia*],"[37] painted priests[38]—indeed, a "plague of the Church [*pestis Ecclesiae*]"[39] and, according to Isa. 5:13–14, the true "people of eternal perdition [*populus perditionis aeternae*]."[40] The satisfactionary distortion of the function of the office and of the intent of consecration induces Luther to conclude that the "*ordo*, which, like a sacrament, ordains this race of men into clerics, is truly, purely, and entirely a fiction born of men who understand nothing of the Church, the priesthood, the ministry of the Word, or the sacraments."[41] For Luther, *that* ordination is a *figmentum* [fiction] which ordains to the ministry of sacrifice without relation to the true *ministerium verbi et sacramentorum* [ministry of the Word and Sacraments] and produces a priesthood which is a different estate from the *officio praedicandi* [office of preaching].[42] It cannot be ignored that Luther's polemic does not apply to ordination generally, but specifically to the ordination for the sacrifice of the Mass, thus the satisfactionary distortion of ordination.

In the treatise *Misuse of the Mass* (1521), Luther wants "to replace the pope's priesthood with the office which Christ gave and committed to the apostles, for a priest is supposed to preach."[43] The office of the apostles was a preaching office, not a sacrificial priesthood. The two are contrary. Christ is the only priest in the New Testament in the proper sense of the word (thus "sacrificial priest"); the Levitical priesthood of the Old Testament is fulfilled in His

---

[32] WA 6:564.1ff.

[33] WA 6:564.1ff. and 10f., 566.10ff.

[34] WA 6:564.20ff. — Luther shows that the Roman ordination did not then include the call to preach from the fact that none of the Roman priests preached "unless he were called again with another call beyond the sacramental ordination" (WA 6:565.1f.).

[35] WA 6:564.11ff., 567.17f., 566.5f., 9, and 32f. Also cf. below, p. 29 n. 47.

[36] WA 6:564.24ff.

[37] WA 6:565.33f.

[38] WA 6:566.5f.

[39] WA 6:567.3.

[40] WA 6:567.10.

[41] WA 6:565.6ff.

[42] WA 6:564.27f.

[43] WA 8:494.36ff.

sacrifice; outside of Him there is no "external, visible priest"[44] in the new covenant; and we have need "of no other priest or mediator than Christ."[45] Scripture does not speak of a special mediatory, satisfactionary priesthood in the New Testament (as the Roman *sacerdotium* tries to be), and "what does not have its origin from Scripture is surely from the devil himself."[46] Thus Luther condemns "this papistic priesthood and sacrifice of the Mass" as the work of the devil,[47] by which the true Mass and the true priesthood, the noblest treasures of the Church, are destroyed.[48] Because of its satisfactionary function—which Christ, as sole Mediator between God and man, supersedes—the Roman sacrificial priesthood is a "damned priesthood,"[49] which takes honor from Christ and negates *His* priesthood.[50]

In his letter to the Bohemians, *Concerning the Ministry* (1523), Luther also alleges of the Roman ordination that it is not given for the "public ministry of the Word by which the mysteries of God are dispensed."[51] The office of the Word is "both the highest and greatest of all things in the Church; in it all the power of the churchly estate subsists since without the Word nothing in the Church exists, and through the Word alone all things exist."[52] The papistic consecration, however, does not make ministers of the Word but only "those who offer Masses and hear penitents."[53] None of them is instructed "to dispense the mysteries of Christ and teach the Gospel and govern the Church of God, which He purchased with His own blood."[54] Through its adulteration with the sacrifice of the Mass, ordination, in Luther's eyes, becomes something abhorrent; it is pervaded by the "highest and most impious perversity [*summa et impiissima perversitate*]".[55] The consecration to the sacrificial priesthood is for him "pure falsehood and mockery of God [*merum mendacium et irrisio dei*]."[56] By it, no one becomes a true priest of God, a minister of the Word, but rather it makes

44 WA 8:486.19f.; cf. also WA 2:211.24ff.

45 WA 8:486.29.

46 WA 8:491.14ff.; cf. WA 8:488.3ff., 489.10ff.; 8:504.33ff. — In another passage, Luther points out that what is today termed "priesthood" is in Scripture called "ministerium," etc., "and in no place 'sacerdotium' . . ." (WA 7:630.12ff.); cf. also WA 12:190.11ff.

47 WA 8:499.17f.

48 WA 8:505.1ff. and 16ff.; 8:538.3ff., 541.4f.

49 WA 8:541.4f.

50 WA 8:489.26ff. Cf. also WA 12:175.9ff. This is why the priests called to offer sacrifices are also called by Luther "hypocrites and anointed idols" (WA 6:407.20f.).

51 WA 12:173.1ff.

52 WA 12:173.4ff.; cf. WA 12:180.5f., 181.17f.; also WA 10/3:170.5ff.; 11:415.26f.; 12:318.28; 22:184.2f.; 26:52.29ff.; 38:231.8ff.; 38:423.21ff.; 53:253.32f.

53 WA 12:174.12f.

54 WA 12:173.21ff. and 31ff.: "In the papacy, the office of the Word is treated as by far the vilest and simplest thing of all and is bestowed on the worst."

55 WA 12:172.32ff.

56 WA 12:174.28ff.

only "masks of falsehood and vanity [*larvae mendacii et vanitatis*]"[57] and "priests of Satan [*sacerdotes Satanae*]"[58] and is to be avoided "under the curse of God [*sub anathemate dei*]."[59] It is evident in the letter to the Bohemians that Luther's whole polemic against the Roman *ordo* is motivated by his opposition to the sacrifice of the Mass and the satisfactory, sacrificial priesthood.

We find precisely the same attitude in the treatise *The Private Mass and the Consecration of Priests* (1533). Here, too, Luther takes up the question: To what purpose are priests consecrated in the papacy? Answer: "To be priests of their own sacrifices, priests of their own works, not priests of the whole Church," like those who preach and administer the Sacraments.[60] This means "being consecrated against Christ,"[61] "more unconsecrated than consecrated"[62]—indeed, "being consecrated a devil,"[63] being made a "public thief of God and robber of the Church" (insofar as the sacrificial priest offers up the Sacrament instead of distributing it).[64] Concerning this consecration of sacrificial priests, it cannot but be the case that it is "patently false, anti-Christian, and utterly vain";[65] "far more worthless and wicked than baptizing bells and consecrating stones";[66] and an "abomination of abominations."[67] "Christ knows nothing of this consecration, that is certain."[68] Of course, Luther says all this not of the consecration per se—to the right use of which, as a call to the preaching office and pastoral office, he certainly assigns proper value[69]—but of the consecration to the sacrificial priesthood distorted by the idea of the sacrifice of the Mass.

B. The Legalistic Distortion

The sacrifice of the Mass has for its path of salvation that of the Law. It is the priest's sacrificial offering, or the participation of individuals in that offering, that is supposed to procure salvation. The ergistic and meritorious understanding of the way in which salvation occurs is intrinsically a teaching of the Law.

---

[57] WA 12:174.20.

[58] WA 12:175.41; cf. WA 12:187.17.

[59] WA 12:176.7f.; cf. WA 12:172.32ff. — Here Luther also opposes the validity of the papistic consecration generally. By virtue of the *ordo* for offering the sacrificial Mass, *sacra ordinatio* [sacred ordination] is destroyed (WA 12:174.16f.).

[60] WA 38:199.29f.; cf. WA 38:203.22ff., 220.16ff.: It is true "that, under the papacy, no priest is ever consecrated as a pastor or preacher, but only as a private priest, which no one can deny"; WA 38:220.30f.

[61] WA 38:199.33 and 28f.: "against Christ's whole ordinance and intent"; WA 38:203.33f.: "against the opinion and faith of the Church."

[62] WA 38:203.34.

[63] WA 38:206.12ff.

[64] WA 38:207.33f.; cf. WA 38:221.15f.

[65] WA 38:199.34f.

[66] WA 38:204.8.

[67] WA 38:199.19ff.; cf. WA 38:228.16f.

[68] WA 38:199.4f.

[69] WA 38:220.15ff. and 34ff., 228.19ff., 238.7ff., 256.3ff.

The Law requires action and recognizes nothing but action. Under this premise, the Gospel, too, is twisted and transformed into a *nova lex* [new Law], causing the office, which in the New Testament is supposed to be an office of the Gospel, to become an office of the letter and of bondage to the Law. In this legalistic distortion, however, it can no longer fulfill its purpose of conveying salvation to believers through the promise of the Gospel. The path of the Law is no path of salvation.

According to Luther, a man remains excluded from understanding the genuine Law of God as long as he views it as feasible outward action and overlooks its true requirement: the perfect righteousness of the heart. The sinner can never be justified with regard to the *genuine* Law of God. Thus the path of the Law ushers him not into salvation and life but either (by a superficial understanding) into hypocrisy and a holy appearance or (by a right understanding of the requirement of the Law) into despair.[70] Either way, those who wish to be justified before God through the Law are still not only under the servile yoke[71] but also under the curse.[72] They cannot sustain the Law's accusations in the long term and perish by the Law.[73]

Granted, this knowledge of being under the Law comes only from the Gospel. Thus Luther's discovery of the Gospel is at the same time his discovery of the distinction of Law and Gospel. The Law, as *opus alienum* [alien work], belongs to the wrathful God; the Gospel, as *opus proprium* [proper work], to the gracious God, who in Christ redeems man from the curse of the Law. The Law works in its judicial capacity so that the sinner, whose self-righteousness has been shattered by the Law, takes refuge in *sola gratia* and through faith in the Gospel experiences justification. Thus the Law is the disciplinarian unto Christ, preparing the way for the working of the Gospel.[74] This interrelationship of the Law and the Gospel—with the strict, natural distinction of both quantities—belongs to the very foundation of Luther's doctrine of justification. Without the distinction of Law and Gospel it cannot exist. Thus Luther regards the "locus of the distinction of Law and Gospel [*locus de discrimine legis et Evangelii*]" as the "height of all Christian doctrine [*summa totius Christianae doctrinae*]."[75] Rightly distinguishing Law and Gospel is "the highest art in Christendom that we should know."[76] "For unless the Gospel is sharply distinguished from the Law, Christian doctrine cannot be kept intact."[77] By the commingling of Law and Gospel, justification *sola gratia, sola fide* is laid waste. If the Gospel is mixed with the Law,

---

70 WA 36:15.28ff.

71 WA 40/2:8, 5, and 26ff.; 40/1:553.3ff.

72 WA 2:516.21f.

73 WA 44:503.27ff.; WA 2:564.32ff.

74 WA 40/1:529.11ff.; WA 2:528.1ff.

75 WA 40/1:209.16f.

76 WA 36:9.28f.

77 WA 40/1:486.26ff. "Whoever does not understand this distinction can distinguish no Christian from a Jew or heathen, for on this distinction everything depends" (WA 36:9.5ff.).

"it will produce nothing but *lex*,"[78] but that in turn means that Christ and the righteousness of faith cannot have dominion since that requires the pure Gospel without admixture of the Law. Those who mingle Law and Gospel by necessity become adversaries of the Gospel and hinder justification proceeding from the grace of Christ.[79]

It is in this light that Luther had to view the Roman office. It was marked by the basic commingling of Law and Gospel, by the elevation of the Law to absolute dominance. All Gospel was turned into Law and laws, all the acts of God into the action of man—whether in the special function of the office or in what was suggested by the office to men as the path of salvation. Priests in their priestly action turned to the path of the Law and led the consciences of men the same way. Against this, Luther defines the true essence of the office as ministry "not of the Law but of the Gospel [*non legis, sed Evangelii*]."[80] In no way does this mean eliminating the preaching of the Law. The preaching office must also declare the judgmental, deadly word of the Law so that the false path of salvation may be cut off. Luther was constantly impressing upon Johann Agricola the necessity of preaching the Law.[81] Without the preaching of the Law, there can be no proper understanding of the Gospel. This is all completely clear. But—and herein lies the *proprium* [characteristic quality] of the Evangelical office—the Law stands in relation to the Gospel in every case under the dominance of the latter, always directed toward the Gospel, serving the Gospel, preparing the way for it, never an end in itself. The New Testament office is carried by the spirit of the Gospel, is a "ministry of the spirit, not of the letter"; it is constantly advancing from the preaching of the Law to the evangelical preaching of grace and therein fulfilling its God-given purpose of being an instrument by which salvation comes to men.[82]

---

[78] WA 40/1:469.11ff.

[79] WA 40/1:114.12ff. (Dr): ". . . because when they mix the Law with the Gospel, they cannot but be subverters of the Gospel. For either Christ shall stand and the Law perish, or the Law shall stand and Christ perish. Christ and the Law can by no means dwell or rule together in the conscience. Where the righteousness of the Law has dominion, the righteousness of grace does not have dominion; and vice versa, where the righteousness of grace has dominion, the righteousness of the Law cannot have dominion." — On Luther's doctrine of Law and Gospel, cf. T. Harnack, *Luthers Theologie* I (1927), pp. 365ff.

[80] WA 6:566.32ff.

[81] Cf. the *Disputations against the Antinomians*, WA 39/1:345ff., and *Against the Antinomians*, WA 50:468ff., as well as the *Lectures on Galatians* of 1519 (WA 2:436ff.) and 1535 (WA 40/1).

[82] In connection with 2 Cor. 3:6ff., Luther says, "The priests, preachers, and preaching of the Old Testament dealt with no more than the Law of God. . . . But in the New Testament, there is preaching only of grace and the Spirit given us through Christ. . . . Therefore, St. Paul here calls the preaching of the New Testament '*ministerium spiritus*,' the ministry of the Spirit, that is, the preaching office by which the Spirit and grace of God are presented and offered to all who are oppressed and mortified by the Law and have become eager for grace" (WA 7:654.21ff.). "Behold, this is called the *ministerium spiritus, non literae* [ministry of the Spirit, not of the letter]—preaching of the Spirit, preaching of grace, preaching of true indulgence, preaching of Christ, that is, the New Testament" (WA 7:655.19ff.).

The legalistic distortion of the office in the papacy becomes especially clear to Luther in its view of the Office of the Keys.[83] The Keys are above all conceived of as the power of jurisdiction. Binding and loosing are thought to signify enacting and dispensing with ecclesiastical laws.[84] The function of the Keys is relegated to the legal domain. At the same time, it is not the divine Law by which consciences are bound, but human laws enacted by the church. Thus both the Gospel *and* the authentic Law, in their pedagogical function directed toward Christ, are concealed.[85] The Keys become a mere instrument of the rule of canon law. The office relates to men on the basis of these ecclesial laws; the priestly works are chiefly "commanding, forcing, threatening, urging, pressing [*mandare, exigere, minari, urgere, premere*]";[86] the comfort of the Gospel in the Keys is completely buried. According to Luther, the Keys are "an office, power, or charge from God given to the Church through Christ to retain and forgive men's sins,"[87] "and whatever else they ascribe to them from the Keys beyond this is sheer invention."[88] The keys of binding and loosing belong together; the one is not to be used without the other.[89] The key of binding performs the work of the Law and brings sin to light; the key of loosing does the work of the Gospel by promising the forgiveness of sins.[90] While the key of binding is concerned with the Law, it is not a binding of ecclesial laws as in the papacy,[91] but a "divine threat,"[92] and "it is directed toward the releasing of the sinner from his sins."[93] The key of binding is even located under the premise of the Gospel, being used only to prepare the way for the key of loosing by leading the sinner to repentance and bringing him to the proper state to receive the Absolution. Thus in Luther the stress is entirely on the key of loosing as the consummation of the Gospel. The minister who employs the Keys is a minister of the Gospel. In the Roman jurisdictional office, by contrast, the emphasis is solely on the key of binding in the sense of binding with ecclesial laws, in which matter the pope claims infallibility. The key of binding is said to be infallible while the key of loosing, as the forgiveness of sins, remains uncertain since it is said to be valid only under the assumption that the repentance was true, about which no certainty

---

83 Cf. on this point G. Hök, op. cit., pp. 158ff., where a thorough presentation of Luther's doctrine of the Keys may also be found; and E. Roth, *Die Privatbeichte und Schlüsselgewalt i. d. Theol. d. Reformatoren* (Gütersloh, 1952), pp. 61ff.

84 WA 12:183.19ff.; cf. WA 6:312.1ff.; 6:543.12ff.; 7:171.11ff.; 7:644.15ff.; 28:478.14ff.; 30/2:436.7ff., 439.32ff., 465.20ff.

85 WA 7:661.1ff.

86 WA 6:564.1.

87 WA 30/2:498.18ff.; cf. WA 30/2:467.4ff., 455.30f., 456.25ff., 503.18ff.

88 WA 6:412.3f.

89 WA 30/2:506.5ff.; also WA 30/2:457.5ff.

90 WA 30/2:503.26ff.

91 WA 30/2:467.10ff.

92 WA 30/2:468.23, 456.29ff., 459.1ff.; cf. WA 30/2:468.22ff.

93 WA 30/2:467.23f.

can be obtained.[94] Thus in the Roman understanding of the Office of the Keys, everything amounts to a requirement of the Law binding the conscience and preventing it from attaining the object for which the Keys were instituted: the certainty of salvation.

Luther's critique of the legalistic distortion of the office, which nullifies the Gospel, is no less sharp than that of the satisfactionary distortion. The keys of the pope contradict Christ, for Christ brings grace and forgiveness with the Keys, whereas the pope requires works with his keys.[95] And because the pope's keys contradict Christ, they are empty and without power or validity,[96] and their use in this legal distortion is an *abusus damnabilis* [abuse meriting damnation].[97] The same judgment which Luther passed on the satisfactionary *ordo* of the sacrifice of the Mass he also pronounces on the legalistic, jursidictional office in the papacy.[98] The burning of the book of canon law before the Elster Gate on December 10, 1520, was thus a pregnant symbolic act declaring that the hegemony of the Law—i.e., of ecclesial laws—over the conscience had to be broken so that the Gospel might have free course.[99]

The power to make laws is the power of a sovereign. Connected to the legalistic distortion of the Roman office was the clerical, hierarchical distortion, which represents the third point of Luther's opposition to the Roman view of the office.

---

[94] WA 30/2:476.31ff., 477.10ff.; cf. WA 30/2:446.17ff., 453.8ff. Luther vehemently assails the notion of the *clavis errans*, the so-called "erring key," which the key of loosing was supposed to become should someone's contrition prove untrue. "Erring key" is for Luther "a cursed, damnable term . . . which the devil himself invented and cast into the church and by it destroyed faith in Christ and took away all comfort and solace from our conscience. For our soul or conscience must truly be perfectly certain of that in which it is to trust, confide, and hope against sin and eternal death. So it must truly confide in the key by which it is absolved and receives forgiveness of sins, yet if this be uncertain and in error, it will truly have to despair and perish and forever" (WA 30/2:453.25ff.). Cf. WA 30/2:449.6f.: "For an uncertain absolution is just the same as no absolution."

[95] WA 30/2:468.3ff.

[96] WA 30/2:484.33ff.; 50:632.26ff.

[97] WA 12:183.26; cf. WA 8:505.22ff.: The true priestly office has been extinguished "and in its place an idolatrous human doctrine and law has been erected."

[98] Cf. J. Köstlin, *Luthers Lehre von der Kirche* (Stuttgart, 1853), p. 27.

[99] Cf. WA 8:459.38f.: "It is therefore impossible for the Gospel to govern alongside canon law." — On Luther's position vis-à-vis Roman church law, cf. R. Sohm, *Kirchenrecht* I (Leipzig, 1892), pp. 460ff. Yet Sohm paints a crude picture, asserting that Luther rejected not only the pertinent canon law but also the whole idea of ecclesial law and the juridical nature of the Church. G. Holstein (*Die Grundlagen des ev. Kirchenrechts* [Tübingen, 1928], pp. 84ff.) showed that Sohm exaggerated Luther's remarks on canon law. Luther never rejected canon law per se. Cf. also G. Törnvall (*Geistliches und weltliches Regiment bei Luther* [Munich, 1947], p. 116 n. 155), who identifies Sohm's thesis regarding the impossibility of church law as a direct consequence of his spiritualistic view of the concept of the kingdom of God. Similarly, W. O. Münter (*Die Gestalt der Kirche 'nach göttl. Recht'* [Munich, 1941], p. 50) sees the root of Sohm's total rejection of church law in his spiritualistic Docetism, which caused him to overlook the true incarnation of God and thus the humanity of the Church. Sohm reads his own ideas into Luther. On the critique of Sohm in recent time, cf. esp. W. Maurer, *Pfarrerrecht und Bekenntnis* (Berlin, 1957).

C. The Hierarchical Distortion

The legal view of the office leads to the perversion of its nature from that of ministering to the congregation to one of ruling over the congregation.[100] The consequence, in turn, from this view of the office is the shift in emphasis from the office's function to its estate, which, by virtue of the satisfactionary distortion of the concept of the office, was furthermore surrounded with an aura of salvific, mediatory qualities. In this way, the spiritual estate as such—thus isolated from its real function—becomes the actual carrier of the Church's spirituality and creates a deeper divide between clergy and laity, the *ordo* and the *populus*. Luther keenly saw that this represented a departure from the New Testament. Particularly since the Leipzig Disputation of 1518, when he had called into question the collective Roman system of authority, he came to regard with increasing clarity the idea of the universal priesthood. On December 18, 1519, he writes to [Georg] Spalatin that the distinction between priests and laymen—whenever he considered it—seems to lie only in the *ministerium*, the ministry of Word and Sacrament (when one disregards the duties which the Roman Curia has imposed on priests).[101] The concept of the universal priesthood from 1 Peter 2 and Revelation 5 was doubtless an influence in this regard.[102] In the year 1520, these insights matured into full clarity.

In the treatise *To the Christian Nobility of the German Nation*, Luther teaches on the basis of 1 Corinthians 12 that any distinction among Christians, who are all members of the single Body of Christ, is found only in the distinct work and office (= service) by which one serves another.[103] The concept of service governs Luther's view of the functions and cooperation of the individual members of the single body. Even the spiritual office has its existence only in ministering or serving. The opposite of this, however, confronted Luther in the Roman form of the office. In *The Babylonian Captivity of the Church*, he most incisively attacks the *tyrannis clericorum in laicos* [tyranny of the clergy against the laity] and censures the papistic clergy for forgetting that the purpose of the office is to serve and—in pharisaical arrogance, with confidence in the anointing of hands and in the tonsure and priestly garments—for thinking themselves superior to the Christian laity (though they, too, are anointed with the Holy Spirit) and regarding them as unworthy dogs.[104] As a result, the *fraternitas christiana* [Christian brotherhood] is disrupted,[105] wolves are made of shepherds, tyrants of servants, hypersecular of the spiritual.[106] The

---

100 The migration of Roman bishops and the papacy into the exercise of political, temporal power should also be understood from a legal view of the office. Whoever does not understand how to distinguish Law and Gospel is also unable to comprehend how to separate the two kingdoms of God.

101 WA Br 1:595.26ff. and 30f.

102 Ibid., line 28ff.

103 WA 6:407.13ff., 408.26ff., 409.1ff.; cf. WA 15:625.7.

104 WA 6:563.31ff.; cf. WA 6:354.15ff.

105 WA 6:564.3f.

106 WA 6:564.4f.

office is then no longer oriented toward the other but toward the self, and in this egocentric posture becomes a ministry of the belly.[107] Against this Luther maintains that the office "is nothing other than ministry."[108] Those who bear the office have no "right of rule, except as much as we willingly grant them."[109] Yet wherever use is made of such a right to rule, according to Luther, there is a falling away from the Gospel and a perversion into what is anti-Christian. By bestowing the power of the Keys, Christ gave the apostles not a *dominium* but a *ministerium*. The Keys are not an earthly dominion but an aid to entering the kingdom of heaven by the forgiveness of sins.[110] The same applies to those who succeed the apostles in the office of the Church. "For bishops and the successors of the apostles do not have rules but ministries." "They are called servants of the Church of Christ, as Paul says in Colossians 1."[111]

The perversion of the office of the ministry into an office of mastery necessarily meant the surrender of the office's functional character in favor of a static understanding. Hand in hand with Luther's attack on the hierarchical distortion of the office, then, is his attack on the Roman doctrine of the spiritual estate, in which Luther saw the legitimizing of depravation. According to Roman teaching, the spiritual estate was founded on an ontologically implanted *character indelebilis* [indelible character] without inner relation to the awareness of the true function of the office. Thus it was possible for the laws and dignities of the spiritual estate to be insisted on while the true function of the office was entirely absent. Luther had in view an office in the papistic church that did not preach, but neglected to administer the means of grace ordained by Christ.[112] For him this is a self-contradiction, for "the duty of a priest is to

[107] WA 38:221.9ff.: ". . . Indeed, they are consecrated for themselves and for their belly alone"; cf. WA 38:199.2ff., 208.35ff.

[108] WA 6:564.13f.; cf. WA 6:564.11f.: "The priests . . . , whom we call, are ministers"; WA 6:566.32f., 567.17f.; 2:676.37: "The power of the pope is servitude, not lordship." Cf. also E. C. Achelis, "Studien über das 'gestliche Amt,'" *Theol. Stud. u. Kritiken* (1889), pp. 34f. and 73ff.

[109] WA 6:564.9; cf. WA Br 5:492.27ff. (Luther's opinion on the question of whether and to what degree bishops may require ceremonies of the church): "A bishop, as bishop, has no power over the church to impose any of his own tradition or ceremony except by the express or tacit approval of the church. For the Church is a free woman and a lady, and the bishops may not exercise lordship over the faith of the churches. . . . For they are merely ministers and stewards, not masters of the Church . . ."; also WA Br 5:493.63ff.; WA 2:677.27ff.; 8:254.17ff. — Regarding the passage WA 6:564.9, W. Brunotte's (*Das geistl. Amt bei Luther* [Berlin, 1959], p. 58) critique of A. W. Dieckhoff's interpretation is likely correct.

[110] WA 45:461.15ff.; cf. WA 1:596.29ff.; 2:248.35ff.: "St. Peter or a priest is a minister or servant of the Keys; the Church is the lady and bride whom he is to serve with the power of the Keys." The "feeding" in John 21 [:15–17] is not governance but proclamation: WA 2:195.19ff.; 6:564.23f.

[111] WA 7:753.28f.; cf. WA 2:678.6ff.; 6:543.28: "For He established in His Church not dominions, not powers, not authorities, but ministries"; WA 8:502.17f.: "not to rule, but to minister to the sheep . . ."; WA 11:271.11ff. — Cf. P. Althaus, *Communio sanctorum* (Munich, 1929), pp. 65f.

[112] WA 38:222.25ff.: "These priests use none of the aforesaid things, which Christ has ordained for the maintenance of the Church. They do not preach, they do not baptize, they do not give the Sacrament, they do not absolve. . . . They are in no office of caring for souls, nor do they do anything for the dying. Rather, they are unprofitable, lazy, idle servants who only handle the Sacrament (as

preach."[113] When Luther says, "The ministry of the Word makes the priest and bishop [*Ministerium verbi facit sacerdotem et Episcopum*],"[114] "makes" ["*facit*"] is to be taken in the strict sense. It means that for Luther the actual exercise of the true function of the office is so integral to the office that without it, it does not exist in the full sense. The office is for him a completely ontological ministry and work functionally defined in its being. As evidence of this, Luther eagerly reclaims the New Testament terminology of the office which uses expressions that constantly point to the function of the office. "Scripture, I say, calls the spiritual and priestly estate a ministry, a caretaker, an office, an elder, a watchman, a tabernacle, a preacher's office, shepherds."[115] To this Luther adds a far-reaching statement. When Paul says "*dispensatio*," "*economia*," "*ministerium*," "*minister*," "*servus*," etc., his intent is "in no case to set up *some estate, order, authority, or rank* (as our men wish) but to commend *only an office and work*, with the authority and rank of priesthood in common with the rest."[116] The opposition to estate, order, etc., on the one hand, and office and work on the other, is telling. The antithesis of the hierarchical distortion of the office in the papacy brings Luther to the point of seeing, in a spiritual estate intrinsically aloof from the laity, an evil that must be resisted. Thus from the viewpoint of the functional specificity of the office, Luther shatters the

they believe) and sell it as a sacrifice and work, and for that they devour the goods of Christian and non-Christian alike . . ."; cf. WA 38:223.11ff.; 41:156.27f.; 41:183.7f.: "Our bishops bear the name but are unwilling to touch the work"; WA 50:248.1ff. — Also cf. above, pp. 9–12. — To the excuse that the preaching and feeding are indeed done by the pope and bishop "*per alios*" ["through others"], Luther admits no validity. Cf. WA 2:[197].6ff.: "This saying" ("feed My sheep") "unavoidably means that either they must be shepherds, loving and teaching personally, or, if they do not love and teach personally, this verse does not pertain to them"; WA 2:670.22ff. and 30ff.: "Unless the priests themselves feed, pray, and govern, they are not priests, and the word 'feed' does not pertain to them at all." Nevertheless, Luther occasionally expressed different sentiments on this point. Thus in the treatise on the episcopal consecration in Naumburg [*Model for the Consecration of a True Christian Bishop*] (1542), WA 53:253.21ff.: "Yet we do not press so rigidly that a bishop must execute this episcopal office in person. We will sincerely and gladly take upon ourselves even before God . . . that they might be following the example of St. Valerius . . ."; so also in his *Exhortation to All Clergy Assembled at Augsburg* (1530): WA 30/2:340.20ff. Yet such sentiments are not to be understood as essential but as considerations of temporary circumstances that are difficult to change and as a concession to them.

113 WA 6:566.5f.; cf. WA 26:52.29ff.: "We have heard that a bishop should have the grace of teaching well and willingly, for this is the chief work of the office of bishop: the ministry of the Word"; WA 50:247.3ff.: A true Christian bishop "provides for the church with God's Word and the Sacraments."

114 WA 6:566.9.

115 WA 7:630.14ff.; cf. WA 8:247.15f.; 41:210.6ff.

116 WA 12:190.19ff. — The Roman hierarchical development arises, according to Luther, when "the names apostle, bishop, and others begin to be not offices or ministries but dignities and dominions" (WA 17/2:256.7f.). Cf. WA 7:28.26ff.: "Holy Scripture gives no other distinction than that those who teach or are consecrated should be called *ministros, servos, oconomos*, that is, ministers, servants, stewards, which are supposed to preach Christ, faith, and Christian freedom to others. . . . But now the stewardship has been turned into such a worldly, external, admirable, fearful majesty and authority that true worldly power can in no way compare to it . . ."; cf. WA 2:234.38, 235.1; 2:196.36ff.; 2:670.11; 12:390.3ff.

Roman conception of an estate and replaces it with the teaching of the universal priesthood of all believers, which Rome had forgotten. The concept of the spiritual unity of the Church also plays an important role for Luther here. The ontological separation of clergy and laity is for him a disruption of Christian unity.[117] "Those who . . . introduced such sects among the Christian people and divided them into clergy and laity . . . : those who devised this have divided and split asunder the Christian people."[118] Bishop and priest are "not the name of a sect but the name of an office."[119] The spiritual office is not a special privileged estate but the particular ministry of the congregation. Especially dangerous in Luther's view is the doctrine of an essential difference between clergy and laity, most of all by the fact that *this spiritual estate, set apart from the laity, is understood ontologically as a means to salvation*. It alone has the power to offer the sacrifice of the Mass by which salvation is concretely realized. Because of its salvific and mediatory privileges, it is assigned a higher level, even before God, and salvation is expected from it rather than from Christ. Here Luther discerns the threat to justification *sola gratia, sola fide*. "Priests should not be greater in God's sight than we, like a prince's officers. We are not supposed to trust in them. . . ."[120] Luther's purpose in resisting the idea of a higher level before God which the *ordo* is supposed to give and which is supposed to represent in itself a salvific value is especially to combat the ontological *ordo in general* and to *replace* it with a functional concept of the office. That it is not necessary for an ontological *ordo* to contradict absolutely the functional specificity of the office remains hidden to Luther because of the dusky image of the Roman office in his time, which, having forsaken its true function, was configured as a privileged, static estate and reshaped as a means to salvation. A further basis for

[117] "From the fact that clergy and laity are separated more than heaven and earth, a confusion of the evangelical communion has arisen" (WA 6:563.29ff.). Luther also sees celibacy (and other peculiarities of the clergy) in terms of an instrument by which they isolate themselves still further from the rest of Christians "as though from the unclean" (WA 6:565.11).

[118] WA 8:503.32ff.; cf. WA 6:408.33ff.: "Christ does not have two bodies nor two kinds of body, one temporal and one spiritual. There is one Head, and He has one Body"; WA 8:429.30ff.: "The Christian people is one, in which there should be no sect at all, no difference of persons, no laity, no clergy, no tonsure, no chrismation, no monk—but all without distinction, each either married or unmarried according to his will, just as we see happens naturally in civil communities. But bishops or presbyters or elders or deacons should not differ in any way from the rest of Christians except only in the office of Word and Sacrament"; WA 8:503.23.

[119] WA 8:504.1ff.; cf. WA 8:430.3. — Nevertheless, it must also be observed that Luther himself, under the auspices of a functional view, absolutely teaches a distinction between pastors and other Christians and personally incorporates the concept of the spiritual estate in the framework of his teaching of the three estates. Cf. below, pp. 94–98.

[120] WA 10/3:397.1f. Cf. WA 2:196.38ff.: "The imposition of the office through the word 'feed' did not confer on him a higher rank, nor could it confer one"; WA 2:482.32ff.; 8:254.24f.: "Thus we have recovered from the robbers of the Church those two names and shown that they are not more the Church nor more priests than all Christians are"; WA 10/3:396.24ff.: "Here clerical privilege would fall apart, and they would be unable to say that they are better than we, for the devil instituted that idea; and thus we were directed to priests and believed that the priests were our means to God and we had to be saved through them."

Luther to combat the doctrine of an ontological clerical estate is the fact that, in the papacy, it sounded as if the *ordo* itself made a man spiritual, that it was tied to a gross devaluation of baptismal grace and a concealment of every man's spiritual character arising from Baptism. The Roman doctrine of the spiritual estate lacked the foundation of the universal priesthood. To restore this, Luther launches an opposition to the doctrine of the ontological *ordo* in general. If one considers all these motivating factors, it will have to be said that the antithesis "*not the estate, ordination, etc., but the office and work* [*non status, ordo, etc., sed officium et opus*]" in Luther is to be understood from the perspective of the distorted Roman *ordo*.

The hierarchical distortion of the office from an office of ministry to an office of mastery depends on the underestimation of the functional specificity of the office and leads the office-bearers to rest on their privileges, which separate them from the people and make the people spiritually dependent on them, and to renounce the proper work of the office. Over against this, Luther's concept of the office bears the characteristics of a concept of the office which stresses as the decisive content of the office its proper function and configures the spiritual office on the basis of the universal priesthood, which bridges the great gap between clergy and laity. —

Luther's teaching on the office can be understood only in the context of the particular situation in which he found himself. It is not merely the product of this situation, yet neither is it to be comprehended apart from this situation. It is integrally rooted in an evangelical basis, in the Reformation understanding of the Gospel, in justification *sola gratia, sola fide*, but it acquired its particular expression in the conflict and dispute with the Roman form of the office that confronted Luther. Naturally, this dispute itself is based in turn on Luther's new understanding of the Gospel and his teaching on justification and is to a great extent a practical application of these. For this reason, the *driving* force of Luther's teaching of the office can be seen only in the internal, factual component: the necessity of ministry in Word and Sacrament from the perspective of justification. The other, external component, rooted in the polemical situation with Rome, comes under consideration only as coformative, yet may by no means be ignored.

As the result of the study of the basic assumptions of Luther's concept of the office, we may note that the ecclesial office for Luther is entirely subordinated to the Gospel; it is the ministry of the Gospel for the transmission of the Gospel's gifts of salvation to men. It has its essence in the factual execution of the Gospel, which awakens faith in Christ's salvific work and thereby leads to the justification of the sinner before God. It rests on the salvific necessity of the *verbum externum* [external Word] (fundamental position of anti-Enthusiasm) and is defined only by this Word, the Gospel of the free grace of God in Christ (fundamental position of anti-Romanism).

Having laid the foundation of Luther's concept of the office, it is fitting for us to examine it in greater detail, taking as our point of departure the universal priesthood, not simply because the line of thought in the first chapter has led up to it, but because the teaching of the universal priesthood in fact yields the basis for the concrete realization of the collective doctrine of the office in Luther, and his concept of the office must necessarily be developed from that. —

CHAPTER II

The Universal Priesthood as the Embodiment of the Office

1. The Spiritual Estate of All Christians

The discovery of the Gospel of justification by faith on account of Christ is followed, in Luther, by that other new discovery which can be summarized in the concept of the universal priesthood.[1] The idea that all Christians are priests and members of the clerical estate received little or no attention in the papacy. Luther presses on to the New Testament view of the priesthood, clearly teaching from 1520 that "all Christians are truly of the clerical estate"[2] and that ". . . we are all priests, as many of us as are Christians."[3] Every Christian who believes in Christ and is baptized is anointed with the Holy Spirit and sanctified in body and soul,[4] is taught by God and anointed a priest,[5] is in faith one with Christ,

[1] The internal connection between Luther's doctrine of the universal priesthood and his teaching on justification has been thoroughly treated by H. Storck, *Das allg. Priestertum bei Luther*, Theol. Existenz NF no. 37 (Munich, 1953), pp. 6–20, also pp. 4f. Also cf. F. J. Stahl, *Die Kirchenverfassung*, etc., 2nd ed. (1862), p. 101; G. Rietschel, *Lehrbuch der Liturgik* II (1909), p. 406; K. Holl, *Luther*, p. 318; G. Niedermeier, "Das allg. Priestertum der Gläubigen u. d. geistliche Amt," *Ztschr. für sys. Theol.* (1930), p. 345. J. Köstlin has shown how the idea of the universal priesthood is rooted in Luther's conception of the church as the congregation of saints: *Luthers Lehre von der Kirche* (Stuttgart, 1853), p. 47.

[2] WA 6:407.13f., 408.28f.; 7:628.7 and 23f., 634.9ff. and 23ff.

[3] WA 6:564.11, 566.27; cf. WA 6:412.20; 7:633.16, 634.9ff. and 23ff.; 8:217.14; 8:250.32; 8:415.23f., 486.27f., 487.10f. and 36f., 488.34, 489.3–6, 492.19ff. and 37f., 555.7ff.; 12:178.28ff.; 12:317.10f.; 25:16.17 and 23; 38:247.21ff.; 41:153.10f., 154.20, 155.10; 49:590.36.

[4] WA 6:566.16f.; cf. WA 41:155.26ff.: "But Christians must all be holy priests and have holy adornment; for here is another man who consecrates them priests, namely, the one High Priest, Christ, . . . and gives another chrism or anointing and priestly consecration, namely, the Holy Spirit, who adorns them in a glorious and holy manner and clothes them with His power and gifts."

[5] WA 11:411.31ff., 412.5ff.

and so is a participant in Christ's priesthood[6] and is consecrated a priest with Christ.[7] In the New Testament, only the priesthood of Christ is valid. "We have only one priest, Christ, who for our sake offered up Himself, and all of us with Him."[8] But the priesthood of Christ results in the priesthood of Christians. "This is a spiritual priesthood shared by all Christians, by which we are all priests with Christ; that is, we are children of Christ, the High Priest."[9] Expounding 1 Pet. 2:9, Luther says, ". . . We are all priests before God if we are Christians. For since we are founded on the Rock, who is the Most High Priest before God, we also have what He has."[10] The Rock is Christ; to be founded on Him means to have faith in Him, and faith means participation in the nature and benefits of Christ. The "holy and spiritual priesthood,"[11] which for Luther is the main question, first designates simply the immediate relationship with God obtained through faith in Christ, communion with God, the state of reconciliation and adoption as children of God, the estate of the Christian.[12] Whoever is a priest has free access to God and is permitted to come into God's presence.[13] This applies to Christians insofar as they are in Christ, who has reconciled them with God. According to 1 Pet. 2:5, they are thus enabled to offer spiritual sacrifices to God. These involve the sacrifices of the body and the praise and thank offerings of the lips and of love in action.[14] These holy sacrifices include confessing Christ, teaching about Christ in order to spread the kingdom of God on earth, and enduring affliction in following Christ.[15] They can be offered only by one who is already in the spiritual estate, that is, "by a Christian who has the Spirit of Christ."[16] These sacrifices of Christians are to be sharply distinguished from

[6] WA 12:179.15ff.; 7:27.17ff.; cf. WA 4:224.21: "All believers are priests through their Priest, Christ."

[7] WA 11:412.1: "Christians, brothers of Christ, who with Him are consecrated priests." In addition, that Christians are Christ's brothers, cf. WA 15:720.15; 38:230.3f. and 7.

[8] WA 8:486.21f.

[9] WA 8:486.27ff.; cf. WA 8:415.22ff.; 41:205.5ff.: "It is a strong definition that we know no other priest or cleric than Jesus Christ, God's Son, our Lord; and after Him all born from Him are called children of priests. . . . He is our Father; we are His children. Therefore, each Christian should be called a priest by birth. . . . Therefore, we do not need to be ashamed of the name and that we are called children of the Priest"; also cf. WA 41:204.29ff.; 49:714.36ff.; 52:567.11ff.

[10] WA 12:317.4ff.; cf. WA 6:567.29f.; 10/3:394.27ff.; 12:307.22f.

[11] WA 12:307.22.

[12] Cf. H. Storck, op. cit., pp. 16f.; R. Josefson, "Das Amt der Kirche," in *Ein Buch von der Kirche* (Göttingen, 1951), p. 392.

[13] WA 12:317.26: "To be a priest means: 'You may approach God . . .'"; WA 16:406.21; cf. WA 12:317.19f.: "To be a priest . . . is only a kind of office that deals before God"; WA 7:28.7ff.; 8:486.31f.; 41:193.17ff., 212.11f.

[14] WA 6:371.21ff.; 8:252.30ff.; 8:420.35ff., 492.16ff. (on Rom. 12:1f.): "No one can deny that he is describing the priestly office here, which is nothing else than offering oneself to God as a reasonable sacrifice . . ."; WA 8:492.21ff. and 31ff., 493.1ff.; 12:185.19ff. On the theme "priesthood and sacrifice" in Luther, cf. V. Vajta, op. cit., pp. 270ff.

[15] WA 41:154.27ff., 211.8ff.: "This sacrificing consists of suffering"; WA 49:714.38f.

[16] WA 12:186.1ff.

the sacrifice of Christ, which alone satisfies and atones for sin. They are another genus of sacrifice. Although they *may* be offered, and even founded, on the basis of that single sacrifice of Christ, they are not sacrificial offerings for sin but thank offerings for redemption from sin.[17]

This interpretation of the priesthood of Christians as a direct relationship with God and the ability to offer spiritual sacrifices pleasing to God is immediately connected in Luther to a *regard for others*, for whom a Christian—following the example of Christ—is to offer himself, interceding before God in a priestly capacity.[18] Paul Althaus referenced this in the course of his examination of the concept of *communio* in Luther.[19] Christians, being made participants in the priesthood of Christ, also enter into Christ's priestly exercise toward others and so become priests.[20] Here the concept of the Christian's uniformity with Christ, emphasized in recent times especially by Hans Storck[21] and Gösta Hök,[22] plays a significant role for Luther. If the Christian can approach God in faith in Christ and offer spiritual sacrifices, he is at once necessarily drawn into Christ's priestly work of love toward others and assumes responsibility for his neighbor, whose priest he then becomes. Thus this "approaching of God" is promptly followed by "praying for others," and then also "teaching others," the proclamation of God's saving works according to 1 Pet. 2:9. As Christians' priestly works, we see side by side in Luther not only approaching God and offering holy sacrifices[23] but also approaching God, praying for others, and preaching or teaching.[24] Yet it

---

[17] WA 41:211.7f.: "We cannot make offerings for sin like Christ—that belongs to Christ alone." Cf. G. Hök, op. cit., p. 158.

[18] Regard for others is the basis, according to Luther, for the distinction of the concepts of priesthood and king: WA 16:407.33f.: "Thus every Christian is a king for himself and a priest for others. The priesthood is higher than the kingship; it spreads farther. For a priest handles the Word not only for himself but also for others"; cf. WA 7:28.6ff.: "Besides that, we are priests—that is much more than being a king—because the priesthood makes us worthy to approach God and to pray for others. For standing in God's presence and praying is fitting for none but priests. . . . Who, then, can fathom the glory and majesty of a Christian man? By his kingship he has power over all things; by his priesthood he has power over God, for God does what he asks and wills."

[19] *Communio sanctorum* (Munich, 1929), pp. 68ff., esp. p. 69: "It is always for others that one is a priest"; "It is precisely by an individual's being placed immediately before God that he receives the power of proxy." — Cf. also J. Köstlin, *Luthers Lehre von der Kirche* (1853), pp. 61ff., who has already emphasized the universal priesthood in Luther. — Recently again in V. Vajta, op. cit., p. 272.

[20] WA 10/3:309.11ff. — Cf. K. Holl, *Luther*, p. 332.

[21] Op. cit., pp. 17f., also pp. 26f., where Storck shows how the priesthood of Christians is manifested as they are ready to take responsibility for their neighbors entrusted to them through their particular office (= vocation). Cf. also E. Vogelsang, *Der angefochtene Christus bei Luther* (Berlin & Leipzig, 1932), pp. 74ff.

[22] Op. cit., p. 156.

[23] WA 41:154.27f.: "those who always stand before God, offering holy sacrifices"; WA 41:212.8f.: "This is the glory: that we through Christ are so highly consecrated that we may pray and offer sacrifices."

[24] WA 7:28.7ff., 54.24f.: "Through the priesthood we are worthy to appear before God, to pray for others, and to teach each other the things of God"; WA 8:487.3ff.: ". . . It" (Scripture) "makes prayer, access to God, and teaching (which is appropriate and fitting as a priest) common to all men";

has to be kept in mind that the primary element in the concept of the priesthood in Luther, from which responsibility for others first arises, remains the immediate access to God, the communion with God won by Christ, of which every Christian is a participant in faith.[25] All Christians are priests, which always primarily means that they are in a spiritual estate before God, redeemed children of God through faith in Christ.

With this teaching of the universal priesthood, Luther went against the prevailing Roman view of the priesthood. The interposition of the mediatorial priest in the Roman system, which is unbiblical and violates the sole mediation of Christ, is abolished. The salvific estate of the Christian has no need of such a mediatorial entity.[26] Every Christian already has immediate access to God through Christ. With his teaching of the universal priesthood, Luther combats the notion that a consecrated and anointed priest is closer to God, of a holier estate, than a baptized Christian, "as though they alone were Christ's possession," as though priests alone had the character, "the spiritual mark in their soul which no common Christian has, only consecrated priests."[27] This priesthood, which views the spiritual estate before God as its sole prerogative, is for Luther an accursed antagonism of the true spiritual estate and serves to empty the latter.[28] Every Christian has the spiritual character in his soul by virtue of his connection with Christ. But by the pope's laws and governance, things went so far "that the precious common terms 'church,' 'priest,' and 'spiritual' were transferred from the common people to the most selective group—which we now

---

WA 12:307.27ff.: "Now Christ is anointed High Priest by God Himself and has offered up His own body for us, which is the office of the high priest. Next, He prayed for us on the cross. Third, He also declared the Gospel and taught it to all men. Therefore, since He is Priest, and we are His brothers, all Christians have the power and charge, and are required, to preach and come before God, to pray for one another, and to offer themselves to God"; WA 12:309.24ff.: "This, then, is the true priesthood which consists of three parts . . . : Offering oneself spiritually, praying for the Church, and preaching. Whoever can do that is a priest"; WA 16:406.19ff.: "What, then, is a priest? He in whose mouth God puts His Word. . . . Likewise, he makes offerings and prays for others. Such a priest may come before God in faith, pray for the people, speak their words, and act on their behalf before God, and then return from God to the people and relay to them God's answer and command . . ."; cf. WA 16:407.14ff.; 25:16.18f. Cf. also M. Rade, *Das königliche Priestertum der Gläubigen und seine Forderung an die ev. Kirche unserer Zeit* (Tübingen, 1918), p. 8. The theme of regard for others in Luther's concept of the universal priesthood is overlooked by Brunotte (op. cit., pp. 149ff.). His polemic against H. Storck (ibid.), V. Vajta (op. cit., p. 151), and P. Althaus (p. 153 n. 124) on this question seems irrelevant to us.

[25] WA 41:210.25ff.: "But if you ask: What, then, does the priesthood of the Christian consist of, or what are the works of their priests? Answer: The very same that were discussed above, namely, teaching, offering sacrifices, and praying. But one must know . . . that Christ is the only High Priest, whose priestly office we must have first as done for our good—indeed, given for our own—before we do such priestly works."

[26] WA 8:486.28f.: "We are children of Christ, the High Priest, and we need no other priest or mediator than Christ"; WA 8:487.8ff.: "Christ alone, and no other, is the Mediator and Instructor of all Christians"; cf. WA 8:415.24ff.

[27] WA 38:227.31ff. and 20ff.; cf. WA 41:205.33ff.

[28] WA 8:459.30f.: "Therefore, by this accursed and execrable priesthood, he transfers and empties our Christian priesthood."

call the spiritual estate and priestly estate—and their things, the things of the Church, when in fact we are all the Church, clerics, and priests, as many of us as believe in Christ."[29] Restricting the spiritual character to the clergy would mean reducing the laity to the profane.[30] The Gospel, however, is not merely given to the spiritual,[31] but is universal, for which reason all Christians are in the inheritance of Christ and are spiritual.[32] The distinctions among Christians which arise from some exercising the functions of a particular office and others not doing so are only before men; "before God there is no distinction."[33] In both their free access to God and their priestly responsibility for others they are all equal since these both proceed from faith, which is only one. The universality of the priesthood is founded on the universality of the faith.[34] And vice versa: if the universality of the priesthood is infringed on, the faith is destroyed, and "the whole covenant of Christian grace, freedom, faith, and all that we have from Christ, even Christ Himself, are thereby taken away. . . ."[35] For Luther, asserting the *universal* priesthood concerns all the riches of the Gospel; negating this doctrine is for him equivalent to negating the Gospel.

More than that, the doctrine of the spiritual estate and the priesthood of all Christians is an attack on the significance of the priestly consecration according to the Roman view. Luther takes what was ascribed to the consecration of priests in the papacy and gives it back to Baptism. It is not the pope who by his consecration makes a Christian "or spiritual man," but he thereby makes only "hypocrites and idols"; but rather Baptism, the Gospel, faith "alone make spiritual

[29] WA 7:634.20ff.; cf. also WA 7:633.16; 7:28.28ff.: "The word 'priest,' 'cleric [*pfaff*],' 'spiritual [*geystlich*],' and the like have been treated wrongly and transferred from the common people to the special group which is now called the spiritual estate"; WA 2:189.27f.: "The Spirit of Christ is also in the laity"; WA 12:317.2ff. and 9ff.: "Therefore, I would very much like this word 'priest' to be as common as calling us Christians. For they are all the same thing: priests, baptized Christians . . ."; WA 8:254.6ff. (contrary to Emser's division of spiritual and physical priesthood): "But St. Peter's words are God's words; they can mean nothing but the one common priesthood. . . ."

[30] WA 6:565.11; cf. WA 7:29.2ff.: ". . . just as though the laity were something other than Christian people."

[31] WA 10/3:394.32ff., 395.30ff.

[32] WA 10/3:396.19ff.: "Priests should not appropriate to themselves alone the riches of Christ; another is just as much in the inheritance as they."

[33] WA 10/3:396.11ff.; cf. WA 10/3:398.19ff.: "But here in the sight of man we must honor our priests and honor them as priests; but not in the sight of God, for in God's sight we are all priests through faith"; WA 12:309.4f. Cf. also V. Vajta, op. cit., p. 201.

[34] WA 6:370.24ff.: "For faith must do it all. It alone is the true priestly office and lets no one be otherwise; therefore, all Christian men are priests and all [Christian] women priestesses, whether young or old, master or servant, mistress or maidservant, learned or lay. Here there is no distinction unless their faith is dissimilar"; WA 7:634.23ff.; 8:539.17ff., 555.7f.; 10/3:398.24ff.: "If I have faith, then I am also a priest; who will deny me this? . . . Therefore, faith brings with it the priesthood"; WA 12:308.34ff.: "a distinction which faith cannot tolerate"; WA 15:720.10f.: "We know what God has, namely, all things. Thus a Christian [is a priest] by faith. There is no distinction, whether man, woman, maidservant . . ."; WA 15:720.29f.; WA 15:720.36: "Let the name of priest and of Christian be shared and held in common." Cf. also V. Vajta, op. cit., p. 272.

[35] WA 7:29.3ff.

and Christian people."[36] Luther proclaims *Baptism as the true priestly consecration*: "Accordingly, we are all consecrated priests through Baptism."[37] Because of Baptism, there is present in all Christians an intrinsic equality in the Christian priesthood.[38] In the treatise to the Bohemians, *Concerning the Ministry* (1523), Luther prefaces the discussion of the Christian priesthood by saying that in the New Testament there is no externally anointed priest, nor can there be, since "in the New Testament particularly, one does not become [a priest] but is born one; one is not ordained one but created one."[39] The priesthood is thus characterized as part of the spiritual act of creation in Baptism: "But he is born not by birth of the flesh but by that of the spirit, namely, of water and the Spirit in the washing of regeneration."[40] That all Christians are priests by virtue of Baptism is so certain for Luther that he continues: "And let it be anathema to assert that a priest is different from him who is a Christian. For that would be asserted apart from the Word of God."[41] When it is believed that a man becomes a priest by external anointing, it is heresy for Luther.[42] "If I call you a Christian, I am also calling you a priest."[43] The two are integrally related. Just like being a Christian, the priesthood, a man's spiritual estate obtained in Baptism, is a prerequisite of the proper consecration and call to the pastoral office, not something that it effects. ". . . The status and power of the priesthood must precede it, being furnished by Baptism and shared by all Christians through faith. . . ."[44] This was completely obscured in the Roman doctrine of the office, according to which the consecration produced a priest in the proper sense. The hypertrophy in the realm of the priestly consecration corresponded to a dystrophy in the realm of Baptism. The priestly consecration overshadowed Baptism and hid its

---

[36] WA 6:407.18f.

[37] WA 6:407.22f.; cf. WA 6:564.6f.: "We are all equally priests, as many of us as are baptized, as in fact we are."

[38] WA 6:370.10f.: "all alike spiritual priests before God"; WA 6:564.6f., 566.27 ("equally [*aequaliter*]"); WA 7:630.10: "Scripture makes us all equally priests"; WA 7:631.28: "all alike spiritual clerics"; WA 12:179.39: "equally [*ex aequo*]."

[39] WA 12:178.26f.; cf. WA 38:230.8: "our congenital, inherited priesthood"; WA 38:230.13ff.: "And this is why in the New Testament the Holy Spirit carefully avoided the name *sacerdos*, 'priest' or 'cleric,' nor gave it to any apostle. Rather, it is the name of the baptized or Christians only, as it were a congenital, inherited name from Baptism"; WA 38:230.26.

[40] WA 12:178.27f.

[41] WA 12:178.28ff.

[42] WA 41:457.10.

[43] WA 15:720.27ff.; cf. WA 8:252.30ff.; 12:317.6f. and 10f.; 41:207.2f.: "Therefore, as common as the name Christian is, so common also should the name priest be"; WA 41:207.30ff. and 37f.

[44] WA 8:253.26ff.; cf. also WA 7:31.33ff.; 7:633.12f.; 38:229.14ff.: "I say again, if we are not true priests already without the bishop and chrism, the bishop and his chrism will never make us true priests"; WA 38:230.17ff.; 41:208.7ff., 209.9f. and 24ff., 210.3f.: "The office, however, does not make me a priest, but I must be one already"; WA 6:407.25ff.: "For if there were not a consecration in us higher than that which the pope or bishop gives, a priest would never be made by a pope's and bishop's consecration, nor could one celebrate Mass nor preach nor absolve. . . ."

operation.[45] In arguing against this doctrine of consecration, Luther sees himself as the defender of baptismal grace.[46] The doctrine of the universal priesthood was supposed to return the glorious gift of Baptism to the light of day. While the Roman *ordo* falsely applied the priesthood to itself in two respects—namely, first, in the satisfactionary sense (thereby reducing and obscuring the priesthood of Christ) and, second, in the exclusive sense (thereby suppressing Baptism and negating and dissolving the priesthood of all Christians)—Luther implements a twofold project of purifying the *ordo*: he separates the *ordo* from the satisfactionary priesthood and gives it back to Christ, and he also unhitches it from the priesthood wrongly described as the true one and gives it back to all Christians. Thus everything is put in its proper place.[47]

2. Basis of the Universal Priesthood on Baptism and Faith

Luther first bases the universal priesthood simply on being a Christian. Whoever is in Christ is also a priest. But when it is asked further by what means being a Christian is constituted and where the universal priesthood is thus concretely grounded, two answers are found in Luther: Baptism and faith. Most of these statements occur in relation to *Baptism*. At first, in the polemical writings of the year 1520, but also later, Baptism is emphasized as the true priestly consecration.[48] Phrases such as "all of us,"[49] "each baptized person,"[50] "as many of us as are baptized"[51] support the idea of the priesthood, according to Luther,

[45] WA 38:227.20ff.: "But this most of all is one of the true abominations against love and blessed Baptism, that they claim in the holy church to make clerics with their chrism and consecration; that is a far, far higher and holier estate than Baptism gives, for a consecrated and chrismated cleric compared with other common, baptized Christians is like the morning star compared with a smoldering wick"; WA 38:229.10ff., 230.24ff.: "Behold, this is another thing . . . by which they have shamed, darkened, and weakened our Baptism and so shamefully and blasphemously suppressed and concealed our glorious, eternal, inborn, inherited priestly honor while they presented to us their dead, horrible chrism as so high and glorious that we had never feared and honored God Himself so highly as this worthless mask and Carnival play of theirs."

[46] WA 6:408.2ff.; 6:563.30f.; 38:230.8ff.: "May we not let this inborn and inherited priesthood be taken, hindered, or obscured, but rather let it be held out, proclaimed, and extolled with all honor so that it gives light and shines like the sun. . . ."

[47] Although Luther opposes the idea that the consecration makes a priest, it is not absolutely essential for him that the name "priest" for the bearer of the office should disappear. He is only concerned that the blurring of the office be eliminated. "It matters not what we are called, as long as the priestly dignity is allowed to remain in Christ, bequeathed to us by Baptism" (WA 41:211.3ff.). Thus, following a naturalized linguistic usage, he himself uses the word *sacerdos* or "priest" for the bearer of the office, e.g., WA 6:407.34ff., 408.19; 6:564.11ff. ("whom we call priests"); WA 17/1:511.5.

[48] *1520*: WA 6:407.22f., 408.11; 6:564.6f., 566.16f. *1523*: WA 12:178.26ff. *1533*: WA 38:229.29ff., 230.23f. *1535*: WA 41:207.26f.

[49] WA 6:407.22.

[50] WA 41:207.26.

[51] WA 6:564.6f.

belonging to the objective effects of Baptism. It is a component of the "unspeakable treasure" which is given in Baptism through water and God's Word.[52] When Luther, following Titus 3:5, calls Baptism the "washing of rebirth,"[53] one is to think at the same time of "rebirth as a priest." The priestly privilege and dignity belong to that which lies in Baptism *per sese*[54] and which is not simply categorically negated by the absence of true faith.[55] What Baptism promises and brings is "victory over the devil and death, forgiveness of sins, the grace of God, the whole Christ, and the Holy Spirit with His gifts,"[56] "for by these we are sanctified and saved."[57] Certainly the priesthood is included here. Being sanctified and saved means, of course, being in the communion of God and having free access to Him as His reconciled child. Having Christ and the Holy Spirit means nothing different. Since denying a baptized Christian the priesthood is equivalent for Luther to denigrating baptismal grace[58] and to shaming, obscuring, and weakening Baptism,[59] the priesthood is clearly regarded by him as an integral part of (objective) baptismal grace.

At the same time, Luther also bases the universal priesthood simply on *faith in Christ*; indeed, he identifies faith itself as the true priestly office.[60] He even uses the exclusive wording that "they alone are the holy and spiritual priesthood who are true Christians and built on the rock," that is, on faith in Christ.[61] "Whoever does not have faith is no priest."[62] Since Baptism and faith do not always accompany each other in actual practice—indeed, the unbelief of the baptized child or adult must always be taken into account—it is possible that someone could be baptized and yet, lacking faith, not be a priest. Thus the priesthood cannot be regarded as an *objective* gift of Baptism. This appears to contradict those statements of Luther in which he simply unites Baptism and the "new birth as priest."

The difficulty which emerges here thus concerns the relationship of Baptism and faith and must be resolved using the entire body of Luther's teaching on

---

52 WA 30/1:215.13f., 216.14f.

53 WA 30/1:215.19.

54 WA 30/1:216.14f. ("in itself").

55 WA 30/1:218–20, esp. 220.1ff.: "Therefore, it is conclusive that Baptism always remains proper and complete even if a man is only baptized and does not truly believe in addition."

56 WA 30/1:217.17ff.

57 WA 30/1:217.36f.

58 WA 6:563.30f.: ". . . with unbelievable harm to baptismal grace"; cf. WA 6:408.2ff.

59 WA 38:229.3f., 230.25f.

60 Cf. the passages indicated above on p. 27 n. 34, as well as WA 6:370.8, 371.22f.; 7:27.17ff.; 10/1.2:239.11ff. and 17; 11:96.25; 10/3:394.27ff., 395.5ff. and 31ff.; 12:523.5f.; 16:406.26ff.; 41:203.33f.

61 WA 12:307.22f.

62 WA 12:316.26f.; cf. WA 7:57.25: "These . . . are the offices of priests, which can be granted to no unbeliever." — H. Behm (*Der Begriff des allg. Priestertums* [Schwerin, 1912]) ignores such passages in Luther when he tries to see the universal priesthood in the sense of Luther's *allein* [alone] based on the *character indelebilis* [indelible character] of Baptism. Cf. p. 28: "All Christians have received the consecration of the priestly estate; not believers alone, but the priestly people of God. . . ."

Baptism. The objectivity of baptismal grace is clearly taught by Luther[63]—granted, only in connection with that other axiom that the spiritual gifts of God can only be appropriated to salutary effect *per fidem* [by faith]. Otherwise *sola fide* would fall and Baptism would work salvation *ex opere operato* [by the pure outward action]. The baptismal treasure is objective, independent of the baptized person's faith or lack of faith, through the Word in the water; it does not need faith first to bring it about. It is also brought to men objectively through the legitimate administration of Baptism according to its divine institution. The fact of Baptism leaves such an indelible impression on man that he can always return to his Baptism.[64] But "faith alone makes the person worthy to receive the salutary divine water *to his profit*";[65] "without faith it is unprofitable . . .";[66] "without faith it could not be taken hold of."[67] Faith is the organ by which the objective gift of Baptism is so apprehended that it may unfold its benefits and have its salutary effect. Applied to our question, this would mean: the priesthood is given objectively to every baptized person, but it has power and effect only on those who have faith. It might also be formulated thus: from the bare performance of Baptism, the baptized person receives the inauguration to the priesthood objectively (without respect to faith or lack of faith) while this inauguration is effected in his actual life only through faith.[68] In this way are satisfied both the concern with the objectivity and enduring power of Baptism which Luther so vigorously defends[69] and the *sola fide*. It will be necessary to have this understanding in mind as we interpret the uncritical inclusion of both ideas in many of Luther's statements on the universal priesthood: we all become priests through Baptism and through faith.[70] Luther sees Baptism and faith together. They both jointly—not one without the other—place a person into the spiritual priesthood. Thus

---

[63] WA 30/1:216.14f.: "in itself a divine, extraordinary treasure"; WA 30/1:220.1ff.; cf. WA 26:165.7ff.: "But whoever is baptized at God's Word and commandment, even if there is no faith, yet Baptism is true and certain, for it is done as God commanded it. It may not be profitable to the unbelieving candidate because of his unbelief, but it is not therefore wrong, uncertain, or nonexistent."

[64] WA 30/1:222.2: "The ship does not break."

[65] WA 30/1:216.10f.

[66] WA 39.1:216.13f.

[67] WA 30/1:216.25f.

[68] So also G. Niedermeier, op. cit., p. 350: "Every baptized person *can* become God's priest, but he is not one until he has faith." Nevertheless, Niedermeier is not giving God's objective act in Baptism its due.

[69] WA 30/1:219.3ff.

[70] Cf., e.g., WA 6:407.17ff.: "This all causes us to have one Baptism, one Gospel, one faith, and to be equal Christians, for Baptism, Gospel, and faith alone make spiritual and Christian people"; WA 8:253.26ff.: "priesthood . . . brought along from Baptism, shared by all Christians through faith"; WA 10/3:395.3ff.: "We are as much baptized as the pope is; we have the same God as he. So if I have Christ, I have his authority too. . . . For where there is faith, there follows all that is Christ's"; WA 41:207.28ff.: "For St. Peter is a priest because he became a believer in Christ, as am I. Thus we all . . . became children of the Priest in Baptism. Therefore, as common as the name Christian and child of God is (namely, to all who believe in Christ), so common should the name priest be, and be understood to be."

the statements that *all* the baptized are priests, as well as the other statements that whoever does not have faith is no priest, are to be viewed together in a higher unity. This much is certain in Luther's view: that "believer" who does not think Baptism is necessary is not in a Christian priesthood, for "whoever rejects Baptism rejects the Word of God, the faith, and Christ, who directs us and binds us to Baptism."[71] On the other hand, it is also certain that he who is baptized but does not believe the promise of salvation offered him in Baptism is not a priest in the full sense, at least not in the context of his life being lived out; for without faith he cannot take hold of what God has given him fundamentally in Baptism. Thus the proposition in Luther that *all* the baptized are priests may not be pressed so far that by it the necessity of faith is obscured, nor, conversely, may the proposition that unbelievers are not priests be pressed so far as to deny that, in Baptism, the inauguration into the priesthood is objectively given to all.

There is still a certain difficulty here for Luther's view of the office as being founded on the universal priesthood. By tying the priesthood to faith, the objectivity of the office, which is understood by Luther as the exercise of the priesthood, is endangered.[72] While Luther bases his rejection of Donatism not on an indelible priestly character imparted in Baptism and effective in faith but on God's Word and commandment that is inherently valid and effectual regardless of the unholiness of the minister,[73] he also reiterates that only a spiritual (= clerical) man—i.e., a priest—can do spiritual, priestly works, and the priesthood is prerequisite to the exercise of the office.[74]

3. The Universal Priesthood and the Authority of Word and Sacrament

To say that all Christians are priests is for Luther not merely to teach a spiritual estate of all Christians, in which all by Baptism and faith can have free access to the throne of God, offer spiritual sacrifices in Christ, and intercede before God on behalf of others. This is only the first and most basic element in Luther's understanding of the universal priesthood. To this is added a second crucial element: *the fundamental qualification, authorization, and power for every function of Word and Sacrament.*[75] We have found so far, as the content of the universal priesthood in Luther (and this is certainly the most foundational!),

---

[71] WA 30/1:216.3ff.; cf. WA 30/1:212.28ff., 215.36f.

[72] M. Schian already pointed out the difficulty here in "Das 'allgemeine Priestertum' und die kirchliche Praxis," in *Studien z. Reformationsgeschichte und z. Prakt. Theol., Festschrift for Kawerau* (Leipzig, 1917), pp. 126f. — Also cf. T. Harnack, *Die Kirche, ihr Amt, ihr Regiment* (1947), p. 48.

[73] WA 26:163.15ff., 165.32f.; 50:634.20ff.

[74] WA 12:186.1ff.; 38:229.14ff., 230.8ff. Cf. above, p. 28 n. 44.

[75] H. Storck, as a result of his study of the concept of the universal priesthood, identifies three topics encompassed by it in Luther: the immediate relationship of the Christian to God, the sacrifice of the Christian for one's neighbor, and the Christian's power to perform all the spiritual acts of the office (op. cit., p. 53). These are a natural consequence, as are the two elements emphasized here.

that it all depends on the internal realm and the individual's standing before God.[76] But Luther does not stop there. As Karl Holl shows,[77] he really expands the concept of the universal priesthood to include all the functions pertaining to the ecclesial office in the external order of the Church. With Luther, the universal priesthood is *also* the embodiment of the office of Word and Sacrament, the latter, according to Luther, proceeding from the former.[78] The question of the content of the universal priesthood causes Luther to make all Christians' spiritual estate prior and foundational and to see all the official functions of Word and Sacrament implicit in the universal priesthood.[79]

In *The Babylonian Captivity of the Church* (1520), Luther writes: "He who is a Christian has Christ; he who has Christ has all things which are in Christ and can do all things [*Qui Christianus est, Christum habet, qui Christum habet, omnia quae Christi sunt habet*]."[80] This sentence shows how both elements in Luther's concept of the universal priesthood are interrelated. The second depends on the first. Connection with Christ brings one into possession of all that is Christ's. "To have Christ through faith is equivalent to having all the riches of Christ."[81] The riches of Christ include above all the Word, the Sacraments, and the Keys, by which means salvation is effected. Every Christian, by virtue of his spiritual priesthood, by virtue of his connection with Christ, has the power over

---

[76] Cf. above, p. 24 n. 13.

[77] *Luther*, p. 318; also, p. 318 n. 5.

[78] F. J. Stahl's claim that Luther nowhere teaches "that the ministry of the Word is itself a component or product of the universal priesthood" (op. cit., p. 101) cannot be supported. Stahl can only be endorsed in the sense that Luther does not teach it so as to exclude the positive divine institution of the office (p. 101). Stahl believes Luther's doctrine of the universal priesthood can be summarized in the following two points: "The use which Luther makes of the idea of the universal priesthood is . . . only twofold. He uses it, first, to oppose the doctrine of a particular, personal quality and a particular estate of grace on the part of the cleric . . . and, second, to oppose the doctrine of a power (the Keys) imputed to the clergy alone. It is that essential similarity of Christians and that solidarity for divine authority which he derives from the universal priesthood" (p. 101). In the second point, however, the expression "solidarity for divine authority" does no justice to Luther. In Luther, the main focus is really on the equality of the factual authority held fundamentally among all Christians, on which Luther in a sense goes on to construct the whole concept of the office. Cf. our chapter 3, esp. the section on the *delegatio* by the congregation, below, pp. 62–69.

[79] Only the "ruling" or "feeding" of the congregation, which in Luther are clearly classified as functions of the office, do I find nowhere attributed to the universal priesthood. Yet it must be kept in mind that for Luther all ruling and feeding in the Church is done only by Word and Sacrament, and this function is only too clearly given to the universal priesthood. Cf. WA 6:440.34f.: "to rule the flock and congregation . . . with preaching and the Sacraments"; WA 6:564.23f.: "to feed, that is, to teach"; WA 12:387.5f.: ". . . to wield spiritual rule, that is, to preach and to provide for the Christian congregation."

[80] WA 6:567.29f.; cf. WA 12:523.4ff.: As God gave all power to Christ, "He has also placed us into the same power, that those who believe should have all power over heaven and earth."

[81] Cf. WA 2:208.25ff.: "Faith has with it all the things which follow faith: the Keys, the Sacraments, the power, and everything else"; WA 10/3:120.12f.; 10/3:213.18f.; 10/3:394.26ff.; 12:307.23ff.: "For since Christ is the Bridegroom and we are the bride, the bride has all that the Bridegroom has, even His own body. For when He gives Himself to the bride, He gives Himself to her in all that He is . . ."; WA 15:720.10f.; 16:406.26ff.

these riches; he is *omnia potens* [one having power over all]. In this way Luther comes to the statement: "Let him therefore be certain and acknowledge himself, whoever acknowledges that he is a Christian, *that we are equally priests, that is, that we have the same power in Word and Sacrament*."[82] The concept of the priesthood in Luther is also filled with this very power over Word and Sacrament. In another passage it says, "If I call you a Christian, I am also saying by the same token that you are a priest and have the power *to administer the Sacraments*, to intercede before God, and to judge doctrine."[83]

Again, in the treatise *To the Christian Nobility of the German Nation* (1520), the expression that all Christians are of the spiritual estate is directly connected with the other statement that they are all fundamentally qualified for the functions of the office. When Luther says, "Anyone who has been baptized can declare that he has been consecrated a priest, bishop, and pope,"[84] attention should be given to this sequence of the three concepts of priest, bishop, and pope. Luther means to say not only that every Christian has been given the spiritual estate by Baptism (though that is, of course, fundamental) but also—as implied by the other two concepts of bishop and pope—that the very thing which had previously been reserved for priests, bishops, and pope (the power of Word and Sacrament) belongs to everyone who is baptized.[85] Being baptized means having the power of Word and Sacrament, although the actual use of this power is another question. There is no other distinction among laity, priests, princes, and bishops besides the actual exercise of the function; with respect to their qualification and authorization they are all equally "truly priests, bishops, and popes."[86] This idea is also presupposed in Luther's appeal to temporal power for the work of the Reformation. Rulers, too, are members of the Body of Christ by virtue of their Baptism. As all members are to serve one another, each by his peculiar work, rulers are also to

---

[82] WA 6:566.26ff. The stipulation "yet no one is allowed to use the same except by consent of the congregation or by the calling of one greater [*verum non licere quenquam hac ipsa uti nisi consensu communitatis aut vocatione majoris*]" does not negate the prefixed principle. The *potestas in verbo et sacramentis* [power of Word and Sacraments] is already given in the universal priesthood. The use of this *potestas* is another question which is beyond our scope here. Also cf. WA 6:407.30f.: "who all have the same power"; WA 6:408.15; 10/1.2:239.18: "Every Christian has the same power that the bishops, clerics, and monks have"; WA 10/1.2:239.28f.: "while we all have this power" (yet this is followed by the same limitation of the public use of this power to those who are called); WA 10/3:170.24ff., 171.5ff.; 10/3:398.37ff.; 12:309.7: "one does not have more power than another"; WA 12:309.20f.: ". . . no distinction of power"; WA 15:720.32f.: "If we are" (i.e., priests), "we have power to speak the Word of God, to baptize, as women also do, which is the office of a priest . . ."; WA 15:720.37f.; 8:248.2ff.: "It is well-known what kind of power the priesthood entails, namely, to preach, say Mass, administer the Sacrament, and use the Keys of heaven"; WA 8:253.34: "The name" (priest), "with all its power and privilege and whatever pertains thereto, is shared by us all."

[83] WA 15:720.27ff.; cf. WA 12:522.21f., 524.10.

[84] WA 6:408.11f.; the concession "although not everyone is fit to exercise this office" (WA 6:408.12f.) lies primarily outside the domain of fundamentals. Cf. above, n. 82.

[85] Also cf. M. Schian, op. cit., pp. 125f.

[86] WA 6:408.29; also WA 6:409.5ff.: "A shoemaker, a smith, and a peasant each have the office and work of their trade and yet are all equally consecrated priests and bishops. . . ."

do so by exercising against evildoers the office of punishment and the sword entrusted to them by God. They are to let their work proceed free and unhindered against all the guilty, including bishop and pope, and according to their power they are to curb corruption even in the church, if pope and bishops use their power to injure and offend Christians rather than to correct them. But fundamental for Luther in all this is the acknowledgment that those who bear the power of rule also stand in the universal priesthood on the basis of their Baptism and are therefore "fellow priests, fellow clerics, having power with the others in all things."[87]

In the treatise *Misuse of the Mass* (1521), Luther wishes to show "that the only proper and true preaching office, like the priesthood and offering of sacrifices, is shared by all Christians," and he cites 2 Cor. 3:6 in support of this.[88] The apostle's words are "addressed to all Christians, that he might make them all ministers of the Spirit."[89] Luther has the same understanding of 1 Pet. 2:9 and 1 Cor. 14:27ff., esp. v. 31. Of course, for the sake of order, all men cannot and should not preach, but that does not negate their fundamental right to do so: "although they have all power."[90] All Christians, according to John 6:45, are taught by God, and "all certainly have the Spirit and the Word of God,"[91] and they, too, are included in Luke 10:16: "Whoever hears you, hears Me."[92] Even women, whom Paul forbade to speak in the congregation in accordance with Gen. 3:16, nevertheless have the fundamental right to preach by virtue of their priesthood, which in certain situations can even become operational.[93] From Scripture Luther is completely sure "that there is no more than one office of preaching God's Word, shared by all Christians, so that each person might speak, preach, and judge, and the others are all obliged to listen."[94]

In his treatise to the Bohemians, *Concerning the Ministry* (1523), Luther demonstrates in very explicit terms how the priesthood given in Baptism includes the functions relating to Word and Sacrament. There Luther unfolds the concept of the priesthood in the particular *officia sacerdotalia* [priestly duties] and enumerates seven: [1] teaching, preaching, and proclaiming the Word of God; [2] baptizing; [3] consecrating or administering the Eucharist; [4] binding and loosing sins; [5] praying for others; [6] offering sacrifices; and [7] judging the doctrines and spirits of all men.[95] These priestly functions are all shared by every Christian. Luther demonstrates this with regard to each.

---

87 WA 6:413.27ff., 408.8ff., 409.31ff., 410.3ff.

88 WA 8:495.12f.

89 WA 8:495.16f.; cf. WA 8:488.33ff.

90 WA 8:495.25, 497.25: "although each one has the power to preach."

91 WA 8:497.7; also cf. WA 17/1:509.3ff.

92 WA 8:496.20ff.

93 WA 8:498.13f.

94 WA 8:498.15ff. — Cf. Harleß, *Kirche und Amt nach luth. Lehre* (Stuttgart, 1853), pp. 14–16.

95 WA 12:180.2ff.

The first and highest priestly work is the proclamation of the *Word*.[96] That the *verbi ministerium* [ministry of the Word] is shared by all Christians is taught preeminently in 1 Pet. 2:9.[97] Those who have been called from darkness to light are not merely the "tonsured and chrismated masks [*rasae et unctae larvae*]," but all Christians, and the "proclamation of the virtues of God" which is here directed at Christians is surely "nothing other than the preaching of the Word of God."[98] The interjection which Hieronymus Emser and others made in the explanation of this passage—that a twofold priesthood should be distinguished, the *spirituale et commune* [spiritual one shared by all] and the *speciale et externum* [particular, external one], and that Peter is speaking here only of the former—is countered by Luther's assertion that the work of the particular and external priesthood (i.e., the ecclesial office) is predominantly to proclaim the *virtutes dei*, but what Peter says here is addressed to all Christians in the universal priesthood. Thus the particular priesthood is at its core no different from the universal priesthood.[99] Here Luther expressly rejects the idea of a distinction between the proclamation in the ministry of the Word and the universal proclamation of the *virtutes dei* according to 1 Pet. 2:9.[100] "There is no priesthood other than the spiritual one shared by all men."[101] In the institution of the Holy Supper, the Verba ("This do in My remembrance") are spoken not only to those who have been tonsured and chrismated, but to all Christians, and this remembrance is simply "preaching the Word," proclaiming the Lord's death (1 Cor. 11:26); thus Christ would, by these words addressed to all Christians,

[96] WA 12:180.5ff.: "First . . . and greatest of all, on which all else depends, is teaching the Word of God. For by the Word we teach, by the Word we consecrate, by the Word we bind and loose, by the Word we baptize, by the Word we offer sacrifices, through the Word we judge all things." Cf. above, p. 11 n. 52.

[97] WA 12:180.17ff. On the idea that all have the power to preach, cf. WA 10/3:170.24ff., 171.5f.; 10/3:395.31 and 39, 396.7ff., 397.16f.; 11:411ff.; 12:309.16ff., 318.25ff.; 41:212.24ff.

[98] WA 12:180.20ff.; also cf. WA 8:253.8ff. — In his exposition of 1 Peter (1523), Luther clarifies the proclamation of the *virtutes dei* from 1 Pet. 2:9 in such a way that in it one should properly see only the (private) promise of God's Word from one brother to another and the public proclamation to *such* as do not yet know the wonderful light to which Christians are called. The statement "It belongs to a priest that he is God's messenger and has the command from God to proclaim His Word" (WA 12:318.25f.) is followed by the example: "And your sermons should be preached in such a way that one brother proclaims to another the mighty acts of God, how you have been delivered by Him from sin, hell, and death, and from all adversity, and called to eternal life. In the same way, you should teach other people how they, too, may come to this light. For it is all directed to the intent that you may know what God has done for you and may consider your most important work to be to preach this publicly and to call everyone to that light to which you have been called. Where you see people who do not know it, you should instruct them and also teach them as you have learned . . ." (WA 12:318.29ff.). However, these restrictions are not discernible in the exposition of this passage in his treatise to the Bohemians [*Concerning the Ministry*].

[99] WA 12:180.20ff.

[100] WA 12:180.29f., 189.40ff.

[101] WA 12:180.31f.; also cf. WA 7:634.13ff.

be applying the ministry of the Word equally to all.[102] Even 1 Cor. 14:26 ("each one") and v. 31 ("you can all prophesy") are addressed not merely to some Christians but "to the whole Church and to every Christian."[103] In these passages it is for Luther most clearly stated that there is only one office of the Word in the Church, and it is shared by all Christians.[104] The same goes for the other priestly works. That Baptism, at least in cases of emergency, can be performed by all Christians is universally acknowledged.[105] From this universal right to perform emergency Baptism, Luther concludes that all Christians—even women—are priests "even without tonsures and the episcopal character," who are authorized and qualified for all the functions relating to Word and Sacrament. "Therefore, women also, when they baptize, are fundamentally carrying out the office, and that not in a private action, but in the public and ecclesial ministry belonging to the priest alone."[106] Likewise, according to Luther the administration of the Holy Supper, the power to consecrate, is common to all, for Christ says the words "This do" to all His people both "present and future" who would eat this bread and drink this cup. "Whatever, then, was given there was given to all."[107] When Paul writes in 1 Cor. 11:23 that what he received from the Lord he delivered to the Corinthians, he had in mind all the Christians in Corinth, "making them all such as he himself was, i.e., consecrators."[108] The power to consecrate, incidentally, is for Luther the lesser (*id quod minus est*) compared to the power of proclaiming the Word and baptizing (*id quod majus est*). If the latter has been given to all, then the former has properly been given first.[109] The same applies in Luther's view to the *binding and loosing of sins*. "All of us who are Christians have this office of the Keys in common."[110] In Matt. 18:18, all Christians are addressed; the power to bind and loose is given to them all.[111] Likewise, praying for others is assigned to all.[112] Christians' priestly *sacrifice* is related not to the sacrifice of the Mass but to the spiritual sacrifices which are offered through the Word, which is shared by all—for which reason it, too, must be the sacrifice.[113] Luther places special stress in this connection on the right to judge doctrine, which he nevertheless teaches as being given to all Christians.[114] On the basis of

[102] WA 12:180.33ff., 181.5f.: "Christ here confers the ministry of the Word on all alike and equally."

[103] WA 12:181.11f.

[104] WA 12:181.15ff. and 17ff.; also cf. WA 8:496.4ff.

[105] WA 12:171.18f., 181.23f.

[106] WA 12:181.30ff.; cf. WA 12:182.36ff.

[107] WA 12:182.25ff.

[108] WA 12:182.32f.

[109] WA 12:183.12ff.

[110] WA 12:183.30f.

[111] WA 12:183.32ff., 184.11ff.; also cf. WA 8:173.28.

[112] WA 12:186.21ff.

[113] WA 12:185.16ff. and 34ff.; cf. also WA 12:308.11ff.

[114] WA 12:188.29ff.

John 10:27; Matt. 7:15; and other passages which warn against false prophets, he concludes that every Christian is a "most free judge of all those who teach him, being taught inwardly by God alone."[115] This is again supported by reference to 1 Cor. 14:30ff., according to which we "can all prophesy one by one," which includes the ability to judge doctrine.[116]

All these priestly works are thus ascribed to all Christians, and thus all have the full priesthood. So because priests in the particular ecclesial office have no different duties from all those held in common,[117] neither do they have any "different priesthood from laymen"—or else other duties are designated for them (as in Rome), but this results in a *sacerdotium Satanae* [priesthood of Satan].[118] Thus Luther showed that there is only the one priesthood shared by all Christians, which possesses all the power of Word and Sacrament. The particular office thus appears only as a usage of the power of the function of Word and Sacrament already possessed fundamentally in the universal priesthood.[119] The

---

[115] WA 12:188.15f.; cf. WA 12:188.17ff.: "Therefore, let everyone teach what he teaches. You must see to your own supreme peril or convenience what you believe"; and WA 12:188.38ff.: "A Christian is so certain as to what he should believe and not believe that he would even die for it, or at least be ready to die." Also cf. WA 11:410.13ff.

[116] WA 12:188.20ff. — On the right to judge doctrine, cf. esp. the treatise *That a Christian Assembly Has the Right to Judge All Teaching*, from 1523 (WA 11:408ff.). Here esp. WA 11:409.20ff. Cf. further WA 6:412.20ff.: "Besides, we are all priests. . . . All have the same faith, the same Gospel, the same Sacrament. How, then, shall we not also have the power to test and judge what is right or wrong in the faith?"; WA 6:412.32f.; 8:496.4ff.; 10/2:217.14ff.: "Discerning and judging doctrine belongs to each and every Christian, and it belongs in such a way that if anyone infringes on this right one whit, let him be accursed"; WA 10/3:173.33ff.: ". . . Judgment is granted to every Christian personally so that such power is not human, but we have been divinely given power to assess and judge all things"; WA 10/3:174.31ff.; 15:720.29. — E. Sommerlath has pointed out that Luther, in granting the right to judge doctrine to every Christian, primarily means the ability to distinguish the voice of the Good Shepherd from that of the false prophets (one might incidentally compare the following passage: "Not only the whole flock of sheep but also every individual sheep for himself has the right and power to flee from wolves wherever it can," WA 53:245.5ff.) and that he asserts this right with an eye to the state of emergency in which the congregations actually stood ("Amt und allg. Priestertum," pp. 76f.). Yet it must be remembered that, in Luther's sense, the right to judge doctrine is not merely a right in case of emergency, but a Christian's fundamental right which, while manifested only in cases of emergency, is nevertheless given fundamentally with the universal priesthood.

[117] Cf. WA 12:189.40ff.: "We firmly hold that there is no other Word of God than that which all Christians are commanded to proclaim, there is no other Baptism than that which every Christian is able to confer, there is no other remembrance of the Lord's Supper than that wherein any Christian is able to make what Christ instituted to make, that there is no other sin than that which any Christian may bind and loose. . . ." However, when Luther explicitly emphasizes the works of the particular office as being no different from these *officia sacerdotalia* of the universal priesthood, which he has shown to be shared by all, Brunotte disregards it so that his critique does not answer R. Josefson and J. Heubach (op. cit., p. 83 n. 63).

[118] WA 12:189.28ff.

[119] Cf. WA 12:189.34ff.: "For to bear such fruits publicly or privately does not demonstrate different priesthoods, but different uses of the same priesthood." — Also, Brunotte repeatedly notes in his interpretation of Luther's thought process in writing *Concerning the Ministry* that Luther proves that there is only one priesthood fundamentally shared by all Christians, whether they are in the

man wielding it is not to be referred to as a priest in the particular sense, but only as a minister.[120]

We have accordingly shown how, in these foundational writings of the earliest period of the Reformation, Luther sees all the functions of the office of Word and Sacrament implicit in the universal priesthood, which qualifies every Christian, and in doing so abolishes the distinction between the functions of the particular ecclesial office and of the universal priesthood. It must be further noted that, even in later years, Luther never retracted the basic tenets of his doctrine of the office which he laid out here.

It is therefore incumbent on us at this point to note especially the forceful way in which Luther here *teaches the power of the Keys in particular as the universal property of every believing Christian.* To this end, a few testimonies from various years:

> *1520*: It is "quite obvious that the Keys are not given only to St. Peter but to the whole congregation."[121] *1522*: ". . . Here the Gospel clearly states that we may all absolve."[122] "Thus wherever a Christian has faith, he may absolve, preach, and do all other things which belong to a priest. . . . I have just as much power to forgive and absolve sins as the pope. And we should not let this power be taken away from us, but stand firm on it."[123] *1523*: (on John 20:21) "And this power is given not only to clerics, although the apostles are being addressed, but to all believers. . . . This power is in the mouth of every Christian spiritually."[124] "This is a power which every Christian has."[125] *1526*: (on John 20:22f.) "All Christians are here given this power." Pope, bishops, clerics, and monks "say publicly and unashamedly that this power is given to them alone and not to the laity also. But Christ speaks here of neither clerics nor monks but says, 'Receive the Holy Spirit.' Whoever has the Holy Spirit, this power is given to him, that is, to him who is a Christian. But who is a Christian? He who believes; and whoever believes has the

---

particular office or not (op. cit., pp. 84, 88, 92, 93). By doing so, however, he contradicts his own oft-repeated assertion that in Luther the particular office is not derived from the universal priesthood, it is only elevated and distinguished from the other functions of the universal priesthood by the fact that in it the function of the universal priesthood is carried out publicly in the congregation. Additionally, the passage WA 12:191.37 (". . . from ourselves, who have already been born and called to such ministry by Baptism without such [episcopal] election") illustrates how we believe, contrary to Brunotte (op. cit., p. 90 n. 104), that in the baptismal call of the universal priesthood, Luther sees a call, including a call in a fundamental sense, to the ministry of Word and Sacrament in the public office since for him the particular office is only a particular function of the universal priesthood. Yet Luther does not mean to say—and here we agree with Brunotte—that "the call to the spiritual office . . . *is rendered superfluous* by the universal priesthood" (ibid.).

120 WA 12:190.11ff.

121 WA 6:417.37f. ("the whole congregation" in Luther's sense means all believing Christians); cf. WA 6:309.29f.

122 WA 10/3:394.23; also WA 10/3:394.20f.

123 WA 10/3:395.31ff.; also WA 10/3:395.24f. and 28f., 398.35ff.; also cf. WA 10/3:215.17ff., 216.17f.

124 WA 11:96.19ff. and 36ff.

125 WA 11:97.24f.; cf. WA 12:521.35ff., 522.27ff.

Holy Spirit. Therefore, every Christian has the power which the pope, bishops, priests, and monks have—in this case to retain or release sins."[126] *1530*: "Now this much is certain, that Christ gave the Keys not only to the bishops but to His dear Church. . . ."[127] *1536*: "We have power to speak the Absolution, but because He instituted it and gave it to the ministers of the church, apostles, and adherents and to all. . . ."[128] *1540*: (on John 20:21) "The Lord, through the public office, committed to called ministers and to each person privately that they should comfort one another and speak to each other . . ." (the Absolution).[129] "There" (in the words of John 20:21, "I send you") "Christ sanctified us all and made us priests."[130] "Christ instituted it so that as everyone should speak to his neighbor in the name of Christ, Christ would do it."[131]

This survey shows how Luther always taught the Office of the Keys as given jointly to all Christians in the universal priesthood. The power of the Keys belongs not only to the congregation as a whole but explicitly to each individual member of it. "The Keys belong to the whole Church *and to all its members by right as well as by use*, and in every way. . . ."[132] While in other cases Luther strictly distinguishes between *jus* and *usus*, teaching that only the former is given indiscriminately to all Christians in the universal priesthood,[133] this distinction is omitted with respect to the Keys. The opposing argument that springs from the idea that "the right of the Keys belongs to the Church but the use thereof to the bishops" is expressly rejected as frivolous: "Christ here gives the right *and the use* of the Keys to any Christian."[134] The words of Matt. 18:17ff. are addressed "to all absolutely and generally."[135] Still, it should be noted that Luther grants the use of the Keys to all Christians only insofar as by it the administration of the

[126] WA 10/1.2:239.11ff. ("according to the following, only the *public* exercise of this power remains limited to those chosen by the congregation").

[127] WA 30/2:437.21ff.; cf. WA 30/2:456.26, 490.16, 503.38f.

[128] WA 41:543.17ff.; also WA 41:543.13f. and 32. *1538*: WA 38:630.12ff.

[129] WA 49:139.22f.; cf. WA 49:140.6f.: "I am sent, and so is every pastor and every Christian."

[130] WA 49:141.5f.

[131] WA 49:140.39f.; cf. WA 44:713.6f. — E. Sommerlath writes: "Regarding Absolution, Luther, as we know, made many statements assigning the right of loosing to every Christian. However, many of the examples he cites involve the comforting of brethren, the *consolatio fraterna*, in which a Christian, in pastoral discourse, consoles his brother with the comfort of divine grace . . ." ("Amt u. allg. Priestertum," p. 76). This is certainly true. Yet it should not be overlooked that it is the authority for special *absolution* which Luther repeatedly and explicitly grants to every Christian.

[132] WA 12:184.21f.

[133] Cf., e.g., WA 10/3:397.16f.: "We all have the authority to preach, but not all of us should use it"; WA 25:16.23f.: "Christians all have the priesthood, but not all have the function, although all can teach"; also WA 8:250.31ff., 253.8ff. and 29ff.; 8:424.24ff.

[134] WA 12:184.3f. (Matt. 18:17f. is meant); cf. WA 12:184.8: with the "sit tibi" Christ "not only gives the right but commits the use and exercise."

[135] WA 12:184.23; cf. WA 12:184.27ff.: "in which" (i.e., the cited passages, esp. Matthew 18) "the fullest right and most present use of binding and loosing is established, unless we would deny Christ Himself the right or use of the Keys when He is dwelling in the midst of two."

Keys by the spiritual estate is not compromised,[136] i.e., insofar as it is actually exercised only in case of emergency[137] or in the private sphere.[138] We will have cause to return to this later.

Thus the concept of the universal priesthood in Luther, taken as a whole, finds its significance in the fact that in spiritual matters all Christians are fundamentally *able* to do all things and that there is therefore no differentiation with respect to their spiritual *potential.*

4. Every Christian's Right and Duty Derived from the Universal Priesthood

With the spiritual priesthood gained from Baptism, every Christian, according to Luther, has the fundamental *right* to administer the Word and Sacraments, even if the actual exercise of this right is still bound by certain additional requirements.[139] Luther's doctrine strongly emphasizes this fundamental right—for which the term "power," "authority," or "potency" may also be used[140]—signifying a fundamental authorization, received from God in

---

[136] Cf. WA 38:630.9ff.

[137] *1519*: "For this power to forgive sins is nothing other than a priest saying, Yes, it is necessary for every Christian man to be able to say to the other: . . . Be of good cheer, your sins are forgiven you. . . . In the New Testament every Christian man has it" (i.e., the power of the Keys) "when a priest is not present, by the promise of Christ . . ." (WA 2:722.16ff. and 36ff.); "Since" (namely, in Matthew 16 and 18) "He" (Christ) "is speaking to the whole Church, and to each Christian individually" (WA 2:723.1f.). *1529*: WA 28:470.23. *1536*: ". . . placed His word in your mouth in time of need" (WA 41:543.17ff.). *1540*: "In time of need or peril of death, they" (i.e., all Christians) "can all encourage each other" (WA 49:139.7f.).

[138] WA 10/1.2:239.28ff. Cf. more detailed discussion below, pp. 52–54 and 113–15.

[139] Cf. WA 8:253.34ff.; 41:209.18ff., 213.16f.: "An office is only assigned, but the right belongs to all Christians" (Rörer). — Cf. M. Schian, op. cit., p. 120; W. Elert, *Morphologie des Luthertums* I (Munich, 1952), p. 298. The fundamental right and ability to dispense the office and the actual warrant to exercise the same publicly in the congregation must be kept separate. This would be endorsed here by H. Behm, who stressed that Luther in no way uses the concept of the universal priesthood to teach an undifferentiated, universal ecclesial warrant for all Christians to minister (op. cit., pp. 17f.). That would be a misunderstanding of Luther's statements, as though he granted every Christian the administration of the ecclesial office by virtue of the universal priesthood (p. 17); the universal priesthood, according to Luther, would only give the fundamental "personal qualification" for the office (p. 19). Behm also notes that many passages in Luther clearly have the tone of a "canonical view of the universal priesthood" (p. 39 n. 12). In these there is expressed an awareness of the *fundamental* right to dispense Word and Sacrament derived from the universal priesthood, an idea Luther strongly emphasized (cf. below, pp. 62–69). Rudolph Sohm, on the other hand, overlooks Luther's teaching of the fundamental right of every Christian derived from the universal priesthood when he writes: "The universal priesthood does not confer a single legal warrant" (*Kirchenrecht* I [1892], p. 511 and elsewhere).

[140] WA 6:566.28 ("power [*potestas*]"); WA 6:567.30 ("*potens*"); WA 8:253.35 ("authority, right, and property"); WA 8:423.2 ("power [*potestas*]"); WA 8:495.32 ("authority and power"); WA 8:497.25 ("authority"); WA 10/1.2:239.11, 18, and 29 ("authority"); WA 10/3:395.6 ("power"); WA 10/3:395.4 and 35 ("authority"); WA 10/3:398.10 and 15 ("authority"); WA 11:412.6 ("right and

Baptism, for all functions relating to Word and Sacrament. In the argument for this teaching, two explanatory thought processes clearly emerge. First, Luther assumes that, according to generally acknowledged church teaching, every Christian is able to administer Baptism in cases of emergency. How could he do so if the spiritual capacity for the function of Word and Sacrament were tied to a special consecration or to the possession of the particular ecclesial office? This is possible on a fundamental basis since in his view the spiritual capacity for it is already given in Baptism. "*For this reason* everyone is able to baptize and absolve in cases of necessity, which would not be possible if we were not all priests," writes Luther in *To the Christian Nobility of the German Nation* (1520).[141] As already mentioned, he uses the same argument in his treatise to the Bohemians [*Concerning the Ministry*] (1523).[142] If the power and right to the functions of the office in Word and Sacrament are present in cases of necessity, they are fundamentally present and intrinsic in the Christian estate already given.[143] The other explanatory thought process makes reference to the aforementioned scriptural examples of instances when the use of the Word is blessed without a particular call. Luther points especially to Apollos (Acts 18:24ff.), who "without any call and ordination" enjoyed such blessing in his work, and asks, "By what right, I ask, does this man discharge the ministry of the Word except by that general and common right?"[144] He says the same of Stephen and Philip, who were called only to the *ministerium mensae* [ministry of the table], and of the eunuch from Acts 8 who preached at home "by no right except that of his Baptism and faith."[145] Certainly Luther does not overlook the particular circumstances of such teaching activity without a particular call, nor does he use these biblical examples to dispute in any way the necessity of the particular call for exercising the function of Word and Sacrament in the congregational office. He only draws from them the idea that every Christian by Baptism and faith must already be given a fundamental right and capacity for the function of Word and Sacrament. How else would Apollos and the others mentioned be able, without a particular call and consecration, to do what Scripture so plainly describes them doing? They could do so only on the basis of the *jus generale et commune* [general and common right] derived from the universal priesthood.

---

power"); WA 11:412.31 ("power and right"); WA 12:188.28 ("we are able [*possumus*]"); WA 25:16.24 ("be able [*posse*]"); WA 41:211.16 ("right and power").

141 WA 6:408.1f.

142 WA 12:181.30ff.; cf. above, p. 37.

143 Another view of emergency Baptism is given by F. J. Stahl: "That exercise of the power incumbent upon every Christian in case of emergency is to be seen not as a return to the natural exercise of the universal priesthood but as an extraordinary call to the exercise of the office" (*Die Kirchenverfassung*, etc. [1862], p. 112). Likewise, T. Harnack, *Die Kirche, ihr Amt, ihr Regiment* (reprint, 1947), p. 48 (Thesis 100). Cf. P. Althaus, *Die chr. Wahrheit* II (1948), p. 298; and E. Sommerlath, "Amt u. allg. Priestertum," p. 56.

144 WA 12:191.38ff.

145 WA 12:192.8ff. and 22.

A certain difficulty for the assertion of indistinct fundamental right and capacity for the function of Word and Sacrament among all Christians lies in the fact that obviously not all are suited for it. If all have the fundamental spiritual capacity, one would expect that they also have the practical capacity, and so the required gifts, and are equipped for it. But this is not the case, as Luther often notes himself.[146] For instance, he refers to women and children, who while able to "hear God's Word and receive Baptism, the Sacrament, and Absolution" and who are also "true, holy fellow Christians, as St. Peter says," are nevertheless unfit for the teaching office.[147] With respect to the fact that not all have the practical capacity for the function of Word and Sacrament, Luther here comes involuntarily to divide the first element in his understanding of the universal priesthood—namely, that all Christians are holy and in a spiritual estate before God—from the second—that all are fundamentally authorized to exercise the official functions of Word and Sacrament—and states that the latter is not a universal property with respect to practical ability. Yet he fails to draw the principal consequences from this and to reformulate his teaching of the universal priesthood accordingly. Thus we are left with Luther teaching a *fundamental* spiritual, but not practical, capacity for the function of Word and Sacrament among all Christians arising from the universal priesthood—a *fundamental* right to it, but not one which is practically exercisable. This is a paradoxical element.

As we have often observed, the initiating command of Christ to proclaim the Gospel and to administer the Keys and the Sacraments is related by Luther to all Christians.[148] Thus Luther adds to the teaching of every Christian's fundamental right to dispense Word and Sacrament that of the fundamental *duty* to do so.[149] He finds this duty especially valid with respect to the proclamation of the Word, to preaching, for which 1 Pet. 2:9 is again cited: "Accordingly, we all have the power to preach. Indeed, we *must* preach God's name, and we are commanded to, as St. Peter says."[150] Yet it is evident on closer inspection that Luther, in referring to the duty laid on every Christian to preach, does not essentially mean the public proclamation among Christians but rather the individual's

---

146 Cf. below, pp. 59–62.

147 WA 50:633.12ff.; cf. WA 8:497.19ff.

148 Cf. WA 12:180.20ff., 182.27 and 32f., 183.12ff., 184.11ff.

149 WA 38:254.3ff.: "Thus they must certainly have the power and right to preach, baptize, give the Sacrament, forgive sins, etc. Indeed, they are hereby commanded to do so"; WA 8:423.27f.: "All Christians have the right and duty to teach"; WA 12:189.14f. (regarding the *officia sacerdotalis* incumbent on every Christian): "For we are dealing here not with preference or permission but with command and necessity."

150 WA 10/3:170.24ff.; cf. WA 8:422.36ff.: "What Christian has not been called out of darkness? And his is both the right and the power—indeed, the necessity—to preach the mighty power of the One calling him"; WA 12:180.22f.: "Peter gives them not merely the right but even the command to proclaim the mighty works of God, which without doubt is nothing other than to preach the Word of God . . ."; WA 11:412.11ff.: "So that here again it is certain that a Christian has not only the right and power to teach the Word of God, but is indebted to do so or forfeit his soul and incur the wrath of God." — Luther especially stresses the duty of all to judge doctrine; cf. WA 11:411.4ff.: ". . . so that they not only have the power and right to judge everything that is preached but also are indebted to judge it, or else incur the disfavor of the divine Majesty"; WA 12:189.12ff. Cf. K. Holl, *Luther*, p. 319.

personal testimony of the faith, especially before those who do not believe.[151] In this regard, the vocation in which an individual lives plays an additional role for Luther.[152] The duty to proclaim the Word is not open-ended, but exists for the individual in the realm of his vocation, and so for the housefather in his family and domestic community.[153] It will therefore be necessary in Luther to distinguish the fundamental sphere from the practical with respect to the duty of discharging the function of Word and Sacrament. If the *officia sacerdotalia* in Word and Sacrament are fundamentally conveyed to every Christian in the universal priesthood, then—regardless of the duty to testify to the faith personally, which is always a practical one—they become tangible, practical duties only according to the boundaries of the particular vocation which is bestowed on the individual or is bestowed in an emergency situation. Therefore, the teaching of each Christian's fundamental duty to discharge the function of Word and Sacrament deriving from the universal priesthood does not at its core conflict with the existence and necessity of the particular office.[154]

5. The Idea of the Equality of All Christians on the Basis of the Universal Priesthood

The rights and duties of every Christian are equal on a fundamental level since all have the same priesthood and are *ex aequo* [equally] priests.[155] The same

[151] WA 12:521.19ff.: "This is the first and highest work of love that a Christian is to do when he has begun to believe—that he bring others to the faith, even as I have come to it"; WA 12:521.36f.: ". . . commanded all Christians to confess their faith publicly and to bring others to the faith"; WA 12:522.5ff. and 21ff., 523.1ff. and 22ff.; 17/1:509.4ff.: "Every Christian who is baptized and believes receives the Holy Spirit. He now has the power to preach, and it is every Christian's duty to confess God and His Word by mouth, and his own faith, for which reason a Christian should not be silent, but rather speak the Word of God." Nevertheless, Luther distinguishes this proclamation in matter and content as a personal testimony of faith from one man to another, not occurring before the congregation on behalf of the office, which introduces an element of lack of clarity into his teaching.

[152] "Vocation" [*Beruf*], here in the sense of a call to a specific estate in life.

[153] WA 17/1:509.11ff.: "Parents have the duty to teach their children and family with their own mouth. In so doing, parents exercise the office of preacher. If he does this, therefore, he is a priest and bishop. No one should preach the Word unless he is commanded. Parents are commanded; therefore, they are certain that they please God; therefore, all parents have a certain vocation, and it goes well if they teach in faith"; cf. WA 32:303.26ff.; 30/1:392.4ff.; 12:171.17.

[154] Cf. in greater detail below, p. 59. Regarding the concrete limitation of the fundamental right given with the universal priesthood and of the fundamental duty to dispense Word and Sacrament, Brunotte's critique (op. cit., p. 151ff.) of H. Storck's formulations on "the Christian's empoweredness to carry out every spiritual action of the office" is right, but in Brunotte it is not always clear that according to Luther the universal priesthood holds within it the fundamental power to dispense Word and Sacrament even as occurs in the concrete office. Also cf. what was said above, pp. 38–39 n. 119.

[155] WA 12:179.39; cf. WA 41:209.6f.: ". . . Because of the priesthood we are all equal." — The idea of the spiritual equality of all Christians in Luther is examined in detail by F. Lezius, "Gleichheit und Ungleichheit, Aphorismen zur Theologie und Staatsanschauung Luthers," in *Greifswalder Studien*

Baptism, the same Gospel, the same faith produce the same rights, the same power, the same ability.[156] Every differentiation in the sphere of spiritual being is rejected by Luther and abruptly asserted to be the *eadem potestas* [same power] over Word and each Sacrament.[157] The distinctions among Christians related to their different gifts and charisms, ages and sexes, or justified on the basis of their various "offices or works,"[158] the various functions actually exercised, are never viewed by Luther on the vertical plane *coram deo* [before God], but always on the horizontal plane *coram hominibus* [before men].[159] They do not concern one's being before God; in this realm, perfect equality prevails: "There is no distinction there, whether man, woman, or maidservant [*Ibi nullum discrimen, sive vir, mulier, ancilla*]."[160]

The chief motive for this teaching of the existential equality of all Christians is without doubt to be found in the concern to preserve in every respect the righteousness of faith as equal in all people *per fidem propter Christum* [through faith on account of Christ] and to undermine from the outset the concept of the office distorted by satisfactionary, mediatorial, and hierarchical ideas which was then current in Rome in connection with the doctrine of an intrinsic, particular priestly estate.[161] To this is added as a further motive the idea of *fraternitas christiana* [Christian brotherhood]. Matthew 23:8–10 gives Luther the biblical basis to realize this motive. "You have one Master, Christ, and you are brothers. Therefore, we all have the same right."[162] The equality of all Christians with

(Gütersloh, 1895), pp. 285ff. He posits that, in Luther, the spiritual equality of all Christians on the one hand rests "on the identical nature of the spiritual good which qualifies each man personally" (p. 288) and, on the other hand, consists in the "equality of their religious and ecclesial rights and duties" (p. 289). Detailed support is given there.

156 Cf. WA 6:407.18: "equal Christians"; WA 6:567.27ff.: ". . . and joyful liberty will return to us, in which we all know that we are equal with respect to every right"; WA 10/3:396.3ff.: "the authority which I have, another has also"; WA 12:189.22f.: "who have the same right."

157 Cf. above, p. 34 n. 82.

158 Cf. WA 6:408.27f., 409.4 and 8.

159 Cf. above, p. 27 nn. 33–34.

160 WA 15:720.11; cf. WA 12:308.34ff., 309.4f. and 13ff.: "If you want to see Christians, you must see no distinction. . . . They are all the same, an utterly spiritual people." — The distinction of preachers and laity, taught so forcefully against the Enthusiasts in the treatise *Infiltrating and Clandestine Preachers* (WA 30/3:525.18f.), will not, in Luther's understanding, submit to being turned into an ontological distinction. It does not negate the intrinsic equality of all Christians in the universal priesthood. Also cf. below, pp. 97–98 n. 81. — Equality, however, is only posited by Luther with respect to the spiritual life (with the fundamental rights and powers included therein). H. Behm rightly pointed out that Luther "distinguishes the factual, official differentiation of all those in the social membership of the church's body from the spiritual, personal equality of all those in the universal priesthood" (op. cit., p. 16). Herein lies the kernel of truth in R. Sohm's assertion (including with respect to Luther): "The teaching of the universal priesthood of believers does not mean the teaching of the universal equality of believers" (*Kirchenrecht* I [1892], p. 505). This assertion is only false with respect to Luther's teaching when it is used to dispute all believers' intrinsic equality derived from the universal priesthood.

161 Cf. above, pp. 18–21.

162 WA 12:189.8f.

respect to their spiritual privilege entails for Luther that they are all brothers before Christ, who alone is Master. The Christian brotherhood and fellowship does not permit "one to be higher than another or to have a greater share or privilege than another, particularly in spiritual matters."[163] It is rather significant that Luther here coordinates the concepts *jus* [right] and *hereditas* [inheritance]. In doing so, he shows that the doctrine of the intrinsic equality of all Christians is rooted in the teaching of justification. The *jus* of the Christian is seen by Luther as closely linked with the state of grace generally. There is only one state of grace, and so only one brotherhood without grades of dignity before God. All Christians, in the royal priesthood which they possess in Christ, are *fratres aequales* [equal brothers].[164]

6. The Congregation as Bearer of All Rights and Powers

Every individual Christian, according to Luther, has in the universal priesthood the same rights and powers relating to Word and Sacrament. Yet this must not be taken in an individualistic sense. The priesthood in which the individual has these rights binds him both to Christ and to the congregation which is the Body of Christ. Indeed, it gives him these rights only by means of this bond. The royal priesthood of Christians is simultaneously (and primarily) a priesthood of the whole congregation of believers. It cannot be made a matter of the individuals alone, who possess it only as *membra ecclesiae* [members of the church].[165] The congregation as *communio sanctorum* is that to which Christ has given the Word, Baptism, the Supper, the Keys, and all spiritual riches, and which therefore has the sole right and power over them.[166] This becomes especially plain in the power of the Keys, which Luther at the same time vigorously asserts is given to every individual. "The Keys are not the pope's . . . , but the Church's; that is, they belong to the people of Christ, the people of God, or the holy Christian people, as wide as the whole world is, or wherever there

[163] WA 12:189.8ff.

[164] WA 12:192.6f.; also cf. above, p. 28 n. 38. — E. Sommerlath expressed the idea that, in Luther's teaching of the spiritual equality of all Christians with respect to rights, there are also "democratic, egalitarian ideas" echoed in his antithesis of the Roman concept ("Amt u. allg. Priestertum," p. 49). This may be accurate, but it comes into play only as a secondary factor.

[165] WA 12:184.21f.: "The Keys belong to the whole Church and to all its members" (observe the order of the parties!). Cf. Niedermeier, "Das allg. Priestertum der Gläubigen u. d. geistliche Amt," *Zeitschrift f. syst. Theol.* (1930), pp. 348f.

[166] WA 38:237.11ff., 238.7ff., 252.13ff.; 11:413.17ff. — In direct contradiction to this teaching of Luther's, R. Sohm (*Kirchenrecht* I [1892], pp. 500ff., esp. p. 502 n. 33) maintains that the congregation, the Church per se, has no Office of the Keys or office of preaching—indeed, "neither faith nor gifts"; every individual receives faith, gifts, priesthood, preaching office immediately from God. This position has nothing in common with Luther's teaching.

are Christians," says Luther in 1539.[167] He already taught this in 1519 in the *Explanation of the Thirteenth Thesis on the Authority of the Pope*.[168] In his exposition of Matt. 16:18f., a passage that had been improperly related to the primacy of Peter and then of the pope, Luther stresses that the power of the Keys (i.e., the power to forgive and retain sins, not to make laws!)[169] was given here not to Peter alone but to all the apostles.[170] This means in turn that the Keys were given to *the Church*.[171] In Matt. 16:18, Peter is the one to whom the Father revealed the mystery that Jesus is the Messiah, and he confesses the faith in Him *sub totius ecclesiae persona* [in the person of the whole Church]. Thus he represents the person of the Church. It is in this capacity that the Keys are given to Peter, that is, given to the Church.[172] Therefore, since we cannot know for certain whether any private person has received the revelation of the Father and so believes in Christ, it must be said that the Keys are given not to any individual but to the Church, which is known to be the Body of Christ.[173] It is accordingly clear for Luther that "the Keys do not belong to any single man, but to the Church and congregation."[174] He disputes not merely the pope's exclusive right to the power of the Keys, but generally that the power of the Keys belongs to any individual person; it is given to the Church as a whole.[175] Wherever the *ecclesia* appears as the *communio sanctorum* in the assembly of those who confess the pure Gospel of Christ, the power of the Keys is there also[176]—not only in this and that congregation, but in every one.[177]

The same explanation of Matthew 16 is found in the sermon on the power of St. Peter from 1522.[178] The Keys are given to the one who by faith stands on the Rock, Christ, but all believers can also fall. "Therefore, the Keys belong not to any designated man, but to the Church, that is, to those who stand on this Rock. The Christian Church alone has the Keys, no one else. . . ."[179] Likewise, Matt. 18:18 shows, according to Luther, that the power of the Keys is given to the

---

167 WA 50:632.28ff.; cf. WA 50:243.13ff.: "The Keys are an office and authority given *to the Church* by Christ, to bind and to loose sins. . . ."

168 WA 2:180–240.

169 Cf. above, pp. 15–16.

170 WA 2:188.29ff. and 38ff., 189.25f. and 35ff.

171 WA 2:188.25, 189.6f., 190.11ff., 191.10ff., 208.36ff.

172 WA 2:190.5ff. and 38ff., 191.34f., 193.14; cf. WA 2:248.33f.: "It is true, the Keys were given to St. Peter, yet not in his own person, but in the person of the Christian Church."

173 WA 2:190.12ff., 193.8ff.; cf. WA 2:191.8f.

174 WA 2:191.18.

175 WA 2:194.5ff.: "Therefore, what remains is that the Gospel in this passage pertains not to Peter, nor to his successor, nor to any bishop or any single human, but to the communion of saints, which is the Church"; cf. WA 30/2:437.21ff.

176 WA 2:191.24ff.

177 WA 2:191.22f., 192.29, 194.20.

178 WA 10/3:208–16.

179 WA 10/3:215.21ff.; cf. WA 6:309.28ff.: "that the Keys were given to St. Peter in the stead of the whole Church and not for his own self"; WA 6:311.36f., 313.33; 6:411.37f.; 30/1:235.23ff.: ". . . Christ

congregation: "Here Christ gives the Keys to the whole congregation and not to St. Peter."[180] John 20:22f. is understood the same way.[181]

What has been said here concerning the Office of the Keys is, in Luther's scheme, fundamentally to be applied to Word and Sacrament in general. The congregation is the possessor of all the means of grace and of the right to administer them. In the universal priesthood, the individual believer does not have the power of Word and Sacrament in isolation, but only ever as a member of the congregation. This is the important corrective in Luther's teaching of the universal priesthood. It cannot be disregarded, lest the overall picture be distorted. It fights against the idea of the universal priesthood as an individual's personal possession, an individual person's ability and power, and curbs the individualistic view of the Church.[182] Incidentally, when speaking of the congregation, Luther here has in mind the *communio sanctorum*, the *whole* Church, which, while taking tangible form and being present in every individual, local congregation,[183] also encompasses all other congregations. The individual, local congregation, as a manifestation of the *communio sanctorum*, is never detached from the other congregations, but rather is oriented toward them and bound to them. All congregationalism and independentalism are alien to Luther; he always sees the local congregation in the context of a larger ecclesial association.[184] The individual, local congregation for Luther is always the proper nucleus of the function of Word and Sacrament. For where the Church is, there with the priesthood of all believers is also the power to use Word and Sacrament; indeed, there is also the power and right to appoint the particular office of Word and Sacrament, as we might as well note here.[185] This latter point is best shown by the fact that for Luther the congregation is ultimately the actual possessor of all spiritual rights and powers relating to Word and Sacrament. —

We have now examined the teaching of the universal priesthood in Luther, paying special attention to the function of Word and Sacrament, and have found that the universal priesthood for Luther includes the fundamental authorization, qualification, and empowerment to dispense Word and Sacrament, even if this

---

Himself put the Absolution in the mouth of His Christian Church and commanded it to release us from sins."

[180] WA 8:173.24; also cf. WA 2:191.1ff.; 7:170.14f.; 12:184.11ff.

[181] WA 6:309.30ff., 311.15ff., 312.28ff.: "The words of Christ are nothing but gracious promises made to the whole Church, to all Christians"; WA 2:188.23ff.

[182] W. Elert (*Morphologie* I, p. 299) pointed out that "Gemeinde" in Luther's sense does not represent an association-like collection of separate, believing individuals, but a transsubjective reality. The concept of church as association is not Luther's view of the church.

[183] Cf. WA 6:407.34ff.

[184] Cf., in the writing to the Bohemians [*Concerning the Ministry*], the plan of instituting an Evangelical archbishopric of Bohemia (WA 12:194.18ff.) and the preface to the *Instructions for the Visitors* (WA 26:195ff., esp. 200.10ff.). R. Seeberg, *Dogmengeschichte* IV.1, p. 296; G. Holstein, *Die Grundlagen d. ev. Kirchenrechts* (Tübingen, 1928), p. 99; W. Elert, *Morphologie des Luthertums* I, pp. 305ff. and 322ff.

[185] WA 38:252.17, 253.1ff.; 41:241.12ff. and 35ff., 242.5ff. On this cf. below, pp. 122–28.

is only valid for the individual Christian in the sense that he is a member of the Church. This teaching of the universal priesthood provides the basis in Luther's view for his teaching of the ecclesial office. *The priesthood of all Christians is for him the embodiment of the particular ecclesial office insofar as all the priestly functions of Word and Sacrament, which form the content of the particular office, are for him considered already fundamentally bestowed in the universal priesthood*, and he therefore develops the particular ecclesial office from the universal priesthood of all Christians. It is possible, in order to identify the relationship of both entities in Luther, to speak of an "*office per se*" in the universal priesthood and of the *concrete* office, or else of a *universal* office of Word and Sacrament in the universal priesthood and of the particular ecclesial office. In any case, it is evident that Luther bases the concrete *ministerium ecclesiasticum* [ecclesial ministry] on the universal priesthood and derives the former from the latter. In what form and manner this is done by him now constitutes the next subject of our study.

CHAPTER III

The Rationale for the Concrete Office from the Universal Priesthood

1. The Concrete Office as Public Office

When we speak of the concrete office, we mean the office of the Word and Sacrament conferred on specific persons for concrete, regular exercise within the Christian congregation. Luther plainly distinguishes this concrete office from the priestly office shared by all Christians,[1] calling it the "common office,"[2] the "ministerial office,"[3] the "office of preaching or office of ministry."[4] It is called "ministerial office" because it ministers to or serves other Christians with the Gospel and exists for their sake.[5] It rests on the universal priesthood, to which the "office"—that is, the assignment to exercise on a regular basis the function of Word and Sacrament in the ministry—is then added.[6] Luther uses the term

[1] WA 41:210.22ff., 213.14ff. This is noted, e.g., by J. W. F. Höfling (*Grundsätze ev. Luth. Kirchenverfassung*, 3rd ed. [Erlangen, 1853], pp. 55f.).

[2] WA 41:213.35.

[3] WA 41:209.6.

[4] WA 41:210.22.

[5] WA 41:213.14ff.: ". . . The offices are appointed for this purpose; this does not mean the priestly estate, but an office for the other priests, i.e., Christians. . . ."

[6] Luther is eager to emphasize the fact that the priesthood is already present and must be present, and the particular office is then only assigned in addition to it. Cf. WA 41:207.13f.: "The ministers are not priests because of the office, but by birth"; WA 41:208.7ff.: "As here one does not become a citizen when he is elected as mayor, but he is already a citizen, from which he has his civic rights, then he is elected for the office out of the multitude of those called citizens, and thus brings his civic right with him into the mayoral office; he does not find it therein. . . . So a woman does not become a woman because she is married to a husband, unless she was already born one of the woman's sex. . . . She brings the woman's sex into the marital estate, then she receives the key, . . . then the office is added, which is placed upon her . . ."; WA 41:209.8ff.: "Therefore, just as a man must first be a man before he takes a wife, so he must first be a preacher, a bishop, a priest. A pope or bishop does not

"office [*Amt*]" (*ministerium*)—as Gösta Hök has shown[7]—in two senses: first, in the sense of the office of the universal priesthood which all Christians hold and, second, in the sense of the concrete preaching office of the Church possessed not by all, but only by those specially called to it.[8] Essential to this concrete church office is, in Luther's view, the fact that it is a *public office* (*ministerium publicum*). It is only by its public character that the dimension of this concrete *ministerium ecclesiasticum*, this particular office of the Church, is approached.[9] "Behold, in this way every Christian has and exercises this priestly work. But in addition to this is the common office, which handles and deals with teaching *publicly*."[10] Here the church office as public teaching office is most clearly separated from

make a priest. One must be one beforehand; but after he is already a priest, the office is added and makes a distinction"; WA 41:213.15ff.

[7] Op. cit., pp. 149f.

[8] H. Storck's criticism (op. cit., pp. 42f.) of Hök's description of the twofold office in Luther cannot be supported. Hök has undoubtedly observed correctly that Luther makes a material and conceptual distinction of the office in the broad sense (= universal priesthood) and the office in the narrow sense (= ecclesial office).

[9] The public character of the particular office is highlighted by most of those who have worked with Luther's teaching of the office. Cf., e.g., J. Köstlin, *Luthers Lehre von der Kirche* (1853), p. 48; E. Wolf, "Zur Verwaltung der Sakramente nach Luther u. luth. Lehre," in *Peregrinatio: Studien zur ref. Theol. u. z. Kirchenproblem* (Munich, 1954), pp. 244 and 252f.; F. K. Schumann, "Amt der Kirche und Berufung zum Amt," in *Wort und Gestalt* (*Ges. Aufsätze*) (1956), p. 316; V. Vajta, *Theol. d. Gottesdienstes* (1954), pp. 200 and 216; G. Hök, op. cit., p. 150. — A deficiency in Storck's study of the universal priesthood in Luther is found in the fact that he never goes into the public character of the particular office in Luther. Thus the particularity thereof in comparison with the universal priesthood is not fully treated. When Storck writes: "In Luther, no distinction between the functions of the clerical office and those of the universal priesthood can be established" (op. cit., p. 41), it is correct in a material sense—we established the same thing several times in the previous chapter—but in order that the overall picture may not be false, it must be supplemented by establishing the (essential!) formal distinction that the functions of the clerical office are public functions in the congregation while the public character in the sense described does not apply to the universal priesthood. The public character of the concrete office as the demarcation for the universal priesthood of all Christians is also stressed by Brunotte (op. cit., pp. 159ff.). He adds to this factor, as a second characteristic of the concrete office in Luther as distinct from the functions of the universal priesthood, the *relation to the church* (ibid., pp. 161ff.). The functions of the concrete office occur in its assignment to the church and in the name of the church, which is not true of the functions of the universal priesthood. This is an important supplement. We will discuss this in sections 5 and 6 of this chapter. In any case, let us not agree with Brunotte in the *explanation* of the relation of office and church or congregation in Luther. For the debate with Brunotte in this regard, see below, pp. 63–64 n. 79; p. 66 n. 91; pp. 67–68 n. 97; p. 71 n. 108; pp. 71–72 n. 111.

[10] WA 41:213.34f.; cf. WA 12:17.37; 12:189.25f.; 30/3:519.30f.

the universal priesthood.[11] Christ wants the preaching office to be carried out not only "in private or in one place, but publicly throughout the world."[12]

If we ask what sense the term "publicly" has for Luther, we find two elements in it. "Publicly" means both "before all" and "for all" in the context of the congregational body. This public office is directed toward the congregation and is thoroughly an office of the congregation. The one holding this office performs the function of the office *coram ecclesia* [before the church] and *in nomine ecclesiae* [in the name of the church].[13] He acts before the congregation and the congregation acts in him. Publicness is not a purely technical concept with Luther, but it is filled with an objective statement. This is why he who is to wield the public office must be supported by the "consensus of the whole or of the church [*consensus universitatis seu ecclesiae*]."[14] He stands *for* this *ecclesia*. But this also leads to this public office being always related to a concrete congregation and having a parochial character. In Luther's scheme it is not merely a "preaching office," but also most essentially a *pastoral office*.[15] As such, it is the office of the Church in the proper sense. It is the condensation of the concrete congregation, above all with respect to the function of Word and Sacrament, by which it is led and governed by means of this function of Word and Sacrament.[16] If it is accompanied by additional offices in the congregation, they are either extensions of the pastoral office (as, e.g., when preachers function as assistants to a parish pastor) or in any case are somehow attached and subordinated to the pastoral office.[17] The pastoral office is *the* public office of the Church (*ministerium publicum ecclesiae*).

The public realm, in which the pastoral office as a public office works in the congregation, thus stands in contrast to the private and domestic sphere, in which every Christian proclaims God's Word and provides for the priestly

---

[11] WA 41:210.22ff.: "Behold, this is how the preaching office or ministerial office must be distinguished from the common priestly estate of all baptized Christians. For this office is no more than a public ministry which is committed to someone by the whole congregation, who are all simultaneously priests"; WA 41:211.18ff.; WA Br 7:339.29ff.: "For there is a great difference between a public office in the church and a housefather over his household. . . ." — Thus for Luther it is not accurate to see with V. Vajta (op. cit., pp. 215f. n. 69) in the function of the housefather the functioning of "the churchly office" and thus of the public office!

[12] WA 32:351.3; cf. WA 41:213.19ff.: "Then let the offices be distributed so that the multitude do not go astray and that the confession may be done *publicly* since my preaching here does not happen in a corner. . . ."

[13] WA 12:189.22f.; 49:600.11ff.

[14] WA 12:189.26f.

[15] Cf. below, pp. 89–90.

[16] On the logical consequence that the congregation is governed by Word and Sacrament, cf. the passages indicated above, p. 33 n. 79, as well as WA 6:441.24f.; 41:210.15. Also cf. R. Sohm, *Kirchenrecht* I, pp. 484ff.

[17] Cf. P. Brunner, "Vom Amt des Bischofs," in *Schriften des Theol. Konvents Augsb. Bek.* 9 (Berlin, 1955), pp. 27ff.

functions. The conferral upon specific persons[18] of the *public* exercise of the office in the concrete office does not mean that the other members of the congregation do not also exercise priestly functions on the basis of the priesthood shared by all.[19] Only in the latter case these are done in the private realm. Luther divides the priestly functions into public and "private" (*heymlich*).[20] One and the same priesthood is exercised in two spheres (public and "private").[21] If it can be said that the particular office is the universal priesthood implemented publicly, it must also be observed that the particular form and manner of the public exercise of the priesthood produces a new kind of priestly function, which is a mark of the particular office and in which the latter is clearly separated from the universal priesthood. Luther himself says that these two forms of the exercise of the priesthood "are not to be mingled . . . nor divided";[22] that is, they must be distinguished and yet are both functions of the same priesthood.[23]

The domestic, private sphere exists for Luther *only* in relation to the transmission of God's Word from man to man and home instruction by the housefather[24] and the *mutua consolatio fratrum* [mutual consolation of the brethren], including giving Absolution. If my neighbor comes to me and looks to me for the comfort of the Gospel and asks me for the Absolution, "I may freely do it, yet it must, I say, be done privately."[25] Giving Absolution in the domestic, private sphere is not limited to those who bear the office, even though it may be done publicly only by them.[26] The Absolution in the mouth of a good friend—spoken in God's name—is just as valid as that of the office-bearer.[27] Luther can even tell someone to confess to a lay brother: "If your conscience torments you, consult a godly man, cast your burden before him. If he forgives you, you should accept it; he needs no papal bull for that."[28] This is the same attitude we became acquainted

[18] Cf. K. Holl, *Luther*, p. 319: ". . . If all Christians are priests in the full sense of the word, the 'churchly priest' has no advantage except the fact that he alone is permitted to exercise the universal priesthood *publicly*."

[19] WA 41:211.18ff.: "For although we are not all in the public office and call, yet every Christian should and can teach, instruct, admonish, comfort, and rebuke his neighbor by God's Word, when and where anyone has need thereof . . ."; cf. WA 11:412.4ff.; 12:180.17ff.; 12:521.19ff.

[20] WA 10/1.2:239.28ff.; 12:189.25f.; 49:139.22f.: (Christ has commanded comfort to be given by Absolution) "through a public office to called ministers and to everyone privately."

[21] WA 12:189.34ff.: "For to bear such fruits publicly or privately does not demonstrate different priesthoods, but different uses of the same priesthood."

[22] WA Br 7:339.30f.

[23] The distinction of both spheres is also highlighted by Brunotte (op. cit., pp. 56ff.), but Brunotte misses the fact that in Luther only two different kinds of functions of one and the same priesthood are involved. It is a question of "different uses of the *same* priesthood" (WA 12:189.35). The withdrawal of the former from the latter is negated, which Brunotte accepts.

[24] WA 41:212.25ff.; also cf. above, p. 44 n. 153.

[25] WA 10/1.2:239.32f.

[26] WA 10/1.2:239.29f.

[27] WA 10/3:395.25ff.; cf. WA 49:139.20ff., 140.6ff. and 40f.

[28] WA 10/3:398.35ff.; cf. the confession before a "brother" in the LC (WA 30/1:235.18): "confession which is made with one brother alone"; WA 30/1:235.20f.: ". . . that we lament to such a

with in the treatise to the Bohemians [*Concerning the Ministry*], where Luther insists that "the right and the *use* of the Keys falls to all men absolutely and generally."[29] Yet Luther concedes such private use of the Keys only so far as it does not infringe on the official confessional care of the ministers; Luther knows how easily it may lead to the formation of sects and the dissolution of any sort of congregational discipline.[30] The actual hearing of confession—thus the confessional care of the office—is to be granted to called ministers alone.[31]

Here the question arises why Luther is so insistent that the Absolution should be dispensed by the laity in the private sphere in addition to the confessional care provided through the public office. We will probably not go astray in this if we surmise that the boundaries between the comforting word of the Gospel, which naturally must be granted to every Christian, and of the Absolution proper in the Church's praxis are, in fact, often fluid. Also at work here is the teaching of the overflowing riches of grace, which appears in many forms. "God is superabundantly rich in His grace" and distributes it not merely in one way, but in a variety of forms: through the spoken word, through Baptism, the Supper, the Keys, "and even through the mutual conversation and consolation of brethren."[32]

It must also be explicitly noted that, with respect to the sacraments of Baptism and the Holy Supper, Luther does not envisage a similar "private" function in the domestic, private sphere; indeed, he rejects it.[33] Baptism, according to Luther, is to be administered apart from the particular office only in case of necessity while the Holy Supper is not to be administered without that office at all.[34]

The distinction of public and private realm is needed in order to discern correctly the particular nature of the concrete office according to Luther. This office reveals its true contours only when it is regarded in this dimension of public orientation. —

While the concrete office in Luther is based fundamentally on the universal priesthood of the congregation and of every individual Christian, it does not manifest itself concretely until it is conferred on specific persons for public

---

brother." — But Luther of course also urges going to the priest when someone is inwardly distressed: WA 2:249.12ff.; 41:546.16: "You shall go to the parson. . . ."

[29] WA 12:184.21ff.; cf. above, pp. 39–40.

[30] Cf. WA 38:630.9ff., where Luther grants every brother the use of the power of the Keys but points out: "Yet in such a way that the public preaching of the Gospel or Office of the Keys is not condemned; for it must not be permitted in the Church that, because of the freedom of using the Keys privately, their public function should be insulted. For this would be to create sects and to transform the grace of Christ into excess."

[31] Cf. WA 10/1.2:239.23f.: "If everyone tried to hear confession . . . how would that work?"; WA 10/1.2:239.33ff.: "If I tried to seat myself in the church, and another too, and all wanted to hear confession, how would it make sense?"

[32] WA 50:240.30ff.

[33] WA 41:214.27ff.; WA Br 7:338f., etc.

[34] This is demonstrated below, pp. 113–15.

exercise in and for the congregation. We must now ask how the necessity of this concrete office derived from the priesthood of the whole is reasoned in Luther. In the examination of Luther's statements on the subject, two basic lines of thought become apparent: first, a rationale from the universal priesthood of all Christians and, second, one from the divine institution. Here we are primarily concerned with the former.

2. The Motive of Order as Rationale for the Concrete Office

In the rationale for the necessity of the concrete office, the motive of order plays an important role in Luther. The exercise of the function of Word and Sacrament in the congregation must take place in the context of good order. God is not a God of disorder but of peace (1 Cor. 14:33), for which reason Scripture demands that everything in the congregation be done decently and in order (1 Cor. 14:40).[35] But what if everyone exercised the public function of Word and Sacrament in the congregation; what if everyone wanted to preach and distribute the Sacraments or preside over the congregation? "If everyone wished to preach, who would listen? If we all preached at the same time, what a confusion of noise there would be, as there is now among the frogs!"[36] There would truly be a "vile confusion in the people of God [*turpis confusio in populo dei*]"—indeed, the Church would become a veritable Babylon.[37] Thus for Luther ". . . the whole multitude cannot do it, but they must commit it or have it committed to someone."[38] The practical, technical considerations of the congregation's life and the divine Law of order lead to the necessity of a concrete preaching office filled by specific officeholders, to which the function of public Word and Sacrament is exclusively assigned.[39]

Especially drastic is Luther's portrayal of the problem of order in his treatise *Infiltrating and Clandestine Preachers* (1532). He ties to the motive of order the policy that one should not permit "an uncalled layman to usurp the preaching in his parish church"; the public preaching is to be committed to the called

---

[35] WA 12:189.24f.; 30/3:524.5ff.

[36] WA 10/1.2:239.24ff.; cf. WA 10/3:397.17ff.: "If we all preached, it would be like when women go to market; then they refuse to listen to one another, and all want to talk."

[37] WA 12:189.23f.

[38] WA 50:633.5ff.; 7:28.33ff.: "For although we are all equally priests, we could not all minister or manage and preach"; WA 41:209.13: "We could not all have the office"; WA 41:214.27ff.: "For in the congregation they cannot all attend to the office"; WA 49:600.13f.: "There must be a single man who speaks and holds forth."

[39] WA 10/1.2:239.27: "For that reason" (namely, since for the sake of order it works no other way) "it should proceed in this manner: the congregation should choose one man who is capable of giving the Sacraments, preaching, hearing confession, and baptizing. . . ." Cf. V. Vajta, *Theol. d. Gottesdienstes*, p. 210.

prophets and teachers and is to remain that way.[40] If "any given layman tries to get up and preach in church"—how, then, will all things be done decently and in order in the congregation?[41] The liturgical assembly would then take on a tumultuous character:

> What a fine specimen that would be for me if a pastor preached and someone had the power to join in the conversation and argue with him! Then another would join in the conversation and even bid the others be quiet, and after that a drunken sot would leave his tankard and join in talking with these three and bid the third one hold his peace too, and finally the women sitting there would also desire this privilege and bid the men be quiet, and then the women would all do this to one another! Oh, what a beautiful church fair, tavern, and market day that would be! Which pigsties would not be more excellent than such churches? Let the devil be the preacher there instead of me![42]

Similarly, regarding Baptism, Luther portrays the necessity of the concrete office in his sermon on the authority of St. Peter (1522): "If the whole congregation wanted to go up and all perform a Baptism, they would probably drown the child, for there would be a thousand hands trying to do it. This is not fitting. This is why there has to be one minister who attends to the matter in the stead of the congregation."[43] The emphasis on a public minister to undertake the Baptism is simply a practical, technical necessity. In addition, because the Sacraments must be "a public matter," and in order that one might know who is actually baptized (which is by no means guaranteed when arbitrary home Baptisms are performed by the "common man"), and in order that an orderly congregational life may be realized and general confusion not prevail, it is necessary to have pastors exercising the public function of Word and Sacrament in the congregation.[44]

As to the necessity of external order, the Christian congregation is in the same situation as other human social institutions, such as a kingdom or a household. Thus for the necessity of the concrete office in the congregation Luther also draws examples from the political-economic realm. Where there are many nobles, they elect one to exercise government in the name of all the others, "for if they all tried to rule over land and people, how would it go?"[45] In the members of a household, there must be an obligatory order, "for if every heir wished to be lord and rule, it would go poorly. But if the others go and choose one, and they yield and put it in his hands, it goes well. So here, too, one must be chosen so that order is not upset."[46]

---

40 WA 30/3:524.3f.; also WA 30/3:525.12ff.

41 WA 30/3:524.8f.

42 WA 30/3:522.25ff.

43 WA 10/3:216.3ff.

44 WA 41:213.7ff.

45 WA 10/1.2:239.35ff. (also cf. the preceding text in this passage); cf. WA 6:407.32ff.

46 WA 10/3:170.29ff. On the theme of order, cf. also WA 8:424.24ff.: "that order and honor may be maintained"; WA 25:16.23ff.: "that they may not talk at the same time"; WA 28:474.6ff.

The argument for the necessity of the concrete office based on the motive of order is causally connected to the teaching of the universal priesthood. By the fact that it is necessary for the sake of order to appoint the concrete office, "the commonality of the duty to preach is not nullified," says Luther. "Indeed, it is confirmed thereby. For if not all men could preach, and only one had authority to speak, what need would there be to keep and prescribe order? And it is *precisely because* they all have authority and power to preach that it is necessary to keep order."[47] The necessity of keeping order arises directly from the fact that all members of the congregation are fundamentally endowed with the same right and same power of Word and Sacrament. Were the authorization and qualification for discharging the function of Word and Sacrament not shared by all, but limited from the start to specific individuals, the order would already be prescribed and given. Because all Christians have in the universal priesthood the fundamental right and power of Word and Sacrament, the motive of order gains argumentative significance for the necessity of the concrete office filled with specific persons. The rationale for the concrete office for the sake of order is thus one which also stems from the universal priesthood.[48]

---

[47] WA 8:495.28ff.; cf. WA 8:423.6f.: "For order is necessary for speaking because all have the power to speak." Cf. also G. Rietschel, *Luther und die Ordination* (1889), p. 33; and H. Storck, op. cit., pp. 31f.

[48] H. E. Creutzig (*Amt und Ämter i. d. luth. Kirche*, Theologia militans 22 [Leipzig, 1938], p. 18) has rightly pointed out that the rationale from order in Luther cannot be taken in a purely external way since order is *God's* commandment. In fact, by the necessity for the sake of order, a divine necessity is being expressed *indirectly*. In any case, the theme of order leads nearly to a *jus divinum* [divine right] of the concrete office. Brunotte (op. cit., pp. 130ff.) also stresses that Luther sees the theme of order founded on an explicit arrangement of God (namely, in 1 Cor. 14:40 taken as divine command) and does not take it simply as a law of universal custom, as, e.g., Höfling does. Brunotte, however, goes too far when he tries to find a direct divine arrangement in Luther's sense in the command for order expressed in 1 Cor. 14:40, and thus makes the rationale from order completely identical to the rationale from divine institution. Yet they are two different things. We said above: God commanded order; order can—since all have in the universal priesthood the same rights and powers—be maintained only by appointing a particular office; thus this office, too, is commanded by God. — Or else: God instituted and founded the particular office itself. In the first case, the office is only based on God's will indirectly; in the second, directly. In Luther, both ways of rationalizing the office are present, and it is an undue simplification to take both as one and the same. Therefore, Brunotte's polemic against E. Sommerlath and K. Tuchel, who also speak of two ways of rationalizing the office in Luther, is far-fetched. — The same critique could be made of the assessment by Regin Prenter, who likewise identifies the rationale of the office from order in Luther with that from divine institution (*Theol. Lit.ztg.*, 5/86 vol., cols. 325ff.). The texts which we have cited show plainly that here in the idea of order from 1 Cor. 14:40, Luther actually has in view "calm and order" in the external sense and is not—here—thinking of institutional order of the congregation in the deeper sense.

3. The Concept of Brotherhood as Rationale for the Concrete Office

It has already been indicated what significance the concept of brotherhood has for Luther.[49] All members of the congregation are bound together and associated with each other in the *fraternitas christiana* [Christian brotherhood]. In the universal priesthood they are all fundamentally endowed with the same right and same power. Thus there arises in the congregation a *communio juris* [sharing of the right],[50] which means for each individual, practically speaking, that he is not a free lord over his right but must always view it in relation to the whole. Christian love compels him to do so. Beside him stand others who have the same right and toward whom he is oriented as they are toward him. Accordingly, if anyone tried to overstep this relationship toward others and willfully to make public use of his fundamental right of Word and Sacrament without the call and consent of the whole, and thus with respect to the public exercise arbitrarily usurp the right of Word and Sacrament shared by all which for the sake of order is not exercised publicly by all equally, it would be a violation of the fraternal community and an offense against Christian love. "For no one can take for himself what belongs to all without the will and command of all."[51]

Here Luther uses phrases such as "it is not fitting," "it is inappropriate," "it is unsuitable," "one ought not," "one may not," "one cannot," in Latin "*non licet.*"[52] These expressions necessarily have the force of a prohibition in the strict sense. This is also demonstrated by the fact that Luther characterizes the breach of this prohibition with expressions of moral disqualification, such as "presumption," "arrogance."[53] Underlying the prohibition, in any case, is not only the relationship of every individual to the community but also and most important the principle that in spiritual matters one may not begin something on his own initiative, but must rather be called. However, this perspective will be elaborated in greater detail below.[54]

---

[49] Cf. above, pp. 45–46.

[50] WA 12:189.21.

[51] WA 6:408.15ff.; cf. WA 6:566.29f.: "For because it belongs to all communally, no one can take it for himself alone until he be called"; WA 12:189.17ff.; cf. WA 12:309.7ff.; 10/3:395.40ff.

[52] WA 6:408.12f.: ". . . It is not fitting for everyone to exercise this office"; WA 6:566.28: "may not"; WA 6:566.30: "No one can"; WA 8:253.29: ". . . Exercising such power and applying it is not suitable for everyone"; WA 8:495.24: ". . . that many of you should not preach at the same time"; WA 10/1.2:239.23f.: "How would it fit . . . ?"; WA 10/3:395.40: "But this is not suitable for everyone"; WA 10/3:396.3: "It does not belong to everyone"; WA 10/3:397.17: "But we should not all make use of it"; WA 12:189.18: "No one may"; WA 12:189.26: "may not carry it out publicly"; WA 12:309.7: "No one should"; WA 41:210.14f.: "Not all of us should preach or teach and govern"; WA 41:214.28: "Neither is it fitting. . . ."

[53] WA 6:408.14f.; 10/1.2:239.29 ("usurp"); WA 6:566.30 ("take for himself [*arrogare*]").

[54] Cf. below, pp. 117–20.

The organization of the Christian brotherhood renders impossible any irregular public exercise of the priestly right of Word and Sacrament given to all in Baptism. The fact that the rights of all individual Christians in the congregation coincide and belong together necessitates the organized process of selection and calling by which one or more of the collective whole are nominated to exercise publicly the function of Word and Sacrament, who then administer the concrete office in the name of all.[55] Thus the necessity of the concrete office also finds its rationale in the idea of the *fraternitas christiana.*

The concept of brotherhood limits the public exercise of the function of Word and Sacrament to the man called to the concrete office by the congregation. Yet the fundamental rights and duties of Word and Sacrament of the others are not simply negated by this. Rather, Luther conceives of all the fundamental rights and duties of discharging the function of Word and Sacrament of the others as delegated to the man called to the concrete office, and he sees all the remaining members of the congregation as coactive in his discharging the function of the office. Luther is here anticipating an actual, real-life law of representation, by virtue of which the work of the one becomes the work of all, and the work of all is done in the work of the one.[56] In a deeper sense, this is nothing other than the spiritual reality of the Christian brotherhood. Most important in this regard, it becomes plain that any individualistic understanding of the Christian priesthood is excluded in Luther. All rights and duties of the individual are embedded in the relationship to the community in which he stands. The fundamental right and capacity to discharge the function of Word and Sacrament given to every person in the universal priesthood is not condemned to practical insignificance by the concept of brotherhood, but only somewhat transformed into the right and duty to be responsible for the proper appointment of the particular office and the correct exercise of the public function of Word and Sacrament.[57]

4. The Diversity of Gifts as Rationale for the Concrete Office

We have observed above that Luther, with all clarity, teaches that among all Christians there is an equality of spiritual potency with respect to the function

[55] WA 12:189.21ff.: "This sharing of the right means that one—or however many should please the congregation—are chosen or taken to carry out these tasks publicly in the stead and name of all, who have the same right." — K. Holl sees in this situation a confirmation of the fact that Luther really uses the universal priesthood as a constitutional principle (*Luther*, pp. 318f. n. 5). Insofar as Luther bases the spiritual office on the universal priesthood and this represents the backbone of his concept of the church, it is actually possible to say this.

[56] Cf. below, pp. 69–72, where it is demonstrated.

[57] For the shared responsibility arising from the universal priesthood of every Christian regarding the call to the office and the right exercise of the office, see also Brunotte, op. cit., p. 182. Nevertheless, Brunotte declines to recognize the idea of *delegatio* in Luther. On this, cf. treatments of him on pp. 63–64 n. 79; p. 66 n. 91; pp. 67–68 n. 97; p. 71 n. 108; pp. 71–72 n. 111.

of Word and Sacrament.[58] We have also pointed out that a difficulty for this teaching lies in the fact that not all Christians are equipped with the gifts actually required to exercise the function of Word and Sacrament.[59] Nevertheless, Luther does not let this difficulty call into question his teaching of a spiritual potency to discharge the function of Word and Sacrament that is equally present in all. Rather, it only drives him to reason the concrete office from the universal priesthood, and thus becomes a third motive for the necessity of the concrete office: while all are priests, and all have the fundamental right and power of Word and Sacrament, yet since God has not given to all the gifts needed for the practical exercise of this power, it is necessary that all others transfer their right to the one (especially) capable, on whom God has manifestly bestowed the needed gifts, and let it be exercised by him.[60] Only those are to be elected to the public function of Word and Sacrament "to whom God gives the particular gifts and aptitude in order that they may be suitable to the office."[61] Whoever does not have the requisite gifts "ought to keep quiet and let another speak."[62] He places his fundamental priestly right to discharge the function of Word and Sacrament on another person,[63] and this redounds to his own benefit insofar as he receives strength and help from him who now (even in his own stead!) occupies the concrete office, without which he might not survive in trials and temptations.[64] The necessity for the concrete office necessarily arises from the diversity of gifts among Christians.

To this are added the distinctions of age and sex, which likewise render impossible the exercise of the public function of the office by each and every Christian, and thus underscore the necessity of the concrete office. "But it is true that in this article the Holy Spirit has excepted women, children, and unfit persons and selects only capable males for it (except in necessity), as we read

---

[58] Cf. above, pp. 41–42.

[59] Cf. above, p. 43.

[60] WA 41:209.31ff. — The motive of the diversity of gifts as rationale for the necessity of the concrete office has already been noticed by R. Sohm (*Kirchenrecht* I, p. 495 n. 26). He sees in this the divine necessity for the office while in the theme of order he finds only the human necessity. Yet the latter is incorrect. Just as the diversity of gifts is traced back to God, so is the necessity of order, as we have already noted (cf. above, p. 57 n. 48). In both factors, however, the reference of the necessity of the concrete office back to God's will is in essence only an indirect one; the direct one is encountered only in the idea of institution. — On the divine character of the rationale for the office from diversity of gifts, also cf. F. K. Schumann, "Amt d. Kirche u. Berufung zum Amt," in *Wort u. Gestalt* (1956), p. 317.

[61] WA 41:209.30f.; cf. WA 10/1.2:239.27f.; 8:424.24ff., 497.25ff.: "Although everyone has the power to preach, no man should be used for it, nor anyone undertake to do it, unless he is better equipped for it than others."

[62] WA 8:497.33f.

[63] WA 8:424.30: ". . . He justly places his right under another."

[64] WA 12:389.10ff. Luther shows the necessity of the particular preaching office for the sake of the weak and troubled, who need strength and preservation and without it would be defenseless against the wolf.

here and there in the epistles of St. Paul."[65] Luther explicitly limits the capacity for the concrete office to (capable) *men*: "In other words, it is to be an able, chosen man."[66]

That a woman cannot be considered for the church's public office Luther deduces, via the apostolic prohibition in 1 Cor. 14:34 and 1 Tim. 2:12, from the *order of nature and creation*, as expressed in the Law (Gen. 2:18; 3:16) and confirmed by experience.[67] According to Luther, this natural order is in no way nullified by the Gospel, but rather confirmed as "God's order and creation."[68] In his treatise *Infiltrating and Clandestine Preachers* (1532), Luther refers to the apostolic injunction that women in the congregation should not preach as an "ordinance of the Holy Spirit" and, with respect to 1 Cor. 14:37, a commandment of the Lord: "But in the New Testament, the Holy Spirit, by St. Paul, orders that women should be quiet in the church or congregation and says, 'It is the Lord's commandment.'"[69] Naturally, Luther knows that God, in an extraordinary manner, also called women as prophetesses—and that for the new covenant it was promised: "Your daughters shall prophesy" (Joel 3:1f.)—yet he does not infer from that that women are to be admitted to the public preaching office in the congregation. To the contrary: "But in the congregation or church, where the preaching office is, they are to be silent and not to preach. They may still join in prayer, singing, praising, and saying Amen; and read at home; and teach, admonish, and comfort one another and even expound Scripture to one another as best as they are able."[70]

In other (earlier) writings of Luther's we also find the human *perspective of decency and propriety* ("honor and decency," "honestas et ordo") which forbids women to preach—though this, too, is traced back by Luther to the divine order of creation in accordance with the apostolic instructions and their basis in the Law.[71] Luther emphasizes in these writings that the prohibition of the preaching

---

[65] WA 50:633.12ff.

[66] WA 50:633.16ff.; "A woman should not teach among the people" (WA 50:633.16). — Cases of necessity require individual treatment.

[67] WA 50:633.20ff.: "For nature and God's creation also make the distinction that women (much less children or fools) cannot and should not be in charge, as experience shows and Moses says in Genesis 3"; cf. WA 12:309.17ff.: "except that women should not speak in the congregation but let men preach for the sake of God's will that they should be subject to their husbands, as St. Paul teaches in 1 Corinthians 14."

[68] WA 50:633.23f.; cf. WA 12:309.20: "God lets this order stand. . . ." — On the basis of the passage in WA 50:633.20ff., M. Doerne, *Luth. Pfarramt*, Theol. mil. 10 (Leipzig, 1937), p. 13, writes that it was unthinkable for Luther "for a woman to be entrusted with the office of the Word." Also cf. Brunotte, op. cit., pp. 110f., 112.

[69] WA 30/3:524.27ff.

[70] WA 30/3:524.32ff.

[71] *1521:* WA 8:497.34ff.: "Thus Paul forbids women to preach in the congregation where there are men who are apt to speak, that honor and decency may be upheld, since it is far more appropriate and fitting for a man to speak, and he is also better equipped for it. And Paul did not command this from his own head, but he appeals to the Law, which states that women are to be subject. From this Paul was assured that the Spirit was not against him . . ."; cf. WA 8:424.30ff. *1528*: WA 26:46.13ff., 47.22: "proved by divine and human right" (!), after 1 Tim. 2:11ff. — The aspect of decency is emphasized very unilaterally by H. Storck (op. cit., p. 33) in his description of Luther's stance toward

office for women relates to normal congregations which include men as well: "In the congregation where there are men," the apostles forbid women to preach.[72] Accordingly, where there are only women—as, for instance, in nunneries—they were to be permitted [to preach] according to Luther.[73] Likewise, cases of necessity, in Luther's mind, open the possibility of the office being exercised by women.[74] What Luther regards as a case of necessity, should it come to that, is one in which only women are present anyway (which, however, he can scarcely imagine!)[75] or in which no man is ready or able to attend to the preaching office.[76] In such cases, necessity would cause the universal priesthood of the woman with regard to the public function of Word and Sacrament to find practical significance. Luther particularly stresses this possibility in the case of emergency Baptism.[77]

5. The *Delegatio* by the Congregation

According to our study thus far, two things are clear in Luther: (1) Every Christian is a priest and has, by virtue of his priesthood, the fundamental authority of the Word and Sacrament. And (2) because of the divinely desired order within the congregation; and because of Christian brotherhood, to which every individual Christian is duty-bound; and because in view of the diverse distribution of the gifts to those individuals not all are able, practically speaking, to exercise this authority of Word and Sacrament—it is necessary, rather, to select one or more from the congregation for the public exercise of the concrete office. The process which enacts the latter on the basis and precondition of the former is described by Luther as follows: One from among the multitude of those who all have the same authority is taken and is charged with executing this

---

the woman's preaching office. Storck overlooks the fact that, in Luther, this is rooted in a lower level, namely, of the divine order of creation or the Law. The crucial passages in the treatises *Infiltrating and Clandestine Preachers* (1532) and *On the Councils and the Church* (1539) are left unexamined by Storck. The image which he gives of Luther's attitude toward the woman's preaching office is therefore skewed. In the criticism of H. Storck and [W.] Brunotte in this regard, as generally in the idea of the women's preaching office in Luther, we agree with W. Brunotte, op. cit., pp. 195ff. Also, Brunotte points to Luther's quotation of the Lord's commandment concerning this point mentioned in 1 Cor. 14:37.

72 WA 8:497.34, 424.30; *1522*: WA 10/3:171.7f., where, regarding the possibility of women claiming their right to the preaching office derived from the universal priesthood, it reads: "No, St. Paul forbids a woman to preach in the congregation of men . . ."; WA 26:46.25f.: "Where there is a man, there a woman must neither teach, have dominion . . ."; WA 26:46.32ff.: "He does not grant her the ministry of the word . . . always understand: if there are men present."

73 *1523*: WA 12:309.21ff.; 26:46.25f. — Cf. H. H. Kramm, *Bischof, Pastor und Gemeinde*, Lutherthum 13 (Berlin, 1954), p. 28.

74 Cf. WA 50:633.14: "except cases of emergency."

75 WA 10/3:171.10ff.: "If it came to the point (which I don't imagine) that there were no man, but only women, then a woman could step forward and preach to the others as best as she might, not otherwise."

76 WA 8:498.12ff.: "Therefore, order, decency, and honor demand that women remain silent if men speak; but if no man is preaching, it would be necessary for women to preach"; cf. WA 8:425.4ff.

77 WA 12:181.30ff.

authority "*for the others*."[78] For clarification, take the example of the ten princes who, all being equally heirs, then select one "to govern the estate *for them*."[79]

---

[78] WA 6:407.30f.

[79] WA 6:407.32ff.; cf. WA 10/1.2:239.35ff.: "As an example, where there are many nobles, they choose, with consent of the others, one out of them all to oversee the government by himself on behalf of the others; for if each of them wished to govern land and people, how would it go? Although they all equally have the power that he has, he governs. It is the same way with this power to loose sins and retain sins"; WA 10/3:396.21ff.: "So if there were six brothers who must share an estate, they all have a part of it; it is the same here. The power which God asserts here in the Gospel belongs to us—all of us . . ."; WA 12:309.5ff.: ". . . and only for this reason are some men selected from the people to bear and conduct the office in the stead of the congregation, which they all have; one does not have more than the other." — The expressions "for the others," "for them" (WA 6:407.30 and 32) Brunotte interprets incorrectly (op. cit., pp. 38ff.). Brunotte takes them as "for the benefit of the others" (p. 38 n. 44) and totally misses the fact that the first line refers to the aspect of representing the others and of authorization by the others. "For the others" means "instead of, in the name of, for the sake of the others" (cf. all the passages from Luther quoted in this and the next section). This is also clear from the context of the treatise *To the Christian Nobility of the German Nation*. From the priesthood of Baptism they all have the "same power"; one man is selected to execute this power (publicly)—which they cannot all exercise publicly at the same time—"for the others," in their stead and in the name of them all. This passage seems to us insufficiently treated by Brunotte through his distinction of the concepts of "multitude" [*hauffen*] and "whole assembly" (op. cit., p. 39 n. 49, point 2). At most, there could be a distinction here insofar as the term "whole assembly" (in whose stead the bishop functions during the call) includes the aspect of the collective Church while in the term "multitude" only the number of persons of the local congregation is in view. But even this is completely unsure. In this passage, Luther asserts the equal power of all Christians in the local congregation, and the one called must now carry out this power publicly in the name and stead of all the others. (Incidentally, it does not concern the bestowal of power but the right to exercise this power publicly—contrary to Brunotte, op. cit., p. 45 n. 78.) It will nevertheless be necessary to maintain that, according to Luther, the one chosen for the concrete office *also* "acts in the authority of those who have commissioned him," which Brunotte declines to see as valid (op. cit., p. 43). On the other hand, Luther also bases the office on the divine institution, even in the earlier treatise *To the Christian Nobility of the German Nation*, as Brunotte skillfully demonstrates (op. cit., pp. 40ff.). But the delegative element is still present in Luther, even in an accentuated form, contemporaneously with the idea of the institution and in tension with the same. — In explaining the example of the ten princes, Brunotte ignores this delegative element which is unquestionably present in it (op. cit., p. 44). Luther assumes that all ten princes have an equal royal privilege and equal royal power. But since not all of them can actually exercise the royal office, one does it in their stead, "for them." When Brunotte conversely holds that the royal office, according to its nature, belongs to *one*, and as a result they would not all have it, and there could be no question of a delegation of the rights of all to one, it must be admitted that this is where the comparison used by Luther proves weak. In reality, if it is not the case that the princes, being equally enfranchised, choose and delegate one from their midst to exercise the royal office, the succession to the throne is normally regulated *a priori* and not determined by a free agreement among the princes. But what is decisive here is the sense in which *Luther* uses and employs this example in this passage. And there can be no doubt about this: Luther is stressing the equally present authority and power and the conferral of the public power of governance on one selected in the place of the others. The *tertium comparationis* [common aspect of the things compared] lies in the power equally present in all and the delegation of the one selected to the public exercise thereof. Here again Brunotte completely misses the decisive "for them" (WA 6:407.32). — We are thus unable to follow Brunotte in his polemic against Dieckhoff's opinion of the passage and observation that the particular office is derived from the universal priesthood in Luther (op. cit., p. 39 n. 49, p. 44f. n. 78, p. 46 n. 82). Here, regarding the delegative element in Luther, Dieckhoff has seen the facts more clearly than Brunotte, though we are still unable to

This one represents all the others and exercises their rights, according as they have been delegated to him. We are therefore speaking of this process by which one person from among many of equal qualification is deputized for the public exercise of all the rights held in common, as by a *delegatio*.[80]

The subject of the *delegatio* consists in Luther primarily of those individual Christians who form the congregation, the "we all": "How shall I act? Thus: the authority which I have, another has also, as the text reads. Thus I should not go up and say, 'I have as much authority to preach as you!' No, the priests are to exercise *the authority on behalf of us all*, and we are to say, 'We all may have authority to preach, absolve, and baptize, but *we charge you on behalf of us all* to baptize and to preach the Gospel, to forgive sins and to give the Sacrament, and to carry out other things for us. This person shall preside over us all.' "[81] "We should speak to the clerics thus: 'We know that you have the office to absolve, preach, and baptize. It has been left to us no less than to you. But we give you the authority; therefore, preach to us the Gospel, and we will judge.' "[82] This "we" is to be understood as the sum of the individual Christians who form the congregation. In the congregation, the individual Christians, who naturally all have the same rights, are joined together. Thus a *communio juris* is formed in the congregation.[83] Since in this situation not all are able publicly to exercise their right, it must be conferred on one "in the stead and name of all who have the same right [*vice et nomine omnium, qui idem juris habent*]."[84] Thus the individual Christians in the congregation delegate their several individual rights to

accept with Dieckhoff the idea that in the delegative element there is necessarily a contradiction of the institutionary element, in which he agrees with Brunotte. Brunotte reaches his opinion of the passages in question by the observation that, in the treatise *To the Christian Nobility of the German Nation*, Luther also teaches the divine institution of the clerical office, with which the delegative derivation of the office from the universal priesthood is irreconcilable. Cf. op. cit., p. 43: "The nature of the clerical office cannot be derived from the universal priesthood of the ones calling . . . , nor from that of the one called. This is clearly borne out for this treatise by the determination that the spiritual office is based on the command of God." This is an axiomatic assumption, and it is not advisable to make it an interpretive principle if we wish to see the whole complex of Luther's conceptualization. In Luther, both forms of rationale for the office coincide, and it is wrong to formulate Luther's view as though the nature of the office were to be derived from and based on *not* the universal priesthood *but rather* the divine institution (Brunotte, op. cit., p. 46). In Luther, it is both the one and the other.

80 Naturally, this term is not to be forced, and there are incongruencies in it. We use it because it rightly echoes the essential here. W. Elert (*Morphologie des Luthertums* I [Munich, 1952], pp. 301 and 303) also speaks of a delegation of the universal right to the individual in Luther. Rudolph Sohm (*Kirchenrecht* I [1892], pp. 500ff.; also cf. pp. 51ff.) calls the same process *Gestattung* [authorization] by the assembly of Christians. It could also be indicated, in Luther's own terminology, by the term *Verwilligung* [assent] (e.g., WA 10/1.2:239.35; 49:600.14; and elsewhere).

81 WA 10/3:396.7ff.; cf. WA 11:412.30ff.: "But when he is where Christians are present in the place who have the same power and right as he, he should not put himself first, but let himself be called and put forward in order that he may preach and teach in the stead and command of the others."

82 WA 10/3:398.8ff.; cf. WA 15:721.3ff.

83 WA 12:189.21.

84 WA 12:189.22f.

that one who is then to exercise publicly the right common to all "in the stead of us all."[85] It cannot be denied that an element of cooperative social law is present here in Luther's thought.[86] Precisely because every individual Christian in the congregation, by virtue of his priestly right, participates in the process of *delegatio*, a *consensus* is required for the call to the particular office.[87] The election of a person always presupposes a certain consensus among the voters. Here, however, it is not merely considered in this technical sense, but it has materially essential importance. The will of the others is a presupposition to the selection of one to bear the concrete office, who then "exercises the public office by the command and consent of the others."[88]

Remembering, then, that all individuals have their priestly right only *qua membra ecclesiae* [as members of the Church], it becomes clear that the *delegatio*

---

[85] WA 8:424.30: "places his right under another"; WA 6:407.31 ("for others"); WA 10/1.2:239.36f. ("for the sake of the others"); WA 12:309.6 ("instead of the congregation"); WA 10/3:171.1ff.: "But if" (in a household) "others go and choose someone, and *they yield it and put it in his hand*, it goes well"; WA 38:230.19f.: "After that, one is taken and called from these clerics by birth, or they are elected to such offices, who are to execute this office for all our sake."

[86] This was especially highlighted by G. Holstein (*Die Grundlagen des ev. Kirchenrechts* [Tübingen, 1928], pp. 95ff.). On the analogy of the ten princes (quoted by us above), by which Luther tries to clarify the delegative conferral on one person of the particular right to dispense Word and Sacrament, [Holstein] remarks: "This means that the conferral of the office is done by the free, voluntary decision among legally equal associates; in other words, the office is based on cooperative social law" (p. 97); also cf.: "The organization of the empirical church is . . . accomplished from the bottom up through the free and equal associates' unified desire and conferral of the office" (p. 98). Still it must be said that, with such judgments, Holstein is not entirely wrong. Yet the expression "by the free, voluntary decision" does not match Luther's teaching of the ministry since, according to Luther, the congregation is required by the command of Christ to fill the office for the administration of the means of grace. This therefore depends on the obedience of Christ's command and not properly on "free, voluntary decision" (cf. the section on the specificity of the commission of the office, below, pp. 72–74). In addition, Holstein, in his cooperative socio-legal interpretation, has not really done justice to Luther here since in Luther, besides the delegative basis of the office treated by us here, there is another argument found in the institutive ordinance of Christ, which Holstein does not take into account. His assertion that in Luther the institution of a particular office has "its legal roots not in an institutional assignment but in a cooperative call" (p. 97) depends on skewed observations and is not applicable to Luther in this binary formulation. In actuality, both are present in Luther: the cooperative element which occupies us here in this section as well as the institutional one which we still need to treat (cf. below, pp. 85–99). Still, Holstein has observed correctly insofar as there are at least echoes of the cooperative aspects present in Luther's concept of the office.

[87] WA 12:189.26 and 32ff., 191.26f.: "the common consensus of believers [*consensus communis fidelium*]"; WA 6:564.7f.: "committed by our consensus [*nostro . . . consensu commissum*]"; WA 6:566.28f.: "not allowed . . . except by consensus of the community [*non licere . . . uti nisi consensu communitatis*]." Cf. G. Holstein, op. cit., p. 97: "If everyone has the right, they can only delegate it all together." The constitutive construction of the *consensus fidelium* for the appearance of the concrete office in the congregation in Luther was also stressed by W. Elert (*Morphologie* I, pp. 303f. and 322). In Brunotte, this aspect is not sufficiently examined in the discussion of the passage WA 6:564.6ff. (op. cit., pp. 52ff.) as also in the passage in *Concerning the Ministry* (op. cit., pp. 89ff.).

[88] WA 49:600.14: cf. WA 6:408.14f.: "No one may put himself forward without our consent and choosing"; WA 50:633.9f.: "The others are all content with this and consent to it." — Cf. on the nature of the call as the consent of the congregation, F. K. Schumann, "Amt der Kirche," etc., op. cit., pp. 317 and 325.

of individuals is to be regarded simultaneously as the *delegatio* of the congregation, the collective whole.[89] The "total whole [*tota universitas*]" is that which confers the office "by the common votes [*communibus suffragiis*]" on one or more persons "in their stead [*vice sua*]."[90] No one can occupy the office "apart from the common will and command."[91] The public minister is chosen, set apart, and authorized "by the common assembly of Christians,"[92] "by the whole congregation, which are all simultaneously priests."[93] His legitimacy is fundamentally the fact that he "is in the office and is tolerated by the assembly";[94] that is, that the delegation, once it is completed, is in force and upheld by the congregation. The congregation, as the sum of the individual Christians and of their priestly rights, is the entity by which the *delegatio* is enacted and whose delegative will serves as the basis for the authority of the public minister in office. Even pope and bishop derive their authority only from the congregation.[95]

Delegatio means conferring the several rights of the individual Christians—and thus the right of the congregation—on one who is thereby legitimized to exercise this right in the concrete public office. By the individuals delegating their right, the congregation confers it. And the congregation in any locality is the concrete manifestation of the *communio sanctorum*, the community of all believers, the entirety of Christians, which is the Body of Christ.[96] Thus it is also necessary to see in the *delegatio* of the individual congregation in Luther the involvement of the whole Church. First—focusing internally—all the individual members of this individual congregation, on the basis of their priestly right, participate in this process; yet—turning our focus externally to the whole—so do all other congregations, that is, the collective whole of the Church, the *ecclesia catholica*. Thus while the concept of *delegatio* in Luther is, on the one hand (and fundamentally), oriented in a cooperative direction, on the other hand this cooperative element is nevertheless encompassed and to a certain extent constrained within the overall conception of the Church, which is noncongregationalist, so that it cannot be unfolded by analogy to the law of secular cooperatives.

---

[89] On the connection and mutual foundation of both elements, cf. WA 12:190.36ff.: "For where it is demonstrated clearly that each person has the right of administering the Word . . . how much more right and command shall any total whole not have . . . ?"

[90] WA 12:190.40f.

[91] WA 6:408.16. We thus agree with Brunotte that, in the call of the public minister according to Luther, the congregation acts as a *whole* (op. cit., p. 44; also pp. 39f. n. 49, point 3). But Brunotte oversimplifies Luther when on this basis he strikes out the element referring to the sum of the individuals in the congregation. *Both* are present in Luther. In the action of the "congregation" (*gemeyne*), Luther sees here the action of the several individuals who make up the congregation.

[92] WA 41:208.28.

[93] WA 41:210.24f. Also note here the intertwining of two strands: corporatism side by side with the subdivision of the whole into its several individual parts.

[94] WA 50:634.26f.

[95] WA 10/3:215.23f. — It must be kept in mind in all these expressions of Luther's that there is *a single* perspective involved which remains valid, yet not in isolation from the others to be treated at greater length below (cf. pp. 99–104).

[96] Cf. K. Müller, *Kirche, Gemeinde u. Obrigkeit nach Luther* (Tübingen, 1910), p. 46.

Recently, *P. Brunner* ("Vom Amt des Bischofs," in *Schr. d. Theol. Konv. Augsb. Bek.* 9 [Berlin, 1955], pp. 12ff.) has attempted to elicit a new understanding of one of the core passages for the delegative rationale for the office in Luther, WA 12:189.17–27. There, he suggests, Luther does not teach that, on the basis of the concurring rights claimed by the many individuals in the congregation, these many individual rights in the call are conferred on the one called as the mandatary, trustee, and representative of the others so that he may exercise it on behalf of the others. Instead, the ideas of "community, collective whole, right, representation" must be understood on the basis of the pneumatic [spiritual] nature of the ἐκκλησία (*ekklesia*), and the call involves the action of "those who appoint people to the *ministerium* for public exercise . . . as those among whom the one catholic and apostolic Church is present with the *ministerium* instituted for her. Those who are called act in the stead of this one catholic and apostolic Church. The called do nothing other than take in hand, as it were, the *ministerium* instituted for this one *ecclesia catholica* manifested in their midst, as authorized members of this church, and for the sake of public exercise concentrate it on the ordinand, and thus make it concrete in the ordinand" (p. 14). It will at any rate be possible and necessary to accept the interpretation *in bonam partem* that, in Luther's understanding, the *communio sanctorum* and *ecclesia catholica* also act jointly in the delegative action of the individuals, i.e., the congregation. One must ask, however, whether it is justified on the basis of this view to eliminate absolutely the delegative, cooperative element from this passage. To avoid doing violence to the text, we cannot omit in the exposition of this passage the fact that, according to it, it is the concurrence of the several equal rights of individual Christians, "who have the same right [*qui idem juris habent*]" (line 22f.) in the congregation, which is required for the selection of a public minister (cf. line 17ff.: "*For since these are all things held in common by all Christians*, no one is allowed to go up into their midst by his own authority and take for himself alone what belongs to all"; and line 21f.: "*This community of right requires* that one—or however many pleases the community—are to be chosen or accepted . . ."). The office is here constructed by Luther from the factual equality of priestly rights possessed by all individual Christians in the congregation, by means of the delegative concept. Luther does the same, as we have seen, in various other places as well. Brunner (p. 13 n. 8) himself mentions the section WA 6:407.29, with the analogy of the ten princes, in which Luther suggests a similar understanding. But further passages would also have to be added (with reference esp. to the sections mentioned above, p. 65 n. 85). By comparison with these other passages of Luther, it becomes harder to rule out entirely the delegative, cooperative factor in the passage WA 12:189.17ff.[97] And, indeed, it is present, though constrained

[97] In this opinion of the present passage we have the agreement of E. Sommerlath ("Amt und allgemeines Priestertum," pp. 48f.) and most earlier commentators. The explanation of this passage in Brunotte (op. cit., pp. 85ff.) remains entirely unsatisfactory. Reproducing the term "*communis*" (*jus commune*) with "fundamental" (op. cit., pp. 86f. n. 83) is reckless inasmuch as only one aspect is expressed by this term, not the whole intended content. By this Luther also wishes to refer to the *universality* of this right to the priestly duties: "All have this same right; everyone has the *idem jus*" (line 23). The decisive passage: "who execute this office publicly in the stead and name of all, who have the same right [*qui vice et nomine omnium, qui idem juris habent, exequantur officia ista*

by the idea of the *ecclesia catholica*, which is the *corpus Christi* [Body of Christ], being manifested in the individual congregation. This latter limitation should naturally not be overlooked by any means. On this also cf. F. K. Schumann, op. cit., pp. 315f.; and in the vein of Schumann, H. Thimme, "Welche Folgerungen ergeben sich aus der Lehre der Kirche für ihre Ordnung," in *Schriften d. Theol. Konv. Augsb. Bek.* 8 (Berlin, 1955), pp. 45f. —

Like P. Brunner, *V. Vajta* has also questioned the sociological, cooperative element in Luther's concept of the office (*Theologie des Gottesdienstes bei Luther* [Göttingen, 1954], pp. 211ff.). He rightly stresses that behind the call of the congregation as proper subject, we are to see the call of God, who has given to the congregation the commission of appointing the office. In the context of our study, we will come to discuss this question also (cf. below, pp. 72–74, 117–22). Nevertheless, there is present in Luther a sociological, cooperative element in his view of the office, *including*—as we believe it necessary to maintain contrary to Vajta—the office "as a contract between two individuals" (p. 211), if we can here refer to the various persons assembled and included in the congregation as "individuals." Certainly it is not the only—nor even the decisive—element, being restricted and to a certain extent neutralized by other concepts, yet its presence is undeniable. Vajta says that the passages in which Luther speaks of the office-bearer performing his function in the stead and name of the congregation by no means entail "that the commission to proclaim the Word and administer the Sacraments comes from men" (p. 214) since it is "Christ's commission to all Christians through Baptism, to be His priesthood, through which He Himself works" (ibid.). This is certainly correct. But this does not negate the fact that not all equally carry out this commission of Christ's in actuality; the one who publicly acts in the office is, according to the passages of Luther in question, only empowered for this function delegatively by the congregation. Then "Christ's commission for the whole congregation" is carried out by him with certainty (p. 214), under the assumption that the congregation has thereby commissioned and empowered him for that purpose in a delegative process so that he now performs it "in the stead and name of all who have the same right [*vice et nomine omnium, qui idem juris habent*]." Vajta himself says, "He

---

publice]," which expresses the idea of representation and the principle of delegation, is distorted by Brunotte (op. cit., p. 91 n. 114). Brunotte ignores the "in the stead [*vice*]" when he thinks that no representation of all individuals is presumed here. "All [*omnes*]" really also indicates the sum of the equally empowered individual Christians in the congregation. What else would be meant by the added clause "who have the same right [*qui idem juris habent*]"? Luther also sees the office-bearer as the delegate of all the individual Christians in the congregation. And the passage "this community of right requires [*haec communio juris cogit*] . . ." clearly informs "the necessity of the call to the spiritual office from the concurring rights of the individual Christian" (which Brunotte will not admit: op. cit., p. 93), as Luther's view has been supplemented by such as Höfling. On the whole, there can be no question of this "alone." Yet there can be with regard to an "also." This rationale, too, is visibly present in Luther. — We gladly grant Brunotte that the Christian rights deriving from the universal priesthood in Luther are not understood as "individual rights of an idle individual" (op. cit., p. 142). They do not exist in and with the individual per se, but only insofar as the individual Christian is incorporated into the *ecclesia* as a member thereof. The congregational right is really divided out, according to Luther, into the individual rights of the congregants, who, insofar as they are part of the *ecclesia*, all possess their priestly rights individually for themselves and take them into account when calling a public minister.

has received this commission through the congregation as through the priestly flock, which, for the sake of order in the public worship life of the congregation alone, causes him to proclaim the Word and distribute the Sacraments" (ibid.). By this Vajta acknowledges that, according to these passages of Luther, the universal commission through Christ only becomes the special commission in the midst of the congregation by the commission of the congregation itself, and even then only for the sake of order, namely, on account of the concurrence of the various individual rights, because of the *communio juris*—and this is itself the delegative element. Vajta sees in these passages of Luther an emphasis on the "mediating role of the congregation in the execution of the divine commission" (p. 214), but he also implies that the accent present in them is necessarily "to stress the basis of the pastoral office in the priestly call of all Christians and the equal standing of the pastor with all the other priests" (p. 215)—and by doing so he identifies the very element of the delegative rationale for the concrete office from the universal priesthood. This accent, however, necessarily introduces into the concept of the office a sociological, cooperative thrust, even if this is overlaid by other aspects in the concept of the office and therefore does not come to full fruition. What is false is not the determination of a sociological element in Luther's view of the office, but only an assertion that Luther's view of the office is *purely* sociological. *Such* is not the case.[98]

6. The Office-Bearer as Representative of the Whole

Whoever occupies the public office entered it by means of the congregation's *delegatio*. He neither took this position of his own accord nor was placed into it directly by God without means; the congregation delegated him to this office. He must therefore recognize himself to be at all times the representative of the whole and is obligated at every moment to the congregation as a whole.[99] His official action is the official action of the whole congregation. When he administers the Keys, he does so "not by right, but in ministry to the church (since he is the church's minister)," and uses them "not as given to his own or to himself but to the church."[100] Neither is it the case that the congregation, by the *delegatio*, has fundamentally relinquished its right and he, the office-bearer, is now the only one in possession of this right. Rather, the congregation always remains fundamentally the possessor of all rights and authorities; only the exercise, the public

---

[98] The same could be said, *mutatis mutandis*, against Brunotte's position (e.g., op. cit., pp. 43ff., 76, 85ff., and elsewhere).

[99] The one charged with the clerical office is, according to Luther, in that office *not only in the authority of God*, as Brunotte (op. cit., p. 43) wishes, but quite as much in the authority of the congregation of those who have called and delegated him to the office, who have charged him with the office.

[100] WA 2:191.19f.

use of the fundamental right, is delegated and, as it were, "transferred"[101]—for which reason it is also able, on sufficient grounds, to withdraw a commission previously granted and to annul the *delegatio.*[102] The office-bearer must always be conscious of this fact that his office and his official action are referred back to the collective whole which authorizes and upholds him. "A pastor who tends to the Office of the Keys baptizes, preaches, and gives the Sacrament not for his own sake, but on account of the congregation. For he is a minister (*diener*) to the whole congregation, to whom the Keys have been given. . . ."[103] In his official actions he is merely the congregation's mouth and hand, its instrument. This is especially the case with the conducting of the liturgy.[104] The actual bearer of it, the actual "cleric who performs and sends the work," is the "common priesthood"; the priest at the altar is only the courier and servant, "who carries and brings it."[105]

The relationship of the particular office-bearer to the congregation which delegated him is described succinctly by Luther when he says that this man exercises publicly the priestly works "*vice et nomine omnium.*"[106] If we examine this formula more closely, we see that it expresses two separate ideas. The "*vice omnium*" suggests the element of *standing in the stead of another*, of representation. The office-bearer stands there in the stead of others; as office-bearer he embodies the person of the congregation. This is the first point. The

[101] WA 10/3:171.1ff., and only the "transfer" of the concrete use of the authority is meant. — Also cf. F. K. Schumann, "Amt der Kirche . . . ," op. cit., pp. 315f.

[102] Cf., e.g., WA 12:309.9f.: ". . . One must be brought forward from the multitude and raised up, who may be taken down again whenever desired." — This body of questions is treated at length below, pp. 77–80.

[103] WA 10/3:215.25ff.; cf. WA 10/3:396.3ff.; 8:253.30ff.: "Whoever is called by the people, or by the one who has the command and will of the people, does this work in the stead and person of the people and by common authority."

[104] Cf. the fine passage in the treatise *The Private Mass and the Consecration of Priests* (1533), WA 38:247.23ff.: The pastor approaches the altar and sings the Words of Institution, all the other fellow priests kneel around him, "and in this inborn, inherited priestly honor and adornment we are present, having . . . our gold crowns on our heads, harps in hand, and golden censers. Nor do we have our pastor speak the ordinance of Christ for himself as for his own person, but he is the mouth of us all, and we all speak them with him in our heart and with faith lifted up to the Lamb of God, who is present for us and among us, and who, according to His ordinance, feeds us with His body and blood." Or the other passage from *Sermon at the Dedication of the Castle Church, Torgau* (1544), WA 49:600.11ff.: "For my preaching, when we come together in the congregation, is not my word or doing, but happens because of you all and for the sake of the whole Church. It is only that there must be one man to speak and propound the Word at the command and consent of the others, who by hearing the sermon all confess that Word, and so teach others also. Thus when a little child is baptized, not only the pastor does it, but so do the sponsors as witnesses—indeed, the whole Church does it. For Baptism, like the Word and Christ Himself, is a common possession of all Christians. So, too, they all pray, sing, and give thanks together, and here no one has or does anything by himself alone, but what each person has the others also have." The pastor, especially as liturgist, is the spokesman of the congregation, which speaks and acts in him. Cf. this passage in Rörer's note: "All those who are listening are also speaking" (WA 49:600.1).

[105] WA 7:634.9ff.

[106] WA 12:189.22.

"*nomine omnium*," on the other hand, implies the idea of *authorization*. The office-bearer acts in the name of all, in the name of the congregation; in other words, he is authorized by the others, by the congregation. He personifies the authority of the congregation which it in turn receives from the Lord. This is the second point.

> Both ideas are found frequently in Luther. The pastors conduct their ministry "for us and in our stead" (= *vice omnium*), and they are to "bear the authority on our behalf" (= *nomine omnium*).[107] The public minister is to be selected and called "that he may preach and teach in the stead (= *vice*) and command (= *nomine*) of the others."[108] His function takes place first in representing the others, and then at the command—i.e., in the authority—of the others. People must have pastors or preachers "who publicly and particularly give, administer, and exercise the aforesaid four items or sacred things, on account of and in the name of the church. . . ."[109] Both factors may also be found consolidated in a single expression.[110]

This character of the public office always comes out strongly in Luther as a representation of the collective whole and its authority. All priestly works in this office are done "in our name [*nostro nomine*]."[111] Of great importance,

---

107 WA 10/3:396.1f.

108 WA 11:412.32f., 413.22: "in their stead." — Brunotte seeks to eliminate the idea of representation expressed in these passages by framing the congregation (in contrast to the individual Christians) as the entity in whose stead the office-bearer thus stands (op. cit., p. 67 n. 55; pp. 68–74). Yet this is not what Luther meant, as already shown by the passage WA 11:412.32f., which we have quoted in the text, where it says ". . . in the stead and command *of the others*." Here he focuses on the remaining individual Christians of the congregation. It is extremely hard to see how this passage "explicitly" states "that the one charged preaches by the command and in the stead of the Christian congregation and does not somehow unite in himself the individual rights of the other Christians" (op. cit., p. 73 n. 93). Rather, we must view this as evidence of the delegative view of the office in Luther. The congregation becomes concrete for Luther in the sum of the individual persons who affirm and attend a locality of the pure Gospel. The church as a superpersonal quantity is found only in this bodily assembly of individual Christians. Brunotte makes such expressions numerous times (op. cit., pp. 91, 165f., 179, et al.). Although according to Luther individual Christians do not constitute the Church by their coming together—the Church is constituted by the Word of God which calls the individuals—nevertheless as individuals with their individual rights, they are taken into account by Luther in the conceptual construction of the particular office. Also cf. above, pp. 67–68 n. 97, on Brunotte's statements.

109 WA 50:633.1ff. The continuation "but rather from Christ's institution" will occupy us in greater detail in chapter 4 but can be left out of consideration here. Also cf. WA 8:253.31f.: "in the stead and person of the multitude and power of the congregation"; WA 49:600.12ff.: "for the sake of the whole Church—by the command and consent of the others."

110 "On account of [*von wegen*]": WA 10/1.2:239.36f.; 10/3:215.26; 38:230.20: Certain persons must be set apart "to bear the teaching office . . . [and] handle the Sacraments on account of the congregation"; WA 41:214.31f.: "who on account of us all are to execute this office." "in the stead of [*anstatt*]": WA 10/3:216.1, 396.6–8; 11:413.22; 12:191.1, 309.6f. "For [*fur*]": WA 6:407.29, 31, 33. "in the name of [*im Namen*]": WA 6:564.12.

111 WA 6:564.12. Additionally, regarding this passage in *The Babylonian Captivity of the Church* (WA 6:564.6ff.), Brunotte's thesis that no delegative rationale of the office and no idea of conferral is expressed here is inaccurate. On the basis of the priesthood and its authority which all have in common, a public minister is set apart from among those in the priesthood, and the (public)

however, is that Luther adds to these conclusions yet another: if the priestly function of Word and Sacrament is done in the public office in the name and stead of the congregation, "then the Church does it; if the Church does it, *then God does it. . . .*"[112] The characterization of the office-bearer as representative of the congregation thus happens in Luther's thinking not in opposition to or even detachment from the fact that he is also representative of the Lord God.[113] The congregation, in whose name he functions, which he represents, is not simply an earthly association but at the same time the *communio sanctorum*, which is the Body of Christ. In it, the authority of Christ is active and is also personified in the office-bearer, who stands there *vice et nomine omnium* [in the stead and name of all]. Here we have before us a juncture in Luther's teaching, where the derivation of the authority of the office from the congregation and that from the institutive will of God are in direct contact.

7. The Specificity of the Office's Commission in View of Christ's Command

The idea of the cooperative *delegatio* is bounded in Luther, first, by the fact that in the delegating congregation he sees the activity of the *communio sanctorum* as the Body of Christ, and yet further by the fact that the congregation, in its activity of delegating the office, is only complying with Christ's command to proclaim the Word and to administer the Sacraments.[114] The collective whole of the Christians in the congregation is the recipient of this command.[115] It is therefore responsible for its execution at all times. Thus it has not only a *jus*, but a *praeceptum*, a "command to commit what belongs to the office . . . to one or more persons."[116] It is obligated to do so on pain of eternal damnation.[117] For this reason it delegates the office and assigns to one (or more) from its midst the duty to exercise in its stead and in its name the priesthood with respect to the public function of Word and Sacrament.

---

ministry is conferred ("*ministerium commissum*"!) on him "by our consent [*nostro consensu*]." The conferral is equivalent to an approval or assent that this man executes the ministry for the others. Therefore, he does all things in his office "*nostro nomine*," as representative, mandatary, delegate, and commissioner of the "we." With that "we," however, Luther is by no means thinking only of a superpersonal, holistic quantity of church, as Brunotte intends (op. cit., p. 59), but also of all the individuals ("*nos omnes*"!) who are all equally priests in the association of the congregation. — In this place we must, however, regard as justifiable Brunotte's polemic against Dieckhoff on the interpretation of the words ". . . right of authority, except as much as we freely allow [*jus imperii, nisi quantum nos sponte nostra admitteremus*]."

[112] WA 10/3:216.1ff. (in the subsequent text there appears a rationale for putting forward a public minister for the sake of order!).

[113] Cf. V. Vajta, op. cit., p. 215.

[114] Cf. Vajta, op. cit., pp. 213f.

[115] WA 2:190.5ff.; 30/2:498.18ff.

[116] WA 12:190.40f.

[117] WA 11:411.24ff., 413.23ff., 414.11ff. and 30ff.

In the *delegatio* by the congregation, then, no rights and powers detached from Christ or inherent in the congregation irrespective of Christ are conferred on the man who enters the public office, but simply Christ's commission to preach the Gospel and administer the Sacraments. That man's office is entirely specified by Christ's commission, which comes to him *through* the congregation, yet ultimately from Christ Himself.[118] It stands and falls with this commission, which, though already fundamentally given to the individual with the universal priesthood in Baptism, is now released for public exercise by the congregation's *delegatio*. Thus we must speak of a specificity of the office's commission.

The content of this commission is delineated in very strict terms. The flock of faithful Christians in the wilderness, of which Luther speaks in the treatise *To the Christian Nobility of the German Nation* (1520), chooses a man and charges him not with representing them in a general way in all possible matters, but with "the office of baptizing, celebrating Mass, absolving, and preaching."[119] The "officers and ministers" are "appointed to preach and distribute the Sacrament in the congregation."[120] Regard must be had to the command "that every man who is called to the preaching office has the power and authority to preach, baptize, and absolve."[121] The office-bearers are to dispense not their own mysteries, but God's.[122] The commission, which is actualized in the congregation's *delegatio*, is none other than that of exercising publicly in the congregation the function of Word and Sacrament instituted by Christ. Luther sees the office so firmly bound to this commission that he counts as invalid any call to the office issued in disregard of it.[123] It is an essential mark of the ministers in the public office ". . . that they handle the Word of God and the Sacraments; this is their work and office."[124]

By this emphasis on the specificity of the office's commission, the borders are drawn within which the congregation's authorization and *delegatio* of the concrete office-bearer remains and must remain. The congregation is bound to Christ's commission, as is the public minister appointed by that congregation. No arbitrary decision is permitted on either side. The office-bearer may do nothing except what Christ's commission requires; the congregation may expect nothing from the office-bearer except what Christ's commission stipulates. Both parties—the delegating congregation and the delegated office-bearer—are enclosed in the brackets of Christ's commission and precisely defined. Thus the specificity of the office's commission contributes decisively to neutralizing

---

[118] Cf. G. C. A. Harleß, *Kirche u. Amt nach luth. Lehre* (Stuttgart, 1853), p. 19; and E. Sommerlath, "Amt u. allg. Priestertum," p. 42.

[119] WA 6:407.38f.; cf. WA 10/3:396.8ff.

[120] WA 12:317.4ff.; cf. WA 2:249.12: ". . . for that purpose they are consecrated priests" (i.e., to speak the Absolution); WA 6:409.3f.; 8:503.29f.: "to preach God's Word and give the Sacraments"; WA 38:228.26f., 253.11; 38:427.20ff., 428.7ff.

[121] WA 28:470.38ff.

[122] WA Br 3:210.49ff.; cf. WA 10/3:120.13ff.; 38:240.28ff.; 41:241.39f.; 50:634.28ff.; 6:530.24.

[123] Cf. above, p. 11.

[124] WA 6:409.3f.

somewhat the cooperative element in Luther's rationale for the office and preventing a secular, democratic reading of it.

8. The Specificity of the Office's Function

The commission assigned to the office-bearer, which is the existential basis of the office, has as its objective the function as actually performed. An office without function is unimaginable for Luther. The office consists, in his view, precisely of the proper function. A nonexercise of the office's function would be judged as a boycott of Christ's commission and a crime against the Church. We have already cited Luther's harsh words concerning the nonpreaching "Mass-priests."[125] Where the function is not carried out, the true office is absent—indeed, it has become a diabolical contrary of it.[126] ". . . All apostles, bishops, priests, and the whole clerical estate are called and established only for the sake of the Word."[127] In other words, the function of the Word occurs in a real manner. The question of whether the office-bearer actually exercises the function of the office or not is that on which all its authority and power depends.[128] The actual realization of the office's function is for Luther an essential mark of the particular office, which is why we must speak of the specificity of the office's function.[129]

---

[125] Cf. above, pp. 9–12 and 18–19.

[126] Cf. WA 6:564.15ff.: "From whence it comes that he who does not preach the Word, having been called to this by the Gospel, is in no way a priest . . ."; WA 6:566.5ff.: "The priest's offering is to preach. If he does not do it, he is as much a priest as a picture of a man is a man"; WA 6:567.1ff.: ". . . He therefore who does not know or preach the Gospel is not only not a priest or bishop but also is a kind of plague on the Church"; WA 38:199.23ff., 222.25ff., 223.11ff.

[127] WA 7:22.20ff.

[128] WA 10/3:122.22ff. — V. Vajta (op. cit., pp. 196f.) stresses that the office according to Luther "receives its legitimacy from the Word and Sacraments, which Christ wishes to be used. . . . The Word is thus the primary and forms the basis of the ecclesial office" (p. 196). To think of it in reverse, the idea of the office first legitimizing Word and Sacrament would be "completely mistaken from Luther's way of thinking" (p. 197). "The view of the Word as the basis of the office, and the view of the succession as guarantee of the Word" would not share a "both/and" relationship; "a choice must be made between these two possibilities" (p. 198). By this, Vajta has surely interpreted Luther correctly. When Luther stresses the functional specificity of the office in this way, it is really rooted in the fact that the office is carried by the operative Word itself. Cf. WA 39/2:182.1: "The ministry of the Word makes ministers, not ministers the ministry of the Word. The Word [*verbum*] does it."

[129] To denote the function, Luther uses various expressions: "office [*Ampt*]" (WA 6:407.14f.); "work [*werck*]" (WA 6:407.16); "office or work" (WA 6:408.28, 409.4 and 8; 50:248.1ff.); "ministry [*dienst*]" (WA 41:210.24) or [*ministerium*] (WA 6:564.13); "office [*officium*]" (WA 6:564.28). — The specificity of the office's function in Luther may not, however, be viewed in such a way as to sideline the conferral to that function into irrelevance. The term "office," which in Luther often points especially to the actual function, always implies the conferred quality of this function at the same time. Cf., e.g., WA 30/3:521.7f.: "Either he demonstrates the call and command to preach or, briefly put, is silent and forbidden to preach; for it is called 'the office'—indeed, 'the preaching office'—and no one can have an office without and apart from a command or call." On this meaning of the word "office [*Amt*]," cf. A .F. C. Vilmar, *Die Lehre v. geitsl. Amt* (Marburg, 1870), p. 2. In Luther's scheme, the functional specificity of the office may not be turned against the commissional specificity or the necessity and significance of the special call to the office.

It is in the particular function that, according to Luther, the distinction between ministers in the public office and other Christians lies.[130] "In itself"—i.e., in its essence—there is no distinction.[131] By way of illustrating the functional character of the office, Luther uses the analogy of the ministry of a secular official, judge, or mayor, where only the particular function which that man possesses distinguishes him from the other citizens. Here Luther always means to underscore the fact that neither is the ecclesial office bound essentially and indissolubly with the person of the respective minister, but it has its essence in the function as actually performed.[132]

The relationship between the office and the person of the office-bearer is in need of even greater illumination. For Luther, it is most essential that the office and the person be distinguished from each other.[133] To a certain extent he confronts the office as a quantity independent of the person who is called to it without coalescing with it. He confronts it as an ideal quantity, that is to say, as a delegated ministry, as a commission already given by Christ before him and which survives him as an individual office-bearer, falling on one person today, on another tomorrow.[134] The individual person's connection to it is only guaranteed in the function as actually performed, and in this connection only this latter is of importance since it helps the ideal quantity of the commission to become the practical, concrete quantity of the ministry. The office does not change a Christian in his essence; it is "only applied,"[135] "no more than a public ministry which may be committed to a man by the whole congregation,"[136] a *ministerium commissum* [ministry which is committed].[137] It consists of a "single work, namely, giving or handing out the Gospel commanded by Christ to be preached."[138] It is true that the call to the particular office makes a man an office-bearer—though not a priest, which he already is from Baptism, yet certainly a

130 WA 6:408.26ff., 407.13ff.; 6:567.19 ("nothing except in the ministry [*nihil nisi ministerio*]"); WA 12:309.3ff.; WA Br 1:595.29ff.; 2:86.10ff.: ". . . It is necessary that you see nothing between the priest and the laity . . . but that the ministry belongs to the former, not the latter."

131 WA 8:503.26ff.; cf. WA 8:429.34ff.

132 WA 6:408.18ff.; 7:631.30ff.; 8:503.30ff.; 12:309.2, 317.5; 41:208.6ff.; 45:310.2 (Rörer).

133 WA 28:467.29ff., 469.4ff. and 38ff.; 32:316.15: "For I have often said elsewhere that the office and the person must be sharply distinguished . . ."; WA 38:243.10ff.

134 WA 17/1:510.6f.: "Although I am in the office, the office is not mine; tomorrow another may have it"; WA 15:721.13ff.: "Likewise, they must do their ministry, but not forever. . . . The priesthood which we received from Christ is eternal"; WA 38:241.17ff.: "When Judas went to the devil, he did not take his apostolic office with him but left it behind him, and Matthias took it instead of him. The office and sacraments remain forever in the Church; the persons change daily. Just let those be called and installed who can carry them out, and they will certainly continue. The horse is bridled and saddled, so put on him a naked boy who can ride, and the horse will go as well as if the emperor or pope rode him"; WA 41:210.19ff.; 41:457.3: "Pastors die one after another; the office remains."

135 WA 41:213.16.

136 WA 41:210.24f.; cf. WA 12:190.22: "office and work."

137 WA 6:564.7f.

138 WA 38:239.10ff.; cf. WA 38:239.30ff. That the essence of the office is to distribute the gifts of God is noted especially by Vajta, op. cit., p. 205. Also cf. J. Heubach, op. cit., p. 66 n. 1.

servant and minister of the other priests, a "minister and functionary of the common priesthood."[139] However, this new relationship to the congregation in which the office-bearer finds himself is rooted in the particular function with which he is now concerned and is not intrinsic. It can be withdrawn at any time. The office ultimately remains separate from the person of its respective bearer.[140]

This separation of the office from the person is an essential theme in Luther's view of the office and is of service to him particularly in maintaining an anti-Donatistic stance. The function of the office of the proclaimed Word and the administered Sacraments is independent in its operation from the personal condition of the minister occupying the office. "Whether he is Judas or St. Paul, let it be of no concern to you; only distinguish the office from the person and what is holy from the abomination,"[141] "His personal character does not make God's Word and Sacrament better or worse for you."[142] Even a wicked man can be a "minister of the holy and righteous Church,"[143] as long as he properly carries out the function committed to him.[144] Thus the specificity of the office's function helps to ensure its objectivity.

For Luther, it follows from the functional character of the office that it cannot constitute any estate in an intrinsic sense. We have already described how Luther was led to this opinion in his polemic against the Roman teaching of the clerical estate and the *character indelebilis* [indelible character], corrupted by its ideas of satisfaction and hierarchy.[145] Thus Luther knows of only one estate in an intrinsic sense, the Christian estate; all other differentiations among Christians are for him dictated only by their function. When, in the course of his teaching of the three estates or the teaching of the three orders or hierarchies, Luther focuses on those who occupy the ecclesial office and so speaks of the "clerical estate," he does not mean any habitual quality inherent in its essence.[146] He understands by this only a divine order in which certain men have their particular work. The essential nature required for the public function of the office, according to Luther, is given to all Christians with the universal priesthood in Baptism; all that is needed is the call of the congregation so that the function can be performed in the particular office.

---

139 WA 7:633.13ff.

140 Cf. Vajta, op. cit., p. 202.

141 WA 38:243.25ff.; cf. WA 22:186.5ff.

142 WA 50:634.27f.; cf. WA 41:241.38f.: "does not depend on the person."

143 WA 2:193.39ff.

144 Cf. WA 50:634.30; 38:240.1ff.

145 Cf. above, pp. 18–21.

146 Cf. F. Kattenbusch, *Die Doppelschichtigkeit in Luthers Kirchenbegriff*, Lutherana V (Gotha, 1928), p. 346; M. Doerne, *Luth. Pfarramt* (Leipzig, 1937), pp. 6ff.; and H. Storck, op. cit., p. 25. — On the larger question alluded to here, see also below, pp. 94–98.

9. The Ability of the Minister in Office to Be Removed

Since the office is, according to Luther, quintessentially function, it stands or falls on whether the function is exercised in fact and in the proper manner in accordance with the commission. The case may arise where this fails to be done on the part of the office-bearer. It may happen that office-bearers neglect their function, do not preach, do not distribute the sacraments—Luther had this in mind with the Roman clergy of his time—or they may even exercise the function, yet not according to Christ's commission and institution. What must happen in such cases? Does the congregation have the power to remove them?

Given all that has been said up to now, the answer cannot be doubted. Luther teaches that the congregation has not only the right but also the express duty to remove unfaithful ministers in office who neglect the commission of the office, and to set in their place other, faithful ministers.[147] This also applies in the case of an office-bearer who lives an offensive life.[148] "A minister can be deposed if he ceases to be faithful."[149] The continuance of a minister in office depends on whether and in what way he neglects the function of the office. The decision about this falls upon the responsible discretion of the *universitas ecclesiae*. He can be tolerated in the office as long as it pleases the collective whole,

[147] WA 12:172.10ff.: The "congregation of believers [*congregatio credentium*]" is given the "wholly free ability and means to cast down all ungodly ministers and not to call and install any except the fit and godly whenever it pleases [*liberrima facultas et copia, omnes impios ministros profligendi et non nisi idoneos et pios vocandi et instituendi, quoties placuerit*]." — The phrase "whenever it pleases [*quoties placuerit*]" is not to be taken in the sense of arbitrary will. At least Luther does not mean to justify any groundless expulsion by this. Cf. below, pp. 79–80 and 106–7. — *The church in Naumburg*, according to Luther, did right not to accept the bishop elected by the college on the grounds that his doctrine was impure and rather to elect a different and proper bishop contrary to the college: WA 53:231ff. God orders that a false teacher should not teach. In this way his game is stopped, "and he is removed from his bishopric not by pope or emperor—indeed, not by angels—but by the high, eternal, divine Majesty Himself, when He pronounces judgment and thunders this way: You shall not have other gods nor misuse My name" (WA 53:233.34ff.). In this case, they are "not only permitted . . . but compelled by God's commandment to separate themselves from him and to regard him not as a bishop but as a wolf—nay, as a devil. None of this is my word or opinion. . . . It is all God's own word and earnest commandment, confirmed with threats and anger when He says, 'You shall have no other gods'; and in Matthew 7: 'You shall not listen to the wolves, but beware of them'" (WA 53:234.6ff.). Those who wish to listen to a heretical bishop are "condemned to hellfire along with their bishop" (WA 53:234.20). If sheep are to flee and avoid the strangers and not to hear them, "they certainly have the power and right to remove their wolf-bishops by the very fact that they have the right and power not to obey him—indeed, . . . are compelled by God's commandment to resist him, not to mention not to obey him" (WA 53:234.35ff.). ". . . Whoever wishes to be and abide a false prophet, and not to listen or let up, he should not be heard on pain of salvation, but forsaken, shunned, and condemned, not to mention ousted or deposed" (WA 53:242.17ff.); cf. WA 53:235.30ff., 241.25ff., 245.5ff. — WA 11:411.20f.: It is "divine right . . . and necessary to the soul's salvation to remove or shun" bishops who teach contrary to God and His Word.

[148] WA 50:634.30f.: "except that the Church should not and cannot tolerate open vices."

[149] WA 12:190.25f.; cf. WA 6:408.17f. ("was removed through his abuse"); WA 6:409.32f.: "The universal precept 'let him who is guilty suffer' does not spare even the minister of the Word"; WA 6:567.19f.: "It is not impossible to depose someone from the ministry."

that is, as long as it can be answered for by it.[150] In this regard, the churchly office is no different from secular offices in which a civil servant can likewise be in office only so long as he is supported in the exercise of his office by his *fratres aequales* [equal brothers]. The bearer of the ecclesial office cannot be granted forbearance to the degree possible in secular offices. His unfaithfulness has far graver consequences than that of a secular official since the ecclesial office concerns *eternal* goods, which by means of a bad minister in office may be withheld from the people or lost. He is also far more mobile than a secular official. "Therefore, the rest of the brethren must excommunicate him and substitute another,"[151] says Luther in his treatise to the Bohemians [*Concerning the Ministry*] (1523). The brethren who are then to remove him are, according to this passage, not some sort of comrades in the office, the other office-bearers, but rather those *fratres aequales* who have delegated the office to him: other Christians, all of whom equally possess the priestly right with him and as the collective whole are responsible for the correct execution of the ministry of the Word within the congregation.[152] By their ordination to the particular office, ministers are not left to an exclusive, independent responsibility; the congregation, the *universitas ecclesiae*, must always bear it with him since Christ's commission, which is particularly laid on the public minister, applies also to all other Christians and to the whole congregation. The public minister remains in continual submission to the judgment of the *universitas* (assuming that the latter is consistent with Christ's commission). Thus the ability to be removed from office belongs, according to Luther, to the character of the public minister. "We together with the whole multitude are all priests without the bishop's consecration, but through that consecration we become the other priests' servants, ministers, and officers, *who may then be removed and changed*."[153] With

[150] WA 12:190.26ff. The concept of *universitas ecclesiae* not only embraces all Christians of a local congregation but also includes in it the larger aspect of the collective Church. — Also cf. WA 50:634.26f.: ". . . because he is in office and endured by the multitude."

[151] WA 12:190.27ff. and 31.

[152] Yet it must be observed that Luther, in his treatise to the Bohemians [*Concerning the Ministry*], forms his judgment in the context of the acute state of emergency in the absence of a faithful bishop able to remove unfaithful *ministri*. Having this situation in mind, he asserts the right of removal as a basic right of the congregation. Under normal circumstances, however, Luther views bishops as the exercising authority of this basic right belonging to the *universitas ecclesia*. The same is found in the treatise *That a Christian Assembly Has the Right to Judge All Teaching* (1523). While Luther here makes the removal of unfaithful ministers a fundamental right and a fundamental duty of the congregation, yet as a practical case in which the congregation must make use of this right, he describes only one, properly speaking—that in which the bishops present fail to do it and thereby neglect their duty. Luther, too, thought it was *properly* the duty of the bishops (WA 11:411.24ff., 413.28ff., 414.30ff.). This has been demonstrated especially by W. Walther, *Das Erbe der Reformation* 4, *Luthers Kirche* (Leipzig, 1917), pp. 139ff. Bishops were the normal authoritative entity for the removal of unfaithful ministers, according to Luther. It was only when they renounced this duty that it fell to the local congregation. This is not altered by the fact that it is a fundamental right of the congregation to maintain the proper exercise of the office and to remove false teachers.

[153] WA 7:633.16ff. In the "consecration of the bishop," Luther sees the call of the congregation operative which is made through him as the instrument.

this determination not only is the possibility that even a pastor may renounce and fall away accounted for, but for Luther it follows from the specificity of the office's function.

The congregation's right to remove the minister from office when he is unfaithful is tied to its right to judge doctrine. This right is emphatically ascribed by Luther to all Christians and to the congregation, as we have already described.[154] All prophetic and apostolic warnings against erroneous and human teachings "do nothing other than take from teachers the right and power to judge all doctrine and by earnest decree commit them to hearers on pain of forfeiting their soul" so that they not only have the right but also the duty to do it and ". . . are obligated to judge it or incur the disfavor of the divine Majesty."[155] From the duty to judge doctrine, then, there follows for Luther the duty to remove false teachers.[156]

The removal of the unfaithful office-bearer is a measure with the goal of preventing further damage and guaranteeing the execution of Christ's commission under all circumstances. It is a service to the collective whole. All members of the congregation are duty bound to this service. It would be "unnatural, not to mention unchristian, if one member were not to help prevent another's destruction."[157] Likewise, even secular authority, as "a member of the Christian body,"[158] on the basis of the fact that those who bear it are also of the spiritual estate and priests by Baptism, are duty bound to intervene, even with the secular means of power at their disposal, when the church cannot rid itself of an offending office-bearer by its own power.[159] Everyone has the duty and obligation, according to his ability, to confront him "wherever a member governing a congregation acts wrongly and by his action causes great harm and offense to others."[160] The authority of the office-bearer, quite universally, has its boundaries in the general guideline that it can grant him no authority in the church "except only for correction."[161] If he does not exercise it for correction, it is forfeit and he must be removed.

Nevertheless, there is no such thing as arbitrary removal by the congregation.[162] Luther made occasional remarks which might arouse such a suspicion and which sound as if, in his mind, the congregation were given the freedom

154 Cf. above, pp. 37–38 and p. 77 n. 147.

155 WA 11:411.3ff.; cf. before this WA 11:409.20ff., 410.13ff.

156 Cf. K. Holl, *Luther*, 6th ed. (1932), pp. 319 and 338.

157 WA 6:409.13ff.

158 WA 6:410.4.

159 WA 6:409ff. Cf. H. Storck, op. cit., pp. 47f.; also K. Holl, *Luther*, pp. 333ff., 349f., 354, who stresses that this only applies to a case of necessity while Luther would otherwise keep the secular authority out of church matters. But the latter point, according to Luther, does not apply, e.g., with respect to authorities' right to call; cf. below, pp. 135–37.

160 WA 6:413.8ff.

161 WA 6:414.7; cf. WA 10/3:123.8f.: "There is no authority from Christ except that which is for edification."

162 On this, cf. below, pp. 106–8.

to keep an office-bearer or remove him from office at its pleasure.[163] Yet with due consideration of other very clear statements by Luther, even these passages cannot be explained in any way other than that these, too, include the tacit condition: "when the office-bearer becomes unfaithful."[164] The congregation's action in this context remains bound as ever to Christ's commission and the normative rule of His will. It can and may venture to remove a minister only when it has the Word of God on its side.[165]

Luther, however, also allows for the possibility of a minister of the Word resigning from office: "When I am no longer able or willing to preach, I return to the common ranks, am like you, and another preaches. . . ."[166] In this context, the commission of the office would, according to Luther, be removable as well. Yet it is difficult to imagine Luther not seeing such an action by an office-bearer as culpable or at least as a violation of the duty of love toward one's neighbor, which would have to compel one to fulfill the commission of the office.

Thus it fits the functional character of the office, as Luther sees it, that he who has resigned his office or been removed from office is once more "a peasant or burgher like the others,"[167] "no different from any common Christian."[168] He is then "the same as before,"[169] and so in the same condition in which he was before he was called to the office. Nothing of the office which he bore remains in him. A *character indelebilis* is regarded by Luther as a human invention, and he rejects it.[170] —

In the preceding, we have described the rationale of the concrete office from the universal priesthood in Luther.[171] In the public character of the concrete office we showed the essential distinction between it and the universal office given to all Christians in the universal priesthood (1). Then we mentioned the themes by which the necessity of the concrete office is reasoned from the universal priesthood of all Christians (2–4). Finally, the form of filling the

---

[163] Thus WA 12:172.10ff.: "whenever it pleases [*quoties placuerit*]" (cf. above, p. 77 n. 147); WA 12:309.9f.: ". . . who may be removed again whenever desired"; WA 15:721.13ff.: "Likewise, they must bear their ministry, but not forever; we can confer it on him today and take it away again tomorrow."

[164] Cf. esp. the passages cited below, pp. 107–8.

[165] Cf. G. Holstein, op. cit., p. 99.

[166] WA 41:209.11ff.; cf. WA 41:210.18ff.

[167] WA 6:408.20f.

[168] WA 41:210.20f.; cf. WA 6:567.17ff.

[169] WA 6:408.18.

[170] WA 6:408.22ff.; cf. WA 6:567.22, 562.30ff.

[171] On the rationale of the office from the universal priesthood in Luther, cf. esp. Höfling, *Grundsätze ev. luth. Kirchenverfassung*, 3rd ed. (Erlangen, 1853), pp. 57ff., whose description of *this* thought process of Luther's must be reckoned accurate. Höfling's picture of Luther's teaching of the office only becomes distorted when he ignores the other rationale of the office in Luther, in the divine institution. — For more on the derivation of the office from the universal priesthood in Luther, also cf. M. Rade, *Das königl. Priestertum d. Gläubigen* . . . (Tübingen, 1918), p. 9; and M. Doerne, *Luth. Pfarramt*, p. 13.

concrete office was identified from the perspective of the universal priesthood as *delegatio* (5), and four assertions concerning the concrete office thus realized were added: it is a representation of the collective whole (6), it is specifically defined by Christ's commission (7), it is essentially function (8), and it is therefore not bestowed irrevocably (9). In these formulations we have attempted to clarify that while the reasoning of the concrete office from the universal priesthood in Luther is not devoid of the element of cooperative rights, yet these rights are so bound by other factors that they cannot be brought to bear in the sense of the rights of a secular cooperative, nor do they result in any purely democratic structuring of the office. The delegative view of the office, which is predominant here in Luther, is interwoven with the teaching of the Church as *communio sanctorum* and with Christ's previously given commission (wholly regardless of the connection with other rationales for the office with which we have yet to concern ourselves). Still, this rationale of the particular office from the universal priesthood is to be identified as a rationale "from below," "from the perspective of the congregation."[172] In it, the stress falls on the dependency of the public minister on the congregation, on his constant reference back to the latter. His standing "in the stead and name of all [*vice et nomine omnium*]" is therefore the briefest and most fitting formula.

We could not describe this strain of thought in Luther without repeatedly confronting the fact that behind the *universitas ecclesiae* which acts and calls to the office, there are *divine* realities which determine this activity of the congregation. In order to form a complete picture of Luther's teaching of the office, we will now focus thematically on the viewpoint that the concrete office is traced back to a *jus divinum* and treat it by itself, separately from the teaching of the *delegatio*. The following chapter will thus be concerned with the divine character of the concrete office.

If we have seen in the previous examination that, according to Luther, the roots of the concrete office lie in divine truths, yet this was always made clear only by means of intellectual inference: The concrete office must exist because order demands it. Order is God's will. Therefore, God also wills the concrete office. Or: The concrete office must exist because the brotherhood of equally authorized priests is present and demands that one exercise the public function of the office for all. The brotherhood and priesthood of each individual is from God. Thus God also wills the concrete office. Or: The concrete office must exist because not all possess the gifts needed to exercise the office. That not all have these gifts rests on the will of God, from whom the gifts come. Therefore, God must also will the concrete office. In this way the divine institution of the concrete office could, up to this point, be developed by consecutive facts. Now we will take a new approach and proceed not from the congregation and its necessities, but directly from Christ and His institutive will. In this second strain of thought, also distinctly present in Luther, the office is reasoned from above,

[172] W. Elert, regarding this one rationale of the office in Luther, has noticed parallels with Marsilius of Padua (*Morphologie d. Luthertums* I, p. 299).

directly from the standpoint of Christ. Indeed, one must say that in all of Luther's teaching on the office, there is greater stress on reasoning in this fashion.[173] It is connected with his teaching of the universal priesthood and the rationale of the office from that perspective, and this leads to the features characteristic for Luther's teaching of the office.

[173] Cf. H. E. Creutzig's (*Amt und Ämter in der luth. Kirche*, Theol. mil. 22 [Leipzig, 1938], p. 10) observation: "Speaking numerically, these expressions . . ." (which derive the power of the office from the universal priesthood) ". . . are miniscule next to those which acknowledge the office as divinely ordained. . . ." — We do not, however, agree with Creutzig that the reasoning of the office from the universal priesthood is to be seen only as a product of dispute. It, too, represents an original and independent concept of Luther's.

CHAPTER IV

The Divine Character of the Concrete Office

1. The Divine Institution of the Function of the Office

We began by discussing the necessity of the ministry of the Word in connection with justification and Luther's sharp antithesis against the Enthusiastic spirits who sought to obtain the Spirit apart from the Word and external means.[1] For Luther, the Church is founded on the Word and cannot stand without it[2] since it is only by Word and Sacrament that Christ is present with it, and only by Word and Sacrament that the salvation which Christ procured for it can come to men. By the function of the means of grace "Christ's *passio* and *resurrectio* come into use [*in usum*]."[3] There is no other way of salvation. But, of course, the function of Word and Sacrament is by no means to be regarded as merely a postulate of the doctrine of justification; rather, it *is based positively on Christ's institution.* Christ instituted Word and Sacrament and commanded them to be put to use.[4] As elements "which Christ ordained for the maintenance of the Church,"[5] they belong to the essence of the Church and are its characteristic mark.[6]

---

[1] Cf. above, pp. 3–8.

[2] Cf. WA 12:191.16ff.; 41:124.8ff., 148.28.

[3] WA 34/1:318.16; cf. WA 34/1:319.17: "Here the Passion of Christ is put to use"; WA 28:476.12ff.; 41:541.15f.: "The Lord could not wait a long while but wishes to bring the use and power of the resurrection into all the world"; WA Br 3:210.51: ". . . through whose word the mystery of God comes to the Church."

[4] WA 31/1:196.9ff.; 41:543.17–23, 544.15f.; 49:139.22: "The Lord commanded . . ."; WA 49:140.39f.: "Christ endowed it . . ."; WA 50:647.6ff.

[5] WA 38:222.25ff.; cf. WA 38:223.11ff.; 38:240.28ff.: "In summary, the office and Sacrament are not ours but Christ's. For He ordained it all and left it in the Church to be exercised and used until the end of the world, and does not lie or deceive us. Therefore, we cannot turn it into something else but must follow His command and keep it."

[6] WA 50:628ff.; cf. WA 41:124.4. — Also cf. above, pp. 4–5.

Word and Sacrament, then, are not a static phenomenon but must be functional so that they may come to men.[7] Thus Christ instituted and commanded them as functions. "But we are speaking of the external Word [given] through men, as *orally preached* through you and me";[8] of the holy Sacrament of Baptism, "when it is *taught, believed, and used* rightly according to Christ's ordinance";[9] of the Sacrament of the Altar, "where it is *given, believed, and received* rightly according to Christ's institution";[10] of the Keys, where they are *used* publicly.[11] Through the institution of the means of grace, a function is established by Christ which we may summarize simply by calling it the function of the office.[12] The content of this function (the "what" of the function) is based, like its execution (the "that" of the function), on the will of God. It is possible and necessary to be sure "that both the Word and office are divine and commanded by God."[13]

Because of the institution, the means of grace are so fixed that it is God's will that the functions of the office be discharged in the Church. But this is not yet a prescription of the manner in which the function of the office, given by God, is itself to be exercised—whether by all Christians or only specific persons, whether according to strict rules or "by the random personal intercourse," as K. Holl, responding to R. Sohm, thought it was possible to conclude from a passage of Luther's.[14] Is it left to the discretion of the congregation to judge specifically the form and manner in which the function of the office instituted by Christ is concretely realized? The motives referenced in the previous chapter for conferring the office (and thus the function of the office) on specific persons grew out of sociological realities in the congregation and are therefore properly

---

[7] WA 50:634.24f.: "For it is all given not to the one who has it but to the one who is to receive it through his office."

[8] WA 50:629.16ff.; cf. WA 12:518.28ff.; 41:124.22f.: "Now this scepter is nothing more than the bare word or oral preaching and a physical voice"; WA 47:191.38ff.: "The office has been endowed by God so that people may preach and the power of the Keys may be used." — H. Storck, op. cit., pp. 9f., pointed out that the term "word" in Luther indicates, first, the content of the word and, second, the form of the function in proclamation and teaching. In both respects, the word is determined by God.

[9] WA 50:630.22f.

[10] WA 50:631.7f.

[11] WA 50:631.36ff.

[12] Three senses for the term "office" can be accounted for in Luther in the context of his doctrine of the office: (1) "Office" denotes a (liturgical) rite commanded by Christ: e.g., WA 30/2:498.18ff.; 38:240.28. (2) "Office" denotes the actual performance of that rite, the function of the office in action, thus preaching and the distribution of the Sacraments: e.g., WA 19:233.5f. and 15f.; 34/1:318.15; 47:191.38ff. (3) "Office" (particularly "preaching office") denotes the institution of the office in which the work commanded by Christ is carried out on the basis of the particular call, thus the concrete office in the narrow sense: e.g., WA 28:470.39; 50:632.35f., and the passages cited in the next section. For the most part, all three aspects are present in Luther's use of the term "office," with a greater emphasis of one or another at any given time.

[13] WA 19:233.5ff.; cf. WA 34/1:318.15: "There He commands the office, which is preaching and the Gospel."

[14] *Luther*, 6th ed. (1932), pp. 324f. n. 3. Holl and Sohm's interpretation of the passage in question, WA 6:297.13ff., cannot be maintained, particularly if we take into account the multitude of other passages of Luther's which speak directly of the office. Cf. the following section.

motives of human law—and could in any event be considered only indirectly as having divine legitimacy. The question which we must now pursue is whether there is, according to Luther, a divine mandate for the function of the office being tied to specific, distinct persons who are appointed to exercise it for a period of time. In other words, the question is whether, according to Luther, the *concrete* office, the public preaching office as an institution of the Church, rests directly on Christ's institution.

2. The Attachment of the Function of the Office to Specific Persons: The Institution of the Office

The numerous statements in Luther to the effect that the congregation has a command from God to call preachers and to appoint the concrete office[15] indicate where we must look for the answer to the question of the divine institution of the concrete office in Luther. *Luther understands the concrete office conferred on individuals as a permanent institution belonging to the essence of the Church and traces this instituted entity immediately back to the divine will, to Christ's institutive act.* Not only are the Word and Sacraments divinely instituted, but so is the office, the latter being ordained to be administered publicly in the congregation.[16] Not only are the means of grace (the Word, Baptism, the Supper, the Keys) themselves marks of the Church, argues Luther in his treatise *On the Councils and the Church* (1539), but "fifth, the Church is recognized externally by the fact that it consecrates or calls ministers, or has offices to appoint, which give, pass, and exercise publicly and particularly the aforenamed four items or holy things for the sake and in the name of the Church, yet more so by the institution of Christ, as St. Paul says in Ephesians 4."[17] That the Church calls officers who attend to the function of the office "publicly and particularly"[18] is not a matter of human administration but is so ordained by Christ.[19] This is quite clearly the meaning of this passage. In this context, Eph. 4:11ff. is understood by Luther to mean that Christ instituted and founded the office or offices

---

[15] Cf. above, p. 72, esp. nn. 116–17 with the passages there referenced; in addition, WA 41:456.14 and Enders, *Luthers Briefwechsel*, vol. 11, p. 279, line 23.

[16] That the Word and office do not simply coalesce but are vividly distinguished as two things in Luther is evident, e.g., from WA 47:193.5: ". . . the Word of God, on which the office is established." Here Word and office are plainly distinguished. The Word is the foundation on which and for which the office is established. And by "office" here, in the context, we are clearly to understand the concrete, instituted entity which calls for specific officers. Cf. WA 47:193.3f.: "Therefore, we see that one is called; then he is in an office."

[17] WA 50:632.35ff.

[18] WA 50:633.1. "Particularly [*sonderlich*]" here means "in pastoral care of individuals." These two terms "publicly [*offentlich*]" and "particularly" appear in this sense during Luther's discussion of the Keys in this treatise.

[19] Cf. P. Brunner, "Vom Amt des Bischofs," pp. 16f. n. 11.

for the edification of His Body, and they are to be filled with specific persons by the Church.[20]

> In an epistle sermon on 1 Cor. 12:1ff. from 1535, Luther says, "It is easy to understand what offices are. 'Office' means something ordered, as there must be in every government, that it may have various appointed and commanded duties for the sake of the one in charge. . . . So, too, in the Church there are various offices so that one is an apostle, another an evangelist, another a teacher, etc. . . . So there are now ordered and distinct offices: pastors, preachers, ministers, or priests who hear confession, give the Sacrament. . . ."[21] Here (as in the previously quoted passage from the treatise *On the Councils and the Church*) Luther characterizes all the offic*es* more precisely as varieties and subdivisions of the single *ministerium ecclesiasticum* [*ecclesial ministry*]. Thus this plurality of offices fundamentally involves one concrete office. These offices, then, are expressly *distinguished* by Luther from the powers and gifts under discussion in the same passage.[22] When Luther here speaks of offices, it is not simply a matter of the "charisms," but rather of the official institution to which those persons belong to whom the office is committed.[23] Concerning the filling of *these* offices with certain persons, the passage reads: "That Christ is Lord to whom the offices belong and who ordains and preserves the same, and to that end God gives His powers and the Holy Spirit His gifts."[24] "For to give spiritual offices and spiritual gifts belongs to no creature, nor can anyone do it but God alone."[25] In this sermon, the ecclesial office is pictured very distinctly as Christ's ordinance and institution.

There can be no doubt that, according to Luther, Christ's institutive act is the basis on which the Church selects specific persons from the collective whole,

---

[20] Rudolph Sohm's attempt to distort this passage of the treatise *On the Councils and the Church* in this way, as though Luther were here trying to trace the various gifts and charisms in the Church back to a divine institution but not to establish the divine institution of the public preaching office as such (*Kirchenrecht* I [1892], p. 499 n. 31), must be judged unsuccessful. In Luther's explanation, the gifts from Eph. 4:8 are not simply and strictly the subjective charisms but the offices and officers themselves. F. J. Stahl sees the matter far more truly in Luther's sense when he maintains: "The divine or supernatural aspect of the office consists not only in God's giving the gift (the charisma) for the office, which continually cares for the Church, but also in the fact that He gave the positive command for the appointment of the office and its first institution and that He bestows the power and promise on the office appointed according to this command" (*Die Kirchenverfassung* . . . [1862], p. 114). It is in this latter sense that Luther understands the divine institution of the preaching office according to Ephesians 4. Also cf. Brunotte, op. cit., pp. 106ff. But when Brunotte asserts in another place (p. 127) that Ephesians 4 is adduced by Luther only *in*directly for the divine institution of the office, we cannot agree with him. In this place, WA 50:632.35ff., Luther sees the direct divine institution of the office expressed in Ephesians 4.

[21] WA 22:183.22ff.

[22] WA 22:183.33ff.

[23] WA 22:184.1ff.: "For these things to be carried out and executed, people are required . . ."; WA 22:183.34f.: ". . . only those to whom it is committed."

[24] WA 22:184.7ff.; cf. WA 22:184.36ff., 181.24f.: ". . . Christ, the Son of God, from whom all the offices proceed as the Head of the Church"; WA 22:186.31f.: "if He" (God) "had not Himself ordained and given it" (the office, gifts, and powers).

[25] WA 22:181.34ff.

calls them to the office, and confers on them the power of discharging the function of Word and Sacrament in the instituted office. *In Luther's view, the concrete office is* de jure divino *[by divine right].*[26]

This instituted office as Luther sees it is to be viewed within the context of the *divine order of salvation.* Remembering that the salutary good won by Christ's Passion and death is conveyed to men through this office, Luther says that the pastor's office belongs to the Lord our God, "who won, gave, and instituted it for us by His blood *for our salvation.*"[27] The office as an institution is embedded in the process of salvation, by which God wills to bring the sinner to justification. For "through this office and Word we are freed from sins, justified, and saved in God's sight if we have faith in the Word, which the pastor proclaims to us in the stead of Christ."[28] Christ, by the salutary institution of the office in Word and Sacrament, applies to us the fruits of His redemption,[29] for which reason it is a "very great thing and necessary . . . to all churches."[30] Christ's "whole kingdom and government" is found in this order "to the extent that it may be seen and handled externally";[31] our life and salvation are enclosed by it.[32]

---

[26] Stahl's statement "it is the *positive 'command of God'* that it exist" (op. cit., p. 110) also accurately reflects Luther's meaning. The divine institution of the office is taught in many places in Luther: WA 28:470.39ff.: ". . . that this office is not of men but of the Lord Christ, who institutes and ordains this office and commits it to men"; WA 28:468.6ff., 470.16, 476.6 (". . . instituted . . ."); WA 28:479.31f. ("an office of the Holy Spirit"); WA 30/2:598.33f.: ". . . God did not ordain the preaching office for that purpose . . ."; WA 38:240.24ff.: "We must believe and be certain that the preaching office is not ours but Christ's"; WA 38:243.29f.: "the pastoral office, which is not his office, but Christ's"; WA 41:241.39f.: "The offices are Christ's, who instituted them"; WA 41:543.17ff.; 41:456.24: ". . . instituted a public *ministerium*"; WA 41:457.5f.: "the office made by Christ and 'His'"; WA 47:191.38 ("instituted"); WA 47:193.5 ("instituted"); WA 50:647.6ff.: (Word, Sacrament, offices) "commanded, instituted, and ordained by God. . . . God's own Word, Sacrament, or forgiveness, office"; WA Br 10:255.18ff.: "I hope you will have so much Christian understanding that the pastoral office, preaching office, and the Gospel do not belong to us or any man, nor even to an angel, but to the Lord our God alone, who . . . instituted it . . ."; WA Br 10:257.87ff.: "You have . . . instituted nothing, but only God's Son has." — The positive divine institution of the clerical office in Luther is particularly noted by Brunotte (op. cit., pp. 118ff.). Brunotte also shows how at all times and in all facets of his life Luther maintained the divine character of the institution of the office.

[27] WA Br 10:255.21ff. Ruben Josefson ("Das Amt der Kirche," in *Ein Buch von der Kirche* [Göttingen, 1951], p. 395) pointed out that according to Luther the institution of the office is founded not only in the specific words of Jesus (the Verba) but immediately on the fact of the atonement through Christ's blood. Cf. esp. WA 30/2:530.1ff.

[28] WA 28:479.36ff.

[29] WA 49:141.33: The Lord "instituted it so that" (the Gospel's riches of grace) "may be conveyed to us through ministers." G. Törnvall (*Geistliches und weltliches Regiment bei Luther* [Munich, 1947], p. 19) stresses that the preaching office in Luther is not simply a function but is itself "the blessing that the Gospel desires to impart," and in support of this refers to WA 40/1:387.4ff.

[30] WA 38:423.21ff.

[31] WA 41:123.37f.; cf. WA 34/2:245.24ff.: "God could certainly govern the world without all the offices if He wished, but He does not wish to but has appointed the offices to be His helpers."

[32] WA 28:466.13ff.: ". . . what the preaching office is, namely, such an office in which our life and blessedness consist. . . ."

From this perspective, the institution of the office takes on special significance in Luther's teaching.

For Luther, Christ is the *founder of the office* in the historical sense as well as in the immediate sense. He "personally founded and introduced this public preaching office of the Gospel on earth and charged the apostles to spread it into all the world until the Last Day."[33] Additionally, He Himself acts in the *vocatio ministrorum* [calling of ministers], which He has "left behind" as a permanent ordinance of the Church.[34] The "call or ordination to the pastoral office, preaching office, or curacy" belongs to the "ordinances and fruits of Christ."[35] Because Christ Himself calls people to the office, He is also the *preserver of the office*. This is a *ministerium a deo solo datum et conservatum* [ministry given and preserved by God alone].[36] Through every change of individual officeholders, the office remains as long as the Church exists since it is God's endowment and creation.[37] God has preserved it at all times, even under the papacy,[38] and will continue to do so. Without this office, the Church cannot even exist; it *must* be appointed, or the Church is lost: "The Church cannot exist without these bishops, pastors, preachers, and priests, nor can they without the Church; they must go together."[39] So firmly does the concrete office—i.e., the public preaching office filled with specific officeholders—belong to the essence of the Church that when they are present, the Church is demonstrably there; indeed, the Church cannot be imagined apart from the officeholders. At the same time, the office in Luther's thinking may not be conceived as detached from the *persons* holding the office. While we have seen above that Luther separates the office from the person of the office-bearer on a fundamental level,[40] this does not imply a docetic-spiritualistic sublimation of the office into the realm of the nonconcrete. For Luther, too, the office manifests its reality only as an *appointed* office, i.e., in the persons holding the office, who then also exercise it in fact.[41] This in turn necessitates the functional character of the office. It is important to bear in mind that Luther uses the

---

[33] WA 41:187.26ff.; cf. WA 41:123.34ff.; 49:140.32ff.

[34] WA 41:456.14; cf. WA 28:472.26ff.

[35] WA 38:221.25ff. and 31ff.; cf. WA 47:192.5ff., where Luther says of the commission to the office: "For God commanded them."

[36] WA 38:432.23ff.; cf. WA 22:184.8f.; 30/2:530.3ff.

[37] WA 41:456.38ff.: "If there is no institution, there is no Gospel. No matter who may die, the ministry remains, for it is God's alone; as long as the Church exists, the Gospel, Baptism, the Keys, the Sacrament, and the preaching office also remain here. Pastor after pastor dies, but the office remains"; cf. WA 41:195.26ff.: "The preaching office of the Gospel, Baptism, and Sacraments—and the power thereof—shall continue as long as the world stands."

[38] WA 38:243.28f.

[39] WA 50:641.18f.; cf. WA 50:634.11f.: "So since the apostles and prophets have ceased, others must have come in their place, and still come until the end of the world. For the Church shall not cease until the end of the world; *therefore*, the apostles, evangelists, prophets must remain, and those who attend to God's Word and works, whatever they are called"; WA 12:191.16ff.

[40] Cf. above, pp. 75–76.

[41] Cf. V. Vajta, op. cit., p. 196; also A. F. C. Vilmar, *Die Lehre vom geistl. Amt* (1870), p. 2; and W. Löhe, *Neue Aphorismen.*, *Ges. Werke*, vol. V.1, p. 537.

terms "offices [*Empter*]" and "officers [*Amptleute*]" interchangeably: "So where you see offices or officers, know that the holy Christian people must certainly be there. . . ."[42] If God founded the office, it means that in the congregation He "has appointed His priests and preachers, to whom He has committed the office, that they may teach, admonish, rebuke, comfort, and, in short, handle the Word of God."[43] Regarding Num. 11:16ff., Luther says, "Likewise, He" (God) "also chose for that purpose" (i.e., the ministry of Word and Sacrament) "a portion of men—namely, pastors, preachers—who are scarcely a seventieth part. These He also ordained, that there may be a particular day and specific person and place."[44] With the concrete office a quantity of specific officers is necessarily given. The attachment of the office's function to the specific officers especially called to that purpose is referred back to God's will and arrangement and is thus *de jure divino*. This is what Luther plainly teaches.

It should be noted further that in Luther's writings this concrete preaching office embedded by Christ in the Church always has reference to the parish. It is a *pastoral office*, that is, an office with a parochial jurisdiction, a domain of pastoral care, to which it is assigned and within which it has responsibility.[45] Already in 1520 in his treatise *To the Christian Nobility of the German Nation*, Luther maintains "that according to the institution by Christ and the apostles, each city is to have a pastor or bishop, as Paul clearly writes in Titus 1. . . . For a bishop and pastor is the same thing in St. Paul."[46] The "*pastoral estate*" is that "which God has instituted, which must preside over *a congregation* with preaching and the Sacraments, dwell and keep house with *them* temporally. . . ."[47] The concrete office possesses a concrete congregation, whose pastor is the office-bearer, who is to govern it with the Word and Sacraments. Luther expresses this idea in the treatise *Misuse of the Mass* (1521). There, too, he finds explicit in Paul's guidance to Titus to appoint presbyters in every city (Titus 1:5) the divine institution of the parochial pastoral office. Through Paul, the Spirit of Christ is speaking here, and whoever believes this would certainly recognize "that this is a divine institution and order, that in every city there should be several bishops, or at least one."[48] The office founded by God is for Luther an office in a city, that is, in a specific, parochially defined congregation. Luther especially stresses the parochial character of the office in the treatise *Infiltrating and Clandestine*

[42] WA 50:641.16ff.

[43] WA 31/1:196.6ff.

[44] WA 34/2:296.5ff.

[45] And it is precisely of the *pastoral* office that the divine institution is asserted by Luther: WA 38:243.22f. and 29; WA Br 10:255.18f.

[46] WA 6:440.21ff.

[47] WA 6:441.24ff.

[48] WA 8:500.16ff. Cf. WA 8:501.3ff.: ". . . Paul's bishops are honorable and married men in a city, as many as are needed to attend to the people. These are words . . . of the Holy Spirit and Jesus Christ—indeed, of the divine Majesty"; WA 8:501.18f.: "The Holy Spirit has instituted many bishops *in one city*." On Luther's view of Scripture brought to light in these passages, cf. Brunotte, op. cit., pp. 41 and 123.

Preachers (1532).[49] In the congregation, the pastor "has charge of the pulpit, Baptism, and the Sacrament, and all pastoral care is committed to him" (i.e., in his parish).[50] All Christians who live in the parish are obligated on pain of forfeiting salvation to hold to their pastor and to report infiltrators who turn the people away from their pastor. "For where they do not do this, they help the messengers of the devil and infiltrators secretly to steal from the pastor (yea, from God Himself) his preaching office, Baptism, the Sacrament, and pastoral care, as well as the parishioners, and so devastate and destroy the parish (*which God ordained*)."[51] The parish is a divine ordinance, and so the preaching office, too, is a parochial office *de jure divino*. The call to the office places a pastor into a specific congregation. He is the minister of the Word *there*; he determines who he will allow or not allow to preach *there*.[52] According to Luther, the pastor's direct responsibility does not extend beyond his parish. To the Christians in Strassburg, Luther writes: "So, my dearest friends, I am not your preacher, nor is anyone obliged to believe me. . . ."[53] In defining the character of the pastor, Luther says, "Besides his being a Christian and a priest, he must also have an office and a ecclesial jurisdiction entrusted to him. . . ."[54] It must be observed that this relation of the concrete office to the parish, being founded on Scripture, has for Luther the force of a *jus divinum* [divine right].[55]

---

[49] See W. Elert, *Morphologie* I, p. 305, also p. 302.

[50] WA 30/3:519.3f.; cf. WA 30/3:519.30ff. The full explanation, WA 30/3:518ff., portrays the parochial character of the preaching office as divine right. Also cf. WA 28:475.1ff.

[51] WA 30/3:519.20ff. Cf. WA 30/3:520.21ff.: "Why do you leave your church—where you were baptized, taught, and instructed and to which you belong through God's ordinance—and steal away secretly?" WA 31/1:211.18f.; also WA Br 10:257.82ff. and 87ff., where Luther asserts the divine institution of parishes [*Pfarrhen*] as well as of the preaching office.

[52] WA 30/3:519.1ff.; 31/1:211.4ff.: "Every bishop or pastor has his specific jurisdiction or parish, which St. Peter (1 Peter 5) also calls a *kleros*, or portion, since to each pastor is committed his portion of the people, as St. Paul also writes to Titus. In this parish no one else nor any stranger is to venture to teach his parishioners either secretly or openly, without the pastor's knowledge and wishes." Also cf. *Theses against the Whole Synagogue of Satan* (1530), no. 15: "The Christian Church, however, signifies the number or multitude of the baptized and believers *belonging to a pastor or bishop*, whether in a city or in an entire country or in the whole world" (WA 30/2:425.22ff.; cf. WA 30/2:421.19ff.). The parochial character of the pastoral office is also at the root of this.

[53] WA 15:393.6f. Also cf. below, pp. 119–20.

[54] WA 31/1:211.18ff.; cf. WA Br 1:595.37ff.

[55] This point is the basis of, among other things, R. Sohm's error in his understanding of Luther's view of the office. Sohm acknowledges that, according to Luther, the office is divinely established and that it is a divine ordinance that individuals are called to this office (e.g., *Kirchenrecht* I, p. 472), but he rejects the corollary, that there is also a divinely given ecclesial law present there according to Luther's teaching (pp. 473ff.). "But the regularly called teaching office as such constitutes *no* legally appointed teaching office. . . . Indeed, the legal ordinance of the teaching office is *excluded*" (p. 475). This might be possible only if the instituted office bore no parochial character. According to Luther, however, it has one by virtue of the divine ordinance, with which the legal ordinance of the office is necessarily given as well (also cf. W. O. Münter, *Die Gestalt der Kirche "nach göttlichem Recht*," Kirche und Amt II, Beitr. z. Ev. Theol., vol. 5 [Munich, 1941], p. 60). Luther's teaching of the ordained office as a parochial pastoral office is completely missed by Sohm. For a critique of Sohm's legal concept, cf. above, p. 16 n. 99. — The parochial character of the ordained office in

Thus the attachment of the public function of the office to specific officers set apart for that purpose in the sense of a parochially defined pastoral office is taught by Luther as a divine ordinance embedded in the structure of the Church. The concrete office is no human institution, but a *divine institution*.[56] This is why he calls it a "holy and divine ministry";[57] Christ's "holy, dear pastoral office"[58]—indeed, "this most holy ministry"[59]—which would all be impossible if the divine character of the office's institution were not firmly fixed for him.[60]

The idea of the divine institution of the concrete office in Luther is either totally overlooked or else misinterpreted by many researchers. Let us first look at the *nineteenth century*. Here *J. W. F. Höfling* (*Grundsätze ev.-luth. Kirchenverfassung*, 3rd ed. [Erlangen, 1853]) unilaterally emphasized the rationale of the concrete office in Luther in the practical realities of the priestly congregation (and—it must be added—thereby identified "Luther's view" on this point for several generations). He bases the necessity of the office on a fourfold rationale: (1) the right of the community, (2) the universal law of order, (3) the charismatic classification of the Body of Christ present, and (4) the internal nature of the office itself (i.e., not all may be both subject and object simultaneously) (pp. 67f.); but he denies the positive divine establishment of the office (even with respect to Luther) (p. 75). For him, only the universal office of the priesthood of all Christians—which is to say, the function of Word and Sacrament—is divinely instituted (pp. 7ff.). — Also, *G. C. A. Harleß* (*Kirche und Amt nach luth. Lehre* [Stuttgart, 1853]) sees in Luther only the divine institution of the function of the office, of the ministry of Word and Sacrament (cf. pp. 21 and 25), which, however, necessarily leads then to the appointment of the concrete office. But he does not attempt to relate this necessity back to a positive divine arrangement. — In *W. Preger's* (*Die Geschichte der Lehre vom geistlichen Amt* . . . [Nördlingen, 1857]) section on Luther, we find

Luther is also overlooked by S. Schöffel ("Das Predigt- u. Hirtenamt," in *Credo ecclesiam*, festschrift for W. Zoellner [1930], pp. 200f.) when he makes such a sharp distinction between the preaching office and the pastoral office, attributing the divine institution, evangelically understood, only to the former. Luther thought otherwise. — While W. Elert (*Morphologie* I, pp. 324f.) writes that the existence of the pastoral office in the Church is a matter of divine right according to Luther, he then explains that the differentiation of the office's activity into separate, locally bound parochial offices happens "for practical reasons" and that the local organization of the Church into parishes is *juris humani* (p. 325). This is opposed by Luther's statements which we have quoted.

[56] This cannot be contradicted by the passage from the treatise *Answer to Emser* (1521), in which Luther speaks of the "church's priesthood" and defends this designation by the fact that this priesthood "came from the Church's order and is not based on Scripture" (WA 7:631.25f.; cf. WA 7:635.4ff., 636.19ff.). By this, Luther does not mean to question the positive divine institution of the particular office. Rather, he has in mind here *that* priesthood marked by the distortion of the office in Rome ("the bishops which there are now": WA 7:631.19f.), which thus uses the clerical estate for itself alone and denies the laity a clerical or spiritual character, etc. (cf. WA 7:635.7ff.).

[57] WA 38:425.1f.

[58] WA 38:243.29.

[59] WA 41:763.16.

[60] H. H. Kramm (*Bischof, Pastor und Gemeinde*, Luthertum 13 [Berlin, 1954], p. 35) has the great merit of pointing out that the term "ministerium" contains not only the functional but also very much the institutional character of the office.

nothing about a divine institution of the office. — *H. Heppe* (*Dogmatik d. dtschen Protestantismus i. 16. Jh.*, vol. 3 [Gotha, 1857]) asserts manifestly that, even for Luther, "... it is only for the sake of good and necessary order that the public administration and delivery of the Word is required to be undertaken by separate, specific persons on behalf of the ecclesial community" (p. 325). Heppe also knows that the *ministerium ecclesiasticum* in Luther and the Lutheran fathers is to be seen "not as a congregational ministry dependent on the will of the congregation for its existence and authorization," but as "a ministry of the Church resting simply on the institution and authority of Christ" (p. 325). He regards the *function* of the office as instituted. Yet he fails to see that according to Luther the conferral of this function on individuals also rests on the divine will. In Luther, the fact "that the priestly calling belonging to all believers can be exercised publicly only by individuals" is to be traced back not merely to "the needs of the communal life of the Church" but to Christ's positive arrangement. — *H. Jacoby* (*Die Liturgik d. Reformatoren* I [Gotha, 1871]) writes: "It was by reflecting on the activity of the Church and the structure of the community's external, religious-moral life that he" (Luther) "first developed the concept of the office and the office's constitution" (p. 162). How far from the real Luther this assessment is! — *G. Rietschel* (*Luther und die Ordination*, 2nd ed. [Wittenberg, 1889]) thinks that Luther sees a divine institution in all "that happens in and through the congregation correctly according to God's will" and that he only calls the office a "divine institution" insofar as Word and Sacrament were immediately instituted by Christ, which in turn necessitates separate, individual administrators of Word and Sacrament and thus the appointment of a particular office (pp. 41f.). This is in essence to recognize the divine institution only of the *function* of the office and then to derive the divine character of the office from God's will for order. In this way, Rietschel also explicitly questions Christ's special institution of the concrete office and distorts Luther's clear discussion of the institution of the clerical estate which he quotes as though it taught only the preaching office as being given with the institution of Word and Sacrament and with God's will for order, not its positive institution by God (p. 42; also cf. *Lehrbuch der Liturgik* II [1909], pp. 410ff.). But this is not Luther's intention there.[61] Entirely misleading is Rietschel's assertion that for Luther the question whether the office is *de jure divino* or *de jure humano* is totally nonexistent and that all human orders here on earth are for Luther also divine orders (*Lehrbuch d. Lit.* II [1909], p. 410). — Curiously, this assertion of Rietschel's is replicated by Graff in the new edition of Rietschel's compendium: [Göttingen, 1952], ibid., p. 480). The distinction between what here on earth is *de jure divino* and what is only *de jure humano* [by human right] always held the greatest import for Luther. —

On the other hand, other men in the nineteenth century elevated the teaching of the divine institution of the concrete office, even strongly emphasizing the idea that Luther clearly disseminated this teaching. Here we may name *W. Löhe* (*Ges. Werke* [Neuendettelsau, 1954], vol. V.1, pp. 549ff.); *F. J. Stahl* (*Die Kirchenverfassung* ... [1862], pp. 399ff.); *T. Kliefoth* (*Liturg. Abhandlungen* I [1854], pp. 341ff.); and, above all, *A. W. Dieckhoff* with his in-depth study

[61] Brunotte (op. cit., p. 108 n. 53) also happily opposes this false explanation by Rietschel.

Luthers Lehre von der kirchlichen Gewalt (Berlin, 1865) (esp. pp. 98, 106f., 116f., 149ff.); and, finally, *J. Köstlin* (*Luthers Lehre von der Kirche* [Stuttgart, 1853], p. 74: "Everywhere he defines it as instituted by God"). Later, however, Köstlin (*Luthers Theologie* II [1901], pp. 266f.) fairly unilaterally emphasizes Luther's other rationale of the office, that for the sake of order: "And also the fact that the congregation is to call these office-bearers, and no one take the position without this call, is not grounded by Luther on Christ's direct prescription or promise, but instead he appeals to a universal need for order, of which all must naturally be aware" (p. 266).

In the *twentieth century*, the idea of the divine institution of the office in Luther is also ignored by many in the field. This is especially true for the scholarship of the post-World War I period, in which a universal, democratic feeling is perceptible. *M. Rade* (*Das königliche Priestertum der Gläubigen u. seine Forderung an die ev. Kirche unserer Zeit* [Tübingen, 1918], pp. 11f.) sees the pastoral office of one man against the background of the royal priesthood of all, as found in Luther, only as a demand of "good sense," of "natural law" (p. 11). "The final authority is the unanimous understanding of all parties on the basis of experience" (p. 12). "And only on account of *order*, that all things may go *according to custom*, and because 'what is common may not be assumed by anyone without the will and command of the congregation,' this is why it is better in practice for one man, as the approved and elected representative of all, to undertake the function, where all who gather visibly in public are priests" (p. 28). So, too, the office resting on the basis of reason would be susceptible to change. Rade sees only one side of the rationale for the office in Luther, and thus his overall assessment is completely false. Likewise, *W. Zoellner* (*Das allg. Priestertum d. Gläubigen und die Bedeutung des Gnadenmittelamtes* [Leipzig, 1919], pp. 5f.) mentions only the rationale of the concrete office for the sake of order in Luther. And in *K. Holl* (*Luther*, pp. 318f.), the idea of the institution of the office in Luther is completely passed over; likewise, in *R. Seeberg* (*Dogmengeschichte* IV.1, *Die Lehre Luthers*, 2nd and 3rd ed. [Leipzig, 1917], pp. 292ff.). Seeberg thinks he represents Luther when he says: "The congregation, for the sake of order, confers the proclamation of the Word and the administration of the Sacraments on specific persons whom it regards as suitable" (p. 292), and ". . . there is no sense of a dogmatic necessity of the office in Luther's thinking" (p. 294 n. 2). Also, *F. Kattenbusch* (*Die Doppelschichtigkeit in Luthers Kirchenbegriff* [Gotha, 1928]) only presents the rationale of the concrete office for the sake of order in Luther (cf., e.g., p. 343: ". . . calls for order . . ."); likewise, *Erich Seeberg* (*Luthers Theologie* II [Stuttgart, 1937], p. 441: "only for the sake of order"; *Luthers Theologie in ihren Grundzügen*, 2nd ed. [Stuttgart, 1950], p. 170: "only on account of order"; p. 175: "only for the sake of order are pastors necessary"). No different is *G. Niedermeier* ("Das allg. Priestertum der Gläubigen und das geistliche Amt," *Zeitschr. f. syst. Theol.* [1930], pp. 337ff.). Also, *H. Asmussen* (*Warum noch luth. Kirche* [Stuttgart, 1949], p. 90) mentions, as regards Luther, only the rationale of the office "for the sake of a formal order." —

At the same time, however, researchers may be named who in more recent times have seen the doctrine of the divine institution of the concrete office in Luther and clearly emphasized it. Thus especially *W. Elert* (*Morphologie des Luthertums* I [Munich, 1952], pp. 301ff. and 321). Elert quotes several passages of Luther and concludes: "If it" (namely, the idea of the divine institution) "is discussed for the most part only incidentally, it must be concluded that Luther regarded this view as self-evident" (p. 301). Further, *M. Doerne* (*Luth. Pfarramt* [Leipzig, 1937], pp. 5ff.). *E. Sommerlath* ("Amt und allg. Priestertum," op. cit., pp. 49f.) also stresses that in Luther's view the office, as a conferral on individuals, may itself be traced back to the will of the Lord of the Church; likewise, *P. Brunner* ("Vom Amt des Bischofs," op. cit., pp. 16f.). Additionally, the latest Swedish scholarship on Luther's teaching of the office by *Gösta Hök* ("Luthers läran om kyrkans ämbete," in *En bok om kyrkans ämbete* [Uppsala, 1951]) clearly identifies this line in Luther, e.g., p. 150: "the office of the Church and its origin from divine Law . . ."; "the office of the Church is a divine ordinance independent of and prior to the universal priesthood." *H. Storck* (*Das allg. Priestertum bei Luther* [Munich, 1953], pp. 39f.) also speaks of the "divinely instituted ordinance of the office," but does not take seriously the *jus divinum* of the concrete office in Luther when he suggests that one could, in Luther's thinking, place the ordinance of the clerical office in the church under Luther's statement concerning the ordinance of worship, that this external ordinance is not important in the sight of God, but because it may be useful for one's neighbor, we should respect it out of love (p. 40). According to Luther, a Christian must respect the particular office in the church for the sake of love, not only as any other human ordinance—such is necessary to assert against Storck—but as a divine ordinance calling for unconditional obedience.[62]

The attachment of the office's function to specific officers set apart for and called to this ministry is especially underscored by the *doctrine of the clerical or spiritual estate*. For the term "spiritual office," Luther can also use that of "spiritual estate," thereby teaching the divine institution of the spiritual estate along with that of the office.[63] In so doing, Luther has in mind the guiding principle of the *ordinance of the three estates of all Christians*.[64] The priestly office, the marriage estate, and secular government are "the holy orders and true institutions founded by God,"[65] the "three hierarchies ordained by God,"[66] the "three

---

[62] As the most recent work, we should also mention here that of Wilhelm Brunotte, *Das geistliche Amt bei Luther* (Berlin, 1959), which particularly stresses the divine institution of the clerical office in Luther (op. cit., pp. 40ff., 118ff., and passim).

[63] WA 6:441.24: "I will speak of the pastoral estate, which God instituted"; WA 7:22.20ff.: "Also every apostle, bishop, priest, and the whole clerical estate is called and instituted for the sake of the Word alone"; WA 30/2:526.17ff.: "I hope that believers, and all who want to be called Christian, know well that the clerical estate is instituted and founded by God"; likewise, WA 30/2:530.1ff. For the comparison of office and estate, cf. WA 30/2:530.13: "clerical office and estate"; WA 30/2:531.7: "preaching office and clerical estate."

[64] On Luther's doctrine of the three estates or hierarchies as institutions of God, cf. F. Kattenbusch, *Die Doppelschichtigkeit in Luthers Kirchenbegriff*, pp. 314ff.; and E. Wolf, "Politia Christi," in *Peregrinatio: Studien z. reformat. Theol. u. z. Kirchenproblem* (Munich, 1954), pp. 232f. As textual support for this doctrine, see esp. F. Lezius, "Gleichheit und Ungleichhheit: Aphorismen z. Theol. u. Staatsanschauung Luthers," in *Greifswalder Studien* (Gütersloh, 1895), p. 292 n. 1.

[65] WA 26:504.30f.; cf. WA 30/1:397.1f. ("all manner of holy orders and estates"); WA 49:611.20; 50:652.36 ("of these blessed divine estates and privileges"); WA 26:508.25f. (marriage and the priestly office [are] "holy orders in themselves").

[66] WA 50:652.18, 653.3 ("God's three hierarchies"); WA 43:524.22ff. ("*tres hierarchiae*").

institutions or orders" which "are contained in God's Word and commandment."[67] The doctrine of the three estates is elaborated in Luther's thought in distinct antithesis to the Roman monastic estate, in which the estate was simultaneously conceived as a "way to salvation" and thus regarded as meritorious.[68] According to Luther, "no such order is a way to salvation, but there remains one way above all these, namely, faith in Jesus Christ."[69] The orders or estates are only the paths prescribed by God in which faith is to be exercised in obedience and in love toward one's neighbor, "for God desires such works from us for His praise and glory. And all those who are saved in the faith of Christ do such works and keep such order."[70] Thus it is clear that the doctrine of the three orders or estates in Luther is oriented toward the particular work performed in them commensurate with God's will and arrangement. This also finds expression in Luther's discussion of the "common order of Christian love" which pervades these three orders and is ordained prior to them, in which everyone is to show mercy to his neighbor.[71] These three orders indicate three specific, divinely ordained realms of function to which Christians are called by God. Luther here intends the separate estates to include their associated spheres of life so that the marriage estate includes the widow's estate and the virgin's estate,[72] and the priestly estate includes those who furnish the lower ministries of the church, such as sexton, schoolteacher, and other assistants.[73] However, these assistants belong to the clerical estate only as adjuncts of the one *ministerium ecclesiasticum*, thus only by virtue of their relationship to the clerical office itself.

Luther stresses that all three estates are equally holy estates, thus opposing the Roman limitation of holy and spiritual works to the *religiosi* and *clerici*. From this formal equalization, however, we are not to conclude that Luther supported a leveling of the essential distinction that exists between the clerical estate, on the one hand, and the two other estates, on the other. This essential distinction is present in the origin, content, and purpose of the estates. In these three respects, the clerical estate as Luther sees it differs from the two other estates and is of an entirely higher genus. In contrast to the secular estates, the clerical estate is instituted and founded by God *through the blood and death of the only-begotten Son of God, our Lord Jesus Christ*. By this fact it is set apart from the secular estates.[74] It is thus endued with its second and higher purpose: while the secular

[67] WA 26:505.7ff.; cf. WA 31/1:217.10ff.: "Therefore, these estates which are instituted with God's Word are all called holy, divine estates, even though the persons are not holy."

[68] Cf. esp. his *Confession concerning Christ's Supper* [1528]: WA 26:504ff.

[69] WA 26:505.16ff.

[70] WA 26:505.21ff.

[71] WA 26:505.11ff.

[72] WA 26:505.23ff.

[73] WA 26:504.34f.; 38:255.27ff.; 30/2:528.11ff. (the subsequent biblical exemplification, in which only the preaching office is countenanced, plainly shows that by "clerical estate" it is properly the office itself which is meant, and the auxiliary ministries are to be added to this only derivatively).

[74] WA 30/2:554.2ff.: "And, first, it is true that the temporal authority or office is in no way to be compared with the spiritual preaching office, as St. Paul calls it. For it has not been dearly and highly

estates serve only for temporal, perishable life and convey earthly goods, the clerical estate—as it is founded "for our salvation"[75]—serves for eternal life in the kingdom of God and bestows imperishable gifts. "Insomuch, therefore, as eternal life excels the temporal, so far and high does the preaching office surpass the secular office, as it were a shadow compared with the body itself."[76] While the other two estates belong to God's secular government, the clerical or spiritual estate serves exclusively for God's spiritual government. This is a fundamental distinction. Thus the spiritual estate's content—that is, its authority—differs from that of the other two secular estates. In the latter, external power must be used while in the spiritual estate only the spiritual power of the Word is valid.[77] We must therefore take into account the way in which the doctrine of the three estates in Luther is integrated with that of the two kingdoms of God, which results in a distinct and separate appraisal of the spiritual estate in contrast to the other estates.[78] The spiritual estate is that into which the officers, who exercise

---

adorned by the blood and death of God's Son as the preaching office has . . ."; cf. WA 30/2:527.1ff.: (The clerical estate was instituted and founded by God) "not with gold or silver, but with the precious blood and bitter death of His only Son, our Lord Jesus Christ. For from His wounds truly flowed . . . the Sacraments, and truly and dearly adorned it, that throughout the world people might have this office to preach, baptize, loose, bind, give the Sacrament, comfort, warn and admonish with God's Word, and whatever else belongs to the office of caring for souls"; cf. WA 30/2:583.5ff., 530.1ff., 532.3ff.

[75] Cf. WA Br 10:255.21f., 256.53f.

[76] WA 30/2:554.4ff. and 9ff. — This higher assessment of the preaching office in comparison to the secular offices is ignored by G. Wingren (*Die Predigt* [Göttingen, 1955], pp. 135 and 138), who is only able to see the particularity of the pastoral office for Lutheranism in the fact "that it presents a special case in the great abundance of various calls" (p. 135). The differentiation of the two kingdoms of God and their consequences for the assessment of the preaching office is neglected in Wingren in this regard. — This consideration is also absent in H. Storck (op. cit., pp. 21ff.) and E. Wolf ("Zur Verwaltung der Sakramente nach Luther und luth. Lehre," in *Peregrinatio* [Munich, 1954], pp. 247f.). E. Wolf's particular concern (pp. 247f.) to understand the divine institution of the clerical office in Luther in a purely formal way from his doctrine of the three estates, but not objectively from the administration of the means of grace (for the purpose of justification and eternal salvation), cannot be judged as consonant with Luther's intention. When Luther speaks of the clerical estate, its relationship to Word and Sacrament is specifically included. Cf., e.g.: "I mean that estate which has the preaching office and ministry of the Word and Sacrament, which gives the Spirit and all blessedness . . ." (WA 30/2:528.8ff.).

[77] Also cf. WA 47:246.37ff.; 49:137.10ff., 138.1ff.; EA 3:450; and on the distinction of the individual estates generally: J. Köstlin, *Luthers Theologie* II (1901), pp. 304ff., and *Luthers Lehre von der Kirche* (1863), pp. 166ff. On the doctrine of God's spiritual and secular kingdoms in Luther, cf. E. Kinder, *Geistliches und weltliches Regiment Gottes nach Luther* (Weimar, 1940), and G. Törnvall, *Geistliches und weltliches Regiment bei Luther* (Munich, 1947).

[78] V. Vajta (*Theol. d. Gottes.*, pp. 200ff.) maintains: "The preaching office thus has its place among the various offices with which God rules His secular and spiritual kingdoms. The various offices are equated to one another, but distinguished from one another. The distinction rests on the fact that God cares for the temporal well-being of men through authorities . . . while He gives eternal gifts through the preaching office" (pp. 200f.; cf. p. 203). This is accurate, though it should be noted that the equal placement is only valid before God with respect to the underlying divine arrangement and with respect to the quality of the office-bearer's life. When, in response to Törnvall (*Geistl. u. welt. Regim. b. Luther*, p. 85), Vajta further views the distinction between the secular offices and the

the function of the particular office, are related. They constitute an estate in the Church on the basis of their equally exercised, particular ministry.[79] Whoever occupies this office belongs to a particular, divinely instituted and established order and division of the Church which is immediately given with the institution of the office itself since, of course, it involves the concrete office appointed with actual persons. All office-bearers, according to Luther, are in an *ordo*, though this is not meant by Luther in an intrinsic sense with *character indelebilis* [indelible character] and *habitus spiritualis* [spiritual condition].[80] Still the office, as a holy order, differentiates among Christians.[81] This difference is expressed most

---

spiritual office in the secular office's administering "power reserved to God" (pp. 203f.), we cannot readily agree with him. Vajta explains this distinction by saying that the prince is "an actual authority who is appointed as ruler over men," but in the realm of spiritual government there is "no other authority than God Himself through His Son, Jesus Christ, who is the only Lord of the Church. Christ Himself has the power, and not the one holding the office" (p. 203). These are concerning statements. The phrase "power reserved to God" suggests the idea that, in wholly un-Lutheran fashion, God's actual activity is not implicit in the activity of the office-bearer, as though, for example, a Baptism could be performed without God guaranteeing that He worked through it. This gives way to Reformed ideas of the separation of Word and Spirit, and nothing is less Lutheran. For Luther, the activity of the office-bearer in his office—insofar as he keeps to God's Word and commission, and so administers the means of grace according to their institution—is always understood objectively as the activity of Christ Himself, and therefore also, e.g., the Absolution in an exhibitive sense. The concept "power reserved to God" signifies a distancing of God's power from the activity of the office-bearer, the latter being in some sense *God's* activity only conditionally. But that would not be Luther's view. By the phrase "power reserved to God" Vajta certainly did not mean to teach this, but only that the office-bearer could not arbitrarily dispose of the authority entrusted to him. Yet in fact the phrase tends in that direction and is completely unsuited to describing the particularity of the spiritual office in contrast to the secular office of authority. The passages which Vajta cites from Luther to support this testify directly to the essential involvement of Christ in the activity of the office-bearer and thus call into question the term "power reserved to God" (see p. 204).

[79] Cf. C. Mahrenholz, *Begleitwort* [*zur*] *Agende f. ev.-luth. Kirchen u. Gemeinden*, vol. IV (Berlin, 1952), pp. 13f. — In the last century, F. J. Stahl already rightly saw that, in this light, Luther teaches a divinely instituted clerical estate (*Die Kirchenverfassung* . . . , p. 110). W. O. Münter's critique of Stahl's thesis that a particular estate is founded along with the office (*Die Gestalt der Kirche nach "göttlichem Recht"* [1941], pp. 51ff.) fails insofar as [Münter] overlooks the fact that Stahl never allows the bearers of the clerical estate to be separated from other Christians by any particular qualification but by their particular activity of the office. Neither does Stahl conceive of the office-bearers apart from their function of the office.

[80] Cf. WA 26:504.31ff.: "All who are found in the pastoral office or ministry of the Word are in a holy, true, good order and estate acceptable to God, such as those who preach, give the Sacrament. . . ."

[81] In the treatise *Infiltrating and Clandestine Preachers* (1532), Luther, expounding 1 Cor. 14:29ff., emphasizes that St. Paul here "makes a sure distinction between the prophets and the people. The prophets speak; the congregation listens" (WA 30/3:525.11f.). St. Paul is said there to be speaking of preachers "and not commanding the congregation to preach, but dealing with preachers who preach in the congregation or assembly . . ." (WA 30/3:523.6f.). "It is clear enough that he commits listening and improvement to the congregation here, not the office of teaching or preaching. He then makes an even clearer distinction and calls the congregation laymen. . . . Once again, preacher and layman are here distinguished . . ." (WA 30/3:525.18ff.); cf. WA 30/3:525.30ff. — In this passage, incidentally, Luther advocates the opposite of what he had written while expounding the same text in 1521 and 1523 in the treatises *Misuse of the Mass* (WA 8:495.24ff.) and *Concerning the Ministry*

simply and succinctly in the formula: "All Christians are priests, but not all are pastors."[82] The distinction is based, like the office itself, on the *jus divinum* of Christ's institution. —

We must also say a word about the gradation of the office. There is one divinely instituted office according to Luther; individual grades of the office are not instituted with the office. Scripture knows of no such grades, according to Luther. The scenario of "one man ruling over several pastors" is "established by common Christian ordinance," and so by human right.[83] The colleges of bishops are not instituted by God.[84] Bishop and presbyter (pastor) are made equal according to divine Law.[85] The same goes for the grades above bishops, even up to the pope.[86]

If the gradation of the office is *de jure humano*, it by no means follows that Luther discounts it. On the contrary: to the Bohemians, who were obliged to reappoint their office, he recommends that the newly elected bishops choose one or more among them to visit the others and to be their "superiors [*majores*]."[87] The gradation of the office is human in his view, and yet constitutes good order.[88] Luther wishes to see the Bohemian church organized, if at all possible, as an (Evangelical) archbishopric in the traditional sense, despite the lack of a divinely prescribed order.[89] As the core of the episcopal office, Luther sees the office of overseer or visitor.[90] He knows from Scripture "how divine and salutary a work

---

(WA 12:181.11ff.). On this also cf. A. W. Dieckhoff (op. cit., pp. 152ff.) and W. Elert (*Morphologie* I, p. 303). — Further, cf. the following passages: WA 41:203.34ff.: "But here we must distinguish the office or ministry of bishops, pastors, and preachers from the common estate of Christians . . ."; WA 41:209.10f.: "A man must be one" [i.e., a priest] "beforehand; but once he is" [born] "a priest" [by Baptism, then] "the office comes and makes a distinction" [between him and other Christians] . . . (cf. WA 41:209.26ff.).

[82] WA 31/1:211.17f.; cf. WA 33:551.41f.: "I was not born into it, but made and ordained a preacher"; WA 38:230.17ff. — Cf. P. Brunner, "Vom Amt des Bischofs," p. 25.

[83] WA 6:440.29; cf. WA 6:300.25ff.: "one being over another by human ordinance in the external church." — Cf. H. H. Kramm, op. cit., pp. 54f. (further passages there).

[84] WA 6:441.22f.

[85] Cf. Luther's endorsement of Jerome's teaching on this point (cited WA 2:227.32ff., 229.29ff.): "The opinion stands that bishops are superior to presbyters not by truth of divine dispensation but by custom of the church" (WA 2:230.9f.); ". . . It is clear . . . that bishops are in fact equal to each other and with presbyters, and that it is only by the custom and for the sake of the church that one is to be preferred before another" (WA 2:230.21f.); cf. also WA 25:16.25ff.

[86] E.g., WA 50:213.1ff.

[87] WA 12:194.14ff.

[88] Cf. P. Brunner, "Vom Amt des Bischofs," pp. 27ff. Rather significant are Brunner's elaborations of Luther's view of the character of the pastoral office as an office of governance and the evaluation derived from that of a superior episcopal office of oversight, pp. 30ff. On this also cf. A. W. Dieckhoff, *Luthers Lehre von der kirchl. Gewalt* (1865), pp. 108ff. and 122ff. On the episcopal office in Lutheran thinking generally, cf. O. Söhngen, *Kirchenregiment, Bischofsamt u. Predigtamt*, Kirche in dieser Zeit 8 (Berlin, 1948), pp. 10ff.

[89] WA 12:194.18f.

[90] WA 26:196.5ff.: "For properly a bishop means an overseer or visitor—and an archbishop, he who is over the same overseers or visitors—because each pastor is to visit, attend to, and oversee

it is for pastors and Christian congregations to be visited by wise, capable men,"[91] and from his experience he must confess that he would "be glad to see the true episcopal office and visitor's office restored since it is extremely necessary."[92] And he also saw to its actual establishment (if only through the territorial princes).[93] Still, it remains fixed for Luther that the concrete office is instituted by God as essential and that the grades in it are fundamentally *juris humani.*

3. The Office-Bearer as God's Minister and Legate

If the office rests on God's institution and arrangement, and if the content of the office (Word and Sacrament) is also given by God, then the office-bearer really confronts the congregation not merely as a private person nor merely as its delegate. Rather, in his office he embodies the authority of God. He is in that office not by human power (*ex humana potentia*) but by the command of Him (*ex ejus befelh*) who sent him,[94] "placed into it" (the office) "by divine command."[95] He is the messenger of the Lord[96] and God's legate.[97] Preachers are "like the officers of a prince," says Luther.[98] They represent the Lord, speaking not their own word but His Word. They proclaim the Gospel "in the stead of Christ."[99] Thus they are owed obedience and honor for the sake of their

how his parishioners are taught and live. And the archbishop is to visit, attend to, and oversee how such bishops teach. . . ."

91 WA 26:195.4ff.

92 WA 26:197.12ff.

93 K. Holl has shown how Luther viewed the territorial church governance only as an emergency solution and strove for a visitation office of real bishops (*Luther*, pp. 375ff.).

94 WA 49:139.4f.

95 WA 28:472.27f.

96 WA 12:318.25; cf. WA 41:123.29ff.

97 WA 40/1:56.24ff.

98 WA 10/3:397.1f.

99 WA 28:479.38f.; cf. WA 28:478.35ff., 477.3; 37:381.13ff. ("in Christ's stead"); WA 49:138.37, 141.42ff. Yet the idea that Christ is actually absent and has Himself thus represented *in absentia* is a far cry from Luther. The ministers in the office personally represent the Lord only so far as His visibility is concerned; invisibly, He is already present among them. Also cf. the next section. — K. Frank, *Histor., dogmat. u. krit. Beiträge . . .* , dissert. (Greifswald, 1913), gets Luther's view entirely wrong when he makes Luther see "the pastor merely as an officer appointed by the congregation or even collaborating with it, who must carry out the church's rites perceptible by everyone else in accordance with his call" (p. 12).

office.[100] The pastor, in his office, must be listened to not "as a man, but as God."[101] Whoever despises the pastor acts "contrary to God"[102] and must expect punishment;[103] he is to be counted among the blasphemers and enemies of Christ's Church.[104] Luther lays great stress on recognizing and honoring the authority of God in the pastor while at the same time distinguishing the person as such from the office.[105] The authority of the office-bearer lies in the office itself which is conferred on him, in the Word which he preaches, and in the Sacraments which he handles. His authority is that he represents Christ, independent of his personal character in other respects. The congregation is therefore not to look at his person, his human characteristics, but ". . . to pay attention to this command, that everyone who is called to the preaching office has the power and authority to preach, baptize, and absolve. They are to acknowledge that this office is not of men but of the Lord Christ."[106] On the basis of his commission to the office and his authorization in that office, the office-bearer appears in the authority of Christ when he does the works of his office.[107]

---

[100] WA 6:408.20: "Because he is in the office, he has preeminence . . ."; WA 28:469.7ff.: "The office is to be feared and honored and the person obeyed in all that he does according to the office, for 'he who despises, despises not men, but God. . . .'" Also cf. WA 30/1:155.3ff. in LC 3, the Fourth Commandment: the spiritual fathers "who govern and guide us through God's Word" are to be given double honor.

[101] WA 49:140.38. — H. Storck neglects this when he writes (op. cit., p. 40): "The respect of the called pastor on the part of the equally enfranchised brethren is an act of love," or when he also calls this a requirement of reason (ibid.). The much stronger and weightier argument for the authority of the pastor lies, according to Luther, in the fact that in his office he confronts the congregation in Christ's stead.

[102] WA 31/1:210.25f.

[103] WA TR 6:194.20ff.

[104] WA 30/3:519.6f.

[105] Cf. WA 30/3:570.37ff.: "I would like the young and the people to be trained to say not only 'Worthy Sir,' but also 'Holy Sir,' 'Holy Father,' and to be made to call confession holy, Absolution holy, preaching holy, and all that pertains to the Word holy . . ."; WA 30/3:571.1ff.: "I expect it will not break any of their bones or cause any great heresy since such honor is given not to the person but to the office and the Word of God. If there were no error in the papacy except that the pope were called Most Holy, I would call him Most Holy thrice over. . . ." — Luther describes the dignity of a pastor in the highest terms, calling him "an angel of God, a true bishop before God, a savior of many, a king and prince in Christ's kingdom, and a teacher in God's nation, a light of the world. And who will or can tell all the honor and virtue which a true and faithful pastor has before God? There is no dearer treasure, no nobler thing on earth and in this life than a true and faithful pastor or preacher" (WA 30/2:533.4ff.).

[106] WA 28:470.38ff.

[107] R. Sohm claims one-sidedly that the administration and exercise of the teaching office according to Luther is only ever "possible by virtue of a *free assent* on the part of the assembly" (*Kirchenrecht* I [1892], p. 474), though the office itself comes from God (p. 474 n. 31). In Luther, however, this is only one component—that derived from his delegative concept of the office as a product of the universal priesthood. The other, which has the office and its authority based independently on God's institution, will come into play much more in Luther to justify the authority of the office-bearer vis-à-vis the congregation. According to Luther, the office-bearer is not *merely* a delegate of the congregation, but above all—even simply in the exercise of the office—the mandatary

4. The Office-Bearer as God's Instrument

The office-bearer stands in his office in Christ's stead. And Christ, whom he represents with Word and Sacrament, is He by whom God acts in a justifying and redemptive way toward men.[108] Thus the office-bearer, in his performance of the office, is God's instrument of salvific action. "A preacher is God's minister and instrument, which God uses for His work. When I preach, baptize, absolve, give the Sacrament, God uses my mouth and my hand externally for His work which He wishes to perform internally. . . ."[109] The pure instrumentality of the minister in the office is best expressed in the formulation: "Indeed, He" (God) "Himself preaches through me."[110] Since the content of the office's function was not invented by men, the function itself is not a function of men either.[111] "What he" (the minister) "says or does is not his own, but it is Christ your Lord and the Holy Spirit who speaks and does it all. . . ."[112] The minister in the office only lends

---

of the Lord God. The assent which Luther describes as operative in the calling of a minister of the Word is not a *free* assent, but one that thereby binds itself to respecting God's authority in the one who has now been called.

[108] H. E. Creutzig ("Amt u. Ämter i. d. luth. Kirche," in *Luthertum* [1938], pp. 114ff.) rightly emphasized that in the office, a "realization of the saving Christ" takes place.

[109] WA 45:310.26ff. (Dr); cf. WA 41:543.28f.; 41:455.1ff.: ". . . We are only the instrument and means through which Christ speaks and acts to your honor. . . . We are the spoon; He gives drink through us, the food and drink of the Lord. . . ." (We are) "organs of God through which He works"; WA 41:456.32: "I, an instrument"; WA 45:312.5f.: "God's instrument"; WA 47:451.21: "Christ is the head preacher; these" (doctors and preachers) "are His instruments and tongues"; WA 11:99.2f.: "instrument and mouth of God"; WA 12:524.8ff.; WA TR 3:671.8ff. (no. 3868): ". . . We . . . are only the instrument and assistants of God through whom God acts and works"; WA TR 4:531.16ff. (no. 4812): "God, the Maker of heaven and earth, speaks to you through His preachers; He baptizes, catechizes, absolves you through the ministrations of their sacraments"; WA TR 5:2.23ff.: ". . . preaching office . . . this is the instrument and conduit by which God the Holy Spirit touches the heart. . . ."

[110] WA 45:310.37f. (Dr).

[111] Cf. WA 38:239.2ff.: ". . . A pastor or preacher does not make the Gospel, nor do his words become Gospel through his preaching or office. . . . But he only gives and conveys the Gospel through his preaching. For the Gospel exists beforehand and must exist beforehand. Our Lord Christ made it, brought it, and left it behind . . ."; WA 38:239.27ff.: "Our action, however, only gives and conveys this Baptism ordained and made by Christ's command and institution. Therefore, He alone is and remains the only true, eternal Baptizer, who through our activity or ministry apportions His Baptism daily until the Last Day. . . ."

[112] WA 50:634.28ff. (on the appended condition "insofar as he continues to teach and act rightly," cf. below, pp. 104–6); cf. WA 10/3:395.11ff.: "So when the priest baptizes a child, he says, 'I baptize you in the name of the Father. . . .' This is utter Gospel and is as if Christ baptized you Himself. . . ." (And of the Absolution:) ". . . It is not I who do this, but God does it. . . ." (And of the Sacrament of the Altar:) ". . . So if I receive the Sacrament, the cleric speaks the words of Christ in God's stead, 'This is My body' "; WA 28:479.32f.: "Although they are men who preach, baptize, forgive sin, yet in the preaching office the preaching and baptizing is being done by the Holy Spirit, whose work and office it is"; WA 34/1:395.15f.: "In the preaching office, God speaks with us"; WA 41:188.11f.; WA Br 3:210.49ff.

the Lord his voice and tongue for the purpose.[113] In the celebration of the holy Sacrament, we hear the Words of Consecration ("This is My body," etc.) not "as spoken in the person of the pastor or minister, but as from Christ's own mouth."[114] Our speech and action would truly be unable to make the bread the body of Christ and the wine the blood of Christ,[115] but in the person of the minister at the altar, it is Christ Himself who speaks and acts, who engages the pastor's own person such that the human person is no longer a concern, only the office which that person bears.[116] Thus the words of the minister in the office—when spoken in obedience to the institution of Christ—become the words of Christ Himself. "We hear Christ Himself speaking with and directing us through the pastor's mouth."[117] "When I myself preach, He" (i.e., Christ) "preaches in me."[118] "When you hear the Word, you hear God."[119] Christ, in giving and committing to one man the Office of the Keys, thereby guarantees that He is working through this man: "Peter's mouth is My" (i.e., Christ's) "mouth; his office, My office; his Keys are My Keys."[120] For this reason, he who has received the Absolution may say, "It is not the pastor who has absolved me, but God has spoken through him."[121] When the minister in the office lays his hands on me, Christ does it

---

[113] WA 45:310.38f.: "The word is His, although I lend my tongue and voice for it . . ."; cf. WA 22:186.23ff.: ". . . gift, office, or work . . . which are God's alone, and yet are accomplished through the mouth and hands of men"; WA 45:310.6ff. (Rörer): "Therefore, I call myself a tool. Thus when I preach, I speak the true Word; God takes my tongue and voice and preaching. It is not that I come into the soul with my word; my word does not renew the soul. Rather, it is God, who . . . instituted and willed to give life and the Holy Spirit through a man as a tool."

[114] WA 38:240.14ff.

[115] WA 38:240.11f.

[116] WA 30/2:534.8ff.: "Not that he as a man does it, but his office ordained by God for that purpose does it, as does the Word of God which he teaches. For he is the instrument for that same purpose."

[117] WA 38:240.20f.; cf. WA 43:70.5ff.: "It is therefore the great glory with which the divine Majesty adorns us that thus works through us so that He may call our word His, and our actions His, so that you may truly speak in this way: 'The mouth of a faithful teacher is the mouth of God . . .' "; WA 47:213.20ff.: "I hear . . . the voice of the pastor, but the words which he speaks are not his own . . . but the high Majesty of God speaks through them"; WA 47:298.36: "When the preacher is heard, God Himself is heard." — K. D. Schmidt ("Luthers Lehre vom Hlg. Geist," in *Schrift und Bekenntnis,* festschrift for Simon Schöffel [Hamburg-Berlin, 1950], p. 155) pointed out that Luther teaches, in sharp contrast to such as [Heinrich] Bullinger (who said, "The man preaches . . . the Holy Spirit works," conceiving of the process in a parallelism), that *God* preaches, threatens, comforts, baptizes when the preacher does it. "The proclaimed Word is in the fullest sense the instrument of which God makes use to establish His dominion. This interlocking of Spirit and Word rests on God's ordinance" (p. 155). — Cf. V. Vajta, op. cit., p. 207.

[118] WA 20:350.6 (Rörer); 42:194.19f.

[119] WA 37:136.16.

[120] WA 30/2:455.18ff.; cf. WA 30/2:497.25ff., and esp. 498.5ff.; also WA 10/3:395.14ff.; 37:381.14f.

[121] WA 49:139.16f.; cf. WA 2:249.18f.: ". . . He will loose it in heaven when the priest looses"; WA 11:97.2f.: "If I say, 'Sins are remitted,' it is God's word, not mine"; WA 45:460.6ff.: ". . . God Himself stoops down and ordains with divine authority that a man's absolving should be God's own absolving. Thus he who hears the man absolving should be certain that he is absolved by God Himself in heaven"; WA 49:142.26ff.: "I well know that the pastor is a man, but the words which he

Himself.[122] The mouth and hand of the minister are the mouth and hand of God.[123] Otherwise the office as Luther sees it could not be performed.[124]

In this context, the universal concept in Luther serves as a basis for the idea that *God does not deal with us nakedly but through masks, in coverings*. Word and Sacrament are indeed such masks of God, yet so are the ministers in the office. "My hand and mouth are His instrument and masks, and yet He Himself is acting."[125] Without it being externally apparent, God acts in a hidden manner in the one serving in the office.[126] Thus Luther also calls the preaching office the "foot of Christ," after Ps. 68:24.[127]

In the instrumental nature of ministers in the office we see a specific divine order of salvation which should not and cannot be circumvented. God wishes to deal with us through external means, through His Word and Sacrament; but since He has entrusted these to an office which is exercised by specific persons, we are pointed *by God's order* to the ministers, who are here "fellow helpers and fellow laborers" of God.[128] Of course, God could convey the salvific good even without the office-bearers, but "He does not wish to abolish the preaching office and do something special for each person," so He directs everyone to the pulpit, to the pastor: "Wait, I will arrange it for you, send you an angel. Go, hear the Gospel from your pastor; you will find it there";[129] and concerning the Keys: "I have no other, nor do I know of any other. . . ."[130] Office and office-bearer are Christ's instrument in *this sense*: that everyone who wants to be a participant

---

speaks to me are those not of a man but of God, of Christ, who committed them to him and said, 'Go, strengthen your brothers' "; WA 49:148.20ff.; WA TR 3:671.6ff. (no. 3868): "We say that the Word, Absolution, and Sacrament of a man, the preacher, is not the work of a man but the voice of God, the cleansing and work of God. . . ."

122 WA 49:140.10f.: "If the minister lays his hand on you, so does Christ Himself."

123 WA 43:600.26f.; cf. WA 8:683.13ff.; 37:381.13ff.: "This is a great thing, that every pastor's mouth is Christ's mouth."

124 WA 41:456.34ff.: "If I do not know that God is preaching, absolving, etc., through me, I will never do it. I cannot join man and wife if I do not know that God is doing it"; WA 49:148.24f.

125 WA 41:456.12f.

126 WA 41:456.9ff.: "Thus discern that Christ is His Church's supreme Bishop and Pope who performs all the offices by His ordinance; for from Him we hear the Gospel, are absolved, receive comfort, etc., except that masks are pulled over the eyes, for we do not see Him."

127 WA 8:24.13.

128 WA 17/2:179.21ff.; cf. WA 41:458.25f.: "We are God's stewards [*dispensatores*], His servants, and apportion His treasures"; WA 44:658.30f.: "Paul calls the apostles God's fellow workers [*cooperatores*]. He Himself works, yet through us"; WA TR 3:671.6ff. and 9 ("God's fellow workers [*cooperarii*]"). — Cf. V. Vajta, op. cit., pp. 206f., who explains that *cooperatio* in Luther does not attribute a salvific meaning to human powers: ". . . *Cooperatio* does not imply that the gift of grace exists from the cooperation of divine and human powers, but it is entirely God working here; man only occupies the position of servant. . . . *Cooperatio* is thus only an expression for the idea that, as long as this world endures, we do not encounter God face-to-face, but only through His *larvae* [masks], in which He keeps His working concealed" (p. 207).

129 WA 37:269.18ff.

130 WA 30/2:455.20, 498.7f. This does not apply exclusively to the Office of the Keys which the pastor exercises *publicly*, but to the Office of the Keys generally, which according to Luther may be

in salvation is referred to these entities.[131] To the question for what reason the preaching office was instituted and what it is supposed to accomplish, Luther responds: ". . . For the same reason that Christ came into the world, for which He was sent by the Father, and which He accomplished. This is the most glorious aspect, that He" (Christ) "not only gives to the apostles and their successors the authority and power to preach, and calls and sends them to exercise the Office of the Keys in His kingdom . . . , but He even sends them in every respect as He was sent by the Father, and *places the strength and the work of His resurrection in the mouth of the apostles and of all preachers (who have the office and Word)*, and makes sin and righteousness, heaven and hell subject to them that they may step in with authority, either absolving from sins or burdening with sins, either opening heaven or closing it."[132] In this respect, the "whole kingdom and government" of Christ's Church is also found in the public preaching office.[133]

5. The Attachment of the Office-Bearer's Authority and Instrumentality to Word and Doctrine

Accordingly, both the instrumentality and authority of the minister in the office are attached to an assumption, which is the office-bearer's obedient integration into the office conferred on him.[134] If in his official function the office-bearer deviates from Christ's commission and ordinance, he stands fundamentally outside the office,[135] and so forfeits all authority and can no longer be God's instrument. The congregation must then avoid him as a false prophet. It is from this perspective above all that Luther's opinions of the Roman clergy in his day are to be understood.[136] By corruption of the office of the Word into a satisfactionary office of sacrifice, Christ's institution was broken. Luther therefore regards those who carry out this office of sacrifice as standing outside the true

exercised in the private, domestic sphere by any believing Christian. In the latter case, too, the one speaking the Absolution is God's instrument. Cf. WA 49:140.40f., 146.9f.; 10/3:395.25ff.

[131] Cf. WA 49:139.29f.: "Without faith it is no help to you; for if you regard me as a man, you have been justly served. In this way you cannot be helped."

[132] WA 28:476.7ff.; cf. WA 28:478.25ff., 479.24ff.: "Through your mouth you are to make people righteous; namely, by your proclaiming forgiveness of sins in My name"; WA 34/1:318.15ff.; 49:142.32ff.

[133] WA 41:123.37; cf. WA 41:195.35f.: "And in" (the Church, Christ) "governs as Priest or true Pope through the preaching office and by means of the Holy Spirit. . . ."

[134] WA 28:469.29ff.: "When the pastor deals with you according to his office . . . according to Christ's Word and command, then you are to receive it in all fear, humility, obedience, and faith. . . . But when he deals with you contrary to his office, without God's Word and command, and abuses his office . . ." (then not!); WA 28:470.1ff.: "You must be certain as to when your pastor and teacher remains in his office and when he steps out of it so that you know when you are to obey him and when you are to avoid him . . ."; also WA 28:470.17ff., 471.1ff.

[135] Cf. K. Thieme, *Die Augsburg. Konfession und Luthers Katechismen* (Gießen, 1930), p. 12.

[136] Cf. above, pp. 9–12.

office; their authority has ceased, they cannot claim to be true priests of God. They must be fled from and removed wherever possible.[137] It is better, according to Luther, to have no pastor at all than to have an ungodly, sacrilegious one who spurns God's Word and true doctrine. The harm done by him in the church is worse than when the office is not filled for a time.[138] This is how seriously Luther takes the attachment of the minister of the Word to the content of the office established by the divine institution. There is no nebulous function of the office designed by God, but an entirely specific one: both "the office and the Word of the office" are "comprehended in divine command."[139] Hence it is clear that the office-bearer's authority is not based simply on the function of preaching, but on the right content of his preaching. The office-bearer has authority and is God's mouthpiece only by preaching in accordance with Scripture. "*When I preach God's Word rightly, then* God uses my tongue and voice for the preaching of His Word. . . ."[140] The pastor's speech and action are Christ's speech and action only "*insofar as he continues to teach, and rightly.*"[141]

There is, then, no absolute authority possessed by the office-bearer, according to Luther. The obedience due the office-bearer is only to be rendered conditionally, on the assumption that the minister in the office, with his official activity, remains within the institution of his office.[142] The case of a minister's deviation from his office must always categorically be called to account, for the office does not irresistibly determine the personal character of its bearer but continually demands his new obedience. Every minister in the office stands or falls with respect to his authority and his instrumentality for

---

[137] WA 11:411.18; 50:634.6ff.: "Therefore, in the same sense that they are churches, they are also apostles, evangelists, and prophets, that is, they are the devil's apostles, evangelists, and prophets. For the true apostles, evangelists, and prophets preach God's Word and not against God's Word"; WA 53:246.23ff.: "It is decided by God's decree: A wolf shall not be a bishop in His Christian Church"; WA 2:452.26ff.; WA Br 3:210.61ff.: "If there are those who dispense or teach another than this mystery of God, these are neither apostles nor bishops, but thieves and robbers who destroy the sheep, whom Paul curses (Galatians 1)." — Luther's position toward the pope is also conditioned by this. Because he persecutes God's Word and does injury to the Church, his power and authority are gone; he must be removed: cf. WA 2:677.3ff.; 6:409ff. Also cf. above, pp. 78–79.

[138] WA 12:172.6ff.

[139] WA 19:233.6f.

[140] WA 45:310.36f.

[141] WA 50:634.30.

[142] WA 28:469.11ff.: "But when the person does something not according to the office but contrary to the office, he should not be obeyed, for the Holy Spirit does not do so"; cf. WA 28:469.32ff.; 10/3:122.20ff.: "When the bishop or official preaches to you the Gospel, you are to listen to them; if they do not preach it, they have forfeited their authority. If they preach the Gospel, they have authority; if they do not preach it, their authority is already over"; WA 10/3:174.11ff.: "I am the sheep of God, whose Word I desire and wish to receive, and if you will give me that Word, I will regard you as a shepherd, but if you add for me a secondary teaching and do not give me the Gospel in its purity, I will not regard you as a shepherd nor receive your voice, for this office extends no farther than as far as the Word goes"; WA 10/3:398.11ff.: "It should be thus: if he does not preach the Word of God, another should stand up and preach. We are to hear the Word of God and none other."

God's salvific action in accordance with his faithfulness to the Word "on which the office is founded."[143]

6. The Office-Bearer's Freedom from the Congregation

When the office-bearer deviates from his office—that is, from the institution and ordinance of Christ—and persists in the deviation, he can and must be removed, as has already been established.[144] Neither does the divine character of the office hinder this; indeed, on the contrary, it demands that it be done this way. At the same time, however, it protects the office-bearer unconditionally from the arbitrary will of the congregation and gives him internal freedom despite them, which is essential for the right exercise of the office. The minister of the Word, according to Luther, is the servant not of the congregation but of Christ, and it is *His* commission that is absolutely binding on him.[145] This obligation to Christ's commission constitutes an entirely *personal responsibility of the minister in the office before God*,[146] in which he also confronts the congregation and which may not be diminished by the fact that every congregant is involved in it. Luther sternly takes to task those who frivolously pass judgment on their pastor and abandon him: "Who told you to despise your pastor, to pass judgment on him, to condemn him behind his back before he has been examined or charged? How have you become such a judge over your pastor—yes, and your own judge too?"[147] If the pastor has not been clearly convicted of a transgression, no congregant is entitled to pass judgment on him.[148] This arbitrary, frivolous passing of judgment on the pastor returns upon the person who commits it and judges him. The pastor possesses the preaching office; if a layman (anyone who

---

[143] WA 47:193.3ff.; also cf. WA 7:22.20f. — W. Elert, *Morphologie* I, p. 325. — These connections are also the underlying reason why the ordination examination and ordination vow play an important role for Luther. Also cf. M. Doerne, *Luth. Pfarramt*, pp. 14ff.

[144] Cf. above, pp. 77–80.

[145] In full agreement with Luther's opinion, Simon Schöffel ("Das Predigt- u. Hirtenamt," op. cit., p. 211) writes: (The preaching office) "is tied to God's Word, and no congregation can dissolve or loosen this bond or give the office a different content: the preacher is free and independent from his congregation, responsible only to the Lord, who appointed him to the ministry of the Word." The congregation's requirement of the office-bearer also can, according to Luther, only be that he preaches God's Word purely.

[146] Cf. H. Liermann (*Grundlagen des kirchl. Verfassungsrechts nach luth. Auffassung*, Luthertum 11 [Berlin, 1954], p. 13), who mentions as a sign of the Lutheran concept of the office that it "is unthinkable apart from an utterly personal responsibility before God" (p. 13). Excellent also, and in agreement with Luther's meaning, is the formulation that "the pastor serves the congregation, but he is not their servant" (p. 17).

[147] WA 30/3:520.25ff.

[148] WA 30/3:522.12ff.: "Hence the infiltrators who come into the church think that they have power and right to judge the preachers and to preach differently. But that is far, far wrong . . ."; cf. WA 30/3:523.23ff., 524.1ff.

is not himself called to the preaching office) interrupts him, it must be judged as "infringement on another's office," which Scripture does not tolerate.[149] The congregation, therefore, is by no means the pastor's lord and master. Rather, through his office he confronts the congregation in the authority of God. It has no power over him except as he deviates from Christ's ordinance and institution.

In this connection, *Luther's letter to the Officer Georg von Harstall and the Council of Creuzburg from January 27, 1543*, is relevant.[150] The latter wanted a pastor to be removed from his office because he had become odious to them through his zealous repentance sermons. In his letter, Luther points them first to the divine character of the office. It is instituted by Christ. "For this reason, He" (Christ) "judges very harshly those who despise it and says, 'He who despises you despises Me.'"[151] Then Luther shows them that Christ "shares with them His Word and Sacrament—that is, His blood, death, and life—through His faithful, godly minister, your pastor, in such a pure and abundant way."[152] They are to give thanks for this and not resist their pastor, which would have grave consequences. Churches are built and parishes established not "so that those who wish to teach and hear God's Word may be cast out of them, and those brought in who do not need nor wish to hear God's Word, but they are built and established for the sake of those who hear it gladly and cannot do without it."[153] Luther then asserts the inner freedom of the pastoral office: "You are not lords over the pastors and preaching office, you did not found them, but God's Son alone. Neither have you given anything to it, but you have far less right to it than the devil to heaven. You are not to lord it over them or teach them, nor to prevent their rebuking. For it is God's rebuke, and not man's, who desires that it not be prevented but rather commanded."[154] ". . . For what you intend is a bad example, and it does no good for every officer, judge, or councilman to try to expel a pastor (for which they have no right, power, or cause) maliciously and at whim."[155] Here every political claim made by the congregation over the office, and every unspiritual interference with preaching, is rejected by Luther on the basis of the divine character of the office. The office stands as a divine institution in the congregation; the behavior of the congregation toward its pastor must be regulated accordingly.

Likewise instructive for our purposes is an event referred to by W. Walther.[156] In 1531, the council of Zwickau, without reasonable cause, removed a preacher by the name of *Lorenz Soranus* and replaced him. In several writings to the council

[149] WA 30/3:524.37ff.; cf. WA 30/3:519.32ff. We observe in the treatise *Infiltrating and Clandestine Preachers* the strict distinction between preachers and laymen: WA 30/3:524.1ff., 525.23ff. Also WA TR 4:166.19ff. With an eye to rebellion against the pastor, Luther also speaks of the "masses" ["*pobel*"]: WA 30/3:522.17, 525.30.

[150] WA Br 10:252–58.

[151] WA Br 10:255.22f.

[152] WA Br 10:255.32ff.

[153] WA Br 10:257.82ff.

[154] WA Br 10:257.87ff.

[155] WA Br 10:257.118ff.

[156] *Das Erbe der Reformation*, book 4: *Luthers Kirche* (Leipzig, 1917), pp. 141f.

and to the electors,[157] Luther criticizes the council for acting without cause or due process[158] and, "without knowledge and consent of the pastor"[159] (i.e., the parson, Nicholas Hausmann, to whom the preacher was subordinate), removing Soranus and replacing him and dispensing of the revenues of the parish, which did not belong to the council. In another letter he suggests that the parson, Nicholas Hausmann, go before the council regarding this matter and protest it,[160] and calls the council's action a sacrilege.[161] This relates equally to removal without cause and consideration of the responsibility of competent pastors. We will return to this event below in connection with a different point.[162] In this case, too, Luther defends the freedom and independence of the office over against the arbitrary act by the congregation, and this is what he did in every instance.

The state of obligation to God's commission, according to Luther, involves the pastor's internal independence from the congregation and his responsible freedom to confront it in the authority of God by virtue of his commission. If the minister of the Word does this in full obedience to his Lord, who is also the Lord of the congregation, he is in fact sacrosanct in the handling of the office (in this respect!). —

Let us summarize: The divine character of the concrete office is taught in Luther in a fully accentuated and distinct way. The function of the office, Word and Sacrament, is instituted by Christ. And no less instituted by Christ is the office itself, by which the exercise of this official function is attached to specific, called persons set apart for the purpose. The officers who administer the institution of this office confront the congregation in the Lord's authority; through their ministry of Word and Sacrament, Christ deals with the congregation in a justifying and salvific manner. The divine character of the office demands of its officers sure obedience to the office itself, but then, with this condition, gives them the firm, objective support which they need for successful execution of the office.

In all this, Luther's rationale of the office "from above," in the Lord's institution, is set forth. If this is compared with Luther's other rationale of the office based on the sociological necessities of the priestly congregation, two independent lines of thought in Luther must be postulated which only when taken together form his concept of the office. In Luther's statements—depending on the recipient of his speech or writing—first one and then the other line of thought comes to the fore without one being completely absorbed by the other. For an accurate assessment of Luther's concept of the office, a combined view of both thought systems is an indispensable prerequisite.

---

157 WA Br 6:45–47, 47–48, 48–49.

158 Cf. WA Br 6:77.16f.: "neither accused nor convicted before any judge."

159 WA Br 6:46.5f.

160 WA Br 6:77ff.

161 WA Br 6:77.19.

162 Cf. below, pp. 132–33.

In the nineteenth-century discussion of the office, an error was made by seeing only one side of Luther's doctrine of the office and then making this one absolute. In recent times, W. Elert in particular has emphasized both methods of arguing the concrete office in Luther (*Morphologie* I, pp. 298ff.).[163] Elert points to the fact that in Luther the rationale from Christ's institution is bound together with the purely practical, almost utilitarian, one, without Luther sensing in the former a contradiction to the practical rationale (p. 301). This observation is very important. It will not be possible to interpret the two methods of arguing the office in Luther in a contradictory, mutually exclusive way. For Luther, the concrete office stands on the basis of the universal priesthood of all Christians and of the Christian congregation. As a rationale of this concrete office with respect to its necessity and its essence, Luther uses (1) the sociological derivation from the universal priesthood that he may then (2) bolster this all the more by tracing it back to the positive institution of Christ. It will perhaps be possible to classify the first kind of rationale as an external view, so to speak, but the second as the proper, internal view. To a certain extent this is a matter of two aspects of one and same thing. The concrete office carries a divine necessity as well as a human one; it has both a sociological and an institutional aspect. —

A presentation of the uniformity of Luther's concept of the office despite its two strains of thought—the sociological and the institutional—has lately been attempted by V. Vajta through his elaboration especially on the idea of *cooperatio* in Luther (op. cit., pp. 208f. and 211f.). "In the call, the congregation cooperates with God"; "the call of the congregation [is] a call proceeding from God" (p. 212). "Luther's view of God's activity in the world through the *cooperatio* of various instruments of creation thus finds application to his concept of the office as well" (p. 213). This is at least a constructive thought. Yet it cannot be said that Vajta was entirely successful in keeping the two sides in Luther's rationale of the office untangled, each with all its peculiar qualities. *And yet this is necessary if an inaccurate oversimplification is to be avoided.* Still, Vajta's attempt must be judged positively as a quite worthwhile conceptualization. —

Now that the universal priesthood and the concrete office have been examined in their mutual relationship in Luther, it will be necessary to outline the action by which a person attains to the concrete office. This is the call or ordination. We must therefore proceed to examine this part of Luther's doctrine of the office.

---

[163] Likewise, K. Tuchel ("Luthers Auffassung vom geistl. Amt," *Lutherjahrbuch* [1958], pp. 61–98). Tuchel sees as the midpoint in the parallel of the rationale of the office contingent on order and the rationale contingent on the institution in Luther's writings Luther's view of the Christian as "*simul iustus et peccator* [simultaneously righteous and sinner]," and so traces the twofold foundation of the office in Luther back to the theme of the doctrine of justification (pp. 87f.).

CHAPTER V

The Call to the Office as Legitimization of the Office-Bearer

1. *Vocatio Generalis* and *Vocatio Specialis*

In Baptism, a man is called to the Christian estate (*vocatio generalis*), where he is installed in the universal priesthood and receives the rights and duties of a priest. As we have seen,[1] this includes, first, the free access to God and the ability in Christ to offer spiritual sacrifices to God and to come before Him on behalf of others. But it also carries with it the fundamental ability to perform the priestly office of Word and Sacrament. All Christians are "born and called unto this ministry through Baptism."[2] In Baptism, according to Luther, they are given a *jus generale* [general right] to preach the Gospel and administer the Sacraments. It was on the basis of this general or universal right and the universal baptismal call that Apollos, Stephen, and Philip preached, and it is on this basis that every Christian is able to exercise this office in cases of necessity.[3]

To be distinguished from this *vocatio generalis* in Luther is the *vocatio specialis*, the call to the public preaching office, to the concrete ecclesial office.[4] It is a new and more extensive call beyond the baptismal call and is added to the baptismal call. In *Ordination of Ministers of the Word*, Luther calls it "second sanctification [*altera sanctificatio*]" and contrasts it with the "first sanctification through the Word and Sacrament of Baptism."[5] Through the former, one

[1] Cf. above, pp. 23–25.

[2] WA 12:191.37.

[3] WA 12:191.38ff.

[4] Luther also sees other secular callings which a Christian can occupy on the basis of a particular call. Cf. H. Storck, op. cit., pp. 25f. and 38f., as well as G. Wingren, *Luthers Lehre vom Beruf* (Munich, 1952). Frequently in Luther, *vocatio* is simply the calling or occupation wherein someone has a particular job. But regarding the preaching office, Luther, by "*vocatio*," means "not the office as such," but the "action through which one actually enters the office" (Wingren, p. 15). Also cf. W. Maurer, *Pfarrerrecht und Bekenntnis* (Berlin, 1957), p. 121.

[5] WA 38:424.21ff.

is made a "a good creation" in Word and Sacrament, that is, one is justified and adopted as God's child. Through the latter, one is called "to the holy and divine ministry," that is, to the public preaching office of the Church here.[6] The fundamentally accessible right to exercise the function of Word and Sacrament is engaged by this particular call so that it can become effectual in the public function.[7] Thus this particular call constitutes to a certain degree an authorization to exercise the fundamentally possessed priestly rights and faculties with respect to the public function of Word and Sacrament.[8]

According to Luther, a pastor not only requires the priestly consecration in Baptism but also the regular call to the concrete office.[9] Only through this is one who is already a priest by Baptism also made a preacher and pastor.[10] "The call and command make a pastor and preacher."[11] It must be strongly emphasized that in Luther the priest and pastor are not of the same class; they refer to two mutually distinct calls which must not be confused. Being a priest is a result of the baptismal call, a specification of the Christian estate, while being a pastor is a result of the particular call to the concrete office (although being a priest is the prerequisite for this).[12] Luther never denied the distinction between the two categories. Even in the writings against Hieronymus Emser, in which Luther vehemently stresses the idea of the universal priesthood, he distinguishes the "ecclesial priesthood" which only encompasses those who are specially called to the concrete office from the spiritual priesthood, which comes from Baptism and in

---

[6] WA 38:424.21ff. In the example of *Ordination of Ministers of the Word* extracted by G. Rietschel from Rörer's anthologies (marked with "J" in WA) in Jena, which Rietschel regards as the oldest recension (cf. G. Rietschel, "Luthers Ordinationsformular in seiner ursprünglichen Gestalt," *Theol. Stud. u. Krit.* [1895], pp. 169ff.), it reads: "But you, since you are not only the creatures of God but also those already sanctified through the Word and Sacrament of Baptism at the first holy call of God, and now again at the second call to the holy and divine ministry . . ." (in Rietschel, *ThStKr* [1895], p. 171, and WA 38:424.21ff. nn. 12–13). Rietschel explicitly confirms: "The juxtaposition of Baptism as the first call with the *vocatio altera ad sanctum et divinum ministerium* is entirely of a piece with Luther's conception" (ibid., p. 175).

[7] WA 12:189.25ff.; 17/1:509.18f.: "Because I am called, I possess my function with boldness."

[8] Cf. K. Holl, *Luther*, pp. 318f. n. 5; and R. Seeberg, *Dogmengeschichte* IV.1, *Die Lehre Luthers*, 2nd and 3rd ed. (Leipzig, 1917), p. 293.

[9] WA 38:247.12ff.: "There before the altar stands our pastor, bishop, or minister in the pastoral office, rightly, truly, and regularly called, yet first consecrated, anointed, and born a priest of Christ in Baptism. . . ."

[10] WA 12:178.9f. and 26f.; cf. WA 33:551.41f.; 38:230.17ff.: "For in Baptism none of us is born an apostle, preacher, teacher, or pastor, but we are all only born priests and clerics; then some of those who are born clerics are also chosen and called or elected to these offices."

[11] WA 31/1:211.19f.; also previously, WA 31/1:211.4ff. Cf. V. Vajta, op. cit., pp. 210f.

[12] WA 25:16.15f.: "Although all . . . are priests, yet not all are ministers"; WA 25:16.17ff.: "All Christians are priests . . . yet not all are presbyters, i.e., ministers, as he advises Titus"; WA 25:16.23f.: "All Christians have the priesthood, but not all the function thereof"; WA 31/1:211.17f.; 41:209.4f. and 13, 213.14ff.; 10/3:170.24ff.; 22:183.33f.: "These offices cannot and should not all be conducted and exercised in common where there are Christians; but only those to whom it is committed to do so. Therefore, they are distinguished from the other two things called powers and gifts."

which all true Christians participate.[13] He explicitly rejects Emser's accusation that he had eliminated this distinction.[14] The *vocatio generalis* to the Christian estate and the *vocatio specialis* to the concrete office are thus to be kept clearly separate in Luther.

2. Exercise of the Function of the Office without the Particular Call

Luther recognizes an exercise of the function of Word and Sacrament even without the particular call. This is true, as we have seen, first with respect to the domestic, private sphere, for the teaching of the Word at home by the father of the household and the *consolatio fratrum* [consolation of brethren] among Christians, including the Absolution.[15] Yet it is also the case for specific functions of the *public* preaching office. Here Luther anticipates that in specific cases any Christian can have the right and duty to exercise functions which are properly reserved for the particular office. A common consideration for this is an emergency or the existence of a state of necessity. Where necessity demands, every Christian, even without the particular call to the office, is authorized and obligated to exercise specific functions of the office. "In an emergency, let whoever wishes exercise [the office].[16] . . . Any Christian is obligated to do it, if he sees that it is necessary for the Word and is suitable, even if the whole Church does not call him."[17] But when does a necessity or emergency occur in a concrete sense?

A case of necessity for Luther results when regularly called pastors are unavailable or cannot be procured in time.[18] This gives rise to emergency

[13] WA 7:629ff.; cf. WA 8:250.31ff.: "In all my writings I have meant no more than that all Christians are priests, and yet not all are consecrated by bishops, nor do all preach, celebrate Mass, and exercise the priestly office unless they have first been ordained and called to do so. This is the thrust of my intention."

[14] WA 7:629.17: "In addition, I have not said that all Christians are churchly priests"; WA 7:647.7ff.: "You" (Emser) "are also lying by saying that I have made all laypeople bishops, priests, and clerics *in the sense that* they may at once *perform* the office without being called, not to mention . . . that I write next to it that no one is to presume to take the office without being called, except in the most extreme necessity."

[15] Cf. above, pp. 39–41 and 52–54.

[16] WA 12:189.27.

[17] WA 12:192.4ff.; cf. WA 41:211.20.

[18] WA 2:722.36f.: ". . . where a priest is not present"; WA 45:313.17ff.: "indeed, and certainly in an emergency, where a priest cannot be obtained, by the word of common Christians and brothers who believe in Him."

Baptism[19] or lay absolution of the dying.[20] In the same way, the teaching of the Word is temporarily fulfilled by the housefather at home instead of the public teaching in the preaching office, until the latter is filled again.[21] A case of necessity also arises when the available minister of the Word lapses into false doctrine and neglects his office contrary to Christ's institution. In this case, every Christian, even without the particular call to the office, can and must speak out publicly and stand up for the truth, nevertheless observing the rule "that it be done according to custom and with decency."[22] These two kinds of necessity are addressed in tandem by Luther when he says that every Christian has the right and duty to exercise specific functions of the office "if he sees that *those who teach are absent, or those who are present do not teach rightly*."[23] As in a fire everyone who sees the danger must join in and put it out without waiting to be summoned by the burgomaster or others, so in a case of necessity, every Christian is obligated to come to the aid of the office with his own ministry and exercise specific functions of the office,[24] "for necessity is necessity and has no measure."[25]

Of great importance for Luther here is the *aspect of salvific necessity*. An emergency is characterized by an inability to obtain from a called pastor something *necessary for salvation*.[26] The thing necessary for salvation must in this case be administered by someone without a call. And according to Luther,

---

19 Luther stresses, as we have seen (cf. above, p. 37), that emergency Baptism by a layperson does not happen "by private work" but "by the public ministry of the Church" (WA 12:181.30ff.). Baptism is always a public ceremony. A domestic, private sphere cannot be stipulated for it in distinction to the public (as with the teaching of the Word or with the Absolution). It is therefore always to be regarded as a function of the public office.

20 Hearing the confession of the dying is, in Luther's thinking, not normally considered a part of the *consolatio fratrum* in the domestic, private sphere, but an element of the public administration of the Keys of the office, a special function of the office. This is demonstrated, for instance, by Luther's description of the giving of the Absolution by laymen in such cases as an emergency. Cf. the passages cited above on p. 41 n. 137, and WA 41:456.20ff.: ". . . A Christian—whether a maid, a servant, or a master and in danger—ought to say: The Lord God forgive you all your sins. Go in the name of God. It is meet and right. But when someone is healthy, he should not despise the church, where it is fitting, for when he is out of danger, [the church] would wish to baptize or absolve his family. This is why a public ministry has been established . . ."; WA 41:543.18f.: ("in necessity"); WA 41:546.10ff.: "Do not stare at the heavens when you want your sins forgiven. You have that here below. If there is a pastor or neighbor when you are in need, you do not have to get absolution from above . . ."; WA 41:546.16: "Go to the pastor; in time of need, tell your neighbor to speak the Absolution in the name of Jesus Christ. Then you have the Word; when they do it, Christ has done it"; WA 49:139.20f.: "pastor or neighbor in need."

21 Cf. WA 12:171f. Yet this can really only be valid for time of transition.

22 WA 11:412.33ff.

23 WA 12:190.38; cf. WA 11:413.12f.: ". . . St. Paul gives every Christian the power to teach among Christians when there is need" (with reference to 1 Cor. 14:31).

24 WA 6:413.33ff.

25 WA 11:414.8; cf. WA 11:413.6.

26 WA 38:494.13ff.: "Besides these, the necessity may arise in which brothers who are to be baptized, taught, comforted, or exhorted are placed in the midst of the enemy. Here anyone should intervene, being called, as it were, by the necessity of brotherly love, and *do all those things which are necessary for the salvation of souls*."

"necessary for salvation" includes only the Word of the Gospel, which is to say, the Absolution and the Sacrament of Baptism—not, however, the Holy Supper.[27] An "emergency Supper" analogous to emergency Baptism, administered by someone not called to the public office, is *not* recognized by Luther; indeed, he forbids it.

In the treatise to the Bohemians [*Concerning the Ministry*] (1523), he advises that, in the great necessity in which the Bohemians found themselves, where no orthodox priest could be obtained, every housefather could teach and baptize his children, even though he must do without the Eucharist.[28] Since the Eucharist is not absolutely necessary for salvation—even if only the Gospel and Baptism are available!—a Christian housefather acts rightly "if he forgoes the Eucharist until God, having mercy from on high, releases him from his bonds or provides a suitable minister of the Word."[29]

The same position is found with even greater clarity in Luther's letter to the pastor of Jessen, Wolfang Brauer (*December 30, 1535*). Luther writes to the pastor that he should tell his friend Sigmund Haugreuter, who had inquired about the possibility of lay Communion in an emergency, "that he is not obligated to undertake such a rite to commune himself and his household; moreover, that it is unnecessary since he is not called nor commanded to do it, and besides that, if the tyrannical church ministers who ought to be doing it refuse to give it to him or his family, he can still be saved in his faith through the Word. It would also cause great offense to give the Sacrament here and there in people's homes and ultimately would not end well, and nothing but divisions and sects would arise, for the people are now mad and the devil is maniacal."[30] The housefather is also supposed to teach his family God's Word, "and the Word is committed to each one. But the Sacrament is an open confession and should have open, called ministers since it states, as Christ says, that we are to do it in remembrance of Him. . . . And it also says there that we are to gather together, and it harshly rebukes those who wish to partake of the Lord's Supper by themselves individually. . . . For there is a great difference between a public office in the Church and a housefather over his household, so they are not to be mixed up or isolated. . . ."[31] "Accordingly, since

---

[27] WA 12:171.21f.: "For in time of danger the Eucharist is not necessary for salvation; but the Gospel and Baptism are enough since faith alone justifies and love alone lives well."

[28] WA 12:171.17ff.

[29] WA 12:172.3ff.; cf. WA 12:171.38ff.: ". . . A housefather can provide his family with necessary things through the Word and, while he is in bondage, forgo unnecessary things for a time in pious humility." — On multiple occasions, Luther uses the expression "of which Eucharist he *neither would dare nor could partake* [Eucharistia . . . , quam sumere *vel non auderet vel non posset*]" (WA 12:172.3f., 171.20f.). This might sound as if Luther sees it only as weakness of faith when someone does not dare to handle the Sacrament without being called, as though in time of necessity this were not also permitted to someone who is not called. Yet it must be kept in mind that in 1535 Luther fundamentally and categorically rejected the administration of the Sacrament of the Altar by laity even in time of necessity. Cf. what follows. Thus one would do well not to try to draw too much from that passage.

[30] WA Br 7:338.1ff.

[31] WA Br 7:339.18ff. — One must thus be careful not to view the function of the housefather, or even the teaching of a noncalled Christian among pagans, as simply the operation of the churchly

there is no emergency or call here, no one should undertake anything here at his own discretion without God's certain command, for nothing good would come of that."[32] Luther here negates the possibility of an emergency Supper administered by laymen with a threefold argument: it is not absolutely necessary for salvation; the Sacrament, according to Christ's will, is a public ceremony that is only to be done by ministers called to the public office; and it would cause offense and foster the formation of sects.

In another testimony from the year 1536, we read: "By no means let yourselves be persuaded that every master of a household may give the Sacrament in his house! For I can teach at home, but I am not a public preacher unless I am called to it. . . ."[33] "Therefore, you cannot say, 'The Sacrament is made by the Word, so I can make it in my house'; for *that is not God's ordinance and command. Rather, He desires that the Sacrament be administered by the public office.* For the Sacrament is instituted as a public confession. . . ."[34] With greatest clarity he refers people to God's ordinance and command, maintaining that the Sacrament is only to be administered by the public office!

Luther makes a similar judgment in a *table talk* (no year provided) where, in response to the question whether a housefather may give his family the Holy Supper *in casu necessitatis*, he says: "By no means [*Nequaquam*]"! And he supports this by arguing that (1) he has no call [*vocatio*] to do so, and (2) an offense might result.[35] There can be no doubt that Luther saw the administration of the Holy Supper as limited to the one called to the public office.[36]

Concerning this, it must also be added that, according to Luther, necessity further demands that each Christian teach *publicly* whenever he finds himself *alone among pagans*. In such a case, a Christian does not wait "to see if he may

---

office, as V. Vajta does (op. cit., pp. 215f. n. 69). According to Luther, there is "a *great difference* between the public office in the Church and a housefather over his household"! Vajta does not quite represent Luther's view when he says, "There is only one office in operation, and the fact that any Christian is able to exercise the duties of this office when the opportunity presents itself is not evidence for an emergency office but for the breadth and outward orientation of the ecclesial office, of the Word, which overleaps the barriers of a statically conceived consecration office and stands in the ministry of the living Christ" (p. 216 n. 69); or: "The ecclesial office functions just as truly without ordination in the congregation, at home, or among the pagans . . ." (ibid.). The teaching of a housefather at home or of a (noncalled) Christian among pagans is, according to Luther, not simply the function of the ecclesial office, but the function of the universal priesthood, which naturally includes the concrete ecclesial office on a fundamental level but is not it. The public ecclesial office is, according to Luther, a new one added to the universal priesthood, and this particular form of the public office is, according to Luther, not already in the teaching of the Word in the domestic sphere or among the pagans by someone who is not called. Cf. above, pp. 52–54.

32 WA Br 7:339.31ff.

33 WA Br 7:366.36ff.

34 WA Br 7:366.42ff.

35 WA TR 5:621.26ff. (no. 6361). — Cf. against "home Communion" (yet without addressing the question whether *a layperson* may administer the Sacrament at home): WA Br 5:528.17ff.; 7:167f. — On the whole issue, cf. W Maurer, *Pfarrerrecht und Bekenntnis* (Berlin, 1957), pp. 117f.

36 So, too, Brunotte, op. cit., pp. 80 and 167f.

be given a command or letter from a prince or bishop."[37] The spiritual need of others here demands a testimony about Christ, and it is the duty of brotherly love to perform it.[38] "When he" (a Christian) "is in a place where there are no Christians, he need have no other call than that he is inwardly called and anointed a Christian by God."[39] Thus the Ethiopian eunuch bore witness at home "by no right save that of his Baptism and faith, especially since there were no others there."[40] It is plain that this public teaching by a baptized Christian among pagans is seen by Luther as a function of the universal priesthood, not as a special function of the public preaching office of the Church exercised by noncalled Christians in an emergency capacity. The latter, according to Luther, is only among Christians in a Christian congregation. And as soon as such a congregation is formed, it must also provide for the preaching office in its midst. Thus a Christian's public instruction among pagans is not considered an exercise of the function of the particular preaching office.

If we thus separate the functions of the universal priesthood from those of the particular office—the domestic, private realm, in which every housefather teaches his family the Word of God and in which Christians comfort each other with the Gospel and the Absolution in the *consolatio fratrum*, from the public realm of the office in the congregation, in which the called minister publicly teaches, publicly gives Absolution, publicly administers the Sacraments—and we ask in what case Luther permits the exercise of special functions of the particular public office in the congregation by those who are not called, we find that he ultimately limits this to the three cases of emergency Baptism, lay absolution of the dying,[41] and the public refutation of a pastor's public false teaching. If aside from these special, clearly defined cases anyone without the particular call takes on the exercise of the public function of the office in the congregation, Luther regards it as reprehensible presumption, which is of the devil.

---

[37] WA 11:412.24ff.; cf. WA 16:35.31ff.: "But if one were to enter a population where there were no Christians, one could do as the apostles and not wait for a call, for they have no office for preaching there" (i.e., the concrete office does not yet exist there), "and one might say: There are no Christians here. I will preach and teach them about Christianity. . . . Yet as soon as a body of people is assembled, there follows the election and call of a minister to the office." Cf. further WA 17/1:509.24ff.: "But if I were among the Turks, I would certainly preach to my host—and if a group of people gathered, I would do likewise—since a Christian should also preach the name of Christ among these people."

[38] WA 11:412.18ff.; cf. WA 11:412.27ff.: "Thus love is obligated to help where there is no one else who helps or should help"; WA 11:414.7ff.

[39] WA 11:412.16ff.; cf. WA 12:319.3f.

[40] WA 12:192.22f.; cf. WA 12:189.20f.: "Rightly assume that power and exercise it, where there is no one who wields the same power"; WA 12:192.8ff.: Stephen and Philip preached when they saw that it was needed, without a particular call, simply "on their own impulse and by universal right"; WA 11:412.20ff.; 12:191.38ff.

[41] Cf. above, p. 113 n. 20.

3. The Necessity of the Call to the Public Office

The necessity of the call to the concrete office is properly implicit already in the concrete office itself. If the concrete office exists and not all Christians possess it, then those who are to possess it must enter it by a specific act; that is, they must be called to it. Since the concrete office not only proceeds from the practical necessities of the congregation but also is founded on Christ's institutive will, the call to the office, too, is not only an imperative of human reason but *de jure divino* [by divine right].[42] The church must fill the office—that is, call someone to the office—by reason of a "divine mandate."[43] *God commanded* the sending of men into the office.[44] "Belonging to this office . . . is the sending."[45] Christ enfolds "the preaching office in the command and divine call." He not only gives office-bearers "equal authority and power to preach, to loose and retain sins—He has done so—but also secures them in their office through a sure command, call, and sending."[46] Thus the necessity of the call to the office is given even with the *jus divinum* [divine right] of the concrete office; indeed, according to Luther, it rests directly on Christ's positive arrangement.[47]

But also with respect to the individual person who is to bear the office, and to its subjective prerequisites, the call to the office rests on a divine necessity; for "God desires nothing to be done on the basis of a person's own choice or thinking, but all on the basis of a command and call, especially the preaching office."[48] God Himself initiates the work as He does salvation, but especially in so vital an office as the preaching office. Thus one must wait until God calls one to the preaching office through men and may not embark upon it oneself.[49] In

---

[42] Cf. P. Brunner, "Vom Amt des Bischofs," pp. 16 and 19.

[43] Cf. Enders 11:279.23 (ordination certificate): ". . . The Church calls ministers by divine decree"; Enders 7:131.20ff. (ordination certificate): "It is divinely commanded . . . that churches examine and ordain ministers of the Gospel and set suitable governors over other churches."

[44] WA 47:192.8; cf. WA 28:473.40; 38:221.25–32f.

[45] WA 28:479.33f.; also cf. WA 41:184.21ff. (referring to a true priest): "He is an angel of the Lord, being sent by God Himself and receiving from Him the call and office of teaching the people. . . . Therefore, the first office belonging to a priest, for which he is called, consecrated, and anointed by God Himself, is to teach the people this doctrine and Word, which are not his own, but God's Word"; WA 47:192.1ff.: ". . . The persons do not remain, but die, so they must continually have new preachers. This does not happen except by means . . . ," i.e., by the concrete call.

[46] WA 28:471.5ff.

[47] H. Storck points out a further rationale for the necessity of the call to the office, namely, the "presence of men . . . who require the spiritual love of neighbors" (op. cit., p. 32). Also cf. W. Elert, *Morphologie* I, pp. 304f.

[48] WA 31/1:211.31ff.; cf. WA 47:192.11ff.: "Therefore, each man should know that he must be sent; that is, he must know that he is called and not sneak in, but it must be done openly. This, then, is called a sending from God, and yet occurs through men." — Regarding the necessity of a call in Luther, W. Elert, *Morphologie* I, p. 304, points out the analogy to secular callings. Also cf. V. Vajta, op. cit., p. 210.

[49] WA 10/3:170.17ff.: "The call is very important, for no one is to go forward and preach by his own presumption without the command of the others"; WA 10/3:170.23f.: ". . . that no one

support of this Luther cites Rom. 10:15. Preaching can occur only when God has sent.[50] Christ must first assign the office and command a person to preach to others before it can proceed.[51] "Know"—says Luther in a sermon on Acts 13:1ff. from 1524—"that no one must act for the sake of God unless he be called and ordained by God so that he can say with a sure conscience: I am certain that God wills this and wants me to do this. Otherwise he is not authorized, nor will he be, nor will he succeed."[52] Only he who has been called to the office in due manner can work profitably in it, according to Luther.[53] Whoever teaches without being called only does harm since Christ is not with him then.[54] If anyone thinks that he has to preach even without a call, or that he feels perhaps an inward call of the Spirit to do so without being called outwardly, he is being deceived by the devil.[55] If he actually does it, he does it maliciously[56] and is a false prophet,[57] who, according to Jer. 23:21, runs without being sent by the Lord.[58] Then he is

should force his way in, even though his own inclination prompts him to do so without the call of the others"; WA 12:390.19ff. "It is true, no one should force his way into the office without a call. But when he is called and asked, he should willingly go up and do what his office requires"; WA 16:32.12f.; 17/2:263.16f.: "yet not before we are asked to do it"; WA 17/2:255.14ff.

50 WA 17/2:256.12ff. — The sending in John 20:21 also plays a role here for Luther. He justifies God's activity via human absolution on the fact that the one speaking the Absolution is sent by Christ for that purpose: WA 49:139.1ff., 140.1ff., esp. 140.4ff.: "'I send'; that is, I commission or call you. You are not to do it on your own. *Since I truly call of My own accord, I also do it Myself.*" Cf. WA 49:146:28ff.: ". . . God has spoken and done this through him" (namely, the pastor in the Absolution), "of this I am certain, for my Lord Christ has commanded it and said, 'As the Father has sent Me, so send I you.'" Cf. WA 49:141.41: ". . . I would not dare to go without this command, even if I knew nothing could help and aid you."

51 WA 28:468.6ff., 472.21ff.; 49:612.13: "Who made me another preacher? . . . He who is above . . ."; WA 47:193.11ff.: "No one should think that God's Word comes to earth by human imagining. If it is God's Word, it must be sent. Otherwise it is impossible that Holy Scripture could be understood or explained by personal inclination or arbitrary choice. It is not valid for someone to speak and not be called, for God's Word comes only by God's sending it. . . . If He had not sent the Word and the office, we would have nothing. For that reason, no one should say or hear anything except the Word of God."

52 WA 17/1:508.10ff.; cf. WA 17/1:509.16ff.: "I preach in that name because I was ordained for this. Why would I dare, when I see others who have more of the Spirit than I? Yet since I am called, I boldly maintain my function"; WA 33:551.17ff.: "I preach by command and the bidding of others; otherwise let the devil preach"; WA Br 10:436.7f.: "But because it happens apart from the call, it is doubtless without faith and is annulled (*dissolvitur*)."

53 WA 16:32.4f.: "where God calls, urges, and compels, and then a great work is done"; WA 17/2:262.19f.: ". . . But those who are called do great deeds, no matter how weak, lowly, and simple they are."

54 WA 2:455.3f.: "He who . . . teaches without being called does not teach without harm to both himself and his hearers since Christ is not with him"; WA 17/2:259.10ff.

55 WA 17/2:255.24ff.

56 WA 17/2:257.13f.

57 WA 17/1:360.1f.: "And it is the nature of false prophets to force their way into preaching"; WA 17/1:360.16f.; 17/2:259.12f.

58 WA 30/3:521.20ff.

sent not by Christ but by Satan[59] and opens a window for the devil.[60] "In short, the infiltrators and clandestine preachers are the devil's apostles which St. Paul laments everywhere."[61] Circumventing and despising the regular call to the preaching office is for Luther the characteristic mark of Enthusiasm. He also sees it as an instantly satanic phenomenon as well.[62] Conversely, the call, according to Luther, causes "the devil great pain."[63]

It is thus indisputably fixed for Luther that "without the call and command, no one is to take the office upon himself."[64] Giving freedom to everyone in the congregation to preach and "bark contrary to the regular preacher" is "greatly mistaken" in Luther's view.[65] "Either he gives evidence of his call and orders to preach or, briefly put, remains silent and is forbidden to preach."[66] Not even the strongest inner compulsion to preach can alter this. "Although you can convert the whole world and know how to raise the dead, you may still not teach unless you are called and your call has been certified."[67]

The call, the necessity of which Luther so vigorously maintains, is in his view a concrete call to a specific, concrete, parochially defined congregation and relates to this. It does not grant the power to administer the office everywhere,

---

59 WA 17/1:360.6 and 23; 30/3:518.9 and 18ff.: "Even if such infiltrators had no other vice and were holy in every other way, yet this one thing (that they sneak in without command and uninvited) can forcefully prove that they are the messengers and teachers of the devil. For the Holy Spirit does not sneak in, but openly flies down from heaven . . ."; WA 30/3:518.31, 519.11 and 32ff.: "But these foreign interlopers and assassins cannot claim to do so, but must confess that they come from elsewhere and seize and usurp another's office. This cannot be the Holy Spirit, but must be the heinous devil"; WA 30/3:519.38, etc.

60 WA 40/1:61.16ff.

61 WA 30/3:527.6ff.; 28:472.9ff.: "This is how you know who are Christ's apostles and who are the devil's: the call and the sending. Christ's apostles are called by Christ and sent and come openly. The devil's apostles are not sent by God or men, but sneak in secretly like snakes and vipers, without call or command."

62 Cf. above, pp. 6–7.

63 WA TR 1:34.18ff. (no. 90).

64 WA 28:479.33ff.; cf. WA 2:453.31ff.; 8:250.33f.; 16:34.20f.: "But whoever is not elected here to the preaching office stands back and does not preach . . ."; WA 17/1:509.9ff.: "But among Christians, where Christ's name is known, honor must be given to the Holy Spirit, lest anyone claim for himself above others the duty of teaching unless he is called"; WA 17/2:257.12ff., 262.16f.; 28:471.18ff.: "There it reads: no one is to presume the authority to forgive and retain sin openly to be exercised in the Christian Church unless he is sent and called to it by a sure command. Whoever has no command to preach, baptize, absolve, and give the Sacrament should be content and not presume this office"; WA 30/3:523.33ff.: "Are we then to tolerate a foreign tramp to sneak in to our land, or a burgher to force his way in uninvited and rebuke or lord it over the burgomaster? Nothing good would come of that . . ."; WA 30/3:524.1ff.: "Much less should we allow a foreign interloper to worm his way into the spiritual council—that is, into the preaching office or seat of the prophets—or a layman, uncalled, to take it upon himself to preach in his parish . . ."; WA 32:303.1ff.; WA TR 1:400.24f. (no. 827): "No one should take anything upon himself unless called."

65 WA 30/3:522.9f.

66 WA 30/3:521.7f.

67 WA 17/1:508.20ff.

even in other congregations, without further ado.[68] As a divine ordinance, the parochial structure of the Church and the consequential parochial character of the call to the office is so fixed for Luther that he even deprecates exceeding the boundaries of the local call even if it is to keep false doctrine from other places. No preacher, "however pious or true he may be, is to be allowed to preach or secretly to teach a Papist's or heretical pastor's people without that pastor's knowledge and consent; for he is not commanded to do so. And what is not commanded is to be avoided."[69]

Luther sees the call to the concrete preaching office (as the parochial pastoral office) so anchored in the nature of the Church that, for him, the Church stands or falls, to a certain extent, on its existence as an organized community. "Otherwise, if people did not stand firmly and insist on the call or command, there would finally be no Church left anywhere."[70] There would be never-ending dissolution, disintegration, and devastation as a result.[71] The particular call to the office has for Luther the character of an absolute necessity in every respect.

4. *Vocatio Immediata* and *Vocatio Mediata*

When someone comes desiring to preach, according to Luther, the congregation is to ask, "Where are you from? Who sent you? Who gave you orders to preach to me? Where is your seal and certificate that you have been sent through men? Where are your miraculous signs that God has sent you?"[72] Luther distinguishes here the sending through men from the sending by God—the latter

---

[68] WA 40/1:59.29ff.: "I am not allowed to go outside of this jurisdiction into another city where I am not called and preach there, to the extent that I am a preacher"; cf. WA 40/1:59.12ff.; 12:169.12f.: "for when my ministry does not permit me to go farther than where another authority calls me"; WA 16:34.14ff.: ". . . If I tried to go to Leipzig and preach at the castle there and say, 'The Spirit urges me, I must preach,' that is wrong"; WA 28:475.20ff.

[69] WA 31/1:211.11ff.; cf. WA 32:303.1ff.: "In order to fend off infiltrators and vagrants, one should simply not permit anyone to preach if he has not been charged with it and appointed to the office, nor should anyone, even if he is a preacher, upon hearing a false preacher leading the people astray in a papistic or other church, presume to preach against him, nor go and insinuate himself into people's homes and give special sermons in secret, but remain at home and attend to his office or preaching station, or else be silent if he will not or cannot ascend the pulpit openly. For God does not wish people to go astray with His Word, as though the Holy Spirit drove someone and he must preach and so seek out cities and taverns or preaching stations where he has no office"; WA 33:359.2ff.: "Without a call I am not to preach, I am not to try to go to Leipzig or to Magdeburg and try to preach there, for I have no call or office there, and even if I heard that sheer heresy were being preached in Leipzig, let them keep doing it, it is not my concern. However they may be preaching, I have sown nothing there, so I need not reap anything there either"; WA 40/1:10ff: "[. . .] even if I heard that false things were taught, and souls were led astray and damned, and I was able to deliver them from error and damnation with my holy teaching. But I must commit the matter to God, who in His own time will find occasion for legitimately calling ministers and giving the Word."

[70] WA 30/3:520.34ff.

[71] WA 30/3:521.1ff.; cf. WA 38:495.21ff.

[72] WA 30/3:519.12ff.; cf. WA 28:473.10ff.

of which can only be demonstrated by special miraculous signs.[73] This is in no way to say that the former manner of calling, which happens through men, is not also by God. Rather, Luther only means by this to distinguish the direct (*vocatio immediata*) and indirect call (*vocatio mediata*). "There is accordingly a twofold call to the preaching office: one is done without means by God, the other through men and yet also by God."[74] *Both* kinds of call are *divine* in character; this is just as true of the indirect as of the direct.[75] The sending to the office via the indirect call is one "*through* men and not *by* men."[76] It is this indirect sending to the preaching office through men which Luther sees as founded on the divine institution;[77] it has its "basis in Scripture [*fundamentum in scriptura*]";[78] God commanded it. And "if people assist to that end, then He Himself is sending laborers into His vineyard, and yet doing it through men."[79] Those men involved in the indirect call are only God's masks and instruments in the process.[80]

Luther thus teaches a "twofold divine call [*duplex vocatio divina*]."[81] To differentiate between the two calls, he also likes to identify the direct call as a *vocatio fidei* [call of faith], ". . . which comes from a superior" (also the "high sending"[82]); the indirect, a *vocatio* "*charitatis* [call of love], which comes from an equal"[83] (also *fraterna vocatio* [brotherly call][84]). The indirect call for Luther

[73] Also cf. WA 16:33.21f.: "This call must have an external sign and testimony"; WA 17/1:360.24ff. — Luther knows very well, however, that miraculous signs are not an absolutely trustworthy mark of a divine call since deceiving miracles may also occur through false prophets, for which reason, as a further mark of the direct call, the agreement of teaching with the Word of God is added to the miraculous signs: WA 17/2:254.23ff.

[74] WA 17/2:254.22f.; also cf. WA 17/2:255.7ff.; 38:493.39ff.; WA TR 1:400.25ff. (no. 827).

[75] WA 16:33.20ff.: "The other call is also divine, but it happens through men"; WA 17/1:509.22f.: "We are called with men mediating, and yet by God"; WA 26:5.8ff.; 40/1:59.23: "And this is the *vocatio mediata*, which happens through man, and yet is divine." — Cf. R. Josefson, "Das Amt d. Kirche," in *Ein Buch von der Kirche* (Göttingen, 1951), p. 399.

[76] WA 47:192.5f.

[77] WA 47:191.38ff.: "The other sending is also from God but happens through men and means, according as the office in which preaching is done and the power of the Keys used is founded by God."

[78] WA 16:34.1f.

[79] WA 47:192.7ff.; cf. WA 12:191.25f.

[80] Cf. V. Vajta, op. cit., pp. 211f. K. Tuchel has pointed out that Luther, in emphasizing God's activity in the call, "wishes to express not only God's will for order but also His will as founder of the preaching office" (op. cit., p. 91).

[81] WA 40/1:59.3ff.

[82] WA 47:191.36f.

[83] WA TR 1:400.25ff. (no. 827); cf. WA TR 5:431.14ff. (no. 5998); WA 17/1:362.1ff. and 13ff. — Luther also frames the distinction between direct and indirect call in the words: "This one" (*vocatio mediata*) "is an urging, a calling. The other" (*vocatio immediata*) "is a sending"; WA 17/1:362.5. Cf. WA 17/1:362.20ff. (Dr): "This one is known as being taken, called, and urged. The one that comes from heaven is known as being sent, when the Holy Spirit comes and gives a sign along with it."

[84] WA 26:5.8ff.

involves the divine commandment of love.[85] To comply with the call through men is a duty of brotherly love.[86] At the same time, however, it is necessary to hear and see God's own positive call to the office directly in that call.

He who is to attend to the preaching office in the Church must, according to Luther, have one of these two kinds of call.[87] Yet no promise has been made that God will still issue direct calls to the office today. The direct sending of the apostles "was the last of all."[88] Since that time, God has ceased to call directly. The current situation may be described thus: "God calls us all to the ministry by the call through man, and it is a divine call."[89] Our further study of this subject will therefore concern itself exclusively with the indirect divine call to the preaching office through men.

At times, Luther, citing the church father Jerome, also refers to a fourfold call. Thus in his *[First] Lectures on Galatians* (1519) and in the *Festival Postil* (1527), four kinds of apostles are distinguished: (1) Those who are called not by men nor through men but through God Himself, such as the prophets and apostles. (2) Those who are called by God through a man, such as the disciples of the apostles, who, as bishops and priests, legitimately succeed the apostles until the end of the world. (3) Those who are called by men, but not by God (here we should think of those who received a call through intrigues and human favor). (4) Those who are not called by God or men, but rather by themselves, such as the false prophets and false apostles (cf. Jer. 23:21).[90] Of the fourth kind Luther says: "Of this evil we must take great heed."[91]

5. The Call through the Congregation

We have ascertained that, according to Luther, the concrete preaching office requires an additional, particular call over and above the general call to the Christian estate and that, since the apostolic era, this call happens only indirectly, namely, "through men in the stead of God."[92] We ask further: through which men?

---

[85] Cf. WA 16:35.9ff.: "The other call which happens through men was confirmed beforehand by God's command on Mount Sinai: Love God, and your neighbor as yourself. When this commandment drives you, you need no sign; for God has commanded it before, and I must do it. . . . Thus I preach without any sign, and yet it is the call of God. For it comes from the commandment of love and is compelled by God"; WA 16:35.21f.: "But this is my boast and confidence: that I know that I do rightly and am called to it through the commandment of love. This is my boast."

[86] WA 17/1:362.15ff.: ". . . For I and you are obligated to each other: Love your neighbor as yourself. Thus he needs me and requires me, and I am obligated to do it . . ."; cf. WA 12:192.6f. and 14f.

[87] WA 38:494.2f.

[88] WA 47:191.35ff.

[89] WA 40/1:59.4ff.

[90] WA 2:454.3ff.; 17/2:257.25ff.

[91] WA 2:454.21.

[92] WA 30/3:521.23.

This much is clear: it can only be those men who form the Church or in which the Church acts. In Luther, the Church as *communio sanctorum* is—as we have described above[93]—the proper possessor of all rights and powers. It alone can confer the office, call to the office.[94] *The call to the office in Luther's conception always happens through the Church.*[95] Yet this can take different forms *in concreto*. In Luther, two different lines of thought in this respect may be noted.[96] The first stresses the call through the local congregation by the route of election; the second requires a calling entity consisting of persons occupying a higher official rank, through whom the call is concretely realized.[97] In both cases, however, the Church as *communio sanctorum* is acting in the call. We will first treat the call through the local congregation.

The congregation as a concrete manifestation of the *communio sanctorum* has the power and right to call suitable persons to the concrete office;[98] indeed, it has a command to do so.[99] The office is instituted by Christ, and it is His will that it be filled through the call. Neither is it at all possible for the congregation to live without the execution of the office.[100] There may be no doubt "that the congregation, which has the Gospel, may and should choose and call among itself one to teach the Word in its stead."[101] Inasmuch as the congregation does this, it is only acting "according to Scripture."[102]

The call through the congregation is viewed by Luther as the given since the persons for the office are taken from the congregation itself[103] and then minister

[93] Cf. above, pp. 46–48.

[94] Cf. WA 2:194.8: "*This* . . . can commit the Keys"; WA 2:196.26: "from which, as it were the minister, the priest receives. . . ."

[95] Cf. V. Vajta, op. cit., pp. 209f.

[96] That Luther does not here elevate a specific mode to absolute law has been frequently noted. E.g., A. W. Dieckhoff, op. cit., p. 174; R. Sohm, *Kirchenrecht* I, p. 493; H. Storck, op. cit., p. 34.

[97] Cf. WA 6:566.28f.: "it is not permitted . . . that unless by consent of the community or call of a superior"; WA 38:493.40ff.

[98] WA 6:407.34ff.; 12:172.10ff.: "Those who believe and know the truth have the most free faculty and power of rejecting all wicked ministers and of not calling or installing any except the suitable and godly, as many as may please them"; WA 38:252.17, 253.1ff.; 41:241.12ff. and 35ff., 242.5ff.: "Thus the Christian Church always has the right and call to it."

[99] WA 11:411.13ff.: "Not only right and power . . . , but obliged . . . on pain of their soul's salvation, according to their pledge which they made to Christ in Baptism"; WA 12:190.40f.: "right and command."

[100] WA 11:411.22ff.; 12:191.16ff.

[101] WA 11:413.20ff.; cf. WA 38:237.11ff., 238.7f., 252.14ff.: "Are we then to be the holy Christian Church and have the greatest and most needful things—such as God's Word, Christ, Spirit, faith, prayer, Baptism, Sacrament, Keys, office, etc.—and not have the smallest thing also, namely, the power and right to call some to the office to give to us the Word, Baptism, Sacrament, forgiveness . . . and serve us therein? What kind of Church would that be, I wonder?"

[102] WA 11:411.28; cf. WA 11:413.7ff. and 17ff.

[103] WA 6:564.12; "elected from among us"; WA 7:631.30ff.; 12:190.34ff.: "For here by light more clear and faith more certain we have whence priests or ministers of the Word are to be sought, that is to say, out of the same congregation of Christ and nowhere else"; WA 38:230.19f.: "One chooses from among these born priests and calls or elects them . . ."; WA 41:208.28ff.: "set apart from the

to the congregation.[104] The congregation is best able to judge its members' aptitude for the office since it knows them best. Therefore, it should also call them itself.[105] At very least, it must give its consent to the call of an office-bearer.[106] The consent of the congregation to the office-bearer personally is also required if for no other reason than the fact that they are all *fratres aequales* [equal brothers] and that the fundamental right of priesthood shared by all can be exercised publicly in the congregation only with the consent of all to that one.[107]

With the authority of the congregation for the call thus clarified, we now inquire further concerning the nature and manner thereof. Then we meet the decisive meaning of the *electio personae* [election of the person]. In his treatise *To the Christian Nobility of the German Nation* (1520), Luther shows how he imagines the call through the congregation. For the sake of clarity, he cites an extreme example: If there were a flock of pious (lay-)Christians in the wilderness who had no priests consecrated by a bishop, they would choose one and commit to him the office of baptizing, celebrating the Mass, absolving, and preaching, and "he would be a priest as truly as if all the bishops and popes had consecrated him."[108] Accordingly, the call consists of the election and the commission of the office through the congregation. "Thus we clearly learn from the apostle" (according to Titus 1:5) "that things should be conducted in the Church such that every city elects from the congregation a learned, pious citizen, commits to him the pastoral office. . . ."[109] Luther sees the ordination in this connection as a

---

common flock of Christ, just as someone in secular government chooses and appoints certain officers from among the whole citizenry or community."

[104] WA 2:248.36ff.: "St. Peter or a priest is a minister of the Keys; the Church is the wife and bride to whom he is to minister with the power of the Keys . . ."; WA 7:631.29ff.

[105] WA 12:172.22ff.; cf. WA 2:231.2ff. and 26ff. Luther here cites favorably Cyprian's statements from the fourth letter to the presbyter Felix, where he describes and explains the election of priests, saying that it is determined "by divine authority that the priest be chosen in the presence of the people, under the eyes of all, and be proved worthy and suitable by public judgment and testimony" (WA 2:231.8ff.). "The people must be present since they know best the character of the individuals" (WA 2:231.26ff.), and "lest someone, being unworthy, sneak into the ministry of the altar or the place of the priest" (WA 2:231.25f.). V. Vajta calls it "a matter of course for Luther that these (namely, the preachers) must be taken through the congregation itself and out of the congregation" (op. cit., p. 210).

[106] WA 11:414.12ff.; 12:172.22ff., 191.1. Also cf. below, pp. 133–34.

[107] WA 12:189.17ff.

[108] WA 6:407.34ff. — It should, however, be observed that Luther is here illustrating the congregational or lay right of calling for a clear case of necessity, citing a fringe case in order to expose the ultimate consequence of his idea. The description of the consecration by the bishop in the preceding sentence shows that it is not like Luther to form a principle solely from a call of this kind through the lay congregation. In the following (WA 6:408.1ff.), emergency Baptism is referred to as if parallel. There, too, it plainly reflects a state of necessity. How Luther sees the congregational call under normal circumstances is apparent from the statement in WA 6:408.4ff.: "In this manner Christians long ago chose from the flock their bishop and priests, who were then confirmed by other bishops without all extravagance." Luther also knows very well that the episcopal confirmation is normally joined to the congregational election.

[109] WA 6:440.31ff.

kind of consummation of the election and commission to the office, as "a kind of rite of electing a preacher in the church."[110]

Of exemplary significance, then, is *the call process as proposed by Luther to the Bohemians in 1523* [*Concerning the Ministry*], although he did not intend it to be elevated to law[111] since he was aware that this act of calling can only proceed from faith.[112] It is to be carried out by those who believe and confess the Gospel.[113] The election rite, according to Luther's instruction, is to be begun with earnest private and public prayers. With fear and trembling the congregation is to confess its sins before the mercy seat, Jesus Christ, and is humbly to implore the Holy Spirit to grant both the desire and the fulfillment.[114] Each person is then to believe firmly that God gives as He is asked, and so to be certain that now, in the election rite, it is not human volition and human initiative alone which are at work, but that God Himself is guiding the voters.[115] The voting assembly is to be convened freely and is thus composed of those whose hearts God has moved to participate in it.[116] Then, prayerfully, by means of a vote ("*communibus suffragiis* [by the common votes]"), one or more who are worthy and suited are to be elected. The elected are then to be confirmed by the most respected persons ("*qui potiores inter vos fuerint* [those who are more prominent among you]") with prayer and the laying on of hands, and presented and commended to the *universitas [ecclesia]* [Church as a whole], and then to be recognized as true bishops, ministers, and shepherds of the congregation.[117] This act of calling through the "common consent of the faithful who know and confess the Gospel" is to be regarded as indubitably performed

[110] WA 6:564.17.

[111] WA 12:194.4ff.

[112] WA 12:192.24ff.: "It remains, therefore, O most glorious men, that you wear the firm faith to which you counsel your Bohemia—a bold faith, I say, is here required. For we write these things to those who believe; those who do not believe do not receive such things."

[113] WA 12:191.26f. Also cf. W. Walther, *Das Erbe d. Reform.*, book 4, *Luthers Kirche* (Leipzig, 1917), p. 137.

[114] WA 12:193.22ff. and 30ff.: "For if this thing is to begin prosperously and continue salutarily, it is necessary that it be done in you by God's power, which God ministers. . . ."

[115] WA 12:193.33ff.: "Then, when you ask in this way, have no doubt that He whom you ask is faithful, that He will give what you ask for, open to those who knock, and be found by those who seek, that you may be very certain that *you are being acted upon in this matter, not acting yourselves.*"

[116] WA 12:193.35f. — P. Brunner ("Vom Amt des Bischofs," pp. 22f.) has pointed out that the convention of voters is still clearly differentiated from the people by Luther here. The electoral action is not necessarily carried out by the collective whole, the *numerical* whole, but by a unit within that whole (p. 23). Brunner sees in this "unit qualified by spiritual competence to judge . . . the preliminary outlines of an office of overseer and governor" being sketched out (p. 22 n. 23). "That narrower unit . . . acts effectively in a representative capacity for 'the bishops' in a presumed case of necessity" (pp. 22f. n. 23). This is in fact the case (contrary to Brunotte, op. cit., p. 94 n. 127), though it is even more descriptive of the narrow*est* unit, isolated in turn from the convention of voters: the *potiores*, who carry out the confirmation act with the laying on of hands.

[117] WA 12:191.22ff., 193.35ff.

by God.[118] However, this *consensus* must not be accounted a purely technical one. Luther understands it in the light of agreeing in prayer, in accordance with Matt. 18:19–20. It is thus a consensus of the prayers of the faithful, the power of which consensus lies in the divine promise given to it. God acts through it; thus it happens in the hearing of a prayer, and this in turn in the fulfillment of a promise. The whole call process is subjected by Luther to this promise in Matt. 18:19–20, and in faith in it the people are assured that Christ Himself is at work in this act.[119] Considering that the act of calling is so plainly oriented here around prayer, and that its divine character is based on the confidence that that faithful prayer is heard, any comparison of this voting action with a democratic vote, which involves a merely technical decision by the majority, is impossible. This vote described here by Luther is a thoroughly pneumatic phenomenon and excludes every attempt to draw parallels with superficially similar processes in the secular realm. Looking at the whole call process which Luther here recommends to the Bohemians from the perspective of where the decisive matter occurs in it, it becomes apparent that the point at which the person of the prospective office-bearer is laid hold of, so to speak, the act of calling is the vote occurring in the context of prayer, and the action through which that vote is ultimately and openly ratified is its liturgical confirmation by prayer and the laying on of the hands of the *potiores* [prominent men], which is to be seen as conforming with the commissioning of the office—the subject under discussion in the treatise *To the Christian Nobility of the German Nation.*

Luther calls this act of calling a "free and apostolic rite of installing a priest."[120] He does not intend that it should be introduced by force everywhere since no one should be compelled to faith.[121] The example of those who employ it is to encourage others gradually to imitate it.[122] Once several cities have elected bishops in this

---

[118] WA 12:191.25ff.: ". . . believing with indubitable faith that whatever the common consent of the faithful, who know and confess the Gospel, shall have performed and done in this respect is performed and done by God"; cf. WA 12:195.4ff.: "Thus it is false for you to think that you are not the Church of God, even if there are only ten or six people who have the Word. But whatever two will have done in this matter, even with the agreement of the rest who do not yet have the Word, plainly it is certain that Christ has done it; they will have performed the thing only with humility and prayers." — W. Elert (*Morphologie* I, pp. 303f.) has pointed out that "the participation of the collective believers and confessors is precisely what brings the certainty that the act of installation is directed and accomplished by God." The *consensus fidelium* is to some extent the guarantee that God is actually working here. At the same time, however, attention will have to be given to the perspective of prayer mentioned by us in the following.

[119] WA 12:191.32ff., 192.34ff. Cf. generally the prayer of the congregation, WA 49:593.25f.: ". . . Prayer is never so mighty and powerful as when the whole flock prays together with one accord"; WA 49:594.16: "how much more should the whole congregation of Christians take comfort in the promise when they join with one accord to ask for something."

[120] WA 12:194.21f.; cf. WA 12:192.35f.: "This manner of electing bishops is the most ancient and is approved by the examples of the apostles and their disciples." — Luther attaches importance to the call in the Church being undertaken according to the *apostolic* mode. Cf. WA 25:17.13ff.: "We say that we are bishops by the apostolic rite."

[121] WA 12:194.4ff.

[122] WA 12:194.12ff.

manner, these bishops are then to elect one or more among them to the archiepiscopal office of visitation. Thus Bohemia is to become a legitimate Evangelical archbishopric once again.[123] Luther also desires by this appointment of the office, necessarily coming from the congregation, nothing less than to abolish the episcopal constitution of the Church.[124]

We encounter the same picture of a call through the congregation in a sermon from 1524, in which Luther says, "If . . . we know that a man is godly, we set him apart and, in the power of the Word which we have, give him the authority to preach the Word and give the Sacraments. This is ordaining."[125] The election and assignment of the office also, according to this, are equivalent to the ordination to the office, that is, the appointment of the office.[126] In this sermon, Luther sees the election as the fundamental act. "If, therefore, we agree that this one or another is ordained to the office, he is certainly ordained."[127] The congregation's election can, according to Luther, also be legally binding under certain circumstances even when an episcopal confirmation is omitted. For instance, if a bishop hostile to the Gospel refuses to confirm the election of an orthodox preacher, it is Luther's opinion—assuming the election has been conducted in a Christian and legitimate manner—"that he is nevertheless confirmed through the common call."[128] In the treatise *The Private Mass and the Consecration of Priests* (1533), Luther says that if the bishops refuse to confirm the Evangelical preachers, which has often been requested of them, we will see "how we get pastors and preachers from Baptism and God's Word without their chrism, ordained and confirmed through our electing and calling."[129] The election and call through the congregation without episcopal confirmation is, in the case of necessity, also a valid call. But it must be strongly emphasized that this applies only to an emergency.[130] It is significant that Luther always speaks of the call through the congregation when he is presented with an emergency situation that has arisen from the fact that the proper Roman bishops refused the call and installation of true Evangelical preachers.[131] This is true especially of the trea-

[123] WA 12:194.14ff.

[124] Cf. esp. below, pp. 132–34.

[125] WA 15:721.3ff.

[126] The juxtaposition of these two elements, election and commission of the office, is observed repeatedly in Luther: WA 6:407.37f., 440.32; 11:413.22, 414.3f.: "elect and call"; WA 16:35.36: "elected and called"; WA 38:236.32: "by our electing and calling"; WA 41:210.16f.: "some . . . elect, to whom such office is commended"; Enders 11:40.19: "to elect and constitute"; Enders 11:41.55: "calling and election" (on the question whether this text may be ascribed to Luther, cf. below, p. 135 n. 177).

[127] WA 15:721.8f.; cf. WA 15:721.12f.: "By ordination he is constituted from the election. . . ."

[128] WA 11:414.14f. and 32f., 415.13f.: "Why should a Christian congregation not also make a preacher by its calling alone?"

[129] WA 38:236.30ff., also 236.17ff.

[130] Cf. F. J. Stahl, op. cit., pp. 102f.

[131] Also cf. the dispute around the appointment of the preacher's post at Altenburg and Luther's position on that as described by K. Müller, *Kirche, Gemeinde, Obrigkeit nach Luther* (Tübingen, 1910), pp. 103ff.

tises to the Bohemians (*Concerning the Ministry*) and to the Leisnigers (*That a Christian Assembly Has the Right to Judge All Teaching*).[132] Both treatises address the call of preachers in this concrete emergency situation and relate thematically to that subject.[133] While the right of the congregation to call preachers is taught in them as a fundamental right and not only as a right in a state of necessity,[134] nevertheless the *practical application of this right* in the form of the lay act of calling is required by Luther *only with respect to a state of emergency*.[135] Even under the most difficult constraints, Luther was never moved to urge the call through the congregation as a fundamental and general aspect.[136]

6. The Call through Spiritual Office-Bearers

The call directly through the congregation is only one form of the act of calling for Luther, and he speaks of it properly only with respect to a state of necessity. Practically speaking, stronger preference is shown in Luther's works for the other strain of thought which envisions the *call through higher-ranking officers*, through whom Luther then naturally sees the Church also acting.[137] If

---

[132] This circumstance is wholly overlooked in G. Rietschel, *Luther und die Ordination* (1889), p. 43. It is explicitly noted in turn by W. Walther, *Luthers Kirche*, pp. 137f., and V. Vajta, op. cit., p. 209, and even earlier by G. Plitt, *Einleitung in die Augustana* II (Erlangen, 1868), pp. 375f.

[133] WA 12:171ff.; 11:411.13ff., 413.10f., 414.30ff.: "But now in our times there is an emergency, and there is no bishop to supply Evangelical preachers. . . ."

[134] In this, G. Holstein (*Grundlagen des ev. Kirchenrechts* [Tübingen, 1928], p. 96) and W. Trillhaas ("Die luth. Lehre 'De potestate ecclesiastica,'" *Zwischen den Zeiten* 11 [1933], p. 503 n. 13) have certainly had the correct view.

[135] We must therefore agree with T. Kliefoth when he writes: "We must stop speaking provocatively on the basis of this letter" (to the Bohemians) "as some kind of Magna Carta or canon law of the Lutheran Church," yet only insofar as he refers to that which must be done not in the [normal] order but in extreme necessity (*Liturg. Abhandlungen* I [1854], pp. 365f.). Cf. W. Löhe, *Neue Aphorismen*, *Ges. Werke*, vol. V.1, pp. 549ff.

[136] Brunotte, op. cit., pp. 179–82, shares this judgment. Cf. A. L. Richter, *Geschichte d. ev. Kirchenverfassung i. Deutschld.* (Leipzig, 1851), p. 16, who calls it "simply an error when, in recent time, the demand for the congregational right of free election has appealed to Luther's statements in order to gain authority for itself in his name." Also cf. K. Holl, *Luther*, p. 378: Luther would not conclude "that every congregation must have the right of electing pastors." Also F. J. Stahl, op. cit., p. 105. — W. Elert has shown that while Luther understands the call as proceeding from the local congregation, he does not tie it exclusively to that body but really has in mind the larger association of the Church and its responsibility for the individual local congregations (*Morphologie* I, pp. 305f.). Elert brings this to light especially with regard to Luther's thoughts concerning the further development of Bohemia toward a restoration of Bohemia's archbishopric with the power of visitation possessed by *majores* under the bishops (op. cit., pp. 306f.). Elert also notes that all of Luther's suggestions for executing the institution of the pastoral office on the part of the local congregation derive "from considerations of expediency." "Thus they cannot be evaluated as provisions of a divine constitutional law for the Church" (op. cit., p. 324).

[137] The representation by R. Seeberg, *Dogmengeschichte* IV.1, *Die Lehre Luthers* (1917), pp. 292f., gives the impression that Luther taught only the call through the congregation. This creates a false picture. The election of the preacher through the congregation is a possibility in Luther, but not the only, nor by any means the dominant, one.

any private person comes and calls me to preach, I cannot comply with this *privata vocatio* "since through it the window is opened to Satan's ministers."[138] For the act of calling to be a real one by which God works, it must come from the agency of those who occupy a true, official function[139] and are authorized for that purpose by the collective whole as well as by God.[140] Those who invest the public offices are eligible for this.[141] It must involve "men appointed to high rank or authority"[142] so that the call is at least a *vocatio majoris*, the call of one occupying higher authority and power.[143] Consequently, these persons occupying higher public positions, who would thus be authorized to carry out the act of calling in the name of the Church, can, according to Luther, only be *spiritual or temporal office-bearers*, thus either bishops, on the one hand, or princes (i.e., magistrates, patrons) on the other.[144] Here we will first treat the *call through bishops, or spiritual office-bearers.*

From Scripture Luther knows that the apostles called ministers to the office.[145] They had the command from Christ to appoint bishops and presbyters in order to fill the concrete office in the congregation, and Christ also promised to be active Himself through their call.[146] The apostles' own disciples, especially Timothy and Titus, likewise appointed presbyters at the apostles' bidding. Luther does not ignore those passages of the New Testament which demonstrate this.[147] For instance, he interprets Titus 1:5 in such a way that Paul here says to Titus: "If you see cities in which there are no pastors, appoint and ordain presbyters yourself. . . ."[148] ". . . Imitate my ways. You have seen me ordain a certain number of presbyters in every city. You do likewise."[149] Luther obviously recognizes the propriety of such calls through the apostles or other spiritual office-bearers in the New Testament; indeed, he even refers to the presence of a chain of succession extending from the apostles to our time and beyond until the Last Day: The apostles were directly called by Christ Himself. "The apostles afterward called their disciples, as Paul did Timothy, Titus, etc., who

---

138 WA 40/1:61.16ff.

139 WA 40/1:61.15f.: "through the mouth of a man who is in a legitimate function."

140 Cf. W. Elert, *Morphologie* I, p. 304.

141 WA 40/1:61.5f.: "who bear public offices."

142 WA 38:493.40f.

143 WA 6:566.28f.

144 WA 38:493.40ff.

145 WA 38:494.1ff.; cf. WA 12:387.10ff. (on 1 Pet. 5:1ff.): When St. Peter and the others apostles came into a city where there were Christians, "they elevated an old man or two who behaved honestly, had a wife and child, and understood Scripture. . . . They were called presbyters."

146 WA 49:140.32ff.: "Therefore, I send, that you may run throughout the world and appoint others as preachers, who also may run, preach, and do what I and you [do] until the end of the world"; cf. WA 47:192.5ff.

147 Cf. WA 11:413.23.

148 WA 25:16.13ff.; cf. WA 25:16.21f.: "The first in kind he commits to Titus, that he may appoint presbyters; then he prescribes such ones."

149 WA 25:17.16f.

then as bishops called their successor bishops (as Titus 1), until our times, and from now until the end of the world."[150] Although it is impossible to establish from this passage a doctrine of a consecratory succession in the specific sense in Luther, or even of a necessity of such a thing,[151] it must be maintained that Luther here has in mind the continuing connectivity of a *chain of calls through spiritual office-bearers* originating from the apostles and extending beyond the present to the Last Day.[152] For this reason it will also have to be understood that Luther normally assumes that, *properly*, the bishops, the spiritual office-bearers, are to see to the institution of new ministers of the Word, whether by calling them themselves or by confirming the call made through the congregation. He not only leaves this possibility of the right of calling through bishops free,[153] but views this call as the given and regular one inasmuch as he speaks of the other

---

[150] WA 40/1:59.18ff. (Dr.) — In this statement, Luther obviously depends on a passage of Jerome which he likes to cite in connection to the discussion of various kinds of calls, and without that critique of the idea of succession which it contains; cf. above, p. 122. The second kind of call is the call through men, yet from God, as in the "disciples of the apostles, and those who legitimately succeed the apostles as bishops and priests until the end of the world. And this kind cannot exist without a first from which it has its origin" (WA 2:454.6f.). Cf. the similar German: ". . . such as the disciples of the apostles and all who until the end of the world truly enter the preaching office in the stead of the apostles, as bishops and priests. And these could not exist without the first, from which they all began" (WA 17/2:257.29ff.). Similar ideas are also encountered elsewhere in Luther in his own words: cf. WA 50:634.11ff.: "If the apostles, evangelists, and prophets have ceased, others must have come in their stead and still come until the end of the world. For the Church shall not cease until the end of the world. Therefore, apostles, evangelists, and prophets must continue, whatever they wish to be called or may be called who carry on the Word and works of God." In this context, it will also be observed that Luther speaks of the ministers of the Word, the pastors and preachers, as the "*successores*" or "successors" (*Nachkomen*) of the apostles: WA 21:284.11ff.: "the apostles and their *nachkomen*, pastors, preachers, teachers . . ."; WA 28:471.5ff.: "*Nachkomen*" (the apostles); WA 38:494.1ff.: "*successores*"; WA 41:123.35: "apostles and their *nachkomen*"; WA 49:145.18f.: "you apostles and your *nachkomen* until the end of the world." — Luther's sense is, as Simon Schöffel writes ("Das Predigt- u. Hirtenamt," in *Credo ecclesiam* [1930], p. 207): "There is probably an unbroken lineage of the office, of the conferral of the power to administer the Gospel, traced back to the apostles. From generation to generation this conferral has been passed down, and thus the office has remained alive."

[151] Luther does not share the Roman idea of the necessity of an *ordinaria successio*, but rather rejects it: WA 53:74: ". . . Thus in the Church the succession of bishops does not make the bishops, but the Lord alone is our Bishop, sustaining the bishops where, whom, and when He wills, as we see in Jerome, Augustine, Hus, and ourselves, disregarding the succession, which the Papists reject."

[152] The same idea is present when Luther says of Gal. 1:1f. ("not called by men"): "All of which things extend so far that you may see with what care Christ has instituted and fortified His Church, lest anyone presume to teach by chance without being sent by it or by those sent by it" (WA 2:453.31ff.; cf. WA 17/2:257.12ff.). Herewith Luther means the apostles, or their successors, and thus all truly called office-bearers. Accordingly, Christ has made provision for a call through office-bearers in His congregation. Also cf. WA 47:192.5ff.: "There is another sending, which is through men but not by men. Thus we are sent, and we elect others also and place them in the office, that they may preach and give the Sacraments." Luther also here identifies the sending proper as prerequisite to legitimization for sending others into the office. — Also H. Storck noted these ideas in Luther, cf. op. cit., p. 29: "Luther knows of a successive series of spiritual offices."

[153] Cf. WA 8:502.37ff.: "Christian bishops are honest and married, experienced, brave men, instructed in the Word of truth, several in a city, who are elected *by the neighboring, surrounding*

possibility of the call through the congregation alone as one to be put in practice only in extraordinary cases of necessity.[154]

That in the course of development the call through bishops came increasingly to be neglected in practice and delegated to other entities (particularly government) was solely because of the fact that the Roman bishops did not join the Reformation, but rather became enemies of the Gospel and so could no longer be recognized as the apostles' successors. "If our bishops and abbots, etc., sat in the apostles' seat, as they claim, one might well hold that they be allowed to do what Titus, Timothy, Paul, and Barnabas did by appointing priests, etc.,"[155] but if they have now become wolves who refuse to teach the Gospel, and instead sit in the devil's seat, "they are no more fit for the preaching office and care of souls among Christians than Turks and Jews are. Let them urge donkeys and lead dogs."[156] Only because "in our times there is necessity, and there is no bishop to supply Evangelical preachers, this example of Titus and Timothy does not apply here."[157] It was the heresy of the Roman bishops which here brought other entities into play as emergency assistants and led to solutions in the Evangelical camp that did not correspond to Luther's *proper* intentions.

How strong and fundamental Luther's support was for the appointment of offices through bishops is demonstrated especially by the fact that, on his own initiative, he made provision for the call through spiritual office-bearers (bishops) in the second phase where it could not be obtained from such in the first phase and had to be undertaken through the congregation itself.[158] Thus he

---

bishops, or by their people. . . . This is a divine decision and the Holy Spirit's form and manner of appointing bishops"; Latin: WA 8:429.6ff.

154 Also cf. J. Köstlin, *Luthers Lehre von der Kirche* (1853), p. 77. — In Brunotte (op. cit., pp. 180f.) this is not emphasized sufficiently. Regarding Luther, it is too little when Brunotte says, "The call can, under certain circumstances, be made through church superiors, that is, through bishops, who according to the church's existing legal system are qualified for the call by office-bearers" (p. 180). Luther does not leave this form of call free only "under certain circumstances," but sees it as the normal, given one.

155 WA 11:413.28ff.

156 WA 11:413.31ff.

157 WA 11:414.30ff. Cf. V. Vajta, op. cit., p. 209.

158 Luther, in his treatise to the Bohemians [*Concerning the Ministry*], also mentions the possibility of the Bohemians having the new ministers called and confirmed through the priest Gallus Cahera, who had been consecrated by a papistic bishop, but he only makes this provision in the event that the Bohemians are too weak for his suggested free and apostolic rite of appointing a priest and did not dare to put it into effect (WA 12:194.21ff.). It is almost as if Luther would fundamentally not care whether the call happens through spiritual office-bearers, as if he saw this only as a concession to the weakness of the Bohemians' faith and their scrupulousness. Yet this would be a false interpretation. Luther sees the possible weakness of the Bohemians' faith not in their continuing to think that office-bearers must properly be installed by office-bearers, but in their continuing to prefer consecration by *papistic* bishops for the one who does the calling and confirming. Cf. WA 12:194.23ff.: ". . . let us permit that you accept those now ordained by the papistic bishops, such as that Gallus of yours and his ilk, and use those in place of the papal bishops, that they may call and elect as well as confirm. . . ." Also cf. WA 12:172.9f., where Luther identifies as weakness and scrupulousness the opinion that it is necessary to have priests consecrated by *papistic* bishops

writes to the Bohemians [*Concerning the Ministry*] that the congregation—in the given emergency—has the right and duty to confer the office *communibus suffragiis* on one or more "in their stead [*vice sua*]," and continues: "*And these then upon others*, accompanied by the same prayers."[159] Thus even if the new ministers in the first phase were elected and installed by the congregation, it was the office-bearers thus called who were *then* to call further office-bearers, not the congregation again.[160] In such further calls through the newly elected bishops, the congregations are only to participate by means of their *suffragia*. Here we also begin to see the idea of a vocational succession with which Luther's line of reasoning eventually merges. As his model, he has in mind the Evangelical archbishopric of Bohemia, in which Evangelical bishops also call the ministers of the Word. The end that he would most like to see attained in Bohemia would be the whole of that land returning "back to the legitimate and Evangelical archbishopric."[161] From Luther's suggestions to the Bohemians, it is plain to see that he properly judges the episcopal constitution of the Church, as well as the episcopal right to call pastors, as the legitimate, normal, and most desirable system.[162]

> In this connection we must also note the position which Luther took with respect to the council of Zwickau in 1531, when without regard for the city pastor, Parson Nicholas Hausmann, it removed the preacher Soranus and replaced him with another.[163] Luther here states plainly and without restraint: "For what else is it to depose and replace pastors than to wish to be a pastor and to assume the ministry of the Word for oneself? And this is what those sacrilegious men have done."[164] Here Luther regards the installation and expulsion of preachers as a function of the pastoral office, of the *ministerium verbi*, and the usurpation of this function by others (in connection with the fact that this act was done arbitrarily) as a sacrilegious presumption. Naturally, the assumption here is that the pastor is a faithful minister of the Word, not an enemy of the Gospel. It must also, of course, be noted that this does not directly involve the appointment of the pastoral office, but the call to a subordinate preaching office which ranked below the pastor. Still, this is the *ministerium verbi*. Luther sees the pastor as the local bishop

---

(who had forced the Bohemians to send their priestly candidates to Italy). On the other hand, Luther views it entirely as the duty of an Evangelical bishop to ordain priests, even regarding it as prescribed by the "voice of the apostles" (WA Br 11:156.25ff.; cf. below, p. 192 n. 284). Only this much is clear here: Luther assumes no unconditional *jus divinum* for the call through spiritual office-bearers.

159 WA 12:191.2.

160 Up till now, this has for the most part been insufficiently considered and frequently overlooked entirely. Thus, e.g., in W. Walther, op. cit., pp. 125f., and in W. Elert, *Morphologie* I, pp. 297ff., there is no reference to it. Yet this factor in Luther was already plainly emphasized by W. Löhe, *Neue Aphorismen*, *Ges. Werke*, vol. V.1, p. 551.

161 WA 12:194.18ff. This passage was not noticed by F. Lezius when he opined ("Gleichheit und Ungleichheit" [Gütersloh, 1895], p. 316) that Luther never conceived of a Protestant kind of episcopal constitution.

162 Cf. K. Müller, *Kirche, Gemeinde u. Obrigkeit nach Luther* (Tübingen, 1910), p. 60.

163 Cf. above, pp. 107–8.

164 WA Br 6:79.88ff.

to whom the church is committed. Without him, nothing may be undertaken, including the installation or removal of ministers of the Word: "For the church is entrusted to you; wherefore no one is permitted to govern her without you."[165]

When Luther endorses the episcopal right of calling, he by no means wishes to see congregations incapacitated and silenced. They are to give their *suffragia*, and the bishop is to appoint no one "without the congregation's decision, will, and calling."[166] From Acts 6:1ff., Luther concludes that the apostles did not appoint office-bearers without the vote of the congregation either,[167] any more than Timothy or Titus did.[168] Still, Luther also accounts for the case of necessity in which the bishop, without hearing the congregation, may appoint an office-bearer in order that the souls may not perish "for lack of God's Word."[169] In his treatise *Against King Henry of England* (1522), he says of the call and institution of an office-bearer: "Whether this be done by the authority of an apostle or bishop alone, or with the people electing and consenting at the same time, makes no difference. Although it would be more proper with the people electing and consenting."[170] This "makes no difference" shows that Luther does not assume a *jus divinum* for the election and assent of the congregation. Yet this statement was permitted to stand in relative isolation. Regardless of emergencies, Luther elsewhere strictly calls for the *suffragia* of the congregation.[171]

This leads us to ask how the office-bearer's legitimization to act in the call process is rationalized generally. First, it rests with certainty on the office which he has himself received, on the sending through Christ in which he has participated and which he can pass on,[172] and then especially on the bishops in their superior station, which provides the best conditions for exercising the powers of the right to call. But in all this, it cannot be overlooked that the office-bearer extending the call to the office acts as an *instrument of the church* on the

---

[165] WA Br 6:77.34f.

[166] WA 11:414.12f.; cf. WA 11:414.2ff.; 12:172.22ff., 192.2. Also cf. K. Holl, *Luther*, p. 378.

[167] WA 11:414.22ff. and 25ff.: "Therefore, if the apostles did not dare by their own authority to institute this kind of office that is only concerned with assigning temporal livings, how could they be so eager to confer the highest office of preaching on anyone by their own authority without the knowledge, will, and call of the congregation?"

[168] WA 11:414.16; 10/2:221.2ff. "For when Paul commends Titus to ordain presbyters, nevertheless it does not follow that Titus did it alone by his own authority, but that he instituted them by the apostles' example through the people's prayers. Otherwise Paul's words will conflict with the apostles' example"; cf. WA 10/2:240.27ff.

[169] WA 11:414.4ff. — On this cf. W. Walther, op. cit., p. 138, who very rightly deduces from this that Luther may "not be classified as an opponent of the autonomy of the individual congregation."

[170] WA 10/2:220.36ff. — W. Walther, op. cit., p. 141, stresses that Luther, in the appointment of pastors in which he was involved, always had three things in mind: (1) only true preachers could be installed, (2) the existing orders and powers had to be observed, and (3) no pastor could be forced upon a congregation against its will.

[171] The phrase "makes no difference" has its counterpart, however, in the phrase "it depends" in another passage: cf. WA 53:257.4ff.: "It depends on whether the church and the bishop agree, and the church is willing to listen to the bishop, and the bishop is willing to teach the church."

[172] Cf. WA 47:192.5ff.

basis of an explicit or tacitly stipulated commission to do so by the (collective) congregation. He is the one "who has the flock's command and consent" to call someone,[173] who does so "in the stead and person of the whole assembly."[174] In the right of calling, according to Luther, he does not act on his own personal authority, but represents the church in his own person.[175] And this is why it is only reasonable that the bishop is not to call an office-bearer without the approval of the congregation. If the bishop falls into heresy or tries to call a false teacher to the office, he can no longer be an instrument of the church, and the right to call reverts to the congregation.[176]

If we dissect the whole call process into its constituent elements and ask which entities are particularly responsible for each, Luther refers the election of the person to the congregation (or its representatives, e.g., rulers), the confirmation of the election by prayer and the laying on of hands to the pastors.[177] We may therefore see in the call process the same doctrine of equal cooperation between office and congregation as is evident in the ancient Church's rite of the call.[178]

---

[173] WA 8:253.30f.

[174] WA 6:407.29f. Cf. V. Vajta, op. cit., p. 209.

[175] Also cf. G. Plitt, *Einleitung in die Augustana* II (Erlangen, 1868), p. 375.

[176] Cf. WA 53:242.27ff.: If the cathedral chapter (in Naumburg) elects an idolatrous bishop who neither can nor will be bishop, the congregation may not accept him. "And if the church in Naumburg had to say, 'Dear lords of the chapter, elect however you wish, and elect again, elect a thousand times,' we will never acknowledge your election nor bishop."

[177] Enders 11:40.10ff. and 17ff.: (Both are taught in Acts 1:23ff. and 1 Tim. 5:22,) "that is, it belongs to the church to elect and appoint some in whom it sees the gift of the Spirit, doctrine, and an approved life; then it belongs to other pastors to lay on hands, approve, and to testify as suitable . . . "; cf. End. 11:44.173f. and 45:204ff.: ". . . Christ, sitting at the right hand of God the Father, . . . gives the church the authority to call and elect and consecrate and in its name, with the other pastors, the right to approve and to confirm that this doctrine is truly in accord with Scripture—indeed, the very Word that Christ and the apostles spoke." — On the question whether this memorandum *Ob in Erfurt die wahre Kirche Christi sei* [Whether Christ's true Church exists in Erfurt] (1536), represents a genuine work of Luther's, the following may be noted: Clemen accepts as most probable that the signature of this memorandum ("D. Martinus Lutherus, Philippus Melanchthon, D. Pomeranus, Justus Jonas think and have subscribed to the same. Frider. Myconius") only implies that [Friedrich] Myconius is sure that Luther, Melanchthon, [Johann] Bugenhagen, and Jonas agree with the memorandum issued by him (WA Br 7:509). Yet the language (". . . have subscribed [*scripserunt*]"!) permits no other interpretation than that those mentioned have in fact signed it themselves. Enders has the same interpretation (11:48 n. 1), accepting Myconius as the author, as does Clemen; the others would then have explicitly confirmed and endorsed the contents of the report by their signature. If instead of "think and have subscribed to the same" we read "thinks and has subscribed to the same," then the last phrase applies only to Myconius, and Luther, etc., would be regarded as authors. However one may decide it, it is sure that Luther has fully endorsed the contents of the memorandum.

[178] Luther calls the ancient Church cooperation, described in a letter from Cyprian to the presbyter Felix (WA 2:231.2ff. and 26ff.), a "most sacred and ancient rite of divine Law, unchanging through all things" (WA 2:232.4f.). The opposing view by E. Seeberg (*Luthers Theologie in ihren Grundzügen*, 2nd ed. [Stuttgart, 1950], p. 175) is false: "Yet one does not become a pastor through the call made through bishops . . . , but through the congregation." Thus Brunotte's statement: "The responsibility of specific church entities for the individual aspects of the call ceremony is not debated by Luther" (op. cit., p. 190), cannot be supported.

7. The Call through Christian Rulers

When Luther suggests that the call is to be done through persons who hold *public offices*, who are appointed to a *high position or authority*,[179] he has in mind not only spiritual officers but also temporal ones, especially Christian rulers. "*The prince or magistrate*,"[180] "the *carnal powers and magistrates*"[181] are cited by him in these passages as calling authorities. If it be asked how Luther arrives at the teaching that Christian rulers are authorities with the right to call, we have already identified the most essential cause:[182] the practical failure of bishops, which compels Luther to look for other authorities for appointing the office. And Christian rulers in particular were naturally considered for this, to the extent that they were persons in superior offices whose authority was universally accepted. Rulers were very important for the work of the Reformation generally. Already in 1520, Luther found it necessary to direct his appeal for reform to the Christian nobility of the German nation since the spiritual authorities failed to do so.[183] In emergencies, rulers had to be invoked to manage church affairs. Over the whole course of the Reformation, Evangelically minded members of the ruling class offered the power-political backing without which the whole work of the Reformation would have been a lost cause. It was therefore only natural that church regulations be carried out only with the closest dependence on the territorial princes along with the land's governing authority, if not directly by the territorial lord himself. This is true of the wholesale transformation of the church's structure and especially of the establishment of visitations, which Luther requested from his sovereign because that was the only authoritative entity with a God-given office extending over the whole territory since the bishops, on account of their heresy, were no longer eligible.[184] Luther saw himself compelled to take this approach through the circumstances of the case. The rulers were the only authority able to execute the reorganization of the church's structure, and thus the acute state of emergency in which the church found itself was made to justify the rulers' interference in churchly affairs.[185] In principle, on the basis of his teaching of the two kingdoms, Luther always neatly divided the two authorities of the spiritual and secular and decried the

---

179 Cf. above, p. 129.

180 WA 40/1:59.24ff.; cf. WA 40/1:60:5ff.: "But if the chief or magistrate calls, then I can boast that it is done by the command of God through the voice of a man. There is the command of God through the mouth of the prince; these are still called true calls."

181 WA 38:494.2.

182 Cf. above, p. 131.

183 On this cf. K. Holl, *Luther*, pp. 326ff., and W. Elert, *Morphologie* I, p. 327.

184 WA 26:197ff.

185 K. Holl has strongly emphasized that for Luther the involvement of rulers in churchly matters represents an emergency right. Op. cit., pp. 354, 375; also cf. pp. 333ff., 349f., and in general the whole section on the territorial church government, pp. 326ff., as well as G. Ritter, *Die Neugestaltung Europas i. 16. Jh.* (Berlin, 1950), p. 117. — Cf. also R. Seeberg, *Dogmengeschichte* IV.1, *Die Lehre Luthers* (1917), pp. 301f.

mingling of them as the worst evil.[186] Here, then, in the interest of the work of the Reformation and because of necessity, he was left with no other choice than to entrust secular authority with ecclesial responsibilities. Yet this involvement of rulers in churchly things was facilitated for him by his doctrine of the universal priesthood and the new evaluation of the secular estate in general which it entailed. Those who occupy governmental office also belong to the spiritual estate and are fellow priests, co-responsible for all that takes place in the church. Authority, too, is an office "which pertains and is profitable to the Christian congregation."[187] Those in that office are obligated to dispose of the authority which they have received from God as rulers, for the good of the people.[188] Thus it was advisable for Luther for various reasons to grant to rulers powers in the church. That he included in this the right of calling was necessitated by two additional factors. First, the people were far too immature for—even incapable of—the functions of a true Christian congregation (one being the election and call of true preachers);[189] second, the right of presentation had in any case often been left to the magistrates, the princes, or even the nobility (patronages!) since the Middle Ages. What, then, should prevent permitting the calling of Evangelical *ministri* to be exercised now by the rulers, whose power was certainly from God, instead of the (still infantile) people and instead of the Roman bishops who had become heretical? Thus Luther recognizes Christian government as a proper agent for the right of calling.[190]

Yet it should be kept in mind here that in the call process, according to Luther, rulers act only as a *commembrum ecclesiae* [a fellow member of the

---

[186] According to R. Sohm (*Kirchenrecht* I, pp. 548f.), there was only one Christian Church for Luther, in which there were two different authorities (two swords), the spiritual and secular, both instituted by God, both envisioned with the task of governing the Christian Church, yet by different means on different planes (earthly welfare—eternal welfare). Also cf. G. Ritter, op. cit., p. 117. — K. Holl opposed the idea of a *corpus Christianum* encompassing the two authorities in Luther (cf. *Luther*, pp. 339ff.), as does E. Schlink (*Theologie der luth. Bek.schriften*, 2nd ed. [Munich, 1946], p. 317 n. 8).

[187] WA 6:408.10f.

[188] WA 6:413.30ff.: ". . . especially since they, too, are now fellow Christians, fellow priests, equally spiritual, equally empowered in all things, and their office and work, which they have received from God for everyone, should be allowed to proceed freely wherever it is necessary and beneficial that it do so." Cf. A. W. Dieckhoff, op. cit., pp. 130ff.; E. Foerster, "Fragen zu Luthers Kirchenbegriff aus der Gedankenwelt seines Alters," festschrift for J. Kaftan (Tübingen, 1920), pp. 95f.; R. Seeberg, *Dogmengesch.* IV.1, *Die Lehre Luthers*, pp. 296ff.; K. Holl, *Luther*, pp. 326ff.; H. Storck, op. cit., pp. 48f.

[189] One may also refer to Luther's admonition not to carry out Francis Lambert of Avignon's *Reformatio Ecclesiarum Hassiae* (1526) with its congregational principle.

[190] K. Holl has noted that the cooperation of rulers in the appointment of the preaching office happens not by virtue of their governmental office but out of brotherly love for the neighbor (*Luther*, p. 356 and p. 354 n. 4). — This is accurate insofar as it must be brotherly love, according to Luther, which causes the one occupying the governmental office to use his authority to call and to install true preachers in the congregation. But on the fundamental understanding of the ruler issuing the call, see esp. the following.

church].[191] In doing so, they represent or embody the Christian congregation. The latter properly only make the call *through* them.[192] The later teaching of the *praecipua membra ecclesiae* [prominent members of the church] is already incipient in Luther. At times, Luther refers to congregation (or church) side by side with rulers as calling entities.[193] But this correlation is as a rule more of an interrelation. Church and ruler are not thought of here as two distinct, independent quantities since the ruler, operating in the call as *commembrum ecclesiae*, is representing the church. When Luther says, "This is by definition a sending from God and is nevertheless done through men, *such as a city, prince, or a congregation*, who elect and set apart one man,"[194] it is characteristic that he addresses the city (= magistrate) and prince also as "congregation" (which follows from the words "or a congregation [*oder sonst ein Gemeine*]"). The persons in government represent and embody not only the secular community but also the Christian one (which in those days overlapped) at the same time.

Naturally, both entities—congregation and government—can go their separate ways; namely, when rulers by their actions oppose the Christian congregation in an internal conflict, they cease to be a *faithful* member of the congregation. This happened, for instance, in Erfurt in 1536, when the city council unjustly sought to expel the preachers who had been called. In this case, it has to be made clear the rulers can exercise the powers to call only as a faithful member of the church. "You are not made ministers of Christ" (as the assailed preachers were described) "because five old men called you, but because the Holy Spirit anointed you, *the church called you*, the other men know the Word of Christ preached to the church of God."[195] The act of calling is properly managed by the congregation and spiritual office-bearers; the rulers may in the process embody the congregation and act in its place, but when they cease to be a faithful member of the congregation, they automatically resign their position as an entity of the call process.

---

[191] Enders 11:41.55ff.: "Calling and election of ministers . . . does not properly and chiefly belong to magistrates but to the church. If a magistrate is faithful and a fellow member of the church, he calls not because he is a magistrate but because he is a fellow member of the church."

[192] This is rightly pointed out by G. Rietshel, *Lehrbuch der Liturgik* II (1909), p. 416; 2nd ed. (Graff, 1952), pp. 844f.

[193] WA 17/1:362.13f.: "The other call is when the congregation and the ruler ask for it." — In *Ordination of Ministers of the Word*, WA 38:427.25ff. (F), it reads: (the ordinands are to be certain that they are called by God Himself) "because the *church* which sends you, *and the temporal ruler*, have called and requested you. For what the church and ruler do in this matter, God does through them."

[194] WA 47:192.13ff.

[195] Enders 11:44.169ff.

8. A Person's Worthiness and Fitness as Prerequisite for the Call

The call is also tied to specific prerequisites with respect to the candidate's personal qualities.[196] According to 2 Tim. 2:2, to which passage Luther likes to make reference in this connection, the teaching office is to be committed only to those who are capable and fit for it. For this reason Luther impresses on the Bohemians that those who are to be elected must be "worthy [*digni*]" and "suitable [*idonei*]."[197] But what constitutes worthiness and fitness for the office? Luther adheres to the apostolic rules in the Pastoral Epistles.[198] Regarding the call to the preaching office, Paul taught Timothy and Titus "to look at a person's life and teaching and make sure his teaching is pure and sound and his life without offense, and that he is apt to teach."[199] Here the three elements of fitness are indicated: *doctrinal unity (orthodoxy),*[200] *ability to teach, and testimony of a Christian way of life.*[201]

> The ability to teach encompasses spiritual and natural gifts. As spiritual gift, Luther especially emphasizes "the grace and knowledge of Scripture in order to teach others,"[202] which he also simply identifies as "Spirit."[203] As natural gifts, a strong voice, good pronunciation, eloquence, and good memory are mentioned.[204] These gifts must be present in substantial degree so that the candidates surpass the rest in these areas; only the best are to be called to the preaching office.[205] This is understandable since the office places high demands; it involves not only the communication of the right doctrine but also its defense against adversaries.[206]

---

[196] Cf. WA 25:17.17f.: "Then I desire that you not ordain anyone indifferently" (Luther has Paul say to Titus).

[197] WA 12:193.38; cf. WA 12:191.3ff. and 23; 10/1.2:239.27f.: (The congregation should select one [man]) "who is capable of the task"; WA 50:633.16f.: "It should be a skilled, chosen man"; WA 15:721.3: "a godly man."

[198] Cf. Enders 11:140.24ff.

[199] WA 52:568.15ff. On the authenticity of this sermon from the *House Postil*, cf. below, p. 181 n. 234.

[200] Cf. WA 53:242.25ff.

[201] Cf. Enders 11:40.20: "the gift of the Spirit, teaching, an acceptable life"; WA 53:258.17ff.: "He is also richly gifted by God, instructed and well-versed in Holy Scripture . . . furthermore, has a decent way of life and a trustworthy, upright heart . . . and is above reproach in accordance with Holy Scripture, as St. Paul describes a bishop in Titus 1 and 1 Timothy 3."

[202] WA 49:591.11f.; cf. WA 11:411.29f.; 41:208.4f.: ". . . should be able to know white from black and be versed in Sacred Scripture"; WA 41:214.30: "capable of preaching and familiar with Scripture."

[203] WA 8:497.31, 424.28.

[204] WA 8:497.31ff., 424.29: "voice, eloquence, memory, and other natural gifts"; cf. WA 22:184.3ff.

[205] WA 8:424.25: "better suited than others"; WA 8:497.27; 41:209.30f.: "those to whom God gives particular gifts and aptitude, that they may be good for the office."

[206] WA 41:214.31.

Fitness in this sense is a *conditio sine qua non* [essential condition] for the call.[207] Establishing fitness is therefore directly pertinent to the call process and an integral part of it. The candidate's character can best be judged by the congregation from which he is taken, as can his gifts to some degree. We have already mentioned that this is why Luther values the *suffragia* of the congregation, which is supposed to approve the candidate as suitable, and why he rejects the call performed without at least a consultation of the congregation.[208] On the other hand, it is critical that the candidate's purity of doctrine and aptitude for the teaching office be judged by other office-bearers who are themselves in the office. This is accomplished by the *examination*, which, according to Luther, is an indispensable part of the complete call process. It is to be conducted by clergy who themselves have the aptitude to teach; Paul's instruction to test teaching competence applies for Timothy and Titus as ministers of the Word personally holding the office.[209] The people of Erfurt were told in writing that it falls to other *pastors* to attest (*testari*) that those called are suitable (*idoneos*).[210] In the whole memorandum to those in Erfurt, the recognition of the candidate by other ministers of the Word appears as an essential element of the call.[211] The ordination rite later instituted in Wittenberg is always preceded by the theological examination for aptitude in teaching and orthodoxy in belief, which is conducted by the theological faculty, which is to say, the ordaining ministers.[212] The chief importance of this examination lies in determining fitness. The judgment of the congregation regarding a candidate is only a preparatory act; in the examination conducted by spiritual office-bearers, the determination of fitness is then validated, whereupon the ordination can then be performed.[213] In the historical records of ordinations, the person in question is always described as having been examined by the ordinators and then, after the determination of his orthodoxy and aptitude for teaching, being ordained.[214] On October 24, 1535,

---

207 Naturally the inner worthiness remains known only to God; all that may be determined is the worthiness *coram hominibus* [before men], yet that it be determined is indispensable; WA 2:194.9f.: "This" (church), "then, can commit the Keys now to a worthy man, now to an unworthy; unworthy, I say, before God since it does not know whether he is worthy before God, else it should not commit the office except to the one worthy before men."

208 Cf. above, pp. 123–24, 133.

209 WA 52:568.15ff.

210 Enders 11:40.21f.

211 Enders 11:42.96ff., 44.169ff., 44:174ff., 45.211ff.

212 Cf. WA 41:762.20ff.: "Our elector . . . has decreed that they be sent to us from all dioceses . . . and examined and confirmed. . . ." — Hardly credible is the supposition expressed by Brunotte that, in Luther's view, the examination was assigned to the theological faculty only "for practical reasons" since the necessary quantity of theological attainments "could be determined better through the theological faculty than through individual congregations or patrons" (op. cit., p. 191). The determination of a man's ability to teach prior to his ordination, according to Luther, belongs *fundamentally* to the spiritual office. Cf. also below, pp. 192–93.

213 Cf. the beginning of *Ordination of Ministers of the Word*: "The examination being done . . ." (WA 38:423.6f.).

214 E.g., Enders 11:227.15ff.; 11:278.6ff.

Luther writes to Friedrich Myconius: "We send back your Johann *called and elected by you and also examined and publicly . . . ordained* and confirmed . . . *by us*."[215] The examination is here classified as an *essential* part of the call process.

Since the examination and subsequent ordination are performed by ministers of the Word, a proper call process, according to Luther, normally requires the continuous assistance of other spiritual office-bearers. This may be noted especially in his teaching of the call through Christian rulers. Although a ruler may be the one calling, this is not conceived by Luther in such a way as to exclude the spiritual office entirely from this call process. Rather, Luther assumes in this process that the other ministers of the Word will first examine the candidate and then confirm and approve him so that the spiritual office also has its function in the process. A call which must be executed entirely free from any kind of minister of the Word who currently holds office is for Luther always an emergency call. Fundamentally, the ability to teach must be determined by those who themselves possess the teaching office. And for this reason, Luther again envisions in his treatise to the Bohemians [*Concerning the Ministry*] the call through the bishops occurring in the second phase.[216]

9. The Spiritual Significance of the Call for the Office-Bearer

The call, according to Luther, has a great spiritual significance for the bearer of the spiritual office, which becomes especially clear in tribulation. The minister of the Word must have the certainty that he is not prosecuting his own affair, but holding the office in the name of God and by His assignment.[217] However, no *vocatio interna* [internal call] can give him this certainty since that can become a casualty of his tribulation and so grow dubious or even be doubted in fact. A man may come to the pastoral office through an array of motivations, and no confidence can be placed in these inner processes which lead him to the office. What is required instead is a fact originating from outside himself and independent of his own inner being. This is answered by the *vocatio externa* or *mediata* [external or indirect call], which the man to be called has not personally devised, discerned, or asserted himself but which others have conferred on him, and in these others God Himself. The certainty of being actually called by

---

215 WA Br 7:302.2ff.

216 W. Elert has shown how it is precisely the necessity of the examination before the induction into the office and the assignment of this examination to those with right of visitation (namely, the pastors and bishops or—as in the treatise to the Bohemians [*Concerning the Ministry*]—the *majores* among them) which clarifies that in Luther there can be no question of the right to call being *fundamentally* restricted to the candidate's future parishioners (*Morphologie* I, p. 307; also cf. pp. 322f.).

217 WA 40/1:56.5ff.: "that everyone may be certain of his call, that he may boast before God and men that he preaches and is sent, as a legate of a king glories and boasts that he comes not as a private person but as one sent from the king"; cf. WA 40/1:56.21ff.

God is founded—today, when the direct call no longer occurs—on the *vocatio externa* through the church.[218]

The called minister of the Word, according to Luther, is to extol this call and celebrate it, that his authority may be recognized. In so doing he honors not himself, but God who sent him.[219] He is also to be mindful of his call continually so that he can hold his office with "faithfulness [*fiducia*]"[220] and have comfort in tribulation.[221] When he stands firm on it, the devil must depart from him.[222] "When a call is insisted on, the devil can be frightened."[223] Luther does not know how else the office is to be conducted "without a call [*sine vocatione*]."[224] For him, the call is the basis which makes the preaching office possible, not only objectively but also quite subjectively for the office-bearer himself. —

In the foregoing, we have treated the call to the preaching office in Luther's teaching and discussed its necessity as well as its proximal conditions in a general way. In so doing, we have focused on the overall process of the call to the office, but we have also encountered a division of that process into its individual actions.[225] The call as such is a complex process. Yet amid this whole process

---

218 WA TR 1:400.27f. (no. 827): "Both" (*vocatio immediata* and *mediata*) "are great and necessary for assuring the conscience"; WA TR 5:431.17ff. (no. 5998): "Either call is necessary for confirming the conscience. Let no one therefore attempt it unless he be called."

219 WA 40/1:56.9ff.; 40/1:57.1ff.: "It also behooves him to boast of this before the people, that he may assert his authority before the people, as an ambassador must boast of his legation, for there we do not boast of ourselves but of Him who sent us, whose authority we would have sacrosanct"; WA 40/1:63.6ff.: "You see, then, how necessary is the boasting of our ministry. . . . This boasting avails to the glory of God, to the honor of our ministry, and to the salvation of the people. We do not go around to be something in the world through boasting, as if to be considered great. Rather, it is because I am in a call and the people have a need; this is a most holy pride and a true humility which humbles itself before God against the devil"; WA 30/3:519.30ff. Also cf. K. H. Rengstorf, *Apostolat und Predigtamt*, 2nd ed. (Stuttgart, 1954), p. 46.

220 WA 40/1:56.21ff.

221 WA 40/1:56.11ff.: "He who is a preacher and pastor has the consolation that he is in a holy and heavenly office and can stand against all the gates of hell; but it is a fearful thing when the conscience says that he has done it without a call."

222 WA 22:187.7ff.: "Upon this office, work, and gift I can in faith boast and glory against the devil and his gates of hell, when otherwise I would be unable to stand against him one moment . . ."; WA 22:187.18ff.: "'What I do, I do by His command and His strength,' then he will have to depart from you at once; and he does not flee from your person or doing, but Christ's office and gift which he finds in you"; WA 28:471.22ff.; also WA 28:471.35ff.

223 WA 30/3:519.29f.

224 WA 40/1:62.12ff.; 17/1:509.11ff. — Most meaningful for Luther in the implementation of his reformatory works was his call as a doctor of Holy Scripture. He himself confesses: "I have often said, and say still, I would not take the riches of the world for my doctorate. For I would at last have to waver and despair in the great, heavy matter which lies upon me if I had begun as an interloper without call or command. But now God and all the world must bear witness that in my doctoral office and preaching office I have begun it and have brought it thus far, by God's grace and help" (WA 30/3:522.2ff.). Also cf. W. Walther, *Luthers Beruf*, Luther im neuesten römischen Gericht 3, Schriften d. Reformationsvereins 8.31 (Halle, 1890).

225 Cf. above, pp. 124–27, 133–34.

with its various components, one act in particular emerges in which the whole enterprise ultimately reaches its valid conclusion, and this is the act of *ordination*. It will not be possible accurately to judge the call as Luther sees it—particularly in his more mature view—without taking a closer look at this ordination act in its special significance and in its connection with the other acts of the call process. As the development of Luther's teaching leads from emphasizing the call over against the Enthusiasts to the establishment of the specific ordination in Wittenberg, so his doctrine of the call comes to focus more narrowly on the doctrine of ordination. It is therefore only logical that we begin to examine and delineate Luther's doctrine of ordination.

This also involves ordination in the narrow sense: the liturgical act in which the call is finalized. Luther's language with respect to ordination is not uniform. Frequently he uses the term "ordain" (*ordiniren*) or "consecrate" (*weihen*) for the collective call process as well, thus giving *pars pro toto* [part for the whole],[226] but then he also uses these terms strictly with an eye to the specific liturgical ordination act.[227] In the interest of clarity, let us observe that the following chapter deals with ordination only in the latter, specific sense. What Luther teaches regarding the specific liturgical ordination act will be of significant importance, particularly as this teaching is to be gathered from the more mature stage of the 1530s and 1540s. Thus it will be necessary for us to pay particular attention to it. —

[226] E.g., WA 15:721.3ff.; 38:221.1 ("ordain or call"); 38:221.6 and 25 ("call or ordain"); 38:236.17ff. and 30ff.; 50:247.18f. ("of the consecration and call"); 50:632.36 ("consecrates or calls").

[227] Evidence for this is sufficiently furnished by the following chapter. — G. Rietschel's assertion that Luther, by the terms "ordination" and "ordain," at least until 1535, was always thinking of the call in the most general way, not of a specific liturgical act (*Luther u. d. Ordination* [1889], pp. 49f., 52), is inaccurate, as will be demonstrated in the following chapter. Twenty years later (*Lehrbuch d. Lit.* II [1909], pp. 419f.), Rietschel himself says in passing that "the particular use of the name '*ordinatio, ordinieren*' for the liturgical ceremony was already common prior to 1535."

CHAPTER VI

The Meaning of Ordination

1. Luther's Stance toward the Roman Ordination

For Luther's concept of ordination, his position on the Roman ordination is of primary importance. This can be described as overwhelmingly negative. Why does Luther reject the Roman ordination?

Above all, one may refer to the *false intent for ordination*, which results in ordination having a false content. At the beginning of our study,[1] we showed how Luther fought the Roman consecration of priests since that is not an ordination to the preaching office, to the administration of Word and Sacrament, but a consecration to the sacrificial priesthood, which then concerns itself with private Masses.[2] Through this corruption of ordination's intent, the true *ordinatio* becomes a "false ordination of the devil [*inordinatio diaboli*]."[3] Luther

---

[1] Cf. above, pp. 9–12.

[2] WA 6:524ff.; 12:172ff.; esp. WA 6:564.20ff.: "Be certain, therefore, that he who is not an angel of the Lord of hosts, or is called to something other than being an angel, as I might say, is not a priest at all. . . . Wherefore those *who are ordained only to say the canonical Hours and offer Masses* may be papistic priests but not Christian priests since not only do they not preach, *they also are not called to preach*; indeed, this is done so that this kind of priesthood may have a different rank from that of the preaching office"; WA 12:173.6f.: "Papists . . . do not even dream of this ministry of mine" (i.e., of the Word) "in their ordinations"; WA 12:173.20ff.: "Say, I pray, that I am inventing a fiction or lying, if you could find one man ordained by these ordinations who would dare say that, during his ordination, he was commanded to dispense the mysteries of Christ, teach the Gospel, and govern the Church of God which He bought with His blood. Clearly no one ever hears this or thinks it belongs to him"; WA 12:173.39ff.: "After these things, the wrath of God turns these ridiculous masks of bishops so that not only do they mock the ministry of the Word and in its place ordain an office of sacrificing, but they also get rid of life-giving Baptism, by which living men and rational souls are sanctified for eternal life . . ."; WA 52:569.5ff. and 22ff. — With particular clarity, the disconnection of the Roman priestly consecration from its relation to the office of the Word is seen in the fact that preaching was thought to require a new, additional power, "another call beyond sacramental ordination" (WA 6:565.1f.; 38:220.18ff., 235.2ff.). "Indeed, it continues to be as strictly forbidden for him" (the consecrated priest) "after consecration as before to dare to undertake public preaching in the church and pastoral office without a further particular ordination and call" (WA 38:220.31ff.).

[3] WA 54:428.1f.: "The rite of ordaining Mass-priests—that is, crucifiers of Christ—is a false ordination of the devil [*inordinatio diaboli*]."

sees chrismation as a symbol of this false priestly consecration and attacks it furiously.[4] To him it embodies yet another false intent of ordination in the Roman consecration: it is only by this that a man is supposed to be made a priest, in the sense of a spiritual man, when in reality this has already happened in Baptism. The anointing with chrism in the priestly consecration then becomes the inverse of the anointing of the Holy Spirit in Baptism.[5] Thus Luther views the Roman priestly consecration as blasphemy since it casts aspersion on the Word and Baptism.[6] To this is added a third error in ordination's intent. The Roman priestly consecration lacked any relation not only to the preaching office but also specifically to the pastoral office since it was bestowed absolutely, and so without a specific call to a preaching station, a specified congregation, a parish. Luther's incisive polemic is also directed against this.[7]

On the basis of these distortions, Luther judges the Roman priestly consecration to be invalid and void.[8] By it, no one obtains the ability to do the works of the ecclesial office, to baptize, consecrate, or preach, since it is performed *sine verbo* [without the Word].[9] Nevertheless—and this deserves to be noted—Luther calls for no reordination of the one consecrated papistically[10] and adheres firmly to the idea that even under the papacy Christ had

---

[4] Cf. WA 38:198ff. Consecration and chrism, or even chrism and private Mass, are regarded as a unit by Luther. WA 38:220.34 ("consecration or chrism"); WA 38:205.32 ("private Mass and chrism"); WA 38:205.35 ("chrism and Mass").

[5] WA 38:228.6ff.: "These are the true, fine words and mighty workings of the devil with which the holiness and power of holy Baptism are diminished so that their spiritual chrismation of God, which is the Holy Spirit Himself, was made to be worthless compared to the physical and temporal chrism of the Papists invented by the imagination of man"; WA 38:230.24ff., 234.24ff.: "But that holy, stinking chrism had to be thus polished with lies and guileful looks, to the disgrace and dishonor of holy Baptism . . ."; cf. WA 41:155.20ff.; 50:631.15ff.; also WA 12:179.8ff.: ". . . They make no one a priest unless they first deny that he is a priest. And thus by their making a priest, they actually separate from the priesthood so that their ordination is actually a jest before God, and yet it is the truest and most serious degradation. For what does it mean to say, 'I am ordained a priest,' except to confess that I was not, am not yet, a priest?" — Also cf. above, pp. 23–29.

[6] WA 15:721.11f.: "He, therefore, who wishes to make a priest so that he should become a minister of the Word blasphemes God since he already is one."

[7] WA 12:172.27f.

[8] Cf. the relevant passages cited above, pp. 9–12.

[9] WA 12:174.25ff.: ". . . Let those who have been ordained up till now mourn that they have been thus deceived through masks of falsehood. For if ever they consecrated [the Sacrament] or performed the office of the ecclesial ministry, they certainly did so not by virtue of their holy ordination, which is utter falsehood and mockery of God, but by virtue of their faith and the Spirit of the Church which tolerated them in the place of this ministry and was forced to admit them"; WA 15:720.16ff.: "I was anointed by their custom, I did Mass, but in the same manner I would not willingly administer one sacrament or give a sermon. Now I confess before the world that I do not desire such to be here. Unless I hear the Word of Baptism and Word of God in those whom they have ordained, I do not think that they have ever consecrated the Sacrament. It is no *ordo* since it is done without the Word, nor may any be said to be ordained by virtue of this ordination. And if someone permits himself to be ordained in this way, a priest of God shall become a devil."

[10] WA 12:174.33ff.: "And he who comes to the place of ministry through these masks, come then—let him accept the ministry, and then administer it purely and worthily, forsake the office of

"continually maintained the office and the call to the preaching office among His saints," even if this latter is to be ascribed not to the performance of the papistic consecration but to the fact that, beyond the consecration, parishes had also been granted.[11]

Luther's negative stance toward the Roman priestly consecration is also especially exacerbated by the fact that in Rome it was purported to be a sacrament of the new covenant. If he attacks the Roman consecration with the accusation of perversion, he must properly begin by raising opposition to its being imbued with a sacramental character. Already in 1519 he had begun to doubt the sacramental character of the *ordo*, as he says in a letter to [Georg] Spalatin.[12] In 1520, he clearly acknowledged that the *sacramentum ordinis* [sacrament of ordination] is a human invention, a *figmentum ex hominibus natum* [fiction born of men].[13] This is corroborated for him by the fact that a sacrament of the new covenant calls for a divine institution and the promise of grace, neither of which is found in Holy Scripture for this sacrament.[14] Whatever is to be an article of faith must be founded on clear scriptural testimonies, "which we cannot demonstrate in the slightest in the present sacrament."[15] If this promise of grace is absent in Scripture, neither can the Church postulate one and so create a sacrament on its own since it is not *supra Deum* [above God].[16] In addition to the divine institution and promise of grace, this sacrament also lacks the external sign, as found in Baptism and the Supper. Because of all this, it is demonstrable to Luther that the *ordo* cannot be a sacrament in the same sense as Baptism and the Supper.[17] Indeed, giving the perverted Roman ordination the dignity of a sacrament is nothing other than mocking God.[18] This is then a matter not of a *sacramentum*, but—as Luther says derisively—of an "*execramentum* [accursed thing, execration]."[19]

---

sacrifice, teaching the Word of God and governing the church, and, moreover, condemn and detest with all his heart the anointing and the whole ordination by which he entered."

[11] WA 38:236.7ff.; also WA 38:221.18ff., 243.20ff.: In one consecrated in the papacy, the chrism is not to be regarded, "but let him see to it that he has possession of the pastoral office, which is not his but Christ's office."

[12] WA Br 1:595.32f.: "And we are fairly perplexed whence the *ordo* received the name of a sacrament. Is this not perplexing to you too?"

[13] WA 6:565.29f.

[14] WA 6:560.21ff.; cf. WA 54:428.3f.: "The *ordo* is not a sacrament. . . . It does not have the promise of the remission of sins."

[15] WA 6:560.29f.

[16] WA 6:561.19f., 563.7ff.

[17] WA 10/2:220.34ff.: "I have denied that the *ordo* is a sacrament, that is, a promise and attached sign of grace, as is Baptism and the Bread"; WA 6:560.20f.: "The Church of Christ does not know this sacrament, and it is invented by the church of the pope."

[18] Cf. WA 12:173.39ff., 174; also WA 12:172.35.

[19] WA 12:170.5.

2. The Positive Sense of the Canonical Rite of Ordination

On the basis of Luther's negative position toward the Roman ordination delineated above, one might get the impression that Luther would entirely reject traditional canonical ordination and declare it void and irrelevant, as if he were constructing his doctrine of the call to the office in exclusive opposition to the Roman ordination. This is how Georg Rietschel saw it,[20] and most of the more recent interpreters have followed him. Yet this impression depends on what the texts do not say. This view is false and must be abandoned. Luther does not reject canonical, traditional ordination as such, only the abuses attached to it in the papacy.[21] Luther knows and acknowledges a true use of the ordination rite at the root of the Roman priestly consecration dating back to the apostolic era, as demonstrated by the New Testament.

In the same writings in which Luther vehemently attacks the Roman distortion of the ordination, he also unearths the original positive sense of the apostolic and ancient Church's ordination. This happens, for instance, in the treatise *To the Christian Nobility of the German Nation* (1520). In all the polemic against the false claim that the consecration makes a priest, we find the emphasis of the authentic sense of the churchly ordination: "Therefore, the bishop's consecration is nothing other than when he . . . selects one from the flock . . . and charges him with exercising the same authority. . . ."[22] In ordination, a Christian is set apart from the whole flock and the office is committed to him. With keen vision Luther recognizes the essence of the ancient Church's ordination: the people selected their bishop, "who was then confirmed by other bishops without any pomp."[23] Ordination is a confirmation of a previously held election, documenting the latter as having been performed in a legitimate manner and therefore valid and binding. It is thus a selection of a person from the whole flock and a committal of the preaching office.[24]

Even in the treatise *The Babylonian Captivity of the Church* (1520), the tone of which is really set by its passionate polemic against the Roman distortion of ordination, Luther is still not inclined to condemn the Church's ordination rite practiced for so many centuries,[25] but he maintains its original definition as a "rite of electing a preacher in the Church [*ritus quidam eligendi concionatoris*

---

[20] *Luther und die Ordination* (1889), pp. 48ff.

[21] Also cf. Brunotte, op. cit., pp. 184f., who likewise stresses that Luther does not oppose the traditional ordination act per se, but only the specifically Roman view of it.

[22] WA 6:407.29ff.

[23] WA 6:408.6.

[24] If Luther envisions the emergency event of a flock of lay Christians electing one from their midst for the office and committing the office to him, he certainly does not imagine this committal of office (as the treatise to the Bohemians [*Concerning the Ministry*] in particular shows) without a special ordination rite in which some lay on their hands and pray over the electee.

[25] WA 6:560.24f.: "Not that I would judge condemnable that rite celebrated through so many ages."

in ecclesia]"[26] or a "rite of calling someone to the ministry of the Church [*ritus quidam vocandi alicujus in ministerium ecclesiasticum*]."[27] If *ordination* (here in the narrower sense of "ordination rite") is a rite of selecting a person, of calling a person, it is then conceived as the rite which effectively finalizes the call process as a whole. In it, the election, which must naturally be held beforehand, is given public representation and through it receives the validity and obligation which its general recognition confers.[28] As another positive sense of the Church's rite of ordination, Luther then goes on in this treatise to speak of the equipping of the person for the office.[29] Thus his concern in *The Babylonian Captivity of the Church* is by no means an absolute negation of the canonical rite of ordination! Two years later (1522), Luther says in his treatise *Against King Henry of England*, referring to his statements in *The Babylonian Captivity of the Church*: "I have denied that the *ordo* is a sacrament, that is, a promise and attached sign of grace, which Baptism and the Bread are. I have not denied—nay, I have asserted—the call and appointment of the minister and preacher. . . ."[30] This was for him the positive sense of the canonical rite of ordination: the calling and appointment of preachers. That Luther in *The Babylonian Captivity of the Church* does not aim at the *ordo* as such but only the Roman abuses of it is plainly deduced from the fact that he does not directly and categorically warn against receiving the Roman consecration but rather allows the possibility of receiving it, and then of using it correctly in Evangelical exercise of the office and a generally correct understanding.[31]

In his writings against Hieronymus Emser from 1521, Luther disputes the idea that consecration makes priests, arguing that that is already done through Baptism. While he thus takes *one* (namely, the false) component from the Roman ordination, yet he confirms another (namely, the true) element: "Thus consecration does not make priests, *but it makes* servants of priests."[32] "All of us, including the whole flock, are priests without the bishop's consecration. But *through the consecration we become* the servants, ministers, and officers of the other priests."[33] How is it possible for someone (with Rietschel) to miss the fact that, according to

---

[26] WA 6:564.16f.

[27] WA 6:566.30ff. Also cf. Brunotte, op. cit., p. 51.

[28] G. Niedemeier ("Das allg. Priestertum d. Gläubigen," in *Ztschr. f. syst. Theol.* [1930], p. 352), in connection to this passage, accurately calls ordination in Luther's thinking a "consummation of the call to a specific office of the Church accompanied by prayer and the laying on of hands." Also cf. C. A. G. v. Zezschwitz, *Systm d. Prakt. Theologie* II (Leipzig, 1876), pp. 310f.; and W. Diehl, "Zur Geschichte der Ordination: Halte was du hast," in *Ztschr. f. Pastoraltheol.* (Berlin, 1900), p. 594.

[29] WA 6:561.32f.: ". . . for certain offices they are prepared as vessels or instruments."

[30] WA 10/2:220.34ff.

[31] WA 6:566.10ff.: "Flee, therefore, by my counsel, whoever among you would live safely; flee, young men, and be not initiated into those sacred rites *unless* you are willing to preach the Gospel, or *unless* you can believe that you are not made superior to laymen by this sacrament of ordination."

[32] WA 7:633.12f.

[33] WA 7:633.16ff.

Luther's view, the rightly understood ordination makes a minister in the office?[34] Consecration is here conceived by Luther as appointment to the office.[35]

Yet in his writing to the Bohemians, *Concerning the Ministry* (1523), Luther penetrates more deeply. There, in the midst of the polemic against the Roman *ordo*, he formulates the concept of a *sacra ordinatio* and speaks of an institution of this ordination in Scripture: The ordination is instituted by the authority of the Scriptures, then by the example and decrees of the apostles, "that he should appoint ministers of the Word among the people."[36] From this results the demand: "The public ministry of the Word, I say, where the mysteries of God are dispensed, should be instituted through holy ordination."[37] Through this *sacra ordinatio*, the public preaching office is to be appointed, that is, filled with persons. This is its original sense intended by God, which Luther rediscovered under the rubble of papistic abuses and wishes to see brought to light. It does not consecrate to the sacrificial priesthood but appoints to the preaching office. When Luther then recommends to the Bohemians themselves a liturgical rite of confirmation with prayer and laying on of hands following the election, his intent is nothing other than the renewal and readoption of the original "procedure for calling and appointing a pastor of the Church [*ratio vocandi instituendique pastoris Ecclesiastici*]" attested in Scripture and approved by the example of the apostles and of their immediate disciples.[38] With his concrete suggestions for the shaping of a new ordination ceremony, Luther consciously draws on the original purpose of canonical ordination.

The next year, in 1524, Luther declares that the Roman bishops, with their consecration, are poorly imitating the apostolic example in Acts 13, but that it is still necessary to appoint priests and, what is more, that they should be prayed for *coram ecclesia* [before the church] and the preaching of the Word be conferred on them; for that was the method of "making priests [*formandi presbyteros*]" at that time.[39] Luther, viewing the consecration rite from Acts 13:1ff. as worthy of imitation and distinguishing his position utterly from the Roman abuse of consecration, holds firm to the idea (as the positive sense of Acts 13) that the appointment of priests should be done within the liturgical ordination rite with accompanying prayer and a committal of the office *coram ecclesia*. In a sermon also in the year 1524, Luther defines true ordination, over against the distorted papistic *ordo*, as

---

[34] Also cf. T. Kliefoth, *Lit. Abhandlungen* I (1854), p. 412.

[35] This is completely overlooked by G. Hök (op. cit., pp. 144f.) when he cites this passage to support the idea that the consecration in Luther has no bearing on the call to the office.

[36] WA 12:173.1f.

[37] WA 12:173.2ff. — Cf. Brunotte, op. cit., p. 81.

[38] WA 12:169.5; cf. WA 12:169.23ff.: "We seek a pure and genuine procedure prescribed by divine Scripture . . ."; WA 12:192.34ff.: "It is a new thing (they say), and without precedent, to elect and create bishops thus. I say: Rather, it is a most ancient thing, approved by the examples of the apostles and their disciples, though abolished and quenched by Papists with their contrary example and destructive teachings. Hence a greater effort must be made in order that you may expel the recent, diseased example and recall the original wholesome example."

[39] WA 17/1:511.3ff.

an appointment to the office. "To ordain is this": to set a suitable person apart and to confer on him the "authority to preach the Word and give the Sacraments."[40]

If we add to this, then, the great diatribe *The Private Mass and the Consecration of Priests* (1533), it becomes quite clear that Luther is waging a war against the papistic consecration of priests not because he rejects the *ordinatio canonica* but rather because he wishes to restore this to its original form. Chrismation represents for Luther—as we have seen—the perversion of the original ordination in the papacy. Luther of course knows that the fathers introduced the anointing, but he expressly points out that the fathers only meant to use it to "adorn and paint" the Christian pastoral office "as a distinction from others who are not called."[41] And it is in this that he sees the true, original character of consecration given: "For at its core, the consecration (to treat it properly) should not and cannot be different from a call or command of the pastoral office or preaching office."[42] Here Luther rightly defines the content of the ancient Church's ordination which had been corrupted in the Roman Church. In that ordination, the call to the preaching office is expressed and the command to exercise the office is assigned to one man—and in the process, the local call to a specific, concrete pastoral office is *pre*supposed.[43]

Accordingly, *G. Rietschel*[44] expressed the opinion that Luther, in this treatise *The Private Mass and the Consecration of Priests*, inserts "the ordination not into some ecclesial rite of consecration but into the call and command of the preaching office itself." Everyone who is elected regularly from the multitude of baptized Christians, who are priests, "already has the true consecration through this call" and needs no other special consecratory act in addition to it. "In place of the ordination of the Roman Church, Luther posits the rite of the proper call to the pastoral office as the true ordination."[45] How do these things relate? Before we go on and pursue the train of thought in the treatise *The Private Mass and the Consecration of Priests* from the standpoint of this question and examine the passages on which Rietschel particularly relies, we must note that Rietschel himself is forced to modify his account in the subsequent section of his study (on the basis of Luther's treatise *Concerning the Ministry*) by saying, "All this taken together (namely, the examination of fitness, election, confirmation with laying on of hands before the congregation, and prayer) is the *ordinatio* or true evangelical *ordo* according to Luther."[46] This is something entirely different. Saying,

---

[40] WA 15:721.3ff. — If in the same sermon Luther states that ordaining is not the same as consecrating, he means by this especially to negate the conferral of an intrinsic priestly quality, which he was sure was already given through Baptism, and to stress that the true ordination is the appointment of the preaching office. Also cf. V. Vajta, op. cit., p. 217.

[41] WA 38:228.19ff.; cf. WA 41:457.19.

[42] WA 38:228.27ff.; cf. WA 38:238.7f.: "'Ordaining' ought to mean and be the call and committal of the parish office"; cf. also the Latin translation by [Justus] Jonas: "The true sacrament of the *ordo*, true ordination, is the call to the pastoral curacy" (cited by Drews in his introduction to Luther's *Ordination of Ministers of the Word*, WA 38:401).

[43] Cf. WA 38:220.15ff., 222.25ff.

[44] Op. cit., p. 50.

[45] Ibid.

[46] Op. cit., p. 52.

"*Not* the liturgical act of consecration, *but rather* the election and call are the true ordination," is of course quite different from saying, "The election, call, *and* the liturgical, congregational act are together the true ordination." — If Rietschel had regarded the texts chronologically (first the treatise to the Bohemians, then the treatise *The Private Mass and the Consecration of Priests*), he would perhaps not have proposed the earlier model defining the ordination *in contrast* to the liturgical act of consecration. However, even from the treatise *The Private Mass and the Consecration of Priests* alone it must have been clear to him that Luther does not here form his concept of the true ordination in contrast to a liturgical act of consecration generally but only wishes to emphasize its true character as the act of the call to the preaching office, thus orienting himself solely in opposition to the corruption of the consecratory act in the Roman Church.

For the confirmation of this let us now turn to the line of reasoning in the treatise *The Private Mass and the Consecration of Priests*. Luther had established the true character of the consecration as the "call or command of the pastoral office or preaching office."[47] From this point of departure he continues: "The apostles, without chrismation, only laid their hands on and prayed over those whom they called to the office or sent. . . ."[48] Chrismation first came into use by the "dear fathers," certainly with good intentions, but eventually led to the true priestly consecration in Baptism being obscured. The true consecration as the call to the pastoral office or preaching office was performed among the apostles without chrismation—and perhaps therefore "not as a liturgical consecration act" (as Rietschel hopes)? By no means! The apostles, according to Luther, carried out the call and sending to the office without chrismation, yet with the laying on of hands and prayer, naturally *coram ecclesia*! Thus the apostolic consecration and call to the office to which Luther intentionally resorts involves a liturgical, congregational act with laying on of hands and prayer. Luther does not remotely oppose the liturgical consecration act as such, only its corruption in Rome by the false intent in consecration. The true consecration in Rome "no longer *remained* a consecration to the call or pastoral office" (as it was originally after the apostolic model) "but *became* a private consecration" (namely, in the historic process of distortion and perversion) "for ordaining private priests for the private Mass."[49] And this perversion of the true consecration in Rome correlates with the need for its reformation: "And if the papistic consecration were to work properly, it would do nothing but call these born priests to the pastoral office."[50] It may be noted here that Luther does not desire the elimination of consecration, but its proper use. It—the consecration ceremony—ought to call to the pastoral office and preaching office. Then it would be a true consecration; then it would be once more "the

[47] WA 38:228.28f.

[48] WA 38:228.29ff.

[49] WA 38:229.4ff.; cf. WA 38:230.32f. and 34f.; WA 38:234.30ff.: "But we have shown above how the chrismating bishops, with their consecration, do not call pastors or preachers, but only make nothing but sayers of private Masses."

[50] WA 38:230.21ff.; cf. WA 54:428.3f.: "The *ordo* is not a sacrament, but the ministry and the calling of ministers of the Church"; WA 54:437.1f.: ". . . a commandment, committal, and call to the office of the Christian Church."

fathers' consecration . . . for they consecrated pastors."[51] Thus this true, ancient, and apostolic use of consecration, tragically "abandoned"[52] in Rome, must be recovered. Through the false intent of ordination, "they in the papacy have left the call or the pastoral office or preaching office completely unattended . . . ,"[53] and thus the pope "distracted the ministry and the vocation, call, and true consecration to the preaching office or pastoral office through his shameful private chrismation."[54] Yet in the process, Christ "continually maintained the office and the call to the preaching office among His saints. For the pastors or preaching offices were always granted aside from and in addition to the chrismation, through princes, lords, and cities, and also conferred by bishops themselves, abbots, abbesses, and other estates, and by such conferments the call and the true consecration to the ministry or office continued."[55]

Here G. Rietschel finds confirmation of his view that the true consecration according to Luther is the call and the conferment of the parish, not the liturgical consecration act, and to support this brings the following passage to bear: "Besides this, such called pastors, which received these fiefs and offices, were also 'presented,' that is, directed to the private bishops and caused to be 'invested' or introduced, although this was not the call or fief but confirmation of this call and was not necessary. For the called pastor could also have performed his pastoral office without this confirmation. . . ."[56]

If we examine the passage more closely, we find, first, that the confirmation or investiture by the bishops—which, according to Luther, was not so absolutely necessary that a called pastor could not also perform his office without it—cannot be compared with the priestly consecration and thus the liturgical consecration act, but rather represents the ecclesial authority's confirmation of a parish conferment, an ecclesio-legal act.[57] In Rietschel's inclination to an ecclesio-legal interpretation of ordination, it is understandable that he does not keep this distinction in mind. What Luther thus says here of the confirmation of the call has no correspondence to the liturgical act of consecration to the office. Yet does Luther not say earlier that "the true consecration to the ministry or office" was left intact by the conferment of parishes (by all possible authorities) and, by saying so, distance the true consecration, thus true ordination, from the liturgical consecration act as such? No, this is only an apparent distancing, as shown by two noteworthy factors: (1) Luther knows very well that in the papistic church only those already consecrated could be appointed to parishes.[58] In the calls being issued in the papistic

---

[51] WA 38:230.33f.

[52] WA 38:230.35f.: The pope has ". . . forsaken the fathers' consecration and in its place set up his own consecration for sayers of private Masses."

[53] WA 38:234.35f.

[54] WA 38:236.5ff.

[55] WA 38:236.9ff.

[56] WA 38:236.13ff.

[57] Cf. WA 38:220.18ff.: ". . . not enough that he had been consecrated and received chrismation, but he had to be called or ordained anew, and be invested and introduced, in order to receive and assume such a pastoral office."

[58] WA 38:221.2ff., 243.18ff.

church of which he speaks here, the liturgical consecration act is assumed to have taken place already. (2) If the true consecration in the papistic church is "disturbed" by the chrismation—that is, the false intent for ordination—then the false aspect of the Roman consecration is necessarily corrected by the ensuing conferment of parishes, by which the focus on the preaching office again became apparent. Naturally, it was a very critical state of necessity when the consecration in its proper performance was overlaid with false elements so that the proper focus on the preaching office was not realized until afterward through the additional act of conferring a parish. Yet it was also sufficient that under all the perversion in the papacy, the true consecration to the preaching office remained intact. Certainly, then, it has to be purified, the false relation to the sacrifice of the Mass has to be eliminated, the call to the preaching office must once more determine the course of the consecration rite proper. Luther, however, does not wish to dispute the liturgical consecration rite's significance for the call to the office. When Luther goes on to say, "We will see how we obtain pastors and preachers from Baptism and God's Word without their chrismation, ordained and confirmed through our electing and calling,"[59] this electing and calling is in no way envisioned as separate from a liturgical consecration act with laying on of hands and prayer. This emerges quite clearly from the subsequent reference to the Roman recognition of the ordination of heretics, by which Luther claims the Romans, following their own rules, would have to recognize our Evangelical ordinations as valid, if they regard us as heretics also, which we are not. "Therefore, they should allow our consecrating and ordaining to be correct. . . ."[60] In saying this, Luther clearly knew that, according to canon law, what was recognized as valid was not those call ceremonies by heretics which designate a person to the office in a random, arbitrary form, but naturally only those which were observed with prayer and the laying on of hands by the bishop. If it is to be reasonable for Luther to demand the recognition of Lutheran ordinations on the basis of the aforesaid laws effective in the Roman Church, he can naturally have in mind only liturgical consecration rites with prayer and the laying on of hands, not random designations arising, as the case may be, in a purely bureaucratic manner through a city's councilmen in city hall. It is therefore clear that Luther uses the phrase "our consecrating and ordaining" to mean not simply any kind of election or call in an arbitrary form, but the call which is made in the liturgical consecration rite with prayer and the laying on of hands.

Now, as an accepted objection to his argument from the validity of ordaining heretics, Luther cites only the previously cited "even if they claim that heretics who consecrated were bishops. . . ."[61] Yet Luther knows how to counter this one by referring to the New Testament and the familiar passage of Jerome: "Bishop and pastor were one thing."[62] St. Augustine, for example, is supposed to have had a parish approximately no larger than that of the pastor of Wittenberg. "And the same little pastor or bishop St. Augustine consecrated and ordained many pastors

[59] WA 38:236.30ff.

[60] WA 38:237.4ff.; cf. WA 50:248.16ff.; 53:257.1ff.

[61] WA 38:237.19.

[62] WA 38:237.22f.

or bishops in his little parish . . . , who were requested and called by other cities, as we may ordain and send from our parish in Wittenberg to other cities which request them and have none. For ordaining ought to mean and be the call and commendation of the parish office. . . ."[63] The ordination performed by the pastor in Wittenberg is no different from the ordination performed by St. Augustine. Of course, this is the ordination performed with prayer and the laying on of hands and thus liturgical. According to Rietschel, Luther located the ordination proper not in the liturgical act but in the preceding election through the congregation. But here, contrary to this view of Rietschel's, the local call of the person is distinguished from the ordination act, which is carried out by the pastor (bishop) of the city on the basis of this local designation of the person, the latter action being termed "ordaining": The "ordaining and sending" to which we in our parish in Wittenberg have the power and right is precisely the liturgical consecration act with prayer and the laying on of hands, which confirms the local call, validates it, and represents the actual sending to the office.

For Rietschel, it is "indubitable" that in this passage Luther "by this 'ordaining' did not mean some kind of liturgical consecration rite of the Church"—indeed, such a churchly celebration is not once implied here in the word "ordaining."[64] It is "indubitable" for him because—as he thinks—these rites could not yet have been performed in Wittenberg in 1533; ordination was not properly introduced as a liturgical celebration until 1535. But Rietschel—quite apart from his disregard for the context of the passage—overlooks the fact that Luther says, "As we *may* ordain and send from our parish in Wittenberg. . . ."[65] This is, of course, not to say that such ordinations were actually performed in Wittenberg in 1533, only an assertion of the freedom and right for them to do so.[66] On the other hand, it is by no means a guarantee that scattered ordinations had not been performed for other congregations in Wittenberg.[67] Be that as it may, Rietschel could not but have

[63] WA 38:238.1ff.

[64] Op. cit., p. 56.

[65] WA 38:238.5ff. Drews also disregards this (WA 38:405).

[66] Also "our consecrating and ordaining" (WA 38:237.8) is essentially directed toward the receipt of regular ordinations in Wittenberg, then already considered established by Luther.

[67] Compare the dating, nevertheless possible, of the ordination certificates for Wenzeslaus Kilmann to the year 1529, proposed (contrary to his two printing templates, which both read "1539") by Enders (Enders 7:131f. Kawerau—*Theol. Stud. u. Krit.* [1899], p. 137—dates this certificate to 1536; cf. Drews, "Einleitung z. Ordinationsformular," WA 38:406), and the observations in Luther's sermon from May 21, 1531: "Likewise, when we ordain a pastor, since it is done in obedience to the church to which he is committed" (WA 34/1:437.16ff. [Rörer]); and: "So today, the Papists sit in the true office; they baptize, give the Sacrament, ordain priests, consecrate spouses, *even as we do*" (WA 34/1:432.5ff.). However, it will not be possible to view this passage as evidence for the *regularly* practiced ordination rites for other congregations in Wittenberg, which opinion we share with P. Drews (WA 38:404ff.) against G. Buchwald (WA 34/1:437 n. 2; 34/2:574). The latter opposes especially the passage in the sermon from May 9, 1535, which speaks of the solemn ordination rite as something yet to be instituted: "It is our intent, first, to ordain with a public service. You now have a German Baptism, Sacrament, preaching, and catechism and whatever belongs to a Christian. Although we retain the preaching office and call, nevertheless we also bring them into the German language . . ." (WA 41:240.33ff.). In this passage there also remains a certain possibility to interpret it in such a way that here Luther is only thinking of ordination *in the German language*,

noted in the parallel which Luther draws here to the ordinations of St. Augustine that it is precisely the liturgical celebration that Luther means here by the term "ordaining."

We believe that we have demonstrated that Luther, even in the treatise *The Private Mass and the Consecration of Priests*, did not use the term "ordaining"—as Rietschel supposed—in contrast to a liturgical consecration ceremony with prayer and laying on of hands, but rather directly in response to one which he interprets to mean the "call or commendation of the pastoral office or preaching office," as the sending to the office.[68] In addition, the treatise *The Private Mass and the Consecration of Priests* shows us that Luther does not reject canonical, traditional ordination outright as a liturgical consecration rite, but only wishes to see it purified from the abuses which crept into it in the papistic church.

Luther's reformatory work with respect to ordination was to bring it to light again in its original (apostolic and ancient) sense amid the Roman abuses. Here, too, he was not the *revolutionary who tears down what is before him*, but the reformer who takes what is original and genuine in what he encounters and frees it from its later depravation.[69] Yet it could not stop at the true *doctrine* of the ordination; it had to continue to the practical presentation of true Christian ordination. We must now describe the path which Luther takes in this respect. In the process, it is necessary first to examine Luther's advice to the Bohemians, and then above all the ordination rite itself which he instituted in Wittenberg.

3. The Ordination Act in *Concerning the Ministry*

Luther is fundamentally unwilling to reject or abolish ordination as a liturgical rite in which a call is issued to the office of the Word. This is demonstrated

---

and with a more solemn service, while ordinations in the Latin language and in simpler form than already in practice are assumed. Yet the subsequent text in this sermon creates difficulties for such an interpretation insofar as ordination is plainly discussed in a general sense there.

[68] V. Vajta has likewise detailed how Luther's critique of the Roman ordination was only directed against "the fact that this was not a call to the preaching office but a consecration to a particular estate which did not exist in the Church of Christ" (op. cit., p. 217), namely, to the estate of the sacrificial priesthood (cf. p. 218). Vajta also shows that for Luther "the actual ordination" "is the call to the preaching ministry accompanied by the laying on of hands and prayer" (p. 218). Against Drews, Vajta rightly declares: "It can in no way be thought that Luther . . . wished to renounce the ordination accompanied by prayer and laying on of hands as a liturgical act before the congregation. Ordination was not viewed by Luther as any sort of purely juridical act" (p. 218 n. 80). With these words, Vajta (implicitly) joined the position against Rietschel, who sought to pit the call against ordination in Luther. Vajta frequently says that ordination, according to Luther, is the "public call to the ecclesial office" (pp. 216ff.); thus he thinks that, according to Luther, the call is carried out publicly in liturgical ordination with prayer and the laying on of hands. In this we entirely agree with Vajta. Yet it would be preferable if Vajta had clearly expressed how his interpretation of the corresponding passages of Luther contradicts Rietschel.

[69] Cf. WA 41:458.36ff. (regarding the ordination rite instituted in Wittenberg:): "We have not instituted a new thing . . . but, like a good housemaid, gotten rid of the pope's rubbish and swept it out."

particularly by his suggesting to the Bohemians in 1523, in their particular state of necessity, that they not only elect suitable ministers but that they also then ordain them solemnly, with prayer and the laying on of hands in a subsequent liturgical act before the whole church. It is necessary—so he says in his treatise to the Bohemians [*Concerning the Ministry*]—"to convene an assembly and . . . elect suitable men, and to *commend* and *confirm* them to the whole church with prayer *and* the laying on of hands, and then to recognize and honor them as legitimate bishops and ministers of the Word";[70] and again: "After the election has been held, then, with hands laid on them by those who are prominent among you, *confirm* and *commend* them to the people and the church or the whole, and by this let them be your bishops, ministers, or pastors. Amen."[71]

The content of this liturgical ordination rite occurring after an election is expressed in the terms "commend" and "confirm" (*commendare* and *confirmare*). Both terms include a tacit reference to the election, yet also introduce something new in addition to the election. The confirmation via laying on of hands serves not only as public acknowledgment of the electee but also affirms that the preceding election of that person has been conducted rightly (Latin *ritè*) and definitively joins the commission of the office to the person of the electee;[72] the commendation act commends him to the *universitas* as a current office-bearer and shepherd.[73]

Distinctly inherent, therefore, in this liturgical act of confirmation and commendation is an intercongregational aspect relating to the Church as a whole. It is at least probable that Luther is also thinking of the collective Church of Bohemia when he refers to the "people and church or collective whole [*populus et ecclesia seu universitas*]" as the authoritative entities before which or for which confirmation and commendation of the electee occur.[74] Along the same lines, Luther's thoughts expressed in the following section point to the institution of an archbishopric of Bohemia both legitimate (i.e., corresponding to the traditional division of the Church into bishoprics) and Evangelical, in which inspection is conducted by the bishops or the archbishop chosen by the newly elected ministers from among themselves.[75] Quite apart from any congregationalist, individualist ideas, Luther unmistakably has in mind the context of the whole Church and vigorously pursues its regulated organization. In the first phase, the confirmation act during the call process is to be done, in the absence of true bishops,

---

[70] WA 12:191.22ff.

[71] WA 12:193.38ff.

[72] Luther also views the laying on of hands in Acts 13:3 as a confirmation of the election and call. After the Holy Spirit has chosen and called the parties concerned, they confirm this call (WA 17/1:511.4). — The aspect of the public nature of this ordination act is especially emphasized by Vajta (op. cit., pp. 216f.).

[73] The differences between *confirmare* and *commendare* have been stressed by G. Rietschel (op. cit., pp. 61f.). In the term *commendare* we are to see the commendation or committal to the congregation, but in the term *confirmare*, a kind of confirmation of the call by the Church as a whole.

[74] WA 12:193.39f.

[75] WA 12:194.14ff.

by the *potiores*, the most prominent in the congregation. Yet when Luther makes the provision that in the second phase *these* new office-bearers (= the elected men) should call further ministers to the office,[76] the result is that *these* (= the office-bearers) then naturally carry out the confirmation act also. In this case, however, they are from the neighboring congregations and thus embody the relationship to the whole Church. The similarity of the Bohemian ordination act pursuant to the canonically established ordination from the Council of Nicaea, Canon IV, is not lost on Luther. Luther's desire here is the same as what is later stressed so emphatically (at least with Luther's endorsement) in the memorandum *Ob in Erfurt die wahre Kirche Christi sei* [Whether Christ's true Church is in Erfurt]: that the neighboring pastors' approval of a local call is of great importance for the call process.[77] The confirmation act recommended by Luther to the Bohemians already has in it the tendency to become an ordination act with respect to the Church as a whole and in this way may also prove substantially significant in an ecclesio-legal context. Luther deems it necessary for the integrity and legality of the call. The confirmation act, too, is included under the word "to be necessary [*oportere*]," by which Luther makes the performance of the call process compulsory for the Bohemians.[78] "Then," says Luther, after the election *and* confirmation have occurred with prayer and laying on of hands, those who have been thus called are to be regarded as legitimate bishops and ministers of the Word and to be respected as such.[79] "By this," namely, the confirmation act with prayer and the laying on of hands, they are bishops, ministers, or pastors.[80] The liturgical act of confirmation in Luther's treatise to the Bohemians is plainly intended to be that in which the whole call process reaches its definitive conclusion and obtains universal public recognition by the Church as a whole.[81] It is the appointment into the office properly speaking.[82] In this confirmation act *coram ecclesia*, with prayer and the laying on of hands, we should see those parts which Luther was unwilling and unable to discard from the Roman consecration, the parts of the apostolic model which seemed to him absolutely essential for the call, and what was then given practical form by him in the newly instituted ordination in Wittenberg.

---

[76] WA 12:191.2: "And those then do so to others."

[77] Cf. Enders 11:40.21f., 42.96ff. (On the memorandum, cf. above, p. 134 n. 177.)

[78] WA 12:191.22. Cf. W. Elert, *Morphologie* I, p. 322.

[79] WA 12:191.24ff. ("and to acknowledge and esteem them *then* as legitimate bishops").

[80] WA 12:193.38ff.

[81] Cf. P. Brunner, "Vom Amt des Bischofs," p. 15.

[82] Cf. WA 17/1:511.5ff. (ordination as act of appointment); WA Br 5:700.13f. ("to ordain or to appoint ministers").

4. The Institution of the Ordination Rite in Wittenberg

In the first years after the Reformation, all the regions taken by it were still inhabited by pastors who had been consecrated under the papacy. With increasing urgency, however, the reformatory churches in all places faced the question of the new Evangelical form of the call to the office.[83] On May 23, 1524, Luther says in a sermon on Acts 13: ". . . *Again* priests must be appointed so that in the congregation prayers may be said for them and they may be commended to them to preach the Word of God."[84] Luther here has in mind the institution of a specific liturgical ordination rite of Evangelical character. Some months later, in a sermon from October 16, 1524, Luther is emphatic that every Christian who has received the Word of God is already fundamentally an heir and brother of Christ by faith and possesses all things, i.e., including, on the basis of the universal priesthood, all authority for the function of Word and Sacrament, and he continues on: "This is necessary for us to believe since priests are disappearing.[85] Those consecrated in the papacy acting as priests among us are dying off. The Roman bishops will not consecrate one of our people except he deny the Gospel. We must therefore ordain preachers soon, for which reason I want you to be certain that whoever is a Christian is Christ's brother, if he has His Word."[86] What is meant here by "ordain preachers" Luther explains with a distinction from the papistic consecration: "We will preach and anoint differently from those bishops. But we, who now have ministries, will commend to our ministry. . . . Therefore, if we know a godly man, we set him apart and, by virtue of the Word which we have, give him authority to preach the Word and give the Sacraments. This is ordaining."[87] Ordaining thus encompasses the election of a person ("we set him apart") and the transmission of authority to proclaim the Word and administer the Sacraments ("give him authority," etc.). That this transmission is envisioned by Luther in the way he described some months before in connection to Acts 13—namely, in a public ordination rite in the liturgy of the congregation—there is no doubt.[88]

On May 14, 1525, Magister Georg Rörer was inducted by Luther into his office as deacon of the parish church of Wittenberg during the liturgy before the congregation with prayer and the laying on of hands. This rite involves the public liturgical confirmation of a call to the preaching office. Rörer emphasizes his ordination itself in the preaching transcript of the pertinent Sunday.[89]

---

[83] Comparable to the subsequent account is the introduction to Luther's *Ordination of Ministers of the Word* by P. Drews in WA 38:401ff., though we cannot agree with it in every point.

[84] WA 17/1:511.5ff.

[85] WA 15:720.11f.

[86] WA 15:720.13ff.

[87] WA 15:721.1ff.

[88] Cf. P. Drews, WA 38:402.

[89] WA 16:226.6 (footnote); 17/1:243 (footnote). Also cf. [Johann] Aurifaber's observation in the supplement to *Luthers Schriften* (published 1564) in the overview of the events of the year 1525: "On

Yet no extant reports are preserved for us concerning further ordinations in Wittenberg in the years after 1525.[90]

Until the Diet of Augsburg (1530), the possibility was not yet excluded that the Roman bishops might call and ordain Evangelical preachers. After 1530, it was clear that this possibility was no more.[91] The lack of pastors was pressing. On December 16, 1530, Luther writes to the Roman priest Peter Hackenberg, who wished to join the Reformation but wondered whether he would be able to receive an office: "There is such a great lack everywhere of faithful pastors *that the time is near when we will be forced to ordain or appoint ministers* by our own rite, without tonsure, without chrismation, without fillet, without gloves, without staff, and without thurible, and, finally, without these bishops."[92] Luther views as imminent the fixed institution of a *proprius ritus ordinationis* [peculiar rite of ordination] without the Roman bishops. Such an ordination seems essential to him as a way to guarantee the orderly appointment of the preaching office.

The circumstances in Electoral Saxony and other territories around this time would have to be imagined as somewhat disorderly. Since 1528, at Luther's instigation even, visitations had been instituted by the provincial lords and superintendents appointed to provide oversight.[93] The superintendents also had the task of examining newly elected ministers of the Word for fitness, but had no authority for episcopal confirmation and no right to ordain. Ordination in many cases simply ceased. The call through the congregation or the authorities (magistrate, patron), who possessed the right to issue calls only locally, as well as the examination by the superintendents, would have been all that there was.[94] Yet this did not agree with Luther's intentions.

Cantate Sunday (of the year 1525), Dr. M. Luther reinstituted the ordination of preachers according to apostolic manner after the early service in Wittenberg and M. Georg Rörer was the first ordinand" (quoted from G. Rietschel, op. cit., p. 55). But against this it should be maintained with T. Kolde ("Zur Geschichte d. Ordination und Kirchenzucht," *Theol. Stud. u. Krit.* [1894], p. 241 n. 1) that Rörer himself construed this act at least as ordination in the medieval sense and that he "was attached by that act to the other clergy of Wittenberg with the same rights" (Kolde, ibid.); also cf. E. Hennecke, *Zur Gestaltung der Ordination m. besond. Rücksicht auf d. Entw. Innerh. d. luth. Kirche Hannovers*, Forschungen z. Gesch. Niedersachsens 1.1 (Hanover, 1906), p. 5.

[90] But cf. *inter alia* the ordination certificate of Wenzeslaus Kilmann, above, p. 153 n. 67.

[91] Cf. G. Rietschel, op. cit., p. 61.

[92] WA Br 5:700.12ff. Some months later (March 1, 1531), Luther writes to Johann Sutel: ". . . There is a great dearth of suitable men here, nor can I encourage them except by great force, so that even in this city we are starting to have a deficiency" (WA Br 6:43.7ff.).

[93] Cf. E. Sehling, *Die ev. Kirchenordnungen d. 16. Jahrhunderts*, vol. 1 (Leipzig, 1902), pp. 140ff., 149ff. And W. Elert, "Das Visitationsamt in der kirchlichen Neuordnung," *Jahrb. D. Martin Luther Bundes* (1948), pp. 66ff.

[94] G. Rietschel (op. cit., pp. 55ff. and 63; *Lehrbuch d. Liturgik* II [1909], pp. 420f.) accepted that even in this time in individual congregations there were liturgical acts of introduction with laying on of hands and prayer. Yet this is uncertain. Cf. T. Kolde, "Z. Gesch. d. Ord.," etc., op. cit., p. 233 n. 1, and especially P. Drews, "Die Ordination, Prüfung u. Lehrverpflichtung der Ordinanden in Wittenberg (1535)," *Dtsche. Ztschr. f. Kirchenrecht* 15 (Tübingen, 1905), pp. 66f.

In Göttingen, Johann Sutel was made a preacher at the church of St. Nicolai through the call only, without public liturgical ordination or prayer and the laying on of hands. He asked Luther whether he could administer the Holy Supper without priestly consecration. Luther answered his question in a letter dated March 1, 1531: He had received the impression that the people of Göttingen were not serious about the Gospel. If that were the case, he should continue to refrain from administering the Sacrament. But if the people of Göttingen were actually serious about the Gospel, he should first have himself publicly endued with the "testimony [*testimonium*]" (most likely of his ability to teach and of his call) and the "authority for handling the Supper [*auctoritas cenae tractandae*]" by the other ministers with prayer and the laying on of hands before the altar.[95] Luther thus regards the liturgical ordination as mandatory at least for the full office with administration of the Sacrament. This public ordination rite which Luther suggested to Sutel is a public attestation of the legitimate call and bestowal of the authority to administer the Sacrament, both performed by the other ministers of the Word.[96] This statement of Luther's is in line with what we have seen up till now in his writings. The liturgical ordination rite, in Luther's view, is the act by which the office of Word and Sacrament is actually delivered. The logical consequence of this suggestion to Johann Sutel would be the

[95] WA Br 6:44.15ff. ("... then publicly before the altar, by the other ministers with prayer and laying on of hands, you shall receive the testimony and authority to handle the Supper"). — Enders' interpretation of the passage (End. 8:368 n. 5), as if it were saying, "If no importance is placed on it, I would like you to keep it as before" (i.e., tonsure and chrismation); "but if it is thought important, you will do well to be given testimony by the other preachers with prayer and laying on of hands and be given the authorization to administer the Supper," is refuted by O. Clemen in the Weimar edition of Luther's works. Clemen points out (WA Br 6:44 n. 9) that "*serium*" in line 17 is to be explained by "*serio*" in line 15, and attention is to be given to the connecting particles "*quare*" and "*nam*." According to Clemen, the sense of the passage is: "This fact that the Göttingers are burdened when they are to pay the clergy a little more income is not what you call seeking the Gospel earnestly. Therefore, (since I have suspicions that the Göttingers are not serious about it), I cannot (definitively) answer your question whether you should distribute the Supper without priestly ordination. The answer must depend on whether the Göttingers are serious or not. In the latter case, I would wish that you would refrain, as before, from distributing the Supper, but in the former case you should. . . ." Clemen also points to WA Br 5:569.14ff.: "To the preacher of the prince may you give many salutations in my name. And you shall tell him by no means to attempt to give the Eucharist clandestinely since he is not a minister called for this work, lest occasion be given to our opponents, or . . . those who are outside [the church] be given cause to blaspheme"; and Enders 9:211.3ff. (= WA Br 6:338.2ff.): "I have advised a man, whenever he may be called as a preacher and there should be a danger on account of the administration of the Sacrament, he should abstain meanwhile, and let the pastor administer in his usual manner, and himself be content to teach." Clemen's interpretation is the accurate one. In order for Sutel to administer the Holy Supper, Luther, in his memorandum, calls for him to receive ordination with prayer and laying on of hands.

[96] In the memorandum *Ob in Erfurt die wahre Kirche Christi sei* [Whether Christ's true Church exists in Erfurt] (1536), the greatest emphasis is laid on the recognition of the called man made by the other pastors. The Erfurt preachers are legitimately called because the church desires them and the pastors of the surrounding cities have recognized them as true ministers (End. 11:42.96ff.: "[They] approve their doctrine and confirm them, as it were, with a certain laying on of hands"; End. 11:44.169ff.).

liturgical ordination of all those who were called but had not yet received consecration in the papacy.

Two years later, in 1533, in the treatise *The Private Mass and the Consecration of Priests*, Luther—as already shown[97]—speaks very distinctly of an ordination act in Wittenberg through which ministers of the Word are to be called and sent for other congregations. In the development of an organized Evangelical church structure, ordination, as a public confirmation from the collective Church, could not do without the local call for long. The examinations of elected men in Electoral Saxony had been promptly transferred from the superintendents to the electoral court.[98] It was only natural, then, that a public ordination rite expressing recognition of the collective Church also be instituted in Wittenberg, the ecclesial headquarters for all those responsible (Luther, the theological faculty, the prince). In his sermon from May 9, 1535, Luther says (as already referenced in the notes): "It is our intent first to ordain with a public service. . . . Although we retain the preaching office and call, nevertheless we also translate them into German."[99] Clearly he is contemplating the publication of a German ordination formulary to pave the way for a fixed ordination rite in Wittenberg. When it was no longer possible for preachers to be ordained by Roman bishops,[100] and the lack of pastors steadily increased,[101] instituting ordination was an unavoidable necessity. Luther derived the right to do so from the fact that "we are here the Christian Church and have all that belongs to the Church: Baptism, the Gospel, Sacraments, faith, the Lord's Prayer, the Ten Commandments, and the office too: We also are in the office. I have been called by you as a preacher.[102] . . . We . . . are in the office, and it has been committed to us to act in this way. Therefore, the Christian Church always has the right and call to do so" (i.e., to ordain).[103] Significant in this sermon is, first, the fact that Luther connects the necessity of calling true preachers with the necessity of ordination and, second, the fact that he bases the right to perform ordination also on the presence of the office, that is, properly called office-bearers being among us. Luther is at least increasingly absorbed in the ordination to be instituted, and it is hardly imaginable that he would not have also influenced the elector in this respect.

---

97 Cf. above, pp. 151–53.

98 The transfer of examinations to the electoral court was ordered already by the visitation articles of 1529 and 1533. Cf. G. Rietschel, op. cit., p. 62; P. Drews, "Die Ordination, Prüfung u. Lehrverpflichtung," etc., op. cit., pp. 82ff. From 1535 at least, the examinations of ordinands took place in Electoral Saxony before the theological faculty in Wittenberg. Cf. P. Drews, "Einleitung z. Ordinationsformular," WA 38:409.

99 WA 41:240.33ff.

100 WA 41:241.1ff.: "We made frequent and numerous offers to the bishops to have ourselves confirmed as pastors and preachers. . . . They refuse to do it."

101 WA 41:241.12ff.: ". . . The flock is increasing, and I am growing weak. Chaplains are asking to be excused from giving the Sacrament, visiting the sick. One after the other disappears."

102 WA 41:241.14ff.

103 WA 41:242.4ff.

Accordingly, on May 12, 1535, Elector John Frederick, by edict, ordered the visitors of Meissen and Vogtland to inform the superintendents that those who desired an office in the electorate without having received the episcopal consecration would henceforth be required to seek ordination in Wittenberg. The theological faculty received orders "to ordain and so to bestow the power and authority of their priestly and diaconal office."[104] According to the elector's edict, ordinations for other congregations would be accommodated in Wittenberg, in which local calls would be publicly confirmed with prayer and laying on of hands in a liturgical act before the collective Church, and thus the power to preach and administer the Sacrament would be definitively conferred. We have clear evidence that in the next months of the year 1535, at least before August, several ordinations took place in Wittenberg.[105]

Luther references the elector's edict in a sermon of October 20, 1535, which is unquestionably an ordination address.[106] In it, he argues that when pastors are lacking, new persons must be appointed to the office. "If there is no institution, there is no Gospel. No matter who may die, the ministry remains, for it is God's alone, as long as the Church exists. . . . Pastor after pastor dies, but the office remains. Since this is so, we may appoint others in their stead."[107] That Luther here has in mind the ordination appointed by the elector follows from the fact that he mentions that the Papists, in ordination, confer a chalice, shear the head, and chrismate the hands; and then he goes on: "Not we. . . . We willingly give the office, but we appoint one thing to this office, which is the former way: we only accept the person, which is to be a laborer."[108] Luther discusses ordination, and this is the bestowal of the office, appointment to the office, acceptance of a person into the office founded by Christ. It is performed without chrismation so as to avoid suggesting that the person becomes a priest through ordination. "This is by way of a preface since we are about to ordain someone for another

---

104 The edict is found in print in P. Drews, "Die Ordination, Prüfung, u. Lehrverpflichtung," etc., op. cit., pp. 288f. Also cf. Drews, "Einleitung z. Ordinationsformular," WA 38:407, and E. Wolf, "Zur Neuordnung der Ordination," *Ev. Theol.* 4 (1937), p. 377.

105 In the *Corpus Reformatorum*, there is a record of examination for a certain Hieronymus Hirscheyder dated August 14, 1535, which was presented by the rector of the University of Wittenberg (then in Jena because of the plague). In it, a statement of Melanchthon's (who himself was forced to depart hastily) is quoted in connection with the ordination of this Hieronymus Hirscheyder. There it reads: "And because he sought to be ordained by us, as they call it, since the bishops do not allow our men to teach, and yet it is necessary for order in the Church to retain this rite, we have followed Philip Melanchthon's opinion, who thought that the same thing could more conveniently be done in Wittenberg which by the will of our most illustrious prince was done in this place so often before" (CR 2:901f.). On this cf. P. Drews, "Die Ordination," etc., op. cit., pp. 78ff.

106 WA 41:454–59. In the introduction to the sermons of the year 1535, WA 41:xxix, it reads: "This sermon was held on the occasion of the ordination of a preacher N., called and elected by the congregation in Gotha."

107 WA 41:456.37f., 457.1ff.

108 WA 41:457.9ff.; cf. WA 47:192.6ff.: "Thus we are sent, and we elect others also and set them into the office so that they may preach and give the Sacraments."

church."[109] With this statement Luther characterizes the new ordination rite presently instituted in Wittenberg. Magister Georg Rörer had already been ordained in 1525, but for the Wittenberg city church. Here, the ordination is now carried out *for other congregations too.* "Previously we did not do it, lest the Papists [. . .] and in your presence, that you might be witnesses."[110] These separate fragments recorded by Rörer might be arranged so as to say: Previously we did not ordain before other congregations since we were still waiting to see whether the Roman bishops would confirm our preachers. But since this has proved hopeless, we do it now—and, indeed, before the church, which has the office of bearing witness in this process. The prince has ordered[111] that priests are to be consecrated nowhere *nobis ignorantibus* [without our knowledge].[112] To avoid disorder and the deception of congregations with false doctrine,[113] all those receiving calls are to be sent to Wittenberg, examined there, and then ordained. Then Luther calls on the congregation, which accompanies the ordination as a witness, to pray for the ordinand and all office-bearers[114] and concludes the sermon with the statement: "We therefore confer the office on this man, who has been sent hither by command of the prince."[115] The ordination act is for him the conferral of the office on a person who has been called. Thus the ordinand has not yet received the office by his local call; only through ordination is the whole call process brought to its final conclusion and the office actually conferred.

In another Latin version of the same sermon (WA 41:762f.; also cf. below, p. 165) it reads: "Our elector has ordained necessarily that learned and pious men be here elected and ordained minsters of the Word of God, and no one stand up and teach without our knowledge. Therefore, he desires and has decreed that from all dioceses of Franconia, Meissen, etc., they should be sent to us and examined and confirmed, and sent wherever they are to be sent. You are to be witnesses of that public rite, to pray most fervently to God that He would give us godly and true preachers of His Word. . . . Therefore, esteemed brothers, pray for that great ministry of the Gospel" (WA 41:762.20ff., 763.1ff.). In this version, the ecclesio-governmental aspect of the newly instituted ordination rite

---

[109] WA 41:457.33f. It is from these words, incidentally, that it becomes clear that we are dealing with an ordination address.

[110] WA 41:457.34f.

[111] "The prince may appoint it because he, as ruler, has the office of governing, with which he must serve the Church. He exercises the church government's episcopal functions according to legal provisions for emergencies since the lawful bishops renounce it" (also cf. pp. 135–37). The prince in this case is to be regarded as "emergency bishop." The expression "emergency bishop" (*Notbischof*) is encountered in the following passages: WA Br 8:395.15ff., 396.14; 53:255.5; WA TR 4:378.25f.; also cf. W. Walther, *Das Erbe d. Ref.* IV, *Luthers Kirche* (1917), pp. 122f., who nevertheless only cites two passages.

[112] WA 41:457.37f.

[113] WA 41:458.1ff.

[114] WA 41:458.9ff. In individual phrases of this request for the congregation to pray, there is an echo of the wording in *Ordination of Ministers of the Word.*

[115] WA 41:459.10f.

is particularly emphasized. The prince, through the theological faculty, exercises the ecclesio-governmental office of inspection in examination and ordination of electees. Ordination is the ecclesio-governmental episcopal confirmation of the call before the collective Church on the basis of the examinations passed, as well as the sending to the office,[116] the transmission of this office.[117]

Much in this sermon lends credibility to the assumption of G. Buchwald ("Wann hat Luther die erste Ordination vollzogen?" *Theol. Stud. u. Krit.* [1896], pp. 151ff.) that the ordination for which this address is given represents the first ordination performed in Wittenberg for another congregation. Yet such an assumption can only be held if the ordinations referred to by the examination testimony of August 14, 1535, in CR 2:901f., are viewed as such for their own city of Wittenberg, which is highly improbable.

Four days later, on October 24, 1535, Luther writes to Friedrich Myconius in Gotha (apparently in regard to the ordination performed on October 20): "We are sending back to you your John, called and elected by you and also examined by us and ordained and confirmed for your ministry publicly before our church among prayers and praises of God, in accordance with the command of our prince,"[118] and adds an observation from which it appears that [Johann] Bugenhagen was not in agreement with the new Wittenberg ordination: ". . . Although D. Pomeranus was not very agreeable to this, as he still thinks that anyone in his church should be ordained by his priests."[119] Bugenhagen wanted

---

116 Cf. WA TR 5:111.24f.

117 Cf. in the decree: ". . . to give the power and authority of their priestly and diaconal office" (WA 38:407). — The ecclesio-governmental aspect of the ordination instituted in Wittenberg has been stressed (rather one-sidedly) particularly by Rietschel (op. cit., pp. 61ff.).

118 WA Br 7:302.2ff.

119 WA Br 7:302.6ff. — From a sermon of Bugenhagen's dated April 23, 1525, it seems that he was critical of establishing a liturgical ordination with the laying on of hands as the confirmation of a call. There it reads: "I could do it" (i.e., laying on of hands), "but since various fanatical ideas would result, I do not wish to. Whoever is elected by the church and accepted is ordained" (G. Buchwald, *Ungedruckte Predigten Bugenhagens aus den Jahren 1524–1529* [Leipzig, 1910], pp. 217.31ff.; cited from Drews, "Einleitung z. Ordinationsformular," WA 38:403). This stance accounts for the fact that Bugenhagen, in his Braunschweig church order (1528), appoints no liturgical rite for confirming the call (cf. E. Sehling, *Die ev. Kirchenordnungen des 16. Jahrhunderts*, vol. VI.1 [Tübingen, 1955], pp. 348ff.). Not until the later church orders for Hamburg (Sehling V, pp. 502ff.), Lübeck 1531 (Sehling V, pp. 350 or 502ff.), and Pomerania 1535 (Sehling IV, pp. 328ff.) does he incorporate an ordinationlike rite of introduction to the respective congregation. The Pomeranian church order of 1535 (concluded in December 1534, at the provincial diet of Treptow, issued in print by Bugenhagen in 1535; cf. Sehling IV, pp. 305f.) is of particular importance in the sense that here the act of an episcopal confirmation of the call is separated from the introduction to the congregation with prayer and the laying on of hands. Bugenhagen arranges the call process in this church order as follows: The candidate is examined, whereupon the congregation, or whoever has right of patronage, takes him and presents him to the bishop; the bishop charges him with his duties and sends him back to the congregation. Then the one thus confirmed is received by other clergy and committed to the church in the liturgy before the congregation. During this rite, not only clergy but also "some of the congregation" are to lay hands on him (Sehling IV, p. 332). G. Rietschel opined that Bugenhagen's dissolution of the element of the episcopal ecclesio-governmental confirmation from the investiture in the congregation should be regarded as the starting point for the development of

every ordination to be done in the respective congregation from which the person had been called. Luther remarks: "That will happen eventually, should this new affair and ordination take deeper root and the usage become more firmly entrenched."[120] Luther, at any rate, thinks it well for the ordination at first to be firmly planted in Wittenberg as the center of the Church, and later to consider permitting it to happen in the congregations. However, things progressed in such a way that no return to the issue was ventured.[121]

From all these testimonies it is clear that Luther fully endorsed the ordination mandated by the elector and that it reflected his own intentions.[122] From the ordination records subscribed to by Luther—as well as from the treatise *The Private Mass and the Consecration of Priests* (1533)[123]—it may also be noted that Luther sees the establishment of an ordination for other congregations occurring at an ecclesial headquarters as supported by medieval canonical practice as well. He makes repeated reference in this regard to the decree of the Council of Nicaea, using it to justify the Wittenberg ordination rite.[124] It also confirms that the ordination newly established in Wittenberg was in no way forced upon Luther but was actively pursued by him. From a report by the papal nuncio Vergerius on the discussion which he had with Luther and Bugenhagen on November 7, 1535, it is clear that ordination was being practiced in Wittenberg in November 1535.[125] Yet it is surprising to see that the Wittenberg registry of

---

the Evangelical ordination then introduced in Wittenberg (op. cit., pp. 60 and 63ff.; *Lehrb. d. Lit.* II, p. 422). And P. Drews says, "When the act of that ecclesio-governmental confirmation and committal of the office was carried out in liturgical form, the Evangelical ordination was . . . complete" ("Einleitung z. Ord.form.," WA 38:406). Yet it should not be assumed that Luther was inspired by this notion of Bugenhagen's to set up an ordination rite in Wittenberg. It is readily gathered from Luther's letter to Myconius that Luther was in disagreement with Bugenhagen regarding the ordination in Wittenberg. Furthermore, we have shown how the ordination rite instituted in Wittenberg is based distinctly on Luther's concept of the call of true preachers. Luther was the actual driving force in the establishment of the Wittenberg ordination; Bugenhagen was only gradually (at first quite reluctantly) brought by Luther's influence to go along with the ordination in Wittenberg, and then (especially after 1539) even to ordain.

120 WA Br 7:302.8ff.

121 Cf. G. Buchwald, "Wann hat Luther," etc., op. cit., p. 156.

122 F. Rendtorff's opinion ("Luthers 'ungefährliche' Kirchenbräuche," in *Studien z. Reformationsgesch. und z. Prakt. Theol.*, festschrift for Kawerau [Leipzig, 1917], pp. 153f.) is thus inaccurate when he claims that Luther only affirmed ordination reluctantly against his own convictions, as is P. Drews' claim (WA 38:408) that ordination before 1535 did not figure into Luther's thinking about [the ministry]. The texts show the opposite.

123 Cf. WA 38:238.1ff.

124 Cf. Enders 7:131.22ff.: "And the Council of Nicaea has piously and very wisely decreed that neighboring churches should seek ordination from neighbors"; End. 11:227.22ff.; 7:132.28ff.: "Therefore, by divine authority and the testimony of the Council of Nicaea, it is certain that our ordination is valid"; cf. End. 12:197.12ff.; 16:275.19ff. (= WA Br 11:156.15ff.); 18:52.13ff.

125 According to Rietschel, op. cit., pp. 68f. — When Luther then after the report says to the papal legate concerning the ordination in Wittenberg: "We are compelled to do thus" (namely, to account for the circumstances, to care for our souls, and to give the authority of ordination to one from the theological faculty with the approval of many good men, that he may administer this office in the stead of the bishop), this may not be taken to mean that Luther viewed the adoption of

ordinands does not begin until July 29, 1537.[126] Rietschel suspected that, because of Bugenhagen's resistance in the years 1535–37, ordination in Wittenberg was not carried out fully, but only in a tentative manner, especially since Bugenhagen had been designated an ordaining minister by the theological faculty. And only after Bugenhagen traveled to Denmark in July 1537 did Luther make ordination fully operational in Wittenberg. This would explain why the record of ordinands begins in July 1537.[127] There is a great deal of probability in this proposal, yet it is also firmly established that ordinations were already being performed for other congregations in Wittenberg from 1535 on.[128]

5. Luther's *Ordination of Ministers of the Word* [*Ordinationsformular*]

In early January 1537, Spalatin sent Melanchthon a note (written in Spalatin's hand) with a memorandum to the effect that—should the bishops continue to persecute the Gospel—"it is of utmost necessity to prepare the ordination. For all informed Christians are aware that no one is to teach publicly without a call, for which reason special and sizable importance is placed on such a call."[129] This document gives the impression that in early January 1537 the true form of ordination in Wittenberg had not yet been given clear articulation. In light of the elector's edict of May 12, 1535, this can refer only to the liturgical form of ordination in the agenda and the other finer points thereof. From this document as well as from the fact that, according to evidence from the Wittenberg ordination record from July 1537, ordination had been implemented consistently in keeping with the church order, G. Rietschel deduces that the appearance of Luther's *Ordination of Ministers of the Word* is to be placed in

the ordination rite in Wittenberg only "as a compromise with human frailty" (Drews, "Einleitung," WA 38:408f.), as though he would really have preferred to dispense with it. Rather, the meaning of "[we are] compelled"—as clearly gathered from the report of the legate—is that Luther and his fellows in office were compelled to conduct ordination themselves so long as the Roman bishops refused to do so. The remark "we are compelled to do thus" is not an expression of an underlying indifference with respect to ordination, but precisely the opposite: the conviction of the necessity of ordination, which must be performed by pastors instead of bishops only because of the dire necessity. If ordination were regarded as unnecessary for the appointment of the office, it is difficult to see why one should then be compelled to conduct the ordination on his own initiative. If that were the case, it could simply be omitted.

126 The earliest ordination certificate signed by Luther and handed down to us is from June 11, 1536: Enders 17:356ff. And the ordination certificate for Jakob Siegel, dated October 7, 1537 (which Rietschel regards as the earliest: op. cit., p. 72), reads concerning the *publica ordinatio*: "which is accustomed to be done in our church . . ." (End. 11:278.4).

127 Rietschel, op. cit., pp. 71f.

128 Cf. the evidence already cited.

129 CR 3:235 and 236. On this document cf. P. Drews, "Die Ordination, Prüfung," etc., op. cit., pp. 73ff.

the first half of 1537.[130] Yet it has been shown by Drews that the earliest copy of *Ordination of Ministers of the Word* originates with reasonable certainty in the year 1535. The copy of *Ordination of Ministers of the Word* found in the municipal library of Hamburg is prefaced with an excerpt of an ordination address,[131] and its close similarity to an ordination sermon given by Luther on October 20, 1535,[132] particularly in its conclusion, has been convincingly demonstrated by Drews.[133] It likely represents a digest of this sermon. The *Ordination of Ministers of the Word* immediately following this is itself characterized in its first sentence as being written at the same time as the preceding address. From this it appears that *Ordination of Ministers of the Word*, so closely linked to this address in excerpted form, is very probably from the year 1535 as well. We have already seen that as early as May 1535, and thus before the elector's edict, Luther was contemplating translating the ordination rite "into German,"[134] and thus publishing a German ordination formulary. It is very possible and probable that the reformer immediately embarked upon this plan, and in this way *Ordination of Ministers of the Word* appeared, so that what we have in the Hamburg copy (marked "H" in the WA) is the original form. Spalatin's note from January 1537 can then be understood to mean only that this *Ordination of Ministers of the Word* of Luther's was not fully implemented and in steady use until early 1537, perhaps because of Bugenhagen's resistance.

Agreeing in large part with the Hamburg exemplar of *Ordination of Ministers of the Word*, save for a few phrases, is the exemplar found by Rietschel in the Jena university library, in the collection derived from the Rörer estate (marked "J" in the WA), which Rietschel regarded as the earliest.[135] Differences nevertheless exist between the two copies, and Drews used these to demonstrate that the Hamburg exemplar is earlier.[136] The Jena copy would be regarded as the second earliest.

The copy of *Ordination of Ministers of the Word* which Melanchthon gave to two preachers of Culmbach as coming from Luther is dated to the year 1538 (marked "C" in the WA).[137] This in turn agrees almost exactly with another copy found in the city archive of Freiberg (Saxony) and also dated to 1538[138] (marked "F" in the WA). Finally, we may mention the leatherbound personal copy

[130] Op. cit., p. 74.

[131] Reproduced in WA 41:762f.

[132] WA 41:454–59.

[133] WA 38:412ff. Also cf. P. Drews, *Dtsche. Ztschr. f. Kirchenrecht* 15 (Tübingen, 1905), pp. 291ff., where this copy of *Ordination of Ministers of the Word* was printed for the first time.

[134] Cf. above, p. 160.

[135] G. Rietschel, "Luthers Ordinationsformular in seiner ursprünglichen Gestalt," *Theol. Stud. u. Krit.* (1895), pp. 168ff.; E. Sehling, *Kirchenordnungen*, vol. I (Leipzig, 1902), p. 25.

[136] "Einl. z. Ord.form.," WA 38:414f.

[137] Cf. T. Kolde, "Z. Gesch. d. Ord. u. d. Kirchenzucht," *Theol. Stud. u. Krit.* (1894), pp. 217ff., where this version is published for the first time.

[138] Cf. E. Sehling, *Kirchenordnungen* I, p. 459.

located by Rietschel in the parish archive of Wittenberg, which comes from the year 1539 and shows a few corrections, probably originating with Bugenhagen.[139]

That the text of *Ordination of Ministers of the Word* is from Luther himself can be regarded as certain.[140] In several church orders it is printed with the title "Form of Ordination Appointed by the Reverend Dr. Martin Luther."[141] Even Bugenhagen incorporated this *Ordination of Ministers of the Word* of Luther's into his later church orders.[142] Yet it cannot be determined with complete certainty which edition retained the original Lutheran conception with greatest purity. Presumably, this would be true of the earliest edition (H). But it is clear that the formulary underwent a development process characterized by Luther's own hand or by Bugenhagen's hand with Luther's consent.[143]

For foreign students incapable of understanding the German, Luther also produced a Latin edition of *Ordination of Ministers of the Word*, which is not so much a literal translation of the German exemplar as a free reproduction. In the formulation of the specific ordination prayer spoken during the laying on of hands, it has significant enlargement in comparison to the German text, describing the ordination rite as a *confirmatio vocationis* [confirmation of the call].[144]

Ordination of Ministers of the Word includes *seven rubrics* regulating the procedure of the ordination rite.[145] It assumes that the examination of the candidates has been conducted with success (*examinatione facta*).[146] The first rubric specifies that the congregation (after the sermon) is to pray for the ordinands and all ministers of the Word, that the Lord would send laborers into His harvest and preserve them in the sound doctrine. (In H, a reference is added to the necessity of the office, which is given and preserved only by God.) The ordination rite proper begins with the second rubric. The ordaining minister,

---

139 Cf. G. Rietschel, *Luther u. d. Ordination*, pp. 12ff.; "Luthers Ordinationsformular in seiner urspr. Gestalt," op. cit., pp. 168ff.; and T. Kolde, "Z. Gesch. d. Ord.," etc., op. cit., pp. 236ff.; P. Drews, "Einl. z. Ord.form.," WA 38:420.

140 Cf. Drews, "Einl.," WA 38:410: "That Luther proposed the *Ordination of Ministers of the Word* himself cannot be doubted."

141 So esp. the Mecklenburg church order of 1552 (E. Sehling, *Kirchenord.* V, pp. 161ff., 193), which was personally edited by Melanchthon. Thus Melanchthon, at least, is convinced of Luther's authorship. Of course, he also sent that *Ordination of Ministers of the Word* to the Culmbach preachers as the one originating with Luther.

142 So the Braunschweig-Wolfenbüttel church order of 1543 and in the Hildesheim order of 1544 (E. Sehling, *Kirchenord.* vol. VI [Göttingen, 1955], pp. 188f. and 535ff.).

143 Cf. Drews, "Einl.," WA 38:410.

144 E. Sehling, *Kirchenord.* I, p. 28; Drews, "Einl.," WA 38:421.

145 The text with critical apparatus is in WA 38:423–31.

146 On the examination of ordinands and the doctrinal vow likely attached to it, cf. P. Drews, "Die Ordination, Prüfung u. Lehrverpflichtung d. Ordinanden i. Wittenberg 1535," op. cit., pp. 82ff. and 273ff. — In the ordination certificates it is always made clear that orthodoxy was established before the ordination: e.g., End. 11:227.16ff.: "We have determined that he understands the sum of Christian doctrine rightly, and embraces the pure and catholic understanding of the Gospel which our Church professes, and abhors all the fanatical opinions condemned by the judgment of the catholic Church of Christ"; End. 11:278.9ff.

the whole presbytery (the other ministers of the city), and the ordinands kneel before the altar to pray for the Holy Spirit. The choir sings "Veni sancte Spiritus" ["Come, Holy Spirit"]. This is followed by a Versicle (*Cor mundum crea in me Deus* [Create in me a clean heart, O God]) and the Collect for the Holy Spirit. Third, lessons from Scripture are read by the ordaining priest from the altar (in H, a longer prologue is added in which the importance of Baptism and the call for the office are emphasized and the duties of the office are detailed), these being 1 Tim. 3:1–7 and Acts 20:28–31. Fourth, the ordaining minister adds an exhortation to the ordinands to remember that they are appointed to feed the congregation of God, to defend them with the pure Word of God against wolves and sects, and to lead an exemplary life themselves. This address culminates in the appended question: "Are you prepared to do so?" to which the ordinands are to respond with a simple "Yes."[147] Integrated into the question in F is a reference to the legitimacy of the ordaining minister ("by the command of the Church through our office") and to the work of the ordaining minister subsequent to the question ("to ordain and confirm . . ."). In the fifth rubric, there follows the laying on of hands on the ordinands[148] by the ordaining minister and the

[147] Implicit in this pledge is the vow of pure doctrine. An express doctrinal vow, however, did apparently occur at the conclusion of the theological examination before ordination. The ordination certificates mention not only the assessment and determination of orthodox belief before ordination but also a specific pledge to cling firmly to the pure doctrine which is confessed by the ordaining ministers and—as the examination has confirmed—is also the confession of the ordinand: cf. End. 7:131.13ff.: "He was asked to show that he will be diligent and constant in teaching, and in good faith pass on without corruption the doctrine which our Church professes"; End. 11:227.20ff. and 11:278.16ff.: "He promised that he would pass on purely and defend that doctrine of Christ's catholic Church which we profess"; End. 14:252.8ff., 286.15ff.; 15:87.8ff., 142.14ff. (= WA Br 10:297.11f.); 16:63.11ff. (= WA Br 10:621.9f.); 18:32.12ff., 52.11ff. — A doctrinal vow regarding specific, enumerated symbols—i.e., the three ancient symbols and the AC—which according to CR 12:6 was incorporated in Wittenberg from around 1533, probably had its place in the doctoral promotions (cf. the Wittenberg doctoral oath according to the statutes of the theological faculty issued in 1533). On this cf. G. Rietschel, op. cit., pp. 82f.; P. Drews, "Die Ordination, Prüfung u. Lehrverpflichtung," op. cit., pp. 273ff.; O. Ritschl, *Dogmengeschichte des Protestantismus*, vol. 1, pp. 212ff. and 240ff. An *ordination* vow regarding specific confessions appears not to have been instituted until later. Note, however, W. Elert's finding (*Morphologie* 1, p. 307): "While *Melanchthon* also could have had a substantial share in the ordination vow of confessional subscription which appeared in the meantime, the requirement of a doctrinal vow is still a natural application of Luther's doctrine of the church. It makes the connection between the Evangelical approach and his doctrine of the office and congregation."

[148] Evidently, the laying on of hands was suspect to the preaching friars in Onolzbach, who prepared an opinion on the report of the two Culmbach preachers concerning their consultation with Luther and Melanchthon on ordination and other matters. They write, namely, that they are not opposed to the Lutheran ordination in principle, but it should only be done with examination and the authorities' presentation and appointment, and add: "which we then regard as a true, regular call and consecration no less than the laying on of hands" (T. Kolde, "Z. Gesch. d. Ordination," etc., op. cit., p. 233; also cf. p. 220). Luther must have known that in some places an aversion to the laying on of hands had arisen, and yet consciously included it in the ordination act, apparently as something not entirely unimportant to him (as we believe contrary to Kolde, op. cit., pp. 242ff.). Cf. Drews, "Einl.," WA 38:420: "The chief parts of Luther's formulary are the Scripture readings and the prayers with the laying on of hands. He consciously borrows this rite from the biblical model."

whole presbytery, and the ordination prayer consisting of the Lord's Prayer and a prayer paraphrasing its first three petitions, in which the Lord is implored, with reference to Matt. 9:37–38, to give the Holy Spirit richly to these His ministers (and to the whole *ministerium*) and to restrain all opposing forces which hinder the course of God's kingdom. The sixth rubric brings the committal of the office with the words of the apostle in 1 Pet. 5:2–4, while the seventh forms the Benediction with the sign of the cross and words of blessing.[149] The congregation sings "Nun bitten wir den heiligen Geist" [Now let us beseech the Holy Spirit],[150] a presbyter intones the Lord's Prayer, and the celebration of the Holy Supper follows with communion of the ordained.

We thus find in Luther's *Ordination of Ministers of the Word* the following seven elements of the ordination rite proper: (1) prayer of the congregation for laborers for the Lord's harvest, (2) "Veni sancte Spiritus," (3) Scripture readings focusing on the duties of the office, (4) vow, (5) laying on of hands with ordination prayer consisting of Lord's Prayer and additional prayer for the Holy Spirit for the ordinand, (6) committal of the office, and (7) Benediction.

Completely incomprehensible, on the other hand, is Brunotte's wish that the laying on of hands in ordination be entirely omitted in our time, "by which ordination, as Luther views it, would find its fullest expression without distortion" (op. cit., p. 202). Brunotte's intention certainly has nothing in common with Luther's here!

149 T. Kolde (op. cit., pp. 237f.) and G. Rietschel (*Luther u. d. Ordination*, p. 16, and "Luthers Ordinationsformular i. s. urspr. Gestalt," op. cit., p. 176) regard the Benediction with the sign of the cross as a later addition of Bugenhagen's. Since this element does not appear in H and F, it is in the realm of possibility that such is the case. Yet in one of Luther's table talks (WA TR 5:111.17ff., no. 5376), a blessing is found in the description of the ordination of M. Benedict Schumann on April 22, 1537—a relatively early ordination rite. After the ordination prayer it reads: "Wherefore I pray benediction and prosperity for you, my brother, that you may walk in the fear and confidence of the Lord" (WA TR 5:112.12ff.). For this reason, it cannot be accepted without question that the Benediction is not from Luther. And if, at most, Bugenhagen added it, Luther nevertheless supported and endorsed it, nor was it against his understanding of ordination, or it would not have been accepted in the personal liturgical copy (R) actually used in the ordinations in Wittenberg. Neither should it be overlooked that the Latin formulary also has the Benediction, of which Luther is unanimously accepted as the author (cf. Rietschel, *Luther u. d. Ordination*, p. 24, and E. Sehling, *Kirchenord.* I, p. 26).

150 T. Kolde (op. cit., p. 238) thinks it is a liturgical monstrosity to have "Nun bitten wir den heiligen Geist" sung again at the closing of the ordination act and, not believing Luther capable of doing it, tries to have this rubric originate with an editor (namely, Bugenhagen, of all people!). Yet it is hard to see how it is a liturgical monstrosity after the completion of the ordination act to pray for "the true faith" for the ordinands! Besides this, the chorale "Nun bitten wir den heiligen Geist" is also sung as the Hymn of the Day or even as the post-sermon hymn (remember that the ordination rite was inserted after the sermon within the course of the divine service). Cf. G. Rietschel, "Luthers Ord.-form. i. s. urspr. Gestalt," op. cit., pp. 17ff. This line of argument by Kolde is adequately addressed by this.

6. The True Sense of Ordination according to Luther's *Ordination of Ministers of the Word*

Collecting what has been ascertained thus far concerning Luther's teaching of ordination, we can posit the following semantic content for ordination: it is the rite in which the election and call to the office are realized;[151] it is the testimony by other ministers of the Word that the called man has a legitimate call and the ability to teach;[152] it is the effectual confirmation of the local call previously extended;[153] and thus the committal to the spiritual office,[154] the conferral of the office,[155] the transmission of the *auctoritas praedicandi et dandi Sacramenta* [authority to preach and to give the Sacraments],[156] the acceptance of a specific person to the office,[157] the appointment to the office,[158] the sending to a specific office,[159] and the preparation[160] and blessing[161] of the person for that office. It will therefore also be necessary to establish that *Ordination of Ministers of the Word* actually comes from Luther and realizes Luther's own personal intentions, and whether the sense of the ordination arising from *Ordination of Ministers of the Word* agrees with what we have previously learned in this regard from Luther's writings.

What is the true sense of ordination according to Luther's *Ordination of Ministers of the Word*? We can establish three points: *The ordination is the public confirmation of the call held before the Church as a whole, it is the effective sending into the office, and it is the blessing to the office.*

(1) The local call of the ordinand to a specific congregation is clearly assumed in *Ordination of Ministers of the Word*.[162] It is stressed (esp. in F) that in the call of the church (= congregation) and of the authorities who have sent the ordinand to Wittenberg for ordination, the call of God has already been

---

[151] WA 6:564.16f., 566.30ff.

[152] WA Br 6:44.15ff.

[153] WA 6:408.6; 12:191.22ff., 193.38ff.; 17/1:511.4; WA Br 7:302.4ff.

[154] WA 6:407.29ff.; 17/1:511.3ff.; 38:228.27ff.

[155] WA 41:459.10f.

[156] WA 15:721.3ff.; 41:457.15; WA Br 6:44.15ff.

[157] WA 41:457.15.

[158] WA 10/2:220.34ff.; 12:173.2ff.; 17/1:511.5ff.; 41:457.9ff.; 47:192.6ff.; WA Br 5:700.13f.

[159] WA 38:238.5ff.

[160] WA 6:561.32f.

[161] WA TR 5:112.12ff.

[162] On this also cf. the ordination certificates, in which the local call is always mentioned as a prerequisite of the ordination, e.g., End. 11:278.1ff., 227.12ff., etc. Likewise, cf. the Wittenberg ordinand certificate, where the local call is always indicated next to the name. Even after that, however, as the same ordinand certificate shows, there were ordinations in Wittenberg in which a special local call was still lacking (cf. Rietschel, loc. cit., p. 80). Yet this was contrary to Luther's actual intent.

received by the ordinand.[163] However, the ordination in Wittenberg does not constitute any kind of investiture into the specific, local office to which the ordinand has been called by the congregation or authorities. This is unavoidably clear—as Rietschel noted[164]—from the fact that *Ordination of Ministers of the Word* envisions the simultaneous ordination of multiple ordinands with various local calls. Rather, this ordination represents a public confirmation of the lawfully issued local call, with that confirmation being performed before the Church as a whole through the collective Church's ministers designated for that purpose: "Thus we will ordain and confirm you through our office by the command of the Church. . . ."[165]

The two phrases "through our office" and "by the command of the Church" are significant. When Luther refers the ordinatory action of the ordaining minister to the command of the Church,[166] it can hardly mean the will of the local congregation expressed in the local call of the ordinand, in which the ordained man is then to enter his office, since the congregation has nothing to "command" the ordaining ministers in Wittenberg. Otherwise it would have to say "at the request of the church*es*," in which *kirchen* would have to be seen as the plural in light of the multiple ordinands from various congregations. Rather, in the expression "by the command of the Church" there is a reference to the decree from the elector, who had in fact committed ordination to the theological faculty.[167] In that case, Luther sees, in the elector, the Church acting in the collective sense and commanding or committing ordination, and in the command of the elector the command of the collective Church is received by the ordaining minister. This is in line with the opinion which Luther expresses on the ecclesial functions of the ruler, the territorial prince, in the state of necessity resulting from the absence of the bishops.[168] The prince, who as the instrument of the collective Church commands ordination, here serves as emergency bishop. Under normal circumstances, the regular bishop would take his position, who would then either perform the ordinations through his appointees or act in them himself, yet strictly in the name of the Church, the Church as a whole.[169] The Church *must* command ordination since it has God's command to call ministers to the office, and this must be done in the form of ordination according to apostolic example. Luther thus traces the Church's concrete command to ordain, now executed through the elector, back to Paul's command to Titus and

---

163 WA 38:427.24ff. (F); cf. also WA 38:424.25ff. (H). T. Kolde stressed that this passage in F must immediately strike every Luther enthusiast "as coming from Luther" ("Z. Geschichte der Ordination und Kirchenzucht," op. cit., p. 237).

164 Op. cit., p. 74.

165 WA 38:428.25ff. (F).

166 Cf. also WA 34/1:437.16f.: "Likewise, when we ordain a pastor, since it is done in obedience to the church to which he is committed," etc.

167 Cf. above, p. 161.

168 Cf. above, pp. 135–37.

169 Cf. above, pp. 133–34.

Timothy to appoint priests in the cities and to commit the Word to those who are capable, and to teach others.[170]

The apostle's command obligates the Church to do the same today, and even—as then, so today—by the spiritual office. Therefore, Luther emphasizes that the ordaining and confirming occur "through our office." St. Paul gave the command to Titus and Timothy to appoint priests because they, as office-bearers, were in a position to determine their suitableness. So today, the ordaining is carried out by bearers of the office since they (on the basis of an examination) are able to attest that the ordinands are suitable, apt to teach, and orthodox in belief.[171]

If Luther attaches importance to the ordaining minister's mandate of office being brought to bear in ordination,[172] this cannot be conceived as in any way disconnected from the Church. The office embarks upon its ordaining function "by the command of the Church." In ordination, the ordaining minister embodies the Church to a certain extent; he ordains not only as office-bearer but also as instrument of the whole Church.[173] The whole Church participates in the ordinatory action. The whole Church (through the office) confirms the call. Therefore, it is only logical that Luther designates ordination as a public, liturgical act of the congregation.[174] The congregation is to be present not only as witness, as we have already noted,[175] but also in a cooperative capacity through its prayer, which introduces the whole rite. While Luther does not permit the congregants to lay on their hands (as Bugenhagen does in his Pomeranian church order of 1535), this being reserved for the ordaining office-bearers alone, nevertheless the invocation of the Holy Spirit upon the ordinands is also a matter belonging to the congregation. The congregation in Wittenberg before which the ordination takes place—since Wittenberg is the ecclesial headquarters, where the ordinations are to be done as desired by the territorial prince—stands for the Church as a whole. In the Latin *Ordination of Ministers of the Word*, in the great ordination prayer, it reads: "We beseech You that You would deign to grant . . . the Holy Spirit . . . to these who seek from

---

170 WA 38:428.29ff. (F): ". . . ordain and confirm, as St. Paul commands Titus and Timothy, that we should appoint priests in the cities and commit the Word to those who are capable of teaching others." It is the general command from the apostles which the Church passes on to the ordaining minister.

171 Cf. above, pp. 138–40.

172 Cf. below, pp. 192–94.

173 Cf. in the ordination certificates the expression that the ordination is done in the authority of Christ's Church: End. 17:357.17f., where it says of ordination: "what was committed to us by the authority of Christ's Church and the command of our superiors"; End. 11:279.19: (the ordination is carried out) "according to the Word of God by the authority of our Church."

174 In other passages also, Luther, as we have seen, places importance on the ordination happening *coram ecclesia*: WA 17/1:511.6f.; WA Br 7:302.2ff. ("publicly before our church"); WA 53:257.21f.: "Also the church and the people as well as the territorial princes and protectors are personally present." In the ordination certificates, there is an emphasis on the ordination being "*publica*": End. 11:227.14, 228.1, 278.14, 279.19.

175 Cf. above, pp. 162–63.

this church the confirmation of their calls"[176]—thus the local congregation in Wittenberg ("from *this* church"!) is understood as the embodiment of the collective Church before which the confirmation of the call is to take place. The ordination is the public and solemn confirmation of the local call being done through the spiritual office and before the collective Church, by which said call is validated in a general and public manner.

(2) Prior to ordination, the ordinands are not yet appointed to their office, though they have already received a call from God in the call through the congregation and authorities. The actual appointment to the office is merely introduced by this call and its subsequent examination, but now in ordination it is to *take place*. The congregation begins by praying for the ordinands that God would deign to send laborers into His harvest, etc.[177] Thus the ordinands have not yet been sent; this sending will not occur until the ordination. This petition is made to the Lord in regard to this ordination rite just beginning, that He might (presently!) send laborers into His harvest. In the first lesson (1 Tim. 3:1–7) it reads: "If anyone *desires* a bishop's office. . . ."[178] The ordinands who were addressed by this lesson have not yet received the office; they first desire it. Before they receive it, the duties of such an office are laid before them through the lessons from Holy Scripture and in a special exhortation by the ordaining minister, and then the question is posed to them: "If you are willing and ready to *accept* this office and to exercise it faithfully, then we will . . . ordain you. . . ."[179] If the ordinands already *had* the office, the question would be illogical, but they still do not *have* it; only now do they take possession of it and for this purpose express their readiness to assume it and to exercise it faithfully. Luther explains "ordaining and confirming"—as we already saw—by reference to what Paul assigned to Titus and Timothy: to appoint priests in the cities and to commit the Word to those who are capable of teaching others.[180] Only here in ordination—and, indeed, in the appended act of the ordination prayer with laying on of hands and the committal of the office—are the ordinands appointed as priests and is the Word committed to them. It is here, then, that they obtain the office of the Word. Thus, according to the whole system of *Ordination of Ministers of the Word*, the decisive act is the great ordination prayer with the laying on of hands, which coalesces with the express commission of the office with 1 Pet. 5:2–4: "Go, therefore, and feed the flock of Christ which *is* committed to you."[181] Indeed, the flock of Christ *is* now committed to them, the commission of the office *is* now laid upon them, they *are* now in the office, validly and effectively

176 WA 38:433.11f.; Sehling, *Kirchenord.* I, p. 28.

177 WA 38:423.13ff. (R); cf. WA 38:429: "the ordination prayer."

178 WA 38:425.18ff. (R); cf. WA 38:428.21 (F).

179 WA 38:428.22ff. (F).

180 WA 38:428.29ff. (F).

181 WA 38:431.2ff. (R).

sent to those congregations that had desired them.[182] Now, by ordination, the call to the ecclesial office is "realized."[183] The ordination is, according to Luther's *Ordination of Ministers of the Word*, the effective sending into the office. —

(3) The whole ordination rite also involves equipping the ordinands properly for the office. This consists above all of imparting the Holy Spirit, who sustains them in pure doctrine and makes them true evangelists and [enables them] to stand fast against the devil, the world, and their own flesh.[184] The ordination rite is filled with prayer for the Holy Spirit. In the beginning, the people kneel and pray for the coming of the Holy Spirit: "Veni sancte Spiritus." The lesson, Acts 20:28–31, highlights the fact the Holy Spirit appoints people as bishops. Most notably, the great ordination prayer, which expands on the first three petitions of the Lord's Prayer, has as its content the invocation of the Holy Spirit upon the ordinands; it concerns the apportioning of the Holy Spirit.[185] Nevertheless, He is not transmitted in a purely ritualistic way (only in the horizontal plane, so to speak), but is invoked from God (in the vertical plane). This also finds expression in the fact that the ordaining minister includes himself and those assisting the ordination in the petition of the ordination prayer.[186] All who hold the office are constantly in need of the renewed gift of the Holy Spirit, but He is especially invoked now on those to be newly ordained. Additionally, at the close of the service stands the Benediction by the ordaining minister, which also brings the horizontal aspect to the fore: "Let the ordaining minister bless them with the sign of the cross. . . ."[187] J. Heubach has noted that Luther is very familiar with real benedictions.[188] Thus he says in the Genesis lectures (1535/1545)[189] concerning the blessing of Isaac (Gen. 27:28f.): "Neither is this benediction merely the empty sound of words nor some verbal imprecation. . . . In Holy Scripture there are real benedictions, not merely imprecations, but indicative, constitutive blessings which bestow and bring the very thing

---

[182] Cf. WA TR 5:111.24f.: ". . . to which we call and send you by God's authority, just as God sent us." — H. Asmussen says, "The Lutheran ordination formularies make it clear that they wish to see the ordination itself—and not some official action—regarded as the birth hour of the concrete office" (*Warum noch lutherische Kirche* [Stuttgart, 1949], p. 186). This is true especially of the prototype of the Lutheran ordination formularies, namely, that of Luther himself.

[183] W. Künneth, *Politik zwischen Dämon und Gott* (Berlin, 1954), p. 569. By this word, Künneth hits precisely on the actual interpretation of Luther's Ordinationsformular as well. Also cf. C. Mahrenholz (*Begleitwort d. Lit. Ausschusses*, z. Bd. IV *d. Agende f. ev. luth. Gem. u. Kirchen* [Berlin, 1952], p. 12), who says of the ordination instituted in Wittenberg in 1535: "The focus of this act is on the determination of suitability" (combination of formation and examination!) "and in the conferral of the spiritual office in general. . . ."

[184] WA 38:430.5ff. (R) among others.

[185] WA 38:429.26ff.: ". . . We heartily beseech You to give Your Holy Spirit richly to these Your servants . . ."; cf. WA 38:433.11ff.

[186] WA 38:430.1ff. (R): ". . . will give Your Holy Spirit to these Your servants, together with us and all who are called to Your Word. . . ."

[187] WA 38:431.18ff. (R).

[188] *Die Ordination zum Amt der Kirche* (Berlin, 1956), pp. 108f.

[189] Yet on the Genesis lectures, cf. what is said below, p. 183 n. 245.

sounded."[190] It is in this sense that the blessing in the ordination rite as well as the ordination prayer with laying on of hands, which is performed with the intent of benediction, are understood according to Luther. The gift of the Holy Spirit is not merely prayed for but is—insofar as the prayer of faith has the sure promise of being heard—actually and really allocated as well. The ordination prayer is efficacious, effectual. It gives the Holy Spirit in such a way that He is—to include another Luther passage here—"always with us for our office when we preach the Gospel, baptize, absolve, give the Sacrament according to the Holy Spirit's institution and ordinance."[191] Thus the ordination is in Luther's sense also a blessing for the office.[192] —

The ordination rite appointed in Luther's *Ordination of Ministers of the Word* is therefore not to be regarded as any mere human activity. In all that is done by the ordaining minister and his assistants in the ordination *coram ecclesia*, not only is the Church acting but so is God Himself, calling, sending, blessing the ordinands.[193] The ordaining minister is God's instrument in this: "We are there God's masks and our Lord God's netlike hand," says Luther in the ordination sermon from October 20, 1535.[194] "*God* makes and ordains ministers"[195]—this sentence from the Genesis lectures could easily serve as the motto for Luther's whole ordination rite.

This view of ordination as the confirmation of the call and effective sending to the office, as the ultimately effectual conferral of and appointment to the office, which we have found in Luther's *Ordination of Ministers of the Word*, is impressively confirmed by the *ordination certificates*, on all of which Luther's signature appears first. In what we believe to be the earliest ordination certificate in our possession, that of Joachim Pogan dating from June 11, 1536, it reads: "We have judged him to be fit for the ministry of the Gospel, and we have declared our judgment by the testimony of public ordination . . . , and we accept him according to the command of Christ, that he may purely and faithfully teach the Gospel and administer the Sacraments."[196] In the ordination, the finding by the other office-bearers that the concerned ordinand is capable of teaching is

[190] WA 43:524.32ff., 525.3ff. This is followed by a comparison with the exhibitive Absolution! The Benediction is also exhibitive. Cf. WA 43:525.16f.: "Benedictions are therefore not imprecative but collative"; and WA 43:525.25f.: "The Benediction is a statement [*sententia*] that finishes and concludes something, a final pronouncement or judgment."

[191] WA 28:468.34ff.

[192] The factor of the Benediction in ordination gains prominence in Luther especially in the last years of his life (*Lectures on Genesis* [1535–45]; treatise on the bishop's consecration in Naumburg [*Model for the Consecration of a True Christian Bishop*] [1542]; *House Postil* [1544]). We will return to it in the treatment of the laying on of hands and the ordination gift. Cf. below, pp. 185–88 and 194–99.

[193] Cf. WA TR 5:111.24f.: "to which we *call and send you by God's authority*, just as God has sent us"; WA 47:192.6ff.: ". . . and yet this sending is also from God."

[194] WA 41:457.4f.

[195] WA 43:600.26.

[196] End. 17:357.15ff.

declared by public testimony, and the preaching of the Gospel and the administration of the Sacraments is committed to the ordinand. Hence ordination is the approval of the called person by the other office-bearers (and in this sense a confirmation of the call) and the committal to the office. Likewise, the two ordination certificates for Benedict Schumann of April 22, 1537, and for Jakob Siegel of October 7, 1537, show the content of ordination to be the public confirmation of the call and the conferral of the office to preach the Gospel and to administer the Sacraments.[197] From that time, the standard formula in the ordination certificates is something to the effect of "That the call may be confirmed by public testimony, we have examined his understanding and confirmed him as rightly holding the sum of Christian godliness and comprehending the doctrine of the Gospel. . . . Wherefore, according to the teaching of the apostles, the ministry of teaching the Gospel and administering the Sacraments instituted by Christ is hereby conferred on him. . . ."[198] Ordination, according to Luther's ordination certificates, is not only the public confirmation of the call by the office-bearers who conduct the examination and ordination but is also by the same token the appointment to the office, the effective transmission of the office.[199]

Having thus examined *Ordination of Ministers of the Word* and the ordination certificates pertaining to it, we can establish that the content of the ordination expressed here agrees with what we have already found in Luther's other writings. The true sense of ordination is, according to Luther: (1) the public confirmation and enactment of the call before the collective Church, (2) the appointment and sending to the office, and (3) the consecration or blessing for

[197] End. 11:227.12ff. (for Benedict Schumann): "Since the church of Naumburg has called him to the work of teaching the Gospel and has asked that that call be confirmed by public ordination . . . (we have assessed him and found him pure in doctrine, and he has pledged to be faithful). . . . Wherefore since our office must not be without neighboring churches, and the Council of Nicaea has piously decreed that ordination should be sought from neighboring churches, we have committed to this Master Benedict, by public ordination in the Church, the ministry of teaching the Gospel and administering the Sacraments instituted in the Gospel . . ."; End. 11:278.3ff. (for [Jakob] Siegel): ". . . requested that by public ordination . . . the ministry of teaching the Gospel and administering the Sacraments should be committed to him . . . (he had the testimony concerning his call, was examined and found pure in doctrine, promised to be faithful in the office). . . . Therefore, in accordance with the Word of God, by the authority of our Church, the call has been confirmed by public ordination, and to this Jakob the ministry of teaching the Gospel and administering the Sacraments has been committed."

[198] End. 14:286.18ff.; cf. End. 7:131.16ff.; 12:22.12ff., 197.14ff.; 15:142.16ff. (= WA Br 10:297.12ff.); 16:63.13ff. (= WA Br 10:621.10ff.), 275.29ff. (= WA Br 11:156.23ff.); 18:32.14ff., 52.15ff.

[199] The transmission of the office, according to the ordination certificates, is valid for the jurisdiction for which the ordinand receives the call. This is apparent in the fact that it typically reads: "We have committed the ministry of teaching the Gospel and administering the Sacraments according to the call" (End. 11:228.4; 12:22.14, 197.16; 7:131.19; 15:142.19 [= WA Br 10:297.15]; 16:63.16 [= WA Br 10:621.13], 89.15; 18:53.18ff.). Cf. End. 14:252.15ff.: "committed to him to preach the holy Gospel and to administer the holy Sacraments *where he was called*"; likewise End. 15:88.14ff. and 17:357.19ff.: "We have accepted . . . that he should teach the Gospel purely and faithfully and administer the Sacraments *in the manner that his call demands*. . . ."

the office, in all three of which elements God is to be seen as the actor.[200] Insofar as the whole call process reaches its consummation in the ordination rite, it is logical for Luther to summarize it simply with the term "ordaining."[201]

Previous scholarship on Luther's concept of ordination has unduly focused on the public approval of the call and more or less ignored the other two elements: the effective appointment and sending to the office and the consecration for the office. Thus *G. Rietschel*, held to be the foremost scholar on Luther's doctrine of ordination, lays the stress rather lopsidedly on the public ecclesio-governmental confirmation of the call, particularly in his dispute with Theodor Kliefoth,[202] although he also mentions in passing that ordination gives the authority for the office as well as being the conferral of the office.[203] Nevertheless, he restricts the latter proposition to the legal sense, as though only the *right* of preaching and administering the Sacraments were conferred.[204] When he attacks Kliefoth's thesis that ordination causes a man to become a pastor—saying that it does not make a pastor but only confirms before the congregation the call in the name of the Church and the triune God, and attests this in the context of the ecclesial office, assuring the ordinand that his call has been carried out according to God's will and the Church's order[205]—this opposition should be judged at least as not reflective of the sense of Luther's *Ordination of Ministers of the Word.*

Likewise in more recent works, which on the whole are almost entirely dependent on Rietschel regarding this question, we find only the unilateral emphasis on the aspect of confirmation. Thus *E. Wolf* describes the essence of ordination in the narrow sense, according to Luther and the Lutheran fathers, as consisting merely of the public declaration of the call.[206] *H. Storck* writes: "The act of ordination represents the public approval of the call,"[207] and thus abandons the question of ordination in Luther. The effective appointment to the office and the consecra-

---

[200] J. Heubach's opinion (op. cit., p. 77) that "the Church of the Reformation adhered fundamentally to these three basic elements of ordination (i.e., *vocatio, benedictio, missio* [call, blessing, sending])" is accurate for Luther. — When *G. Werner* (*Tröstet euch der Ordination*, Bek. luth. Kirche 13 [Neuendettelsau, 1954], p. 17) says, "However much people are involved in the task of the Church, including the various stages of the call, the moment must come some day when it is made unmistakably and unambiguously clear to the man called to the office that, here and now, God Himself is standing, that Christ, who does the sending, is manifesting Himself with His Word and Spirit. From now on, the man who is called . . . may use the apostles' argument for carrying out his office: he represents Christ"—this moment in Luther's scheme must doubtlessly be identified as ordination. — Also cf. G. Wehrung, "Zu Augustana VIII," *Ztschr. f. syst. Theol.* (1937), pp. 7f.

[201] Cf. above, p. 142.

[202] Op. cit., pp. 101ff.

[203] Op. cit., p. 74.

[204] Op. cit., p. 75.

[205] Op. cit., p. 105. So, too, R. Sohm (*Kirchenrecht* I, p. 497 n. 28). Also Sohm misses the fact that, according to Luther, the actual conferral of the office happens in ordination, for which reason his contrast of the meaning of the Roman Catholic ordination and Evangelical ordination is distorted and falls short.

[206] "Zur Verwaltung der Sakramente nach Luther u. luth. Lehre," in *Peregrinatio: Studien z. reformatorischen Theol. u. z. Kirchenproblem* (Munich, 1954), pp. 251f.

[207] Op. cit., p. 35.

tion for the office nevertheless remain ignored when, in response to G. Hök,[208] he maintained that, according to Luther, the called man receives "no special power or gift of grace."[209] What, then, does it mean for Luther to say that the "authority to preach the Word and give the Sacraments" is *bestowed* in ordination or that the office is *conferred* in ordination? Is this not also the impartation of a new power, a new concrete authority?[210] According to Luther, the power to handle Word and Sacrament is certainly present fundamentally from Baptism, yet it is only in ordination, through the specific call, that it is given an official authority for practical application! And yet one cannot ignore the fact that for Luther a real spiritual gift is mediated through the ordination prayer. We must make this response to *G. Hök*, who places all importance on the call in contrast to the consecration (= ordination) and asserts of the office of the Word: "The office is received not through consecration but through the call to the ministry."[211] This opposition of the call and ordination is not found in Luther's writings. According to Luther's *Ordination of Ministers of the Word* and his statements elsewhere, if the two acts of call and ordination are to be compared, it is *ordination*, through which the office is actually transmitted and received, that places someone in the office. Hök writes: "The consecration according to Luther's view is only a public confirmation of the call,"[212] and expressly denies—as already noted—the reception of a special gift of grace or a special power. This leads to a distorted picture. The word "only" is the cause of the distortion. For Luther, ordination, as public confirmation of the call, is also the effective appointment to the office, the authorization and consecration for the office.[213] On the next page, Hök himself formulates in passing that the elected man "is appointed to the office by the bishop or the person who performs the consecration"; "by this the call is confirmed and publicized";[214] and again: "The bishop sets the called person into the office through the consecration to confirm publicly that the call has been done legitimately."[215] In these formulations, the electee seems to be not yet appointed to the office after the election but is only appointed to the office by the consecration (= ordination), which is certainly *another* public confirmation of the call. Hök's initial devaluation of the consecration compared with the call does not agree with this and puts a false accent on his representation of Luther's teaching. Luther sees both elements as related to each other and clings firmly to the fact that the ordination is the actual appoint-

[208] G. Hök, op. cit., p. 145.

[209] Op. cit., p. 39.

[210] Cf. A. W. Dieckhoff, op. cit., p. 84, and P. Brunner, "Vom Amt d. Bischofs," p. 14.

[211] Op. cit., p. 144.

[212] Op. cit., p. 145.

[213] Rather, R. Josefson's statement ("Det andliga ämbetet i Svenska kyrkans bekännelseskrifter," in *En bok om kyrkans ämbete* [Uppsala, 1951], p. 185) may be accepted: "According to the Lutheran view, the priest, through the consecration, gets no other qualifications than those which every Christian receives, nor does he have a *more* direct access to God's grace," although the bestowal of the power to exercise the office publicly could also be called a qualification. Still, according to Luther, it does not rise to the level of an intrinsic quality that cannot be relinquished. To this extent it would be possible to follow Josefson in this observation.

[214] Op. cit., p. 146.

[215] Op. cit., p. 148.

ment to the office. When Hök says, "The consecration according to Luther is not constitutive; whoever has received a proper call possesses the office independent of the consecration,"[216] this may hold true for Luther at best with respect to the Roman priestly consecration, but not with respect to the Evangelical ordination. Hök later limits his position by saying, "*In the case of necessity*, the congregation can call without the cooperation of the bishop or consecration."[217] This comes closer to what is actually gleaned from Luther: regarding the case of emergency, Luther speaks of the expendability of the *episcopal* confirmation, but he wants to see a confirmation act carried out even in an act of necessity, only by the congregants; cf. his treatise to the Bohemians [*Concerning the Ministry*]. Significantly, the instances quoted by Hök to prove that not the consecration but the call places a person into the office, and that the consecration is strictly the public confirmation of the call, not the bestowal of a new authority,[218] are wholly incorrect. None of them actually says that for which Hök references them.[219] —

Our examination of Luther's idea of the true sense of ordination thus leads, partly in contradiction to the authors cited, to the positions recently taken by J. Heubach in the ordination debate.[220] Rietschel's vision of Luther's idea of ordination, which previously held the field without objection, was justly criticized and called into question by Heubach.[221] Luther possessed much more theological understanding for the specific ordination rite than Rietschel perceived. It is

---

216 Op. cit., pp. 144f.; cf. p. 148: "The office is held by the one called, even when the consecration is omitted."

217 Op. cit., p. 146.

218 Op. cit., pp. 144f.

219 The latest study by Brunotte does not in essence venture beyond G. Rietschel's position. According to Brunotte, Luther views the ordination act as "a modest procedure which has its great significance in the fact that God is making use of His own people for the divine commission" (op. cit., p. 189). According to Luther's *Ordination of Ministers of the Word*, the liturgical ordination rite is meant "not as a bestowal of a special gift on the office-bearer, but as the public commission to exercise the spiritual office" (ibid.). The ordination in Luther is, by virtue of its specific sense, "the public declaration or public acknowledgment of the call of the office-bearer, carried out by the true Church" (ibid.). According to Brunotte, the meaning of liturgical ordination in Luther is thus centered on the first aspect referred to by us, the public confirmation of the call (in which the intercongregational, collective Church aspect of ordination is at very least ignored by Brunotte). Insofar as he says that it is the "public commission to exercise the spiritual office," we also hear an echo of the second aspect which we mentioned, the effective sending and appointment to the office. Nevertheless, the third element, the blessing, is negated. In this way, Brunotte not only ignores the Benediction indicated as the last rubric in *Ordination of Ministers of the Word* but also mistakes the meaning of the ordination prayer in Luther's *Ordination of Ministers of the Word*. It will surely not be fair to Luther's intention if the meaning of ordination in his view is expressed in the contrastive proposition: "*not* a bestowal of a special gift on the office-bearer *but* a public commission to exercise the spiritual office." In Luther's view, the commission to the office is also accompanied by a real spiritual gift, namely, the authority of the office or the gift of the Holy Spirit, if not simply horizontally by means of the laying on of hands understood in a distinctly sacramental way, yet by means of the ordination prayer (occurring with the laying on of hands) and its assured reception. — On this cf. below, pp. 186–88, where the benedictory function of the laying on of hands in Luther is discussed.

220 We are thus unable to join in Brunotte's critique of J. Heubach's position (op. cit., p. 185 n. 66).

221 Op. cit., pp. 33ff., 77f., 102, 105f.

time to reorient ourselves by reference to the sources of Luther's understanding of ordination and to dispense with biased opinions.

7. The Elements of the Ordination

Luther fights against *false elements* of ordination in the Roman priestly consecration, including the committal to the sacrificial priesthood and the elevation to a special priestly estate intrinsically distinct from the other baptized. This is why the symbolic signs of this false content in the ordination—namely, the tonsure [*rasura*] and chrismation [*unctura*]—are to be combated as well.[222] These things are a "portentous sign [*portentum*]" for Luther.[223] The apostles called men to the office "without chrism."[224] Chrism is "only a human invention" and has "no order or command from God";[225] it is not to be regarded.[226] The true call to the office happens legitimately "without the tonsure, chrismation, and other masks set up by human audacity in place of the holy and necessary things."[227]

Tonsure and chrismation are unnecessary, false pomp.[228] The mark of true ordination is that it is done "without any splendor."[229] Yet Luther himself, regarding the ordination rite to be introduced in Wittenberg, speaks of a "public splendor."[230] By this he means the *publicus ritus* [public rite] of the liturgical ordination which is to be performed in Wittenberg with a certain degree of solemnity and thinks of the ceremonies pertaining to the ordination rite in the good sense,

---

[222] Cf. WA 6:566.10ff. Also cf. above, p. 144 nn. 4–5.

[223] WA 12:178.11ff. and 17 ("that portent of tonsure and chrismation"); cf. WA 38:228.6ff.

[224] WA 38:228.29ff.; cf. WA 38:253.10ff. (on 2 Tim. 2:2): "There is no chrism or butter here. There is only the command to teach God's Word . . ."; cf. WA 38:254.7; 12:191.3ff.

[225] WA 38:228.17f.; cf. WA 38:197.5ff., where Luther speaks of God's ability to purge away even "the awful chrism introduced apart from His will through mere human imagination."

[226] WA 38:243.20.

[227] WA 54:428.5f.; cf. WA Br 5:700.14f.: "without tonsure, without anointing, without fillet, without gloves, without staff, and without thurible, and, finally, without these bishops"; WA 53:231.41ff. (Luther says in an ironic tone that we would have committed a great sin) "if we had ordained and consecrated a bishop in the Naumburg cathedral without any chrism, or without butter, schmaltz, bacon, pitch, grease, incense, coals, and whatever other things are of great sanctity. . . ." — Luther, however, would not have so categorically opposed the rite of anointing and tonsure if it had not been an expression of the consecration to the sacrificial priesthood. Cf. WA 41:214.23f.: "I would have my head shaved and myself consecrated as he" (i.e., the pope) "wishes, if he would only let Christ remain Christ and not make himself a king of 'justice and peace' nor make a new priesthood, law, and doctrine. These are the priests of Baal and priests of the devil. . . ."

[228] WA 12:191.2f. ("the pomp of shearing and anointing and ordaining").

[229] WA 6:408.6. While Luther, in the Smalcald Articles, allows consecration by the Roman bishops if they are true bishops and willing to stop persecuting the Gospel, he nevertheless adds the stipulation: "Yet let all masks and specters of unchristian ways and pomp be left behind" (WA 50:247.27ff.).

[230] WA 41:240.33f. ("We intend to ordain once with a public ceremony").

without becoming pomp and *abusus* [abuse], and therefore may be found in Holy Scripture. Which are those?

Luther commends to the Bohemians the confirmation of the election with *prayer and the laying on of hands.*[231] The ordination of which he speaks to Sutel is to be done "with prayer and the laying on of hands [*cum oratione et impositione manuum*]."[232] In this, Luther consciously follows the apostolic manner of ordaining office-bearers. The laying on of hands and prayer—says Luther in 1533—are the rites which the apostles used in calling and sending people to the office.[233] In the same tenor, Luther speaks in greater detail in a sermon on St. Andrew's Day (from the *House Postil* of 1544).[234] According to St. Paul's direction, Timothy and Titus first examined the life, teaching, and aptitude of the ordinands, then, after the election, "called together the elders and laid hands on them; these were all the ceremonies."[235] That prayer is not neglected in this is shown by the next sentence: "Then" (namely, during the laying on of hands) "the people prayed that God would enlighten, govern, and direct the elected man by His Holy Spirit, for the welfare of the Christian Church."[236] From this primitive Christian custom, there arose in the ancient Church a practice approximately as follows: "When no deficiency was found in their teaching and life, these capable persons were called to the ministry of the Church, whereupon, with the laying on of hands, the office was publicly committed to them in the church by certain bishops and pastors in the vicinity."[237] As examples of this, one may cite Ambrose and Augustine. There was no "shearing, smearing, and other foolery."[238] This new method of ordaining was introduced by the pope because he wished to consecrate people to the sacrificial priesthood. "Christians, however, should know that ministers, bishops, pastors, chaplains, or whatever they may be called require nothing more than to be above reproach in conduct and to have a good understanding of Christian doctrine, and to be able to communicate it clearly. If this is the case, no more is needed than that those persons be called by author-

[231] WA 12:191.22ff., 193.33ff.

[232] WA Br 6:44.18f.

[233] WA 38:228.29ff.: "The apostles only laid their hands on the head, without chrism, and prayed over those whom they called or sent to the office."

[234] On the authenticity of the sermons of the *House Postil*, compare the introduction in WA 52:viif. The sermon on St. Andrew's Day is found only in the Dietrich collection, not among Rörer's transcriptions (cf. WA 52:xxiii: "R offers no sermon for this day"). It is thus somewhat uncertain. Dietrich occasionally included in the collection sermons derived from others or even his own (WA 52:xi). Yet the present sermon from St. Andrew's Day may be regarded as an authentic Luther sermon since its body of thought is also demonstrable in Luther's writings (cf. here the relation to the apostolic and ancient examples of the ordination of ministers, the stress on the ordination prayer and its being heard, the emphasis on the visible gifts of the Spirit in the apostolic laying on of hands, etc.). An argument nevertheless may be ventured for the ideas from this sermon not corroborated elsewhere.

[235] WA 52:568.15ff. and 20ff.

[236] WA 52:568.23ff.

[237] WA 52:568.34ff.

[238] WA 52:569.5.

ities and have the preaching office and other church ministry publicly committed to them. Then the laying on of hands may be used, and prayer accompany it. Thus are Christians to consecrate their ministers; then they are following the example of the apostles and the early Church."[239] True ordination happens, according to the example of the apostles and early Church, by means of a public committal of the office with the laying on of hands and prayer (not—as Luther reiterates—with anointing and tonsuring, not for sacrificial service, not with the vow of celibacy, by which the false elements of the Roman ordination are indicated).[240]

Accordingly, if we ask whether the laying on of hands and prayer are for Luther elements of ordination *jure divino*, the answer is an unqualified affirmative with respect to the prayer. How could any liturgical act of ordination be imagined without prayer? In view of all the statements about ordination which we have found in Luther up till now, it is beyond all doubt that the prayer in ordination is for Luther *juris divini*.[241] Things are not quite so clear with respect to the laying on of hands. Luther certainly acknowledges from the New Testament—as we have seen—that the apostles ordained with laying on of hands and also directed their successors to ordain with the laying on of hands. He also knows that the ancient Church's ordination was performed by the laying on of hands by the neighboring bishops. Luther discusses the ancient Church's act of calling and ordination according to Cyprian's letter to the presbyter Felix,[242] according to which the election by the people is joined by the *judicium* [decision] of the bishops, who confer the episcopacy (the office) with laying on of hands. Here he calls this whole act of calling and ordination a "most sacred and

---

[239] WA 52:569.11ff. The wording "may [be used]" is not to be interpreted to mean that it does not matter, as though laying on of hands and prayer were permitted but were unnecessary things that have been added on. This is proved by the fact that "may" also refers to "and prayer accompany it," and the prayer during ordination is absolutely obligatory for Luther and by no means left free. — Also cf. WA 6:549.21ff., where Luther, in the discussion of confirmation as a biblical custom, also mentions the laying on of hands, saying that the apostles ordained presbyters through it. And probably to be understood without specific reference to confirmation is another sentence: "And if only there were such a laying on of hands in the Church as there was in the time of the apostles!" (WA 6:549.31f.). Cf. to this passage W. Maurer, *Gemeindezucht, Gemeindeamt, Konfirmation*, Schriftenreihe d. Pfarrervereins Kurhessen-Waldeck 2 (Kassel, 1940), p. 55 n. 14 — In the sermon on Acts 13:1ff. from 1524, already frequently cited, Luther mentions particularly as elements of the appointment act only the public prayer and committal of the office (WA 17/1:511.5ff.); in the letter to Myconius on the ordination performed in Wittenberg on October 20, 1535, Luther identifies as elements the public prayer and the praise of God (WA Br 7:302.2ff.: "ordained and confirmed for your ministry publicly before our church among prayers and praises of God . . ."), yet it is in no case to be assumed that this ordination was done without laying on of hands (cf. *Ordination of Ministers of the Word*). The laying on of hands was also used by Luther at the episcopal consecration in Naumburg in 1542 (WA 53:257.6ff.).

[240] WA 52:569.22ff.

[241] One need only compare the fundamental meaning of the prayer in the whole call process that Luther recommends to the Bohemians [in *Concerning the Ministry*].

[242] WA 2:231.2ff. and 26ff.

ancient right *and completely in keeping with the Law of God*."[243] If, in doing so, Luther was not focusing particularly here on the specific rite of the laying on of hands, it is still included in the ordination act executed according to *divine* right through the phrase "*per omnia*" ["through all"]. It is, at least, in Luther's view, harmonious with the divine right to use the laying on of hands in ordination. Luther uses it for that purpose—indeed, designates its general use in his *Ordination of Ministers of the Word*—and without question counts it as an apostolic pattern and example pointing the way for every era.[244]

In the Genesis lectures (1535/1545),[245] on Gen. 28:17, there is a statement by Luther that places the laying on of hands during ordination in direct parallel to the external elements in Baptism and the Supper and expressly denies that the "laying on of hands [*impositio manuum*]" is a "human tradition [*traditio humana*]," but rather that *God* makes and ordains the ministers.

> After aligning the ordination to office with Word and Sacrament in this passage of the Genesis lectures,[246] Luther goes on: "It is a great . . . dignity and majesty when one says: This is the Word of God, I hear the voice of a man, I see human actions, bread and wine in the Supper are bodily things. In ordination, the laying on of fleshly, human hands occurs. In Baptism, water is water—carnal sight only recognizes there the external, but these external rites are bound up with the Word of God. If the Word of God is regarded, then they are 'God's house and the gate of heaven'—the Spirit is to see the water and the hand and Word of God, and God Himself, in the water. The flesh sees only so sharply as to judge water to be water and rules out God, just as the Sacramentarians and Anabaptists do. It must therefore be learned, contrary to the carnal eye, that it is not a simple word or only an empty sound, but it is the Word of the Maker of heaven and earth. *Thus the laying on of hands is not a human tradition, but God makes and ordains ministers*."[247] This line of thought is extended to the Absolution: "Neither is it the

[243] WA 2:232.4f.

[244] "It is a ceremony of the fathers, prophets, and the whole Church observed in all ages" (WA 44:695.21ff.).

[245] However, the text of the Genesis lectures, composited from the transcriptions of Rörer and [Caspar] Cruciger by Veit Dietrich, [Michael] Roting, and [Jerome] Besold, and (apart from the first volume) not further edited by Luther himself, is not really guaranteed as coming from Luther in every sense, including the literary-critical sense. On this cf. E. Seeberg, *Studien zu Luthers Genesisvorlesung* (1932); *Luthers Theologie* II (Stuttgart, 1937), pp. 423ff.; and above all, Peter Meinhold, *Die Genesisvorlesung Luthers und ihre Herausgeber* (Stuttgart, 1936). Still, to a certain extent, a body of thought genuinely representing Luther (in content if not in form) may be acknowledged here when there are no obvious indications for a different origin in a given passage.

[246] WA 43:599.28f.: ". . . When sermons are preached there" (i.e., in church), "when the Sacraments are administered, and when ministers are ordained to teach, then say, 'There is the house of God and the gate of heaven.'"

[247] WA 43:599.36ff., 600.21ff.; cf. WA 44:407.37–40: "With ministers we lay on hands and at the same time pour out prayers to God, simply to testify that ordination is divine not only in these but also in all other estates of the church, politics, and household"; also cf. WA 43:521.33ff. As parallel to the passage from the Genesis lectures cited in the text, we may cite WA 41:457.4f.: "There we are the masks of God and our Lord God's netlike hand." Through this parallel, the validity of the Genesis commentary is considerably enhanced.

pastor who absolves you, but the mouth and hand of the minister is the mouth and hand of God."[248]

Assuming that this is an authentic passage of Luther, against which no concrete argument can actually be proved, this statement is of unique significance. It is then a testament to the fact that Luther conceived of ordination to the office in the greatest possible proximity to the Sacraments and saw it as parallel to them in the sense that, in ordination, God deals with men through an external rite (the laying on of hands). In this way, the same role is ascribed to this external rite of the laying on of hands as is played by the element of water in Baptism and the elements of bread and wine in the Holy Supper. It would be overinterpreting the passage if it were assumed that Luther wished to teach the divine institution and designation of the specific rite of the *impositio manuum*. It is more probable that the term "*impositio manuum*" is a synecdoche for the whole ordination rite, through which God acts and calls to the office as through an external, physical event.[249] But even so, it remains rather significant that Luther can take the laying on of hands as the characteristic mark of the whole act and compare it to the sacramental elements in Baptism and the Supper. Obviously for him it is (accompanied by prayer and God's Word, of course) the point at which God's activity in the ordination resorts to an external element as a medium and is made concrete in it. And for this reason it (with the whole ordination, and yet as specific rite) is not to be regarded simply as *traditio humana* either.

A sure, positive *jus divinum* is to be assumed for the specific rite, but it is rendered difficult by the fact that, in many places in which Luther would have had to mention the laying on of hands if he considered it divinely ordained, he does not refer to it, and that the last-cited passage from the Genesis commentary is not entirely certified as an authentic Luther text. What is sure is that Luther generally held to the laying on of hands as an apostolic rite and a rite of the universal Church and did not wish to see it omitted without cause, and also that he regards it—when used in the right way—as also being *embraced* by the *jus divinum* of the ordination. Perhaps we best reflect Luther's view if we say with Gottfried Werner that it is not actually constitutive of the office and yet belongs to the concrete reifications "without which God never makes Himself known and never wishes to work, and to the signs to which our weak faith clings."[250]

---

[248] WA 43:600.26f.

[249] Cf. G. Rietschel (*Lehrbuch d. Lit.* II [1909], pp. 425f.; and 2nd ed. [1952], p. 852), who, regarding the whole sixteenth century, says, "In the rite of ordination, the action of the laying on of hands is used so that this laying on of hands is so closely connected with the ordination rite that the name 'ordination' and 'laying on of hands' were probably also used indiscriminately." This holds true for Luther too, as we see here.

[250] Op. cit., p. 20; also cf. J. Heubach, op. cit., pp. 108f., who judges Luther's view similarly. At least matters are not so simple here in Luther as G. Hök (op. cit., p. 149) thinks when he simply asserts: "The laying on of hands is not necessary. It is not taken up as a divine command. It is used not *jure divino*, but *jure humano*, as a pious custom from the apostolic era." Hök does not include the passages cited by us. Hök is right, however, in that the emphasis in Luther is more on the prayer than on the laying on of hands (op. cit., p. 149).

Yet this can only hold true in Luther's scheme for *that* laying on of hands which is tied to prayer and the Word of God, as we have already suggested and as is really self-evident. Only when the laying on of hands is conducted by virtue of the Word and supported by prayer can it be more than a mere human, symbolic ceremony, namely, a medium of divine action. The *Word of God* is for Luther the natural, basic element of ordination. An ordination in which the Word of God is not involved is no ordination, remarks Luther in a sermon from 1524.[251] The office is transmitted in ordination "by virtue of the Word."[252] Thus we must number the true elements of ordination in Luther as three: the Word of God, prayer, and the laying on of hands. But we will still have to concern ourselves in greater detail with the specific sense which Luther ascribes to the laying on of hands in ordination.

8. The Understanding of the Laying on of Hands in Ordination

The laying on of hands in ordination, according to Luther, has primarily a *declarative, testimonial sense*. It publicly declares that this person is the one elected and properly called. It expresses the *approbatio personae* [approval of the person] by the other ministers of the Word and indicates the transmission of the office.[253] In the Genesis lectures, Luther characterizes the laying on of hands as the "the most ancient rite and ceremony of the fathers," which was taken over from the Old Testament into the New and always used when an office (*munus*) or any function (*administratio*) was conferred on anyone.[254] The laying

[251] WA 15:720.20f.: "There is no ordination since it is done without the Word. . . ."

[252] WA 15:721.4.

[253] WA 52:568.22f.: Laying on of hands is "a public sign . . . of the preaching office being transmitted"; cf. End. 16:275.29ff. (= WA Br 11:156.23ff.): "by apostolic rite, with the laying on of hands, we declared (our testimony concerning him), and we committed to him the ministry of teaching the Gospel and administering the Sacraments"; End. 11:42.96ff.: "Also all pastors of all the churches of Christ, of cities both great and small, acknowledge those as Christ's true disciples and ministers when they commune them, approve their doctrine, and, as formerly, confirm them with the laying on of hands." — The laying on of hands is a sign of the approval and confirmation itself.

[254] WA 44:695.19ff.: "The rite of the laying on of hands is the most ancient and taken over by the fathers into the New Testament also, as evident from Paul, when he says, 'Lay hands on no one prematurely.' Moses lays hands on Joshua. And it was a ceremony of the fathers, the prophets, and of the whole Church used in every age, when they committed to anyone any office or ministry." But W. Maurer (*Gemeindezucht, Gemeindeamt, Konfirmation*, op. cit., p. 56 n. 15) remarks on this passage: "Purely legal, and therefore probably not from Luther, is the view of the laying on of hands in the Genesis commentary on Gen. 48:13." In fact, one might surmise even a Melanchthonian influence here, although this expression for the laying on of hands, that by it an office is committed (*mandare alicui munus*), is not found in Melanchthon (cf. below, pp. 323–26). In Luther, however, the committal of the office plays a constant role in the theology of ordination (cf. the sixth rubric in *Ordination of Ministers of the Word* and the passages discussing the committal of the office above, p. 170 n. 154, as well as WA 26:83.8ff.). Thus it is probable that we have an authentic Luther text in this passage. — C. Mahrenholz says of the laying on of hands in the ordination according to

on of hands serves as the rite of conferring and committing the office. In ordination, it also simultaneously confirms the legitimate conduct of the collective call process before the whole Church.[255] Thus Luther stresses in his treatise on the episcopal consecration in Naumburg [*Model for the Consecration of a True Christian Bishop*]: "The laying on of hands—they bless, confirm, and testify to this, *as a notary and witness testify to a secular matter.* And as the pastor who blesses the bride and groom confirms or testifies to their marriage which they previously undertook and openly declared. . . ."[256]

In this passage, Luther regards the laying on of hands in particular as the *rite of public testimony of a prior consensus*, namely, between the church and the recipient of the call, that "the church will hear the bishop and the bishop teach the church."[257] To this extent, the parallel to marriage is especially close. This statement about the laying on of hands accordingly refers to a rite that was not properly ordination by itself but also included the investiture (introduction) to a specific concrete office in a specific place. This explains the greater focus here on the consensus between the congregation and the recipient of the call. In the actual ordination, it is more the legitimacy of the collective call process and, in particular, the examination conducted which is to be testified to and confirmed by the laying on of hands. Nevertheless, it still features a local call, and thus a consensus between a specific congregation and the ordinand.

While the laying on of hands in ordination has a testifying, to a certain extent notarial, significance according to Luther, this should not be regarded as exclusive. The laying on of hands in ordination in Luther's view also has a benedictory function. This is why, in his report on the episcopal consecration in Naumburg, it reads: "*The laying on of hands—they bless*, confirm and testify to this. . . ." The benedictory function even comes first.[258]

Luther (op. cit., p. 23): "This early Church . . . practice was retained by Luther because it reflects the common tradition of the Church, is a public sign of the office committed, and constitutes a strong assurance of the person called, on whom the office is quasi-physically bestowed by the laying on of hands."

[255] Cf. WA 26:99.18ff.: "Surely it is a dangerous estate; that is, do not easily entrust any office to any man. Then ministers were ordained in this way: the confirmation of ministers was done in the presence of the church."

[256] WA 53:257.6ff. We also encounter the comparison to marriage in the Genesis lectures: WA 44:407.34ff.: "It is senseless, therefore, that they prohibit peculiar rites in the church for marrying spouses, likewise for ordaining ministers of the Word. We bless husband and wife, recite the words of the divine institution, call upon God that He would protect this order. With ministers we lay on hands and at the same time pour out prayers to God, etc." — On the episcopal consecration in Naumburg in detail, cf. the new study by Peter Brunner, *Nikolaus von Amsdorf als Bischof von Naumburg*, Schriften des Vereins für Reformationsgeschichte 179, vol. 67.2 and 68 (Gütersloh, 1961), esp. pp. 60ff.

[257] WA 53:257.5f.

[258] WA 53:257.6ff. — Regarding this passage, P. Brunner believes that Luther did not incorporate the Benediction into the confirmation performed in ordination until 1542 ("Vom Amt. d. Bischofs," p. 15 n. 10). Yet the element of the *benedictio* is already found in Luther's *Ordination of Ministers of the Word*, and it is noteworthy that Luther already teaches in his exposition of 1 Timothy in

This benedictory force is imparted to the laying on of hands by its connection to the prayer. In the sermon on St. Andrew's Day 1544, Luther says of the early Christian ordination according to the Pastoral Epistles: "Now this laying on of hands was not only a public sign of the preaching office being transmitted, but it was accompanied by prayer. . . . This prayer was not in vain; for through this laying on of hands and prayer, the Holy Spirit came, sometimes visibly, upon the ministers being ordained, as in Acts 19. And Paul tells us twice how Timothy, by such laying on of hands, received the election of the Holy Spirit . . . (1 Tim. 4:14; 2 Tim. 1:6)."[259] Luther holds this effect of the laying on of hands during prayer as operative in the present. Although the Holy Spirit no longer comes with visible signs as at that time, the ordination prayer will nevertheless "not be fruitless, but [will] accomplish that for which it is done according to Christ's promise: 'Where two or three are gathered in My name, whatever they ask the Father, that will He give them. . . .' "[260] From this text two things are evident: first,

1528 that, according to the New Testament, a spiritual gift is given through the laying on of hands (WA 26:83.6ff.).

259 WA 52:568.22ff. Similar thoughts are also found in other writings of Luther's. In the treatise *Against King Henry of England* (1522), the content of the *impositio manuum* in the apostolic age is characterized as a "visible gift of the Holy Spirit [*donatio visibilis Spiritus sancti*]" (WA 10/2:221.8f.). In any case, Luther in this treatise does not say this with respect to ordination; indeed, he denies that the laying on of hands in the Timothean passages refers to the *sacramentum ordinis* [sacrament of ordination]. In so doing, he is motivated by the polemic against King Henry, who in expositing this passage taught that with the laying on of hands in the priestly consecration a spiritual gift of grace is imparted (Walch, 1st ed., vol. 19, pp. 277f.). Luther counters: "What he draws from the laying on of hands for the sacrament of ordination—little boys see that it in no way relates to the sacrament of ordination, but by his papistic method he thus makes from Scriptures whatever seems right to him. Then the laying on of hands was a visible giving of the Holy Spirit" (WA 10/2:221.5ff.; cf. WA 10/2:240.15f.). Here Luther has obviously allowed himself to be pressed into an interpretative error by his polemical task, yet he does not give up the idea that the laying on of hands at that time had as its result the gift of the Holy Spirit with a visible sign. In 1528, by contrast, Luther, in expositing 1 Timothy, to a certain extent tacitly corrects these statements against King Henry. On 1 Tim. 4:14, namely, he says, " 'Charisma': a free gift. What kind of gift it was supposed to be it does not say, but I think that it was an ability to teach and exhort" (WA 26:82.35f.). "The Lord has adorned you with an extraordinary gift, which someone else cannot [do]" (WA 26:83.3f.), ". . . He has this gift from the laying on of hands. At that time, the Holy Spirit was also given visibly, when they laid their hands on, as in the early Church in Acts" (WA 26:83.6ff.). The parallel with the passage from the *House Postil* is obvious. Luther goes on: "This laying on of hands was nothing other than the reception and assignment of those to whom some office was committed, as in Acts 13. Such was done to Timothy" (WA 26:83.8ff.). The office was committed to Timothy by the laying on of hands, and by it he received the gift of the Holy Spirit, which Luther himself explains as a particular capability to perform the office, and so a particular grace of the office. The connection of the committal of the preaching office with the gift in the laying on of hands also demonstrates the relationship of both texts as well as the connection of the laying on of hands with the prayer: "What the prophecy is that is used in addition to the prayer I have said above, and certain prayers spoken from Holy Scripture" (WA 26:83.10ff.). These Luther passages are completely ignored by Brunotte (op. cit., pp. 18ff.) when he maintains that, according to Luther, no particular gift is imparted in ordination.

260 WA 52:569.18ff. — Obvious here, in turn, are the parallels to Luther's further explanations in his treatise to the Bohemians [*Concerning the Ministry*] (cf. above, pp. 125–27). This correspondence also substantiates the authenticity of the sermon for St. Andrew's Day in the *House Postil*.

that for Luther the *benedictory function of the laying on of hands is rooted in the ordination prayer connected to it* and, second, that through the ordination prayer with laying on of hands *a real,*[261] *spiritual gift is actually given.*[262] The difference between the laying on of hands in the early Christian period and that in the present day lies, according to Luther, in the fact that the Spirit's gift was formerly given with visible signs while today it is bestowed on the ordinand as an internal aptitude. The reality of the gift, however, is the same, then and now. The laying on of hands is the *ceremonia externa* through which the spiritual gift requisite for the office is given out by means of the prayer.[263] Luther assigns to the laying on of hands in ordination a benedictory significance alongside the notarial one.

9. The *Minister Ordinationis*

Who is to perform ordination? Are only bishops or other bearers of the clerical office eligible—which is to say, only carriers of the clerical office—or unordained congregants as well?

Fundamentally, Luther always assumes that the available Roman *bishops* are to perform the ordination. In addition to this is the condition that they cease imposing improper vows in ordination[264] and persecuting the Gospel. Directly

---

[261] Cf. WA 44:407.37f.: "With ministers we lay on hands and *at the same time pour out prayers to God. . . .*"

[262] Cf. above, pp. 174–75 on the benedictory reality in Luther. — For G. Rietschel (op. cit., p. 53), "Benediction [*Segnen*]" is only "an expression of the intercession made in the same liturgical act of the congregation." The fact that a real, spiritual gift is given in it has been entirely ignored by Rietschel (op. cit., also pp. 111f.); likewise by E. C. Achelis (*Lehrbuch der prakt. Theol.*, vol. 1 [Leipzig, 1911], p. 139), who sees in the laying on of hands in Luther only the "gesture of intercession for the person." The benedictory laying on of hands with prayer during ordination is more than simply a "gesture of intercession." It is the effective impartation and endowment. The same can be said against H. Heppe (*Dogmatik d. dtschen. Protestantismus i. 16. Jh.*, vol. 3 [Gotha, 1857], p. 325). — J. Heubach accurately concludes that, according to Luther's view, "the impartation of the Holy Spirit, and with Him His gifts requisite for the exercise of the office," are to be, as it were, " 'displayed' through the laying on of hands and 'enacted' through the external action" (op. cit., p. 109). Brunotte's critique of Heubach has already been dispelled above, p. 179 n. 220. Brunotte, in his representation, shows no understanding for the benedictory function of the laying on of hands in Luther (op. cit., pp. 188ff.). His call for the laying on of hands in ordination to be omitted in our time "so that ordination according to Luther's view may take full effect and not be distorted" (op. cit., p. 202) must appear absurd.

[263] WA 43:521.33ff. (on Gen. 27:28f., the blessing of Isaac): "For external spiritual things cannot be administered without external ceremonies. The five senses and the whole body have their actions and rites under which the body must live as if under certain masks. This is why he [Isaac] blessed not only in the heart but also with the external senses and ceremonies. It was necessary for those sons seeking the blessing to bring their father such fine food and wine. . . . After the ceremony was observed, Moses again says, 'And he blessed him,' namely, externally, when he had smelled the odor of his clothes. For a sense which moves the Holy Spirit is always present, and the Holy Spirit moves hearts through external things, such as the Word, ceremonies, and objects, which move the heart through an external sense."

[264] Namely: the renunciation of the true doctrine of the Gospel, celibacy, the vow to celebrate the sacrifice of the Mass, to administer Communion under one kind, etc.

traceable to Luther's influence was the practice of Evangelicals always to attempt first to have their preachers consecrated and ordained by the available Roman bishops under these conditions.[265] Only when it was *impossible* to obtain such an ordination were they compelled to take the act of calling, and with it the ordination also, into their own hands, that is, to handle it without the bishops, through simple ministers of the Word.[266] In the event that episcopal ordination becomes impossible, Luther appeals to the right of *all ministers in the office* to perform ordination.

But if the necessity becomes more pressing, since not only had the bishops become enemies of the Gospel but, besides that, there were no other orthodox ministers of the Word in the vicinity who were able to ordain, Luther goes a step further regarding the identity of the *minister ordinationis* [minister of ordination] and, in light of such a situation, as we saw, stipulates in his treatise to the Bohemians [*Concerning the Ministry*] that *congregants also* perform the confirmation act with prayer and laying on of hands, namely, those congregants "who are more prominent among you [*qui potiores inter vos fuerint*]."[267] The most prominent, most respected ones are then to ordain.[268] It should, in any case, not be forgotten that this direction is to be regarded only as pertaining to the specific case of necessity in Bohemia and in no way as a rule to be effective for

---

265 WA 38:195.17ff.: "We have always very humbly assured the pope and bishops, especially at the Imperial Diet at Augsburg, that we did not wish to seize their church rights and authority, and if they would not force upon us unchristian articles, we would gladly be consecrated and ruled by them and also help to exercise their rights and authority, but we were unable to ascertain or acquire it . . ."; cf. WA 38:236.23ff.; 41:241.1ff.: "We made frequent and numerous offers to the bishops to have ourselves confirmed as pastors and preachers, even though they are our enemies and we are not obliged to do so since they are not Christians nor do they wish to be—just as I would do obeisance to the Turk if he was the lord of the land, which God forbid!—They refuse to do it"; WA 50:247.20ff.: "If the bishops would be true bishops and take up the cause of the Church and the Gospel, it might be possible, for the sake of love and unity, though not from necessity . . . to let it be granted so that they would ordain and confirm us and our preachers." The added phrase "though not from necessity" shows that the *episcopal* ordination does not constitute a *divine* Law for Luther. On this cf. P. Brunner, "Vom Amt des Bischofs," pp. 42f., as well as Brunotte, op. cit., p. 180, who, however, makes too little of Luther's essentially positive appraisal of episcopal ordination.

266 WA 50:248.11ff.: "Therefore, as the ancient examples of the Church and of the fathers teach us, we will and should ordain (able) persons to this office; and in this they cannot forbid or prevent us . . ."; WA 52:569.33ff.: "Therefore, we have good cause since they refuse to yield their office to us true ministers of the church because we do not care about their apery and popery, but ordain and elect ministers ourselves, as Christ, the apostles, and all the true Church elected and ordained them"; also cf. WA Br 6:113, 111f.

267 WA 12:193.39.

268 When W. Elert (*Morphologie* I, p. 303) writes: "But the confirmation is also performed by the congregation since its content is the recognition that the rights granted to the collective Church are now delegated to individuals," it must be countered that the *potiores*, while themselves acting as congregants and organs of the church, are set apart by the *universitas* in the ordaining rite and stand in contrast to it precisely in the fact that they confirm the electees for the *universitas* and commend them to it. The entity that performs the confirmation proper is the narrower circle of the *potiores*, which in its ordaining action takes the place of the bishop whose absence is the cause of the necessity. Also cf. P. Brunner, "V. Amt d. Bischofs," pp. 22f. n. 23.

the long term. It is clear from this that Luther—as we already mentioned several times—envisions in the second phase the call (and ordination) of further ministers through the newly elected and ordained pastors.[269] If they are to perform the call, then it is only right that they may do the ordination also. When Luther simultaneously thinks of a higher-ranking archiepiscopal office of oversight and visitation in Bohemia and of the restoration of the legitimate episcopacy of the Bohemian Church, it is also clear that ordination is intended to become a specifically *episcopal* function again. Thus it is beyond doubt that Luther envisions an ordination through congregants not holding an office only in the most extreme case of necessity[270] and otherwise maintains that *ordination is the function of the spiritual or clerical office, and specifically of the bishop.* Of the same tenor are Luther's other statements on the question of the *minister ordinationis* through which we have yet to sift.

In 1531, Luther writes to Pastor Sutel in Göttingen that he should be ordained by the other ministers publicly at the altar with prayer and the laying on of hands and should be given the authority to handle the Supper [*auctoritas cenae tractandae*]. Obviously ordination appears as a function of the spiritual office in this letter of Luther's.[271] In the treatise *The Private Mass and the Consecration of Priests* (1533), Luther cites the ancient call process ordered by the Council of Nicaea, a process which always had an orthodox meaning for Luther, especially for the ordination which was to be newly implemented in Wittenberg. In this process, however, the ordination through the laying on of hands is naturally performed only by the bishops, even though the people elect those to be ordained and give their *placet* [endorsement]. Augustine consecrated in his own parish many pastors for other cities; therefore, "we, too, may do so, and in our parish in Wittenberg ordain ministers of the Word for other cities."[272] By the term "we," Luther refers to himself and his colleagues in the pastoral office in Wittenberg. If Augustine ordains as a municipal bishop, the pastor of Wittenberg (quite like Augustine in his actual position!) has the right to do so. When in the same treatise Luther wishes to see ordination restored to the church, he means by this that the power to ordain should be given not only to the greater bishops (now merely calling themselves such) but also to the lesser, municipal bishops, the pastors in the larger cities, but by no means does he wish to advocate, or even to elevate to the status of principle, an ordination by the congregants who do not hold office.[273]

---

[269] WA 12:191.2.

[270] Namely, only as a temporary measure until the office is reinstated.

[271] WA Br 6:44.18ff.

[272] WA 38:238.2ff.

[273] WA 38:252.4ff.: ". . . [Christ] here desires that they begin . . . to assign and give back to the Church the call or true consecration and ordination to the pastoral office, as the Church had it from the beginning, which the greater bishops wrested for themselves alone and took from the lesser bishops or pastors." — And this is the sense in which WA 41:241.38f. is be understood when it says "it does not depend on the person."

In the ordination address of October 20, 1535, Luther says, "We willingly give the office,"[274] and repeatedly uses the first person plural with respect to the action of ordination. Here—as in the treatise *The Private Mass and the Consecration of Priests*—he means himself and the other ministers of the Gospel in Wittenberg, which is to say, his colleagues in the theological faculty, to whom the task of ordination was assigned by the elector and who were at any rate always bearers of the spiritual office.[275] This cannot be taken otherwise since in the same address the "we" is contrasted with a "you," by which the congregation is meant.[276] The congregants are only invited to be witnesses and to join in prayer; the performance of the ordination itself as confirmation of the call, as conferral of the office and blessing for the office, is conceived as the action of the ordaining office-bearers. So is it also in *Ordination of Ministers of the Word*. The ministers with the ordaining minister are lifted up by the congregation in that they alone are with the ordinands at the altar, and they alone act in an ordaining capacity. Only the ordaining minister and the other ministers lay their hands on the ordinands and speak the consecratory prayer.[277] The same picture is also presented by the episcopal consecration of Naumburg [*Model for the Consecration of a True Christian Bishop*] (1542).[278] ". . . Not only was I at this consecration and laying on of hands, but so were the following bishops or, as they wish to be called, pastors: Doctor Nicholas Medler, pastor and superintendent of Naumburg; Master Georg Spalatin, pastor and superintendent of Altenburg; Master Wolfgang Stein, pastor and superintendent of Weissenfels. According to the usage of the ancient Church and as the ancient canons teach—viz., that a bishop is to be consecrated with the bishops of the nearest cities—so was it all done here."[279] In accordance with the canonical ordinance, only bishops (superintendents, pastors) participated in the laying on of hands; the people were merely "in attendance."[280]

274 WA 41:457.15.

275 Compare the signatures on the ordination certificates: "Pastor and ministers of the Gospel of the Church of Wittenberg" (End. 11:279.29; 12:197.21ff.; 14:252.1, 253.26ff.); or: "Pastor of the church of Wittenberg and other ministers of the Gospel in the same church. Martin Luther, Johann Bugenhagen Pomeranus, etc." (End. 7:132.36ff.; 14:287.45ff.; 15:88.39ff., 143.45ff. [= WA Br 10:298.36ff.]).

276 WA 41:457.34f. ("in your presence, that you might be witnesses"); cf. WA 41:763.3ff.

277 WA 38:424.1ff., 429.1ff. In J, in the ordination address before the readings, it reads: "We also bestow our office conferred upon us, that you with us and we with you may be the more sanctified, and we add our word and prayer, as it is written: 'He who is holy, let him be sanctified still'" (WA 38:425 n. 7).

278 The proceedings of the episcopal consecration in Naumburg are found described by G. Rietschel, "Luthers Ordinationsformular i. s. urspr. Gestalt," op. cit., pp. 176f. (after *Neue Mitteilungen aus dem Gebiete hist.-antiquar. Forschungen* II, 2., pp. 178ff.) and by T. Kolde, "Z. Gesch. d. Ord.," op. cit., pp. 238f., and recently in detail by Peter Brunner, *Nikolaus von Amsdorf als Bischof von Naumburg* (Gütersloh, 1961), pp. 60ff.

279 WA 53:257.13ff.

280 WA 53:257.21f. The *Agende IV f. ev.-luth. Kirchen und Gemeinden* (Neuendettelsau, 1951), which envisions only ordained office-bearers as assistants in ordination, must thus be cleared of

In the treatise to the Erfurt preachers,[281] the functions in the call process, with appeal to Scripture, are divided between the people and the office-bearers. The election and appointment of suitable persons belongs to the church while the laying on of hands, approval, and attesting of fitness belong to other pastors.[282] In his lectures on the Epistles of Titus and Philemon (1527), Luther mentions that in the apostolic era ordination was not done as "our people" (i.e., Roman bishops) do it, but the *senes* [elders] assembled with the laying on of hands.[283] This is how Titus and the *senes* ordain. But who are these *senes*? While it might be possible here to take the term *senes* as the "prominent men [*potiores*]" in the congregation, this is prevented by the fact that in his sermon on St. Andrew's Day (1544) Luther gives a contradictory gloss. There he says that, by the elders (*Ältesten*) who were convoked by the apostles (which is to say, Timothy and Titus), "other ministers of the church (*Kirchendiener*)" are meant.[284] Agreeing with this pattern from the apostolic era is the ancient Church usage: ". . . and the office was afterward publicly committed to them" (the electees) "with the laying on of hands by certain bishops and pastors who were in the vicinity."[285]

We can summarize by saying that for Luther—apart from the case of extreme necessity in which no true ministers are available—the legitimate *minister ordinationis* is a bearer of the spiritual office and specifically, in normal, orderly circumstances, the bishop.[286]

Brunotte's charge that it does not agree with Luther's view of ordination in this respect (op. cit., p. 202). Rather, it wonderfully agrees with it in this respect as also in the fact that it maintains the laying on of hands, which Brunotte urgently wishes to see abolished in order to replace it with "the vow of the ordained by handshake" (ibid.). It is regrettable that Brunotte's book on the spiritual office in Luther, which contains so many good and worthy observations, closes with these suggestions.

[281] Cf. above, p. 134 n. 177.

[282] End. 11:40.18ff. — On the basis of this passage, W. Elert (*Morphologie* I, p. 311) confirms that in Luther's view the actual practice of ordination being performed liturgically only by ordained men is without fault. Also cf. End. 11:45.209ff.: "Christ . . . gives to the Church the authority to call and elect and consecrate, and the right, in its name, to approve and confirm by other pastors that this doctrine is truly in harmony with Scripture—indeed, the very word that Christ and the apostles spoke."

[283] WA 25:17.18.

[284] WA 52:568.20f.: "The elders (that is, other ministers)." — The ordination certificate for Prince George of Anhalt from August 2, 1545, which was even drafted by Melanchthon (and thus evinces rather Melanchthonian language), yet fully endorsed and signed first by Luther, reads: "Since Paul commanded Titus to appoint presbyters to teach and govern the churches in different places, let this ordained man know that he also is commanded by the apostolic voice in this function, to ordain priests to teach and direct the churches and to examine their doctrine and life" (End. 16:275.32ff. [= WA Br 11:156.25ff.]).

[285] WA 52:568.35ff. The relationship of the account here with, e.g., that in the treatise on the episcopal consecration in Naumburg [*Model for the Consecration of a True Christian Bishop*] again supports the idea that that sermon on St. Andrew's Day 1544 is an authentic Luther sermon.

[286] When H. Storck opines that Luther gives the right of ordination to "all true Christians" (op. cit., p. 35), it is not an accurate representation of the facts in Luther. Only in the most extreme emergency are the *potiores* of the congregation to ordain; in every other case, the ministers personally holding the office do so. When Storck says further: "The power of ordination according to Luther's view is not reserved to certain ecclesial office-bearers but is available everywhere the Gospel

Yet let us further ask why ordination as Luther defines it should (except in a necessity) be undertaken by a minister in the office and what reasons Luther gives for seeing ordination as a function of the spiritual office. We must mention first, as a formal cause, the agreement with the apostolic and ancient example. We may also begin with the general observation that, since not all can ordain simultaneously, this function must be conferred on certain individuals. Because the ministers are at least the public trustees of all things ecclesial, it is self-evident that they also perform the ordination. Yet there are specific arguments in Luther's writings. First, ordination is the testimony of the examined man's aptitude to teach. Assessing the aptitude to teach and testifying to it are matters belonging to the office of the Word. The bearers of this office therefore assess and admit men to the office.[287] But then Luther delves even deeper into the argument for ordination through ministers of the Word, tracing it back to the mandate of the ordaining minister's office. Thus he says in the sermon from 1524 already familiar to us: "We will preach and anoint differently from those bishops. But we, who already have ministries, will commit to our ministry. . . . By virtue of the Word which we have, we give the authority to preach the Word and give the Sacraments."[288] The conferral of the office in ordination has as its prerequisite that those who confer it themselves possess it.[289] Also in the sermon from May 9, 1535, Luther vigorously stresses as a requirement of ordination that rightly called office-bearers must be present.[290] In his table talk concerning Benedict Schumann's ordination, Luther says to the ordinate: "My dear brother Benedict, you are ordained by God to be a faithful minister of Jesus Christ there in Naumburg, to invoke His holy name with the pure teaching of the Gospel, to which we call and send you by God's authority, *just as God has sent us. . . .*"[291] The divine sending to the office occurring in ordination is founded on the prior divine sending of the ordaining minister. Since we ourselves are in the office and sent by God, we are able to call and send you to the office "by God's authority." Clearly there is an underlying idea of a succession to the office here, as we also found in our discussion of the call.[292] Against this backdrop,

---

is rightly and purely preached" (ibid.), it can only apply in the sense that Luther does not bind the right of ordination exclusively to *certain* ecclesial office-bearers (i.e., the bishops), but grants it to *all* pastors, yet not in such a way that it is the same to him whether it is exercised by office-bearers or those not holding the office. — On the whole matter also cf. E. Kinder, *Ev. Glaube u. d. Kirche* (Berlin, 1958), pp. 188ff.

287 Cf. above, pp. 138–40 and F. K. Schumann ("Amt der Kirche," etc., op. cit., p. 326): "The office must testify to the office."

288 WA 15:721.1ff.

289 On this passage also cf. H. H. Kramm (op. cit., p. 45), who shares our understanding "that those who have the pastoral office hand it on."

290 WA 41:241.14ff.

291 WA TR 5:111.22ff. (no. 5376); likewise, WA 47:192.6ff.: "Thus we are sent, and we elect others also and set them in the office, that they may preach and administer the Sacraments."

292 Cf. above, pp. 129–30. Nevertheless, a specific theory of the propagation of supernatural powers and abilities from person to person, such as lies at the root of the doctrine of apostolic succession in the Roman-Anglican understanding, is foreign to Luther.

it becomes more significant that the formula in *Ordination of Ministers of the Word* reads: "by command of the Church and *through our office*, we will ordain you. . . ."[293] And yet it must be kept in mind that the ordaining minister acts not only as office-bearer but also as instrument of the whole Church.[294] Thus in the case of necessity (cf. the Bohemians[*Concerning the Ministry*]), the authority of the whole Church may even stand for the mandate of office absent in those performing ordination.

10. The Ordination Gift

We have found in Luther that ordination is not without a real effect. Ordination definitively places a person in the office, gives the authority to preach the Word and administer the Sacraments [*auctoritas praedicandi verbum et administrandi sacramenta*], and is thus the transmission of the office. At the same time, however, it is also a blessing for the office and thus (by means of the laying on of hands and the ordination prayer) gives a spiritual gift which equips the person for the office. This gift is most accurately described as the *gift of the Holy Spirit*, for which prayer is made during the ordination.

> Here the gift of the Holy Spirit as the grace of justification, as appropriation of the adoption as sons of God and the foundation of the estate of grace, which has as its purpose the eternal salvation of the person in question, must be distinguished from the gift of the Holy Spirit as a particular equipment for the office, as the charisma of the office, which is given to the person in question only for the office which he is to bear. In a sermon from 1529 on John 20:21ff., Luther explains that there are two manners of having the Holy Spirit: one for oneself, for one's own person, and, second, "not for oneself or for one's own person, but for the office."[295] Luther thus knows of the gift of the Holy Spirit as an equipment for the office in contrast to a personal gift of grace.[296] In this sermon on John 20:22

[293] Cf. above, pp. 170–72. Thus when Luther refers the performance of ordination to those bearing office, it is a deeper argument than the formal one which states that ordination occurs in the context of public worship and that "public proclamation is the object of the spiritual office," as evident in Brunotte (op. cit., p. 191).

[294] Cf. above, pp. 133–34 and 171–73.

[295] WA 28:468.2ff. and 28ff.; also WA 28:467.40ff. — The distinction between having the Holy Spirit for oneself and for the office is also made by Luther in his sermon on 1 Cor. 12:1ff. (1535): WA 22:179.15ff.: "For he" (the apostle) "is mainly speaking here of the office which preaches about Christ and carries His command. Wherever this office goes and points to Christ (as to the Lord), that is for certain the preaching of the Holy Spirit, even if he who bears this office does not have the Holy Spirit for his own person. For the office belongs directly to the Holy Spirit"; cf. WA 22:183.5ff.

[296] In *The Babylonian Captivity of the Church*, when Luther says of the *ordo* that it has no promise of grace put anywhere in it (WA 6:560.21f.), his focus is on forgiveness. This kind of grace is not promised to the *ordo*. But the idea that a spiritual charisma is imparted in the true, Evangelical ordination, which occurs by virtue of the Word, lies entirely within Luther's field of vision (particularly in later years). Cf. WA 43:524.32ff.; 52:568.22ff., 569.16ff.; 53:257.6ff. — The question is whether it is justified to conflate Luther with Höfling in this regard; cf. P. Brunner, "Vom Amt des Bischofs," p. 13 n. 7: "He" (i.e., Höfling) "no more than Luther saw a charisma *bestowed* in ordination." Rather, one

("Receive the Holy Spirit"), he explains that Christ is giving the Holy Spirit to the apostles for their office (as the sending in v. 21 is also construed as a commission of the office).[297]

Accordingly, Luther teaches that this ordination gift is an *objective* one. It is independent of the internal character of both the ordaining minister and the ordinand. Time and again, Luther cites approvingly the ruling of the ancient Church that the ordinations of heretics are valid.[298] With this ruling he confronts the Romans, who regard the Lutherans as heretics, to demonstrate to them that their own canons compel them to acknowledge Lutheran ordinations as legitimate. "They must therefore allow our consecrating and ordaining to be true."[299] In his treatise in defense of the episcopal consecration of Naumburg [*Model for the Consecration of a True Christian Bishop*], Luther explains: "Even if it must be accounted for that the bishop of Naumburg allowed these hostile heretics and apostates of the papal church to consecrate or lay on their hands,"[300] and puts the emphasis on the objectivity of the ordination *rite*, which is right and valid independent of the pastor's character. "Whether the pastor is an angel or a devil, since the service has taken place, the bride is blessed."[301] All that matters is that the person who performs the ordination is "in the office" and carries out the function of the office. "Indeed, even if the devil were in the office and did it . . . ," the ordination would be right and valid.[302] If the ordaining minister is in the office and performs the ordination in due manner, it is a valid act of God, and the gift of ordination is still given by it.[303]

At the same time, the character of the one receiving the ordination gift cannot negate it either. Luther explains in the sermon from 1529 cited above that

---

might agree with Brunner's formulation (op. cit., p. 15 n. 10) that, in the Reformation understanding of ordination, there is "insufficient recognition" of the fact that a charisma is bestowed in ordination through the speaking of the Word, laying on of hands, and prayer, though it must be said that the idea of a transmission of a spiritual gift in ordination plainly emerges in Luther. This is entirely overlooked by Brunotte (op. cit., pp. 188ff.); also cf. above, p. 179 n. 219.

297 WA 28:466.22f.: "He sends them, just as He is sent from the Father and gives them the Holy Spirit for this sending and office"; WA 28:468.14ff.: "And this is why He does not relate the Holy Spirit to the apostles' persons . . . but to their office"; WA 28:470.21ff.: "For here Christ gives the Holy Spirit to His whole Church and all Christians, to the apostles and the apostles' successors, pastors and preachers, that they may preach, teach, comfort, and forgive and retain sins, and, in short, be sent as the Father sent Him."

298 E.g., WA 38:237.4ff.; 53:257.1ff.; cf. WA 34/1:432.1ff. (Cyprian's re-ordaining of those who had been ordained by heretics is deprecated): "But this was not right. Just as today the Papists sit in the true office, baptize, give the Sacrament, ordain priests, consecrate spouses, even as we do. And yet I say, he who receives their Sacrament truly receives it, and whom they ordain a priest, let it be so, even though they themselves do not grant that we do so."

299 WA 38:237.8f.

300 WA 53:256.10ff.

301 WA 53:257.10f. The same train of thought is found in the sermon of October 20, 1535: WA 41:456.13ff.

302 WA 53:257.4.

303 WA 41:456.12ff., 457.5.

having the Holy Spirit "for the office" is a "dangerous way" of having the Holy Spirit. This is because this possession of the Holy Spirit will be for the judgment of the one who is unfaithful in the office, in accordance with Matt. 7:22–23.[304] It is not simply invalidated by a false inner quality in the office-bearer. It must be maintained that wicked priests, too, have the Holy Spirit on account of the office; this is an objective fact.[305] Luther here positions himself in sharp contrast to Donatists, Anabaptists, and Enthusiasts.[306] He expressly teaches that the Holy Spirit is not always with us for own sake, "but for our office: whenever we preach the Gospel, baptize, absolve, administer the Sacrament according to the Holy Spirit's institution and ordinance, the Holy Spirit is always with us."[307] The gift of the Holy Spirit is so bound up with the office (i.e., the concrete office as conferred on a person) that it is always operative when the office is being discharged. There is only one condition to stipulate here, which is that the office is discharged "according to the Holy Spirit's institution and ordinance," and thus *ritè* [duly]. If this condition is fulfilled, the Holy Spirit is objectively effectual through the office-bearer.[308] If it were otherwise—if God's Word and office depended on human worthiness—"everything would be uncertain: the Word, Baptism, the Keys . . . ,"[309] and then the true sense of the means of grace would become void. But such is not the case. Christ founded the preaching office and objectively bound to it the gift of the Holy Spirit.[310] And this is so much a reality that it asserts itself in the function of the office even in opposition to a wicked minister's personal character: the Holy Spirit is active even through a Judas.[311]

---

304 WA 28:468.8ff.

305 WA 28:468.2ff.

306 WA 28:466.29ff.

307 WA 28:468.29ff. and 34ff.

308 WA 28:467.9ff.: "To the extent that the preaching office and the Word of the Gospel and the Sacraments, which is the Holy Spirit's ordinance, is present whole and intact, there is also forgiveness of sins, life, salvation, and all that Christ gives and promises to give through the preaching office and the Word, even if unbelievers and wicked men hold the office and handle that Word"; also WA 28:467.14ff: "Therefore, note well to what extent the Holy Spirit is present and to what extent the Holy Spirit is not present. If the Holy Spirit's ordinance is kept, the Holy Spirit is present. But if the Holy Spirit's ordinance is not allowed to remain, the Holy Spirit is not present. When the Gospel is preached and the Sacraments administered as the Holy Spirit ordained and established them, the Holy Spirit is present, even if he who preaches and baptizes is personally an unbeliever and ungodly"; cf. WA 28:467.32ff.; 38:241.6ff., 242.21ff., 243.13f.; 47:192.42ff.: "So it may also happen that a man is called and occupies an office and yet is a rogue. . . . Thus we see that if someone is called, he is in an office. If he preaches what his office requires and he preaches the Word of God on which the office is founded, it proceeds properly. . . ."

309 WA 28:470.26ff.; cf. WA 28:467.37ff.

310 WA 28:470.30ff. and 41f.: "Therefore, if a man who is called to the preaching office acts according to the office, the Holy Spirit is certainly present"; cf. WA 28:466.22f.

311 WA 38:243.25ff. Also cf. above, pp. 75–76. In addition, WA 41:455.11ff.: ". . . Look to the gift and the true giver, not the instrument by which it is given, lest it be the kind that does not give what God commanded. . . . But if he is a true instrument, allows the Gospel and Sacraments to remain, let nothing move; whether he is a thief or a godly man, if he gives the Gospel, Sacrament, Baptism, Absolution, there is truly what they are through his dignity . . ."; WA 41:456.3f.: "He" (i.e., Christ)

Thus the ordination gift is, in Luther's view, independent of the personal character of the ordaining minister as well as that of the ordinand.[312]

But it must now be observed that the objective ordination gift does not penetrate the ordinand's nature. It is, according to Luther, always active *only by the function of the office actually being done* and only so long as the person is actually in the office. It is possible for the office-bearer to lose it, namely, when he is removed from the office. We have already discussed this removability of the minister of the Word according to Luther.[313] Luther knows of no *character indelebilis* [indelible character] as a persistence of personal specification given through the ordination.[314] This is a consequence of his functional view of the office.[315]

"also baptizes through the hand of the traitor as through that of St. Peter"; WA 50:634.22ff.; WA TR 1:137.28ff. (no. 342): "Concerning ministers of the church one should think thus: The office is not Judas's but Christ's, the only one. When He says to Judas, 'Go, baptize,' He Himself is the baptizer, not Judas, since the command comes through Him from above, even though it goes through a stinking conduit. The office is not affected by the minister's own unworthiness. . . . The office and person are to be differentiated. Thus the pope has the true ministry, even though he misuses it; he does not deny the Word, Baptism, or the Sacrament, but only misuses these. . . . He denies not the thing but the use of the thing. It is only a distortion. He ought to grab the knife by the handle, but he grabs it by the blade. The Enthusiasts do not do so; they toss the knife away and say, 'There is no knife.' . . . Enthusiasts take away the substance; the pope only takes away the accident. So, too, the name of God is true in the abuse . . ."; WA TR 1:285.7ff. (no. 605); WA 38:241.2ff.: (Even if the devil snuck into the office and exercised the office) "we would still confess that the Sacraments were real, we had really received Baptism, really heard the Gospel, really received the Absolution, really took Christ's body and blood. . . ." — Luther even maintains the validity and salvific efficacy of the function of the office in the event that an uncalled, unconsecrated minister infiltrating the office dispenses the function of the office, assuming he dispenses it strictly according to Christ's command and ordinance. Cf. WA 38:241.6ff.: (Our faith and Sacrament do not depend on whether the person) "is good or bad, consecrated or unconsecrated, called or infiltrator, the devil or his mother. . . ." Thus it is impossible to say that Luther would make the validity and efficacy of Word and Sacrament directly *dependent* on the presence of the ordination gift. Where ordination *has* taken place, the gift of the Holy Spirit proceeding from ordination is objectively efficacious with the salvific efficacy of the function of the office, even despite the disbelief and moral unworthiness of the office-bearer's person. And if the ordination is somehow culpably omitted and an unordained man (without the congregation knowing it) is actually occupying the office and is tolerated in the office (cf. WA 50:634.22ff.), the Word and Sacrament are nevertheless valid, operative, and salvifically efficacious in and of themselves, even without the ordination gift. — G. Wehrung ("Zu Augustana VIII," op. cit., p. 10) has detected in Luther "a deep-rooted inclination toward the objective."

312 G. Hök's statement "call and consecration do not work *ex opere operato*" (op. cit., p. 149) raises a few questions, if by saying so he means that, according to Luther, the call and ordination do not *ipso facto* place a person into the office and give him the Holy Spirit for the office independent of the subjective character of ordaining minister and ordinand.

313 Cf. above, pp. 77–80.

314 WA 6:408.21ff.: "Thus truly is a priest no more a priest when he is removed. But now they have invented *characteres indelebiles* and babble that a removed priest is nevertheless different from a plain layman—indeed, they dream that a priest can never be anything other than a priest nor become a layman. This is all man-made sayings and statutes."

315 WA 6:567.17ff.: "Therefore, as much as we are taught from the Scriptures, since the ministry is that which we call the priesthood, I do not really see why a layman cannot become one again after he has been made a priest since a priest is no different from a layman except by his ministry, and

Yet beside the functional specificity of Luther's thinking on the office, other factors must be taken into account which play a joint role here in his rejection of the *character indelebilis*. Luther found the doctrine of the *character indelebilis* in the Roman Church embedded in the Roman doctrine of ordination, which distorted the true concept of the office. *For this reason* the doctrine of the *character indelebilis* strikes Luther as a support for the sacrificial priesthood. In the Roman Church, of course, the *character indelebilis* was ascribed not to the office of the Word but to the consecration to the sacrificial priesthood.[316] The *character indelebilis* served to stabilize and distinguish it, even to the exclusion of the office of the Word! It is *for this reason* that it strikes Luther especially as in line with the "greased and oiled fingers, the tonsured head, and the pharisaical garments of the wretched clerics."[317] The general dispute against the sacrificial priesthood also encompasses the *character indelebilis*. Perhaps Luther would have judged it differently if it had not been combined with the sacrificial priesthood.

The second motive for Luther to attack the Roman *ordo* generally—that is, the fact that the priestly consecration was described as transferring a person to the clerical estate, by which the grace of Baptism was obscured and infringed upon—plays a role in Luther for his assessment of the *character indelebilis*. The *character indelebilis* which Luther attacks is that which, because of the false theology of the *ordo*, conceals the true *character indelebilis* which every Christian has from Baptism.[318] If the spiritual estate of all Christians had been clearly taught in Rome at that time, and the *character indelebilis* of ordination had been interpreted only as the particular thing given in ordination to the office of the Word and Sacraments, Luther's assessment might have been different. But it

---

it is not so impossible to be removed from ministry, but that punishment is now observed against culpable priests, in which case they are either suspended temporarily or deprived of their office forever"; WA 12:190.24f.: ". . . If they are only ministers, already that *character indelebilis* perishes and that eternity of the priesthood is nothing but an invention." When Luther says, "For this is a pretty papistic invention, . . . that he uses *character indelebilis* to make his priests perpetual and unable to be removed by anything except a crime" (WA 12:172.12ff.), it seems as if he confuses the *character indelebilis* with priests' immunity to removal. But Luther is naturally aware that the irremovability of priests is known and practiced in Rome also (cf. the passage WA 6:567.20ff. just cited). In this passage he only wishes to condemn the fact that the congregation's right to dispense with bad priests has been excised from the doctrine of the *character indelebilis* (cf. WA 12:172.10ff.). — Also cf. V. Vajta, op. cit., pp. 218f. Vajta thinks that Luther would call for a new ordination for an ordained pastor who, being removed or abdicating the office, wished to take up again the exercise of the ecclesial office (p. 219), and he supports this with the statement: "Everything depends on the ministry and the office, not the person" (ibid.). In consideration of Luther's functional idea of the office, this is quite possible, yet clear evidence for this is lacking, nor does Vajta offer any, nor does Brunotte, who expresses the same view as Vajta (op. cit., p. 186).

[316] WA 12:173.31ff. and 36ff.: [Papists say that] ". . . dispensing the mysteries of God and feeding souls is an office utterly without a *character indelebilis*, nor is there a sacrament of the *ordo*" (i.e., in the Roman perspective!). "But consecrating and sacrificing Christ—this has a character, this is truly the sacrament of the *ordo*."

[317] WA 8:504.12f.

[318] WA 38:227.32ff.: "likewise . . . the character, the spiritual mark in the soul, which no common Christian is supposed to have, only the consecrated priests."

may be that even then, his belief in the functional specificity of the office would have prevented him from recognizing a *character indelebilis* from ordination.[319]

Nevertheless, it must also be seen—as J. Heubach has worthily pointed out[320]—that Luther also knows of an irrevocable blessing (if we may trust that the relevant passage from the Genesis lectures is authored by Luther). In connection to Gen. 27:33, where Isaac declares the irrevocability of the blessing bestowed on Jacob ("He will also remain blessed"), Luther asks why he could not revoke the blessing and answers: ". . . he knew that this blessing was simply the *immovable* and *immutable* work and gift of God. Thus if I give someone Baptism, my soul and will are altogether certain that I will truly baptize. Even if he who is baptized acts in deceit, nevertheless I have administered true Baptism, which is not mine but is in truth the work of God. In the same way, Isaac said, 'I have blessed also, and he shall be blessed.'[321] In that benediction, Isaac was certain, after careful consideration, that he was voicing a definitive judgment, pronounced and confirmed by divine authority.[322] Such judgments cannot and may not be changed: for God does not change His gifts. He does not revoke Baptism, Absolution, *or other things which He bestows through His Word. . . .*"[323] Would not ordination have to be included among these "other things"? Here, at any rate, is a starting point for the doctrine of an Evangelical *character indelebilis* in Luther, even if Luther did not expressly apply these ideas to the ordination gift.

[319] Luther would regard as valid and efficacious any other functions of the office of a removed pastor who resumes the office against the will of the church (with the assumption that he carries it out according to the ordinance of Christ), even if he would support it with the innate power of the Word and Sacraments rather than a *character indelebilis*.

[320] Op. cit., p. 112 n. 124.

[321] WA 43:531.12ff.

[322] WA 43:531.19f.

[323] WA 43:531.22ff.; cf. WA 43:521.3ff. (on Gen. 27:23b, "and he blessed him"): "Isaac, when he had touched and felt Jacob's hands, was taken completely by surprise, struck dumb and out of his mind, and concluded this blessing and confirmed in his heart that it had to be certain and firm, as though he should say, 'The blessing has already been made and certified.' Just as below he will say to Esau: 'He will be blessed.' For the Holy Spirit is He who is blessing through Isaac. This is why it was impossible to revoke or change anything. Here was the impulse and operation in the Holy Spirit alone by which Isaac decided within himself, after he touched the hands and neck, that he would bless his son. Neither did he change his judgment despite many arguments to the contrary . . ."; WA 43:521.13f.: ". . . The Holy Spirit does not revoke His movements, 'neither is He one who changes,' as Malachi says . . ."; WA 43:521.16f.: "When God has made any decision, He does not change or retract it, as men are wont to do"; WA 43:530.37ff. (on Gen. 27:33): "Neither, however, is He moved, that He should change a blessing once it has been conferred. But whoever he ultimately may be who received it, He says, 'He is blessed, and shall be blessed,' for the gifts of God cannot be revoked"; WA 43:532.33ff. (on Gen. 27:36): "Therefore, you, being born first, are not greater, but the buyer is and has the blessing by the supreme right, which it is impossible to take back from him since it is the gift of God, which is not changed"; likewise cf. WA 43:535.27f. and 537.9ff.: "If . . . a blessing has once been pronounced, it is not in our will to recover it, but in God's giving it is given freely, and in such a way that it may not be moved by the tears, cries, or labors of any man."

11. The Necessity of Ordination

What did Luther think of the necessity of the specific ordination rite? This question has already been touched on in various ways in previous sections. We will try here in summary to form a clear overall picture of this question.

In *The Babylonian Captivity of the Church*, when Luther vehemently attacks the sacramental nature of the Roman sacrament of the *ordo*, stressing that the *ordo* has no promise of grace and no divine institution in Scripture and cannot therefore constitute an article of faith and is not necessary to salvation;[324] and when he wishes to have the *ordo* count only as a "rite observed through so many ages,"[325] as a "a kind of churchly rite introduced by the fathers of the church"[326]—we cannot automatically apply this to the ordination Evangelically purified after the apostolic model nor conclude that Luther knows of no divine institution but regards it as a human, ecclesial rite without any requirement based on God's Word.[327] In his treatise to the Bohemians from 1523 [*Concerning the Ministry*], regarding the original apostolic ordination which he wishes to deliver from the Roman distortion and institute afresh, Luther speaks of *sacra ordinatio* as of a rite instituted "by the authority of the Scriptures, then by the example and decrees of the apostles."[328] In no way, then, is true ordination for Luther the *ritus ecclesiasticus* introduced by the church fathers, but *the institution founded on Scripture and on apostolic example and apostolic design*. Otherwise Luther would be unable to call it *sacred* ordination.[329] The apostolic example has a sense of obligation for Luther. "We are called by apostolic rite and are bishops," he stresses in 1527.[330] In his treatise *The Private Mass and the Consecration of*

---

[324] WA 6:560.20ff., 563.3ff. Cf. above, pp. 9–10.

[325] WA 6:560.24f.

[326] WA 6:561.26f.: "Therefore, I grant that the *ordo* is a certain churchly rite; many such others were also introduced through the church fathers, as consecration of vessels, houses, garments, water, salt, candlesticks, herbs, wine, and similar things, in all of which no one posits that there is a sacrament, nor is there any promise in them. Thus anointing a man's hands, shearing the scalp, and doing other things of that kind is not giving a sacrament since nothing is promised in them, but they are only performed for certain offices, as it were vessels and instruments." — If this passage is examined carefully, it becomes evident that Luther ultimately has the outward ceremonies of the Roman priestly consecration in mind when he compares the *ordo* with those other rites introduced by the church fathers, and precisely those ceremonies which had become the very symbols of a false ordination content: chrismation and tonsure (on this cf. WA 38:228.29ff.). When Luther speaks here only of a "church rite introduced through the church fathers," he means primarily the external *habitus* of the degenerate Roman ordination rite.

[327] Also cf. above, pp. 146–47. K. Tuchel pointed out from Luther's lecture on Romans (1515/16) how, despite his low regard for the spirituality of his time, Luther "never questions the necessity of the consecration" there, "which must needs precede every priestly action and also preceded Luther's own address" (op. cit., p. 66). He refers, e.g., to the passage WA 56:172.11ff.: "Likewise, no one can do the works of a bishop or priest unless he has first been consecrated and sanctified for that purpose."

[328] WA 12:173.1ff.

[329] Also cf. above, p. 148. On the expression "free and apostolic rite of appointing a priest" (WA 12:194.21f.), cf. above, pp. 126–27.

[330] WA 25:17.13.

Priests (1533), he makes a strong appeal to the apostolic ordination over against the Roman consecration,[331] as happens in *Ordination of Ministers of the Word.*[332] In the sermon on St. Andrew's Day 1544, he concludes his account of apostolic ordination with the sentence "This is how Christians should consecrate their ministers; then they are following the example of the apostles and the early Church."[333] The apostolic example and pattern lies for Luther practically on a level with a command of Holy Scripture, occupying a divine rank. This is demonstrated in a number of ordination certificates where ordination is traced back to God's command in Holy Scripture.[334]

If repeated reference is made to the practice of the early Church, especially of the Council of Nicaea,[335] it may not be thought that Luther saw ordination as founded only on church tradition. Rather, he references the canonical ordination of the early Church to show how the apostolic example from Scripture still defined ordination practice in the early period of the Church before the foreign Roman influence gained dominance. The evidence of tradition only undergirds and strengthens the testimony of Scripture.

Luther regards the ordination from Scripture as necessary. This is shown not only by the practical instruction which he gives to the Bohemians regarding the call,[336] and the request that Sutel submit to ordination before beginning to administer the Holy Sacrament,[337] but also and above all by the establishment of the ordination rite in Wittenberg itself. It must be asked why Luther would pursue this at all and write the *Ordination of Ministers of the Word* for it if he did not think ordination necessary.[338] How could he then have written to Peter Hackenberg: "*We intend* to ordain or appoint ministers by our own rite"?[339] The

---

331 E.g., WA 38:228.29ff.; cf. above, p. 149.

332 WA 38:428.29ff.

333 WA 52:569.21f.

334 In the ordination certificate for Wenzeslaus Kilmann, it reads that it "has been divinely commanded that churches should choose and ordain ministers of the Gospel and set them as suitable governors over other churches" (End. 7:131.19ff.). The subsequent reference to the decision of Nicaea shows plainly that Luther has that specific ordination act in mind here. Cf. further End. 14:252.12ff.: "Therefore, the aforesaid Baldasar Haußmann has been publicly ordained here in the church according to the command of Holy Scripture . . ."; likewise End. 15:88.33ff.: ". . . according to the command of divine Scripture." — In the ordination certificate for Jakob Siegel from October 7, 1537, it reads: "Therefore, according to the Word of God, by the authority of our Church, the call has been confirmed with public ordination" (End. 11:279.18ff.). In others it reads instead: "according to apostolic teaching" (End. 14:286.18; 15:142.16f. [= WA Br 10:297.13]; 16:63.14 [= WA Br 10:621.11]). Also cf. the memorandum for the Erfurt preachers, in which the approval of the recipient of the call through the laying on of hands on the part of other pastors is also defended by reference to Scripture: End. 11:40.17ff., 44.174ff., 45.204ff.

335 WA 53:257.19ff.; End. 11:227.22ff.; 12:197.12ff.; 7:131.24ff.

336 Cf. above, pp. 154–56.

337 WA Br 6:44.15ff. Cf. the very definite demand by Luther that the Holy Supper be administered only by called ministers (above, pp. 114–15).

338 Cf. C. Mahrenholz, "Begleitwort," op. cit., p. 16; and G. Werner, op. cit., p. 28 n. 31.

339 WA Br 5:700.13ff.; cf. above, p. 158.

unavailability of the Roman bishops as ordaining ministers would occasion the adoption of a peculiar ordination rite only if ordination as such was deemed indispensable.[340] In the ordination address from October 20, 1535, Luther says quite clearly: "You know that the ordination of the Church with its rites *is necessary*."[341] Likewise, in the report of the conversation of the two Culmbach preachers with Luther and Melanchthon in 1538 concerning the question of ordination, among other things, it is emphatic that Luther and Melanchthon deemed ordination necessary.[342] Of significance in this regard is also the fact that in his Genesis lectures Luther says of the laying on of hands—and so, indeed, of ordination—"it is no human tradition, but God acts through it."[343]

Incidentally, Luther remarks that episcopal confirmation of the call is not necessary, namely, in the event that the bishops have become hostile to the Gospel and refuse to grant the confirmation, contrary to their duty.[344] Yet this episcopal confirmation of the call cannot simply be equated to ordination, nor can the dispensability of ordination be inferred from these statements, since the episcopal confirmation to which Luther refers may also denote the church-governmental act of confirming the granting of a parish, and the latter is quite obviously meant in one case.[345] And even if it is not, it would only be an absolute denial of the necessity of an *episcopal* ordination and an assertion that the episcopal participation in the call process can even be omitted in an emergency.[346] That Luther does not wish to see ordination omitted outright in such a case, but rather performed by pastors or, in the most extreme necessity, by the *potiores* of the congregation, is shown by his treatise to the Bohemians [*Concerning the Ministry*] and by his introduction of pastoral ordination to Wittenberg.

We can establish in summary that ordination, as the act of initiation to the spiritual office founded on Scripture and committed to the Church by apostolic example and apostolic order, is regarded by Luther as necessary.[347]

---

340 Cf. above, pp. 164–65 n. 125.

341 WA 41:762.18.

342 Here it reads: "To this (our question whether it would not be good to engage and ordain able teachers as priests) they gave us this answer: that they have ordained a great number of teachers as priests; but they regard it not only as good, but necessary, that they be publicly ordained or consecrated with a public form according to the example of the holy apostles" (T. Kolde, "Z. Gesch. d. Ord.," etc., op. cit., pp. 221f.).

343 WA 43:600.25f.

344 WA 11:414.14f. and 33f.; 38:236.17ff.

345 Namely, in the passage WA 38:236.17ff. Cf. above, pp. 149–54.

346 Cf. Luther's general axiom: "Necessity is necessity and has no measure" (WA 11:414.8).

347 This at least must be adjoined to Brunotte's continually rehearsed finding: "*How* the call process is appointed in its details is a matter of human law according to Luther, as long as an external rite is performed" (op. cit., pp. 184, 186, 190).

12. The Relationship between the Call and Ordination

It would be mistaken and incongruous with Luther's scheme to define the relationship of the call and ordination in such a way that the one act competes with the other. According to Luther, we cannot say: "The call, not ordination, is the decisive factor" nor "Ordination, not the call, is the decisive factor." The question "the call or ordination" is irrelevant. According to Luther, the call and ordination are so bound together and interrelated that they are mutually dependent on each other.

The call demands ordination. If there is an election of a person for a specified office, it must be confirmed as legitimate by ministers of the Word, and the electee must be approved on the basis of an examination. The local election and call must further be publicly recognized and put into effect by the whole Church, for no congregation is so independent, so to speak, as to disregard the concern of the larger community of the Church in which it lives. A congregation's call to the office of the Church cannot be "handled within its own ranks." Not until the designation of the person for an office has taken place is the whole process of appointment to the office begun. This points beyond itself to the liturgical rite of ordination, in which the intercongregational aspects of conferring the office come into play and the designated pastor is then received to the office by those already occupying the office. The local call possesses within itself the tendency to manifest itself in the liturgical ordination act and to be given the divine seal of its validity in that act. The call demands ordination as the concretizing of the *divine* sending to the office and blessing for the office. A call without ordination must be regarded in Luther's scheme as an incomplete process and temporary measure.

On the other hand, *ordination in turn assumes the call.* Luther rejects ordinations given absolutely, that is, without a preceding, concrete call to a specified office. Ordination is for him essentially and primarily the confirmation of that local call. If this call does not occur, nothing can be confirmed or ordained according to Luther. The congregation always takes part in the local call. It may either nominate the person of the pastor itself, or—if this is done through particular parties chosen from the congregation—at least express a preference for a designated person and join in assessing his doctrine, conduct, and gifts (even if the actual decision regarding doctrine rests with the ministers). While ordination assumes the concrete call to a specified office (including the relevant *placet* of the congregation), it is fitting that the congregation's stake in the total call process be taken into account.

Thus the call and ordination go together and are not to be divided or torn apart. One alone without the other is not constitutive for the reception of the office. If ordination occupies the foreground in comparison to the call—as through it the whole process of the appointment in the office is brought to its ultimate conclusion and it is the act through which the office is definitively transmitted—and the Lord Himself sends to the office, nevertheless the vocation as the local call is the objective prerequisite for it and therefore is jointly constitutive with it. For this reason it is also understandable that Luther likes to use the dual term "call and ordain" to identify the whole process of appointment to the office.[348] In Luther's teaching, both acts are organically intertwined. Whoever tries by force to dissolve this bond by favoring one or the other act destroys the whole vocation in the sense in which Luther conceives it as legitimate. —

We have sought in this chapter to present Luther's doctrine of ordination in its differing viewpoints (considering it in its historical derivation and systematically). It is only comprehensible against the background of the Roman priestly ordination encountered by Luther, and the justified criticism thereof, for which reason we began there (1). Then the individual elements of the doctrine of ordination proceed from Luther's positive assessment of the ancient canonical ordination rite (2), from the advice regarding ordination which he makes to the Bohemians (3), from the practical conception of ordination introduced to establish the ordination rite in Wittenberg (4) and which lies at the root of Luther's *Ordination of Ministers of the Word* (5). In the provisions of *Ordination of Ministers of the Word*, we find the individual strands of Luther's doctrine of ordination brought together in a focused way, revealing the true sense of ordination with greater clarity (6). For further clarification, we have also mentioned various individual questions: the elements of ordination (7), the understanding of the laying on of hands in ordination (8), the question of the *minister ordinationis* (9), the ordination gift (10), and, finally, the necessity of ordination (11), in order to conclude by appending a summary consideration of the relationship between the call and ordination (12). From the whole, we get the impression of a closed doctrine of ordination organically incorporated into the overall structure of the doctrine of the office as its finishing capstone and underscoring its most essential concern: to guarantee the function of the means of grace by tying the ministry of Word and Sacrament to specific persons called and set apart for that purpose. With internal consistency the doctrine of the call leads to the doctrine of ordination, in which the general provisions from the doctrine of the call find their concrete realization in the liturgical act. That Luther sees in ordination not only a human activity, not only an activity of the Church, but also the activity of God throughout makes the character of the office clear as one that is divinely instituted and keeps his doctrine of the institution of the office from remaining in the realm of theory. By virtue of the effectual ordination, the office of which Luther speaks stands as a powerful reality of God's salvific activity in the congregation and, with the means of grace, embodies a reference to God's condescension manifested in Christ for the salvation of the world.

[348] Cf., among others, the passages cited above on p. 142 n. 226.

CHAPTER VII

Summary

1. The Bipolarity of Luther's Doctrine of the Office

If we attempt an overview summarizing all that has been found in Luther concerning the office and ordination, two poles of the doctrine of the office emerge around which everything is grouped: the universal priesthood of the Christian congregation on the one hand and the concrete office based on the divine institution on the other. These two poles are not confined to the basic theological rationale of the office. The lines drawn from one or the other pole become evident in all individual parts of the doctrine of the office, including the doctrine of the installation in the office. The rationale of the office from the universal priesthood and needs of the priestly congregation is reflected by the call through the congregation while the rationale from Christ's institution is reflected by ordination as the conferral of the office through those already holding the office. Both trains of thought, however—in this part, as we have just outlined, as well as otherwise—are connected and correlated. In their intertwining, they produce that concept of the office peculiar to Luther.[1]

The polarity naturally present between the two lines can nevertheless lead to their diverging and becoming opposites. Church history shows several examples of such processes. The Roman system may be understood as the first line rendered independent and absolute, which causes the office reasoned from Christ's institution and through ordination to be passed on exclusively, while the other line may be seen as ascendant in the spiritualist sects of the Middle Ages and of the Reformation period, and then in the congregationalist communities emerging later from Calvinism. In each case, it is an operation of rivalry, so to speak, in which one line is exaggerated at the expense of the other and played off against the other. This is not in Luther's scheme, the essence of whose doctrine of the office consists precisely of maintaining a separation between both poles and of preserving the intertwining and interpenetration of both lines.

This does not, however, prevent signs of an incipient exaggeration of one line from appearing even in Luther from time to time, though without Luther

[1] Also cf. G. Hök, op. cit., pp. 150f.

proceeding to the fundamental elimination of the other. If in some of Luther's writings one line is unilaterally emphasized, the balance is generally reestablished when the other writings are consulted.

One line, isolated and made absolute, would produce the following scheme: By means of the universal priesthood, the congregation of believers, as well as every individual Christian, has the office of the Word and Sacraments with the fundamental authorization to exercise all the functions thereof. Only because it is impossible on grounds of order for all to preach, baptize, etc., simultaneously in the congregation, the public function of the office is delegated to a mandatary who exercises it for all and in the name of all. For the realization of this delegation occurring *de jure humano*, only one person need receive from the collective whole an election and call, which would nevertheless be revocable at any time. The minister in the office is then merely a functionary of the priestly congregation, dependent on it in all things, strictly its minister and instrument. The office as Christ's institution, and the ordination through other ministers in the office as conferral of the office, would be excluded from such a scheme. But it cannot be denied that in some extreme statements, Luther approaches such a picture, and this in the nineteenth century caused Höfling, e.g., to describe that one line, in its absolute form, as the genuine representation of Luther; yet at the same time, it must be observed that Luther on the whole avoided this scheme in his teaching.

The other line, isolated and made absolute, would produce the opposite scheme: The office is instituted by Christ and transmitted to designated officers, who then hand it down in turn through the chain of ordinations going back to the apostles (apostolic succession!), in which the congregation remains solely a spectator. The office appoints the office without the congregation bearing co-responsibility for it, not to mention collaborating in it. The office-bearers stand before the congregation in the authority of God in such a way that it cleaves to them unconditionally and is only an object of their exercise of the office. In this way Christ's institution of the office is unmoored from its living relation to the priestly congregation in which the office is naturally embedded, and the priesthood of all Christians is dangerously curtailed. Luther could not be said to be in danger of becoming one-sided in this direction, which would rather be true perhaps of certain Lutherans of the nineteenth century.[2] But this probably depends less on a strong, belief-like inclination toward the first aspect, that of the universal priesthood, than on the historic circumstances in which Luther lived and which affected his doctrine.[3]

These two lines are present in Luther, but on the whole lack the exclusive traits. They do not diverge in his thinking but are held together by a higher

---

[2] We must agree with H. Storck when, regarding the two tendencies in the theology of the office of the last century, he opines: "The two views do not coincide with Luther's understanding of the office of the Word, although they both contain a kernel of Luther" (op. cit., p. 41 n. 183).

[3] Cf. below, pp. 208–10.

principle.[4] It becomes especially plain in a passage of the treatise *On the Councils and the Church* (1539) in which Luther says that the calling of church ministers, the appointment of the preaching office, is a mark of the true Church and continues: "For people must have bishops, pastors, or preachers who publicly and particularly give, extend, and exercise the aforenamed four articles or holy things *on account of and in the name of the Church, yet much more so because of the institution of Christ. . . .*"[5] Here, the rationale of the office from the universal priesthood of the congregation is placed side by side with that from the institution of Christ, and in their relationship the first rationale is surpassed by the second ("much more"!). In the subsequent text, the same bipolarity is found again with respect to the method of appointing the office: "For the flock cannot do this as a whole, but must commit, or have it committed, to one man. . . ."[6] In the active verb "commit" is the call in the narrow sense, emphasizing the congregation as agent; in the passivistic construction "have it committed" is ordination, in which it is particularly the ministers of the Word which act while the congregation only acknowledges this action and accompanies it with their prayer. The arc of tension that ties together these two poles in Luther's doctrine is the actual pillar on which his doctrine of the office rests.

2. Development in Luther

Now and then in the history of interpreting Luther's doctrine of the office, there has been an attempt to relieve the tension between universal priesthood and instituted office by citing a development or even change of viewpoint in Luther.[7] Yet this approach is not feasible.[8] It cannot be denied, of course, that there is a development in Luther, yet it does not involve an open revision of

[4] W. Elert pointed out that Luther did not sense an opposition between the rationale of the office from Christ's institution and the purely practical one with the delegatory idea (*Morphologie* I, p. 301; cf. above, p. 109) and writes that this is only intelligible "if he" (Luther) "in the term 'office' is thinking only of the purely functional one, not the personal apparatus of the organization of the pastoral office" (p. 301). The fact that the functional idea plays a large role in Luther is doubtless certain, yet we would have reservations about balancing the tension inherent in the coexistence of the two different lines in Luther by adopting a *purely* and thus *exclusively* functional view of the office. We have found (cf. above, pp. 89–91) that Luther also traces the *parochial* pastoral office back to the divine arrangement. Christ's institution, in his sense, cannot be limited to the purely functional. For this reason there remains a rationally unsatisfying tension in Luther's philosophy of the office which is at the same time characteristic for him. — Cf. E. Sommerlath ("Amt und allg. Priestertum," p. 41): "No perfect balance or theological clarification has ever been obtained for these trains of thought." Nevertheless, Brunotte views Luther's doctrine of the office too simplistically when he supposes that it contains absolutely no "unbalanced tensions, internal contradictions, or theological loopholes" (op. cit., pp. 199f.).

[5] WA 50:632.36ff. M. Doerne (*Luth. Pfarramt*, p. 11) also regards this passage as a "classic expression of the bipolarity of Luther's understanding of the office."

[6] WA 50:633.3f.

[7] So, e.g., A. W. Dieckhoff, op. cit., pp. 149ff., and elsewhere.

[8] Cf. M. Doerne, *Luth. Pfarramt*, p. 9.

previously held positions. In his early writings (esp. of the years 1520–23), the accent is placed strongly and relatively one-sidedly on the universal priesthood and the delegative origin of the concrete office from the same; in his later writings, the institutive character of the office receives greater emphasis. Parallel to this, the call through the congregation comes to the fore in the earlier period while later—especially with respect to the introduction of the ordination rite to Wittenberg—greater weight falls on ordination and on the office's part in appointing the office. There is one path from the discovery of the universal priesthood in 1519 via the foundational disputes with the papistic church and theology in the 1520s and 1530s and the struggle with the Enthusiasts, up to the episcopal consecration in Naumburg in 1542; and the Luther of the Genesis lectures is different from that of *The Babylonian Captivity of the Church*[9]—but it cannot be shown that Luther altered his view in the doctrine of the office in any distinct way or later corrected or retracted any statement from the early period. Development is seen only in his nuancing and more balanced elaboration of his doctrine of the office.[10]

3. The Situational Conditionality of Luther's Doctrine

In speaking of a development in Luther, it will be necessary to explain it from the various circumstances of his life. Luther was constantly involved in various new struggles and conflicts, and his doctrine was formed in relation to these. This is especially evident in his concept of the office since one's view on the office always affects the concrete order of congregational life and one's view on the Church, and therefore has a great number of concrete, practical relationships. The actual conditions of the Church for which Luther had to account in

[9] In the great Galatians commentary from 1535, Luther testifies that, over the course of the year, he had deepened his view of the office in the direction of holding it in higher esteem. Luther says there, after extolling the call [*vocatio*]: "When I was a new theologian, I thought that Paul was jesting and playing the fool through these boasts" (that he boasted in his call to the apostolic office); "I did not know what he meant. I did not know that the ministry of the Word was such a great thing" (WA 40/1:63.6ff.). This suggests that the more mature Luther saw the spiritual and divine character of the preaching office more clearly than the younger one. Is it a coincidence that this statement comes from the same year that the ordination rite in Wittenberg was firmly established?

[10] Thus Dieckhoff's view is inaccurate that the later Luther acknowledged his earlier delegation theory, and thus the derivation of the particular office from the universal priesthood, as an error and disposed of it (op. cit., p. 151). One need only compare *Sermon at the Dedication of the Castle Church, Torgau* from October 5, 1544 (e.g., WA 49:600.11ff.). Dieckhoff was right only in seeing that the later Luther, unlike the Luther of 1520–23, shifts the accent so that in later time the emphasis in his rationale of the office lies on the divine institution of the office. — A shift of accent in Luther in this regard is also discussed by H. H. Kramm (op. cit., p. 23). — That Luther was fundamentally unchanging in this view of the office in its essential points has been affirmed by various scholars. Thus Höfling (*Grundsätze*, 3rd ed. [1853], p. 55); J. Köstlin (*Luthers Lehre von der Kirche* [1853], p. 48); K. Holl (*Luther*, 6th ed. [1932], p. 378); H. Storck (op. cit., p. 4); P. Brunner ("Vom Amt d. Bischofs," p. 6 n. 2).

various ways are reflected in the stages of the development of his doctrine of the office.[11] It is necessary to speak of a *situational conditionality* of his doctrine of the office. Luther never speaks or writes as an abstract thinker contemplating a subject "per se." He always speaks or writes about a concrete situation that demands his response. This can be easily demonstrated in all his writings, and especially regarding the exegetical writings and sermons.

With respect to the doctrine of the office, there is a group of Luther's writings entirely defined by the polemic against Rome's false concept of the office.[12] In laying out Luther's doctrine, we have always repeatedly sought to consider the polemical accent of Luther's statements in these writings and to take into account the situation of conflict which dominates in them. Luther's statements about the universal priesthood are strongly characterized by their contrast with the Roman idea of the estate and understanding of consecration,[13] and the same holds true for many of his statements on ordination. The dark shadow of Roman positions against which Luther is forced to maintain his position in an existential struggle is always looming in the background, even when he speaks positively about the office and ordination.

On the other hand, writings characterized by the polemic against the Enthusiasts and clandestine preachers may also be identified.[14] Here the pendulum swings the other way in Luther, and in emphasizing the distinction of called preachers and the congregation, he goes to the limit of what is defensible for his doctrine of the universal priesthood. While, when confronting Rome, he was most emphatic about teaching the equality of all in the Christian priesthood and fought all distinctions in the Church, when confronting the clandestine preachers, he places great value on the fact that not all Christians are the same and that a distinction exists between preachers and laymen. When Luther makes clear use of the term "laymen" against the clandestine preachers, this plainly suggests in such contexts that not all Christians are able to speak in spiritual matters, which in turn borders on a refutation of what Luther taught against Rome in other passages, e.g., in the treatise *That a Christian Assembly Has the Right to Judge All Teaching*. We have already noted that, regarding the explanation of 1 Corinthians 14 in the treatise *Infiltrating and Clandestine Preachers* (1532), Luther represents exactly the opposite of what he taught in 1521 and

[11] W. Elert makes the same interpretation when he identifies as the two formal marks of Luther's doctrine of the office: first, the endeavor to protect at all costs the correlation of the doctrine of the office to Evangelical principles and, second, "the practical flexibility which has its basis in the transitional character of his era" (*Morphologie* I, p. 308).

[12] E.g., the three main writings of 1520 (*To the Christian Nobility, The Babylonian Captivity of the Church, Freedom of a Christian*), the writings against Hieronymus Emser, *Misuse of the Mass* (1521), *Concerning the Ministry* (1523), *That a Christian Assembly Has the Right to Judge All Teaching* (1523), *The Private Mass and the Consecration of Priests* (1533), among others.

[13] Cf. E. Sommerlath, "Amt u. allg. Priesterum," pp. 41–49; and "Das Wesen d. Amtes nach luth. Auffassung," in *Die Kirche Jesu Christi u. d. Wort Gottes* (Berlin, 1937), p. 155. — Also, R. Sohm noted this (*Kirchenrecht* I, p. 495 n. 26).

[14] So esp. the treatise *Infiltrating and Clandestine Preachers* (1532).

1523.[15] This is to be explained solely by the different opponent whom Luther is addressing in each case. Toward the clandestine preachers, he speaks and thinks otherwise than toward Rome. The havoc which the Enthusiasts wrought (particularly against the grim backdrop of the Peasants' War and the Münzerite movement) showed Luther plainly the practical limits that were set for a doctrine of the universal priesthood and of the right and power of every Christian, which he did not always keep in mind in his struggle with Roman ideas, and which caused him to emphasize much more the office as divine institution—and therefore also the necessity of the call to the office and of ordination—than had been the case in the dispute with Rome. In this way, Luther's doctrine is strongly conditioned by the situation.[16] It can also be understood through the lens of a "two-front battle" (namely, against Rome on one side and Enthusiasts on the other), as M. Doerne has done.[17]

Besides this, it must be remembered that some items of Luther's doctrine of the office are based on the Church's acute case of necessity, which he saw had to be dealt with. Many things would certainly have developed in a very different way if the Roman bishops, or even a percentage of them, had not renounced the Reformation and the episcopal structure had been kept intact everywhere. The institutional element in Luther's doctrine of the office would without doubt have emerged much more strongly. He would have been spared any recourse to territorial authority in organizing and shaping the circumstances in the Church, among other things. Thus Luther was compelled to maintain his fundamentally conservative stance amid a maelstrom of revolutionary conflicts and in an existential struggle for life and death with the traditional ecclesial authorities. In the process, some things crumbled away and were lost which would otherwise have been preserved. Throughout Luther's doctrine of the office, it is necessary, in order to make an accurate assessment, to keep in mind the emergency situation by which his teaching is often informed.

4. Luther's Constantly Operative and Underlying Philosophy

Even if Luther's doctrine of the office exists as a bipolarity strongly conditioned by the respective situation and progressively elaborated, it is not without its deep, internal unity. This can be seen in the *importance of the Word* governing everything. For Luther, the Word does not exist for the sake of the office, but the office for the sake of the Word. The Word for Luther always has absolute priority and superiority in the Church. "The Word of God . . . is incomparably above the

---

[15] Cf. above, pp. 97–98 n. 81. — W. Elert, regarding such passages in the treatise *Infiltrating and Clandestine Preachers*, says, "The danger of such a recourse" (in Luther) "is almost tangible here" (*Morph.* I, p. 303).

[16] This is also referred to by G. Hök, op. cit., p. 150

[17] *Luth. Pfarramt*, p. 5.

Church."[18] Luther always assumes that "nothing exists in the Church without the Word, and all things exist through the Word alone,"[19] and that therefore the office of the Word "is the highest and greatest of all things in the Church."[20] If Luther teaches the universal priesthood as the epitome of the office and uses it for the rationale of the concrete office, he does so in order that the Word may not be held hostage by a nonpreaching priestly estate which claims for itself alone the authority to teach, without also the function of doing or without the power of doing. It is not the power of the pope or any bishop that governs the Church, but the Word of God, which is bound to no one, most free of all, the King of kings and Lord of lords.[21] Luther derives the office from the universal priesthood in order to pave the way for the Word, that it may have free course and bring forth fruit in the Church. But when the *spiritus enthusiastici* [Enthusiastic spirits] arise to distort the Word with their doctrines of men and to put it in the opposite prison, Luther confronts them with the ordained, instituted office of the Word and demands clear proof of a legitimate call. When he sees the Word hedged about by the walls of a false view of the *ordo*, he tears them down with the right and duty of the universal priesthood and raises the banner of the call through the congregation. When the call of the congregation no longer guarantees the purity of the Word, he places next to it ordination *in virtute verbi* [by the virtue of the Word]. The magnetic field emitted from the two poles of his doctrine of the office and defined by their mutual relationship is the living Word, the *viva vox evangelii* [living voice of the Gospel]. That *it* may be executed rightly is for him the most basic meaning of the office and of ordination.

[18] WA 6:560.36.

[19] WA 12:173.5f.

[20] WA 12:173.4f.

[21] WA 2:676.34ff.

PART II

THE OFFICE AND ORDINATION IN MELANCHTHON

CHAPTER I

Foundations for the Concept of the Ministry

1. Gospel Ministry and Its Necessity to Salvation

In order for us to unfold Melanchthon's concept of the ministry correctly, we must begin with his doctrine of the Gospel. Since human reason is blind to the mysteries of redemption, God's system of grace can be learned only by revelation, i.e., understood from Scripture. And Scripture consists of two elements: *Law and Gospel.*[1] These are the "principal components of Scripture to which every part is to be judiciously referred."[2] Distinct are the work and ministration of the Law, on the one hand, and of the Gospel, on the other. "The Law reveals sin; the Gospel, grace. The Law indicates the disease; the Gospel, the remedy. The Law is the handmaid of death . . . the Gospel, of life and peace."[3] The Law leads to the knowledge of sin, unsettles the conscience, and through the wrathful judgment of God terrifies man and condemns him.[4] But only by such means is a man disposed to hear the Gospel and by it to obtain the grace of God. The Gospel is the "promise of grace or divine mercy, and so of the remission of sin, and the testimony of God's kindness toward us."[5] In the Gospel, God reveals His gracious will toward us and shows us Christ as the atoning sacrifice for us, for whose sake He wills to pardon us.[6] The Gospel is God's word of promise, pointing us to Christ and assuring us of righteousness. It came into the world

---

1 CR 21:139: "The two parts in all of Scripture are the Law and the Gospel."

2 CR 21:149.

3 CR 21:139.

4 CR 21:152: "The proper work of the Law is the revelation of sin"; CR 21:153; 21:405: "The chief and proper office of the divine Law is to show sins, to accuse, to terrify, and to condemn consciences."

5 CR 21:140; cf. CR 21:157.

6 CR 21:416.

immediately after the fall of Adam, regarding the woman's Seed who would crush the head of the serpent, and is one and the same in every age,[7] always the promise of grace *propter Christum* [on account of Christ], and in every age demands faith as its own possession. But this faith is nothing other than "faith in divine mercy promised in Christ."[8] By faith the conscience is pacified and the inward man renewed.[9] "We are justified, therefore, when, being put to death through the Law, we are raised again by the Word of grace promised in Christ, or by the Gospel that pardons sins, and we cling to that faith, not doubting that Christ's righteousness is our righteousness, Christi's satisfaction is our atonement, Christ's resurrection is ours."[10] By faith in the gracious promise of the Gospel of Christ, the sinner is justified and all the riches of Christ's salvation become his own.

This Gospel, then, which calls for faith, is joined by the *signa sacramentalia* [sacramental signs] instituted by God Himself in the New Testament: Baptism and Communion. They are "sure testimonies of the will of God toward us," guaranteeing that we have actually received what God promised.[11] They have the function of underscoring the divine promise of the Gospel and awakening and strengthening our faith in it.[12] They are attached to the Gospel and have their continued existence in the Gospel. "Thus we join together Sacrament and promise," says Melanchthon, thereby intending to emphasize this relationship.[13] Also belonging to the right use of the Sacraments, therefore, is faith in the promise of the Gospel.[14] The Gospel comes to people in its most concentrated form in the Absolution, which Melanchthon also includes among the Sacraments.[15] This, too, is a promise and can only be received by faith.[16]

As the Gospel and Sacraments appeal to faith, through which alone they can be appropriated for salvation, faith in turn depends on the Gospel and Sacraments in that it is first awakened and aroused by them as by instruments

---

[7] CR 21:416: ". . . And there is one and the same Gospel in which all saints from the beginning of the world have been saved in every age."

[8] CR 21:163.

[9] CR 21:154: "If the afflicted conscience believes in the promise of grace in Christ, it is renewed and revived by faith."

[10] CR 21:159.

[11] CR 21:208.

[12] AC 13.1 (*Bekenntnisschriften* [Göttingen, 1930], pp. 65f.): ". . . instituted to awaken and confirm faith in those who use them."

[13] CR 21:468.

[14] AC 13.2 (*BKS* 66); CR 21:468: "Just as the promise is to be received by faith, so also in the use of the Sacraments faith must be added, which thus causes us truly to touch those things which are propounded in the promise."

[15] CR 21:485: "For practical purposes, the sacrament of repentance also is counted among the Sacraments"; Ap 12.41 (*BKS* 259): "And the Absolution properly can be called a sacrament of repentance"; Ap 13.4 (*BKS* 292): "Baptism, the Lord's Supper, and Absolution, which is the sacrament of repentance, are truly sacraments."

[16] Ap 12.39ff. (*BKS* 259).

and is inconceivable apart from them.[17] The gracious will of God revealed in the Gospel implies a *specific manner of appropriating the benefits of salvation.* Melanchthon, in his *Commentary on Romans* (1529), on [Rom.] 10:14–15, points to the "gradation of the means of justification or cause of faith taught in the passage."[18] There is a specific mode appointed by God "by which the benefits of the Gospel come to us":[19] namely, *through the Gospel, the external Word, and the Sacraments.* The Word is the efficient cause of faith.[20] Through "the voice and perceiving of the Gospel," God gives the Holy Spirit, who produces faith,[21] all the benefits of salvation, righteousness, and eternal life.[22] Moreover, the Gospel is the *exclusive* way of salvation.[23] There is no other possible way to obtain faith and salvation than through that Word. "Without the Word, the Holy Spirit does not come."[24] It is necessary to know that "God desires His will concerning sin and grace to be known and apprehended in no other way than in the Word and that the Holy Spirit is efficacious through the Word."[25]

This "in no other way than in the Word" as the divine order of salvation is one of the most important fundamental axioms of Melanchthon's theology and serves as a basis for the incisive *Antithese zu den Schwärmern* [Antitheses to the Enthusiasts], identified by Melanchthon as "fanatical spirits"[26] and "heretics."[27] Their "most grievous error" is that they despise the "spoken Word [*verbum vocale*]" of the Gospel and think the Holy Spirit is given without the external Word.[28] They seek illumination "apart from the Word of God and outside the

---

17 AC 5.1f. (*BKS* 57); CR 21:485: "But faith uses instruments, the Word and Sacraments, which testify that the benefit of Christ is ours."

18 CR 15:478; cf. CR 15:477: "When Paul wished to show the cause of faith, he used a progression thus: No one calls, no one believes. No one believes unless he has heard the Word. He cannot hear the Word unless it is preached. The Word cannot be preached unless God send people to preach the Word."

19 CR 15:694; cf. CR 12:349: "By wonderful . . . counsel and a most certain decree, God instituted the salvation of mankind by the voice of the Gospel given through the Son from the bosom of the eternal Father and sounding through the apostles, and not otherwise."

20 CR 15:478: "Therefore, the efficient cause of faith is the Word, by which God impels and moves the heart to believe."

21 CR 15:429; cf. CR 26:354; 21:470.

22 CR 21:555; cf. CR 21:834; AC 28.9 (*BKS* 122).

23 CR 5:711: "by the voice of the Gospel and not otherwise"; CR 12:349; 21:470; 21:853: "We know . . . that God in His great goodness has made His will known in the Gospel, nor are other lights to be sought, but faith and invocation are to be stirred up by this Gospel revealed to us."

24 CR 15:478; cf. CR 12:490.

25 CR 15:695.

26 CR 21:470.

27 CR 15:478.

28 CR 12:349: "They either diminish and despise the spoken Word, or they teach that violent seizures should be awaited to the neglect of the Word"; cf. CR 12:109: "We execrate Stinkfeld's [i.e., Caspar von Schwenkfeld] fanatical absurdities, who turns hearts from the Gospel and with an awful noise contends that God communicates to them in the thoughts of their minds without the Gospel"; CR 12:490; 15:430, 478, 694f., 991; Ap 13.13 (*BKS* 294).

Gospel" and with their teachings lead men away from the Word of God and entrust them to their own opinions and fantasies.[29] Because of their "wicked doctrines," which wreak "endless destruction" in the Church, they are condemned.[30] "Enthusiasts are to be shunned and accursed."[31]

Accordingly, if God apportions the forgiveness of sins and eternal salvation only through the Gospel, the salvation of men depends on the Gospel being purveyed, that is, proclaimed in its purity, and the Sacraments being administered "in accordance with the Gospel."[32] The character of the Gospel as the exclusive means of grace necessarily demands the *service of the Gospel.* It cannot be left to chance or the current spiritual inclinations of Christians whether the Gospel is proclaimed or not. The service of the Gospel must be constantly maintained in the Church. This leads to the necessity of a *ministerium* [*ministry*] *of the Gospel,* a concept in Melanchthon that designates not simply the function of the Gospel but precisely the ministerial function, the ministerial service, of the Gospel.

W. Thomas has observed that in Melanchthon *ministerium* is frequently equated to the spoken word generally.[33] H. Busch speaks in the same manner concerning a *ministerium* in Melanchthon in the widest sense of the word, as the voice of the Gospel heard, read, or meditated upon, while Melanchthon in later times almost exclusively intends the public ministry occupied by officers specifically appointed to it.[34] Certainly it is undeniable that in Melanchthon passages appear in which *ministerium* (or *ministerium Evangelii*) and *Evangelium* [Gospel] are used interchangeably, and *ministerium* seems to mean simply the function of the Gospel, the audible rendition, the proclamation and recitation of the Gospel.[35] However, we must pay attention to the context of the time, by which it becomes evident in the individual passages that, in Melanchthon's use of the term *ministerium Evangelii,* there is at least a simultaneous intimation or intention of the personally occupied ministry of the Church (already concrete then). If we take the two passages cited below from the *Loci* of 1543 (CR 21:833–34), we find in the preceding text the reference to Rom. 10:14f. and Eph. 4:11. God's giving of ministers (apostles, prophets, shepherds, teachers) is equated to the "ministry of the service of the Gospel" (CR 21:833). When a few lines later it then says that the Church is a "congregation bound to the voice or *ministerium Evangelii,*" there, too, it can only mean that "voice of the Gospel" which is made

[29] CR 26:354f.; cf. CR 12:603, 617; 14:892; 21:470.

[30] CR 26:354f.

[31] CR 15:695.

[32] Cf. AC 7.1 (*BKS* 59f.).

[33] *Die Lehre Melanchthons vom geistlichen Amt*, dissertation (Leipzig, 1901), p. 10.

[34] *Die Lehre von der Kirche bei Melanchthon*, dissertation (1918), p. 59.

[35] CR 12:616: "the benefit of God, who desires the Church to be tied to the ministry of the Gospel or to the voice of the Gospel heard, or read and contemplated . . ."; CR 12:628f.; 12:682: "When Isaiah refers to faith—and likewise defines faith as a firm, certain thought—he certainly requires the preaching of the Word of God or ministry of the Gospel . . ."; CR 12:492; 21:833: "We know, therefore, that the Church, the assembly of God, is bound to the voice or ministry of the Gospel . . ."; CR 21:834: ". . . that God is truly efficacious through this ministry, that is, through the voice of the Gospel heard, read, contemplated."

audible through those ministers placed into the ministry by God, and thus the ministerial proclamation of the Gospel. In the following text it may be denied that the *ministerium* is to be equated with the bishops standing in regular succession, yet it is quite plain that *ministerium* is thought of in the sense of the concrete ministry: "The Church is bound to that same Gospel of God which sounds aloud in the ministry; God then awakens certain men who teach rightly, as said in Ephesians 4 . . ." (CR 21:834). The emission of sound—that is, the pure function of the Gospel—and the *ministerium* are here two different things. It is not primarily for the sounding of the Gospel but for the sounding of the *ministerium* that God gives ministers. Likewise in the following: "The voice of the Gospel and ministry is therefore to remain, and the Church of God shall be a visible assembly, and yet as a scholastic assembly. It is an order, it is a distinction between teachers and hearers, and there are gradations. Some are apostles, some pastors, some doctors . . ." (CR 21:835). The term *vox ministerii* [voice of the ministry] prevents understanding *ministerium* as pure function. That Melanchthon, in the word *ministerium*, has the concrete ministry in view is demonstrated further by his reference to the distinction between teachers and hearers as a permanent order of the Church. When all these passages are read in connection to one another, it becomes clear that *ministerium Evangelii* in Melanchthon *is never treated as pure function being performed in an unspecified manner*, but always used for the ordained ministry. At first it seems difficult to see in the "voice of the Gospel heard, *read, and contemplated*" (CR 21:834; 12:616) a reference to the public ministry. It would be easier here to think simply of the words of the Gospel with no regard to the concrete ministry, [words] which can be read and meditated upon just as well as heard; yet we must be clear that Melanchthon sees the voice of the ministry (namely, of the apostles) being sounded even in Scripture. In the *heard* voice of the Gospel, it is the ministry's present proclamation of the Word in the congregation that is under consideration, whereas in the read and considered voice of the Gospel, it is a matter of the written, deposited Word of the apostle; yet in either case, it is the "voice of the Gospel sounding in the ministry." Compare his words in CR 15:991 on Rom. 10:14f.: "This verse clearly shows that Paul affirms that God, as the voice of the Gospel sounding in the ministry and contemplated by the one hearing or reading, is efficacious . . ." (and thereafter). In CR 21:825, he discusses the "visible Church, in which the voice of the Gospel sounds and in which the ministry of the Gospel is *perceived*." Here W. Thomas himself responds: "In this distinction between 'voice of the Gospel' and 'ministerium,' which 'is perceived,' we can clearly see that here *ministerium* is meant in the sense of the public ministry."[36] But Melanchthon, by the term *ministerium Evangelii*, not only here but in every instance, is thinking of the ministerial institution of the ongoing proclamation of the Gospel and administration of the Sacraments in the congregation. Here, however, we must keep in mind that the ministry characterized in

[36] Op. cit., p. 13; also cf. the following passages in which *Evangelium* and *ministerium Evangelii* are distinguished as two different concepts: CR 14:892: "That the Son may be efficacious through the Gospel, it is necessary for there to be a ministry of the Gospel"; CR 15:317: "I say that the Church is bound to the Gospel and to the ministry of the Gospel"; CR 21:832: "neither the voice *nor* the ministry of the Gospel"; CR 21:834: "It is necessary for both the voice *and* the ministry of the Gospel to be in the Church."

this way is wholly determined by the function actually being carried out (despite the fact that the functional character meanwhile negates the institutional one!).

It is just when Melanchthon speaks of the Gospel as an exclusive means of grace that he also comes to speak of the *ministerium Evangelii*, or ministry of the Gospel, and deduces the necessity of the ministerial office from the necessity of the Word.[37] Since God does not wish to reveal Himself except through the Word—"*for this great reason*, let us bestow all honor on and defend the ministry of the public Word."[38] Thus the mode by which God causes the riches of salvation to be shared by men is simply described as "the ministry of the Word."[39] Likewise, the Enthusiasts' scorn is directed not only against the Word but also against the ministry of the Word and against ordination, by which it is constituted.[40]

It is in the divine institution of the Gospel that the ordained service of the Gospel, the ministry of proclaiming the Gospel, has its basis. It exists in order to bring the Gospel to men for the effecting of salvation. With this, the essential groundwork of the concept of the ministry in Melanchthon has been laid. It will assume proper clarity, however, only when we examine its place in Melanchthon's general concept of the church.

2. The Anchoring of the Ministry in the Concept of the Church

In the Augsburg Confession, Melanchthon describes the Church as "the congregation of saints in which the Gospel is purely taught and the Sacraments are rightly administered."[41] The stress lies on the pure proclamation of the Gospel and right administration of the Sacraments. Melanchthon does not understand

---

[37] CR 21:853: ". . . We know that God in His great goodness has made His will known in the Gospel, nor are other lights to be sought, but faith and invocation are to be stirred up by this Gospel revealed to us, and God wants there to be a public ministry, and miraculously preserves it and continually purifies it, that we may know that the Church is bound to this Gospel which has been revealed. Paul says this in Ephesians 4 . . . with these words: 'The ministry of the Gospel is instituted that the Gospel may be preserved. . . .'" It should be observed here how the revealed Gospel is always spoken of as implicit in the institution of the public ministry. Cf. W. Thomas: "With the necessity of a means of salvation, the necessity of a man's constant service of mediation is also given" (op. cit., p. 11). Also cf. CR 12:490: "Neither does God save without that ministry, which He Himself ordained."

[38] CR 15:695; cf. CR 15:991: "But since we know that the ministry of the Gospel is *necessary*, much more do we honor and cherish the ministers of the Gospel."

[39] CR 12:349: "St. Paul regarded the manner in which these heavenly and eternal goods are communicated to us, which are not given us otherwise than through the ministry of the Word"; cf. CR 15:694; 21:850: "We know that eternal goods are revealed to us through this ministry."

[40] CR 15:478; 21:852.

[41] AC 7.1 (*BKS* 59f.). — On Melanchthon's concept of the church in general, cf. H. Busch, *Die Lehre von der Kirche bei Melanchthon* (1918), and O. Ritschl, *Dogmengeschichte des Protestantismus*, vol. 1 (Leipzig, 1908), pp. 310ff.

the Church in the congregationalist sense of arising from the gathering of the faithful and those confessing the Gospel, even though it is called a *congregatio*, a "gathering." These concepts are here meant *in a passive sense*, which is underscored by the relative clause "in which . . .": The Church is an "assembly of those who truly believe, who have the Gospel and the Sacraments, and are sanctified by the Holy Spirit,"[42] "an assembly . . . in which the voice of the Gospel sounds without corruption,"[43] ". . . in which God is efficacious through the ministry of the Gospel."[44] Through the Gospel and Sacraments, in which the Holy Spirit works, the assembly of those who confess the Gospel is called together and held together. This is also expressed by the term "assembly of the called [*coetus vocatorum*]."[45] Before the called there is the call, the Gospel itself. By Gospel and Sacrament, and not otherwise, God gathers His Church for Himself.[46] Only after Gospel and Sacraments are present is the Church constituted as *congregatio*. The Gospel has absolute priority since it is by the Word that the Church is founded, fed, nourished, cared for, and governed.[47] Melanchthon's doctrine of the church must be understood alongside his doctrine of the Gospel. In it, the living voice of the Gospel is dominant. If the Holy Spirit works in a faith-creating and salvific way only by the external Word and Sacraments, the Church, too, can have its subsistence only in the Word and Sacraments. Therefore, the "pure Word of God and the legitimate use of the Sacraments" are the ever-present marks of the true Church.[48]

If the Church's existence is found in the Gospel and the Sacraments, it can, *as a community of people*, consist only of those who depend on the Gospel and Sacraments, who accept and confess the pure doctrine of the Gospel and use the Sacraments. The Church is thus an "assembly of those who embrace the Gospel of Christ and rightly use the Sacraments."[49] However, the inner relationship of the members of the Church to the Word and Sacraments is not for all the same one specified by saving faith in the Gospel. There are many "hypocrites and evil persons" who belong to the Church outwardly but inwardly lack true faith. Thus Melanchthon, in his view of the Church as a community of people, distinguishes the Church in the proper sense (*proprie*) and in the broader sense. The Church in the proper sense, then, is, as Melanchthon says in AC 8, only the "congregation of saints and true believers"; the Church in the broader sense also includes

---

[42] CR 23:597.

[43] CR 12:400.

[44] CR 28:409; cf. CR 12:399, 431; 21:826.

[45] CR 21:825.

[46] CR 23:xxxv; 5:585; 8:284, 429; 8:371f.: (Christ) "surely gathers for Himself an eternal Church in mankind by the Gospel and not otherwise."

[47] CR 1:410; cf. CR 15:696; 12:482f.: "It is most foolish to imagine that the Church precedes the Word of God. For it is certain that since the beginning of the world men have been called and reborn through the Word of God, just as Adam was called when the promise was heard."

[48] E.g., CR 21:506.

[49] CR 21:826; cf. CR 12:399, 431, 433; 28:409.

"hypocrites and evil persons mingled therewith."[50] The same distinction is also found in the *Loci* of 1535 and following. In Scripture, the Church may sometimes (as Melanchthon expresses it) be generally described as "the congregation of all who profess the Gospel and are not excommunicated, in which good and evil persons are mingled together."[51] But properly and principally, the Church signifies the "congregation of the righteous, who truly believe in Christ and are sanctified by the Spirit of Christ."[52] However, this Church never exists purely in the proper sense; there are always many evil persons and hypocrites mingled with it here on earth.[53] It is probably in consideration of this last fact that Melanchthon, in later editions of the *Loci* (1543 and following), finds cause to dispense with the distinction of Church in the narrower and broader sense and to define the Church simply as the "assembly of the called [*coetus vocatorum*],"[54] in which assembly God, through the ministry of the Gospel, regenerates many unto eternal life and in which there yet exist many who are not regenerate who nevertheless outwardly confess adherence to the true doctrine.[55] Especially for later Melanchthon, the boundaries of the Church as a community of people are defined by this "consenting to the doctrine of the Gospel," regardless of whether it concerns a mere outward acknowledgment or one of true faith.

We have thus surveyed two basic provisions in Melanchthon's concept of the church (with respect to the institutional side of the Church as well as to the sociological): the Church is founded entirely on the Word and Sacrament and is therefore to be characterized as the "assembly of the called." Melanchthon accordingly places greatest emphasis on the *visibility* of this assembly of the called amassed around Word and Sacrament.[56] The Church is no Platonic idea, but a concrete quantity in this world, perceptible to the senses.[57] With the doctrine of a visibility of the Church, Melanchthon does not desire any greater proximity to the Roman concept of the church, in which the Church comes

---

[50] AC 8.1 (*BKS* 60); Ap 7.12ff. (*BKS* 236ff.)

[51] CR 21:505f.

[52] CR 21:506.

[53] Ibid.

[54] CR 21:825: "Whenever we think of the Church, we contemplate the assembly of the called. . . ."

[55] CR 21:826: "Let this be our definition: the visible Church is the assembly of those embracing the Gospel of Christ and rightly using the Sacraments, in which God through the ministry of the Gospel is efficacious and regenerates many unto life eternal, in which assembly, however, many have not been reborn but are in agreement concerning the true doctrine." Cf. *Mel.s Werke*, ed. R. Stupperich (*Stud. Ausg.*), vol. VI (1955), p. 285.

[56] O. Ritschl calls this visibility a "fundamental characteristic in his concept of the church" (op. cit., p. 311); also cf. H. Busch, op. cit., pp. 42f.

[57] Ap 7.20 (*BKS* 238): "Neither, indeed, are we dreaming of a Platonic state"; CR 12:139: "We do not speak of the Church as a Platonic idea, but we teach a visible assembly"; CR 12:619; 15:314: "The invisible Church is not an imaginary thing, as if a Platonic idea"; CR 21:825: "the assembly of the called . . . which is the visible Church . . . nor do we imagine another Church, invisible and inaudible, though of men living in this life; but both eyes and heart perceive the assembly of the called, that is, of those who confess the Gospel of God, and we know that the voice of the Gospel must sound among men publicly. . . ."

to stand as an "external polity or monarchy" or a "pontifical kingdom."[58] The Church is not to be likened to a worldly kingdom.[59] Rather, the Church is visible insofar as the Gospel and the Sacraments are audible and visible in it, and it is of course the gathering of concrete persons around this audible and visible Word and Sacrament. The Church is never without the audible Gospel and the visible Sacraments and therefore is always the *coetus visibilis* [visible assembly].[60] Gospel and Sacraments are the Church's *notae* [marks] and *signa* [signs] in which it is chiefly visible and by which it is externally recognized.[61]

Before 1552, Melanchthon always speaks of two *notae* or *signa ecclesiae*: "the pure Word of God and legitimate use of the Sacraments."[62] In this arrangement, the first *nota* is the most important since what determines a "legitimate use of the Sacraments" is precisely the pure teaching of the Gospel.[63] The "pure doctrine of the Gospel" is the chief mark of the Church.[64] Here it should be observed that for Melanchthon the Gospel is the same as the *doctrine* of the Gospel.[65] The Gospel is for him not some nebulous message of salvation but a clear, defined teaching with a fixed content. It holds the dogmas of the Church as they are contained in Holy Scripture and comprehended in the symbols of the ancient Church.[66] By the "doctrine of the Gospel" in Melanchthon, the articles of the faith are to be understood. They form the "sum of Christian teaching"[67] or

[58] Ap 7.23ff., 26 (*BKS* 239f.); CR 21:835: "It must be granted that the Church is a visible assembly. At the same time, however, it is not the kingdom of the pope."

[59] CR 12:527; 15:314; 28:412.

[60] CR 12:365ff., 367: "It is clear that this assembly may be distinguished by the eyes and ears from all those which emit a different voice"; CR 12:601: "But since we are speaking of the Church . . . we do not imagine a Platonic idea, but we refer to the Church which can also be heard in mankind and seen and distinguished from all people and sects . . ."; CR 12:635: "God wishes the Church to be seen and heard in mankind"; CR 28:412: "although . . . the Church is the assembly, which may be seen and heard. . . ."

[61] CR 12:139: ". . . We refer to a visible assembly, which through certain signs is distinguished from other men"; CR 12:619: "We refer to it" (the Church) "whatever and wherever it may be, and we refer to signs, not to lies, that the true Church may be distinguished from other gatherings, which are enemies of the true doctrine."

[62] CR 21:506; cf. CR 21:843 ("the uncorrupted Gospel and the legitimate use of the Sacraments"); CR 15:526 ("confession of the pure Gospel and the legitimate use of the Sacraments"); AC 7.1 (*BKS* 60); Ap 7.5 (*BKS* 234): "the pure doctrine of the Gospel and the administration of the Sacraments in accordance with the Gospel"; Ap 7.20 (*BKS* 238): "the pure doctrine of the Gospel and Sacraments." — On the *notae* of the Church in Melanchthon, cf. H. Busch, op. cit., pp. 43f.

[63] Cf. AC 7.1 (*BKS* 60) [German]: ". . . and the holy Sacraments are given *in accordance with the Gospel*."

[64] CR 21:507: "most sure and notable marks, the pure teaching of the Gospel"; CR 8:430: "only the assembly which sounds aloud the true teaching of the Gospel. . . ."

[65] Cf. Ap 7.8 (*BKS* 235): "the fellowship of the same Gospel or doctrine . . ."; and the citations given in n. 62. On this and the following, also cf. O. Ritschl, op. cit., pp. 300ff.

[66] CR 7:394; 7:578; 9:1024; 12:646, 658; 21:334; 24:367.

[67] CR 23:600.

the foundation of Christianity.[68] The concept of the *fundamentum* [foundation] plays an important role in Melanchthon. It signifies that which belongs unconditionally to the essence of Christianity. The articles of the faith and the Decalogue are concrete. Where the foundation is kept, the true Church still exists, even if hay and straw are erected on this true foundation.[69] The assertion of Scripture that the Church is the pillar and foundation of the truth (1 Tim. 3:15) applies to that Church which preserves the foundation.[70] In every age there have been men who held firm to the foundation. This is why there is a consensus of the true Church in every age and in every place (by which Melanchthon especially has in mind the consensus of the ancient Church in its symbols). Conformity with this consensus of the true Church of all ages also belongs to pure doctrine.[71]

If Melanchthon speaks of the pure doctrine of the Gospel as a mark of the Church, he always has in mind the pure doctrine proclaimed in life and presented publicly in the Church. From this perspective it is understood that the Church may be compared to a *coetus scholasticus* [educational institution][72] or *honesta schola* [honorable school].[73] Regarding its visibility in the publicly presented doctrine of the Gospel, Melanchthon makes the Church fit this comparison. The Church can be seen, namely, as an "honorable aristocracy [*honesta aristocratia*] or godly assembly [*pius coetus*] of those who teach and learn the Christian catechism [κατήχησιν]."[74] At any rate, this visible assembly is not "enclosed within the same walls" but is "scattered" throughout the whole world[75] and stationed under the cross.[76] But God cares for it so that people are always present who preserve the foundation so that everywhere in the world

[68] CR 21:837: "the foundation . . . that is, where the articles of the faith are delivered whole and without corruption and where the manifest cults of idols are not defended"; cf. CR 13:798; 14:991; 15:975, 1067, 1347; 23:600; 28:394, 405, 411.

[69] CR 12:433: ". . . Only those men and those assemblies are members of the Church which embrace the uncorrupted doctrine of the Gospel, and though some may have more light, others less, nevertheless it is necessary . . . to keep the foundation, and all the articles of the faith, the doctrine of the Decalogue, even if some build gold upon the foundation and others stubble."

[70] CR 15:1347: "When . . . Paul says the Church is the pillar and seat of truth, we know that he is speaking of the true Church which retains the foundation, even if some have, and will have, more light and others less, and meanwhile saints built stubble on the foundation"; Ap 7.20 (*BKS* 238); *Mel.s Werke, Stud. Ausg.*, vol. 6 (1955), pp. 285, 292.

[71] CR 12:488: "He who departs from this consensus (of the saints concerning the doctrine of all ages) disagrees with the catholic Church."

[72] CR 21:835 ("the Church is an assembly similar to an educational institution").

[73] CR 15:314 ("similar . . . to an honorable school"); CR 15:344 ("similar to a godly school"). Cf. H. Busch, op. cit., pp. 57f. In such expressions, a strongly intellectualist conception of Christian teaching and of the Gospel plainly emerges, resulting from the humanist strain in Melanchthon's nature.

[74] CR 12:367; cf. CR 28:412 ("the Church is no secular kingdom, and yet in it there is an order, namely, between teachers and hearers").

[75] CR 12:367; cf. CR 12:527: "the Body is scattered, which spreads over all the earth"; Ap 7.20 (*BKS* 238): "the truly believing and righteous men scattered throughout the whole world."

[76] CR 12:434; cf. CR 25:46f.

the pure doctrine of the Gospel and the right administration of the Sacraments is alive.[77] In these articles, the true unity of the Church is also founded.[78] The mark of the Church of the pure doctrine in all places and at all times, of the *ecclesia catholica* of which the Apostles' Creed speaks, is the "agreement in the doctrine of the Gospel, even if [the Church] is scattered throughout the world and has various human rites."[79] Outside of this *ecclesia catholica* of the pure doctrine there is no salvation.[80] Nowhere else are the elect and heirs of eternal life found than in the visible *coetus* [assembly] of the Church, and nowhere else has God revealed Himself than in the visible Church, "in which alone the voice of the Gospel sounds."[81]

Over against this true Church of the Gospel there is accordingly an *ecclesia hypocritica*, a false, hypocritical church, which claims the name of the church and often surpasses the true Church in number and prestige and other external advantages, but in truth is the devil's instrument and attacks and persecutes the true Church.[82] One must break away from it and join the true Church of the pure doctrine. It is God's commandment that one clings to the true Church and takes part in its divine services.[83] Everyone who wants to have eternal salvation must take it most seriously and be certain that he is a member of the true Church.[84]

In the concept of the church described thus far in Melanchthon, the decisive element is the pure teaching of the Gospel and the rightly administered Sacraments. The Church proceeds from the pure Gospel and is sustained by it, and by it the true Church is distinguished from the false church. By this it also becomes clear what unique significance the *office of the Gospel and of the Sacraments* must have in Melanchthon's concept of the church. The office is

---

[77] CR 23:599: "There remains . . . some true Church, which retains the articles of the faith . . ."; cf. CR 28:411.

[78] AC 7.2ff. (*BKS* 60); Ap 7.30 (*BKS* 241).

[79] CR 21:506; cf. AC 7.

[80] CR 21:298: "that there is no salvation outside the Church, where there is neither Word nor Sacraments . . . for us it is sure that salvation is in the Church. . . . But that there is no salvation outside the Church since the Church is the kingdom of Christ"; CR 21:473: "There is no . . . salvation outside the Church, where there is neither Word nor Sacrament."

[81] CR 21:825, 833; cf. CR 5:596: (It is eternal truth) "that there are no people of God, no elect, save only in the flock where the voice of the Gospel and the Sacraments are."

[82] CR 21:506f.: "In the Scriptures two bodies are described: one of the true Church, the other of the hypocritical church, which wages war against the true Church"; cf. CR 12:484ff.: "the distinction between the true Church and the false church"; CR 12:485: "It pays a great deal, therefore, to keep the fact that there are always two peoples in the world who strive with each other for the title of the church. One people is truly the Church. The other claims the name church for itself when in fact it is not the Body of Christ."

[83] CR 12:368f.: "You know that it is God's commandment that you be joined to the true Church by faith, confession, invocation, and the offices which God commanded to be done for its maintenance"; CR 12:602: "It is God's command that all men be joined to the true Church."

[84] CR 12:431f.: "and that it behooves everyone to be joined to the true Church by the confession of its doctrine and the invocation of the Son of God, and to establish oneself as a member of the true Church wherever it is."

inserted in its place in the concept of the church, on which the Gospel and the Sacraments stand, and it is regarded together with them. The Gospel is simultaneously the *ministerium Evangelii*, and the Sacraments are simultaneously the *ministerium administrandi sacramenta* [ministry of administering the Sacraments].

> The concept of the office underlying this is without doubt defined in a strongly functional way, as we have already mentioned.[85] An office as a static authority, even regardless of the proper function of the means of grace, is unknown to Melanchthon. The *ministerium evangelii* is the office that actually preaches the Gospel and thus is intrinsically the ministry of the Gospel. But this should not mislead us into thinking that, for the characterization of the ministry of the Gospel happening in this way, it belongs quite decisively to the preaching of the Gospel that this ministry, this preaching, takes place in the *ministerium* on account of the office. The concept of the Gospel stipulates not merely that it is proclaimed in some way, but that it is proclaimed in the Church in a regular, orderly manner in accord with the institution and the office. As this office is entirely oriented toward the function of the Gospel, the Gospel requires that office for its proper function. Both concepts—*ministerium* and *Evangelium*—are mutually dependent. It is in the sense of this twofold relationship that the *ministerium Evangelii* should be understood.[86] Melanchthon never thinks of the office without the Gospel nor of the Gospel without the office.

Thus it is understandable that Melanchthon, in defining the Church, often uses the word "office" in place of "Word and Sacrament": the Church is "a visible assembly . . . in which God regenerates many through the *ministerium*."[87] If God raises someone to new life through the Gospel, He does so through the office of the Gospel. If God gathers the Church through the Gospel, He does so through the office.[88] If God reveals Himself through the Gospel, He does so through the office.[89] If He distributes eternal goods of salvation through the Gospel, He does so through the office.[90] In Melanchthon's thinking, Gospel and Sacrament are inseparably joined with the office. "If this, then, is the definition of the visible

---

[85] Cf. above, p. 220.

[86] On the former relation from the office to the function of the Gospel, cf. CR 11:760: "the ministry of the Gospel, where sounds the voice of the doctrine of the Son of God and the rites handed down by it are kept"; Ap 7.20 (*BKS* 238): the *notae* of the Church are identified (in the German translation by Justus Jonas) as "the preaching office or Gospel and the Sacraments"; CR 12:616 and 21:834 (the text of this passage is quoted above on p. 217 n. 35). On the latter relation of the Gospel to the office, cf. CR 21:825: "that the voice of the Gospel should sound publicly among men—it is necessary that there be a public ministry of the Gospel and public congregations"; CR 21:833: "We therefore know that the Church of God is the assembly bound to the voice *or* ministry of the Gospel"; as well as the passages indicated above on p. 218 n. 36.

[87] CR 12:431; cf. CR 12:399: "visible assembly embracing the Gospel, in which assembly the Son of God, the Mediator, is efficacious through the *ministerium*"; CR 21:826; 28:409.

[88] CR 5:585; 23:xxxv.

[89] CR 21:825: "the *ministerium* of the Gospel, through which God has revealed Himself and through which He is efficacious."

[90] CR 21:850.

Church," he says in the *Commentary on John* (1536), "the Church is the assembly of those who embrace the Gospel, and are joined together in the sharing of the Sacraments and of the ministry of the Gospel, and are born again by the Holy Spirit."[91] Word, Sacrament, office are in a line; they constitute the institutional element in the concept of the church around which the assembly gathers. In the articles against the Regensburg Book in 1541, Melanchthon writes, after determining that God always sustains the one unanimous Church and the same Gospel through the office: "The unity of the Church therefore consists of this association under one Head through the same Gospel and same *ministerium* to which it owes obedience. . . ."[92] Not only the same Gospel but also the same office is a criterion of the Church's true unity. From 1552 on (the *Examen ordinandorum* [Examination of ordinands]), *Melanchthon also counts the office as one of the marks of the Church* [*notae ecclesiae*]. He now identifies three of them: "(1) consensus with the uncorrupted teaching of the Gospel, or the *fundamentum*; (2) the legitimate use of the Sacraments; and (3) due obedience to the ministry according to the Gospel."[93] Consensus in these three things is necessary for the true unity of the Church.[94] Thus the proposition that outside the Church there is no salvation, with the result that all who wish to be saved must adhere to the true Church, also means that they must all adhere to the *ministerium* of the Gospel since it is only by that means that the call of the Gospel reaches them.[95] "The called are those who hear the *ministerium*, are joined to the *ministerium*

[91] CR 15:314; cf. CR 15:317: "I say that the Church is bound to the Gospel and to the *ministerium* of the Gospel."

[92] CR 4:368. It should be noted that both Gospel and *ministerium* are connected by an "and," which shows that the term *ministerium* means something beyond simply "Gospel." The Gospel is bound to the institution of the office, in which designated persons in God's commission declare the Gospel and are therefore deserving of obedience.

[93] CR 23:37; cf. CR 23:lxxv; 24:367, 401, 402: "When you wish to judge whether yourself and others are members of the Church . . . , how do you show this? I ask now concerning signs. For I believe the Creed and use the Sacraments. I am baptized and obey the ministry"; also CR 12:599, 635. Cf. the proof in O. Ritschl, op. cit., p. 317. O. Ritschl finds that Melanchthon's doctrine of the marks of the Church only emerges in finalized form in the *Examen ordinandorum*, in a disputation from 1554 (CR 12:602), in various passages of the so-called *Postil*, and in his *Responsiones ad impios Bavaricae inquisitionis articulos* (C Ph 898 = *Stud. Ausg.*, vol. 6, p. 286). This is formally accurate with respect to the numbering of three marks; yet the same doctrine of the marks is already present in Melanchthon's thinking in 1536 (cf. the passage CR 15:314 cited above in the text, n. 91). Without question, there is an evolution of the concept of the church present in Melanchthon, with a tendency of laying increasing emphasis on the office as a divine institution. It is through the lens of this evolution that the inclusion of the office among the *notae ecclesiae* should be seen. Cf. H. Busch, op. cit., p. 26. The forces pushing Melanchthon in this direction are surely, as Busch notes (op. cit., p. 44), anti-Anabaptist motivations. Also cf. Herrlinger, *Die Theologie Melanchthons* (Gotha, 1879), p. 269. Still, it cannot be forgotten that even in AC 28.22 (*BKS* 124) it says that obedience to the office is required *jure divino*. This is by no means a mere preamble to his later position (as Busch sees it: op. cit., p. 38), but the essence of it even at this stage. The more mature Melanchthon expresses himself even more strongly in this regard.

[94] CR 23:38; 12:433.

[95] CR 23:39: ". . . since God desires all who are to be saved to be implanted in the Church and bound to the ministry of the Gospel."

by external confession of their teaching, and partake of the Sacraments."[96] The office is thus for Melanchthon—as O. Ritschl has said—"the very identifying mark of the Church which summarizes in itself the other two marks."[97]

> This is also made rather plain in a disputation *De obedientia et consensu Ecclesiae* [On the obedience and consensus of the Church] (though from later years),[98] in which Melanchthon directly equates the *ecclesia catholica* with the *ministerium*. The statement in the Apostles' Creed "I believe in the holy catholic Church" demands consensus with the catholic Church and thus obedience toward the office. The "*ecclesia catholica* is the congregation of the godly" who agree not only "in the Spirit" but also in "certain external things," namely, "the *ministerium*." The *ministerium* is the epitome of all that belongs to the essence of the Church, especially of pure doctrine: "the *ministerium* of the catholic Church, the apostolic doctrine given from the apostles themselves and passed down by the holy fathers. *Ecclesia catholica* not only signifies the present ministers but the consensus of the saints concerning the doctrine of all ages."[99] The office is the steadfast rock of this "consensus of the saints concerning doctrine." This is why "those who depart from the *ministerium* of the catholic Church are ungodly and accursed."[100] And: "Wherever . . . the catholic *ministerium* is, there is a part of the catholic Church."[101]

It may be said that the office, in the mature stage of Melanchthon's concept of the office, constitutes the decisive core on which everything centers. The office is for Melanchthon the lifeblood of the Church on which all things depend. Yet the office only has this paramount significance because and insofar as it is the office of the true preaching of the Gospel and administration of the Sacraments.

3. The Significance of the Universal Priesthood for the Office

O. Ritschl has pointed out that in Melanchthon the concept of the universal priesthood recedes noticeably to the background.[102] This is correct

---

[96] CR 25:387.

[97] Op. cit., p. 318.

[98] CR 12:488f.

[99] CR 12:488.

[100] Ibid.

[101] CR 12:489; cf. CR 11:760: ". . . We always know that true Church of God is there where the ministry of the Gospel is. . . ."

[102] Op. cit., pp. 339f. Likewise, cf. H. Jacoby, *Die Liturgik d. Reformatoren*, vol. II (Gotha, 1876), p. 9; Herrlinger, op. cit., pp. 270f.; K. Thieme, *Die Augsburg. Konf. u. Luthers Katechismen* (Gießen, 1930), p. 17; W. Elert, *Morphologie* I, pp. 299 and 309. — The same holds for the Confessions and has frequently been noticed there. Cf. A. L. Richter, *Gesch. d. ev. Kirchenverfassung* (Leipzig, 1851), p. 53; Herrlinger, op. cit., p. 270; E. Sommerlath, "Amt u. allg. Priestertum," p. 75; H. H. Kramm, *Bischof, Pastor u. Gemeinde*, pp. 15 and 20; R. Josefson, "Det andliga ämbetet . . . ," in *En bok om kyrkans ämbete* (Uppsala, 1951), p. 184.

without question. The universal priesthood has no constitutive significance for Melanchthon's doctrine of the office. Still, it would be false to try to assert that Melanchthon had no understanding for this doctrine absolutely.[103] A statement by Melanchthon on this point of doctrine in the religious proceedings of the Imperial Diet of Augsburg served as instigation for this.[104] On July 10, 1530, after the Augsburg Confession had already been presented, Melanchthon produces the memorandum *Cur non plures articuli fidei tradendi sint* [Why no more articles of the faith should be given][105] in which he argues against the fact "that the hateful and unprofitable articles which tend to be discussed in the schools are being stirred up at this time, such as . . . whether Christians are all priests. . . ."[106] According to this, it could seem as though Melanchthon never in fact gave a thought to the universal priesthood. Yet the expression "odious and needless articles" would surely only imply that the universal priesthood is an article that—if it is spoken of—would stir up considerable hatred and which does not belong unconditionally to the fundamental articles and is therefore not needed, at least for the time being, as a subject of settlement proceedings. It is mainly tactical considerations which cause Melanchthon to argue against discussing the universal priesthood.[107] He says that all necessary articles and all abuses in the church which conflict with these articles are treated in the Augsburg Confession. If at this point further articles should be proposed, the emperor would form the impression that the Protestants were concealing many more harmful doctrines which they had not yet divulged, which they would eventually bring to light after they had first submitted the "favorable" articles (in the Augsburg Confession).[108] Still, it is apparent from this memorandum that Melanchthon does not count the doctrine of the universal priesthood among the fundamental articles of the faith. This is why it is not found in the Confession either. One should not, however, be misled by this memorandum of 1530 to deny that Melanchthon had any interest in the doctrine of the universal priesthood. This teaching is thoroughly familiar to Melanchthon, and he himself even takes it up in a positive light.[109] What is important, however, is what content he attributes to the Christian priesthood and how he positions it relative to the particular office. Let us therefore examine this subject.

---

103 This already received due attention from W. Thomas, op. cit., pp. 7f.

104 Cf. that in Herrlinger, op. cit., pp. 270f., and recently in H. Storck, op. cit., p. 3.

105 CR 2:192f.

106 CR 2:183; the questions posed there include "Can a layman consecrate the Sacrament? Does the priestly consecration impress a permanent character? Can a woman consecrate?"

107 Cf. CR 2:182: "First, because the princes would have made their confession regarding the necessary articles of doctrine which are preached to the people publicly in their lands, and it is not necessary to burden them with unprofitable disputations . . . , which belong more in school than to sermons in churches . . ."; CR 2:183: "Since we should not hinder the treatment of these religious matters that has been initiated, it is not at all advisable . . ." (that these articles be addressed).

108 CR 2:182f.

109 He does so especially in the early period, when he was especially under Luther's influence.

As the content of the Christian priesthood, Melanchthon cites the right and ability to perform three functions: *orare*, *offerre*, and *placare* [pray, sacrifice, and please]. As priests, Christians have free access to God by prayer and are able to offer sacrifices to Him.[110] In the *Loci* of 1521, Melanchthon denies office-bearers the title "*sacerdos*" ["priest"] and gives it to all Christians: "And all we Christians are priests, for we offer a sacrifice, that is, our body. For beyond this there is no sacrifice in Christianity; and we have the right to implore God and, indeed, to please Him."[111] This is also how Melanchthon understands the priestly kingdom of 1 Pet. 2:9: "For we Christians are kings since, being free men through Christ, we are lords over all creatures, life, death, and sin. . . . Priests, because we offer ourselves to God, and we implore Him on account of our sins."[112]

The sacrifice of Christians is not the sacrifice of the Mass[113] but the spiritual self-sacrifice in the prayer of faith, the sacrifice of the body for the glory of God, and the praise offering of the lips according to Heb. 13:15. In the *Loci* of 1535, in order to clarify the nature of Christians' sacrifices, Melanchthon introduces the distinction between the propitiatory sacrifice [*sacrificium propitiatorium*] and eucharistic [εὐχαριστικά] sacrifices. By the former, "the remission of guilt and of eternal punishment" is merited, and atonement made for sin before God; it is a "work reconciling God and appeasing the wrath of God on behalf of others, and making satisfaction for guilt and eternal punishment." By the latter, thanks are given to God for the forgiveness of sins and reconciliation already received, which is to say, for other benefits of God as well.[114] There is only one propitiatory sacrifice, the death of Christ;[115] all other sacrifices in the New Testament are eucharistic sacrifices, sacrifices of praise, which are offered through Christ on the basis of the atonement achieved with God. It is the latter which are meant in 1 Pet. 2:9 and Heb. 13:15.[116] The Christian priesthood is expressed in them. Melanchthon enumerates as eucharistic sacrifices "the preaching of the Gospel, faith, invocation, thanksgiving, confession, the afflictions of the saints, and, indeed, all good works of the saints."[117] These can never involve works chosen

---

[110] CR 1:481: "We all . . . are priests. Neither is the priesthood anything other than the right of prayer, or of speaking to God and of making offerings to God" (1521).

[111] CR 21:222.

[112] Ibid. — It must be remembered that here, in the *Loci* of 1521, Melanchthon separates and distinguishes from the function of the particular office the concept of the priesthood as a mark of those spiritual functions before God common to all Christians. We are priests because we offer ourselves to God (as is proper for all Christians), but "bishops, presbyters, and deacons are not, except those who teach, baptize, bless the Supper, and dispense alms" (CR 21:222). Melanchthon—in contrast to Luther—does not see in the office the universal priesthood being (publicly) operative.

[113] CR 21:221.

[114] CR 21:480; cf. CR 12:501ff., 502: "The sacrifices are twofold: first the propitiatory offerings; second, those of praise or *eucharistic* [εὐχαριστικά]"; CR 13:1417ff.; Ap 24.22ff. (*BKS* 355f.).

[115] CR 21:481.

[116] CR 21:482; 12:502.

[117] CR 21:481f. "The preaching of the Gospel" here means not the function of the preaching office, but generally bearing witness to the Gospel as incumbent on every Christian. Further cf. CR 21:483; Ap 24.25 (*BKS* 356).

by men, but only ever those commanded by God.[118] And these sacrifices are not valid *ex opere operato*, but only through faith; they please God "on account of the Mediator, Christ, interceding for us and offering our sacrifices to the Father" according to 1 Pet. 2:5.[119] Their purpose is to render thanks and honor to God and, through obedience, to prove our desire to serve Him as He instructs us.[120] The whole Christian life is to be a perpetual eucharistic sacrifice "in which our knowledge of God, our obedience toward God, and our perpetual celebration of God's benefits should shine forth and be visible."[121]

If Melanchthon stresses the pleasing of God as the content of the Christian priesthood,[122] it is necessary to keep in mind the distinction of *sacrificium alienum* [alien sacrifice] and *sacrificium proprium* [proper sacrifice] commonly used by him.[123] As their propitiatory sacrifice, Christians have only an alien one, that of Christ, and the *placare* [pleasing] is achieved through the faithful reception of the fruit of this sacrifice of Christ's.[124] The eucharistic sacrifices, however, are proper sacrifices, offered by faith in the atoning sacrifice of Christ.[125] When Melanchthon determines that "the right of the priesthood encompasses two duties: pleasing God and offering to God,"[126] faith is implied as accompanying both functions. In the first case, it is the function of faith appropriating the sacrifice of Christ; in the latter case, that of producing fruit in the sanctification of life. For Melanchthon, the Christian priesthood coincides with the Christian's state of salvation, the fact that he is atoned for by Christ, which opens access to God and thus to adoption as a child of God,[127] from which the new life necessarily emerges in spiritual sacrifices. When Melanchthon appeals to the use of the rights of the priesthood, he is only appealing to those expressions of the spiritual life produced by all Christians and arising from the Christian estate:

---

118 CR 13:1420f.: "This kind of sacrifice embraces all works and worships which have God's command . . ."; CR 23:64: "Sacrifice is therefore a work commanded by God"; cf. CR 12:503.

119 CR 13:1419; 21:482: "These avail not *ex opere operato* but on account of faith"; CR 12:503.

120 CR 23:64: (the offering of a work commanded by God) "done in the knowledge of the Mediator and in faith, to the end that honor may be shown to God, that is, that by this work we testify that He truly is God and that He wishes to be served in this way . . ."; CR 13:1420f.: ". . . with the intent of testifying that they know God and give thanks for the benefits received and of rendering Him due obedience in turn."

121 CR 13:1421.

122 CR 12:501: "All . . . believers are priests; that is, they have not only the power but also the command to please God. . . ."

123 CR 12:502: "Every Christian has a twofold sacrifice, the propitiatory and the eucharistic [εὐχαριστικά]. But they have the first as an alien sacrifice; the second, as a proper one. . . ."

124 CR 12:503: "Neither do they please [God] by their own sacrifice but by an alien one, which, however, they do not offer personally but only receive by faith the fruit of that sacrifice."

125 CR 12:503: "Saints have proper eucharistic sacrifices, which avail on account of faith. . . ."

126 CR 12:502.

127 CR 12:503: "Since . . . we have testimony in the Scriptures that we are priests, Scripture testifies that we have the right, given to us by Christ, to please and to pray to God"; CR 12:504: "Neither do men have another greater benefit than the right of the priesthood, *by which they properly become God's sons* and worshipers and God's peculiar people."

". . . Let us use the benefit of God" (i.e., the priesthood) "and the right granted us and show forth our sacrifices: faith, invocation, thanksgiving, and obedience to the commands of God."[128]

In this interpretation of the universal priesthood with which we have been acquainted up to this point, a relation to the particular office is wholly absent. We must now address the question of whether Melanchthon knows of a derivation of the particular office from the universal priesthood, and whether, like Luther, he construes this term to include a fundamental authority over the function of Word and Sacrament in every Christian.

> In his disputation *De Sacerdotio et sacrificio* [On the priesthood and sacrifice],[129] from which we have already drawn several citations, there is the passage: "A priest is properly he who has the right of pleasing God and handling the Word and Sacraments."[130] And of that right it then says, "That right is already given to all believers through Christ."[131] According to this, every believing Christian, by virtue of the priesthood, would also fundamentally have the right to teach the Word of God and administer the Sacraments. But Melanchthon immediately restricts this assertion and distinguishes this function of the universal priesthood from that of the particular office: "Neither, however, may anyone usurp the public ministry in the Church without a call."[132] However, this idea that the priesthood of every Christian also includes the right to the function of Word and Sacrament is not mentioned further in this disputation and is completely absent from another disputation on the same topic.[133] Neither is it taken up in the summarizing final sentence of this other disputation, in which Melanchthon calls for priesthood to be practiced (cited above, n. 128). *Clearly, the argument for this universal Christian right to administer Word and Sacrament on the basis of the Christian priesthood is not of great importance to Melanchthon.* What we have here, then, is an occasional expression which—as far as we see—is without any parallel in the rest of Melanchthon's writing.
>
> In other passages, when Melanchthon argues for the universal Christian right to Word and Sacrament, he places much more emphasis on the Keys as a possession of all Christians. In the *Loci* of 1521, Melanchthon observes that the functions of the presbyter and deacons were formerly not distinct to the extent that it would be a trespass for deacons to teach, to baptize, or to consecrate the Sacrament of the Altar. He continues: "Indeed, all Christians may do these things. For the Keys belong to all (Matt. 18 [:18])."[134] The fundamental permission and

---

[128] CR 12:504.

[129] CR 12:501ff. Undated.

[130] CR 12:501.

[131] Ibid.

[132] Ibid.

[133] CR 12:501ff.

[134] CR 21:222. Later in the text there is hint of a rationale of the particular office on the basis of order, where it reads: "But stewardship" (of the Keys, e.g.) "was entrusted to certain people, that there might be those who necessarily know that the church affairs are to be administered by them and to whom recourse might duly be had if something should happen" (CR 21:222). The universal

authorization for all Christians to administer the Word and Sacraments rests on their sharing of the power of the Keys. Thus in the case of emergency—as Melanchthon explains in his *Treatise on the Power and Primacy of the Pope* (1537), using the Augustinian example of the two Christians in the boat, where the penitent baptizes the catechumen and the latter in turn absolves the former—even laity may baptize and absolve each other and become each other's minister and pastor. This is possible because the Keys are given not only to designated persons (i.e., "in the office") but to the Church.[135] Melanchthon takes the same position in disputation *De iure Absolutionis* [On the right of Absolution],[136] in which he says in reference to the aforementioned Augustinian example: "I stand by Augustine's opinion, for the laity are permitted to baptize and to absolve."[137] But regarding the public office, he goes on: "And yet the public ministry should not be disturbed. Even if the public administration of the power of the Keys belongs to the public ministers of the Gospel, laity may still absolve, not only in the case of necessity but also in other instances. Neither is that absolution uncertain, even if public ministers are the only ones who have the public administration of the Keys."[138] Melanchthon knows of a valid lay absolution not only in the case of necessity but also in other contexts in the life of Christians; only it must be performed in such a way that the public office is not disturbed by it. This is then supported by the fact that "the Keys are given to the whole Church, and it is a general command that we should announce the Gospel to those brothers who seek it, yet in such a way that the public ministry is not disturbed."[139] Here, too, there is no reference to the universal priesthood, but only to the sharing of the power of the Keys. And this lay function of the Absolution (and of Baptism) is clearly distinguished from the function of the particular office.[140]

---

priesthood, however, is not mentioned in this line of thinking. — The passage quoted in our text is not found in later editions of the *Loci*. Cf. H. Jacoby, op. cit., p. 7: "But Melanchthon does not adhere to this view."

135 Tr 67f. (*BKS* 491); cf. Tr 24 (*BKS* 478). On the passage Tr 68, cf. A. F. C. Vilmar, *Die Lehre vom geistlichen Amt* (Marburg & Leipzig, 1870), p. 87, and *Dogmatik* II, unaltered reprint of the first ed. (Gütersloh, 1937), p. 275, who states that this passage describes the Keys only as the property of the whole Church and by no means teaches a derivation of the office from the congregation. This is accurate.

136 CR 12:493f. Undated.

137 CR 12:493.

138 Ibid.; cf. CR 21:220: "As certain as the sinful woman in Luke 7 was . . . that all her guilt was pardoned when she heard Christ's words, 'Your sins are forgiven you,' be just as certain yourself, whoever you are, when you are absolved by a brother."

139 CR 12:494.

140 This also applies to the lay function of the Word. While Melanchthon, in 1521, regarding 1 Cor. 14:30f., still speaks of "the same right to teach" which is given equally to all in the Church (CR 1:336), in his 1551 commentary on the same passage of 1 Corinthians he speaks much more cautiously. There he first speaks of the ministers who are called to the teaching office, and only then, in regard to v. 31 ("you are all able to interpret [*potestis omnes interpretari*]") and Col. 3:16, comes to the permission which is also given to others concerning the free expression of opinion within the congregation, provided it is done in an orderly manner. After mentioning the duty of parents and teachers to teach children the Word of God, Melanchthon refers to Matt. 10:32: "Moreover, a general command is given to all, that they should each exhibit their confession. . . . And this command

We may say that Melanchthon probably knows of a right to Word and Sacrament common to all Christians, but this is relegated only to one passage (CR 12:501) without any emphasis on the concept of the priesthood. There can be no discussion of the particular office being derived from the universal priesthood in Melanchthon.

Yet there are two passages in which Melanchthon references 1 Pet. 2:9 as a basis for the Church's right to appoint the office. In the *Loci* of 1535, Melanchthon teaches that the Church has the command not only to guard itself against false prophets but also to choose godly teachers and place them into office. Where the Church is, there also is the "right of administering the Gospel." The Church may not exist without the Gospel, for which reason it is its most peculiar right to call persons into office according to that verse (1 Pet. 2:9): "'You are a royal priesthood,' which words pertain to the true Church. And the priesthood is the right of administering the Gospel."[141] Included in that priesthood is the right to see that the Gospel is carried out by calling ministers to the office. Because the Church is a royal priesthood, it also has the right to attend to the Gospel by calling persons to the office. One may ask here whether the office is being based on the universal priesthood or even being derived from the universal priesthood. Our opinion: No. This cannot be viewed as a deduction of the office from the universal priesthood, as becomes rather clear when the following text is taken into account. Melanchthon immediately follows 1 Pet. 2:9 with Eph. 4:8ff.: "Likewise, Eph. 4 [:8]: 'He ascended, gave gifts to men.' And he numbers among His own gifts the pastors and teachers of the church. . . ."[142] Pastors and teachers—in other words, the office appointed with persons—(as gifts of God) belong to the Church. On the basis of this divine order, the Church has the right to call ministers, and no one can dispute this right. Nothing else is meant by the reference to the right possessed by the *sacerdotium*, the royal priesthood and priestly people of God, to administer the Gospel. The Christian Church is a *sacerdotium*, a priestly nation, which lives from the Gospel and has the right to make sure that the Gospel is declared to it through the office, and so to appoint persons to that office. No more is being said. The tenor of this passage finds expression in the summarizing statement: "Therefore, where the true Church is, the right of electing ministers must

---

of confession compels the faithful in the congregation, of which Paul is speaking, to declare their opinion when they hear others err in interpretation. But Paul wants all things to be done in order and calmly, not with factious and unruly shouting" (CR 15:1175). Another aspect of order, however, is the presence of certain *seniores* [elders] and *doctiores* [more learned men], who are to function as *judices* [judges] when individuals express opinions and are to show "what they approve and what they reject" (CR 15:1175). The apostle, he says, in this passage forbade both the tyranny of individuals and the tumult of the multitude "and established an arrangement similar to the aristocracy. He wants many learned men and God-fearers to be heard" (CR 15:1176). The most learned and excellent are to have the final word. Similarly, the right fundamentally held by all to judge doctrine (CR 1:336, 349f.; 14:341) is practically limited by Melanchthon to "those capable of judging," to "the pious and learned" (CR 10:702; 11:435; 15:1170f.). "Only such laity are to sit in the council and have a vote" (CR 10:702; 14:341). To my knowledge, a reference to the universal priesthood for the right to judge doctrine is not encountered in Melanchthon. The universal priesthood is not mentioned in the quoted passages on 1 Corinthians 14 either.

141 CR 21:505.

142 Ibid.

also be."[143] The very fact that the necessity to fill the particular office with persons underlies the whole argument of this passage makes it apparent that this is not seen here merely as an exponent of the priesthood but as something that, while belonging to the *sacerdotium*, the priestly nation, is nevertheless not identical to it, and thus is conceived as something distinct from it.

The same train of thought in this passage of the *Loci* (1535) is also found in the *Treatise on the Power and Primacy of the Pope* (1537), where Melanchthon, in arguing for the fundamental right of the Church to elect and ordain its ministers, quotes, among others, 1 Pet. 2:9: "Finally, this is also confirmed by Peter's declaration: 'You are a royal priesthood,' which words pertain to the true Church, which, since it alone has the priesthood, certainly has the right of electing and ordaining ministers."[144] We must agree with H. Bernau that this reference to the universal priesthood in the treatise by no means constitutes "an inwardly directed question concerning the universal priesthood and the appointed office" and that the universal priesthood, according to the whole context, is to serve only as an argument for the Church's right to ordination.[145] No more can really be deduced from the passage than that the Church, on the basis of its character as a priestly nation of God, also has the right to fill the particular office. Concerning the relationship of the universal priesthood and particular office, the most that this can be saying is that the universal priesthood requires the particular office. There is here no actual derivation of the office from the universal priesthood.[146]

The two passages mentioned last are—as far as we know—the only ones in Melanchthon that suggest a link between the particular office and the universal priesthood. In addition to the already quoted reasons, referencing them for a derivation of the office from the universal priesthood is also prohibited by the existence of a statement by Melanchthon in which the two entities of *sacerdotium* and *ministerium* are clearly differentiated and divorced from each other. In his *Commentary on the Psalms*, it reads: "The external ministry and the priesthood differ. For priesthood is the right of individual believers to invoke and sacrifice. . . . But the ministry is the execution of the task of teaching, for which the call is needed. This public ministry pertains only to those who are duly [*ritè*] called. . . ."[147] Office and priesthood are here forced apart so that by this passage it becomes

---

[143] Ibid.

[144] Tr 69 (*BKS* 491).

[145] H. Bernau, "Die Bedeutung der Ordination nach den luth. Bekenntnisschriften," in *Kirche und Amt* I, *Beiheft z. Ev. Theol.*, vol. 2 (Munich, 1940), p. 72 n. 71; also cf. p. 55. A similar assessment of this passage is made by Vilmar (*Lehre v. geistl. Amt*, pp. 90f.), W. Löhe (*Neue Aphorismen*, *Ges. Werke*, vol. V.1, p. 551), T. Kliefoth (*Lit. Abhandlgen* I, p. 342) and F. J. Stahl (*Die Kirchenverfassung*, pp. 411f.).

[146] We must therefore ask whether W. Maurer's formulations (*Pfarrerrecht und Bekenntnis* [Berlin, 1957], pp. 68f.) that Melanchthon, in appealing to 1 Pet. 2:9 in this passage, causes "the ministry to develop from the priesthood" and that "the ministry is a particular form of the priesthood" are suited to the discussion in this passage of the Treatise. Is it not asking too much of Tr 69 to find in it the teaching of the office emanating from the priesthood? Cf. H. H. Kramm, op. cit., p. 15. On the debate with W. Maurer, see the more thorough discussion below, pp. 245–49.

[147] CR 13:1278. The passage nevertheless does not originate from before 1553/55. If it is appraised here together with the passages from 1535 or 1537, this is naturally done with the

completely clear that Melanchthon does not know of an actual derivation of the office from the universal priesthood.[148]

Our study has shown that there is only one passage in Melanchthon in which the priesthood of all Christians is construed as a fundamental right to the function of Word and Sacrament, and that the universal priesthood is related to the particular office consists, according to Melanchthon, only of the fact that the former requires that the latter be filled, and thus a deduction of the office from the universal priesthood is not taught by Melanchthon. It may therefore be said that the universal priesthood has no constitutive significance for Melanchthon's doctrine of the office.

W. Thomas (op. cit., pp. 7f.) notes: Even if the concept of the universal priesthood in Melanchthon is found in lesser quantity, nevertheless its content is all the more present in Melanchthon (p. 7). As objective content of the universal priesthood, he then alleges: "that between a baptized Christian man and a consecrated priest there is no qualitative difference; that the power of the Church belongs not to an individual estate but to the congregation; that these (i.e., the laity) are in no way bound to the 'spiritual estate' either with respect to the administration of the means of grace or with respect to doctrinal decisions; and that, in certain circumstances, they can independently call to the office any Christian whom they regard as capable because he is only to act publicly in that for which he is otherwise authorized privately or within his *vocatio*" (pp. 7f.). Even if these accounts by Thomas, all born from a theory of competition between office and congregation, were accurate, it would still be worth noting that Melanchthon does not attach these contents to the concept of the universal priesthood! But they should not be regarded as such, and in this formulation suggest a false picture. To take only one example, Thomas entirely disregards the fact that Melanchthon teaches that the Church is tied to the office (though not to episcopal succession), that he teaches the continual preservation of the office (the office as filled with persons) in the Church, that he judges the cooperation of the office in the call of pastors to be by divine right, that in doctrinal decisions he sees the laity merely as joint participants, not as actual bearers of doctrinal authority (which for him are the pastors!). Evidence for these facts in Melanchthon will be disclosed by our further study. If we were to try to judge Melanchthon's position as Thomas does, we would have to make quite rare and extreme statements chiefly from the early period—when Melanchthon was still thoroughly under Luther's influence and had not yet evolved in his own individual fashion—as governing explanatory guidelines for all further statements by Melanchthon, which is naturally prohibited. The mature Melanchthon does not think from the perspective of the congregation, and certainly not in the manner of a rivalry between congregation and office, but rather from the perspective opposite that of the office, granted without making the congregation an appendage of the office in the process. Melanchthon's idea of the office is not an absolutizing one because it is underpinned by his preference

---

assumption that Melanchthon did not fundamentally change his view on this point in the intervening period. Incidentally, I owe to F. J. Stahl, op. cit., p. 107, the reference to this passage.

[148] Cf. F. J. Stahl, op. cit., pp. 106f.

for aristocratic forms. Capable laymen are to assist the office. The aspect of the office, however, is so prevalent in Melanchthon that O. Ritschl has the impression that, with Melanchthon's cultivated doctrine of the office, the foundation of the universal priesthood lost "its former significance and its attractive power" (op. cit., p. 339). In saying so, he is likely recalling the significance of this term in Luther. It is by no means incidental, Ritschl further opines, "that Melanchthon also became the theoretical author of the hierarchy of the *ministerium ecclesiasticum*" (op. cit., p. 340). Melanchthon's concept of the office is "a crucial capstone in his construction of an orthodox Church with exclusionary opposition to heresy" (ibid.). Perhaps there is also a certain bias attached to these judgments of Melanchthon's doctrine of the office. Yet it must be said that the characteristic features in Melanchthon are emphasized far more in this interpretation than in the one specified by Thomas.

CHAPTER II

The Office as Divine Institution

1. *Ministerium docendi Evangelium et administrandi Sacramenta*

In Melanchthon's writings, the rationale of the office from the doctrine of the Gospel and the place of the office in the concept of the church show that the office is to be understood entirely as of service to God's salvific will. It mediates the divine offering of grace in the Gospel, calls men to Christ, and thus gathers the Church from the race of man. In accordance with Eph. 4:12ff. (to which Melanchthon often refers), it exists for the edification of the Church, and yet in this purpose it is in every way an office for the mediation of grace since it is only through the Gospel and Sacraments that salvation is mediated. Thus the office in Melanchthon is always defined as the "*ministerium docendi Evangelium et administrandi Sacramenta* [ministry of teaching the Gospel and administering the Sacraments]."[1] Those who enter the office are called "to the office of preaching and the ministry of the Sacrament" and nothing else.[2] ". . . Preaching the Gospel, rebuking and forgiving sin, giving the Sacrament—these alone are to be the office of bishop or priest."[3]

This definition of the nature of the office represents the *antithesis of the Roman office of the sacrificial Mass*,[4] which for Melanchthon is a perverted office that places its occupant on the same level as Jezebel, the priestess of Baal.[5] At the same time, with the office defined as the office of the Word and Sacraments, a

[1] CR 21:470; 15:435; AC 5.1 (*BKS* 57); AC 28.21 (*BKS* 124): "ministry of Word and Sacraments"; also "ministry of the Gospel" (e.g., CR 21:470; 21:825, 826, 833, 850) or "ministry of the Word" (CR 21:470, etc.).

[2] CR 5:596f.

[3] CR 4:1002f.; cf. CR 11:760: "ministry of the Gospel, that is, where the voice of the teaching of the Son of God resounds and the rites handed down from Him are observed."

[4] CR 21:470f.; cf. CR 4:544; 5:585; 15:1334; Ap 13.7ff. (*BKS* 293f.); Ap 28.12 (*BKS* 400): "Those who are now bishops do not perform the offices of bishops according to the Gospel . . ."; Tr 34 (*BKS* 481): "The ministry of the Gospel is forgotten."

[5] CR 21:222; cf. CR 21:852.

contrast is made to the office understood as *potestas politica* [political power].[6] The office of the New Testament is a *ministerium Evangelii* (in contrast to the *ministerium legis* [ministry of the Law]), a *ministerium Spiritus*, an office through which the Holy Spirit is given,[7] and as such is not ruled by corporeal things[8] according to the standards of temporal, political government; much less is it a dominion over the kingdoms of the world.[9] This ministry of the Gospel concerns not physical but eternal things—"eternal righteousness, the Holy Spirit, eternal life"[10]—and is not to be confused with secular things.[11]

Melanchthon always sees the office of the Word and the Sacraments, which for him is the center of everything, in this demarcation from a satisfactionary or political, hierarchical understanding of the office. Part of the essential definition of the office in his view is its public character. The function of Word and Sacrament in the office is always a public rite. "We should know that it is proper for us to sound the voice of the Gospel publicly among men. . . . It is proper for there to be a public ministry of the Gospel and public congregations";[12] "God wills that there be a public ministry."[13] The public character of the office follows from the public character of the Gospel, which, of course, fulfills its purpose only when it is publicized, that is, is proclaimed audibly. Likewise, it goes hand in hand with the doctrine of the Church's *visibility*. It is necessary that it be connected to the Church. In order for it to have that connectivity, it must be visible. In order for it to be visible, Word and Sacrament must be dispensed publicly. The public character of the office is explained by these interrelationships. Melanchthon—as we have already seen—also knows of a private sphere, in which the fraternal consolation of the Gospel occurs and the Absolution of one Christian brother is granted to another.[14] The function of Word and Sacrament, however, is a different genus from that of the office, which is always public.

---

[6] CR 15:435: "The ministry of the Gospel is the command to teach the Gospel and administer the Sacraments; it is not a power similar to the political."

[7] CR 15:164f.; 15:429, 696, 1197.

[8] CR 3:471, 224; 4:1002f.; 14:969; 15:1347f.; 21:501, 503; 22:516.

[9] CR 12:493; 15:426: (Christ) "does not send apostles to seize carnal dominions. And He distinguishes the ministry of the Gospel from dominion"; CR 4:1003: ". . . the apostles have no command of worldly rule, but only of teaching and preaching and the giving of the Sacraments, by which the forgiveness of sins is distributed"; AC 28.1ff. (*BKS* 120ff.).

[10] AC 28.8 (*BKS* 121f.).

[11] AC 28.12ff. (*BKS* 122ff.); also cf. *Stud. Ausg.*, vol. 1 (1951), p. 310.

[12] CR 21:825.

[13] CR 21:853; cf. CR 3:983; 12:490, 493; 21:555; AC 14 (*BKS* 66). On the interpretation of "*publice*" from AC 14, cf. E. Sommerlath, "Amt und allg. Priestertum," pp. 63ff., and W. Maurer, *Pfarrerrecht und Bekenntnis*, pp. 117ff.

[14] CR 12:493f.; cf. above, pp. 232–33.

2. *Institutum Dei*

The absolute necessity of the Gospel for salvation as taught by Melanchthon, and his positioning the ministry of the Gospel in the dominant place in the concept of the church, suggests that the office as Melanchthon conceives it cannot have the character of a merely human-sociological necessity but is related back to the direct, unmediated will of God. And this is taught by Melanchthon most emphatically: "*The office is of divine origin; it belongs to the essential structure of the Church founded by God; it is the institutum Dei.*"[15] God instituted and ordained the office[16] so that it is a *ministerium divinitus ordinatum* [divinely ordained ministry],[17] and as such, a "*most holy* ministry."[18] The terms "institution" and "ordination" imply the proposition that the office constitutes an enduring divine institution. God desires that there *always* be a public office in the Church;[19] He gave it to the Church "for all times."[20] It was His intention in founding the office that we should be wholly "enclosed" within it.[21] This is the more reasonable, according to Melanchthon, as we have seen, as faith can be received only from the Gospel, and the Church is begotten and fed by God's Word.[22] The whole Christian life is embedded, according to God's will, in the operation of the office, which rests on His institution.

---

[15] That public ministers of the Word are charged with the administration of the Sacraments according to Melanchthon "for the sake of order," as W. Thomas, op. cit., p. 32, asserts without any substantiating reference, can be gleaned in Melanchthon from only one passage of the *Loci* of 1521 (CR 21:222; quoted above, p. 232 n. 134). This passage comes from Melanchthon's earliest period and has, as far as I know, no later equivalent. It is demonstrated to be practically meaningless for Melanchthon's mature doctrine of the office by an abundance of other, contrary statements by him. — On the Confessions, cf. E. Schlink, *Theologie der luth. Bekenntnisschriften*, 2nd ed. (Munich, 1946), p. 330.

[16] CR 11:705 ("Let us give thanks to God that He instituted this ministry"); CR 12:381 ("ministry . . . instituted by Him"); CR 12:490 ("ministry which [God] Himself ordained"); CR 14:256 ("The ministry of the Gospel is instituted by divine authority"); CR 21:850 ("God instituted"); CR 21:851 ("this ministry instituted by God"); CR 21:853 ("the ministry of the Gospel is instituted"); CR 21:1049 ("The chief benefice of God is this ministry"); CR 23:188 ("God instituted the ministry"). Also cf. the passages in the following footnotes. — H. E. Creutzig (*Amt u. Ämter i. d. luth. Kirche*, Theol. mil. 22 [Leipzig, 1938], p. 9) rightly concludes that Melanchthon "very clearly supported this doctrine" (of the divine institution of the office) "throughout his life." — E. Sommerlath ("Amt u. allg. Priestertum," p. 60) speaks of the "great seriousness with which Melanchthon isolates the beneficiary character of the office given it by God. The office is an *ordo* commanded by God and instituted by Him."

[17] CR 21:509: "ministry which we acknowledge is a divinely ordained benefice of God"; CR 21:555: "But it is also certain that the public ministry is divinely ordained"; CR 12:489.

[18] CR 11:599; 21:466; 11:325: "The ministry [is] a most holy worship of God"; CR 11:327: "most holy gift"; cf. Ap 15.44 (*BKS* 305): "The preaching office is the highest office in the Church."

[19] CR 21:853; cf. CR 21:1049; *Stud. Ausg.*, vol. 6, p. 288.

[20] CR 5:595.

[21] CR 15:1066: "God with great mercy revealed Himself, gave the Gospel, instituted the ministry of the Gospel, and *God* desired that it should be heard, and we enclosed within it."

[22] CR 1:329; 1:410: ". . . Since the Church is born by the preaching of the Gospel, without a doubt it is to be nourished by the same"; CR 12:482f.

In the Augsburg Confession too, Melanchthon testifies to the divine institution of the office and its character as an instituted entity: "That we may obtain this faith, the ministry of teaching the Gospel and administering the Sacraments is *instituted*" (in the German text: "*Solchen Glauben zu erlangen, hat Gott das Predigamt eingesetzt, Evangelium und Sakrament geben* . . . [To obtain this faith, God instituted the preaching office, to give the Gospel and Sacraments]").[23]

Of importance, then, is what sense is tied to the (intrinsically biased) expression "ministry of teaching the Gospel and administering the Sacraments," and to what the "*institutum est*" is accordingly related. With the phrase "ministry of teaching the Gospel and administering the Sacraments," we cannot simply see an indication of the mere function (however it occurs) of Word and Sacrament. In that case it would have to say "the Gospel and Sacraments are instituted." Even if it said "the ministry of the Gospel is instituted," it would still be subject to being read, at best, in terms of mere function (although in this case we would also relate the ministry to the office). But as the text actually stands—"the ministry of teaching the Gospel and administering the Sacraments"—it can only be interpreted to mean the concrete office itself. The phrase "ministry of teaching the Gospel," etc., is a provision covering those things lying outside the mere function of Word and Sacrament. "Ministry" denotes the office's ministry of Word and Sacrament exercised regularly in the sense of an institution, that is, that ministry of Word and Sacrament which must be publicly exercised by specific persons permanently appointed to that task on the basis of the declaration of God's will to that end. The concrete office of the Word and Sacraments, the *ministerium ecclesiasticum*—as it is called in the heading—is that about which the "*institutum est*" is asserted. According to the linguistic usage of Melanchthon, and of all men at that time, this heading can only mean the concrete, spiritual office of the Church, the public preaching office, discussed in AC 14 and AC 28 and Ap 13.7ff. (*BKS* 293f.).[24] If

[23] AC 5.1 (*BKS* 57).

[24] There is certainly a logical progression from AC 5 to AC 14. While in AC 5 the divine institution of the preaching office is asserted, AC 14 deals with the call to this office and determines that any person who is to enter this office and exercise it publicly is required to have a particular call. AC 5 speaks of the fact of the divinely instituted office and its purpose of bestowing the Holy Spirit; AC 14, of the entrance of those persons into this office. — If we join H. Bernau (op. cit., p. 60) in this distinction that AC 5 relates "to the object of the office" and AC 14 "to the person representing it," it will be possible to understand by the "object of the office" attested in AC 5 not merely the simple function of Word and Sacrament, as Bernau does (pp. 62f.), but the office as an instituted entity. — We must reject the distinction made by T. Harnack (*Die Kirche, ihr Amt, ihr Regiment*, reprint [1947], pp. 39ff. and 44) that AC 5 speaks of the single "office in its essence" existing *jure divino* [by divine right], and AC 14 of the concrete, empirical form of that office, the "officeship," which exists only *jure humano* [by human right]. (On the failed explanation of Ap 13.7ff. proposed by T. Harnack, see below, pp. 318–19 n. 49; on that of Ap 14.1, see below, p. 278 n. 230.) Also cf. W. Maurer, *Pfarrerrecht u. Bekenntnis*, pp. 73 and 119. We must likewise reject G. Hilbert's distinction that the *ministerium* of AC 5 is the ministry of the Word committed to all believers and the concern of the universal priesthood, and that not until AC 14 is there a discussion of the *ordo ecclesiasticus*, which is called to the public administration of the means of grace ("Charisma u. Amt," in *Das Erbe Martin Luthers* [Leipzig, 1928], p. 359). — In addition, E. Kinder, *Der evgl. Glaube und die Kirche* (Berlin, 1958), initially understands the *ministerium* of AC 5 only as the function of Word and Sacrament, the ministry of the Word and Sacrament, which is committed generally to the Church as to each and

comparison is made to the latter passage in the Apology in particular, it is evident that Melanchthon understands by the term "ministry of the Word" (or "of teaching the Gospel and administering the Sacraments") the specific spiritual office entrusted to particular persons. Ap 13.11 (*BKS* 293): "For God instituted and commanded the preaching office . . ."—explained by Ap 13.12 (*BKS* 293f.) [German text]: "For the Church has a divine command to appoint preachers and deacons"—is the parallel expression to AC 5. The preaching office, filled with designated officers called to that office, is the ministry about which AC 5 asserts a divine institution.[25]

Above all, the German text shows that the "*institutum est*" is very specifically connected to the preaching *office*. This would certainly make no sense without the means of grace—Word and Sacrament—likewise given by God. But it must also be distinguished from them since it involves a specific order by God concerning the mode of distributing the means of grace, which represents the very

every person (pp. 146, 151, 152, 153), and the execution of the *ministerium* through specially called individuals is not addressed until AC 14 (p. 153). — Stahl (*Kirchenverfassung*, p. 109) identified a connection between AC 28.21ff. (*BKS* 124) and AC 5: if AC 28 teaches that the ministry of the Word and Sacraments belongs to the bishops *de jure divino*, it also assumes "that the ministers of the Word themselves are such *de jure divino*." This is correct.

[25] The significance of the parallels in Ap 13 for the explanation of AC 5 has been noticed (besides by F. J. Stahl, *Kirchenverfassung*, pp. 401f., and K. Thieme, *Die Augsb. Konf.*, p. 10) especially by *W. O. Münter* (*Die Gestalt der Kirche 'nach göttlichem Recht,'* Kirche und Amt II, Beiträge z. ev. Theol. 5 [Munich, 1941], p. 57). He identifies Ap 13.11f. as "the definitive explanation of Augsburg Confession V." This passage suggests that in AC 5 "not only is the institution of Word and Sacrament taught, but together with it—these two preordained in the sense of the *viva vox* [living voice]—the office, the office that has to work by means of Word and Sacrament, the office that God instituted and the command to fill it which was given to the Church of God." From Ap 13.12 (the Church has God's command to install ministers) it appears "with greatest clarity that AC 5 cannot address the preaching office of all believers since this cannot be filled by the Church through a vote. Rather, the divine institution of the public preaching office is taught here." Münter teaches most plainly that according to AC 5, the particular, public preaching office is a divine institution and exists *de jure divino* (op. cit., pp. 7ff., 27ff., 36, 38, 41). — Likewise, AC 5 is explained as the institution of the concrete public preaching office by A. F. C. Vilmar, *Die Augsburgische Confession* (Gütersloh, 1870), p. 73, and elsewhere (like the other nineteenth-century theologians associated with Vilmar); K. Thieme, *Die Augsb. Confession*, p. 10; F. W. Hopf, *Lutherische Kirchenordnung*, Bek. Kirche 29 (Munich, 1935), p. 11; S. Schöffel, "Das Predigt- und Hirtenamt," in *Credo ecclesiam*, festschrift for W. Zoellner (1930), pp. 201f.; E. Sommerlath, "Amt u. allg. Priestertum," p. 42; F. Brunstäd, *Theologie der luth. Bekenntnischriften* (Gütersloh, 1951), p. 133, cf. p. 202; K. H. Rengstorf, "Wesen und Bedeutung des geistl. Amtes nach d. NT u. d. Lehre d. Luthertums," in *Weltluthertum von heute* (Stockholm, 1950), p. 261; R. Josefson, "Det andliga ämbetet i Svenska kyrkans bekännelseskrifter," in *En bok om kyrkans ämbete* (Uppsala, 1951), p. 184; J. Heubach, op. cit., pp. 70f., 93. — H. Asmussen notices a discontinuity between the flow of the whole article, which only focuses on the means of grace of Word and Sacrament, and the actual wording, which in both the German and Latin suggests an understanding according to which the office, in an unspecified way, has its own existence and is traced back to similar "institutions" such as the Supper; that is, it is "instituted" in the narrower sense (*Warum noch luth. Kirche* [Stuttgart, 1949], p. 88; also cf. pp. 83f.). Here it must be said that in order to elicit what the article actually means, the wording is decisive. It cannot be chosen without consideration. Cf. H. Asmussen, op. cit., p. 90: "The most astonishing thing in our article continues to be the phrase '*institutum est*' ('God instituted'). This formula calls for a very high degree of specificity."

"institution of the office" in the proper sense. In the German text, "*Predigtamt* [preaching office]," on the one hand, and "*Evangelium und Sakrament* [Gospel and Sacrament]," on the other, are plainly distinguished entities and can in no way be equated as the same.[26]

Without doubt the *rest of the article's content* has the particular purpose of arguing, contrary to the Enthusiasts, that the Holy Spirit works through the means of grace—Word and Sacrament—and that justification is obtained through them, not *sine verbo externo* [without the external Word]. This becomes especially clear when the preliminary forms of the article are compared. Marburg Article 8 only states "that the Holy Spirit, normally speaking, gives no man such faith or His gift without a preceding sermon or oral Word, or Gospel of Christ, but through and with such an oral word He works and produces faith where and in whom He wills. Romans 10."[27] The office is not mentioned specifically. Schwabach Article 7 speaks more definitely about the office: "To obtain such faith, or to give it to us men, God instituted the preaching office or oral Word—namely, the Gospel—through which He causes His faith and His power, benefit, and good to be proclaimed, and through the same as through means also gives faith along with His Holy Spirit, as and where He wills. . . ."[28] While "preaching office" and "oral Word" (Gospel) are juxtaposed here as alternatives connected by "or," it is nevertheless clear that the oral Word is not meant here in an indefinite form, but in the form of the office's declaration. The emphasis is the "preaching office," which is, of course, placed first.[29]

---

[26] Vilmar (*D. Augsb. Conf.*, pp. 72f.) attempted to interpret the German translation "*Evangelium und Sakrament geben* [to give the Gospel and Sacraments]" not to mean that another institution of Gospel and Sacrament is being predicated in addition to the institution of the preaching office, but only to indicate the functions of the one preaching office given by God. In our German, it would have to read "*solchen Glauben zu erlangen, hat Gott das Predigtamt eingesetzt, Evangelium und Sakrament zu geben, dadurch er* [to obtain such faith, God instituted the preaching office to give Gospel and the Sacraments, by which He]. . . ." It cannot be denied that this sense reflects much more closely and properly the Latin basis. If we take "*geben*" ["give"] as "*gegeben*" ["given"], the German text would actually contain a new meaning going beyond the Latin, namely, the institution of the Gospel and Sacrament by God. Thus there is much to be said for Vilmar's explanation of the German text. But for a critique of Vilmar's approach, cf. B. Schlunk, *Amt u. Gemeinde i. theol. Denken Vilmars*, Beitr. z. Ev. Theol. 9 (Munich, 1947), pp. 76f. Regardless whether the interpretation of the German text in Vilmar logically follows or not, his general assessment of Article 5 must still be recognized as accurate: "In this it is taught that for the obtaining of faith (1) a particular office (*ministerium ecclesiasticum*, preaching office) is required, that (2) this is instituted by God, that (3) the functions of that office are the proclamation and distribution of the Sacraments, and that (4) by these functions the Holy Spirit is given, who (5) works faith where and when He wills in those who hear the Gospel" (op. cit., pp. 73f.; cf. *Dogmatik* II, p. 275; *Lehre vom geistl. Amt*, pp. 64f.). Likewise, his clarifications on points 1 and 2 must be endorsed: "Accordingly, the *ministerium ecclesiasticum* must be distinguished from the universal priestly office of Christians. . . . This is not something bestowed by men . . ." (*D. Augsb. Conf.*, p. 74). AC 5 cannot be explained otherwise in view of the actual wording.

[27] CR 26:124 (*BKS* 57).

[28] CR 26:155 (*BKS* 57).

[29] The preliminary form of the AC, which was sent to the Nürnberg council on June 3 and retained in German translation ([manuscript] *Na*), already speaks in Article 4, before the treatment of justification, of the obtaining of the Holy Spirit through Word and Sacrament (cf. *BKS* 57); the office is not mentioned. However, in the final version, Melanchthon included the office. On this,

If these precursors to the Augsburg Confession may be employed hermeneutically to find confirmation that the preaching office instituted by God, as intended in AC 5, has a functional character and thus may in no way be imagined apart from the real action of proclaiming the Word and administering the Sacraments,[30] at the same time it cannot be overlooked that in the version finally presented, to which alone a confessional character can actually be ascribed, the text is composed in such a way that, alongside the Word and Sacraments, the office emerges as something exceptional and not simply identical to Word and Sacrament, and it is this which is so specifically asserted to be divinely instituted. This cannot have been done without a clear purpose. Likewise, it cannot be overlooked that the title of the article in the final edition does not read, as in the Marburg Articles, "Of the External Word,"[31] but "*de ministerio ecclesiastico*" ("Of the Preaching Office").[32] AC 5 does not teach merely the divine institution of the function (however it may happen) of the Word and the Sacraments, but very specifically the divine institution of the office, to which the function is tied and through which it must occur.[33]

T. Kolde (*Die älteste Redaktion d. Augsb. Konfession m. Melanchthons Einleitung* [Gütersloh, 1906], p. 50): "By this Melanchthon clearly reverts to Luther's view in Schwabach Article 7. . . ." — Luther, too, had read the AC in its preliminary stages and thought it good, even if it seemed to him perhaps a bit too generous in the assessment of the opposing Roman view (cf. Luther's letter sent to Elector John on May 15, 1530, from the Coburg fortress: "I have read through Master Philip's Apology, which pleases me very much; I know nothing to improve or change in it, nor would this be fitting, since I cannot tread so softly and lightly. Christ our Lord grant that it may bear much and abundant fruit, as we hope and pray. Amen" [WA Br 5:319ff.]) and also endorsed it in its final form (cf. Luther's letter sent to Melanchthon on July 3, 1530, from the Coburg fortress: "Yesterday I carefully reread your whole Apology, and it pleases me greatly" [WA Br 5:435.4f.]). The rebuke following this is probably not directed at the AC but at Melanchthon's personal behavior, cf. WA Br 5:436 n. 4, after Rückert). — On the proceedings of the Imperial Diet of Augsburg and the correspondence between Luther and Melanchthon while it was held, see Joh. v. Walter, *Luther und Melanchthon während des Augsburger Reichstages* (Gütersloh, 1931).

[30] M. Doerne (*Luth. Pfarramt*, p. 8 n. 1) can be supported only where he writes that the preaching office in AC 5 may "not be understood as an estate in a sociological sense, but as a function." Yet note AC 27.13 (*BKS* 112)!

[31] CR 26:124.

[32] The challenge to the heading of the final version of Article 5, "*De ministerio ecclesiastico*," in T. Kolde (*Die Augsburg. Konfession*, 2nd ed. [Gotha, 1911], p. 35 note) clearly has as its only support the fact that *Na* did not include the office. While Kolde states in another passage (see above, pp. 243–44 n. 29) that Melanchthon, in the final version, returns to the form in the Schwabach Articles, which of course speak of the institution of the preaching office, he ascribes this to a new intention in composing the final form of the article, which then warrants a new heading corresponding to this name. It is therefore misleading when M. Doerne (op. cit., p. 8 n. 1) simply says, "The heading of AC V, *De ministerio ecclesiastico*, is not original and gives rise to misunderstandings." Either the whole final version of the AC must be addressed as "not original," or the heading in Article 5, which represents the final and definitive form thereof, must be granted validity and taken seriously as a proposition of our confession.

[33] Thus we must speak against W. Thomas, who writes (op. cit., pp. 9f.) that AC 5 only intends to assert the necessity of the oral Word, and "nothing further" may be gathered from this article "than that God wishes to work faith in us by Word and . . . Sacrament, not by 'private' revelations." If that were truly the case, the mention of the *office* would have been entirely superfluous, and it could have retained a form such as that in *Na* or the Marburg Articles. When Thomas continues: "Who has the right and duty to teach the Gospel and administer the Sacraments is not considered here"

P. Brunner ("*Vom Amt des Bischofs*," pp. 17f. n. 11) wants the *ministerium* discussed in AC 5 not to be viewed as *limited* to the publicly exercised ministry. He agrees that AC 14 and Ap 13.7–13 "are already latent" in AC 5, and that the "*institutum est*" in AC 5 is also asserted of the particular preaching office. "But the domain of the ministry discussed by AC 5 extends farther than that envisaged in AC 14" (p. 17), "AC 5 has room for the one ministering in Word and Sacrament to exercise his ministry in a nonpublic sphere, for which he does not need a call" (p. 18).

A very similar position is taken by *W. Maurer* in his book *Pfarrerrecht und Bekenntnis* (Berlin, 1957). Maurer interprets "the ministry of teaching the Gospel and administering the Sacraments" from AC 5, about which the "*institutum est*" is asserted, as the "general ministerial office of the Christian congregation" and relates it to the universal priesthood of Christians, from which the ordained pastoral office, in reality the preaching office (at least, necessarily), proceeds" (pp. 67ff.).[34] The ministry, he suggests, cannot be limited to the legally organized office; the latter may only exist at all "because and insofar as it is inherent in each Christian within Christianity as a whole" (p. 69). "Ministry" in AC 5 is to be viewed as a "human auxiliary ministry borne by the power of God's Word, which further disseminates this oral Word" (p. 70), and is not equated with the preaching office "in the technical sense" (p. 71). AC 5 "contains absolutely no statement on whether these persons" (i.e., those who exercise the external ministry of the Word) "must possess a designated office in the Church" (p. 72), though there is room in the article for this ministry to occur through an ordained office. In the interpretation of AC 5, "everything depends on the article not being understood simply as a statement about the Evangelical pastoral office, and this office not being simultaneously excluded from the working of the external Word, which cannot exist without the human ministry of proclamation. As a ministerial office, the pastoral office is embedded in this general ministry of the whole Christian

---

(p. 10)—it may be said that it was not in the purpose of *this* article to make any explicit statement on this subject, yet not because the office in the proper sense is not in view here, but rather because there was already a plan to include an Article 14 in the confession and to address this subject there on the basis of the divine institution of the office asserted in Article 5. — H. Bernau, too, sees the office of AC 5 only as a function of Word and Sacrament, claiming that only this function is being attested as "instituted" (op. cit., p. 63). Bernau attempts to bolster his opinion by pointing out that in Ap 13, the promises of God, which are cited there for the *office*, all treat the Gospel alone, the Word in a general sense, by which the office is stressed as a function (p. 63). The grain of truth in this is the strong, functional specificity of the office, which is oriented toward the function and cannot be imagined without it. Yet despite what he says on p. 63 n. 38, Bernau's explanation of AC 5 collapses when confronted by (1) the wording of AC 5, which attests that office is an instituted entity; and (2) the fact that in Ap 13.7ff., which forms the basis of Bernau's argument, not only the office nor only the *ordo* (with which AC 14 is naturally dealing in accordance with the heading) but even the *laying on of hands* is called a sacrament and referred to as a command of God to *appoint* ministers to the office—all of which suggests an appointed office of an institutional nature and exposes *its* divine foundation. — Similar to Bernau are the statements by W. Trillhaas, "Die luth. Lehre 'De potestate ecclesiastica,'" *Zwischen den Zeiten* (1933), p. 502.

[34] So, too, R. Sohm, *Kirchenrecht* I, p. 491 n. 18 and p. 499 n. 31, whose stance on church law, incidentally, is vehemently attacked by Maurer. Quite similar to Maurer's position is that of E. Kinder (*Die evangelische Glaube und die Kirche* [Berlin, 1958], pp. 146ff.).

congregation" (p. 72; cf. p. 68 n. 1). Thus in AC 5, Maurer sees the divine institution of a general ministerial office broadly conceived, which in one way or another (primarily, but by no means *strictly*, through the concrete pastoral office—p. 70) transmits the efficacious power of the Word of the Gospel. In contrast to this, then, it is the pastoral office exclusively which is under consideration in AC 14 (pp. 73ff. and 117ff.). Maurer also conceives of the relationship of AC 5 and 14 in this way: "The *universal* ministerial office of AC 5 is a direct product of the divine right, not tangible institutionally, not limitable by human ordinances. The *public* ministerial office of AC 14 is an instituted entity, a divine institution, whose existence is mandated by divine right and whose earthly historical expressions are subject to the critique thereof" (p. 119). Thus Maurer also sees the ordained public pastoral office as entirely within the realm of the divine institution, yet in the sense that it is likewise contained in the divinely instituted universal ministerial office of AC 5. "The ministerial office, and the pastoral office with it, is by divine right" (p. 78). "And since the Evangelical ministerial office—including the pastoral office—is by divine right . . ." (p. 78). The divine character of the pastoral office, according to Maurer, is consecutive in nature. "This ministry" (i.e., the universal ministry, which is instituted according to AC 5) "does not merely demand the occasional and ever-renewed efforts of all believers; it longs for a constant church order within which it may be carried out continuously and for the whole Church" (p. 112). Thus for Maurer the institution of the concrete pastoral office results as the logical conclusion from the necessities of the instituted universal ministerial office.

However, there is a contradiction in this understanding. If in AC 5 there really is only a universal ministerial function of Word and Sacrament instituted by God (one which is not tangible institutionally, cf. p. 119), and if the question of this ministry necessarily occurring within a specific office order remains excluded, and thus if nothing is determined about it in the divine institution of the ministry according to AC 5 (as Maurer concludes, p. 72), then a concrete divine arrangement for the pastoral office—and only such can be properly identified as an institution—does not exist according to AC 5. Neither, then, can it be called an institution in the proper sense, as Maurer nevertheless does again (p. 119). Then—in consideration of the fact that the universal ministerial function *demands* "a constant order . . . , an institution, for an instituted office" (p. 112)—it is indirectly associated with the divine institution but cannot itself be called a divine institution. The moment the latter happens, it is *ipso facto* an assertion that the concrete pastoral office instituted according to AC 5, with the all-embracing, universal ministerial office, also contains a divine mandate for the concrete pastoral office, a determination about tying the ministry to specific persons called for that purpose. Only the full breadth of the instituted ministerial office could then extend beyond the boundaries of the concrete pastoral office, but even as the Church's concrete preaching office, appointed with persons, is instituted, the nucleus, too, would be mandated, not excluded from AC 5.

Accordingly, if we ask what support there is for interpreting the compass of the "ministry of teaching the Gospel and distributing the Sacraments" (affirmed as instituted in AC 5) more broadly as the Church's concrete preaching office, Maurer points to the "broad use, not restricted to specific officers, which the Confessions make of the term '*ministerium*'" (p. 68). As evidence, Maurer refers to Tr 25f., where the "*ministerium professionis (Petri)* [ministry of (Peter's) confession]" is discussed, and the words "*Super hanc petram* [upon this rock]" from Matt. 16:18 are clarified as "*super hoc ministerium* [upon this ministry]." Yet we might receive the impression from this passage that here, by the term "*ministerium*," it is the specific preaching office which is being discussed. The passage is in the first part of the Treatise, which has the purpose of demonstrating that the pope is not the superior of all bishops by divine right. Melanchthon, in supporting his argument, focuses on showing that all apostles (including Peter) were sent "as equals to the common ministry of the Gospel" (Tr 8, *BKS* 473). Also passages such as Matt. 16:18f. and 18:18 and John 21:17 testify: "the Keys are given equally to all the apostles and that all the apostles are equally sent forth" (Tr 23, *BKS* 478). Peter represents "the whole assembly of the apostles" (Tr 24, *BKS* 478). Then it reads: "However, as to the declaration, '*Upon this rock I will build My Church*,' certainly the Church has not been built upon the authority of man, but upon the ministry of the confession which Peter made, in which he proclaims that Jesus is the Christ" (Tr 25, *BKS* 479). If we tried to see "*ministerium professonis*" simply as the ministry of confession, and therefore as bearing witness that Jesus is the Christ, it is made very difficult by the following sentence: "He accordingly addresses him as a minister, 'Upon this rock,' that is, upon this ministry" (Tr 25, *BKS* 479). In the German, this passage reads: "Therefore, He addresses him as a minister of this office in which this confession and doctrine is to be in operation and says, 'Upon this rock,' that is, this preaching and ministry" (ibid.). Peter is here addressed as a minister—not simply as a believer, a confessor—as a minister of the office, namely, of the preaching office of the New Testament, in which this confession finds its place.[35] The *ministerium* on which the Church is built is the office of the New Testament, the concrete preaching office (which, however, is inextricably linked to the pure teaching of the Gospel).[36] When in connection to this passage it says

[35] In another passage of the Treatise (Tr 67, *BKS* 491), "minister" is compared with "pastor" and is reproduced by Veit Dietrich in the German text with *Pfarrherr* [pastor, parson]. Even though a layman is being discussed in this passage, nevertheless, on account of the emergency situation, he is standing in the stead of the office-bearer and therefore bears his attributes. Maurer says, ". . . Usually 'minister' is simply a translation of *Prediger* [preacher] . . . or of *Kirchendiener* [church minister]" (op. cit., p. 70 n. 4). In the Treatise, it is always the bearer of the preaching office that is meant by the term "minister."

[36] For confirmation of this interpretation of *ministerium* in Tr 25 (*BKS* 479) as meaning the concrete preaching office, the passage CR 21:851 may be cited. Although occurring some years later, it nevertheless shows how Melanchthon uses Matt. 16:18 generally in other places. There Melanchthon speaks of the office being filled with people in ordination and determines that, since it is instituted by God, it can never be destroyed completely. As proof, he cites Matt. 16:18: "For Christ says in Matthew 16 (v. 18): 'Upon this rock I shall build My Church,' that is, upon this ministry; 'and the gates of hell shall not prevail against it.'" Here the rock from Matt. 16:18 is clearly taken by Melanchthon as the concrete office. Also in CR 14:892, the rock in Matt. 16:18 is interpreted as the concrete office, which is "the minister preaching: Thus this saying about the building of the Church should be understood most simply as meaning the true ministry." Also cf. CR 14:427: "'upon this rock,' that is, upon this ministry of the preaching of this voice." The interpretation of Tr 25 (*BKS* 479) as meaning the concrete preaching office is also found, e.g., in W. O. Münter, *Die Gestalt der Kirche 'nach göttlichem Rechte'* (Munich, 1941), pp. 8f. Also cf. O. Ritschl, *Dogmengesch.* I, pp. 317f.

of this ministry of the New Testament that it "is not bound to places and persons as the Levitical ministry,[37] but it is dispersed throughout the whole world and is there where God gives His gifts, apostles, prophets, pastors, teachers" (Tr 26, *BKS* 479), it thereby refutes the pope's claim that the office of the New Testament is bound to himself (to his confirmation, to the seat of the bishop of Rome, or perhaps even to the unbroken episcopal succession), as the Levitical ministry was bound to the tribe of Levi, but at the same time it also makes clear that it does not simply exist everywhere without distinction but is precisely where God furnishes officers (apostles, prophets, shepherds, teachers). When this is contradicted by the subsequent words of the German rendering of Tr 26 (*BKS* 479f.)—"And the person makes no difference for this Word and office commanded by Christ, whoever may preach and teach it . . ."—reference must be made to the original and decisive Latin text of the Treatise, which in this passage reads: "Neither does this ministry avail on account of the authority of any person, but on account of the Word given by Christ." Here the power of this office of the New Testament is founded on the Word (meaning: not on the authority of any person, such as Peter or the pope), which is the same constant among all individual office-bearers, and thus the particular claim of Peter, or of the pope, is rejected but the office of the New Testament is not detached from designated officers.[38] Thus we cannot (at least, not unequivocally) take this passage in the Treatise as evidence for a use of the word "*ministerium*" in the Confessions extending beyond concrete officers.

Maurer further cites Tr 69 (*BKS* 491) (op. cit., pp. 68f.), where Melanchthon has the ministry come from the priesthood. Yet here the universal priesthood of 1 Pet. 2:9 is mentioned solely to demonstrate from that passage also the Church's right to call persons to the particular office,[39] the word "minister" being clearly used here solely of the public minister called to the concrete office. Finally, Maurer refers to Ap 13.7ff. and discusses the equivalence (made there) of the priesthood with the ministry of distributing Word and Sacraments to others (op. cit., p. 69; cf. p. 104 n. 36). Yet in this passage, the term "priesthood" (Ap 13.7 beginning) is not intended to mean the universal priesthood of all believers, but, following the Roman linguistic usage common until then, the particular office (cf. in the German text: "Sacrament of ordination or priesthood": ibid., *BKS* 293), which is interpreted in the Evangelical sense as "the ministry of the Word and Sacraments to be distributed to others." The notion that the *ministerium verbi* [ministry of the Word], the particular office, rests on the *sacerdotium* as the universal priesthood of all believers is not present here.[40]

---

[37] Here, too, in the expression "*ministerium Leviticum*," the *ministerium* is a concrete office of an institutional nature, so to speak. The difference in this Levitical ministry from the ministry of the New Testament does not consist in its being a ministry, of course, but in its being a *Levitical* ministry.

[38] On the interpretation of Tr 24ff., also cf. below, pp. 268–69.

[39] Cf. above, p. 235.

[40] The passages Ap 24.49 and 59 (*BKS* 363, 366), to which Maurer refers, p. 104 n. 36, do not speak of a derivation of the particular office from the universal priesthood either. Maurer also says that the equation of priesthood and ministry here is clarified in the public ministerial office (ibid.). Ap 24.48 ("49" is clearly a typographical error) reads: ". . . With us, priests serve by the ministry of the Word" (*BKS* 363). By "priests," the ministers in the public preaching office are meant, whose

Maurer also refers to Tr 31ff. (*BKS* 480ff.) (op. cit., pp. 69f. n. 3), noting, on the expression "*ministerium evangelii*" in Tr 34 (*BKS* 481), that "the ecclesial office is by no means intended" here (op. cit., p. 70 n. 3). This can be disproved, however, by the fact that, with the proposition "the ministry of the Gospel was neglected," a *function* of the ecclesial office is meant—specifically, the proclamation of the Gospel (as opposed to the false, secular functions which the pope added in neglect of the true function of the ecclesial office), yet certainly a function of the *office*—since it is clearly the concrete spiritual office to which Christ sent the apostles, and its *potestas spiritualis* [spiritual power] (i.e., "the command to teach the Gospel, to proclaim the forgiveness of sins, to administer the Sacraments, and to excommunicate the ungodly without bodily force": Tr 31, *BKS* 480f.) is under discussion in Tr 31ff. (as acknowledged by Maurer himself, op. cit., p. 138, when he addresses the *potestas spiritualis* from Tr 31 as the authority of the *public* minister). —

From all of this, we do not get the impression that there is in the Confessions a use of the word *ministerium* which anywhere avoids the concrete preaching office and only intends a universal ministerial function. It is thus not possible for us to interpret the domain of the *ministerium* meant in AC 5 more broadly than the actual preaching office of the Church, which possibility, in our opinion, anyway is removed by the wording of AC 5—especially in the German text.

Melanchthon teaches the office as a divine institution. For him it is properly the Son of God, Christ, who instituted the office.[41] He Himself exercised it (in Paradise first, and then according to His incarnation), revealed the Gospel, and sent the prophets and apostles to the office. Christ's announcement of sending the apostles in John 20:21 is related by Melanchthon to all office-bearers in the Church. In the sending of the apostles, all true teachers of the Church are sent by Christ, and in it the office has been instituted for all ages.[42] The preaching

---

office is the office of the Word. And in Ap 24.59, the sentence "... The priesthood of the New Testament is a ministry of the Spirit" (*BKS* 366) refers to 2 Cor. 3:6 and means the public preaching office. In neither passage is an allusion to the universal priesthood present.

[41] CR 4:367: "God passed on the Gospel through the fathers and prophets, and afterward through Christ and the apostles, and Christ instituted the ministry"; CR 7:699f.: "God's Son ... instituted the preaching office"; CR 28:408: "The Son Himself instituted ... the ministry." — The fact that the divine foundation of the preaching office in AC 5 is also pictured as having occurred *through Christ* is fittingly emphasized by S. Schöffel (op. cit., pp. 201f.).

[42] CR 7:741: "He" (the Son of God) "brought the Gospel from the bosom of the eternal Father. He instituted the ministry of the Gospel and sent and still sends those who teach it. Romans 10 ..."; cf. CR 4:349; 15:385; 23:xxxv: "And the Son of God Himself was the first preacher and priest in Paradise, and afterward, when He was made man, He sent [men] to the preaching office. As He says, 'As My Father has sent Me, so send I you.' And this is to be applied to every generation as concerning all true teachers who are called to the office. The Son of God sends them...." — This grounding of the present churchly office on that given to the apostles, and the sure application of the commands and promises of Christ given to the apostles to the present shepherds and teachers in the confessional documents, has been noted on various occasions. Cf. A. F. O. Münchmeyer, *Das Amt des Neuen Testaments nach Lehre der Schrift und der luth. Bekenntnisse* (Osterode, 1853), who on p. 43 says of the Confessions: "which speak with assurance of the apostles as of bearers of the same office which bishops and pastors now possess"; E. Schlink, *Theol. d. Bek.schr.*, p. 325 and

office is therefore an office that "springs from the common call of the apostles."[43] It consists of a continuous reference to the office of the apostles and is therefore an *apostolic office*.

The institution and founding of the office mean that the ministerial function ordered by God (preaching the Gospel, giving the Sacraments) is always to be bound to specified persons set apart and called by the Church for that purpose, whose public ministry in the Gospel gathers and sustains the Church.[44] The divine institution of the office is thus synonymous in Melanchthon with the command of God to fill the office, to call persons to the office, and to assign them to the office.[45] In this context, Melanchthon reflects almost always on Titus 1:5, which passage he regards as the concrete mandate of God to fill the office.[46]

---

p. 326; W. O. Münter, *Die Gestalt der Kirche "nach göttlichem Recht,"* pp. 7f. and 38f., and F. Brunstäd, *Theol. d. luth. Bek.schr.*, p. 207.

[43] Tr 10 (*BKS* 424) (which nevertheless only articulates it in the German translation).

[44] On this cf. Melanchthon, in AC 27.13 (*BKS* 112), speaking of the called ministers of the Word as of a God-ordained estate ("... estates which are ordained by God, such as the estate of pastors and preachers ..."). — Fittingly, Münchmeyer (op. cit., pp. 5f.) notes that our church's symbols, when referring to the ministry, always understand two things to be resolved: "(1) the office is only exercised by individuals, not by all members of the communion to which it ministers; (2) there must be some kind of call to the office coming from outside the office, an installation into the office...." Also cf. W. Löhe, *Neue Aphorismen*, *Ges. Werke* V.1, p. 552.

[45] CR 5:585: God "commanded us needy men to call persons who understand Christian doctrine"; CR 5:596: "... Give thanks that God has commanded the Church to elect persons to the preaching office and ministry of the Sacraments"; CR 5:711: "God wants those to be elected who are capable of teaching the Gospel"; CR 5:825: "He gave commands to His Church that it should call capable ministers"; CR 15:1332: "God wants the Church itself to call ministers"; CR 21:470: "The ministry of the Word has the command of God"; CR 21:503: "The Church has the command not to admit ungodly teachers but to seek good ones"; CR 21:850: "the call to the ministry ... all these things are enjoined by the mandate of the Gospel"; CR 23:xxxvi: "But He" (God) "commanded the Church to call and ordain people itself..."; Ap 13.12 (*BKS* 294): "For the Church has a command to appoint ministers." — Höfling altered the sense of this passage to say that the mandate is not to be understood as a positive commandment from God but only as an internal necessity of the priestly congregation, which is endowed with the universal office in all its individual members. It must fill the office because they cannot all exercise it at the same time. It is under these conditions which God has created, wherein all the congregants have the office and yet not all can exercise it, that Höfling sees the mandate to fill the office (*Grundsätze*, pp. 72ff.). W. O. Münter rightly evaluated Höfling's view as being shaped rather by his fear of a new ceremonial law, "but not by findings ascertained from the sources" (*Die Gestalt der Kirche* ..., p. 58). Höfling's scheme here constitutes a "pseudo-Lutheran teaching" (ibid.). — R. Sohm, who had asserted that the Church's appointing of preachers happens according to "human discretion" (*Weltliches und geistliches Recht* [1914], p. 56) has already been countered by K. Thieme (*Die Augsb. Konf.*, p. 10 n. 1): "to appoint 'public preachers' 'by regular call' (*rite vocati*) is God's command [and] occurs 'according to divine right.'"

[46] CR 21:850: "And the mandate is given to the Church to elect ministers or such appointees, as written expressly to Titus"; CR 21:1100: "God wants ... ministers of the Gospel to be called.... Paul enjoins Titus to appoint presbyters here and there in the cities"; CR 5:596: "... as Paul commanded Titus to appoint and ordain priests in the cities"; CR 5:629; 5:825: "Here the ordained man is to know that he has been ordered by the voice of the apostle" (i.e., Titus 1:5) "in this function" (in the episcopal office) "to ordain priests to teach and govern the churches"; CR 15:1332: "These sayings"

Additionally important for Melanchthon is the phrase κατὰ πόλιν in Titus 1:5, by which the relatedness of the office to a specific congregation is expressed. The divinely instituted office, to which specific persons are to be called, is for Melanchthon the parochial pastoral office. Christ desired "that, after the apostles, pastors should be called in all churches, functioning in the office of teaching the Gospel. . . ."[47] "Everyone has his flock."[48] The parochial structure of the office is also *juris divini* for Melanchthon.[49]

Alongside Titus 1:5, Eph. 4:8ff. (esp. v. 11) is for Melanchthon the decisive passage of Scripture for the institution of the spiritual office by Christ.[50] Christ, after His exaltation, gave gifts to men which contained the fruit of His victory. These gifts (*dona propria Ecclesiae* [the Church's peculiar gifts]) are the apostles, prophets, evangelists, shepherds, and teachers (v. 11). They are given by Christ "for ministry, for edification of the Body of Christ, for instructing the saints."[51] The passage, according to Melanchthon's view, means that Christ is continually giving the Church people for the office. But with the gift of officers, He also gives the office itself. The fact that the Church has people for the office and then people in the office, thus the filled office, rests on the will of Christ who furnishes these officers and repeatedly sends new officers into the office. Ephesians 4:11 testifies, according to Melanchthon, that Christ will do this in every age. Thus we are brought to the idea of the *divine preservation of the office*.[52] It is founded by Christ as "a ministry to endure until the end of the

(Titus 1:5; 1 Tim. 5:22; 2 Tim. 2:2) "manifestly show that the Church is commanded to elect ministers"; CR 26:360: ". . . as Paul enjoins Titus to appoint presbyters in the cities."

[47] CR 4:368; 21:1100: "A bishop or pastor is the called teacher . . . *in a certain place*."

[48] CR 21:556; also cf. CR 5:597: "This is said in general of the preaching office, i.e., of all curates who in both teaching and distributing the Sacraments rightly execute their calling, *each in his own place*." — In the passage CR 21:556 (cited in the text) the parochial ordinance of the office is taught, admittedly, as an element of church polity instituted by the Church. Yet for this, too, Melanchthon asserts a *jus divinum*, as the citation shared in the following footnote demonstrates.

[49] CR 12:491: "No one . . . may usurp the ministry without a call. And this is why the distinction παροικιῶν is by divine right since one who is not called may not intrude into another's church." Here, the doctrine of the call plays an assisting role. Since it must also come from the congregation *jure divino*, it must be related to a specific place, a specific congregation.

[50] CR 12:853: "Paul says these things in Ephesians 4 . . . with these words: 'The ministry of the Gospel is instituted that it may preserve the Gospel. . . .'"

[51] CR 21:505. — In a little prayer on the saying of Paul in Ephesians 4 from the year 1559 (CR 12:345ff.), Melanchthon poses the question why the gifts which Christ distributes as fruits of His victory are not identified as forgiveness of sins, reconciliation, the Holy Spirit, hope of eternal life, etc., but as apostles, prophets, evangelists, shepherds, and teachers, and responds: "The reason is very truly that St. Paul was looking at the mode by which these heavenly and eternal goods are communicated to us, which are not given to us except by the ministry of the Word. . . . God decided to save men through the voice of the Gospel sounding through the apostles, and not otherwise" (CR 12:349). Of note is the mutual harmony in which Melanchthon conceives of the Gospel and the office.

[52] CR 4:367f. (on Eph. 4:11): "for He preserves the Gospel and, after the apostles, desired pastors to be called in all the churches . . . , whom He raised up"; CR 5:584: "although God sustains the preaching office and chooses able teachers, as written in Ephesians 4"; CR 5:595f.: "Here St. Paul

world."[53] Christ desires that it should be preserved in every age of the Church and preserves it Himself as He founded it.[54] Part of this is also the fact that the office, which is a "ministry of guarding and passing on doctrine (about the Son),"[55] is continually renewed and purified by Him.[56] Thus a "continuous series" of office-bearers remains, through which God gathers for Himself a Church from the human race.[57]

The teaching of the divine preservation of the office, which in Melanchthon is closely related to that of its divine institution, confirms the character of the office as an institution permanently and essentially inherent in the Church.[58] The two terms *instituere* and *conservare* often appear together in Melanchthon[59] and are practically a constant formula for denoting the divine action in relation to the office. In this, the latter is merely a clarifier of the former. The institution of the office also includes the preservation of it in the Church. If the established office bears this character of a permanent institution,[60] the Church cannot be

---

clearly demonstrates that by Christ the true preaching office is preserved in the Church, namely, so that Christ Himself may continually stir up and sustain true preachers, who teach purely the Gospel which He gave, and if it should be obscured, make it clear again"; CR 12:349f. (the comfort from Eph. 4:11): "The Son of God Himself is the keeper of the Church and preserves the ministry by faithful men and salutary teachers who are continually being raised up. That is why He ascended on high, says Paul, that is why He sits at the right hand of the Father, that is why He reigns—that He may furnish ministers, by whose voice the Church is gathered from mankind"; CR 28:412: (according to Ephesians 4) "the Son of God is the Most High Priest, anointed by the eternal Father, who, that the Church might not perish utterly, gave to it ministers of the Gospel" (chosen in part directly, in part by human call).

[53] CR 4:367.

[54] CR 5:595: "the preaching office, which God gave to the Church for all time, and graciously sustains it Himself in every generation"; CR 5:598: ". . . We know well that the ministry of the Gospel is not built on human will and power, but our Savior Christ desires to preserve it miraculously"; CR 5:580, 584; 7:576: "God preserves . . . the ministry of the Gospel in the Church"; CR 7:699f.: "for that purpose," (God) "instituted the preaching office and miraculously preserves it"; CR 12:381: "the ministry of the Word both instituted and miraculously preserved"; CR 21:850: "the ministry of teaching the Gospel, which He wishes to preserve in the Church by perpetual calling"; CR 21:853; 23:xxxvi: Christ the "eternal priest and preserver of the ministry"; CR 28:408: "The Son Himself instituted and preserved the ministry." Cf. *Stud. Ausg.*, vol. 6, pp. 301f.

[55] CR 28:408.

[56] CR 21:853; 5:596; 21:1049: "By great miracles from God [the ministry is] continually renewed and defended in mankind."

[57] CR 15:1332. — "God Himself preserves the office; so the Church, too, must pray for the preservation of the office, for faithful laborers for the Lord's harvest": CR 12:378f.; 12:381.

[58] Fittingly, H. Liermann, in connection with AC 5 and AC 14, characterizes the office as the "supporting pillar" of church governance, as the "foundational element of Lutheran church polity," as a "true foundational institution of the polity," which is rooted in the *jus divinum* (*Grundlagen des kirchl. Verfassungsrechts nach luth. Auffassung*, Luthertum 11 [Berlin, 1954], pp. 6f.). — Likewise, W. O. Münter, *Die Gestalt der Kirche*, etc., p. 51; cf. p. 9: "In the office, '*jure divino*,' a continuous structural plan is given" to the Church for its ordering and configuration.

[59] E.g., CR 5:595; 5:825; 7:699f.; 12:381; 21:850; 28:408.

[60] CR 5:212: "The abiding Church is the assembly which sounds the voice of the Gospel. Therefore, the ministry also is in that assembly"; CR 12:488f. ("the catholic ministry is always tied to

imagined without it.[61] A church without an office would, in Melanchthon's thought, be a church without a Gospel, which means without forgiveness of sins and eternal salvation. As the Church cannot exist without the Gospel, neither can it exist without the office of the Gospel.[62] And *if* it is without the office, it is simply not the Church.[63] The Church is thus bound to the office of the Gospel.[64]

Yet this does not mean that the office of the Gospel for its part is bound to a specific series of officers or to specific places.[65] "Christ forbade the Church to hold fast to certain persons and to human authority."[66] The ministry of the Gospel must be distinguished from the polity of bishops found in the papistic church, which is bound to places, persons, and the ordinary succession.[67] The ordinary succession of bishops is not a *conditio sine qua non* [essential condition] of the office and the Church, it is not a divine ordinance, as the Papists believe.[68] The office is chained neither to the formal succession nor to the episcopal title.[69] Succession without pure teaching of the Gospel is entirely worthless and has no relation to the essence of the Church,[70] for the true office lives in attachment to the Gospel, to the pure doctrine. As long as the Gospel

---

the catholic Church; where the former is, there is the latter"); CR 21:835: "The voice of the Gospel and ministry will remain. . . . And the Church of God shall be a kind of visible assembly, yet like an educational assembly. There is an order, there is a distinction between teachers and hearers, and there are grades"; also cf. CR 12:195.

[61] Cf. O. Ritschl, op. cit., pp. 318, 321, 338, and Herrlinger, op. cit., p. 256.

[62] CR 8:430f.: "Being without pastors would mean being without the Keys, the Gospel, the forgiveness of sins"; CR 12:490: "Nor can the Church exist if this ministry disappears . . . nor does God save without this ministry, which He Himself ordained"; CR 14:892: "That the Son may work through the Gospel, there needs to be a ministry of the Gospel"; CR 12:519: "Where the Church is, it is necessary that there be a due ordering of ministers"; CR 21:505: "It is impossible for the Church to exist without the Gospel; likewise, without remission of sins. Therefore, this law" (i.e., to fill the office) "belongs to the Church."

[63] CR 14:892: "There is no Church where there is no true ministry"; CR 21:832: "The Church is not in that assembly where there is neither the knowledge of the promise of Christ nor the voice or ministry of the Gospel."

[64] CR 5:596; 5:628; 11:760: "May we always know that the Church of God is present where the ministry of the Gospel is"; CR 14:427; 15:317; 21:833: "May we therefore know that the Church of God is the assembly bound to the voice or ministry of the Gospel"; CR 21:844.

[65] Tr 26 (*BKS* 479).

[66] CR 21:505; also CR 21:506.

[67] CR 5:627: "It is therefore necessary to distinguish from that polity of bishops bound to places and persons and ordinary succession, secular powers, and human laws the very ministry of the Gospel, which God instituted and in His great mercy continually renews and always preserves for His Church, which is not bound to certain places, persons, and human laws, but to the Gospel"; CR 5:595; cf. *Stud. Ausg.*, vol. 6, pp. 290f.

[68] Cf. CR 4:689, 731; 15:981.

[69] CR 15:317: "I say that the Church is bound to the Gospel and to the ministry of the Gospel, but not to the Roman episcopacy and ordinary succession"; cf. CR 5:212; 12:526; 12:602; 15:74, 76, 736; 21:834f.; 21:839, 844; 23:598.

[70] CR 21:844: "Since the bishops do not teach correctly, the ordinary succession does not apply to the Church, but must necessarily be abandoned"; CR 24:402: "The succession of bishops is nothing unless the doctrine of the apostles be preserved"; cf. CR 12:378: "Many men used the pretext

remains, the office also remains—even when the external succession is interrupted. As the true Church is spread over the whole earth, often subject to the cross, and cannot boast of any unfractured form here on earth, so the office of the Church does not always exist in flawless succession, but is "dispersed throughout the whole world," namely, wherever God gives apostles, prophets, shepherds, and teachers.[71]

The proposition that the Church is never without the office, that it is bound to the office, expresses on the one hand the Church's absolute attachment to the Gospel and on the other hand its attachment to the orderly execution of the Gospel by specific persons whom God sends in every age and place. This twofold fact is represented in the following statement by Melanchthon: "The Church is bound to the same Gospel of God so that it resounds in the ministry, from whence God raises up others who teach rightly."[72] It is impossible for the true office of the Gospel ever to fail since it is instituted by God as the foundation and rock of the Church, of which Christ says, "The gates of hell shall not prevail against it."[73] The godly are to know that "remnants of the Church and of the true ministry will remain even if authorities crumble."[74]

3. Instrument of the Holy Spirit

If the office is instituted by God and preserved as a permanent institution in the Church, it must have a decidedly important function. It has already been explained that Melanchthon laid the greatest weight on the God-ordained modes of appropriating salvation through the Gospel and Sacraments and integrated into these God-ordained modes the office of the Gospel and the Sacraments.[75] The significance of the Gospel as medium of salvation is for Melanchthon simultaneously that of the office, with which the Gospel is of course inextricably linked.[76] The office is the ministry of the Gospel and thus has the function of appropriating to men the salvific blessings of the Gospel. This function of the office gains particular weight from the fact that, according to God's will, it

---

of ordinary succession to force their way into church governance and are in truth lazy bellies and only out for money and pleasure."

71 Tr 26 (*BKS* 479).

72 CR 21:834; cf. CR 15:385.

73 CR 21:851: "And there is this great consolation: since this ministry is instituted by God, even if it is always battered in various ways in the world and many men forsake it and perish, yet it cannot perish utterly. For Christ says, '. . . Upon this rock I will build My Church,' that is, upon this ministry, 'and the gates of hell shall not prevail against it' "; cf. Tr 25 (*BKS* 479). Cf. generally above, pp. 246–48; p. 247 n. 36.

74 CR 21:851.

75 Cf. above, pp. 216–20.

76 Cf. above, pp. 218–20 and 225–28. Melanchthon especially demonstrates the importance of the office in the process of salvation by reference to Rom. 10:14f., on which passage he observes: "And this tremendous passage concerning the necessity and worthiness of the ministry should be studied most carefully, that we may know how God is efficacious in us" (CR 15:694; cf. CR 15:477f.).

represents the exclusive means of appropriating salvation (at least as regards orderly, normal circumstances). "By this office, and not otherwise" God gathers for Himself His eternal Church here on earth;[77] "in this way" (i.e., by the appointment and preservation of the office) "He receives us and frees us from sin, the power of the devil, and eternal death, and restores eternal life to us."[78] In the AC it says most clearly of the eternal goods (righteousness, the Holy Spirit, eternal life): "These cannot be taken hold of except through the ministry of the Word and Sacraments."[79] The office is necessary because its function is founded on the will of God, which appoints the way of salvation.[80] When Melanchthon, in the Apology, says of the power of the Keys—naturally exercised chiefly by the office—that it "administers and delivers the Gospel through the Absolution,"[81] he aptly characterizes the nature of the whole office. The Church's office concerns the administration and delivery of the Gospel through the actual function of the means of grace entrusted to the office. By God's will the office is *the guarantee of the delivery of the Gospel and the distribution of grace* to men.[82]

If the office, in accordance with God's will, is to guarantee the delivery of the Gospel, its goal is faith, through which alone the Gospel can be appropriated. Therefore, the purpose of the divine institution of the ministry of teaching the Gospel and administering the Sacraments is indicated in AC 5 with the words "*That we may obtain this faith.*"[83]

As made clear by the next statement—"for through the Word and Sacraments as through instruments, the Holy Spirit is given, who works faith"—what endows faith here is not the office per se, but the Word and Sacraments. Otherwise it would, strictly speaking, have to read: "for through the ministry the Holy Spirit

---

[77] CR 5:585; cf. CR 12:109; 12:349 (also see above, p. 251 n. 51); CR 12:490: "Nor does God save apart from that ministry which He Himself ordained"; CR 15:1332: "This great good must be acknowledged, and thanks given to God, and the comfort be retained that by this means" (i.e., through the call to the office and God's efficacy through the office) "God continually gathers for Himself a Church and is present in the ministry of those who teach rightly."

[78] CR 21:850.

[79] AC 28.8f. (*BKS* 122). "Ministry" cannot be taken here as purely functional since the discussion thematically concerns concrete bishops and episcopal power, and these are equated to the ministry.

[80] On the necessity of the office, cf. CR 5:596: "We confess, even as it is the eternal, immutable truth, that the preaching office and ministry of the Sacraments is necessary and that the Church is bound to it"; CR 15:991: "since we know that the ministry of the Gospel is necessary. . . ." Cf. F. W. Hopf, *Luth. Kirchenordnung*, Bek. Kirche 29 (Munich, 1935), p. 20.

[81] Ap 12.39 (*BKS* 259).

[82] W. O. Münter, with this in mind, called the divinely instituted office according to the Confessions an "institution like the order of salvation" (*Die Gestalt der Kirche* . . . , p. 51).

[83] AC 5.1 (*BKS* 57). Cf. CR 21:519: "And that we may obtain these benefits, the ministry of the Gospel is ordained, through which men are called to the knowledge of Christ." — H. E. Creutzig (*Amt u. Ämter i. d. luth. Kirche, Luthertum* [1938], p. 114) highlighted the fact that the "*ut* [that]" of grammatical purpose in AC 5 demonstrates the close connection between justification (justifying faith) and the office.

is given, who works faith."[84] Faith properly comes not from the office but from the Word and Sacraments. The second proposition of the article—that the Holy Spirit is not given directly apart from external means, but through the Word and Sacraments—functionally carries the former proposition of the institution of the office of the Word and Sacraments.[85] The office is instituted by God not for His own sake but for the sake of the Word and Sacraments, that thereby it may result in faith and so the appropriation of salvation. The institution of the office is oriented toward the Gospel and the Sacraments, toward their actual function, from which it can in no way be abstracted. This is why the office is also called a "ministry of *teaching* the Gospel and *administering* the Sacraments." The verbal form emphasizes the functional character of the office. But in order that it may attain to *that* function of the Word and Sacraments by which faith is worked "where and when it pleases God," and thus according to the counsel and will of God, the office is crucial. The function of the means of grace, according to God's will, is to be carried out continually and regularly in an institutional manner in the Church by specified persons called to do so. And only in this way, to the extent that it agrees with God's salvific will, can it attain to faith through Word and Sacrament. Therefore, God instituted not merely the teaching of the Word and the administration of the Sacraments "that we may obtain this faith," but the *office* of teaching the Gospel and of administering the Sacraments. It is therefore with good reason—indeed, of vital importance—that the obtaining of the faith is designated as the purpose of the institution of the office.

The uniqueness of Melanchthon's view lies in the close *link between the institutional idea and the functional.* Office and means of grace are interrelated according to God's will, making mutual demands without excluding the possibility that in extraordinary circumstances they may diverge in one direction or another. The office may detach itself from the true function of the means of grace, but in doing so it forfeits its true character intended by God. Likewise, the means of grace are not absorbed absolutely into the office, are not tied absolutely to the office, but retain their freedom; in time of necessity (or in the private sphere) there may even be a function of the means of grace without the appointed office—yet their function *in essence always* follows the paths of God's order and institution made for that purpose. This institution is called the office, and its purpose is to guarantee the constant salvific function of the Gospel in the Church. This finds very clear expression when Melanchthon says that the office is instituted by God "that the Gospel may be *preserved* in the world."[86]

---

[84] Yet such formulations are not infrequently found in Melanchthon: e.g., CR 12:349; 15:165; 21:850; cf. above, pp. 225–28. Therefore, it is not possible to draw far-reaching conclusions from this observation either!

[85] This is also made clear in a purely visual manner in the article's syntactic arrangement: "*ut hanc fidem consequamur —> institutum est ministerium <— Nam per verbum et sacramenta donatur spiritus sanctus.*" The statement concerning the institution of the office is enclosed in the others regarding the meaning and purpose of the means of grace. This is likewise suggested by the prior history of the article (in the Marburg and Schwabach Articles).

[86] CR 21:555; cf. CR 21:853. The same idea lies in the characterization of the office as a "ministry of keeping and passing on the doctrine" (of Christ) (CR 28:408).

Since the office is instituted for the exhibition of the Gospel, in order to allow the faith-giving Gospel to take effect to the degree designated by God, the institution of the office is accompanied by a *promise that through the office, through the officers, God Himself will act effectually.*[87] Melanchthon sees this promise expressed first in Rom. 1:16 and Isa. 55:11, the universal promises for the efficacy of the Word,[88] then especially in the word of promise given to the apostles in John 20:22–23.[89] Also cited for this purpose is 1 Cor. 4:1ff., where the apostle shows that "the minister is efficacious through Christ,"[90] and, further, 2 Cor. 3:6; Eph. 4:11; Luke 10:16; and John 15:5; 17:20.[91] God is present in the ministry of those who teach rightly.[92]

The doctrine of God's efficacy in the office is linked to the idea of the *divine sending to the office*. As the Father sent the Son and was efficacious through Him, so the Son sent the apostles and promised to work through them.[93] This also holds true for pastors today: "So even now God sends pastors and teachers, even now He wills that the voice of the Gospel be efficacious; even if the circumstances of the sendings differ, first Paul being called, then Timothy, nevertheless in essence it always is and remains the same, namely, that the Gospel may be

---

[87] CR 5:585: (officers) "through whose voice and ministry in the preaching office and Sacraments He will certainly work and give salvation"; CR 5:596: (God) "desires to be effectual through these persons elected by the Church"; CR 5:597: "the preaching office or ministry of the Gospel, by which God works and is with us"; CR 12:350: "The Son of God, the Logos [λόγος], wills to be efficacious through those men's ministry"; CR 15:1332: "He affirms that He is also efficacious in these men's ministry . . . He is efficacious in their ministry"; CR 21:850: "the promise . . . , which attests that God is truly efficacious through the ministry of those elected by the voice of the Church."

[88] CR 11:325: (In Rom. 1:16, Paul says) "that we establish certainly that the true Gospel also is efficacious"; CR 15:384; 21:850: ". . . as attested by the universal word of the apostles and all who sound the Word given through the apostles (viz., Rom. 1:16)"; cf. CR 28:408: "the ministry . . . , through which He was, is, and shall be efficacious and converts many to Himself, as Paul clearly says, 'The Gospel is the power of God for the salvation of everyone who believes' "; Ap 13.11 (*BKS* 293).

[89] CR 15:426f.: "First, we should know that this verse confirms the ministry of the Gospel and promises the efficacy of God through the voice of all who teach the uncorrupted Gospel . . . just as the Father was with Christ, so certainly He will be with others who function in the ministry of the Gospel"; cf. CR 28:412f.

[90] CR 15:1069.

[91] CR 15:1332.

[92] CR 15:1332; cf. CR 12:203: "The Gospel of all who teach rightly is the same, and the Son of God, the Logos [λόγος] of the eternal Father, is efficacious in the voice of them all"; Ap 13.12 (*BKS* 294): ". . . We know that God approves that ministry and is present in the ministry."

[93] CR 15:426: "As the Father sent Me, and He was efficacious through Me and called and collected the eternal Church, so I send you, I will be efficacious through you, I will call and collect the eternal Church"; CR 15:385: "As the eternal Father sent His Son . . . , and the Son sent the apostles, that the Gospel might be truly efficacious"; CR 28:412f.: "Of the worthiness of the ministry we faithfully teach that nothing more can be said than what the Son of God says, 'As My Father sent Me, so send I you.' And He shows what commands He gives: 'Preach the Gospel,' and He affirms that through their voice He will be efficacious, just as the Father shows that He is efficacious through the Son."

efficacious."[94] From the sending of people to the office through God, it necessarily follows that God will also truly be, and is, effective through them. This efficacy of the office is a *substantial* aspect of the true sending, thus a matter of its substance! There is for Melanchthon no divine sending to the office without divine efficacy in the office. That God Himself works through the office is in the nature of the office, which naturally rests on the divine sending. The office is the *instrument* through which God performs His salvific action toward men with Word and Sacrament.[95] Office-bearers are the "organs through which (the Son of God) imparts to men those heavenly things and those goods that will endure forever."[96] Insofar, then, as conveying to men the salvific goods won by Christ is the particular work of God the Holy Spirit, the office in particular is also an "*instrument of the Holy Spirit*."[97] It is so, moreover, not only on certain occasions but continuously, for "these things in the Church are connected: the ministry, the Holy Spirit, and the forgiveness of sins."[98] The office of the Word and Sacraments is constantly "efficacious and salvific."[99]

If the office is the instrument of God the Holy Spirit, and if God is thus efficacious through it, then the activity of the office is to be regarded as the activity of God. In the office, God Himself is the preacher.[100] In the Absolution, "it is not man . . . who forgives, but God."[101] "The voice of the one absolving is to be trusted just as if it were the voice sounding from heaven."[102] According to Luke 10:16, the human office-bearers in the office do not represent themselves but the person of Christ and deal therefore in the stead and behalf of

---

[94] CR 15:385: cf. CR 23:xxxv: "The Son of God sends them" (the teachers of the Church) "and wishes to work mightily through the Gospel, and thus to gather an eternal Church."

[95] CR 12:399: "the assembly—in which assembly the Son of God, the Mediator, is efficacious *through* the ministry"; CR 12:349: (the teaching from Eph. 4:11 is) "that we should esteem and honor the ministry of the Gospel, and we testify that it is *through* it, and not otherwise, that those heavenly goods are given to us"; CR 21:825: "the ministry of the Gospel, *through* which God revealed Himself and *through* which He is efficacious"; CR 21:826: "God is efficacious *through* the ministry of the Gospel"; CR 21:834; 21:850: "We know that eternal goods are delivered to us *through* this ministry."

[96] CR 12:350; cf. CR 12:349: "Through those" (apostles, prophets, shepherds, and teachers) "sounding the doctrine received from the Son of God, the goods of heaven are conferred and distributed"; CR 12:109: "But at the same time, by that voice" (of the office-bearers), "the Son Himself is efficacious."

[97] CR 15:165: "Through this ministry (of the New Testament) the Holy Spirit is given and is efficacious"; CR 15:350: "Through the ministry the Holy Spirit is efficacious"; CR 15:429: "God is truly efficacious through this ministry and truly gives the Holy Spirit"; cf. CR 15:430.

[98] CR 15:429.

[99] CR 14:256.

[100] CR 12:198: ". . . The ministry of the Gospel, in which the preacher is God Himself, and the train of His ministers conveys His voice to the people."

[101] CR 23:188; 21:220; cf. CR 15:430: "This verse" (John 20:23) "clearly affirms that sin is taken away through the voice of the Gospel, which the minister sounds; that is, God truly approves [that voice] and through it gives His Holy Spirit."

[102] Ap 12.40 (*BKS* 259); cf. CR 12:491; 14:427.

Christ when they exercise the functions of the office.[103] And this fact is objective in nature, and thus is not affected by the human unworthiness of the minister in the office. The Donatistic error, which denies worthiness to the office of a wicked man and forbids it to be used, is consistently rejected by Melanchthon.[104] "We should know that the Gospel and Sacraments are efficacious on account of God's promise, not on account of the minister's character. Christ therefore calls back our minds and our faith from the minister's character to Himself, saying, 'He who hears you, hears Me.' "[105] The promise of God regarding efficacy through the office cannot be overturned by the minister's moral unworthiness. Gospel and Sacraments are effective "on account of Christ and through Christ,"[106] "on account of the mandate and ordering of God, even if the minister's character is evil."[107] Therefore, ministers are not to be abandoned on account of immorality.[108] If the worthiness of the Word and Sacraments depended on the worthiness of the respective minister, we would always be unsure whether Baptism, the Absolution, etc., are really performed in a valid and efficacious manner or not. And this would be contrary to God's intent in instituting the means of grace.[109]

At the root of this emphasis on the objective efficacy of the means of grace in the office is the assumption that the functions of the office are done in accord with the command of Christ, through whom they are instituted. Regarding an office-bearer who falls into false doctrine, Melanchthon says, "When false doctrine is defended and idolatry is established, the ministry itself is altered. Therefore, the ministry of those who corrupt doctrine is to be abandoned."[110] But in so doing, we should not teach that the Sacraments themselves which are distributed by the false teacher are invalid, provided the distribution of the Sacraments is still done according to Christ's institution. "Although the chief part of the ministry is teaching, nevertheless now and then part of the ministry, such as the administration of some Sacrament, may even be possessed by those

---

[103] Ap 7.28 (*BKS* 240): "They represent the person of Christ. . . . When they offer the Word of God, when they offer the Sacraments, they offer them in the stead and place of Christ"; Ap 7.47 (*BKS* 246): ". . . Ministers act in the place of Christ"; CR 4:1002: "in the name and on account of Christ"; CR 15:430: "that in Baptism the minister, in the stead of Christ, receives a man and truly forgives his sins as one acting in behalf of Christ, so in the proclamation of the Gospel." Also cf. F. W. Hopf, *Luth. Kirchenordnung*, pp. 17ff. On the representation of Christ in the office-bearer, cf. below, pp. 286–89.

[104] CR 12:491, 483, 519; 21:508ff., 840ff.; AC 8 (*BKS* 60f.); Ap 7.28f. (*BKS* 240f.); Ap 7.47ff. (*BKS* 246).

[105] CR 21:840; cf. CR 21:509: "Christ refers the authority of the ministry from the ministers to Himself (Luke 10:16): 'He who hears you, hears Me; that is, the ministry is valid on account of Me.' "

[106] CR 21:841.

[107] CR 21:508; AC 8.2 (*BKS* 61); Ap 7.28 (*BKS* 240). Cf. also below, pp. 284–89.

[108] CR 21:510: "Therefore, the present ministers of the churches or of the Church itself are not to be forsaken on account of immorality"; CR 21:842: "We should therefore know that teachers are not to be discharged from the rest of the Church on account of morality, nor schisms to be made if there is no error in doctrine."

[109] CR 21:508.

[110] CR 21:843.

who corrupt doctrine."[111] This applies especially to Baptism. Even Baptism by heretics is a valid Baptism, as long as the words of its institution are retained in their true sense. It is valid because (despite the false doctrine of the minister) it is still done "in behalf of the true Church."[112] A distinction must therefore be made here in Melanchthon's understanding between the office's ministry of the Word and ministry of the Sacrament. God is always working efficaciously in the office's ministry of the Word wherever the Gospel is proclaimed purely and without adulteration and in the ministry of the Sacraments wherever the Sacraments (at least according to the substance) are handled in accord with Christ's institution (even if the doctrine should be impure). We can formulate in conclusion: If the office remains a ministry of teaching the Gospel and administering the Sacraments (thus if it is present according to its God-appointed substance), God, too, is always objectively efficacious through it, and Christians may and should be certain that in the functions of the office God Himself deals with them.[113]

4. The Assignment and Authority of the Office

God's efficacy through the office depends on God's commissioning and authorizing someone for the office. The two are interrelated and interdependent. The authority of the office rests on the commission to the office, and the commission demands the authority. God commands nothing for which He does not give authority. In the commission, therefore, there is also the authorization, the authority of the office. Thus the two concepts, *potestas* [power] and *mandatum* [command], are used synonymously by Melanchthon.[114] The power of the office is more precisely described as *ecclesiastical power* [*potestas ecclesiastica*] or the *power of the bishops* [*potestas episcoporum*] and is equated with the power of

---

111 Ibid.

112 Ibid.

113 B. Schlunk sees the office not as an objective reality but as something that can only become the office now and then "where and when it pleases God"—and means by this the office in the sense of the Confessions (*Amt u. Gemeinde i. theol. Denken Vilmars* [Munich, 1947], pp. 69, 75, 77). This is a terrible misunderstanding of AC 5, by which AC 8 is actually negated, and which manifestly rests on Reformed thinking. The phrase "where and when it pleases God" in AC 5 does not, of course, speak to the validity and capacity of the means of grace in the exercise of the office, but to the formation of faith through the latter. In no way is the objective efficacy of the Holy Spirit, always indwelling Word and Sacrament, thereby put into doubt. This misinterpretation of the phrase "where and when . . ." from AC 5 has also been countered by F. Brunstäd (op. cit., p. 115).

114 AC 28.5 (*BKS* 121): "the power, or command of God"; cf. CR 3:470: "ecclesiastical power is the command of God to teach the Gospel"; CR 12:435; 21:501; 24:370.

the Keys [*potestas clavium*].[115] It is to be regarded as "God's gift and benefice"[116] and sharply distinguished from secular power, the "power of the sword [*potestas gladii*],"[117] which, while also being from God, has different functions. It is exercised as spiritual power, in fundamental distinction to secular power, only in "teaching or preaching the Gospel and distributing the Sacraments,"[118] "without human force, but with the Word."[119] We therefore ask: To what specifically does this spiritual power of the office extend? In what sphere is it legitimately used?

---

115 AC 28.1ff. (*BKS* 120ff.). AC 28.5 (*BKS* 121): "the power of the Keys or the power of the bishops"; AC 28.8 (*BKS* 121, German text): "the power of the Keys or of the bishops"; CR 21:501: "ecclesiastical power and the Keys signify the same thing. . . ."

116 AC 28.18 (*BKS* 123).

117 AC 28.12ff. (*BKS* 122f.): "Therefore, the power of the Church and the civil power must not be confounded. The power of the Church has its own command to teach the Gospel and to administer the Sacraments. Let it not infringe on the office of another; let it not transfer the kingdoms of this world; let it not abrogate the laws of civil rulers; let it not abolish lawful obedience; let it not interfere with judgments concerning civil ordinances or contracts; let it not prescribe laws to civil rulers concerning the form of the commonwealth . . ."; cf. CR 4:1002f.; 21:501f.

118 AC 28.8 (*BKS* 121); cf. AC 28.10 (*BKS* 122); CR 1:595: "There are two kinds of rule: spiritual and physical; spiritual rule is by God's Word alone."

119 AC 28.21 fin. (*BKS* 124); Tr 31 (*BKS* 480f.): "without physical force"; CR 21:501f. — These expressions of the Confessions were especially taken up by R. Sohm (*Kirchenrecht* I, pp. 484ff.) and the character of ecclesiastical power stressed as the power of the Word in contrast to the power of force. Nevertheless, he is guilty of alteration by identifying any force and all binding legal ordinance of the Church with physical force generally and drawing from those passages of the Confessions the rejection of any ecclesiastical law or right. This is entirely absent from the thinking of Melanchthon and of the Confessions. When, for instance, excommunication is required to be done without human force, it means that the ban is to remain an ecclesial penalty (thus denial of the Sacrament, exclusion from the church community) and may not become secular penalty (such as outlawry, exile, imprisonment, etc.) (cf. F. J. Stahl, *Kirchenverfassung*, pp. 146f.). "Without human force" is like "without physical force." This is only to say that obedience to spiritual power may not be compelled by physical power (cf. W. O. Münter, *Die Gestalt der Kirche* . . . , p. 34; *Begriff und Wirklichkeit des geistlichen Amtes* [Munich, 1955], pp. 24ff.). Münter pointed out that the Word—spiritual power naturally being exercised only by the Word!—is also law and as such exerts force (*Begriff u. Wirklichkeit*, p. 25). Münter also refers to the passage Ap 28.13 (*BKS* 400), where it states that every Christian bishop has "authority of spiritual jurisdiction in the church, that is, power and authority to exclude from the Christian congregation." The "*jurisdictio* over public vice" is conceived by Melanchthon as a "spiritual authority and jurisdiction" (Ap 28.14, *BKS* 400). With perfect accuracy, Münter concludes: "Where the Keys are handled only through the Word, as according to Lutheran doctrine, this force [i.e., jurisdiction] is not excluded" (*Begriff u. Wirklichkeit*, p. 26). Nevertheless: "The power of the Keys is not a physical but a spiritual power of force . . . a power of force of its own genus" (ibid., p. 27). Thus Sohm's thesis that the Confessions know of no power of force in the Church and so of no ecclesiastical right is completely mistaken. Additionally, the criticism in the Confessions of the existing canon law is not aimed at the abolishment of the law and all binding church law generally, but rather only at the false equation of Law and Gospel made in it (cf. Münter, *Die Gestalt der Kirche* . . . , pp. 20ff.). On the criticism of Sohm, cf. esp. W. Kahl, "Der Rechtsinhalt des Konkordienbuches," in *Festgabe d. Berliner jurist. Fakultät für O. Gierke*, festschrift (Breslau, 1910), pp. 348ff.; also, generally, G. Holstein, *Die Grundlagen des ev. Kirchenrechts* (Tübingen, 1928). An overview of the criticism of Sohm's thesis is given by Münter in *Die Gestalt der Kirche* . . . , pp. 9–18. Münter has also clearly shown the positive *jus divinum* in the Confessions. — Recently, W. Maurer (*Pfarrerrecht und Bekenntnis* [Berlin, 1957]), in a sweeping reflection, countered Sohm's thesis and demonstrated the divine ecclesiastical right in the Confessions with particular focus on

In the Augsburg Confession, with reference to Christ's commissional directive to the apostles, the content of spiritual power is identified as "to preach the Gospel, to remit and retain sins, and to administer Sacraments."[120] *De jure divino*, and so "according to the Gospel (the mandate of the Gospel)," episcopal jurisdiction includes "the ministry of the Word and Sacraments, remitting sins, rejecting teaching that disagrees with the Gospel, and excluding from the communion of the Church the ungodly whose ungodliness is known, not with human force but with the Word."[121] Special attention should be given to the fact that the judging of doctrine, and thus the decision-making authority in establishing the public doctrine of the church (in the German text it reads: "*Lahr urteilen und die Lehre, so dem Evangelio entgegen, verwerfen* [to judge doctrine and to reject those doctrines contrary to the Gospel]") is numbered among the powers of the office granted *de jure divino*.[122] Naturally, the bishops have no power or authority to establish some-

---

the pastoral office. — Herrlinger, too, succumbed to the same misunderstanding as Sohm, believing that Melanchthon denied *any* power of force, when he calls Melanchthon's view "an idealistic conception of church discipline by which the same is actually canceled" (*Die Theologie Melanchthons* [Gotha, 1879], p. 270).

[120] AC 28.5 (*BKS* 121); cf. AC 28.12 (*BKS* 122): "Ecclesiastical [power] has its own commission to teach the Gospel and to administer the Sacraments"; cf. Ap 12.104 (*BKS* 273): "Ministers in the Church have a command to remit sins"; also CR 14:895; 25:130.

[121] AC 28.21 (*BKS* 123f.).

[122] The judging of doctrines in no way concerns merely doctrinal judgment for one's own person and preaching but is the binding determination of public doctrine, of dogma, as Stahl rightly noted, contrary to Höfling (*Die Kirchenverfassung*, p. 162; also cf. Vilmar, *Die Augsb. Konf.*, p. 199). The designation of the power to judge doctrine as a "command to make judgments of dogmas" in another passage (CR 3:470f.; cf. CR 11:704: "to judge between the controversies of dogmas") confirms that by this Melanchthon means the binding determination of public doctrine (cf. Stahl, op. cit., p. 163), as do the expressions "teaching and governing doctrine . . . presiding over the judgments of the Church" (CR 4:547). R. Sohm views the power of judging doctrine according to these passages from the AC as "a supervisory power over the office of teaching" (*Kirchenrecht* I, p. 489). So does W. O. Münter, who in this power sees the ecclesio-political function of supervising the doctrine of office-bearers (*Begriff u. Wirklichkeit*, pp. 44f.). This is correct insofar as the judgment of doctrine and the determination of the Church's public teaching, as "a rejection of doctrine dissenting from the Gospel," necessarily includes doctrinal supervision and doctrinal discipline (in which the more specific function of bishops as higher-ranking office-bearers is in view). Bishops must keep watch over the pure doctrine in the Church (cf. W. Thomas, op. cit., p. 32; E. Sommerlath, "Amt u. allg. Priestertum," p. 72), and this also belongs to its power of office (and, incidentally, to *all* pastors in general) *de jure divino* (cf. Münter, *Begriff u. Wirklichkeit*, p. 45). Melanchthon calls "punishing false doctrine" "the chief component of spiritual jurisdiction," which is "committed to the bishops in Scripture and to the canons" (CR 4:994). Yet he wants to see learned and godly men from other estates included at councils, making doctrinal decisions in controversies of doctrine: "In controversies of doctrine, bishops should not judge alone, but capable men too should be elected out of the whole body of the Church" (CR 3:472). Yet in doing so, he strongly emphasizes that this should include only those who are exceptional in learning and piety and are therefore especially apt to judge. He is thinking especially of the "princes" and generally of the "most notable persons in the whole body of the Church" (CR 10:702; 11:434; 12:496; 14:915). Also cf. above, pp. 233–34 n. 140. It can never be presumed that Melanchthon regards these laymen at synods as representatives of the congregations. Herrlinger's opinion (op. cit., p. 273) that the synods are in Melanchthon's view to be regarded strictly "as a representation of the congregation," not as an assembly of the hierarchy, is completely incorrect. Melanchthon does not conceive of synods as a representation of

thing *contrary to* the Gospel.[123] This determination in the Augsburg Confession is directed especially against the laws about merits, by which the Gospel was obscured and Christian freedom suppressed.[124] Yet bishops or pastors have the right to make church orders, "that things may be orderly in the Church,"[125] and congregations are obliged to keep these orders "for the sake of love and tranquility, so far that one may not offend another."[126] Obedience to these church orders is distinguished from that rendered to the aforementioned functions of the office since church orders are not promulgated by God's commandment and, in view of this, are not directly binding on consciences, but rather are only for the moral motivation of love and peace.[127]

---

congregations! The driving element in them, according to him, is much more explicitly the pastors and bishops who have the office of teaching. The laity are only adjunct participants. Essentially, they have the function more or less of observers only. When W. Thomas says that, with respect to judging doctrine, Melanchthon grants the office "merely the priority" (op. cit., p. 33), this is too weak an expression. The office is for him the proper bearer of the power of judging doctrine; participating laymen are only to moderate the aspect of the clerical estate's autocracy in questions of doctrine pursuant to the aristocratic ideals which Melanchthon cherishes. If there are laymen present, who on the basis of their learning and piety must actually have important observations on a subject, their voice should be heard and considered. Cf. CR 12:496: "Democracy must stay out of the Church; that is, we must not grant the people indiscriminately the license in all matters to change teachings or make decisions about teachings. For a multitude too, as Herodotus says, is a very cruel tyrant. But a middle way is to be sought. . . . An aristocracy must be established in the composition of which the greatest authority is held by the most learned and excellent."

123 AC 28.23ff. (*BKS* 124f.) and AC 28.34ff. (*BKS* 126ff.).

124 Ibid. Cf. CR 12:435: (among the Roman [Church], the power of the office is falsely designated as though it were) "the power of instituting new ceremonies, the power of binding consciences with mortal sin should one of their traditions be violated, the power of interpreting Scripture with royal authority, the political power of changing the kingdoms of the world"; cf. CR 12:493: "The power of the Keys is not the power of making laws and instituting new ceremonies."

125 AC 28.53f. (*BKS* 129); cf. Ap 28.15 (*BKS* 400); CR 4:369: "The power to make traditions is to be given to the bishops so that all things may be done decently and in order in the church, for instance, regarding certain days, so that the people may know at what time to assemble"; CR 8:705f.: (After the obligations of the office are mentioned, in which there is a command of God, it reads:) "Further, they may in their churches, for good order, establish times and orders for preaching and the administration of the Sacraments, yet with the consent of the church and without the idea that it justifies or is necessary"; CR 21:503: (bishops) "have the authority to appoint ceremonies to the end that things may be done in orderly fashion in the public assembly of the church"; CR 21:511: "Bishops or pastors can make such orders with this political purpose"; CR 22:519.

126 AC 28.55 (*BKS* 129).

127 It is clear that for Melanchthon the office's power to proclaim the Word and to administer the Sacraments, Absolution, and excommunication, etc., which is expressly designated as *de jure divino*, is of a different genus from the power to make church orders. K. Winter ("Die Lehre von der Kirche in den ev.-luth. Bekenntnisschriften," in *Credo ecclesiam*, festschrift for W. Zoellner [Gütersloh, 1930], p. 15) therefore designated the latter as *de jure humano*. Yet F. J. Stahl fittingly expresses the present distinction as follows: "The ritual orders in the AC are not classified among the things ascribed to ministers of the Word by divine right, yet not because ministers of the Word do not have the power to establish them by divine right (about which nothing is said), but because they themselves, that is, their contents, are not equally commanded by God" (*Die Kirchenverfassung*, p. 165). Therefore, regarding the congregation's behavior, the distinction is made that they must follow the bishops in rejecting false teaching or in banning a wicked person according to God's commandment

In the *Apology*, Melanchthon uses the traditional division of ecclesiastical power into the power of ordination [*potestas ordinis*] and the power of jurisdiction [*potestas iurisdictionis*] [128] and reckons to the power of ordination the power to declare the Word and administer the Sacraments, and to the "power of jurisdiction the authority to excommunicate those guilty of public crimes and, conversely, to absolve them if they are converted and seek absolution."[129] This is also the case for the *Loci of 1535*.[130]

---

while in a liturgical order it is for the sake of love and unity. Church orders constitute no direct binding of consciences since they are not given directly by God. The AC, in this article (and others), is of course disputing the error of Roman bishops who claim that their human statutes are binding on the conscience and adherence to them is meritoriously effective. Also cf. Vilmar, *Lehre vom geistlichen Amt*, pp. 68f., and *Dogmatik* II (reprint, 1937), p. 276. Like Stahl and Vilmar, Sohm, too, takes a position on this point: "Nevertheless it is clear that the call [*Beruf*] is appointed to assign such church orders, as included in the office of teaching . . ." (*Kirchenrecht* I, pp. 526f. n. 34). Likewise, W. O. Münter: "Although these ordinances, as such, cannot claim for themselves any *jus divinum*, the authorization by virtue of which they are given is by divine right" (*Begriff u. Wirklichkeit*, p. 46). — Of these two forms of the power of the office (in the domain of Word and Sacrament ordained directly by God, and in the domain of ecclesial order) we must further distinguish the power which bishops possess in a transitional domain (between church and temporal rule), namely, in matrimonial matters and in the collection of tithes (AC 28.29, *BKS* 125), which are only granted them *de jure humano* and may also be taken from them if needed (also cf. F. J. Stahl, op. cit., pp. 145f., and P. Brunner, "Vom Amt des Bischofs," pp. 35f.).

[128] Ap 28.13 (*BKS* 400): "We are pleased by the old division of power into the power of ordination and the power of jurisdiction." — M. Doerne (*Luth. Pfarramt*, p. 18) stressed that it is "not merely an apologetic adaptation to Roman linguistic usage" "when Melanchthon in Apology Article 28 (14) ascribes to the Evangelical pastor the power of ordination as well as the power of jurisdiction. . . ."

[129] Ap 28.13 (*BKS* 400). Cf. CR 2:376: "There is no one who could not know that rebuking manifest and egregious sins belongs to pastors and the Church." Belonging to the power of jurisdiction is the ban of public sinners and exclusion from the Holy Sacrament (CR 26:87) and from the office of godparents (CR 5:605) and, finally, removal from the church (CR 14:915), conceived as formal juridical processes ("ecclesiastical court"); also cf. CR 5:603f. The use of the ban is, according to Melanchthon, a matter of the spiritual office (CR 4:368; 4:547; 8:705: "conducting the ecclesiastical court in orderly manner, everyone in his place"; CR 12:494; 26:186f.; 28:413; Tr 60 and 74ff., *BKS* 489, 493f.). Cf. W. O. Münter, *Begriff u. Wirklichkeit*, p. 29. Yet Matt. 18:17 requires, in Melanchthon's view, the participation of judicious people (CR 14:915), including outside the clerical estate. For more difficult cases, there are the consistories. Cf. CR 8:369: "And although in notorious crimes a pastor may proceed alone without others, first with private warning, then, in an incorrigible case, with public ban, yet there are more cases, namely, grave suspicion, disputed matters of doctrine, marriage vows, divorce, church properties, etc." (and for that reason there must be consistories); CR 8:370: "The ban is committed to this consistory so that not every pastor proceeds to excommunicate without orderly inquiry or due process. For from such private handlings many injustices arise." — The legal process of excommunication according to Melanchthon is described in W. Thomas, op. cit., pp. 35ff. — The power of jurisdiction is of course also tied to the norm of the Word: "But their power is not to be tyrannical, i.e., without a fixed law; nor regal, i.e., above the law; but they have a fixed command and a fixed Word of God according to which they ought to teach and according to which they ought to exercise their jurisdiction. . . . And they have the Word, they have the command, how far they ought to exercise jurisdiction, namely, if anyone would do anything contrary to that Word which they have received from Christ" (Ap 28.14, *BKS* 400).

[130] CR 21:501; 21:494: "The power of pastors is twofold. The first is said to be of the ministry, by which they convey to us the Gospel and Sacraments and proclaim the forgiveness of sins openly

In the *Treatise on the Power and Primacy of the Pope* (1537), the power of the office is described with similar scope,[131] and stress is laid on the fact that the power of the office is *jure divino* the same for all "who preside over churches, whether called pastors or presbyters or bishops."[132] There the power of ordination, too, is objectively ascribed to pastors, namely, where it states that an ordination "by a pastor in his church is valid by divine right"[133] and that in the case of necessity (in the absence of bishops), the churches are also to ordain ministers of the Word "using their own pastors [*adhibitis suis pastoribus*],"[134] which assumes that the pastor's power of office extends to ordination. Clearly Melanchthon sees here the power of ordination included in the power given equally to all pastors.[135] This is confirmed by the fact that in another statement made in the same year, 1537, the power of ordination is described as belonging "to the ecclesiastical power of the office" by "divine command."[136] In the *1538 and 1541 editions of the Loci*, Melanchthon likewise relates the "command to call ministers to the office's power of ordination."[137] In his exposition of 1 Timothy from 1541, the "substance of the ministry of the Gospel" is described in the following terms: "preaching the Gospel, administering the Sacraments, excommunicating the impenitent, absolving those who repent, judging calls to the ministry of the Gospel," and further adds: "judging doctrine may also rightly be added since this is a necessary part of preaching the Gospel."[138] Two things are worthy of noting here. First, the command to call ministers is defined more precisely by the *Loci* than is the judging of calls to the ministry. Judging the orthodoxy and teaching ability of candidates for the office (on the basis of an examination) belongs to the substance of the office, to the immediate domain of the power of the office.[139] In this there is a hint of an objective rationale for the calling of new ministers of the Word being assigned to the competency of the office. Only the office, being in possession of the power of teaching, is able to choose a person for the office on the basis of his aptitude for teaching. The other thing worthy of note in this

---

and privately. . . . The second power is called that of jurisdiction, which is the external judgment of the Church, which pertains only to manifest crimes, excommunicates, and absolves"; cf. CR 12:494.

131 Tr 31 (*BKS* 480): "spiritual power, that is, the command to teach the Gospel, to announce the forgiveness of sins, to administer the Sacraments, to excommunicate the ungodly . . ."; Tr 60 (*BKS* 489): "The Gospel assigns to those who preside over the churches the command to teach the Gospel, to remit sins, to administer the Sacraments, and besides that jurisdiction, namely, the command to excommunicate those whose crimes are known and again to absolve those who repent."

132 Tr 61 (*BKS* 489). In Tr 74ff. (*BKS* 493ff.) it is explicitly stressed that this is related to the power of excommunication. Cf. W. O. Münter, *Begriff und Wirklichkeit*, pp. 9 and 16.

133 Tr 65 (*BKS* 490).

134 Tr 72 (*BKS* 492).

135 This is confirmed by R. Sohm (*Kirchenrecht* I, p. 489 n. 14).

136 CR 3:470f.: "the power of the Church is God's command to teach the Gospel, to administer the Sacraments, to ordain ministers of the Gospel, to announce the forgiveness of sins severally and generally, to pass judgments on doctrine, and to excommunicate by the Word, without physical force, those who live in manifest sins." Cf. H. Busch, op. cit., pp. 62f.

137 CR 21:501 n. 50.

138 CR 15:1347.

139 Cf. W. Thomas, op. cit., p. 32.

passage from the 1541 commentary on 1 Timothy is that the judging of doctrine is regarded as perfectly consequent as a necessary part of preaching the Gospel, and hence located within the domain of the power of the office. The judging of doctrine, which in the Augsburg Confession had already been ascribed to the bishops *de jure divino*, is characterized as flowing from the power to preach. In his *Postil*, Melanchthon locates the judging of false doctrine within the office's power of jurisdiction,[140] thus deriving it from disciplinary power, which has a parallel in the *Artikeln der Protestanten gegen das Regensburger Buch* [Articles of the Protestants against the Regensburg Book] (1541). Here, the power of excommunication, which is assigned to pastors by the command of Christ, is applied not only to the profligate but also and explicitly to false teachers, "who . . . scatter wicked opinions contrary to sound doctrine."[141] "Ordaining as ministers of the Gospel those who have been duly called and examined" appears again in the *Saxon Confession* (1551) as part of the power of the office;[142] likewise in the *Gutachten* [opinion] that Melanchthon sent to the *imperial court preacher Pfauser in 1556*: "Ordaining priests who are regularly called" also belongs to those things for which bishops and pastors have the "command of God."[143] Coming unmistakably from Melanchthon's later years are his *Propositiones*, propositions on the chief articles of the faith, in which the "command to ordain ministers" is reckoned to the "power of ordination,"[144] and the disputation *De politia Ecclesiastica seu de ministerio et ordinationibus* [On church polity or ministry and ordinations], in which five parts of the "divinely ordained ministry" are named "the right of calling, that is, the right to elect and ordain ministers; the command to teach the Gospel, to remit sins, to administer the Sacraments; and jurisdiction"; and these five parts of the office are all "*juris divini*."[145]

The spiritual power given to the office by God, according to Melanchthon, extends to the proclamation of the Word, the administration of the Sacraments, the remission and retention of sins, excommunication and the ban, the discipline of doctrine, the calling and ordination of ministers of the Word, and the

---

140 CR 24:370. "The power of ordination is the command of Christ to teach the Gospel and to administer the Sacraments. The power of jurisdiction is the judgment of outward and known sins; likewise, of corruption of doctrine." — In this passage, a division of the power of ordination into the power of teaching, on the one hand, and the power of administering the Sacraments and directing the congregation, on the other, is also encountered in Melanchthon. The teacher (*doctor*) has the power to teach only, not to distribute the Sacraments and not the directorial functions in the congregation: "The teacher is the person called to teach the Gospel, not to govern the church. . . . He has the power to teach; he does not have the administration of the church. Likewise, he does not administer the Sacraments, even as I do not have the administration of the Sacraments" (CR 24:313).

141 CR 4:368; also cf. CR 28:413.

142 CR 28:413; cf. CR 4:547: "to order and to examine those to be ordained."

143 CR 8:705.

144 CR 12:435.

145 CR 12:489f.; likewise, CR 12:494: "The power of ordination includes the legitimate call and the divine command to teach the Gospel, to forgive sins, and to administer the Sacraments. The duties of jurisdiction are to excommunicate those guilty of manifest crimes and to receive them into grace if they repent. These duties are valid in the Church because of the Word and command of God, but they call for necessary obedience."

establishment of church orders. To summarize these individual realms in the power of the office, it is possible to say that, according to Melanchthon, the spiritual office holds the governance of the Church, the *Kirchenregiment* [ecclesial rule]. By the term *Kirchenregiment*, we are not to think merely of the external power of order in the Church; Melanchthon uses it in an all-encompassing sense to denote the spiritual administration of the Church with Word and Sacrament by means of the spiritual office.[146] Thus it is understandable that in AC 14, the Latin *ordo ecclesiasticus* (by which the concrete pastoral office is denoted) is rendered as *Kirchenregiment*.[147] "With respect to the divine commission, the *Kirchenregiment* is identical to the pastoral office."[148] The pastoral office in the discharge of its function is also *Kirchenregiment*. For this reason, Melanchthon also refers to the power of the office simply by the expression *regere ecclesiam* [ruling the Church] or *praeesse ecclesiae* [presiding over the Church].[149] *Regere* can of course simply be *verbo regere*, ruling by and according to God's Word, though this never once signifies the "legally nonbinding nature" of such ruling, as Sohm wrongly assumed.[150] The *Kirchenregiment* of the spiritual office is a spiritual rule under the absolute dominant of God's Word, a spiritual jurisdiction according to a specific word and mandate, as it is expressed in the Apology,[151] and yet jurisdiction none the less, that is, a binding, concrete power of governance in the whole domain of those functions attributable to the office (according to divine or human right).[152] The fact that external church order is

[146] Cf. F. Brunstäd, op. cit., p. 203: "Church governance [*Kirchenregiment*]—in the linguistic usage of the Confessions, ecclesiastical power—is the spiritual direction of the Church by Word and Sacrament, the function of the spiritual office."

[147] AC 14 (*BKS* 66); Ap 14 (*BKS* 296). Cf. R. Sohm, *Kirchenrecht* I, pp. 484ff., and W. O. Münter, *Begriff und Wirklichkeit*, p. 40

[148] E. Schlink, op. cit., p. 336. — Cf. W. O. Münter: ". . . The bishop, as such, is a pastor and thereby simultaneously an ecclesial ruler according to divine right" (*Begriff und Wirklichkeit*, p. 43); and E. Sommerlath, "Amt u. allg Priesterum," p. 45.

[149] Tr 30 (*BKS* 480): "teach the Word or rule the Church with the Word" (as the sense of "feed" in John 21:17); Tr 60f. (*BKS* 489): "those who preside over churches." — P. Brunner noticed here that "to preside over a church" is a necessary element demanded *jure divino* in the ministry of the Word conferred by the call ("Vom Amt des Bischofs," p. 27). — On "ruling the Church," also cf. CR 11:704: "This is your function, to teach the Gospel of Christ, to maintain the purity of the Gospel, to judge between controversies of doctrines, to rule the Church, and to withstand the ravings of the enemies."

[150] Sohm lays great stress on the fact that the teaching office (preaching office, pastoral office) is "the office of governance in the Church of Christ" (*Kirchenrecht* I, p. 527), that it contains all ecclesio-political power, even that of external church order, so that from the verbal character of this office it is necessary to conclude: "The essence of church government and church order is its legally nonbinding nature" (ibid., p. 533); there is no authority in the Church (ibid., p. 536; also vol. II [1923], pp. 140f.). Compare Sohm's interpretation of the doctrine of the two kingdoms (ibid., pp. 544ff.).

[151] Ap 28.14 (*BKS* 400).

[152] Cf. E. Sommerlath, "Amt u. allg. Priestertum," pp. 70ff.; P. Brunner, "Vom Amt des Bischofs," p. 35. — W. O. Münter found that the AC (like the later confessional documents) used the term *iurisdictio* [jurisdiction] "as a designation for the power of the office granted to the bishops by divine right as well as for the power in temporal matters granted them by human right" (*Begriff u.

included—as we have mentioned—should not be overlooked.[153] W. O. Münter's statement "The functions of administering and leading are ascribed by the Lutheran Confessions to the office-bearers exclusively"[154] is correct. E. Schlink complements this by saying that any other administration of the church is "fundamentally excluded" in the Confessions by their doctrine of the church and the spiritual office,[155] and F. Brunstäd traces this back to the "divine will."[156]

If this ecclesiastical power is the power of the office according to God's will, and thus if it finds concrete manifestation in those who bear the pastoral office, the question arises how it relates to the participation of all Christians in the power of the Keys.

R. Sohm has proposed the radical thesis that the full ecclesiastical power (according to Melanchthon) belongs to every believing Christian according to the measure of his gifts, that every Christian holds the full preaching office with all its powers, and Sohm attempts to justify this especially by reference to Tr 24ff. (*BKS* 478f.).[157] But he has misunderstood this passage of the Treatise. Sohm wants to explain the statement that the Keys are given to the whole Church (Tr 24; *BKS* 478) as meaning that they are given to every individual and in the sense that each individual possesses the full power. He overlooks the fact that the possession of the Keys, which in this passage is assigned to the Church, is directly linked to the *jus vocationis* [right of calling]; "Therefore, He" (Christ) "grants the Keys principally and immediately to the Church, just as also *for this reason* the Church

---

Wirklichkeit, p. 42). As the scope of church governance [*Kirchenregiment*], he lists the following five points: (1) the use of doctrinal discipline, (2) the exercise of the ban, (3) the power to ordain people to church offices (these three by divine right), (4) the permission to make external guidelines for the orderly execution of the administration of Word and Sacrament, (5) the juristic power in matters of marriage and church property (the last two according to human right) (*Begriff u. Wirklichkeit*, pp. 50f.). But on point 4 and its placement among the powers existing by human right, cf. above, pp. 263–64 n. 127.

[153] Cf. W. O. Münter, *Begriff u. Wirklichkeit*, pp. 46f.; F. Brunstäd, op. cit., pp. 202f. Brunstäd speaks of an "internal necessity" by which the appointment and use of the church order must be placed in the hands of the spiritual office (p. 203). This naturally calls for setting apart specific office-bearers for the discharge of the particular function of church governance, narrowly conceived, over a larger area. The Confession thus assumes as the form of church governance "the guidance of the Church by its spiritual office, the episcopal office" (p. 204). The definition of the episcopal office is "the subordination of the collective Church's legal order to the requirements of the spiritual office, which an elevated minister of the office discharges."

[154] *Begriff u. Wirklichkeit*, p. 44.

[155] *Theol. d. luth. Bek.schriften*, p. 339. The statement "in any case, it is certain that only the Church itself has the power to direct the Church, and that this must happen through the spiritual office" follows "as is necessarily recognized by all men from the Confessions today" (ibid., p. 339 n. 31).

[156] Op. cit., p. 206.

[157] *Kirchenrecht* I, pp. 489ff. — According to Sohm, every Christian receives the Office of the Keys and the office of preaching directly from God. The role of the Church—that is, the assembly of Christians—is, according to Sohm, only that it has been *granted* the public exercise of the preaching office received from God. Sohm argues that the Church as such has the Office of the Keys or the preaching office (esp. p. 502 n. 33). These are very un-Melanchthonian ideas.

principally has the right of calling" (Tr 24, *BKS* 478). The fact that the Church has the power of the Keys means that it has the *jus vocationis*, the right to fill the concrete office with people who exercise it publicly. The possession of the Keys compels the Church to fill the office. The power given to the Church properly only becomes concrete in the called minister. This is by no means to say that the Church exercises the power in each of its members so that every Christian possesses the power of the Keys in the proper sense.[158] It only refutes the idea that Peter—which is to say, the pope alone—has the right and power to call persons to the office. It is with this purport (cf. Tr 1 and 5, *BKS* 471f.) that all individual items in Tr 7–30 are to be understood. Melanchthon has not the least interest in leveling the distinction between office and congregation.

The same holds true of the subsequent passage, Tr 25ff. (*BKS* 479f.).[159] Sohm commits the error of reading "apostles, prophets, shepherds, and teachers" from Eph. 4:11, referred to in Tr 26 (*BKS* 479), simply as the charisms.[160] However, these are the offices or officers given by God. When in Tr 26 it states that the office of the New Testament "is there where God gives His gifts, namely, apostles, prophets, shepherds, and teachers," it means that it is there where it finds manifestation as something *appointed*, to which those persons certainly belong who are equipped with the charism of teaching, and yet also the call to the office, which is not to be identified with the charism (as Sohm would wish).[161] Wherever the Church, making use of the power of the Keys bestowed on it, calls people to the God-given office and these officers preach the pure doctrine of Christ, the office of the New Testament is found. And in the process, the validity of this office depends not on the particular authority of an individual man, such as one who has issued the call to the office, not on that of the pope (which involves the subject of Peter's supremacy or dominance!), but on the fact that the office-bearer—after he has been called to the office by the Church—now adheres to the pure Word of Christ. Tr 26 must be interpreted in this way.[162] This does not represent the dis-

---

158 So, too, W. O. Münter, *Die Gestalt der Kirche 'nach göttlichem Recht,'* p. 56; *Begriff u. Wirklichkeit*, pp. 30f. Likewise, F. J. Stahl, op. cit., pp. 411f. Further cf. T. Harnack, *Die Kirche, ihr Amt, ihr Regiment* (reprint, 1947), p. 42, Thesis 85. On Tr 24 specifically, see A. F. O. Münchmeyer, *Das Amt des Neuen Testaments* . . . , pp. 62f. and 64.

159 Cf. above, pp. 246–48.

160 Especially op. cit., pp. 504f. Melanchthon did not take Ephesians 4 this way. Also cf. W. O. Münter, *Begriff und Wirklichkeit*, p. 68, who asserts the same against Sohm.

161 In Tr 67, the conclusion is drawn from Eph. 4:11 that where the true Church is, there is also the right to elect and ordain church ministers. Thus Melanchthon sees the call as belonging to the gift of officers from Eph. 4:11! Also cf. A. F. O. Münchmeyer, op. cit., p. 13, and T. Harnack, op. cit., p. 47. To the argument that the office is already given with the charisms, Harnack answers that the gifts are given by the Lord "not for testifying to the office, but for the proper exercise of the (office) established by Him" (Thesis 95, p. 47); ". . . The Church has an office not because it has believing or spiritually gifted persons but because it has the means of grace and the Lord's mandate" (Thesis 96, p. 47). Harnack also clearly sees that, for the presence of the gifts for the concrete office, the conferral of the Lord's mandate on a talented person, and thus the call to the office, must be added. Likewise W. Löhe, *Ges. Werke*, vol. V.1, p. 544.

162 The question is whether Veit Dietrich's German translation accurately reproduced that of the Latin text when it says for the final sentence of Tr 26: "And the person makes no difference for this Word and office commanded by Christ, whoever may preach and teach it; where there are hearts

solution of the concrete office resting on the particular call, but only negates the pope's ceremonial-legal claim. Nowhere in the whole Treatise is there an idea of vindicating the particular power of the office for all Christians.[163]

Accordingly, in the second part of the Treatise, in connection with the Augustinian example with the two Christians in the boat, it states as an additional reason for the Church having the right to call ministers of the Word: "Here belong the statements of Christ which testify that the Keys have been given to the Church, and not only to certain persons: 'Where two or three are gathered together in My name,' etc." (Tr 68, *BKS* 491). With the expression "certain persons," it is the bishops specifically who are in view, who claimed that they alone possessed the right of ordination (the Keys) by divine right. Melanchthon accordingly says that not only the bishops have the Keys (and thereby the right of calling and ordination), but the Church in general has them so that in the case of necessity, when "the bishops ordinary become enemies of the Gospel" and refuse to give ordination (Tr 66, *BKS* 491), they can call people to the office even without or against the bishops. (Of course, the subject here in the second part of the Treatise is the validity of the call without the bishops, by pastors alone.) The word *tantum* [only] ("not *only* to certain persons") is very noteworthy.[164] The power of the Keys is not *only* given to the bishops such that the Church *jure divino* would be bound absolutely to the episcopal estate and its ordinary succession (which would necessitate that the bishops were unable to err, but there is no promise for this). Yet further than this, neither are the Keys given only to pastors alone (as the previously cited Augustinian example in Tr 67 shows). The power of the Keys is not *absolutely* bound to any certain officeholders at all. In the end, it is present wherever the Church is, that is, the two or three who confess the name of Jesus.

---

who believe and adhere to it, it is done for them as they hear and believe because Christ so commanded it to be preached and called for His promises to be believed" (*BKS* 479f.). A spiritualizing tendency is clearly evident here, which leads directly to a shift in meaning. Significantly, Sohm quotes mainly from the German text of the Treatise since he more readily finds in it echoes of his own idea. But it is necessary to adhere to the Latin text as the original Melanchthonian copy. Similar alterations of meaning by inaccurate translation are apparent in Tr 68 (where the significant word "*tantum*" is disregarded) and Tr 72 (where "*adhibitis suis pastoribus*" is omitted). Incidentally, on the words "*wer da woll* [whoever]" in the translation of Tr 26, cf. W. Löhe, *Neue Aphorismen*, *Ges. Werke*, vol. V.1, p. 554.

[163] Note that in Tr 23f. (*BKS* 478), as well as in Tr 8f. (*BKS* 472f.), the alternative is not worded "the power of the office is given not to Peter alone but to all Christians," but: ". . . not to Peter alone, but to all *apostles*." In Matthew 16 and John 21, Peter represents the common person of the whole assembly of the *apostles*, not of the assembly of all Christians! The words of Christ in Matt. 18:18 and John 20:23 are applied to all apostles, not simply to all Christians. Also in Tr 60f. (*BKS* 489) it reads not "the Gospel assigns to all Christians the command to teach," etc., but: ". . . to those who preside over churches . . . whether they are called pastors or presbyters or bishops." For Melanchthon in the Treatise there is a *jure divino* equality for (1) all apostles or bishops (so that the primacy of Peter or of the pope is demonstrated as incorrect) and (2) all pastors, all who occupy the spiritual office, whether they are called bishops or presbyters or pastors (so that the primacy of bishops ostensibly resting on divine right is demonstrated as incorrect). Beyond this, Melanchthon's thinking does not tend toward any sort of equality of all Christians or any leveling of the God-ordained distinction of the office in the congregation.

[164] A spiritualizing tendency has significantly omitted it, as we already mentioned (see above, [pp. 269–70] n. 162).

This statement betrays no tendency toward eliminating the office. Melanchthon acknowledges, of course, that primarily, the officeholders possess the power of the Keys (also, that normally they alone exercise this),[165] but he wants to express the fact that the power of the Keys fundamentally extends beyond the officeholders, that it appertains to the whole Church in such a way that *in cases of necessity* (when officeholders refuse or are not available), even a layman may baptize and absolve and can thereby stand in the stead of the unavailable minister and pastor. We have found statements along these lines elsewhere in Melanchthon.[166] Thus ecclesiastical power, in Melanchthon's thinking, may not be seen as chained to the officeholders such that in *cases of necessity* it would not be available without them. Ecclesiastical power cannot be characterized as an absolutely exclusive privilege of persons in office.

Ecclesiastical power finds concrete manifestation, according to Melanchthon, in the officeholders, but it is at the same time given to the whole Church and in case of necessity may also become functional outside the office (i.e., without officeholders), whether in the performance of individual acts of Word and Sacrament by laymen or for the reappointment of the ecclesiastical ministry by the Church. The power of the office is consistently to be viewed on the basis of the power pertaining to the whole Church, nor is the latter fully absorbed into the former.

This finds expression, incidentally, in Melanchthon's desire to see suitable individual laypeople involved in the doctrinal decisions at synodical conventions as well as in the execution of church discipline, as we have already mentioned.[167] Here it is important to bear in mind that this always involves a *joint* participation without the central position of the office being in any way leveled by it. F. J. Stahl has rightly grasped the matter in Melanchthon in this regard when he says, "The office of the Word appears everywhere as the primary subject, the actor proper, the congregation or the laity only as joining in, adding their decision. . . . In every statement, the idea is clearly that the lay element is only to reduce the ecclesial rule of the minister of the Word, but not to become the center of ecclesial rule. It is to be a safeguard to keep the ministers of the Word from using doctrine and order to oppress the congregation or from abusing discipline (the ban), but it is not to be a means by which congregations and laymen gain power and decisional sway over the ministers of the Word."[168]

---

165 Cf. Tr 74ff. (*BKS* 493f.).

166 Cf. above, pp. 232–33.

167 Cf. above, pp. 262–63 n. 122, and pp. 264 n. 129.

168 *Die Kirchenverfassung*, p. 172. — W. Thomas says, op. cit., p. 27: "This power of the Church belongs fundamentally to the congregation," and cites as testimony CR 14:195. There it reads: "This power is committed chiefly to the Church, that is, to pastors and prominent persons in the whole body of the Church." For this reason, Thomas's statement that the power of the Church fundamentally belongs to the congregation holds validity only when by the term "congregation" we do not understand the lay congregation with exclusion of office-bearers—which, however, Thomas does on p. 7 ("the congregation, i.e., the laity"). The *ecclesia* to which the power of the Church is entrusted is explained more precisely by Melanchthon as the pastors and the chief persons in the whole body of the Church. Plainly, for him, the proper bearers of the power of the Church are the pastors, to which

5. The Authority of the Office

Since the office is established by Christ and Christ works through it and has given it a spiritual power, the office has authority. The practical expression of this authority of the office is the *requirement of obedience to and reverence for* the office with respect to the office-bearers.[169] Attached to the list of the office-bearers' rights *jure divino* in the Augsburg Confession is the sentence "Herein the congregations of necessity and by divine right must show them obedience according to that verse: 'He who hears you, hears Me.' "[170] Because office-bearers in their official functions "represent the person of Christ" and stand "in the stead and place of Christ,"[171] therefore, according to God's explicit command, in all that pertains to their office,[172] in whatever is exercised by them *jure divino*,[173] in whatever the Gospel commands or forbids,[174] they are due unconditional obedience, as is the Gospel itself.[175] "Disobedience to the bishop is disobedience to God."[176] God's commands in Luke 10:16 and Heb. 13:17, which require obedience to office-bearers, require in essence "the obedience owed to the voice of the Gospel."[177] Office-bearers stand in the office for the Gospel; the minister does not act by his or human authority but only passes along the Word which God Himself has commissioned him to speak.[178] Thus for the Gospel's sake, the people are to be encouraged to esteem and love the office,[179] to honor it with "utmost piety," and to do everything to preserve and strengthen it.[180] God demands no work so earnestly as this; this is "the highest

---

a few prominent lay members are added. From this passage it is absolutely impossible to conclude that the lay congregation (with exclusion of office-bearers) is, according to Melanchthon, the proper bearer of the power of the Church. For Melanchthon, it is the office-bearers who form the core of the *ecclesia* to which the power of the Church is committed.

[169] Cf. W. Thomas, op. cit., p. 15.

[170] AC 28.22 (*BKS* 124); cf. CR 4:368; 21:838f. ("jure divino"); CR 5:597 ("by God's command"); CR 5:629 ("by divine mandate"); CR 12:494 ("by necessary obedience").

[171] Ap 7.28 (*BKS* 240).

[172] CR 21:503 ("which pertains to the ministry"); CR 21:1050 ("in the function of the ministry"); CR 24:367 ("in those things which are proper to the ministry of the Gospel"). To this also belongs church discipline: CR 4:368; 12:433: "I include . . . judgments when I refer to the obedience due the ministry."

[173] CR 21:1048: "in all those things which are by divine right."

[174] CR 21:838f.: "in all things which the Gospel commands"; CR 5:597: "in all matters which the Gospel commands or forbids"; CR 5:629: "in all things which the Gospel commands or denies."

[175] CR 21:503: "As to the Word of God, so to the ministers teaching the Word of God . . . obedience is due"; ibid.: Luke 10:16 demands "the obedience due the Gospel itself." Cf. W. O. Münter, *Begriff und Wirklichkeit*, p. 53.

[176] E. Schlink, *Theologie der luth. Bekenntnisschriften*, p. 346.

[177] CR 28:413; 21:503; Ap 28.20 (*BKS* 402): "This saying" (Heb. 13:17) "requires obedience to the Gospel."

[178] CR 15:430.

[179] CR 5:585; 15:991.

[180] CR 21:555; 12:200; 15:427.

worship of God," which is accompanied by great promises.[181] Daring to diminish the dignity of the office is a sin against the Second Commandment, "for the honor of God's name is injured by contempt for the ministry."[182] By disobedience to the office, a man puts himself at risk of eternal damnation[183] and separates himself from the catholic Church of Christ.[184] Thus Melanchthon later relates not only the office alone but also obedience toward the office among the marks of the Church [*notae ecclesiae*].[185] This obedience is to be rendered even when the office-bearers personally lead a life of less than exemplary character, as long as their doctrine is pure.[186] It especially includes *remaining with the office*: "If the teaching is right and no idolatry is practiced in the churches, all men are obliged before God to remain with the regular, public ministry and cause no division. And whoever in such a case causes a division and establishes new ministries assuredly acts against God."[187] Therefore, the Anabaptists sin, who despise and forsake the public office.[188] When the congregations adhering to the Gospel seceded from the pope on account of open idolatry and false teaching, this was justified, "but there is no true reason why the ministry should be abandoned in our churches."[189] If the teaching is pure, remaining with the office is required *jure divino*.

As much as Melanchthon stresses the duty of obedience toward the office, he also decidedly asserts the boundaries of such obedience. The authority of the office is not infinite and despotic. There is no formal, legal authority of the office which might demand absolute obedience. The authority of the office-bearer is extinguished whenever he oversteps the boundaries of his office, whenever he

---

181 CR 5:597; cf. CR 21:555. — Worldly authorities (*magistratus*), too, must obey the ministry of the Word "and honor it as divine" (CR 3:472).

182 CR 21:509. The despising of the office is also a sin against the Third Commandment (CR 23:133) and against the Fourth (CR 21:509). Cf. O. Ritschl, op. cit., pp. 319f.

183 CR 5:597: "on pain of everlasting condemnation"; CR 5:629: "Obstinacy is punished with eternal torments."

184 CR 12:488: "The article in the Creed 'I believe in the holy catholic Church' not only means that there is one Church but also requires due obedience to the external ministry. For it requires consensus with the catholic Church, and so requires due obedience to the ministry." On the passage, cf. W. Thomas, op. cit., pp. 37f.

185 Cf. above, p. 227–28.

186 CR 21:509.

187 CR 3:198f.; cf. CR 3:983: "But since God wants the ministry of the Gospel to be public, and commands it to be adorned and preserved by all, there is no doubt that God is greatly offended by the obstinacy of all who forsake the assemblies of churches, which are rightly established, or carry others away thence. As Christ says, 'He who denies you, denies Me' "; CR 12:433: (Obedience to the office also means that the people) "do not make divisions from the common fellowship of the Church."

188 CR 12:490; cf. CR 25:387: "They are devilish-minded men who separate themselves from the ministry."

189 CR 3:983.

teaches falsely and so departs from the true ministry.[190] Only for the latter does the duty of obedience apply.[191] In the *Loci* of 1521, it reads: "First, therefore, if they teach Scripture, they should be heard as Christ, according to that verse (Luke 10:16). . . . Second, if they teach something contrary to Scripture, they should not be heard. Acts 5 . . . Third, if they establish something outside of Scripture so that they thereby bind consciences, they should not be heard. . . ."[192] In the event of false teaching, all duty to obey is dissolved. Here congregations have God's command prohibiting obedience in such a case.[193] No authority of man can be higher than the Word of God.[194] The bishops have no "power to establish something against the Gospel"[195] nor even in addition to the Gospel.[196] They cannot institute new articles of faith or new divine service nor issue laws in the realm left fundamentally free by Scripture.[197] They do not have the right to establish at their own discretion a tyrannical dominion outside of Scripture.[198] Their right to make orders for ecclesial life, which serve for peace and good order, is not contested; this is to be obeyed—at least to the extent that the unity of the Church remains intact and no offense is given[199]—but as soon as such orders are issued as necessary and meritorious forms of worship, they must be withstood for the sake of the Gospel.

---

[190] On this cf. R. Sohm, *Kirchenrecht* I, pp. 486f.; W. Kahl, "Der Rechtsinhalt d. Konkordienbuches," pp. 338f.; W. O. Münter, *Die Gestalt der Kirche . . .*, pp. 34f.; K. H. Rengstorf, "Wesen u. Bedeutung d. geistlichen Amtes," etc., p. 263.

[191] CR 4:488: "we understand obedience to the ministry of the true doctrine of the Gospel, and of the administration of the Sacraments, and of the jurisdiction commanded in the Gospel . . . we feel . . . that we owe obedience to the *true* ministry."

[192] CR 21:224.

[193] AC 28.23ff. (*BKS* 124): "But when they teach or establish anything against the Gospel, then churches have the command of God which forbids them to obey." For the scriptural basis, reference is made to Matt. 7:15; Gal. 1:8; 2 Cor. 13:8–10. Cf. Ap 28.20 (*BKS* 402): "Neither should bishops frame their traditions contrary to the Gospel or interpret their traditions contrary to the Gospel. And when they do this, obedience is prohibited"; Tr 38 (*BKS* 483) and Tr 57 (*BKS* 488f.). Cf. K. Thieme, *Die Augsb. Konfession*, p. 11.

[194] Tr 11 (*BKS* 474): "Let the authority of none avail more than the Word."

[195] AC 28.34 (*BKS* 126).

[196] Ap 28.8 (*BKS* 398): "Bishops have no right to institute traditions outside of the Gospel"; Ap 28.20 (*BKS* 402): (For the Word, Heb. 13:17,) "did not institute a kingdom for bishops in addition to the Gospel"; cf. CR 21:501, 503; 21:1048; 28:413.

[197] CR 21:224: "For the bishop cannot bind the Christian conscience"; CR 4:423; 8:705f.; 12:435.

[198] CR 21:225: "Whatever . . . bishops command outside of Scripture is tyranny. For they do not have the right to command"; cf. CR 15:1170.

[199] CR 5:597: "Then there are external orders of seasons and lessons which are made by ministers in true Christian understanding according to the circumstances of each locality. In this the people are obligated to obey to such an extent that they do not act offensively against it and needlessly divide the church"; CR 12:489: "In traditions, too, ministers are owed obedience: in such a way, namely, that they are not forsaken without good reason"; CR 21:503: "Therefore, those traditions are owed obedience which are not a matter of offense; outside the matter of offense, consciences are free"; cf. AC 28.55f. (*BKS* 129f.). Also cf. W. O. Münter, *Begriff u. Wirklichkeit*, p. 51.

Just as Melanchthon regards remaining with the office (provided it continues in the pure doctrine) as required *jure divino*, he also considers it required *jure divino* that people separate themselves from those office-bearers who teach against the Gospel and have become enemies of the Gospel and are thereby to be addressed no longer as members of the true Church. They are not only not to render them any obedience but even to shun them and to renounce them publicly.[200] Thus Melanchthon's teaching on the authority of the office, with striking logical consistency, takes full account of the possibility that those who wield the office may also err and fall away from the Gospel, as the circumstances of the times made quite conspicuously clear.

6. The *Politia Ecclesiastica*

By *politia ecclesiastica* [church polity], Melanchthon understands the whole visible institutional structure of the Church, the external form of the Church.[201] It has two parts: (1) The divinely ordained ministry (encompassing the "right of issuing a call, that is, the right to elect and ordain ministers; the command to teach the Gospel, to forgive sins, to administer the Sacraments; and jurisdiction, that is, that those guilty of crimes may be excommunicated")[202] and (2) the external church order, which regulates the communal life of the Church. The divinely established office is the nucleus of church polity and is unconditionally *juris divini*.[203] The church order regulates the finer circumstances of the efficacy of the office; provides quite generally for εὐταξία, or public harmony, for discipline and peace in the Church;[204] appoints ceremonies, places (parochial boundaries), seasons, and the like;[205] and, above all, establishes the public gatherings, the worship services, which, according to God's will, must take place regularly;[206] and also provides for specific grades of ministers and regulates visitation and inspection, ensuring the preservation of doctrine and discipline in the Church.[207]

---

200 CR 1:766; 6:840; 6:930; 8:430; 11:434; 15:38; 21:834f., 838f.; Ap 7.48 (*BKS* 246); Tr 41ff. (*BKS* 485ff.).

201 CR 12:489; 21:555f.

202 CR 12:489.

203 CR 12:490.

204 CR 12:491; 21:466, 509, 555.

205 CR 12:491; 21:466, 555f.

206 CR 21:511: "that the people may know at what time they should meet to hear and learn the Gospel and for the use of the Sacraments"; CR 21:556; 21:1049: "God wills to sound His Gospel in the public congregation and when honorable men are assembled . . . public assemblies of the church are necessary to preserve the ministry of the Gospel"; CR 23:xxxv: "God wishes thus to gather for Himself an eternal Church . . . which are public, honorable assemblies, in which certain persons present the Gospel to the people and give them the Sacraments"; cf. CR 23:xxxvi, xci; 21:825; 12:199: "God does not will that the Church should always be hidden in secret places, but that there should be public and honorable gatherings and that in these the voice of the Gospel should sound, that it might be heard by all mankind."

207 CR 12:491; 23:xxxv.

Church orders are necessary because the divinely instituted office is a "public and external ministry";[208] without them, the office could not be exercised in orderly fashion nor could the Church exist.[209] Thus they exist for the sake of the office.[210] They accustom men to hearing the Gospel, through which God is efficacious toward them, and they are God's instruments by which He calls men to true godliness,[211] "the chains which join us to the ministers of the Gospel."[212] They are to be treated reverently "because of the most holy ministry,"[213] though in themselves they may by no means be explained as *cultus*, as worship.[214]

On account of its close connection to the divinely instituted office, the church order is described by Melanchthon as a "*holy* and useful thing,"[215] though he sees it fundamentally on the level of *jus humanum*. Church orders depend on the authority of the Church,[216] are made by bishops or by synods,[217] but always by human beings.[218] Still, even as human orders which are only established by the authority of the Church, they are owed reverence and conscientious compliance.[219]

The concept of ecclesiastical polity, in the full sense of the whole ecclesial order with the divinely instituted office as its center, is oriented very strongly in Melanchthon toward the historical, traditional, canonical church order. By this concept, Melanchthon has in mind especially the episcopal structure of the

---

[208] CR 21:555; cf. CR 21:511.

[209] CR 21:556: "When these bonds are broken, the Church will dissolve and break apart. . . . We know that when the church orders are dissolved, the Church also will be in danger."

[210] CR 21:555: "They are of service for the ministry divinely instituted."

[211] CR 12:491.

[212] CR 21:556.

[213] CR 21:466: "The canonical orders and church power are to be held in reverence for the sake of the most holy ministry."

[214] CR 12:491: "The reputation of being a form of worship must be taken away from them"; CR 12:466: "No suggestion of their being necessary should be added"; CR 21:511ff. In a letter to Luther dated July 14, 1530 (CR 2:193–96), Melanchthon distinguishes five kinds of traditions: (1) traditions designed to appease God; (2) traditions thought to be necessary at all times, to be a "mandatory worship" (corresponding to the Old Testament ceremonial law); (3) traditions for the "sake of good order"; (4) traditions as "bodily exercise for the inexperienced"; and (5) traditions as signs of the thanks for grace received, "for the sake of worship certainly, yet following faith." The last three kinds of traditions here receive from Melanchthon the assessment: "[These traditions are] allowed; [there is] nothing of impiety [in them]"—while the first two prove impious. But in this letter, Melanchthon asks Luther for advice regarding how necessity and freedom relate in the last three permitted kinds of tradition; this is unclear to him. Cf. WA Br 5:491ff., and A. W. Dieckhoff, op. cit., pp. 176ff.

[215] CR 2:766.

[216] CR 21:555: "εὐταξία [order] instituted by authority of the Church"; CR 21:556: "εὐταξία [order] instituted by the Church."

[217] CR 12:491.

[218] CR 21:555: "human orders"; CR 12:491: "orders made by human authority."

[219] CR 21:509: "To this same order of the Church which supports public unity we owe honor"; CR 21:555: "We ought to love and maintain these" (i.e., orders); CR 21:1049: "In churches which are taught rightly, let all both love and support the public assemblies and comply with the rightly teaching pastors who designate the times and lessons."

Church with its diocesan organization and gradation of offices, which he rates highly and does not wish to see dissolved.[220]

The *Religionshandlungen auf den Reichstag zu Augsburg* [Religious proceedings at the Imperial Diet of Augsburg] show how Melanchthon was intensely eager to preserve the Church's canonical order and episcopal structure. In the Augsburg Confession, the basic principle proclaims that with respect to traditional church orders, those rites are to be retained "which may be observed without sin and which are profitable unto tranquility and good order in the Church"; only that which is contaminated by ideas of merit and thus contrary to the Gospel is to be abolished.[221] In closing the first part of the Confession, it reads that "among us, in large part, the ancient rites are diligently observed"; that "it is a false charge that all ceremonies, all the things instituted of old, are abolished in our churches";[222] and, further, "only some abuses have been omitted which are new and which have been accepted by the corruption of the times, contrary to the intent of the canons."[223] Stress is laid on the fact that nothing is more suited to fostering piety and reverence in the people than the ceremonies being duly enacted.[224] And in Article 28, the episcopal jurisdiction is not attacked by a single word; its only purpose is that the bishops forsake the tyrannical application of their power and permit the Gospel.[225] Melanchthon does not mean here to criticize the episcopal organization of the Church.[226] His intention in no way concerns an alteration of the Church's episcopal structure; rather, he wishes to see it restored where it has been destroyed: "Oh, if only I might not establish any rule, but restore the administration of the bishops," he says in a letter to Camerarius dated August 31, 1530.[227] On

---

220 On the relationship which the Confessions have with canonical right as such, cf. W. Kahl, "Rechtsinhalt d. Konkordienbuches," pp. 310ff., and especially W. Maurer, *Pfarrerrecht und Bekenntnis*, pp. 84ff. On Melanchthon's position on the episcopacy of the Roman Church and on episcopacy in general, cf. P. Brunner, "Vom Amt d. Bischofs," pp. 43ff. On Melanchthon as an episcopalian, cf. K. Rieker, *Die rechtliche Stellung der ev. Kirche in Deutschlands* (Leipzig, 1893), pp. 93f.

221 AC 15.1 (*BKS* 66); cf. Ap 15.1 (*BKS* 297).

222 AC [Concl. Part 1 (Latin)], 3ff. (*BKS* 83).

223 AC [Pref. Part 2 (Latin)], 1 (*BKS* 83f.); cf. AC 28.72 (*BKS* 132): ". . . which are new and received contrary to the custom of catholic Church."

224 AC [Pref. Part 2 (Latin)], 6 (*BKS* 84).

225 AC 28.77 (*BKS* 132): "This is not an attempt to have the bishops cede some of their dominion" (= jurisdiction), "but all that is asked is that they allow the Gospel to be taught in its purity and that they relax some few observances which cannot be kept without sin."

226 Cf. H. Asmussen, "Das Amt der Bischöfe nach Augustana 28," in *Reformation, Schicksal und Auftrag*, commemorative gift for J. Lortz (Baden-Baden, 1958), p. 211 and passim. Asmussen finds "that the foundational document of the Lutheran Church sees no cause to oppose the existence of bishops as bishops. The AC has not abolished bishops. . . . The whole article" (namely, 28) "becomes pointless, not to mention loses its character as a confession, if it is essentially indifferent whether one has bishops or not" (p. 211). Cf. P. Brunner, "Vom Amt des Bischofs," p. 34.

227 CR 2:334. Cf. P. Brunner, op. cit., p. 35: "Purification of the episcopacy by governmental rule, however, does not mean abandonment of the episcopacy." Thus W. Thomas's statement—"What convinced him" (Melanchthon) "of the latter" (esteem for the episcopal office) "is not the wish to restore the episcopacy in the sense of the Catholic Church but the acknowledgment of the necessity of higher and lower human orders including under the pastors" (op. cit., p. 38)—does not quite fit

September 4, 1530, Melanchthon writes: "By what right . . . will it be lawful for us to break up the πολιτείαν *ecclesiasticam* [ecclesiastical polity], if the bishops grant us those things which it is proper for them to grant?"[228] And on September 6, 1530, to Johann Hess: "Besides, we granted jurisdiction to the bishops and openly acknowledged that we would willingly preserve the ecclesiastical polity, and *desire that bishops should preside over the churches*."[229]

Likewise, Melanchthon speaks clearly in the Apology of 1531. In Article 14, it is testified that "it is our greatest wish to maintain ecclesiastical polity and the grades in the Church, even though they have been made by human authority";[230] "we will gladly maintain ecclesiastical and canonical polity, provided the bishops only cease to rage against our churches."[231] If the "canonical polity, which we greatly desired to maintain," is dissolved in some places, it is only because of the "cruelty of the bishops."[232] Our people are not to blame when the "authority of the bishops" is shaken.[233] And in Article 15, only the traditions and statutes relating to merits, which contradict the Gospel, are renounced, "but we cheerfully maintain the old traditions made in the Church for the sake of usefulness and

---

the case. In Melanchthon's thinking, there is both the objective motive noted by Thomas here *as well as* a historical one in the sense of preserving or restoring the canonical episcopal church order. The latter, especially in view of Melanchthon's strong traditionalist inclinations (not only in this area), should not be overlooked.

[228] CR 2:341.

[229] CR 2:347; cf. CR 2:431: "For neither did we ever ask that ecclesiastical polity be dissolved, only that the bishops would not condemn the Gospel"; CR 2:247: "Neither are our men reluctant to submit to bishops, if only they might accept them"; CR 5:598: "We do not like to see disorder, but heartily desire that the bishops and their co-rulers should do their episcopal duty, and we offer our obedience on condition that they forbear to persecute Christian teaching"; CR 7:29: "we would gladly see the ecclesiastical polity well ordered."

[230] Ap 14.1 (*BKS* 296); cf. in the German text: "that we are most exceedingly inclined to help maintain the old church order and governance by bishops, which is called canonical polity. . . ." — A misunderstanding of Ap 14.1 is present in T. Harnack. Harnack (*Die Kirche, ihr Amt, ihr Regiment*, p. 44, Thesis 89) detaches the church ministry of AC 5 from the church order in AC 14 and attributes *jus divinum* only to the former while he views order, along with the appointed concrete office, as belonging to canonical polity and, according to Ap 14.1, "made by human authority." Yet in Ap 14.1, the term "ecclesiastical polity" or "canonical polity" is in no way meant simply as an expression of the appointed concrete pastoral office described in AC 14, the "church order." We know that Melanchthon is here reacting to the assertion in the Confutation of AC 14 that claims canonical ordination must be used in calling ministers. By "ecclesiastical polity," he means the whole realm of canonical church order (cf. the German text's expression for this: "ancient church order and the governance by bishops, which is called 'canonical polity' "), in which *episcopal* ordination is prescribed. He has in mind here the grades in the Church specifically (esp. the distinction between bishop and presbyter) and asserts that they are "made by human authority"! Melanchthon is not in the least interested in understanding the concrete pastoral office itself—the "order" generally, as treated by him in AC 14—as existing merely by human authority. This applies only to the gradation of the office and other provisions within the canonical polity.

[231] Ap 14.5 (*BKS* 297). By "ecclesiastical and canonical polity," the episcopal organization of the Church is clearly meant. Cf. P. Brunner, op. cit., p. 37; further, A. Kimme, "Doctrina und ordo ecclesiasticus nach luth. Verständnis," in *Schriften des Theol. Konvents Augsb. Bek.* 8 (Berlin, 1955), pp. 72f.

[232] Ap 14.2 (*BKS* 297); cf. CR 5:598.

[233] Ap 14.5 (*BKS* 297).

tranquility. . . ."[234] In Article 28, Melanchthon states that "we do not censure canonical polity" but "maintain its value."[235]

A further testimony for Melanchthon's episcopal inclination is his *Gutachten für König Franz I. von Frankreich de moderandis controversiis religionis* [Memorandum for King Francis I of France, how religious controversies might be moderated], *from August 1, 1534.*[236] Here, to begin, he rejects the opinion that the Evangelicals only wanted "to wrest barbaric liberty from the monarchy of the Roman pontiff and to despise the ancient church orders," declaring: "I have not done this that the authority of the Church may be dissolved, but that other great matters may be argued and explained pertaining to the conscience and the worship of God."[237] Then Melanchthon goes on: "They grant that our ecclesiastical polity is a lawful entity, namely, that there are some bishops who preside over several churches; likewise, that the Roman pontiff presides over all bishops. Of this canonical polity, as I believe, no wise man disapproves, nor ought to disapprove if it remains within its bounds, that is, if the pontiff and bishops do not abuse their authority and oppress the true doctrine."[238] "Concerning the supremacy of the pontiff and of the authority of the bishops there is no dissent. For in the Church there must be governors who examine and ordain those called to church service and who exercise church judgments and inspect the priests' teaching."[239] The necessity of an episcopal office which provides the higher functions of the spiritual office is for Melanchthon so firmly rooted in objective reasons that he states: "And even if there were no bishops, nevertheless it would be necessary to create them."[240] Melanchthon acknowledges in this memorandum the authority for the whole gradation of church offices, including even the primacy of the pope;[241] he only demands that the pope and bishops actually purvey the pure doctrine of the Gospel and ensure that this is not withheld from the congregations.[242]

In his response to the Regensburg Book, the *Articuli Protestantium Caesari traditi* [Articles of the Protestants, submitted to the emperor] *from May 31,*

---

234 Ap 15.38 (*BKS* 304); cf. Ap 15.44 (*BKS* 305): "From this condition of the churches, it may be judged that we diligently maintain church discipline and godly ceremonies and good church customs."

235 Ap 28.12 (*BKS* 400).

236 CR 2:741–75.

237 CR 2:744.

238 CR 2:744f.

239 CR 2:745–46; cf. CR 5:597: (There must be those present) "who have oversight over others"; CR 5:599.

240 CR 2:745–46. From this it is completely clear that Melanchthon calls for the superior episcopal office not merely as a concession to his love for the unity of the Church but from an internal, objective necessity. Cf. P. Brunner, "Vom Amt des Bischofs," p. 44, and W. Trillhaas, "Die lutherische Lehre 'De potestate Ecclesiastica,'" *Zwischen den Zeite*n 11 (1933), p. 504.

241 Cf. also CR 2:745–46: "In my opinion, the monarchy of the Roman pontiff would be advantageous for maintaining a consensus of doctrine among many nations. Wherefore harmony may be easily established in this article of the superiority of the pontiff, if agreement is possible in other articles."

242 Cf. CR 6:840: "I allow the order and the episcopal estate to exist as it is. When the pope has the right doctrine, he should be obeyed; if he does not have right doctrine, obedience must cease"; further cf. CR 2:766f. and 4:927.

1541,[243] he states, after discussing the institution of the concrete office of shepherd appointed by the call, that for the performance of the supervisory function among pastors and for the avoidance of schisms, there appeared in the ancient Church a "useful order, that out of many presbyters a bishop should be chosen to govern the Church by teaching the Gospel and upholding discipline and to preside over the same presbyters. Then several grades were made, namely, archbishop and, above these, patriarchs. . . . These orders, if those who preside do their office, are useful for maintaining the unity of the Church, that is, for convening synods; for issuing lawful judgments of doctrine; for correcting the vices of vagabonds, usuries, and other scandals; for correcting laws; and for punishing those who initiate scandals."[244] The emphasis in these expressions is on the fact that the possessors of these superior offices actually provide the function of their office[245]—and herein lay the fault in the contemporary Roman episcopacy—but it is important to note that, fundamentally, the church hierarchy is not attacked but is acknowledged as a "useful order."

This happens with equal force in the subsequent *Denkschrift Melanchthons zum Regensburger Reichstag de reformatione Ecclesiae* [Memoirs of Melanchthon on the Regensburg imperial diet concerning the reformation of the church] *from July 1541*,[246] which contains a demonstration of the true functions of the episcopal office and its practical necessity. Here Melanchthon mentions four chief duties of the bishop: "teaching and governing doctrine, ordaining and examining ordinands, presiding over judgments of the Church, and visiting churches."[247] The discharge of these episcopal functions is necessary for the Church, as emphasized separately with each particular function,[248] and for Melanchthon this necessity really has the weight of a *jus divinum*.[249] If the present bishops are hindered in their episcopal duties by their worldly jurisdictions, they are, if they wish to maintain their secular rule, to designate trustworthy men to perform the episco-

---

[243] CR 4:348–76.

[244] CR 4:368f.

[245] CR 4:368f.: "But these bishops [*praesides*] serve their call, teach, examine the doctrine and usages of the churches over which they preside, correct errors and vices, exercise the judgments of the Church."

[246] CR 4:542–52.

[247] CR 4:547; cf. CR 5:382 ("episcopal functions: to spread the pure doctrine and personally to preach, to visit the churches, to ordain capable persons, to oversee schooling, to govern marriage courts and other ecclesial courts, to manage Christian discipline"); CR 5:388; 4:368f.; 8:705f. In the Wittenberg Reformation of 1545, the duties of the bishops are traced back to God's commandment (CR 5:601f.): "First, it is acknowledged by bishops that God commanded them above all else to fill the preaching office rightly, either personally or through others, to observe proper Christian ceremonies. . . . Second, they know that it is God's commandment that they conduct ordinations with proper diligence, namely, with due examination and instruction. . . . Third, it is also God's commandment to see to it continually that pastors and preachers teach and govern rightly. . . . Fourth, it is God's commandment that the church courts are conducted as Christ teaches in Matthew 18." Cf. W. O. Münter, *Begriff u. Wirklichkeit*, p. 57.

[248] CR 4:547: "It is necessary . . . that there be certain suitable governors of doctrine and ordination in the Church. It is necessary that judgments be passed on doctrine and in marital controversies and divorces. It is necessary that excommunication commanded in the Gospel be restored. . . ."

[249] Cf. the passage CR 5:601f. cited above, n. 247.

pal functions in their place, for it is an unavoidable necessity "that certain men be chosen in any given diocese to preside over ordination and examination of ordinands; likewise . . . to preside over the judgments of the Church and to visit churches."[250] The primary concern for Melanchthon is that the functions of the supervisory office are actually performed, even if it is done only by a committee.[251] Yet Melanchthon sees the latter only as an emergency solution; properly, the bishops themselves would have to attend to their office.

It is an incontestable fact that Melanchthon would have preferred to keep the canonical polity, the episcopal organization of the Church, in full force[252] and that he expected the worst from its dissolution. "I see what sort of Church we will have if the ecclesiastical polity [πολιτεία *ecclesiastica*] is dissolved. I see that there will be a more intolerable tyranny after that than there ever was before."[253] At the same time, however, it must be maintained that Melanchthon sees the whole gradation of offices in the ecclesiastical polity fundamentally on the plane of *jus humanum*. *The fact that* the superior functions of the office—church government in the narrow sense—are exercised is for him without a doubt "God's commandment,"[254] but the grades of offices themselves are man-made.[255] The divinely ordained ministry is one *jure divino*. The equality of the ministry is true with respect to the *divine* right.[256]

This also applies to the distinction between pope and bishop as well as between bishop and pastor. While in 1530 Melanchthon still counts the question of whether the pope is the supreme bishop by divine right among the inessential articles preferably avoided in religious proceedings,[257] in 1537, in the *Treatise on the Power and Primacy of the Pope,* he represents the *jure divino* equality of all ministers in the office thematically as a doctrine of the church. In part one, he rejects the notion that the pope is superior to the bishops *jure divino;*[258] in part two, he counters the view that the bishops are higher than pastors *jure divino.*[259] These distinctions exist only by human authority. Therefore, in the case

---

250 CR 4:547.

251 CR 4:547: "He therefore discharges the office of the bishop—whether it be someone in a certain place or this body of magistrates [*decuria judicum*]." Also belonging to this committee (as observers) are "honorable, serious, and learned laymen" (ibid.). These ideas laid the groundwork for the establishment of the consistorial organization of the Church. Cf. CR 28:413: "That this may be rightly done, consistories have also been established in our churches."

252 Cf. W. O. Münter, *Begr. u. Wirklichkeit*, p. 56.

253 CR 2:334; cf. CR 2:341; 5:598; 21:466.

254 CR 5:601f.

255 Melanchthon teaches this, although he is aware that various grades of office are mentioned in Scripture: CR 21:835.

256 CR 24:402; cf. CR 8:706; 15:1069.

257 CR 2:183.

258 Tr 1–59 (*BKS* 471–89); cf. CR 1:336; 2:318; 12:203.

259 Tr 60–82 (*BKS* 489–96); cf. CR 1:336; 2:318.

> of necessity, when the bishops ordinary become hostile to the Gospel, ordination by pastors is valid *jure divino*.[260]

Thus we find Melanchthon's teaching of ecclesiastical polity governed by two factors: first, there is the concentration of the divine right on the ecclesiastical ministry, which combined with the functions of clerical church government forms the nucleus of church polity; and at the same time, in the broader realm of ecclesiastical order, belonging to the *jus humanum*, the vigorous endeavor to maintain the canonical polity and the episcopal structure of the church's organization as they have been handed down. —

Having thus delineated the essence of the *ministerium ecclesiasticum* as a divine institution in Melanchthon, we will now proceed to examine Melanchthon's doctrine concerning the call to the office.

[260] Tr 65 and 72 (*BKS* 490 and 492); cf. CR 1:766.

CHAPTER III

The Legitimate Call to the Office

1. The Necessity of the Call to the Office

In the Augsburg Confession Article 14, concerning ecclesiastical order, Melanchthon teaches "that no one should teach in the public office or administer the Sacraments unless he be rightly called."[1] This fundamental expression of

[1] AC 14 (*BKS* 66); cf. CR 2:195: "... No one should offer the body of the Lord except a called presbyter" (this sentence has "nothing of ungodliness"). E. Schlink (op. cit., p. 328) sees the priesthood of all believers behind AC 14: "Because the spiritual office is entrusted to all believers, its exercise is not left to the discretion of every individual believer. Rather, the public exercise is tied to the conferral of the assembly of believers." These ideas, according to which the office is already fundamentally given to each believer and only its public exercise is authorized in the call, are characteristic ways of thinking for Luther but not for Melanchthon. Melanchthon says nowhere that all believers have the ecclesiastical ministry and that in the calling to the office only the public exercise of the office already possessed is authorized (cf. above, pp. 268–70 and on the definition of ordination, cf. below, pp. 310–17). The consequences of these ideas also would include the theory of conferral (that the right to public exercise of the office by the collective membership is conferred on the pastor), about which Schlink himself says, "The idea of the conferral of the rights of the universal priesthood on the person of the pastor is foreign to the Confessions. The Church does not *confer* its office of preaching the Gospel and administering the Sacraments on individuals of its membership but *appoints* them to this office entrusted to it by God, it *calls* them to this office established by God" (op. cit., pp. 330f.). *This* is the perspective from which AC 14 must be understood. There is behind this article no notion of the universal priesthood (which of course finds no mention anywhere in the AC), nor the sociological rationale of the concrete office derived from it, but rather the idea of the divine institution of the ecclesiastical ministry. AC 14 is based on AC 5. Cf. E. Sommerlath, "Amt u. allg. Priestertum," p. 56. — Also important for understanding this article is the fact that by "ecclesiastical order" or church governance, to which the title refers, nothing else is meant than the divinely established ecclesiastical ministry of AC 5, but now with respect to the orderly appointment of this office, which is likewise ordered by God. Cf. W. O. Münter, *Die Gestalt der Kirche* ..., p. 58. Münter also confirms F. J. Stahl's observation that the beginning of the article with the word "*docent* [they teach]" shows that this is not only dealing with a laudable human institution, but a divine institution. "*Docent*" always introduces a dogmatic statement (op. cit., pp. 58f. n. 287). Similarly, R. Josefson ("Det andliga ämbetet i Svenska kyrkans bekännelseskrifter," in *En bok om kyrkans ämbete* [Uppsala, 1951], p. 190) refers to the fact that Article 14 is among the doctrinal articles, not the reformatory articles (pp. 22ff.). This would mean that what is taught in Article 14 does not merely represent a consequence of ecclesiastical law but belongs to the foundation of faith

the necessity of a regular call for the exercise of the public office in the Church is Melanchthon's consistent teaching.[2] It is grounded quite concretely on the divine institution of a particular office filled with people and, more precisely, on the command of God to call people to the office (*mandatum de constituendis ministris*).[3] Since God has commanded the call to the office, the Church must comply with this command of God. It also assumes that not every Christian automatically possesses the office, but that it is only received in the particular call. Thus the necessity of the call without further ado is clear. Since it is based on a divine mandate, this necessity is regarded as *de jure divino*.[4]

Joined, in Melanchthon's thinking, with the rationale for the necessity of the call to the office based on the divine institution is the *motive of order*, which is likewise traced back to God's will. God desires no "barbaric confusions" in the Church, as would arise if everyone were allowed to exercise the public office without a particular call. "God desires the congregation of the churches to be ordered with all honor. As Paul says, 'Let all things be done with decency and order.'"[5] The particular call to the office is also needed because of the divinely commanded order.

In addition to these reasons for the necessity of the call to the office (reasons relating to the nature of the office and the Church) are those oriented toward the person of the office-bearer. The office-bearer needs the *divine sending* to the office. If he is to preach in God's name, he must, in accordance with Rom. 10:15, also be properly sent by God.[6] If he preaches without this, he incurs the judgment of Jer. 23:21.[7] It is the divine sending, however, which results in the particular call to the office. Only in an "external call" with visible testimonies can the office-bearer as well as the Church be assured that God actually did the

itself. The placement of the article shows that through the call to the office, Christ's own conferral is accorded to a man and that the office can be obtained by no other means. — On the explanation of *rite vocatus*, see below, pp. 302–8.

[2] CR 3:184: "It is true that no man is to presume to take the public preaching office without a public call and vocation"; CR 7:742: "We rightly say that no one may function in the ministry without this indirect call"; CR 12:378; 12:491: "No one . . . may usurp the ministry without a call"; CR 12:501: "Neither . . . may anyone occupy the public ministry in the Church without a call"; CR 15:1333; also cf. AC 28.8 (*BKS* 121): "according to their calling."

[3] Ap 13.12 (*BKS* 294); Tr 72 (*BKS* 492): "The churches are in duty bound, . . . according to divine Law, to ordain"; also cf. the passages further cited above, pp. 250–51 nn. 45–46. Cf. W. O. Münter, *Begriff u. Wirklichkeit*, p. 59.

[4] Cf. W. O. Münter, *Die Gestalt der Kirche . . .*, p. 57. Münter emphasizes the connection between AC 14 and AC 5 and the dependence of the former on the latter. He describes the obligation demanded in AC 14—"no one should publicly teach in the Church or administer the Sacraments unless he be regularly called"—as the "other side of the divine command, expressed in the form of a prohibition" which "in its positive form expresses the command to appoint ministers" (op. cit., p. 57).

[5] CR 7:742; cf. CR 4:368; 12:381. Also cf. above, pp. 232–33 n. 134.

[6] Cf. CR 7:741; 15:477f.; 15:694f.; 15:991.

[7] CR 7:741f.; 15:1333.

sending.[8] And only when in such a call the office has been undeniably given to someone by God can it be discharged in blessing.[9]

Finally, Melanchthon's ideas regarding the necessity of the call to the office are oriented toward the *examination of doctrine and life*, which is necessary before entering the office, and the execution of which appears guaranteed only in a regular call process.[10] Melanchthon recoils at the idea that any member of the congregation could simply begin teaching publicly. "What barbarism it would be if men from every which where, uncalled and unexamined, infiltrated the churches! And what great danger there would be!"[11]

For all these reasons, the necessity of the call to the office is obvious. For Melanchthon it is a well-established *jus divinum* so that whoever willfully bypasses the call and exercises the office without it sins grossly.[12] Of further interest, then, is the question whether the necessity of the particular call also affects the *validity and efficacy of the functions of the office.*

In examining this problem in Melanchthon, it will be necessary to begin with the fact that Melanchthon also knows of an efficacious administration of the Word, Baptism, and the Absolution through laity not called to the office.[13] This holds true within specific contexts: in the realm of necessity, when called office-bearers are not available;[14] and, for the Word and the Absolution, in the private sphere of brotherly exchange of Christians with one another;[15] and, with respect to the Word, in the sphere of the office of housefather and schoolteacher, as well as the universal office of bearing witness, which every Christian has toward pagans and unbelievers on the basis of his priesthood.[16] Yet Melanchthon very clearly distinguishes this administration of Word and Sacraments by laity, as we have seen above,[17] from the public ministry of the Church. Our specific question presently is whether the exercise of the function of the specific public office by noncalled persons—that is, by those who have pretended to the office on their own initiative and who, without a regular call, have infiltrated it—may be seen as a valid and efficacious function of the office. We have already been acquainted with Melanchthon's anti-Donatistic stance in the question of the ministry of "wicked men and heretics."[18] The validity of Word and Sacrament depends, for him, on

---

[8] CR 7:741f.; 15:1331f.

[9] CR 12:198: "First . . . ministers receive the doctrine, the Holy Spirit, and the ministry from God. . . . Then . . . they spread abroad the voice of the doctrine."

[10] CR 12:380f.: ". . . Admittance to the ministry and the task of teaching publicly are not open to all, but only to those whose doctrine has been examined and whose life has been inspected, just as Timothy is directed by Paul" (for which reason ordination with examination is necessary).

[11] CR 7:742; cf. CR 12:381.

[12] CR 12:378f.; 7:742; 15:1333.

[13] Cf. above, pp. 232–37.

[14] Tr 67 (*BKS* 491).

[15] CR 12:493f.

[16] CR 15:1175.

[17] Cf. above, pp. 232–37.

[18] Cf. above, pp. 258–60.

the institution and commandment of Christ (AC 8), not on the character of the minister. The minister's personal character may be wicked, but the Word and Sacraments are still effectual. But what if it is not a question of a minister—that is, someone rightly called—but of a usurper who pretends to the office without a proper call? Melanchthon in his anti-Donatistic statements always has in mind the function of people, who, though wicked and not regenerate, are nevertheless rightly called ministers of the Church. But what if the latter aspect also is absent, and noncalled men actually exercise the function of Word and Sacrament?

The answer to this question is difficult to formulate insofar as Melanchthon did not pose it directly, so his stance here must be deduced from his other statements related to the subject. It will be necessary, at any rate, to begin with the proposition that, in the sense of Melanchthon, Word and Sacrament—as long as they are handled "purely, rightly [*rite*]"—are *always* "instruments of the Holy Spirit" and thus salvific and are able to work faith "where and when it pleases God." Without question, in Melanchthon's conception, it can be no different when a noncalled person is sinfully exercising the function of the office either. Such is the case in other situations in which laymen handle Word and Sacrament (cf. the spheres mentioned above). Yet a public function of the office of noncalled persons is clearly distinguished from the lay function of Word and Sacrament in the aforesaid spheres by the fact that it happens without permission, illicitly, as sin. And here without question lies an obstacle for the full efficacy of the Holy Spirit through this function of Word and Sacrament: this has the result that the level of certainty relative to the efficacy of this function of the illegitimate "office" is lower than when there is a proper call to the office. From this perspective, a number of Melanchthon's expressions might be taken into account which expressly emphasize or else presuppose the *call's relevance to the validity and salvific effect of the function of the office* relating to Word and Sacrament.

In the *Apology*, the content of AC 8 is reproduced as follows: "Neither does the fact that the Sacraments are administered by the unworthy detract from their efficacy because, on account of the call of the Church, they represent the person of Christ and do not represent their own persons. As Christ testifies: 'He who hears you hears Me.' When they offer the Word of God [or] the Sacraments, they offer them in the stead and place of Christ. That voice of Christ teaches us not to be offended by the unworthiness of the ministers."[19] The validity of wicked men's administration of the means of grace is based on their "representing the person of Christ," and this is true of them "*on account of the call of the Church.*" The expression used in AC 8—"by reason of the institution and commandment of Christ"—is rendered here in Ap 7.28 as "on account of the call of the Church."[20] Insofar as the ministers have the call of the Church and handle Word and Sacrament as those who are "rightly called," they represent the person of Christ. They stand in the stead of Christ on account of the call of the Church. In the call of the Church,

---

[19] Ap 7.28 (*BKS* 240); cf. the German text: ". . . on account of the call of the Church, they are there not for their own person but as Christ; as Christ testifies: 'He who hears you hears Me.' Thus even Judas was sent to preach. Then they give them [the Word and Sacraments] in the stead of Christ. And the Word of Christ teaches us that in such a case we should not let the unworthiness of the ministers offend us."

[20] Cf. H. Bernau, "Die Bedeutung der Ordination nach d. luth. Bek.schriften" (1940), p. 54.

the person of Christ is linked to the person of these men, the ministers, from which results the objective efficacy of the official actions of these ministers independent of moral worthiness or unworthiness.[21] Here we encounter an interpolation of "the call of the Church" into the train of thought on which the objective validity of the office's functions is grounded, which deserves special attention. If we consider Ap 7.28 as it reads literally, we do not really receive the impression that the call of the Church has any relevance for Melanchthon with respect to the validity of the functions of the office. Rather, *H. Bernau's* insight seems correct when he says on the basis of this passage: "The efficacy (namely, of the Sacraments of wicked priests) is valid because '*they represent . . . the person of Christ*,' and that means: it is valid 'on account of the call of the Church.' . . . This determines the significance of ordination (here in the comprehensive sense equivalent to the call process): the authority and power of the ecclesial office in representing Christ on the basis of the Church's commission depends on that ordination."[22]

A similar passage in Melanchthon's works is also found in the *Loci of 1535*. The godly are to know, he says, in full accordance with AC 8, that the "use of the Sacraments" is valid on account of the "divine command and institution, even if the character of the minister is evil." And further: "We speak of the wicked in the Church, not the openly blasphemous, such as Jews or Turks, to whom the Church has committed no ministry."[23] The first statement is thus not applicable to open blasphemers such as Jews and Turks, who are outside the Church and to whom the Church has committed no office. This can be taken to mean that Melanchthon wishes hereby to exclude from objective validity only the administration of Word and Sacrament by those who are unbaptized or excommunicated. But why does he then add "to whom the Church has committed no ministry"? Lying behind these words is, at least, the notion that the objective validity of the functions of the office are also in some way dependent on the Church's call to the office. In all likelihood, this statement is rooted in the same train of thought which Melanchthon expresses in the Apology.

A further statement which points in this direction is found in his disputation *De autoritate ecclesiae et de dicto Augustini: Evangelio non crederem, etc.* [On the authority of the Church, and on the saying of Augustine: "I would not believe the Gospel," etc.] (from the year 1531?) which reads: "And we may use the Sacraments

---

[21] On this cf. G. Wehrung, "Zu Augustana VIII," *Zeitschr. f. syst. Theol.* (1937), p. 8.

[22] Op. cit., p. 54. — The well-known distortion of Ap 7.28, according to which the function alone is supposed to have any bearing on the validity of Word and Sacrament here ("when they give the Word of Christ or the Sacraments . . .") and the call of the Church is held to be irrelevant, is encountered, e.g., in R. Sohm (*Kirchenrecht* I, p. 503 n. 36). All too clearly, Sohm hints at the motive that brings him to this distortion; namely, he states that the other interpretation of the passage which hinges on the call of the Church is "a Catholic notion." Therefore, it cannot be considered! Sohm's antithesis is inaccurate: "It is not their office, but their word as such . . . that makes them representatives of Christ" (ibid.). Both are required: the right function and the legitimate call of the Church. The complete objective validity of the activity of the office results from *both*, even in the event of personal unworthiness. — Likewise, we must reject B. Schlunk's criticism (op. cit., p. 67) of Vilmar's explanation of Ap 7.28. Schlunk, too, disregards the phrase "on account of the call of the Church" and, from a false view of the office generally, judges it as if it were only existent "where and when it pleases God" (cf. above, p. 260 n. 113).

[23] CR 21:508.

if they are offered by wicked men who are in the ministry of the Church, unless they are openly blasphemous, such as Turks or Jews."[24] The Sacraments may be used (that is, they are objectively valid) with the "wicked who are in the ministry of the Church," who, being rightly called, possess the office. Here, too, the discussion concerns only those who are truly in the office.

As we consider this question in all these passages, we are led to ask in which sense "by reason of the *ordinationem* and *mandatum* of Christ" in AC 8 is actually meant.[25] It may first be assumed that *ordinatio* and *mandatum* denote simply the institution and appointment of Word and Sacrament by Christ, on the basis of which these are then objectively valid. Yet why is this idea omitted in the parallel passage of the Apology (7.28) and replaced by another about representing Christ "on account of the call of the Church"? In the other passage of the Apology which addresses AC 8—i.e., Ap 7.47 (*BKS* 246)—we similarly find only the argument for the efficacy of wicked men's Sacraments from the fact that the ministers represent Christ. The question arises whether AC 8 is even interpreted rightly in the sense indicated, and whether in this *ordinatio* and in this *mandatum* of Christ under discussion here, instead of strictly the institution of Word and Sacrament, we ought not more properly to see in addition the institution of the office and the commandment to appoint ministers, which is then actualized in the call, or ordination, of the Church. This would explain why Melanchthon, in the Apology, renders "*propter ordinationem et mandatum Christi*" as "*propter vocationem ecclesiae*." H. Asmussen reads the passage this way.[26] What Melanchthon says in the *Loci* generally on the objective validity of Word and Sacrament in opposition to the Donatistic error (CR 21:508f. and CR 21:840f.) is not in conflict with such an interpretation. In CR 21:508, the phrase "*propter mandatum et ordinationem divinam*" is taken up in accordance with AC 8, yet is found there—as we have seen—closely linked to the idea of the commission by the Church. In the subsequent text of this passage, it is evident that the efficacy of the ministry of wicked men is also argued (as in the Apology) from the presence of Christ in the ministers: "'He who hears you hears Me'; that is, the ministry is valid on account of Me,"[27] and shortly after that it says, "We owe obedience to that ministry, which we acknowledge to be a divinely ordained benefice of God, and on account of it tolerate even a less-than-suitable morality of ministers."[28] The presence of the office established by God (realized concretely through the call, of course) guarantees the objective validity of Word and Sacrament. When in the corresponding passage of the *Loci* of 1543 it reads: "It must be known that Gospel and Sacraments are efficacious on account of the promise of God, not on account of the person of the minister," it means that very promise that Christ will be present and active in the office-bearers (Luke 10:16) since Melanchthon continues: "Christ therefore calls

[24] CR 12:483.

[25] In the German text these words are absent.

[26] *Warum noch luth. Kirche*, p. 127.

[27] CR 21:509.

[28] Ibid.

back our minds and our faith from the person of the minister to Himself, saying . . . , 'He who hears you hears Me.' "[29]

The words "by reason of the institution and commandment of Christ" in AC 8 will in fact have to be explained in such a way as to refer not *only* to the institution of Word and Sacrament but *also* to the institution of the office connected to it and the legitimate call to the office coming from it. For Melanchthon, then, a valid public administration of the Sacraments requires not only obedience to the institution of the sacramental rite by Christ in the execution of the sacramental action but *also* obedience to the institution of the office appointed for the administration of the Sacrament and thus to the "command to appoint ministers." In other words, the presuppositions of the complete objective validity and effectiveness of the public administration of the Sacraments call for its being discharged by those who are "rightly called" (*rite vocati*). Of course, from this line of thinking, the doctrine of the necessity of the call to the office still receives particular emphasis.

Nevertheless, it is not possible to draw far-reaching conclusions from this. Melanchthon, in his anti-Donatistic argumentation for the objective validity of the means of grace, refers heavily to the "call of the Church" or to Christ's presence in the ministers grounded in the call. He also sees the "ordination of Christ" rooted in the objective validity of the means of grace as one with the institution of the office, but he would unquestionably avoid drawing from this the conclusion that a public function of Word and Sacrament by a noncalled person is void and ineffective. This would be at odds with his conception of the spiritual power residing intrinsically in the Gospel and the Sacraments, of the living, inherently potent voice of the Gospel which is not so bound to the office that it could not be effective extraordinarily outside of it and even contrary to the malice of a wicked man. The *fundamental idea* contained in the AC and the Apology as well as in the *Loci* is obviously that God has concretely instituted Word and Sacrament and established the office for that purpose, and so issued the command to confer the public function of Word and Sacrament on specific persons in the congregation through the particular call [*vocatio*], and that on the basis of this whole institutive and organizational activity of God, which is actualized in the particular call of the Church to the office and then in the particular living function of the office in Word and Sacrament, the Word and Sacrament are objectively valid and efficacious. The consequences which arise from this fundamental supposition are not, however, drawn out by Melanchthon. It is necessary to postulate two separate themes in Melanchthon standing tenuously side by side—that of the necessity of the call for the validity of the means of grace and that of the inherent potency of the Word and the Sacraments.[30]

---

[29] CR 21:840.

[30] If we were to lay as a foundation the aspect of the inherent potency of the Word and the Sacraments and the concomitant, automatic efficacy of Christ in the handling of Word and Sacrament treated rightly [*rite*], we would have to interpret the contrast (repeatedly emphasized in Melanchthon) that the means of grace are valid and efficacious "*on account of Christ*" (or "on account of the divine institution, the divine promise"), "*not on account of persons*" in such a way that not only is the moral character of the ministers explained as irrelevant to the validity of the means of grace but so is their actual relationship to the function performed by them, and thus whether they are called or not. Then, however, the recurring argumentation with Luke 10:16

2. The Direct and Indirect Call to the Office

Melanchthon distinguishes two kinds of call to the office: the *vocatio immediata* [direct call] and the *vocatio mediata* [indirect call]. In both kinds of call, the subject is the triune God. In the *vocatio immediata*, God calls directly; in the *vocatio mediata*, He uses specific men as intermediaries and calls through them.[31]

The direct call is only accorded to prophets and apostles. With His own voice the Son of God called these men, sent them and anointed them with the gifts of the Holy Spirit, and is efficacious through their office. It is also accompanied by manifest testimonies of the call, "nor does He wish such great things to be done in the Church without testimonies." The miraculous signs are particular revelations through which God discloses to others that the people in question are sent by Him (thus, e.g., the call of Samuel was demonstrated to Eli, and that of Paul to the Antiochian congregation).[32] The direct call of prophets and apostles is distinguished from the indirect one occurring today in the Church especially by the fact that it was not tied to a parish and that it was connected with the *donum inerrantiae* [gift of inerrancy].[33]

This direct call no longer occurs after the apostolic era. It is an Anabaptistic error to look for a direct call.[34] Now, the indirect call is the only call to the office of the Church. Without it, no one may function in the office of the Church.[35]

---

which speaks of the apostles as sent—which is to say, the office-bearers as called—and especially of the phrase "on account of the call of the Church" in Ap 7.28, would remain unintelligible. Also compare Melanchthon's teaching that God promises to be effective *through the ministry, in the ministry, through the ministers* (cf. above, pp. 256–60). The promise of God's efficacy through the functions of the office presupposes the sending to the office, the call to the office. This means that full efficacy, according to Melanchthon, is still only on the basis of the call. — It is worth noting that Melanchthon, in his *Responsiones ad impios articulos Bavaricae inquisitionis* [Responses to the wicked articles of the Bavarian Inquisition] (1558), in refutation of Article 18 ("Whether the consecration of the Sacrament is valid when done by those not ordained by bishops") does not—as might be suggested—respond that the Sacrament is valid of itself regardless of the minister's ordination, but argues that "the ordination of ministers of the Gospel in our churches is just" and that the Son of God without doubt is "efficacious in the ministry" established and sustained by Him. The confirmation by the Roman bishops is not necessary, but "it is enough that the election be performed by the church of his locality with the participation of one local bishop or several, in accordance with the Council of Nicaea" (*Stud. Ausg.*, vol. VI, pp. 301f.). This gives absolutely no suggestion that the call to the office was seen by Melanchthon as irrelevant to the validity of the functions of the office.

[31] CR 7:741; 12:379; 15:547; 15:1233f., 1298, 1331; 28:412.

[32] CR 15:1331f.; cf. CR 7:741.

[33] CR 15:547: "And in this place the apostolic call is to be distinguished diligently from the bishop's call. The apostle is called directly by Christ to teach the Gospel and has a sure testimony that his teaching is divine, and is sure that he has the Holy Spirit and does not err in teaching, and can teach in all churches everywhere. But the bishop is called through men to teach the Gospel in a certain place and can err, nor does he need to be certain that he has the Holy Spirit"; cf. CR 15:1233f., 1298; 21:1099f.

[34] CR 15:1333.

[35] CR 15:1333: "Where there is no prophetic and apostolic call, we should know that nowhere is the ministry of the Gospel to be entered without an indirect call"; cf. CR 7:742: ". . . Likewise, the

The *vocatio mediata*, however, is no less divine a call than the *vocatio immediata*, even if it happens through men, through the Church. God Himself wills that the office-bearers be called through *suffragatio humana* [vote of the people][36] and promises that the office of such persons indirectly called will be efficacious.[37] It is to be regarded as a "tremendous benefice of God that He has given men the right to call and approves it."[38] The external vocatory action in the indirect call is the testimony, the demonstration, that God has really issued the call to the office (as are the special miraculous signs in the direct call). In them, the person called can find assurance of the divine call to the office.[39] In the external call, God acts. He directs the human action of the vote,[40] anoints men with the Holy Spirit, lays His hands on them, blesses them, and sends them to the office that He might then work mightily through those thus called and gather for Himself an eternal Church through their performance of their office.[41] It should therefore be carefully noted that, in its essence, the indirect call through the Church agrees exactly with the direct call; through it, God calls to the office; only the *accidentia missionis* [nonessential details of the sending] differ.[42]

By this understanding of the *vocatio mediata* (*vocatio ecclesiae* [call of the Church]), the necessity of the particular call to the office is underscored. When God, by design and promise, permits Himself to be present and active in specific human actions in the capacity of calling and sending, the despising of God's gracious order of salvation can only be evaluated as a sacrilege, and the call is absolutely required by *divine* right before entry to the office.

3. The Concrete Entities of the Call

To the question who may issue the call to the ecclesiastical ministry, the answer in Melanchthon is primarily simply the Church.[43] The Church is the

---

condemnation is very harsh: 'They ran, and I did not send them'" (here related to lacking an indirect call). Cf. above, p. 284 n. 2.

36 CR 21:1100: "It is necessary to consider the testimonies which confirm the call performed through men, and they show that God desires ministers of the Gospel to be called by human vote and to be efficacious through them. Paul (Titus 1:5) directs Timothy to appoint presbyters in the cities in various places. And in 2 Timothy 2 (v. 2) it says, 'This is commended to faithful men who are able to teach others'"; cf. CR 7:741f.; 15:1332.

37 CR 7:741: "God desires that men be regularly called to the Evangelical ministry by the voice of the Church and affirms that the ministry is efficacious even when such men called indirectly through the Church function in it"; CR 15:1336; 28:412: ". . . and He approves the Church's election and in His great goodness is efficacious also through the sounding of the Gospel by those elected by the votes or in the name of the Church"; Ap 13.12 (*BKS* 294).

38 CR 12:490.

39 CR 7:741f.

40 CR 12:379.

41 CR 7:742; 23:xxxv.

42 Cf. above, pp. 257–58.

43 On the whole subject also, cf. pp. 343–48.

possessor of the *jus vocationis* [right of calling].[44] For this, Melanchthon exhibits several arguments.

1. Christ did not give the *Keys* to individual persons but—as Matt. 18:20 teaches—"principally and immediately" to the Church. If the Church, then, has the Keys "principally," it also "principally has the right of calling."[45] But the Church exists where the "pure doctrine" is believed and confessed (no matter by how many!). Where the true Church by this definition exists, there, too, is the right of calling.[46]

2. The true Church, according to 1 Pet. 2:9, has the *sacerdotium* [priesthood]. As a priestly people, it cannot be without the Gospel. Thus while the office itself may not proceed from the priesthood, the right to call to the office ministers of the church does. Of the true Church it may be said: "Since it alone has the priesthood, it certainly has the right of electing and ordaining ministers."[47]

3. Instituted for the true Church is the *ministerium Evangelii* [ministry of the Gospel], and God has promised always to give it shepherds and teachers (Ephesians 4). On this basis, the Church has the power and right to put people in the office given to her, and thus to issue the call [*vocatio*].[48]

4. The Church has God's command not only to proclaim the Gospel and to administer the Sacraments but also to call people directly to the office. "The Church has the *command to appoint ministers*."[49] Christ has "commanded the Church to call and ordain people itself."[50] Scripture commands the Church to guard itself against false teachers (Matt. 7:15; Gal. 1:9). "Therefore, since the Church has the command to reject wicked teachers, it also has the command

---

[44] CR 12:490: "First ... ordaining was Christ's; afterward, the right of calling and electing and ordaining ministers was given to the Church"; CR 4:349; 12:519; 21:505; Tr 67 (*BKS* 491). Cf. W. Maurer, *Pfarrerrecht u. Bekenntnis*, p. 139. — Not representative of Melanchthon is R. Sohm's position that the office is not given to the Church but only to individuals (*Kirchenrecht* I, pp. 500ff.), and it is not the Church which calls, *but* God (in this antithesis): "The 'conferral,' which the public preaching office ensures is, viewed spiritually, *not* a conferral but an approval, a testimony, an acknowledgment of the call given not by the congregation but by God: it is the congregation's *subordination*, from the duty of love, to the *God*-given charism" (ibid. p. 504). One has to ask why Melanchthon then speaks of a "call of the Church" at all. Is that meant only improperly? This is not easy to imagine. According to Melanchthon, the Church calls, and God works in this call of the Church. Only through this call does God's call actually reach the person so that he can be certain of it. Sohm sees the actual call to the office in the equipping for the office. But this is in no way Melanchthon's view. Cf. above, pp. 268–71.

[45] Tr 24 (*BKS* 478f.); cf. Tr 68 (*BKS* 491): "The Keys are given to the Church ..."; CR 21:505. Cf. W. O. Münter, *Begriff u. Wirklichkeit*, pp. 60ff.

[46] CR 21:505; 8:430.

[47] Tr 69 (*BKS* 491); CR 21:505.

[48] Tr 67 (*BKS* 491); CR 21:505; 8:430; 12:519: "Where the Church is, there it is necessary that the right ordination of minsters be since the ordination of ministers is properly among the gifts of the Church, according to Ephesians 4."

[49] Ap 13.12 (*BKS* 294).

[50] CR 23:xxxvi; further passages on this, cf. above, pp. 250–51 nn. 45–46.

to elect good teachers."[51] The command to call people to the office is closely connected with the command to handle the means of grace. Thus we encounter the following association of ideas in the Treatise: "Wherever the Church is, there is also the right to administer the Gospel. *Therefore*, the Church always has the right to call, elect, and ordain ministers."[52] This conclusion is rooted in the idea that the administration of the Gospel and the filling of the concrete office are integrally required and inextricably bound to each other.

This right of calling, granted for the reasons stated, is a perpetual, fundamental right of the Church, a "gift properly given to the Church, which no human authority can take from the Church."[53] This becomes clear especially in times of necessity. When the "bishops ordinary," the possessors of the power of ordination, become "enemies of the Gospel" and refuse to ordain capable people, or only do so on condition that they make certain unrighteous vows, then "the churches retain their right."[54] "Neither therefore is the universal Church extinguished, but the Church remains with us. Where the voice of the Gospel sounds, there also the ministry and right of election and of approval remains."[55] But the Church not only retains the right to elect and call ministers of the church itself when the bishops become heretical, but it is even *obligated* to do so by divine right.[56]

> Nevertheless, it should be kept in mind that Melanchthon is not thinking here of the Church as a pure congregation of laymen without any ministers, or even as opposed to office-bearers. In the referenced passages he is only postulating the event that the bishops fail, not the event that there are no more office-bearerers, as made clear especially in Tr 72.[57]

The Church is the proper possessor of the right of calling; Christ gave that right to it. But this is not saying anything specific about the concrete entities of the call. How, by whom, and through what entities does the Church call?

---

[51] CR 21:505; cf. CR 15:1335: (The true Church has the right of calling) "since 'appoint presbyters' is addressed to the true Church."

[52] Tr 67 (*BKS* 491).

[53] Ibid.; CR 12:519.

[54] Tr 66 (*BKS* 491); Tr 72 (*BKS* 492); CR 21:505. Note in Tr 66, 67, 72 the repeated use of the term "*retinere*" ("retain"). It underscores the character of the basic, inalienable right.

[55] CR 5:212; cf. CR 8:431.

[56] Tr 72 (*BKS* 492f.): "by divine right . . . are compelled"; cf. W. O. Münter, *Begriff u. Wirklichkeit*, p. 31 and p. 59.

[57] Tr 72 (*BKS* 492): "Therefore, when the bishops either become heretics or refuse to bestow ordination, by divine right the churches are compelled to ordain pastors and ministers, *making use of their own pastors*." Cf. Vilmar, *Lehre v. geistl. Amt*, pp. 90f. Likewise, W. Löhe, *Neue Aphorismen*, *Ges. Werke*, vol. V.1; p. 551: no injustice should be done to the Symbols "by limiting the Church to the laity, to the exclusion of the *ministerium*"; also p. 554. — Here we must contradict T. Harnack (*Die Kirche, ihr Amt, ihr Regiment*, p. 45), who in the Treatise wishes to see in the Church exercising the right of ordination not the Church together with its pastors but simply the congregation of believers. The event of a pure flock of laymen calling ministers to the office is not envisioned by the Treatise.

Melanchthon, in the pastoral letters (esp. on Titus 1:5; 1 Tim. 5:22; 2 Tim. 2:2), observed that, according to the New Testament, the apostle Paul commands the *office-bearers* Titus and Timothy to appoint presbyters. Here he finds scriptural testimony that, in the early Church, pastors were appointed by other pastors.[58] "Therefore, these apostles and pastors were calling other ministers."[59] This fact has exemplary significance for Melanchthon. He sees in Titus 1:5 a scriptural imperative for all ministers in the office to call new pastors where required.[60] And in 2 Tim. 2:2, the objective basis, in his view, is indicated for the calling of new ministers to the office to occur through available ministers of the Word: only they are able to undertake the doctrinal assessment through which the applicants' ability to teach others is determined.[61] For this reason we also find in the Treatise the significant expression "by divine right, churches are compelled to ordain pastors and ministers, making use of their own pastors."[62] And in the AC *Variata*, Melanchthon then appends the wording of Article 14 ("no one . . . unless rightly called"): "as Paul also commands Titus to appoint presbyters in the cities."[63] The "rightly called" thus includes the idea that the call is undertaken according to apostolic precedent by (higher-ranking) office-bearers.

Yet Melanchthon cannot therefore exclude the congregation, *the people* (= the laity), from the process of the call since the New Testament offers warnings to all Christians to guard themselves against false teachers, that is, not to admit unfaithful teachers but rather to ensure that there are good ones. Thus the whole congregation shares the responsibility for the call to the office. "Thus by ancient custom, authority to elect ministers came to the Church. . . ."[64] It is from this perspective that Melanchthon explains the call process, which was usual in the ancient Church and prescribed by the Council of Nicaea. "Histories and decrees testify that this was the custom: The people would hold an election, after which authority was given to a neighboring bishop, who approved the one

---

[58] CR 21:503: "This is why there is the testimony of Scripture that pastors are ordained by neighboring pastors, that is, the prefects for other churches"; cf. CR 21:850; 12:490; 5:211; 5:825; 3:471f.; 15:1333; 5:601; 20:653.

[59] CR 7:741.

[60] CR 12:490; 22:524.

[61] CR 15:1333: "It is fitting for godly teachers from the college of ministers of the Gospel to be involved for the sake of examining doctrine, about which command is clearly given to Timothy (2 Timothy 2)."

[62] Tr 72 (*BKS* 492). Cf. W. Maurer, op. cit., p. 113, on the passage "Only with orderly inclusion of appointed public ministers ('*adhibitis suis pastoribus*,' § 72) is the appointment of new ones to occur." — W. Kahl ("Rechtsinhalt . . . ," p. 336) thinks that the Treatise leaves open the question "how the Church should or may exercise its right of calling directly," and only tirelessly repeats "that it is done." But in Tr 72 he is able to discern a more refined provision on the manner of the call, namely: "making use of their own pastors."

[63] CR 26:360.

[64] CR 21:503; cf. CR 5:596.

elected."[65] The appointment of a bishop, as Melanchthon gathers from the words of Cyprian, was accompanied by the "vote of all the brotherhood and the assessment of the bishops who convened in their presence."[66] From this Melanchthon concludes that the call process is an action that takes place *with the cooperation of both the people and the bishops, the office and the congregation.*[67] The people choose; the office confirms. Here it is significant that it involves the bishops of the neighboring churches in which the Church as a whole is thus represented. A call is not the action of one (conceived, where possible, as independent) individual congregation, but of the Church as a whole.[68] In the cooperation of people and office, the church issues the call as the whole Church, as the Body of Christ. Such was Melanchthon's impression of the ancient Church.[69] Moreover, this example of the ancient Church always had normative significance for Melanchthon's own doctrine.

If we compare the current way of handling the call process with that of former times, the following picture is produced for Melanchthon: "Once there used to be this calling or election through the votes of the church, with the involvement of a certain bishop or pastor for the sake of examining doctrine. . . . Now the calling is done by prominent members of the church, such as, in cities, through the council with the involvement of certain of the college of ministers of

---

[65] CR 21:503; cf. CR 15:1333; 22:524f.: "It should be further known that for many hundreds of years since the time of the apostles, the Church has retained the custom of electing priests and laymen from all estates as bishops through the assembly of the prominent persons who confessed faith in Christ and behaved worthily, and to that end two or three bishops from the closest cities were summoned, who heard the doctrine of this elected person and confirmed him accordingly. The congregation had to choose and submit their vote, but the summoned bishops inspected his doctrine and observed the ceremonies of the confirmation with the laying on of hands, as has been stated"; Tr 13ff. (*BKS* 475f.); Tr 70 (*BKS* 491f.): "formerly, the people elected pastors and bishops. Then they were joined by the bishop either of their church or a neighboring one, who by the laying on of hands confirmed the man elected."

[66] CR 21:504. W. O. Münter, in interpreting this passage of Cyprian—which is, of course, often cited by Melanchthon—pointed out that here two possibilities exist for interpretation: (1) the congregation assists the election only while the bishops themselves perform the action of the vote in the presence of the people; (2) the congregation also actively takes part in the election through the suffrage of the whole brotherhood. Münter thinks that Melanchthon, in the Treatise, leaves both interpretive possibilities free (*Begriff u. Wirklichkeit*, p. 71). It is possible to endorse him. What is essential is the coparticipation of the office.

[67] Cf. W. Maurer, op. cit., p. 140. — T. Kliefoth (*Lit. Abhandlungen* I, pp. 349ff.) described this as a mark of the Lutheran doctrine of appointing the office. In Rome, the office is filled by the office alone; in the Reformed Church the office is excluded and the congregation alone issues the call. According to Lutheran doctrine, the call comes from the whole Church, that is, in its divisions, "through the organization of the Church" (op. cit., p. 355). While in Melanchthon we do not find the formulation that the *whole* Church is obliged unconditionally to undertake the call, it really amounts to the same thing when he calls for the participation of the office as well as of the rest of the congregation.

[68] Cf. W. Maurer, op. cit., p. 138.

[69] Cf. CR 3:184; 4:698; 8:431.

the Gospel."[70] Already in the ancient Church, as Melanchthon notes, there was movement away from having a vote of the *whole* congregation. This was because of tumults and riots on various occasions during the people's oral vote for the calling of a bishop, which resulted in the "vote being restricted to fewer men."[71] Certain men appointed by the congregation, especially prominent persons, then undertook the vote[72] while the bishops confirmed it. And this, then, is how it was conducted: the most prominent ones, the "leading members of the congregation [*praecipua membra ecclesiae*]," perform the vote in the name of the whole congregation, and the ministers examine and confirm the one chosen.[73]

By *praecipua membra ecclesiae*, Melanchthon is thinking particularly of the princes or, in cities, of the senates and city councils (magistrates).[74] A Christian government has, according to Melanchthon, a right in two respects to cooperate in the call process: first, as a member of the governing estate (*quia praesunt* [because they preside]), who is obliged according to God's will to ensure that in his realm the ministry of the Gospel is rightly appointed; and, second, as the most conspicuous member of the church (*quia sunt praecipua membra ecclesiae* [because they are prominent members of the church]).[75] If a city senate issues a call, it does not depend, according to Melanchthon, on how many people in the senate pronounce the call, but that those do it who have the *praecipua autoritas* [chief authority] and are members of the congregation to which the respective person is to be called.[76]

---

[70] CR 15:1333; cf. CR 7:742: "In histories we read the call or election . . . was made by the vote of the whole multitude. This was accompanied by the election or call, which now happens through the prominent members of the church, through the princes, senate, with the involvement of the ministers of the Gospel, that they might be inspectors of doctrine." The latter must therefore be present for the inspection of doctrine. Also cf. CR 21:503.

[71] CR 15:1333.

[72] In other passages, Melanchthon views the call process of the ancient Church from the outset as consisting of an election held not by the whole multitude but only by selected, especially suited persons, "to whom the church had committed the matter" (CR 21:503). Cf. CR 3:184: ". . . The regular call was such that the people—that is, the prominent among the people—consecrated a preacher and bishop with the consent of the others"; CR 3:471f.; CR 4:698: "for long ago the election was conducted by the prominent among the people and by the authorities"; CR 5:210: "through the people, that is, honorable persons in all stations"; CR 5:596: "It is known that it was usual for the church—that is, honorable and God-fearing persons of all stations—to call and elect bishops"; CR 12:490.

[73] CR 15:1333f.; 12:379.

[74] E.g., Tr 54 (*BKS* 488); CR 5:210.

[75] CR 5:210f.; cf. CR 5:585. It is worth noting Stahl's (*Die Kirchenverfassung*, p. 195) observation: "By 'prominent member of the church,' Melanchthon is referring to the princes, not as the highest member of the ordered church but only as the highest member of the lay congregation (*reliquae ecclesiae* [rest of the church]), in contrast to the shepherds—not as church rulers, but only as the foremost congregant." R. Sohm confirms this (*Kirchenrecht* I, p. 567 n. 37). — A compilation of the duties of authorities relating to the church according to Melanchthon is found in W. Thomas, op. cit., pp. 39ff. Authorities are obliged (1) to put aside ungodly worship and foster pure doctrine; (2) to use good ministers of the Word to ensure that subjects are instructed rightly in the pure doctrine, to remove bad pastors, to rebuke blasphemers, and to compel church attendance; and (3) to protect the goods of the church (citation in Thomas).

[76] CR 5:211.

When a patron issues a call—right of patronage is expressly acknowledged by Melanchthon—he must first hear from the prominent men of the congregation.[77] It is the duty of patrons (as it is generally of those who exercise the right of the call) to make sure that in the church idolatry is eliminated and the office of the pure doctrine is established.[78]

The concrete entities of the call are, according to Melanchthon, the same as in the ancient Church: people and office, the congregation (or its prominent members [*praecipua membra*]) and the ministers of the Word (*ministri Evangelii*)[79]—and here the stress for Melanchthon is clearly on the office. The office has the main responsibility for the office in the Church,[80] even if the rest of the congregation always retains the right to refuse unsuitable or impious pastors.[81] For the office, God has committed primarily to the bishops, yet also to all pastors, the calling of capable persons to the office wherever needed.[82] If this responsibility is invested in the office by divine command, that office also bears chief responsibility in the appointment of the office by divine right. And when it says in Tr 72: "by divine right the churches are compelled to ordain pastors and ministers, making use of their own pastors," this is safely applied "by divine right" to the words "making use of their own pastors" as well.[83] This is confirmed by a statement of Melanchthon's in his disputation *De politia Ecclesiae seu ministerio et ordinationibus* [On church polity or ministry and ordinations]: "The right of calling and electing ministers does not belong strictly to the people, but Paul orders Titus to appoint presbyters, and to Timothy he writes: 'Lay hands hastily on no man.' Therefore, it is necessary that pastors be ordained by pastors. And by ancient custom the Church, that is, those to whom the Church committed the matter, held an election, and to this was added the judgment and approval of the ordaining bishop. Mob rule [δημοκρατία], in which the people seize the vote

---

77 CR 4:544.

78 CR 7:510.

79 Cf. the judgment of the episcopal election of Naumburg: choice by patron, nobility, city councils (= congregation), public ordination with prayer and laying on of hands "through certain preachers" (CR 4:698); cf. CR 3:471f.

80 Cf. above, pp. 264–66: "the right of calling as an element of the ecclesiastical power of the bishops."

81 CR 4:544; 15:1334: "Afterward it is proper for churches to assess the one elected or called because if the church should learn that he does not believe rightly, it could reject the call, but when it determines that he believes rightly, it confirms the calling."

82 CR 5:601: "First, it is known among them themselves that God commanded the bishops, above all, rightly to appoint the preaching office, either through themselves or others. . . . Therefore, the bishops, in their chapters [*Stift*] and dominions, are to ordain God-fearing, learned men who teach rightly"; CR 5:825: "Let this ordained man know that he is commanded by the voice of the apostle in this function to ordain priests to teach and govern the churches . . ."; CR 22:524: "From this command (Titus 1:5) it is clear that, wherever preachers and ministers are needed and desired, true ministers are commanded to ordain capable persons for those churches and to confirm them with the laying on of hands and prayer. . . . And the command of St. Paul to Titus to appoint priests applies not only to those [with the] title of bishops but also belongs to all Christian ministers."

83 Also compare the links to the previous statements in Tr 70f. (*BKS* 491f.).

for themselves without the judgment and approval of pastors, militates against divine right and the ancient Church."[84] From this there can be no doubt that, according to Melanchthon, bishops or pastors (in any case, office-bearers) must by divine right take part in the call process without infringing on the people's right to vote or call to the office.[85] The latter Melanchthon does not wish to see omitted under any circumstances; the call is not to be done without at least the congregation's consent.

The question regarding the entities of the call, then, is directly related to the other question about the elements of the call process. Thus we are brought to the next subject of our study.

4. The Elements of the Call

The call is a complex process.[86] Melanchthon names as its two principal components the call to the ministry of the Gospel and the public approval of this

---

[84] CR 12:490 (year not given). Cf. R. Sohm, *Kirchenrecht* I, pp. 523ff.

[85] Here it is necessary to expand on the statements of W. O. Münter (*Begriff u. Wirklichkeit*, pp. 61ff.), who thinks that while the true Church, according to the doctrine of the Confessions, is the possessor of the right of appointing the office, it is not possible to name a concrete entity for the exercise of this right: "Aside from the divine right of appointing the office, which belongs to the Church, the separate expression of this right in all phases remains a matter of human right" (p. 65). It is correct that "specified office-bearers in distinction to the lay congregation" or "laymen in contrast to the office-bearers" or "a firmly defined local congregation" or "a provincial or territorial church" could not be named as the agent of the call process *jure divino* (p. 65). But from the provisions of the Treatise, it is possible to conclude that, according to Melanchthon, the call must take place by cooperation between the people and the office, and that this has divine right (Tr 65, *BKS* 490: "Ordination administered by a pastor in his own church is valid by divine right"; Tr 72, *BKS* 492: "making use of their own pastors"). This is only made clear, however, by consulting other passages of Melanchthon's writings (thus, e.g., CR 12:490). Münter's proof suffers somewhat under his failure to interpret the propositions of the Treatise against the background of the overarching Melancthonian teaching, which is understandable in that it only concerns the Confessions. But even regardless of this, it is incomprehensible that he so entirely misses the phrase "making use of their own pastors" in Tr 72—indeed, even thinks that Tr 72 only deals with a lay congregation (p. 64), which is patently false. Münter depends too much on the German text of the Treatise in which these words are omitted, but which—as is also apparent in this passage—has a spiritualistic tinge. If we appraise it hermeneutically in favor of the Latin text, it makes it impossible to relate "*de jure divino*" to "*adhibitis suis pastoribus* [making use of their own pastors]" also. Yet the question is whether the German text can be appealed to hermeneutically, at least if we are trying to determine what Melanchthon wished to say in the Latin text, since the German "translation" comes from another's hand. — W. Löhe says of the Confessions (probably regarding these passages from the Treatise in particular): "In dealings with the Roman bishops, they are always merely defending the call issued by pastors as the last resort, nothing more" (*Neue Aphorismen*, *Ges. Werke*, vol. V.1, p. 551).

[86] The term "vocatio" is used by Melanchthon both for referring to the total call process (CR 7:741; 12:490; 15:1333; 21:503f.) and, in the narrower sense, for the call and nomination of the person by the congregation or its prominent members, and so for the first part of the total call process (CR 5:210; 21:850). — On the entire issue around the elements of the call, also cf. below, pp. 345–46.

call and says that both parts are arranged by the command of the Gospel.[87] For him, these two chief elements of call (or election) and approval (or coapproval) are prescribed by the use of the ancient Church.[88] In referring to the right of calling, the expressions "right of calling and ordaining"[89] or "right of electing and ordaining"[90] (or even "right of calling, electing, and ordaining")[91] are heard.[92] Yet Melanchthon also divides the call process more minutely and enumerates additional components of the call, designating these, too, as by divine right.

In his *Commentary on 1 Timothy* (1541), Melanchthon states that the election of the person through the prominent members of the church must be followed by the examination of doctrine, in which, in accordance with 2 Tim. 2:2, it is determined by other ministers whether the person in question is capable and suited to the teaching office. Then the elected and examined person is to be presented to the congregation so that it has the opportunity to object in the event that it knows, e.g., whether there is any hindrance. Finally, prayer is also to be included.[93] Enumerated as "necessary elements in the ordination" (meaning here the total call process) are: the call to the ministry, examination of doctrine, presentation of the called person to the church, approval of the call, and prayer.[94] Melanchthon counts all these parts as *jure divino*.[95]

Melanchthon also describes the elements of the call process exhaustively in his *Sententia de ordinatione Ecclesiae ministrorum* [Opinion on the ordination of church ministers] (1551).[96] There, by use of Titus 1:5 and 1 Tim. 5:22, he identifies for the first time how the call process was handled in the apostolic era: "The apostles themselves and pastors called . . . other ministers, and with the customary sign, the laying on of hands, declared the call that it might be more sure to the one

[87] CR 21:850 (with an appeal to Titus 1:5).

[88] CR 5:211; cf. CR 3:184; 4:698; 8:431; Tr 70 (*BKS* 491f.).

[89] CR 8:430.

[90] CR 12:489; Tr 67 (*BKS* 491); Tr 72 (*BKS* 492).

[91] Tr 67 (*BKS* 491).

[92] W. O. Münter thinks the terms *vocare*, *eligere*, and *ordinare* were used in the Confessions interchangeably for the same thing—namely, the appointment and call to the office—and thus did not designate different elements of the call process (*Begriff u. Wirklichkeit*, pp. 65ff.). This is basically right insofar as all three terms may also be used for the total process. But when they appear together, connected with an "*et*" ["and"], a reference to the various elements of the total call process is clearly being expressed. It cannot be overlooked either that Melanchthon is guided in his thinking by the example of the ancient Church, according to which the people and the bishops are responsible for different actions: the people for the election, the bishops for the confirmation (ordination), as, of course, is explicitly referenced in Tr (14 and 70) on the basis of this ancient model. It is in no way the case that the term "*ordinatio*" in Melanchthon refers to just any kind of call. Rather, when Melanchthon uses this term for the call he is always thinking of the kind of call to which the specific, liturgical ordination act belongs as its essential component. Cf. e.g., Tr 65 (*BKS* 490): "ordination performed by the pastor in his own church."

[93] CR 15:1333f.

[94] CR 15:1335.

[95] CR 15:1334: "In this ancient usage it must be seen which parts are necessary and by divine right. . . ."

[96] CR 7:740ff.

called and made known to the church."[97] Again, the two principal parts are plainly noted: the call and the public declaration or confirmation of the call. On the latter part, Melanchthon says, "The church must demonstrate the call so that it is manifest, either with words or with some kind of sign. To these called men also it is very advantageous to know their call and to have clear testimonies of the call. . . ."[98] The public confirmation of the call is regarded as a "clear testimony of the call," which fulfills the twofold purpose of giving assurance to the congregation, as well as to the called man himself, that he is truly called and can now bear the office in the name of God. Then Melanchthon comes to the use of the ancient Church, and the current use based on it, in order to establish: "This call, embracing the very nomination or election of the person, the inspection of doctrine, the attestation before the church, and the prayer, is really the ordination referred to here, which God wishes to be carried out by men in the church."[99] He explicitly emphasizes: "These things which I have said, I have no doubt, are all by divine right—calling, examination of doctrine, attestation before the church, and prayer."[100] The "attestation before the church" corresponds to the approval or coapproval of the call; it is above all a testifying by the other office-bearers that the ordinand has the true doctrine,[101] and it may be performed verbally or by a rite.[102]

In a *letter to Christoph Fischer from November 1, 1555*, Melanchthon writes: "We must distinguish and retain the things that are necessary and by divine right, such as the call and examination, publication of the approval, the prayer. . . ."[103] The components of the call process here described as by divine right are the same as those which we have already met before, only instead of *approbationis vocationis* [approval of the call], here it says *publicatio approbationis* [publication of the approval]. Yet the same process is intended since the approval of the call is always conceived by Melanchthon as the public act (which also plays into the concept of *testificatio* [attestation]).

To summarize our findings, we may state that Melanchthon either emphasizes two principal components of the total call process—namely, call and approval (coapproval, declaration) of the call—or else refers to four parts: (1) the call; (2) inspection (exploration) of doctrine (examination); (3) public approval of the call (which includes the "presentation of the called to the church"), which is to say, the attestation before the church or public approval; and (4) the prayer. Melanchthon quite unambiguously teaches the *jus divinum* for all four parts.[104]

---

[97] CR 7:741.

[98] CR 7:741.

[99] CR 7:742.

[100] CR 7:742.

[101] Cf. CR 3:184: ". . . that the elected person may have testimony of his doctrine, as also Paul gives charge to Titus"; CR 4:489: "We approve the ancient Church's custom of ordinands being first examined and instructed, and, with public testimony of certain godly and learned men who preside in the churches, being admitted to the ministry"; also cf. CR 4:503.

[102] CR 7:742.

[103] CR 8:597.

[104] W. Thomas wants to confine the *jus divinum* in Melanchthon to the call in the narrower sense: "Only the call can be by divine right in the full sense of the word" (op. cit., p. 17). On the one

A good deal of importance, according to Melanchthon, falls to the *exploration of doctrine*, the *examination*.[105] The Roman Church's ordination is sharply censured because they ordain "uncouth donkeys" and "admit to the priesthood anyone indiscriminately."[106] "Although the bishops keep the ceremonies of ordination, nevertheless, for all their keeping of them, it is obvious that no true examination, no true instruction, occurs there, and they fill the world with unlearned, reckless, ungodly priests. . . ."[107] Appointing the office rightly requires "inquiry into morals, vocation, and doctrine."[108] The bishops are not to be "unexamined" men, but are to be investigated with regard to "behavior and doctrine,"[109] and ordination is "to be conducted with proper examination and instruction."[110] It is an absolutely necessary part of the call that the ordinands be "questioned and instructed thoroughly."[111] And of utmost importance to this end are schools,

---

hand, he is aware that Melanchthon teaches a *jus divinum* for other parts of the total call process (examination, approval, prayer) (cf. p. 20: "The aforementioned approval or ordination is defined by Melanchthon in various instances to be necessarily *jure divino*"; also pp. 24f.). Yet he argues against Melanchthon meaning this "*jure divino*" in the strict sense and interprets it as follows: "By this he only wished to say . . . that, '*non temere* [not to worry],' the confirmation on the part of other bishops or pastors may be omitted . . ." (pp. 20f.) He claims that the approval is necessary for Melanchthon only because it is "of great value for the tranquility of the mind" (p. 21). The supporting passages cited by Thomas are, however, not conclusive for this (it cannot be deduced from CR 5:210f. that Melanchthon regards the call or election *alone* as necessary; the passage CR 3:184f. finds the rationale of the propriety of exercising the office not only in the congregational call but also and explicitly in the testimony of right doctrine given by other possessors of the preaching office; in CR 12:490f., pastors' judgment and approval is plainly taught as required *de jure divino*). Thus Thomas's stance on Melanchthon's statements about the *jus divinum* of all four parts of the total call process which we have indicated remains unsatisfactory. Also cf. below, p. 343 n. 170. — Likewise dubious is W. O. Münter's assessment: "The call is the central thing, and the Church is in duty bound to execute it regularly *jure divino*. According to the Lutheran Confession, its execution in the election and ordination, and thus in the rite of the call, is left open to the freedom of human arrangement" (*Begriff und Wirklichkeit*, p. 65). In view of the teaching of the AC, its Apology, and the Treatise, such may not be said, especially when these are viewed against the background of other Melanchthonian expressions on the subject, such as those encountered here and in the previous excerpt. Cf. above, p. 298 n. 85.

105 Cf. W. Thomas, op. cit., p. 19: "Thus for Melanchthon the examination is the chief matter in ordination." Even if this formulation appears too strong, yet it is certain that the examination before ordination is tremendously important for Melanchthon. — For the examination, Melanchthon composed his *Examen ordinandorum* [Examination of ordinands] in 1552, which was included in the Mecklenburg church order of 1552 (cf. G. Rietschel, *Luther u. d. Ordination*, p. 81).

106 Ap 28.3 (*BKS* 397).

107 CR 5:601f.; cf. CR 4:533; 4:543f.; 5:614; 7:175; 7:742; 20:653.

108 CR 23:xxxvi; cf. CR 12:380f.

109 CR 4:544, 547; cf. CR 4:489.

110 CR 5:601.

111 CR 7:34; 6:934; 4:689: "Truly, ordination must not be a ceremony only, but high necessity demands an incisive examination and that instruction be given for a few weeks to some who are undistinguished"; CR 8:290.

where the ordinands may be trained for their office.[112] "In our churches," says Melanchthon, "diligent examinations and investigations of their doctrine and life are carried out first, and once they are acknowledged as being fit for it, they are ordained in the church before the whole congregation. . . ."[113] The inquiry into the ordinand's doctrine and the testimony to his orthodoxy during ordination also mean that the examining or ordaining minister possesses the duties of inspection and visitation and thus of further supervision with respect to doctrine and life. Melanchthon was always sensitive to the objective bond between ordination and visitation.[114] —

We must now discuss a specific problem already touched upon—what Melanchthon meant precisely by "*rite vocatus* [*duly called*]" in Article 14 of the Augsburg Confession.

AC 14 is to be viewed against the background of the situation in 1530. It was not yet clear how the Roman bishops would act toward the Evangelicals. For their part, at least, the Evangelicals were ready to grant the bishops their jurisdiction, and with it the ordaining of Evangelical ministers, if they would for their part cease raging against the Gospel. This readiness (and the distinct desire that things would be ruled in this way!) was also present in the composition and presentation of the Augsburg Confession and found its documentation above all in Article 28.[115] Thus Article 14, by "*rite vocatus*," cannot mean something that the canonical ordination by the Roman bishops excludes. This is a foregone conclusion. The phrase "*rite vocatus*" is, in any case, to be construed as to allow for canonical episcopal ordination.

On the other side, however, it is also clear that by the word "*rite*" there was no desire to commit oneself absolutely to the canonical (thus episcopal) ordination as the only possibility given in *jus divinum*. It cannot be denied that there is a

---

112 CR 11:327: "Therefore, schools are needed for the ministry of the Gospel and are a chief part of that most holy duty; for it is necessary, first, to give long and diligent instruction to those to whom the governance of the churches is to be committed."

113 CR 28:524. In a treatise of the Wittenberg theologians (authored by Melanchthon but also signed by Luther, [Johann] Bugenhagen, and [Caspar] Cruciger), the two Pomeranian dukes, Barnim and Philip, who wished to make the young count of Eberstein the bishop of Cammin, are urgently warned against this undertaking. Through passages in the Pastoral Epistles, earnest command is given to choose a person "who is able to perform the office personally" (CR 5:383). What is said subsequently has validity not only specifically for the episcopal office but also generally for the pastoral office: "And no one may, without sin, endorse the naming or election of a person whom he knows to be far from capable for the office and too unstudious to become capable of preaching, teaching, silencing adversaries of the Gospel with the truth of Holy Scripture and defending the pure doctrine, and exercising other churchly offices, etc. For this commandment in St. Paul's writings is not to be put aside and discounted as words which were only said for the sake of appearance, but they are earnest, divine commands, the despising of which is punished with eternal wrath and with temporal afflictions should someone continue in that sin . . ." (CR 5:383f.).

114 CR 4:533f.: "Neither should bishops think that they have fulfilled their duty when they admit the ordained, but after that let them also be inspectors of doctrine and morals, as we shall say below concerning visitation and synods"; CR 5:825f.; 5:601; 6:934: "Likewise, let a diligent oversight of the doctrine and morals of the priests also be performed afterward"; CR 7:34; 23:xxxvi.

115 AC 28.71ff. (*BKS* 131f.).

certain vagueness and universality associated with the phrase "*rite vocatus*" which allows for a certain amount of interpretation. The composers of the Confutation also naturally felt this and requested that "*rite vocatus*" be defined more precisely as follows: "that 'rightly called' ought to be understood according to the form of the law, in accordance with the sanctions and decrees of the Church observed everywhere in the Christian world until this day."[116] Melanchthon, in the Apology, repeats this demand of the Confutation, saying, ". . . They accept it, yet on condition that we employ canonical ordination."[117] Note that by "canonical ordination" he means ordinations by properly consecrated *bishops* in compliance with the canons. Elaborating on the idea of episcopal ordination, he manifests there in the Apology, Article 14, the ardent desire, already frequently expressed in Augsburg, to maintain the church polity and the ranks in the Church, even though made by human authority.[118] In other words, it is his wish and that of the Evangelicals that the episcopal structure of the Church, and with it canonical episcopal ordination, remain intact, even though this rests only on human right. The grades, which are made by human authority, of which Melanchthon speaks here, are the ranks or degrees of the office, primarily the rank of bishop-presbyter. The ordination by bishops instead of by pastors rests only on human authority (yet is by no means to be discounted for that reason) and is not prescribed *jure divino* like the immutable ordering of the Church. Yet the Evangelicals seek most earnestly to preserve it. But if this "canonical polity, which we greatly desired to maintain," is in some places dissolved—that is, if episcopal ordination is no longer retained—the blame and responsibility for this lies exclusively with the Roman bishops themselves, who either compel our priests to renounce the doctrine which they confess—and this "Confession is true, godly, and catholic"—or even murder them.[119] If the bishops would cease "to rage against our churches," our pastors would allow our priests to be ordained by them according to canonical ordination. But if they do not, we would nevertheless know that the Church is among those "who teach the Word of God aright and administer the Sacraments rightly, and not with those who not only by their edicts endeavor to efface God's Word but also put to death those who teach what is right and true."[120] The true Church is with those who teach purely and administer the Sacraments rightly, that is, with the "Evangelical ministers,"[121] who are then authorized *jure divino* to call others to the office and to ordain them. This is the true sense of the Apology, Article 14, the purpose of which is to define the wording of AC 14, and thus "*rite vocatus*," more precisely

116 CR 27:114f.

117 Ap 14.1 (*BKS* 296).

118 Ibid.

119 Ap 14.2 (*BKS* 297).

120 Ap 14.4 (*BKS* 297).

121 The opposing view [that] "the Church is among those who teach the Word of God rightly and administer the Sacraments rightly, and not with those who not only by their edicts endeavor to efface God's Word but also put to death those who teach what is right and true," shows quite clearly that for Melanchthon the issue here is the Evangelical ministers ("*rite vocati*")—others are not to teach or administer the Sacraments publicly, as stated in AC 14!—in contrast to the Roman bishops. That the Church is bound to the Roman bishops *jure divino* is disputed, but that it is bound to the ecclesial ministry generally is not disputed in the least.

in contrast to the Confutation. While the raging of the Roman bishops makes it impossible for us to receive canonical ordination by *bishops*, ordination through Evangelical ministers who teach purely and administer the Sacraments rightly remains valid as *jure divino* since wherever the pure ministry of the Word and Sacraments is, the true Church also is. Thus anyone ordained by an Evangelical minister of God's Word is "*rite vocatus* [duly called]," not only those who have been ordained by the bishops ordinary.

The train of thought in Apology, Article 14, eventually leads to what Melanchthon teaches in Tr 60ff.: The distinction of bishop-presbyter is not *de jure divino* so that ordination by pastors is sanctioned *jure divino*,[122] and congregations are obliged to ordain new ministers to the office, making use of their own pastors, when the bishops ordinary either become "heretics or refuse to bestow ordination."[123]

If we accordingly consider AC 14 from the perspective of this statement in Apology 14 and in the Treatise, it is clearly evident that "*rite vocatus*" makes no allowance for anything beyond episcopal (canonical) ordination and simple ordination by pastors. Thus taking "*rite vocatus*" as its actual content (comprising the divine right for the call of the Church), we may note the following two points: (1) a proper call is always at its core a (liturgical) ordination rite; and (2) being a liturgical ordination rite, it is to be executed at least by ministers of the Word (whether bishops or pastors). Yet it further carries the tendency (*jure humano*, but not therefore irrelevant) that ordination is, whenever possible, to be performed by the bishops (in the sense of canonical ordination). The "*rite*" without question contains a reference to the liturgical ordination rite and at the same time to the order valid in the Church, and finally also to the *ordo ecclesiasticus* itself, to which the governance of the Church properly belongs and under which concept the whole Article 14 of the Augsburg Confession is subsumed. These connections first become readily apparent through the clarification of AC 14 encountered in Ap 14 and are also powerfully confirmed through the phrase added by Melanchthon in the AC *Variata* (1540) to the earlier words: "as Paul commands Titus to appoint presbyters in the cities."[124] The addition, contrary to misinterpretations, expresses even more clearly the original intention of the "*rite vocatus*" in AC 14 as already expounded in Ap 14.[125] Such an interpretation of AC 14 is in harmony with the other statements about the call which we have found in Melanchthon.

---

[122] Tr 65 (*BKS* 490)

[123] Tr 66 and 72 (*BKS* 491f.).

[124] CR 26:360.

[125] Vilmar says of this addition: "It was actually contained very simply already in the words '*rite vocatus*'" (*Lehre v. geistl. Amt*, p. 75) and "As Paul had presbyters appointed through Titus, so also among us shepherds are appointed by shepherds" (ibid.). — P. Brunner explains the addition in the *Variata* by reference to the altered situation of the Church, but understands it as a demand for ordination through office-bearers, namely, through Evangelical bishops ("Vom Amt d. Bischofs," p. 20 n. 17).

The vagueness of the expression "*rite vocatus*" in AC 14, and the fact that it plainly allows for some interpretation, has of course been amply noted.[126] *W. O. Münter* thought that, by "*rite vocatus*," ordination as a particular act of sacramental consecration was to be deliberately removed from its peculiar position and "that, for the Lutheran confession, the concern is no longer performance, but the regular call," for which reason in the Apology, too, the term "ordination" is displaced by the terms "appointment" and "election." These are supposed to designate "the Church's divinely commanded conferral through which the order of the ministry of the Word is provided for while ordination as an individual act of human design recedes."[127] For the content of "*rite vocatus*" in AC 14, Münter will only allow "that the Church has the power of the regular call *jure divino*, from which it follows that he who is '*rite vocatus*' has been called by the Church—no matter whether by office-bearers in the context of the church polity made by human authority or by the lay congregation, and no matter the rite."[128] Much, however, may be brought forward in contradiction of this view. There cannot really be any discussion of a displacement of the term "ordination" by the terms "election" and "appointment" in Ap 13.7ff. (esp. in the Latin text). On the contrary, the emphasis there is on a liturgical ordination since it endorses both a ritual component of the ordination process, the laying on of hands appointed for the total call process, and the designation of this as "a sacrament" under the proviso that the ordination is an ordination to the preaching office.[129] This would be unthinkable if the tendency in Ap 13 were to push the liturgical act of ordination in the total call process into the background. Further, Münter betrays a misunderstanding of the statements regarding church polity or canonical polity in Ap 14 when he opines that Melanchthon there means to place not only the ordination by bishops but also generally the ordination by office-bearers, by ministers of the Word, in the sphere of a church polity existing merely *jure humano*, and so to justify an ordination by the bare lay congregation as remaining within the boundaries drawn by the *jus divinum*. Yet, as we have already mentioned several times, Melanchthon only wishes to designate the *grades* in the Church, and thus the ranks of the office, as made by human authority and therefore not absolutely binding in matters of ordination, and consequently only to maintain the right to pastoral ordination over against episcopal ordination.[130] A fundamental aversion to a particular sacramental act

[126] Cf. e.g., B. W. Trillhaas, op. cit., p. 502; F. K. Schumann, "Amt d. Kirche u. Berufung zum Amt," op. cit., p. 311; H. Asmussen, *Warum noch lutherische Kirche*, pp. 182f., 184; P. Brunner, "Vom Amt des Bischofs," p. 20 n. 17; W. Maurer, *Pfarrerrecht und Bekenntnis*, p. 123 n. 58.

[127] *Begriff und Wirklichkeit*, p. 65.

[128] Ibid.

[129] Ap 13.12 (*BKS* 293f.).

[130] Nothing in the AC or Apology indicates the possibility of an ordination or call by the laity. In the Treatise, the only passage which might possibly be construed this way would be Tr 68 (*BKS* 491). Yet this would only work if the sentence were understood not merely as justification for the laity's right to emergency Baptism and emergency Absolution (which is the subject under discussion immediately before) but also as further justification for the congregation's right to call. But even then it is doubtful whether the provision that the Keys of the Church are given not only to specific persons (in accordance with Christ's saying in Matt. 18:20: "Where two or three," etc.) will not

of consecration is out of the question since Melanchthon explicitly testifies that the Evangelicals would most earnestly like to see the canonical polity preserved, and with it canonical ordination. As Münter overlooks the phrase "making use of their own pastors" in Tr 72 (cf. above, p. 298 n. 85), he also ignores here the fact that this is concerned with the problem of *episcopal* ordination (i.e., ordination by a bishop instead of only by a presbyter). There is in Münter a statement which appears to validate our understanding of AC 14 and Ap 14: "As evident from Apology 14, the thinking in Augsburg (AC 14) concerns a regular call by the episcopal church leadership as by a government exalted by human authority. . . ."[131] Here Münter admits that the "*rite vocatus*" of AC 14 was thought of in very concrete terms with respect to canonical ordination, and it would follow properly from his observation that, according to Ap 14, only the ordination through bishops specifically instead of through a presbyter is characterized as established by human authority, but not the ordination generally through ministers of the Word instead of through the lay congregation. However, Münter does not proceed to draw this conclusion but sticks to the interpretation of Ap 14 that the Church (instead of the bishops) undertakes the ordination *jure divino*.[132] —

P. Brunner does not wish to see the interpretive scope in "*rite vocatus*" in AC 14 limited in any way. Since the question of ordination by the Roman bishops had not yet been decided, AC 14 is thought to leave "all possibilities open with respect to the *form* of the call process. From the situation of unsettled church conflict in 1530, these possibilities in AC 14 move between extremely contrasting poles, namely, between that situation of an emergency right of a scattered flock of Christian laymen and of an episcopal 'consecration' conducted according to the canonical law."[133] Thus Brunner explicitly wishes to see the interpretive scope extended to include calling by the laity without any minister of the Word. To this it must, however, be replied that the Evangelical churches in *this* situation in no way found call processes by the laity necessary when the episcopal ordination could not be obtained; therefore, Melanchthon, in AC Article 14, could have no actual interest in using "*rite vocatus*" to provide for such extreme situations of necessity. Furthermore, this kind of call by emergency right (through laymen alone), as Brunner himself calls it, and which may have its authority as such, can scarcely be found designated by the word "*rite*."

---

fundamentally establish the Church's liberty only from *bishops* and not also from those who bear the office of the Word generally. The "*certae personae* [certain persons]" to whom the Keys (and the right of calling) are not to belong exclusively are still unquestionably the bishops according to the whole thrust of the second part of the Treatise. If in Tr 68 Melanchthon is really supposed to be thinking of a bare lay call process (which, however, is utterly improbable, especially given his statements elsewhere regarding pastoral cooperation in the call process), this can still only have been entertained as a right in extreme necessity, as a sort of authorized exception to the rule. Neither in the overall flow of Tr 60ff. nor in the practical provisions of Tr 70ff. is it possible to find a connection to such an exception for an emergency right. Also cf. W. Löhe, *Neue Aphorismen*, *Ges. Werke*, vol. V.1, p. 554.

131 *Begr. u. Wirklichkeit*, p. 60.

132 Ibid., pp. 60f.

133 "Vom Amt des Bischofs," p. 20 n. 17.

W. Maurer, too, regards the scope of "*rite vocatus*" in AC 14 as unlimited. It is impossible "to fill the concept of the '*rite*' in AC 14 with concrete content from the propositions in the AC and Apology"; "all that was demanded by the word '*rite*' was *that* a public, valid legitimation of the public minister would result; concerning the manner in which it should happen, the Confession was at first able to establish nothing."[134] The fact that, in consideration of the still unsettled situation of 1530, *a certain* scope is consciously left in the "*rite vocatus*" in AC 14 can certainly not be disputed. The question, however, is whether this scope is really meant to be unlimited and whether the possibility of a bare call process by laity is consciously included by Melanchthon. From the perspective of Ap 14, as well as with the enlistment of the provisions of the Treatise and the view universally present in Melanchthon that the call must be made *jure divino* with the cooperation of people *and* office, this is not to be accepted in my view.

The interpretation of "*rite vocatus*" in AC 14 set forth by us has already been represented by *Vilmar.*[135] For him, the essential content of "*rite vocatus*" is that "shepherds can be called only by shepherds."[136] Here Vilmar argues first from the perspective of Apology 14 but also asserts the idea that AC 14 excludes someone making himself a member of the *ordo*; this must be done by others. But in addition to those are considered only those which themselves are in the *ordo* since only they can have the ability to make decisions about whether the aptitude for the office is present in a person.[137] It must be said that these are thoroughly Melanchthonian trains of thought. In particular, Vilmar relies on the later addition from the *Variata.*[138]

It is to *H. Asmussen's* particular credit that he emphasized the aspect of the liturgical form in "*rite vocatus.*" "The next article shows in a limited way what is meant by this" (i.e, the "*rite vocatus*"). "'*Riten*' are the liturgical forms in the broad sense. He is '*rite vocatus*' who has been called to his office according to the liturgical forms."[139] Asmussen also interprets AC 14 on the basis of Apology 14 and therefore determines that "nothing is said against the hierarchical system of Rome. . . ."[140] "Our Confession prescribes . . . the closest possible proximity to the canonical ordination ritual. . . ."[141] The article expects that the liturgical office will result from the liturgical action,[142] and so from liturgical ordination.

These considerations of Asmussen's have been confirmed by *E. Sommerlath,* who in the "*rite*" sees two things preserved: "the call in a liturgical form and the character of this form as one corresponding to the divine institution."[143] "The tendency of Article 14 of the Apology, which embraces the sense of Article 14 of the

---

134 *Pfarrerrecht u. Bekenntnis*, p. 123 n. 58; cf. generally, pp. 117ff.

135 *Dogmatik* II, p. 276; *Lehre vom geistl. Amt*, pp. 69ff.; *Die Augsburg. Confession*, pp. 129ff.

136 *Dogmatik* II, p. 276.

137 *Die Augsb. Confession*, pp. 130f.

138 *Lehre v. geistl. Amt*, p. 75.

139 *Warum noch lutherische Kirche*, p. 182.

140 Ibid., p. 184.

141 Ibid., p. 186.

142 Ibid.

143 "Amt u. allg. Priestertum," p. 57.

AC, is probably not falsely understood if it seems to endorse 'as much proximity as possible to the canonical ordination ritual' (with reference to Asmussen)."[144] —

Now that we have examined Melanchthon's teaching on the vocation in general, we must turn our attention to another specific act within the total call process: ordination, in the narrower sense as liturgical action. An overall picture of Melanchthon's teaching of the call to the office can only be obtained once his understanding of ordination has been studied and considered along with it. Thus we are brought to the next subject of our labor.

[144] Ibid., pp. 57f.; also cf. p. 64. — Likewise, A. Kimme ("Doctrina und ordo ecclesiasticus nach luth. Verständnis," op. cit., p. 65) confirms that AC 14 is focused on the liturgical form. — M. Doerne (*Luth. Pfarramt*, p. 14) saw the ordination rite instituted in Wittenberg as the implementation of a more precise definition of AC 14's *rite vocari* [calling in due manner], "which is simply indispensable for an orderly administration of the preaching office"; also cf. p. 15.

CHAPTER IV

Ordination

1. The Term *Ordination*

In Melanchthon's writings, the term *ordinatio* is used in two ways with respect to the call to the ecclesial office.[1] By *ordinatio* he means, first, the total call process and the individual elements contained in it, as we have learned;[2] and, second, the particular act of the public confirmation of the call or election already carried out insofar as it takes a liturgical form, and so what we call "ordination" today.[3] Where in Melanchthon the word *ordinatio* indicates the total call process, the specific ordination is still conceived as included with it,[4] and where *ordinatio* refers to the specific ordination, it does so in reference to the other related elements of the total call process. For Melanchthon, ordination in the narrow sense of a liturgical ordination rite is never an isolated act effective and efficacious in itself, but only ever one piece in a more extensive

[1] Also cf. G. Rietschel, *Luther u. d. Ordination*, pp. 75f. — Melanchthon's doctrine of ordination is chiefly to be drawn from the following writings: (1) the *Loci*, several eds.; (2) the exposition of 1 Timothy from 1541 (CR 15:1331ff.); (3) the *Judicium de impositione manuum* [Judgment on the laying on of hands] from 1543 (CR 5:209–12); (4) the *Sententia de ordinatione ecclesiae ministrorum*, [Opinion on the ordination of church ministers] from 1551 (CR 7:740–44); (5) the disputation *De politia ecclesiae seu ministerio et ordinationibus* [On the polity of the Church, or of the ministry and ordinations] (CR 12:489–91); and (6) the letter to Christoph Fischer dated November 1, 1555 (CR 8:597f.).

[2] E.g., CR 3:471f.: "But legitimate ordination includes the call or election, which is done by the people, or by those to whom the people have committed it, and the approval of certain bishops"; CR 7:742: "This call embracing" (the various parts) . . . "is by the same fact ordination"; CR 15:1335; 21:470: "the idea of the ordination of ministers of the church"; CR 21:850: "*Ordinatio*, as they refer to it, is the call to the ministry of the Gospel and the public approval of that call"; also cf. the superscription in CR 7:740: "opinion on the ordination of ministers of the church" (by which the total call process is meant). For the Melanchthonian confessions, the all-embracing use of the term *ordinatio* was pointed out by H. Bernau, op. cit., pp. 53ff., though without ignoring the fact that in this overall process designated by *ordinatio*, the specific ordination is always still in mind and that in other passages *ordinatio* also designates the specific ordination by itself.

[3] CR 8:597 ("public rite of ordination"); CR 12:490; 15:1335 ("rite of ordination"); CR 23:1: "rite of public ordination"; CR 28:412; also CR 5:825.

[4] The term *ordinatio* is not, e.g., transferred by Melanchthon to the total call process, in contrast to the liturgical ordination rite, as if to devalue the latter.

whole. In particular, it presupposes the specific call. Therefore, there can be for Melanchthon no ordination bestowed absolutely. Ordination without a specific call to a specific congregation in a specific ecclesial office is for him an *abusus* [abuse] for which he reproaches, e.g., the Roman [Church].[5] The office is for him always an office to a specified locality, to a specified congregation with specified parochial boundaries.[6] Therefore, ordination is not to take place unless the ordinand carries a "a testimony of a call to a certain ministry."[7] Evident in this provision is the way in which the specific ordination in Melanchthon's thinking is closely linked to the other parts of the total call process.

2. The Sense of Ordination

In order to define the sense of the specific ordination rightly as Melanchthon conceives it, it will be necessary to assume in accordance with observations just set forth that the ordination rite enjoys an intimate connection to the preceding specific call. First, it has essentially the character of the public confirmation of the election or call (*approbatio, comprobatio, confirmatio vocationis*),[8] which is to say, the public announcement of said confirmation of the election or call (*publicatio approbationis*)[9] by the clerical office. It is a demonstration of the proper and valid call of a person before the public of the gathered congregation: "attestation before the church [*testificatio apud ecclesiam*],"[10] "declaration of the call so that it may be more certain to the called themselves and also certain to the church [*declaratio vocationis, ut ipsis vocatis notior esset, et nota esset ecclesiae*]."[11] Here we are especially to think of the doctrinal examination tied to the call, the successful conclusion of which is officially confirmed in ordination. Ordination, in Melanchthon's view, shares in its essence an intimate relationship to the preceding examination (as to doctrine, gifts, and way of life); indeed, the latter may be viewed by Melanchthon virtually as a component of the ordination rite.[12] In

---

[5] CR 4:533; cf. CR 4:544: "Bishops . . . ordain no one except for the specific ministries of the Church."

[6] Cf. CR 21:1100 ("in a certain place"); CR 5:597 ("everyone in his place"); CR 15:547, 1233f., 1298; and above all CR 12:491. Cf. above, p. 251 (and nn. 48–49 there, where the text of the latter passage is cited).

[7] CR 4:544. Cf. W. Thomas, op. cit., p. 20.

[8] CR 5:211; 15:1334; 21:850.

[9] CR 8:597. This latter view of ordination as a "publication of the approval" in Melanchthon was given special attention by G. Rietschel, *Luther u. d. Ordination*, p. 77.

[10] CR 7:742.

[11] CR 7:741; cf. CR 5:825; 15:1334: "This sign" (i.e., the laying on of hands in the ordination) "shows the call and the confirmation of the call."

[12] Cf. CR 8:597. — H. Busch (*Die Lehre von der Kirche bei Melanchthon* [1918], p. 60) states: "In ordination, however, the chief matter is not the consecratory act but rather the examination, which concerns doctrine, talent for teaching, and personal conduct. Still, the demonstration of this examination through the laying on of hands accompanied by prayer seems to have some importance." However, it is not correct to value the examination more highly than the attestation of orthodoxy,

ordination, one or several called ministers of the Word in the office publicly attest to the orthodoxy of the ordinand's faith and his aptitude for the office, and thereby assure in a general manner the propriety of the previously issued call.[13]

This attestation or public approval of the call is seen by Melanchthon as a *liturgical act* [*Handlung*], as an *ordination rite* [*Ordinationsritus*],[14] to which the prayer over the ordinand belongs *jure divino*.[15] In his *Judicium de impositione manuum* [Judgment on the laying on of hands] (1543), Melanchthon describes the content of the ordination act in the following terms: ". . . The elected man is placed before the church, commended to God by public prayer, confirmed by the testimony of the college [of clergy]."[16] Thus three elements are noted in ordination: its public character ("placed before the church"), its petitionary character ("commended to God by public prayer"), and its testimonial character ("confirmed by the testimony of the college [of clergy]"). In all three relations, ordination is thought of as a liturgical act in the congregation, and the person of the elected or called stands at the center of all that happens: he is to be publicly placed before the congregation; he is to be commended to God in prayer, the gifts of God for the office to which he has been called are therefore to be implored for him; and he receives the testimony of the collegium, the presbyterium—that is, the other ministers of the Word—that he is pure in doctrine and rightly called. We may now observe in passing that ordination in Melanchthon's view is the *liturgical, public testimony and confirmation of the proper call, accompanied by prayer* (and preceding examination) and given by the office-bearers of the church before the assembled congregation.

Melanchthon sees the true ordination rite corrupted by improper elements among the Romans.[17] Therefore, he hails Luther's establishment of the Evangelical ordination rite in Wittenberg: "Luther acted faithfully when he

---

the ordination rite itself. Both acts have their significance. But if the examination and ordination acts are compared, it must be said that the examination is only a preliminary act while ordination is the valid conclusion, which results in ordination's greater importance.

[13] CR 7:743: "the glorious signs of the call, testimonies of the call"; CR 5:825: "When . . . to this ministry of the Gospel . . . he is duly and piously called . . . , learned and serious men are summoned . . . , that in the same church of Merseburg the call may be augmented by a public testimony thereto"; CR 3:184f. ("testimony of his teaching"). Cf. W. Thomas, op. cit., p. 20. — A distinction between "attestation" (or "declaration") and "confirmation" (or "approval") is perceived by both F. J. Stahl (*Die Kirchenverfassung*, pp. 132f.) and G. Rietschel (*Luther u. d. Ordination*, p. 77). "Attestation" is only the testimony that the minister has been rightly called while "confirmation" is the testimony that the whole Church approves and confirms the call. Yet this distinction between the terms cannot be pressed. When the office gives approval and testifies to the true call, the whole Church does so too.

[14] "Rite of ordination": CR 8:597; 15:1335; 23:1; 28:412.

[15] CR 7:742; 15:1334; 8:597; 12:380 ("in the beginning we gather for prayer . . .").

[16] CR 5:211.

[17] He mentions: "ungodly opinions about offering sacrifice for others, false cults, the unjust bonds of the canons" (probably meaning the obligation of celibacy), "anointings with oil consecrated with sorcerous blasphemies" (CR 7:742; cf. also cf. *Stud. Ausg.*, vol. VI, pp. 297 and 356ff.); to these are added the unjust swearing of oaths and the renunciation of the pure doctrine of the Gospel (CR 15:1334).

transmitted to the true Church not only the call but also this public testimony, which is done by the public rite."[18] For the rationale of the necessity of such an ordination rite, Melanchthon cites various causes.

First, the necessity of doctrinal inspection by ministers of the Word is mentioned: "since surely the inspection of doctrine by ministers of the Gospel must be carried out."[19] This makes clear how closely Melanchthon sees ordination linked to the doctrinal examination, how for him it is a testimony of the ordinand's orthodoxy, but also how it necessarily falls in the realm of the office's function, the object of which is to perform this examination and attestation, and how it also results in the ordaining minister's duty to ongoing doctrinal inspection.[20] But Melanchthon cites yet other "godly and serious reasons for retaining this public rite": it is "honorable" to conduct the "initiation of the ministry" and its relevant prayer in a public rite; it is good for the congregation to see by whom the testimony of the ordinands' doctrine is given and for the ordinands themselves to have "clear signs of their call" (to which they may cling when they fall into tribulation, such as the thought that they were not sent by God, according to Jer. 23:21).[21] Finally, it is also good for the ordained in the true Church of the pure doctrine to be distinguished by public testimony from those who are anointed by the Roman bishops.[22]

Elsewhere, for the demonstration of the usefulness of the public rite of ordination, the following specific reasons are cited: "(1) . . . that there may be clear testimonies of the call and of the approval of the call; (2) . . . that it may be evidenced which church's doctrine the called embraces; (3) that there may be public prayer; (4) this rite itself is advantageous also for the confirmation of many, that they may know that the right of ordination belongs to the true Church; (5) and that they may consider which are the errors of the adversaries (6) and of whose church they wish to be citizens," etc.[23]

From Melanchthon's last year, 1560, we get the following list of reasons: "*First*, that the entry to the ministry and the task of public teaching may not be open to all, but only to those who have been examined as to their doctrine and life. . . . The *second* reason is that God wants those to whom the attestations are given to be seen by the whole Church, that it may be assured of their call, and their doctrine and character be approved by the whole presbytery and by those to whom the governance of the Church is committed. The *third* reason is that these doctors of the Church also may know their call and have clear testimonies of their calling.

---

[18] CR 7:742f.

[19] CR 7:743.

[20] Cf. above, pp. 301–2.

[21] CR 7:741: "Also for those who have been called, it is very beneficial to know their call and to have clear testimonies to their call since the conscience, arguing with them about the call, often torments them severely and rebukes them with this voice: 'They ran, and I did not send . . . them'; there is great danger . . ."; CR 15:1331: "But for those who have been called, it is also very necessary on account of their conscience to have a testimony of their call since their consciences are greatly anguished when they are attacked by that voice: 'They ran, and I did not send them. . . .'"

[22] CR 7:743.

[23] CR 15:1335.

> . . . The *fourth* reason is that God may be thanked in those assemblies for the ministry of the Word both instituted and until now . . . miraculously preserved and that we may pray to God that He would preserve and care for the ministry of the Word which He instituted and send forth laborers into His harvest, that He may anoint them with His Holy Spirit and lay His hands on them, that they may bear much fruit and their fruit remain."[24]

Some of these reasons cited by Melanchthon are purely pedagogical in nature and assert nothing about the factual content of ordination. But if we consider what the other reasons cited by Melanchthon indicate for the sense of ordination, it must be said that ordination (as testimony of orthodoxy, aptitude for teaching, and the orthodox call of the ordinand through the clerical office) is supposed to give both the congregation and the ordained man himself the certainty that God Himself has acted by sending someone to the office. The ordination rite, according to Melanchthon, is the *certain testimony to the fact that God Himself sent a person to the office*, which is why the ordained man is able in tribulation to cling to this physical, tangible, objective rite and find peace in it. The prayer and testimony during ordination are thus to be understood as acts in which the mission of God becomes irrevocably valid and concrete as an objective fact. In ordination, after prayer and testimony are made by the clerical office over a person publicly before the congregation, there can no longer be any doubt that he has truly been *sent by God Himself*. The sense of ordination *cannot* be defined in any other way if by it the certainty is to be obtained that God has sent someone to the office.

Thus Melanchthon knows very well that the Church's ordinatory action is no mere human action, but that Christ Himself is present in it and acting upon the ordinands by means of the prayer and testimony of the office-bearers: "*Meanwhile*" (namely, while the confirmation is being carried out by the testimony of the office-bearers with the laying on of hands and prayer) "without any doubt the Son of God causes this man's ministry to be efficacious, thus He Himself lays His hands on and anoints him."[25] "He Himself . . . anoints the salutary ministers with His Holy Spirit. He Himself lays His hands upon him and blesses the ministry."[26] Here it is clearly stated that in the ordaining minister's laying on of hands, Christ Himself is laying on His hands and in the process truly giving the Holy Spirit to the ordinands.[27] The laying on of hands points

---

[24] CR 12:380f.

[25] CR 15:1334.

[26] CR 7:742.

[27] According to John 20:21ff., it says of the apostles that Christ "gives them the Holy Spirit" (CR 15:426), and this also applies to all ordinands (cf. above, pp. 249–50). Cf. CR 12:198: "First, ministers receive the doctrine, the Holy Spirit, and the ministry from God. . . . Afterward . . . they disseminate the voice of the doctrine." — It must especially be noted that ordination is not *solely* a prayer for the Holy Spirit (though it is that too!) but at the same time the bestowal of the same. In the ordination prayer and the laying on of hands by those ordaining, God acts through the real gift of the Holy Spirit. — We find in Melanchthon the same thing that J. Heubach says on the subject: in ordination "the gift of the Holy Spirit is besought and bestowed" (op. cit., pp. 101ff.).

forward to the benediction event in ordination, which causes the office of the ordained person to be efficacious. This is certainly not a prescription for God that He cannot make a man's office effective in some other way, yet He does it here in ordination *all the same*. Therefore, it is objectively true of those who are ordained: "The Son of God sends them and wills to work efficaciously through the Gospel."[28] Thus it is necessary to speak of an exhibitive and causative character of the ordination rite in Melanchthon, which is to be taken so seriously that Melanchthon even indicates a causal relationship between the efficacy of the office and the benediction and the gift of the Holy Spirit which happen in ordination.[29] Thus in order to describe rightly the sense of ordination according to Melanchthon, we must further add to the provision that the public (liturgical) confirmation of the call comes through the clerical office the fact that, as such, it is at the same time the *effective divine sending to and benediction for office.*

It is therefore only logical that Melanchthon speaks of ordination as a *conferral of the office.*

> The title of the work by which Melanchthon wishes to help ordinands to prepare for the ordination examination is *Examen eorum qui audiuntur ante ritum publicae ordinationis, qua commendatur eis ministerium evangelii* [Examination of those who are heard before the rite of public ordination, by which the ministry of the Gospel is conferred on them].[30] In an academic address, Melanchthon describes the content of ordination in the following terms: ". . . To begin, we join in prayer, and then, with public voice before the church, *we confer the ministry of teaching the Gospel* on those whose doctrine has been examined by us and whose character has been inspected."[31] And in the Saxon Confession it reads: "Therefore, we also retain in our churches the public rite of ordination, *by which the ministry of the Gospel is conferred* on chosen men, whose character and doctrine we first investigate."[32]

In ordination, the office is conferred on the ordinands, that is, the *mandate of the office* is placed upon them. "By this ordination, the preaching of the Gospel and the administration of the Sacraments are publicly conferred on them."[33] But it is very well to note that this conferral of the office happens "by divine

---

[28] CR 23:xxxv.

[29] Cf. above, pp. 283–84.

[30] CR 23:1.

[31] CR 12:380.

[32] CR 28:412. — Cf. the central sentence in the ordination certificate composed by Melanchthon for Laurentius Hunnicus: "for which reason, the ministry of teaching the Gospel and administering the Sacraments, according to the call, is committed to him in accordance with apostolic doctrine by a public and godly rite" (CR 5:721); and in the ordination certificate for Prince George of Anhalt, also composed by Melanchthon: "We, being gathered . . . have declared our testimony concerning him by the apostolic rite, with the laying on of hands, and have committed to him the ministry of teaching the Gospel and administering the Sacraments" (WA Br 11:156.18ff.; Enders 17:275; yet the last clause "and have committed . . ." is missing in CR 5:825).

[33] CR 28:524.

ordinance,"[34] and therefore by the mouth and hand of the ordaining minister God Himself confers and commends the office.[35] Yet *two qualifications* must be made here. Ordination has this effect of conferring the office and appointing people to the office *not per se*, not in isolation, but on the basis of the regular call preceding it and the examination already conducted, and it has it only when the *intention* (of the ordaining ministers) in the ordination rite is directed toward the true office of the Word and Sacraments. "The command of ordination must be oriented toward the preaching office and giving of the Sacraments, not toward offering other works for the living and the dead."[36]

> The charge of ordaining with a false intention for ordination must be laid against the Roman bishops.[37] In Apology, Article 13, Melanchthon uses the discussion of the sacrament of ordination to suggest that the opponents understand the priesthood not as a "ministry of the Word and Sacraments to be given to others," but of "sacrifice, as if in the New Testament it were necessary to have a priesthood like the Levitical one to offer sacrifices for the people and to merit remission of sins for others."[38] In contrast to this, it is our teaching that Christ's sacrifice has made satisfaction for the sins of the whole world, and no other sacrifice is needed; rather, justification is obtained by faith in this single sacrifice of Christ's. For this reason, the priests among us are called "not to offer any sacrifices but to teach the Gospel and give the Sacraments to the people."[39]

Thus it depends on the purpose for which the ordinands are called, the *kind* of office to which they are called. Only when they are called to the office of the Word and Sacraments established by Christ can ordination be understood as God's action (and thus sacramental). But if this is the case, it *must* be construed as an effective divine call event. In it, all the church's activity in the call process reaches an effective conclusion and a person is definitively called to the

[34] CR 22:524: "For this is the consecration and nothing else: After a hearing of the doctrine, to confirm the electee by certain persons of the church laying their hands on his head, committing to him the office by divine ordinance, and praying that God would give Him the Holy Spirit for that purpose and govern him, and that God would be efficacious through his preaching and administration of the Sacraments. . . ."

[35] Cf. Vilmar, *Dogmatik* II, p. 277; W. O. Münter, *Begriff u. Wirklichkeit*, pp. 82f.; G. Wehrung, "Zu Augustana VIII," op. cit., p. 7, and F. W. Hopf, *Luth. Kirchenordnung*, p. 28. The aspect of the effective committal of the office in Melanchthon through the laying on of hands and prayer in ordination was overlooked by W. Thomas (op. cit., pp. 16f. n. 3).

[36] CR 5:585.

[37] CR 15:1334: "They do not intend a call to the ministry, but say that they ordain priests to offer sacrifice, and they invent the idea that a certain group of Mass-priests is needed to offer sacrifices for the living and the dead"; CR 5:585: "But ordination has come to great abuse, wherein the right doctrine is no longer heeded, and the error has infiltrated that there must be priests to offer sacrifices for the people, and the proliferation of this sacrificial offering is the highest worship of God."

[38] Ap 13.7 (*BKS* 293).

[39] Ap 13.8f. (*BKS* 293); cf. CR 21:470f.: "When the others speak of ordination, they do not mention the ministry of the Gospel but think that ordination is a call to offer sacrifices for the living and the dead"; CR 21:852: "Mass-priests, who do Masses for others, invent the idea that ordination is done to give the power to offer sacrifices for the living and the dead. . . ."

office established by Christ. It is very likely on the basis of *this* understanding of ordination that Melanchthon prefers to use the term *ordinatio* for the total call process.

There is one further passage requiring closer examination. In the Treatise, Melanchthon describes the ordination of the ancient Church in the following terms: "Formerly the people elected pastors and bishops. Then came a bishop, either of that church or a neighboring one, who confirmed the one elected by the laying on of hands," and adds "and ordination was nothing else than such an approval" (Tr 70, *BKS* 491f.).[40] Clearly he does this in order to emphasize the true sense of ordination. Ordination was the confirmation of the elected man by the laying on of hands, nothing else. But what is the possible alternative content of ordination that Melanchthon wishes to reject here? This is evident from the following text, which reads: "Afterward, new ceremonies were added. . . . Then more modern writers added: 'I give you the power to sacrifice for the living and the dead' " (Tr 71, *BKS* 492). These "new ceremonies" which were added later and eventually transformed ordination into the consecration of a sacrificial priest are the alternatives which are meant to be rejected by the statement "and ordination was nothing else than *such* an approval." It is important to note the word "such." It contains a reference to the ancient Church's legitimate ordination ceremony of the laying on of hands previously mentioned, by which the approval was carried out, as well as to the election preceding and lying at the root of this approval (naturally [an election] to the office of the Word and the Sacraments). The statement "was nothing else than such . . ." is a sting aimed at the gradual transformation (evident in the "new ceremonies") of ordination from the confirmation of an election to the preaching office made by the clerical office with the laying on of hands into a conferral of the power to offer sacrifices for the living and the dead reserved to the Roman episcopacy. Melanchthon means to say that ordination was originally (and according to its true nature should be today) not a conferral of the "power to offer sacrifices for the living and the dead," as the Roman bishops are able to do and which they alone are actually able to do, but the confirmation, by the laying on of hands, of a man chosen by the people for the ecclesiastical ministry, as every true bishop, also meaning every true pastor (the distinction between bishop and pastor naturally being *de jure humano*: Tr 60ff., *BKS* 489ff.), can perform in his church when the bishops refuse to perform such ordination. To say "and ordination was nothing else than such an approval" is not to question the efficacious character of ordination nor to characterize the bishop's approval with the laying on of hands as a meaningless formality. Neither does this really represent the approval with the laying on of hands as found in the Fourth Canon of the Council of Nicaea. In the broader context, the focus for Melanchthon here is to show that the Church is not absolutely bound to ordination by the Roman bishops. This is also to be demonstrated here by the original and true nature of ordination after the pattern of the ancient Church. This does not require a bishop who can say during ordination: "I give you the power to offer sacrifices for the

[40] Cf. CR 5:634: "The bishops themselves know that this is the old idea of ordination, that it is the proper office of bishops, or that this approval itself of presbyters, which happens by the laying on of hands, is necessary"; CR 22:524f. (cited above, p. 295 n. 65.)

living and the dead" (which the Evangelical pastor naturally cannot do), but only a bishop (or pastor) who with the laying on of hands confirms the pastor-elect in the ecclesial office. Every Evangelical pastor, being *de jure divino* equal to the bishop, is able to do this. To perform the liturgical confirmation by the laying on of hands on the basis of the election by the congregation is not reserved for the Roman bishops but is open to all pastors. Thus the ordination done by the pastor in his church is valid *jure divino* (Tr 65, *BKS* 490), and the churches are able, by means of their own pastors (*adhibitis suis pastoribus*), to ordain new ministers of the Word (Tr 72, *BKS* 492). The concept of an ordination validated *jure divino*, which is used for the ordination of pastors, implies that this ordination has the same efficacious character (what else should "valid [*rata*]" mean?). And ordination in accordance with the Treatise has this efficacious character even when it is performed only by a pastor in his church as opposed to by a Roman bishop with higher consecration. The formulation "and ordination was nothing else than such an approval" only points to the intimate link between the true ordination and the election and call preceding it and contradicts the opinion that ordination confers the office even without regard to the election and call to the ministry of the Word, simply by virtue of the special character of the episcopal consecration (whether or not the true intent for ordination is present),[41] but in no way removes the efficacious character from the approval which occurs within it and is grounded on the preceding election.

We may summarize our findings concerning Melanchthon's sense of ordination in the following way: Ordination is the proper call's public, liturgical confirmation accompanied by prayer, executed by other ministers of the Word before the assembled congregation, in which Christ Himself calls a man to the office, sends him to the office, and blesses him for the office by apportioning the Holy Spirit. It is in all of this the definitive commission of the divine mandate of the office and the effectual conferral of the office.

3. Ordination as Sacrament

The Roman consecration of priests, in that church described as the sacrament of ordination, had to be seen by Melanchthon as an abuse of true ordination on account of its false orientation toward a sacrificial priestly office.[42] Closely linked to the very strong impression felt by Melanchthon in his early period of the true ordination's perversion into the Roman consecration of priests was his disinclination in 1521 to acknowledge a sacramental character in ordination. In the *Loci* of 1521, he is only able to spare the observation: "We wonder what comes into the mind of a Sophist, . . . to count among the sacraments those things of which Scripture makes no mention. For whence was this

[41] We can only follow W. O. Münter (*Begriff und Wirklichkeit*, pp. 79ff.) to the extent that he argues against Stahl's thesis that the right performance of the ordination action already contains its blessing. No doubt it is firm, however, that according to the Lutheran Confession ordination, when it follows a proper election and call, effectively confers the office. Also cf. AC 8 and Ap 7.28.

[42] Also cf. above, p. 311 n. 17.

ordination devised?"[43] Ten years later, however, in the *Apology of the Augsburg Confession* (1531), he adopts a different position. While naturally opposing there the sacramental understanding of the Roman consecration of sacrificial priests, he is ready and willing to acknowledge, in contrast to it, the sacramental character of the true ordination to the preaching office. "But if ordination be understood as applying to the ministry of the Word, we are not unwilling to call ordination a sacrament."[44] In the argument for this he lays as a groundwork the general concept of a sacrament, according to which those rites may be called a sacrament "which have the command of God and to which a promise of grace is added."[45] Accordingly, in designating ordination to the ministry of the Word as a sacrament based on the fact that the ministry of the Word to which a person is ordained has the "command of God" and "magnificent promises,"[46] Melanchthon goes a step further and has no qualms with granting, quite specifically, the laying on of hands (here apparently taken as the core rite of ordination) the designation "sacrament," basing this in turn on the presence of a divine "command to appoint ministers," from which follows the certainty that God endorses the office appointed through ordination and wills to work through it.[47]

The interest that moves Melanchthon to endorse such a superlative term as "sacrament" for ordination or the laying on of hands is the great necessity which had meanwhile arisen [for the Evangelicals] to be distinguished from the Enthusiasts, who despise and blaspheme the preaching office and physical Word. "It is of advantage to adorn the ministry of the Word, so far as can be done, with every kind of praise against fanatical men. . . ."[48] It is clear that Melanchthon grants the designation "sacrament" to ordination and the laying on of hands for the sake of the ministry of the Word instituted by God and furnished with the most exalted promises. Yet this cannot be explained in such a way that the sacramental character properly only applies to the office itself but not directly to the concrete act within it, thus the ordination with laying on of hands.[49] The two

43 CR 21:211; cf. CR 21:221: "What comes into the mind of those who enumerate the *ordo* among the signs of grace?"; CR 21:42: "The *ordo* [is] a fiction." — Since it cannot have escaped Melanchthon that Scripture certainly speaks of proper ordination by the laying on of hands, it is very likely that he uses the term "*ordo* [ordination]," which Scripture does not mention once, to mean the Roman consecration to the sacrificial priesthood, and only means to exclude from this any sacramental character.

44 Ap 13.11 (*BKS* 293).

45 Ap 13.3 (*BKS* 292).

46 Ap 13.11 (*BKS* 293). Cf. Vilmar (*Dogmatik* II, p. 277).

47 Ap 13.12 (*BKS* 294): "If ordination be understood in this way, neither will we refuse to call the laying on of hands a sacrament. For the Church has the command to appoint ministers, which should be most pleasing to us since we know that God approves this ministry and is present in the ministry." On this cf. K. Winter, "Die Lehre von der Kirche i. d. ev.-luth. Bekenntnisschriften," in *Credo ecclesiam* (Gütersloh, 1930), p. 12; and E. Sommerlath, "Amt u. allg. Priesterum," p. 60.

48 Ap 13.13 (*BKS* 294).

49 Thus T. Harnack, *Die Kirche, ihr Amt, ihr Regiment*, pp. 44f., Thesis 90. Harnack misinterprets Ap 13.11. By the formulation "But if ordination be understood as applying to the ministry of the Word, we are not unwilling to call ordination a sacrament," Melanchthon in no way means to

may not, in the sense of Apology, Article 13, be divided and turned against each other as mutually exclusive. With the divine institution of the concrete office, the divine command for appointing the office (*mandatum de constituendis ministris*) is directly given as well, and this is performed tangibly in ordination, ultimately in the act of the laying on of hands.[50] Apology, Article 13, shows how in Melanchthon's thinking a sacramental character of the office necessarily entails the sacramental character of ordination as a concrete liturgical action. Thus it is not a slip of the tongue, so to speak, when Melanchthon speaks of the laying on of hands as sacramental, but it has an objective, substantial basis. By it, the greatest possible concrete realization of the instituted office is documented in the physical act of ordination. Melanchthon could not grant the *laying on of hands* a sacramental character if he did not really intend this concretization as *de jure divino*. Designating ordination or the laying on of hands as a "sacrament" includes, at least, the declaration that God's activity becomes objectively concrete in it.[51] To make *this* declaration in opposition to the Enthusiasts is apparently Melanchthon's basic intent here. Since the focus is on ordination to the *preaching* office, the emphasis is laid chiefly on God's dealing with us by no other means than the physical Word. But it cannot be overlooked here that ordination, for this reason, does not occupy for Melanchthon the same level as the three salvific sacraments of Baptism, the Lord's Supper, and Absolution, which are directly connected to the New Testament promise of the forgiveness of sins.[52] The acknowledgment of a sacramental character means for Melanchthon, with respect to ordination and the laying on of hands, only that God's activity for our salvation (on the basis of the given command and given promise) becomes tangible in them, not, however, the coordination in terms of value with the three sacraments by which the redemption is directly administered.

A very similar position on the question of the sacramental character of ordination is found in the *Loci of 1535ff.* There, in the section "De sacramentorum

connect ordination as the concrete act of initiation to a universal concept of the office without regard for the concrete ordination, and so to acknowledge the sacramental character only of such an office conceived as universal (but not the concrete ordination in addition). Rather, his intent—as is fully and unmistakably clear from the foregoing—is to emphasize the relationship of ordination to the ministry of *the Word* instead of the priesthood (which replaced it in Rome), i.e., the sacrificial priesthood, as the prerequisite for the possibility of calling ordination a sacrament. Besides this, Harnack completely ignores the fact that a sacramental character is acknowledged for the laying on of hands specifically (as a very concrete ordination rite!) and that it is as a rationale for this that the discussion involves the divine mandate for *appointing* ministers (*BKS* 293f.). Harnack is—as it appears—guided by the endeavor to keep his thesis (that the concrete, appointed office according to the Confessions is not *de jure divino*) from being shattered. And it would fall if ordination itself, or the laying on of hands, should be assessed as a sacramental act through which God deals. — In this point, like Harnack, J. W. F. Höfling (*Grundsätze*, pp. 100f.) attempts to evade the statements in the Apology.

50 This idea is confirmed by K. Winter (op. cit., p. 12) as contained in the Confessions. Also cf. J. Heubach, op. cit., pp. 76 and 128f.

51 Cf. E. Schlink, op. cit., p. 331.

52 Ap 13.3f. (*BKS* 292).

numero [On the number of the sacraments]," Melanchthon postulates that many sacraments could be numbered if it were desirable for all the things which have a divine promise to be called a sacrament, such as prayer, tribulations, almsgiving, e.g. But if this term is restricted to "the ceremonies or rites instituted in the Gospel and properly belonging to this chief promise, and the one proper to the Gospel, which is to say, the forgiveness of sins," only three sacraments may be named: Baptism, the Lord's Supper, Absolution.[53] In a broader sense, however, Melanchthon could count ordination among the sacraments: "But I am very pleased to count the *ordo* (as they call it) among the sacraments, as long as it is understood as being both the ministry of the Gospel and the call to this ministry of teaching the Gospel and administering the Sacraments."[54] Here too—as in the Apology—Melanchthon would like to see the *ordo* (by which he means the office of the Gospel and the call to this office) counted among the sacraments since he would like to underscore the ministry of the Gospel and the call to this ministry as the means of God's activity with us. By its designation as "sacrament," people would be given an aid to recognize "that God approves those called by the Church and will be present in their ministry." This "benefice of God"—that in the Church's call God Himself calls and sends to the office and guarantees the efficacy of the office of the one so called—must be dear and precious to us, and therefore "is to be diligently adorned and made clear." And this cannot be done better than by attaching the name "sacrament" to ordination. To count ordination among the sacraments would thus be "most useful, namely, for clarifying the dignity of the ministry of the Word."[55] The office and the act of appointment to the office are to be emphasized as sacramental realities in which God is efficacious through the human actions contrary to the fanatical spirits. This is the driving motivation in Melanchthon. Yet by it he also draws a line between his position and the Roman concept of ordination, in which ordination "without mention of the ministry of the Gospel" is understood as "a call to offer sacrifices."[56]

The same motivation for emphasizing God's activity in the Church's call (i.e., in the call and ordination) lies at the root of the *Loci of 1543ff.*, where Melanchthon says, "It pleases me very much if ordination, as they call it, that is, the call to the ministry of the Gospel and the public approval of that call, be added" (i.e., to the number of the sacraments) "since these things are all prescribed by the command of the Gospel . . . and there is added the greatest and most worthy promise of all with the knowledge that testifies that God is truly efficacious through the ministry of those who have been elected by the voice of the Church."[57] Command and promise for the ordinatory action of the Church are given in Scripture, and therefore it is justified to call ordination a sacrament. This would also be of advantage because the "doctrine of ordination, if it were counted among the sacraments," would recall especially the "efficacy of the ministry," the God-given dignity and

[53] CR 21:469f.; cf. CR 21:849f.

[54] CR 21:470.

[55] Ibid.

[56] Ibid.

[57] CR 21:850.

power, as well as the duties which we have with respect to the office.[58] It is clear that Melanchthon also endorses denoting ordination as a sacrament for pedagogical reasons. But it cannot be overlooked that the main motivation for doing so is to stress God's activity in ordination.

From Melanchthon's statements on the sacramental character of ordination, it will be possible to conclude that, while he regards it as a sacrament in a strict and proper sense (thus in the same manner as Baptism, the Lord's Supper, and Absolution), he attaches a sacramental character to it insofar as God's activity of calling to the preaching office is made tangible in it, and it is his express wish to see ordination referred to as "sacrament" in order that it may be secured against the Enthusiasts and that the dignity and efficacy of the ministry may be clearly manifested.[59]

4. The Elements of the Ordination Rite

According to a statement by Melanchthon from his *Judicium de impositione manuum* [Judgment on the laying on of hands] (1543), which we have already cited, he regards the content of the ordination action thus: "the minister-elect is placed before the church, commended to God by public prayer, confirmed by the testimony of the college [of clergy]."[60] According to this, the ordinand, in the liturgical ordination action, must be placed before the congregation in a way recognizable to all since it is his person which is to be treated now. The proper elements of this rite are *prayer* [*precatio*] and the *testimony of the clergy* [*testimonium collegii*].

Prayer (over the ordinand) is always mentioned by Melanchthon wherever he lists the parts of the total call process that exist *de jure divino*.[61] But it has its natural place in the *publicus ritus ordinationis*, the liturgical ordination rite,[62] and is absolutely essential to it. Ordination is not to be "merely a ceremony and spectacle," but—as the ordinands are first to be "well examined and instructed"—so also it is necessary that "during the ceremony diligent prayer be made."[63]

The second part is the *testimony of the clergy*, the witness of the ordaining ministers of the Word, who confirm the call on the basis of the preceding

---

[58] CR 21:852.

[59] Cf. CR 12:490: "The ancients, in order that they might commit the magnitude and dignity of ministry to men, wisely placed ordination among the sacraments"; cf. CR 6:934: "Concerning the consecration of priests, we are not displeased by its being counted in the number of the sacraments, if it is observed rightly and in a Christian way, and we wish that it would be kept with great care in every land."

[60] CR 5:211. Cf. above, p. 311.

[61] Cf. above, pp. 298–302.

[62] CR 7:743.

[63] CR 6:934; cf. CR 7:34.

examination.[64] The ordination rite is of course to give "clear signs of the call," to be "a public testimony" that the ordinand has the right doctrine, is a properly called minister of the Gospel, and thereby it is to give assurance that he is called by Christ Himself and equipped with Christ's promise to work through his office.[65] This "public testimony" ("attestation before the church") may be given verbally or ritually.[66] The rite that can (properly only) be considered for this purpose is the laying on of hands, "which rite we also still keep."[67] Melanchthon says of the public approval (thus the ordination, specifically the testimony within it): "And it is fitting that this be done by the usual rite, which also was used by the apostles and then by the ancient Church" (which is to say, the laying on of hands). "However, I believe that it was used from then until the first fathers, and this rite can be kept without superstition."[68] The Church has complete liberty to use the laying on of hands in ordination; it is the *proper ordination rite from time immemorial.* Melanchthon speaks of it in different ways so that it is hard to determine whether he really means by it merely the rite of the laying on of hands itself or the whole ordination action, the whole public rite of ordination,[69] or else, as we saw in Apology 13 in the treatment of the sacramental character of ordination, he uses the laying on of hands quite clearly for the entire ordination—indeed, the whole call to the office.[70] This would hardly be possible if he did not regard the laying on of hands as an integral part of the ordination action. In the *Loci* of 1543ff., he appoints the laying on of hands for the ordination action generally and states that it brings the efficacy of the ministry to sensorial expression, among other things.[71] For him it is the given rite through which the testimony of the clergy may be furnished as a clear sign [*signum illustre*].[72]

For the laying of the Gospel book on the head of the ordinand, Melanchthon makes no provision anywhere, although he mentions it with the laying on of

---

[64] The examination in Melanchthon's understanding can be counted along with the elements of the ordination action, but in essence it is only the *prerequisite* to the proper ordination action.

[65] CR 7:743; cf. CR 5:825; 21:470.

[66] CR 7:742.

[67] CR 7:742; cf. CR 5:211: "We still keep this custom, as you know, and I am pleased with the rite"; CR 12:380.

[68] CR 8:597f.

[69] CR 5:211f.; 7:742f.; 15:1335.

[70] Ap 13.11f. (*BKS* 293f.).

[71] CR 21:852: "The doctrine of ordination would remind us of all these things—of the efficacy of the ministry, the prayer for the ministry, the duties owed by them, and the penalties of spurning the ministry—when it is counted among the sacraments; and the rite itself would remind us, when we publicly observe the most ancient custom, indubitably drawn from the first fathers, viz., the laying on of hands . . ."; cf. ibid: "since . . . you will think that this rite was taken over from the first fathers and from the apostles not by chance, not without some meaning, that the soul might be stirred up to acknowledge the efficacy of the office, for reverence, for seeking meanings which remind us of Christ our High Priest and of the duties of this office."

[72] On the question of the necessity of the laying on of hands, cf. below, pp. 327–28.

hands as ceremonies of the ancient Church's ordination.[73] The anointing, as it is in use in the Roman consecration of priests, is regarded by him as a corruption of ordination and is rejected.[74]

As constant elements of the ordination action we see in Melanchthon both prayer [*precatio*] and attestation [*testificatio*], the latter normally being done through the rite of the laying on of hands. Thus when speaking of the elements of the ordination rite, mention is made simply of the laying on of hands and prayer. In his *Judicium de episcopo Naumburgensi* [Judgment on the bishop of Naumburg] from November 1, 1541, it says that after the election "the electee is to be ordained publicly by certain preachers with the laying on of hands and prayer, etc., and no other spectacle is needed. . . ."[75]

5. The Sense of the Laying on of Hands in Ordination

If we wish to describe the sense of the laying on of hands in ordination according to Melanchthon, we must first connect it to what has just been said.

(1) The laying on of hands used in ordination has primarily, according to Melanchthon, the sense of visibly making known by means of a specific rite the approval of the call previously carried out. The apostles used this rite as a "usual sign" to clarify the call.[76] "This sign showed the call and the confirmation of the call."[77] And thus the laying on of hands is also the "declaration and approval of the call" today.[78] It serves the purpose of delivering the "testimonies of the call and approval" in an obvious way[79] and is one of the "clear testimonies of the

[73] CR 15:1335: "There were in the external rite of ordination in the ancient Church the ceremonies of the laying on of hands and the placement of a book on top of the head, etc."; CR 8:597.

[74] CR 15:1334; cf. CR 7:742. — However, in a plan for the Leipzig Interim (1548) in which Melanchthon was at least involved, it is expressed that (if the Roman bishops give ordination without the vow of celibacy and with permission for Communion under both kinds) the anointing in such ordination was not to be opposed. It is only pointed out "that to the anointing it is not presumed or ascribed that any working of divine gifts or grace are given by it" (CR 7:180). A statement by Melanchthon from April 1530 on the ceremonies in the consecration will have to be taken in the same sense: "Counsel is certainly found for the fact that if agreement is had in the chief articles, the bishops agree to yield something. For if they wish to make peace, we should justly yield all that can be yielded with a good conscience for the sake of peace" (CR 4:995). To be reckoned, at least, among these potential concessions relative to the individual ceremonies of the consecration would be the acceptance of the chrismation.

[75] CR 4:698.

[76] CR 7:741: "They used to declare the call by the customary sign, the laying on of hands, that it might be more certain to the called men themselves and certain to the church."

[77] CR 15:1334.

[78] CR 5:211; cf. CR 5:187: "Neither was there afterward another laying on of hands except the public testimony."

[79] Cf. CR 15:1335.

call."[80] In the ordination certificate for Prince George of Anhalt, it is described as the means *through which* the testimony of the presbytery is made clear.[81]

(2) Nevertheless, the sense of the laying on of hands in ordination for Melanchthon is *not merely* a symbolic sense. We have already found Melanchthon teaching that, during the laying on of hands, Christ is working so that the office of the ordinand becomes efficacious; He Himself lays His hand on and anoints the ordinand with His Holy Spirit, He blesses him and his office.[82] In the human laying on of hands in ordination, we are to see a divine one which is in turn synonymous with the anointing with the Holy Spirit. The anointing with the Holy Spirit can only mean that the Holy Spirit with His gifts is really bestowed on the ordinand. Thus the laying on of hands—as clearly demonstrated by the close link in Melanchthon's thinking between the laying on of hands and the anointing of the Spirit—is also the organ of imparting the Spirit (as equipping for the office).[83] For him it is also the *effective rite of benediction*.[84] Through it, the reality of the divine blessing is placed on the called man and his office. This is nevertheless the highest thing that can be said of it, and only from here is it properly intelligible that Melanchthon is ready to refer to the laying on of hands as a sacrament (although he does not himself interpret this inner relationship thusly).[85]

[80] CR 12:381.

[81] CR 5:825: "By the apostolic rite with laying on of hands we declared our testimony regarding him."

[82] Cf. above, pp. 313–14 and the passages cited there: CR 7:742; 15:1334, etc. Additionally, CR 15:1332: "ordination, in which the Son of God both anoints them and lays His hands on them, that is, blesses them, and is efficacious in their ministry"; CR 12:381; 21:852.

[83] Also cf. Melanchthon's observations on the apostles' laying on of hands in the discussion of confirmation: "Afterward, public prayer would be made, and the apostles would place their hands on them. Thus they would be endowed with manifest gifts of the Holy Spirit" (CR 21:853). Regarding Roman confirmation, Melanchthon continues: "But now the rite of confirmation, which the bishops retain, is a very unprofitable ceremony" (ibid.). On Melanchthon's position on the laying on of hands in confirmation which he took during the Interim proceedings, cf. W. Maurer, *Gemeindezucht, Gemeindeamt, Konfirmation*, op. cit., pp. 81ff.

[84] Cf. esp. the expressions "anoints them and lays His hands on them, that is, blesses them" (CR 15:1332); "He lays hands on, He blesses the ministry" (CR 7:742); and the passage from the *Loci* cited on the following page.

[85] When Melanchthon, in his *Judicium de impositione manuum* [Judgment on the laying on of hands] (1543), finds that a properly called man can exist even without the particular rite of the laying on of hands by ministers of the Gospel and can administer Word and Sacrament, and then says, "For the laying on of hands adds no right or power, but it is a declaration and approval of the call, about which it is necessary to be assured" (CR 5:211), this statement, in order to avoid making an open contradiction between it and the other expressions on the benedictory meaning of the laying on of hands, can only be understood as applying to the laying on of hands as an isolated act (detached from the call process). The laying on of hands is primarily a declaration and approval of the call. And only where that is, where it is embedded in the entire call/ordination event, is it a factual benediction and anointing with the Holy Spirit. The right and power are ultimately deduced from the call; only normally they come to the one called through the laying on of hands in the ordination and are definitively bestowed in the act of approval. The gifts which God thus bestows through the laying on of hands in the approval of the call are not further gifts in addition to those

The fact that Melanchthon understands the laying on of hands in ordination not only as significative but also as exhibitive is confirmed by his explanations in the *Loci* of 1543ff. There Melanchthon sets forth two traditional meanings for the laying on of hands: it was always "the sign of the thing destined for the worship of God" and also "the sign of the blessing."[86] It thus served as a designation for that which was isolated from the profane world for the service of God and as the rite of benediction. As biblical examples for it, Melanchthon cites how Jacob blesses the sons of Joseph by the laying on of hands, how Moses ordains Joshua as the leader of the people by the laying on of hands, how Christ blesses the children by the laying on of hands, and how the sacrificial beasts were set apart for sacrifice by the laying on of hands.[87] Christ is depicted in the sacrificial beasts. As hands were laid on the sacrificial beasts, so the Father laid hands on Christ, that is, delegated (*delegit*) Him, blessed (*benedixit*) Him, anointed (*unxit*) Him, subjected Him, laid the inexpressible burden of the sins of the world on Him, and made Him a sacrifice for us.[88] The rite of the laying on of hands points above all to this Christ giving Himself up for us, but it is then related to the ministers of the Gospel (namely, in ordination): "Christ the High Priest placed His hand on them, that is, delegated them by the voice of the Gospel, blessed them, and anointed them with His gifts, as it is written: 'He ascended, He gives gifts to men'—prophets, apostles, pastors, doctors, whom He adorns with the light of doctrine and other gifts. Then He subjects them to Himself, that they teach only the Gospel, they keep only the kingdom of Christ. . . . They, too, are victims; that is, they suffer hatred, miseries, and torments for the true doctrine."[89] Here Melanchthon lists as the different semantic contents of the laying on of hands: setting apart for Christ, consecration, anointing with the holy gifts, subordination to Christ, and preparation for spiritual sacrifice for Christ. These are for him the *significationes* [significative meanings] of the

---

which are already included in the proper call, but the very same. Hence the expression "the laying on of hands adds no right or power"; and earlier: "The called man . . . even without the *other* rite of the laying on of hands, is truly a minister of the Gospel." When, in consideration of confused ecclesial circumstances, the call process was carried out in a period of transition without ordination and the laying on of hands, Melanchthon was confident that God also gave the power and gifts for the office without the laying on of hands. In that case, making up for the ordination ceremony with laying on of hands later would only have formal significance and would add nothing in right or power. This is in no way to say that the laying on of hands does not actually impart power and spiritual gifts when it is used rightly in the total call process. — Likewise, in the dispute concerning Freder's ordination, both the opinion of the Wittenberg faculty as well as the decree of the Greifswald synod disavowed any special power of the Holy Spirit (imparted *ex opere operato*) in the laying on of hands as an *isolated* gesture, but did not deny its potency and efficacy in the entire action. Cf. below, pp. 331–32, 335–36.

[86] CR 21:852. "Sign [*signum*]" is to be taken not only as demonstrative but also as instrumental.

[87] CR 21:852: "By this rite Jacob blesses the sons of Joseph; by this rite Moses ordains Joshua. . . . By this rite Christ blesses the children; by this rite sheep are ordained to the office of being victims." The ablative "by this rite [*hoc ritu*]" expresses the instrumental character of the laying on of hands here. Also cf. CR 5:211.

[88] CR 21:852.

[89] Ibid.

laying on of hands. It is in this sense that the rite of the laying on of hands was incorporated by the apostles and fathers in ordination and is also preserved among us.[90]

We can establish in summary: The sense of the laying on of hands is, according to Melanchthon, a significative one and a benedictory one. Through the laying on of hands, the approval of the call is first made known visibly, but in the process Christ Himself deals with the ordinand through the laying on of hands, sets him apart for holy ministry of the Gospel, anoints him with the Holy Spirit, equips him with the spiritual gifts which are conducive to the office, makes his office efficacious therein, blesses him, takes him into His obedience, and consecrates him to suffer for the Gospel. Both sides belong together in Melanchthon in the understanding of the laying on of hands; they cannot be divided or turned against each other. In harmony they produce the full sense of the laying on of hands as Melanchthon sees it.[91]

6. The *Jus Divinum* in Ordination

We have already repeatedly emphasized that for Melanchthon in no way is the "that" of the call alone governed by a *jus divinum*, but (to a certain degree) the "how," and thus a specific mode for the call process is so governed as well. Among the parts of the call process existing *de jure divino*, besides the call in the narrow sense (= the election) and the doctrinal review, Melanchthon always counts the public approval of the call (the attestation before the church), or the publication of the approval and the prayer.[92] If these two latter elements are taken in tandem as the liturgical ordination action—which it is impossible to do otherwise—it may be said that for Melanchthon the *liturgical ordination action* is *de jure divino*. We place this proposition first regardless of what will be said further on the subject.

What, then, is the *jus divinum* within the ordination action supported by the two pillars of approval (attestation) and prayer? Melanchthon teaches, as we have already mentioned, that the "signs of attestation before the church," the things by which the attestation or approval of the call is publicly made known to the congregation, may be either verbal or ritual.[93] By this he hints at a variableness within the liturgical ordination action for which the *jus divinum* leaves room. It concerns the rite of attestation, i.e., the *laying on of hands*.[94]

For Melanchthon, the laying on of hands is the traditional, good, in every respect profitable, and commendable—and, indeed, where it has been introduced by a church order, obligatory—ordination rite. Melanchthon knows that

---

[90] Ibid.

[91] Thus Herrlinger's pronouncement that the laying on of hands in Melanchthon is "not a giving of testimony before the church" (op. cit., p. 273) does not do justice to all the facts in Melanchthon.

[92] CR 7:742; 8:597; 15:1334f.; 21:850.

[93] CR 7:742; cf. CR 7:741: "to show—either by words or by some sign."

[94] Cf. above, pp. 321–22.

it is not to be viewed simply as a later custom introduced by the Church, but that it is demonstrated in Scripture, even in the Old Testament,[95] then especially among the apostles, who highlighted and confirmed the call publicly by the laying on of hands.[96] The laying on of hands is thus an *apostolic* ordination rite.[97] Moreover, it is also evident that "the apostles handed down this most ancient rite to the pastors who after them acted in the ministry, as written by Timothy: 'Lay a hand on no one hastily.'"[98] The fact that the laying on of hands was used without interruption as the ordination rite in the Church since the apostolic era is traced back by Melanchthon to an order of the apostles. Thus it is for him quite literally an apostolic tradition still validated by actual centuries-long usage in the whole Church.[99]

According to these findings, we might expect Melanchthon to teach a *jus divinum* for the laying on of hands as well.[100] In the case of the examination preceding ordination, which has apostolic injunction in the Pastoral Epistles, this is enough for him to teach it as having the *jus divinum*. Here in the laying on of hands, however, the apostolic example and apostolic injunction do not suffice for him to assert a *jus divinum* for this rite. Thus Melanchthon does not include it among the parts of the call process *de jure divino*, but rather teaches that it belongs to the *changeable* signs [*signa mutabilia*] of the attestation or approval of the call[101] and counts it in the end—when it comes down to the specification of what is necessary *de jure divino*—among unnecessary matters [*res non necessariae*].[102] Someone may be "truly called and ordained even when he has not used this rite, that is, the laying on of hands"; and, likewise, his ministry also is efficacious.[103] Even if in such statements Melanchthon apparently reflects

---

95 CR 7:741: 21:852.

96 CR 7:741.

97 "Apostolic rite [*ritus apostolicus*]": CR 5:825; 8:598; 12:380.

98 CR 7:742.

99 CR 8:598: "I believe that it was used from then until the first fathers . . ."; also cf. above, p. 322. — Under the papacy, the true sense of both ordination and the laying on of hands were distorted: CR 7:742; 15:1334.

100 He also did this indirectly, in my view, by referring to the laying on of hands in ordination as a sacrament (Ap 13), even if this was only supposed to be meant synecdochically. At any rate, the laying on of hands in Ap 13 moves into the direct proximity of a *jus divinum*.

101 CR 7:743; 15:1335.

102 CR 7:743; 8:597; 15:1335.

103 CR 7:743. But Melanchthon explicitly stresses the fact that he is not saying this "in order that the rite may be abolished, and there may be disorder [ἀκαταστασία], and those pastors may be condemned who add this rite to a godly call and doctrinal examination," but only that the distinction between the necessary and unnecessary may be kept in mind (ibid.). Melanchthon speaks similarly (CR 5:211) in his *Judicium de impositione manuum* [Judgment on the laying on of hands]. There Melanchthon laments in this writing, in which he advises Veit Dietrich in his dispute with Osiander (on this cf. CR 5:187 and T. Kolde, "Zur Geschichte der Ordination u. d. Kirchenzucht," *Theol. Stud. u. Krit.* [1894], pp. 242ff.): "the dissipation of discipline, which has invaded us and is apparent also in Osiander's refusal to let the ordination rite with laying on of hands come into the Church." (Osiander considered the laying on of hands necessary, but wished to see it performed only by a

on the exceptional circumstances of emergency periods in the Church—under normal circumstances in the Church Melanchthon always desires and calls for the laying on of hands—it must be held that he expressly excepts this from a strict *jus divinum* in ordination.

Having gained clarity on the question of a *jus divinum* for the laying on of hands specifically, we still have to delve more deeply into the question of the *jus divinum* of the liturgical ordination action itself in Melanchthon's thinking. In order to find a satisfactory answer, it is necessary to look briefly at the so-called "ordination dispute concerning Freder," which Melanchthon himself actively followed and the course and conclusion of which he himself (like the other Wittenberg theologians) decisively determined by his judgment.[104] We therefore include here an excursus on these proceedings.

Excursus: The Ordination Dispute concerning Freder

Magister Johann Freder was called in 1540 by the senate of the city of Hamburg to the Hamburg cathedral as second reader [*lector secundarius*] and second pastor. The superintendent and pastors of the city churches issued the approval, the selection was communicated to the congregation, and prayer was made for him from all pulpits. However, a specific liturgical ordination with the approval of the other clergy accompanied by prayer and the laying on of hands was not observed (probably because of the complicated circumstances at the cathedral, which was still occupied by Catholic canons).[105] In 1547, Freder was called by the council of the city of Stralsund as superintendent to that city and accepted the call. There, in the city hall, the office of superintendent was bestowed on him by the council (!) in the presence of all the preachers of the city. On the following Sunday, this was announced and prayers were said for him from all the pulpits of the city. Once again, ordination was not observed nor was one undertaken subsequently there, though urged by the Greifswald general superintendent D. Knipstro.[106] In Stralsund, although not himself ordained in such a way, Freder ordained a new Stralsund preacher, which increased Knipstro's concern considerably. In 1549, the council suddenly released Freder from his office after

---

bishop standing in ordinary succession; cf. T. Kolde, op. cit., pp. 243f. n. 1, and W. Thomas, op. cit., pp. 22f.) Melanchthon writes: "If he loves this custom as he ought to love it, why does he not renew it? And it would certainly be useful to have it restored in more churches," but then continues: "Yet I also say that the one called or elected by their voice, in whose power lies the right to call the one discharging the ministry of the Gospel, even without the other rite of the laying on of hands, is truly a minister of the Gospel, able to teach and to administer the Sacraments" (CR 5:211), this being followed by the statement that we discussed above, pp. 324–25 n. 85.

[104] The ordination dispute concerning Freder is described at length by G. Mohnike, *Des Johannes Frederus Leben und geistliche Gesänge*, vols. I and II (Stralsund, 1837). Important source documents on it are found in J. H. Balthasar, *Erste Sammlung einiger zur Pommerischen Kirchenhistorie gehörigen Schriften* (Greifswald, 1743), esp. pp. 95ff. Further literature on the dispute concerning Freder: T. Kliefoth, *Lit. Abhandlungen* I (1854), pp. 344ff.; G. Rietschel, *Luther und die Ordination* (1889), pp. 90ff.; the article "Knipstro" in *RE*³ by G. Kawerau. — Naturally, in the context of this work, only the most essential events of the whole dispute can be included.

[105] Mohnike I, pp. 9ff.

[106] Mohnike I, pp. 22ff. and 31f.

he proved unwilling to rein in his polemicizing against the Interim from the pulpit. Freder then went to Greifswald, where by Knipstro's intercession the duke awarded him the administration of a professorship. In 1550, he was entrusted with the superintendency of the island of Rugen, which Knipstro had also previously administered. Since the Kiel Accord of 1543, Rugen lay ecclesiastically under the jurisdiction of the Danish bishop of Roskilde. He had to confirm the new superintendent proposed by the duke of Pomerania. The bishop of Roskilde, however, required that Freder personally appear in Copenhagen to receive ordination and confirmation to the superintendency of Rugen, which the duke of Pomerania in turn forbade him to do.[107] Freder could, nevertheless, receive his ordination from Knipstro if he desired. But apparently he was not very concerned about it. Although he himself had never yet been ordained, Freder ordained a young chaplain on Rugen. This led to an open dispute and, in short time, to a literary controversy between Knipstro and him. Their perspectives are as follows:

Freder declared the laying on of hands an indifferent thing that is nowhere commanded in Scripture and as such is not necessary for the preaching office, and prayer for that office is not obligatory. The laying on of hands, while an ancient ceremony, only expresses that the prayer applies to the person concerned and has no further meaning. Even one who is not himself ordained can ordain others with the laying on of hands. Should the laying on of hands be seen as a necessary element of church order, it would be turned into a snare for the conscience [*laqueus conscientiae*]. — The characteristic part of Freder's position is that he identifies the liturgical ordination with the rite of the laying on of hands and by opposing this isolated act of the rite of the laying on of hands opposes the necessity of the entire specific ordination action.[108]

Knipstro, by contrast, looks at the entire ordination action as it occurs, admittedly after the apostolic model, with laying on of hands. This apostolic ordination is no adiaphoron, neither according to Scripture nor according to the opinion of the Wittenberg theologians. Although the laying on of hands in the New Testament has no explicit command (as [do] the sacraments), the whole ordination to the holy preaching office is still testified to there as God's ordinance. The laying on of hands and the prayer are intimately connected and may not be separated. The laying on of hands is more than a mere sign that the prayer is directed toward the person concerned. Ordination belongs to those who are themselves in the office (not to governing authorities); the acceptance may certainly happen at the city hall, but the ordination is to take place before the congregation, which is gathered in the name of Jesus Christ to hear God's Word, and thus liturgically. Only the call in the narrower sense is a matter of governing authorities; ordination as a liturgical action is exclusively a matter of the spiritual office. When Freder makes use of Melanchthon's statement, saying, "The call is in itself the ordination," and represents as his own opinion that ordination is an unnecessary liturgical action, he ignores the subsequent words in Melanchthon's writing, where Melanchthon clearly says, "The naming of the person is not yet the apostolic ordination." Knipstro, on the necessity of the ordination with laying on of

[107] Mohnike II, pp. 4ff.

[108] Mohnike II, pp. 12f.

hands, asserts: "We do not say that it is a necessity for salvation, only for the maintenance of Christian teachers and the churchly office since it is written thus in the Treptow [Trzebiatów] church order."[109] Knipstro reproaches Freder for having not yet received ordination even though there had often been opportunity for it, and because the church order prescribes it, and above all because he, not being himself ordained, ordained others, although no emergency compelled it. As one who is not a doctor cannot make others a doctor, so an unordained man cannot ordain others since he cannot give that which he himself does not yet possess.[110]

In the course of the dispute, the Pomeranian duke as well as Freder himself applied to the Wittenberg faculty to collect their opinion. The Wittenbergers decided in favor of Knipstro, advised the duke to silence Freder, admonished the man himself to keep peace, and called for him to come to Wittenberg to receive ordination there, if not otherwise. Melanchthon, on February 25, 1551, wrote specifically for the Greifswald faculty his *Sententia de ordinatione ecclesiae ministrorum* [Opinion on the ordination of church ministers][111] (also subscribed and endorsed by [Johann] Bugenhagen), which we have already cited numerous times. In it he gives a brief outline of the doctrine of the call and ordination, designating as *juris divini* and absolutely necessary for the office the following four parts: the call, inspection of doctrine, attestation before the church, and prayer. He strongly emphasizes the church order which must be observed and affirms Luther's readoption in Wittenberg of ordination with the laying on of hands in the reformatory church. Luther did right to confer on the true Church of the pure doctrine this "public attestation carried out by public rite." It is also "honorable by a certain public rite that the initiation to the ministry be done, and prayer said," and there are many "godly and serious reasons" for retaining these "public rites."[112] On the laying on of hands specifically, Melanchthon says that it is an apostolic custom and therefore properly to be used in ordination, even if as a specific ordination rite it is replaceable since the "signs of attestation are changeable." A man may be "truly called and ordained" and efficaciously occupy the office in which the rite of the laying on of hands has not been used. This last, however, he does not say in order that this rite may be abolished and the church order which prescribes it be disregarded, but only so that the distinction between the (divinely) necessary and unnecessary may fundamentally be kept in mind.[113] If public attestation and prayer are taken as liturgical ordination, it may be said that Melanchthon here teaches the *jus divinum* for them. (And it can scarcely be doubted that Melanchthon, by attestation, which is *juris divini*, has in mind that attestation *which is done by public rite*, and thus the *liturgical* ordination.) Only for the laying on of hands as an individual rite is the necessity *de jure divino* negated. In this memorandum, Melanchthon, with his characteristic moderation, placed himself on Knipstro's side. The opinion for Freder was nevertheless a clear word that he had to heed the Pomeranian church order, which

---

109 Mohnike II, p. 24.

110 For the whole presentation of Knipstro's position, cf. Mohnike II, pp. 10f., 13f., and 21ff.

111 CR 7:740–44.

112 CR 7:743. Also cf. above, pp. 312–13.

113 CR 7:743. Cf. pp. 327–28 n. 103.

prescribed ordination with laying on of hands and that he was not permitted to officiate without being ordained.

Yet Freder did not submit to the Wittenberg arbitration, and the duke accordingly withdrew his nomination for superintendent of the island of Rugen. Freder then, despite the duke, went to the bishop of Roskilde in Denmark and had himself ordained by the laying on of hands and confirmed as the superintendent of the island of Rugen. Returning to Greifswald, he continued his literary dispute with Knipstro. An agreement drafted by the duke's chancellor, Citzevitz, was not long-lived. A recess [agreement to suspend dispute] was signed by Freder and Knipstro, according to which ordination with prayer and laying on of hands in accordance with the Treptow church order was to be regarded as "a Christian and necessary article for the maintenance of Christian teaching offices and church offices,"[114] but Freder immediately broke the peace by publishing a new disputation against Knipstro, nor did this go unanswered by Knipstro himself. Finally, the duke applied once more to the Wittenberg theologians. In August 1555, he sent to Wittenberg the Greifswald professor of theology Jacob Runge to present the Wittenbergers with Knipstro's book *Von der Vocation und Ordination, etc.* [On the call and ordination, etc.], several printed treatises of Freder's, and the records of the last Accord of Greifswald, and to collect a second ruling from them.

The Wittenberg theologians gave a new *Theologisches Gutachten* [Theological opinion] dated September 24, 1555.[115] It was signed by Bugenhagen, Melanchthon, Johann Forster, Georg Major, Petrus Prätorius, and Paul Eber, but the chief authors were probably Bugenhagen and Melanchthon. In the opinion, Knipstro's book *Von der Vocation und Ordination, etc.*, is explicitly given a full endorsement in all its parts, and the Wittenbergers' regret over the continuance of the dispute is expressed. Freder is then charged with committing sophistry by "ripping out" an element of the total process of the call and ordination—namely, the laying on of hands (which as a ceremony is "not in itself necessary")—and using the non-necessity thereof to attack the necessity of the "ordination of priests" prescribed in the Pomeranian church order. He uses "the fallacy of division" and makes "a hole in the church order with this subterfuge: since this ceremony, the laying on of hands, is not necessary, everyone may occupy the regular ministry of the Church, whether he has been examined or not examined, approved or not approved, and, in short, the Pomeranian church order is a snare for the conscience which makes unnecessary things necessary. In the Old Testament, the laying on of hands was not necessary; in the New Testament it is not necessary. This is of one piece and only refers to ceremonies."[116] The Wittenbergers opposed removing the laying on of hands from the ordination action and arguing on the basis of this isolated ceremony. "Since Freder uses this clever thinking to dangerous effect, we say that this sophistry is wrong: to thrust the necessary together in a heap with this semblance of what is unnecessary, to tear apart good order and strengthen this disorder, so that unexamined people, infiltrators, and rebellious upstarts occupy the regular

[114] Mohnike II, p. 21.

[115] The memorandum is found quoted in full in Balthasar, pp. 98–102.

[116] Balthasar, p. 99.

ministry in the church."[117] For the Wittenbergers, ordination belongs most intimately to the foregoing examination, the successful execution of which is also testified and confirmed in it. Belonging therefore to ordination, which is designated as "the publication and approval of the call," is an external ceremony without misuse or misconstruing the laying on of hands, as was in use "in the Church from the beginning of the world" and rightly prescribed in the Pomeranian church order. Freder ought not to "call it a snare for the conscience nor encourage others to despise it."[118] The Wittenbergers see the proper *status controversiae* not in the condemnation of a ceremony of the laying on of hands but in the question of the necessity of examination and approval of the call (namely, in ordination) *generally*. In several instances they say distinctly that the laying on of hands in itself, as an individual ceremony pulled out of context, is not necessary, but they sharply condemn the belief that the total ordination with examination and public approval is unnecessary and that the laying on of hands practiced in ordination according to the church order is a snare for the conscience. This opinion lies entirely in line with that represented by Knipstro, which is also expressed in the unreserved endorsement of his book concerning the call and ordination of church ministers. It concludes with the faculty's concern that Knipstro's book *Von der Vocation und Ordination* should be presented to Freder and that he should be silenced and exhorted to apologize to Dr. Knipstro. Should Freder not yield, it is the duty of the authorities no longer to tolerate him in the land, but if he gives way and obeys the decision of the (forthcoming) Pomeranian synod, the duke might well forgive him.

Obviously, Jacob Runge had informed the Wittenbergers of the duke's intention, on account of Freder, to call a general synod of the territorial clergy, who were to end the case of dispute by means of their decision. To this end, reference was made to the consideration of the faculty's opinion. Besides this, Melanchthon wrote personally to Freder on November 1, 1555, admonishing him to submit to the synod.[119] He could do this honorably because the learnedness, piety, and moderation of the men in the synod was beyond doubt. Melanchthon's letter to Freder, however, fell on deaf ears, as did the opinion of the faculty, as evident from a later letter of Melanchthon to Jacob Runge.[120] From the outset, Freder was unwilling to hear the synod's pronouncement unless it decided in favor of his view, which was by no means to be expected.

Melanchthon's attitude toward the dispute concerning Freder is also contained in *a letter of his to Christoph Fischer from November 1, 1555*.[121] It reads: "In

[117] Balthasar, pp. 99f.

[118] Balthasar, p. 100.

[119] CR 8:595f. In the letter it reads: ". . . We are very sorry to oppose you so sharply concerning the rite that you call a 'snare for the conscience,' that custom which by good counsel and without corruption of doctrine is used in your and many godly churches. . . . We lovingly beseech you, for the tranquility of Church and fatherland, that you would lay down this unnecessary war which has gone on so many years and join the consensus of your synod . . . ; we beseech you for the sake of God and the Church and your own fatherland not to resist the synod of your churches, which decrees nothing unjust."

[120] CR 8:723f. The letter is dated March 25, 1556.

[121] CR 8:597f.

Pomerania, concerning the public rite of ordination as is used among us, a great dispute has arisen." More precisely, the point of controversy is characterized in the following terms: "M. Johann Freder, superintendent of the church of Stralsund, has written: 'The laying on of hands was necessary in the Levitical priesthood, but now it is an adiaphoron and to be omitted, lest the adiaphorists be confirmed.' Others" (by which Knipstro especially is meant) "think that the call, examination, publishing of the approval, and the prayer are matters of necessity and should not be omitted." By the publishing of the approval and the prayer, the public ordination ceremony is to be understood, which Knipstro saw as the matter of question. Melanchthon's opinion runs: "It is true that here this gesture of the laying on hands is an unnecessary matter, just as formerly in that rite there was here a gesture of placing a Gospel book on the head of the man being ordained; but this is not proof of this understanding because by this pretext the whole practice of examination and approval and prayer is abrogated since here the gesture is not necessary." This would amount to someone wishing to abolish the liturgy entirely since in the new covenant no specific day of the week has been divinely prescribed for it. "We must distinguish those things which are necessary and *juris divini* and to be retained, such as the call and examination, the publication of the approval, and the prayer."[122] Even if no *jus divinum* can be asserted of the individual gesture of the laying on of hands, there remains the absolute necessity of the existence of the *jus divinum* not only of the call but also of the examination, the publication of the approval, and the prayer.[123] It will not be possible to explain this position otherwise than that Melanchthon here teaches the *jus divinum* of the liturgical ordination action. It is clear that Melanchthon's stance in favor of Knipstro and against Freder succeeded. If the decision, met here in this letter to Christoph Fischer, is to be a decision *in favor of* Knipstro and *against* Freder's position, then it is *necessary* that the term "the publication of the approval and the prayer" be understood as the liturgical ordination and thus the public rite of ordination. Freder's fault was of course not that no publication of the approval occurred with him *at all* or no prayer at all! In Hamburg as well as in Stralsund his call and an approval by the municipal clergy were published from the city's pulpits, and prayers were said for him from the pulpits! Thus there was certainly *a* publication of the approval and *a* prayer for him at his call, just not *the* publication of the approval and *the* prayer that happens in a public rite of ordination (with the laying on of hands). Freder's fault concerned the liturgical ordination. This is what Knipstro called for and its necessity is that for which he fought. And it is the necessity of this liturgical ordination that Melanchthon here wishes to assert, when (contrary to Freder!) he teaches the necessity and *jus divinum* of the publication of approval and of the prayer. No other possibility of interpretation remains.

However, it must be noted that Melanchthon, in asserting the *jus divinum* for the liturgical ordination with the approval and prayer, is thinking of a constituted

---

122 CR 8:597.

123 In this position, Melanchthon distinguishes "*ritus*" (by which he means the whole public ordination action: "in that rite this gesture was done . . .") and "*gestus*" (by which the individual, outward signs of ordination, such as the laying on of hands, e.g., are meant). What cannot be asserted of the *gestus* (action), namely, the necessity *de jure divino*, is nevertheless true for whole *ritus* (rite).

church, such as Pomerania was, and thus of an organized church structure in which inspection exists. This is evident from the further content of his letter to Christoph Fischer. There, Melanchthon, in answer to his addressee, touches on what should be done with those ministers who, in the turbulent period of transition from the papacy to an organized Evangelical church structure, and thus a period when no fixed church order was in place and which is to be regarded as a period of conflict and necessity, were called to the office without a proper ordination action being carried out for them and who have exercised the office until the present.[124] Melanchthon's answer to this question runs as follows: "If they are fit—that is, if they teach rightly—their ministry is valid, and they are not to be compelled to receive the public rite of ordination, lest the churches be brought into doubt concerning their ministry. Only consider those who are suitable, who teach rightly, and who do not live in manifest scandal. But those who do not teach rightly and whose character is scandalous must be removed from the ministry for the reason that they do not teach rightly and that they live scandalously."[125] But he immediately continues: "*But since your churches now have inspection, let no one be admitted any more without examination and the public approval.* And it is fitting for this to be done by the usual rite that was used by the apostles and thereafter by the ancient Church. Indeed, I believe it was customary from that time until the first fathers, and this rite may be kept without superstition."[126] While Melanchthon maintained the *jus divinum* for the call, examination, publication of the approval, and the prayer, in which the *jus divinum* of the liturgical ordination is included, he was apparently unwilling to see the divine right of the latter understood in such a way that it could not grant a dispensation in times of extraordinary necessity and general confusion of the Church, or that God could not under such circumstances recognize as a minister one who was called and approved only by the judgment of those calling and who administers the office rightly but was not ordained by public rite. If in such a case Melanchthon advocates that a minister who teaches rightly and lives honorably should not be forced to receive the public rite of ordination, he does so less for the dogmatic motivation of the public ordination action being unnecessary than for the pastoral motivation: "lest the churches be brought into doubt concerning their ministry." Melanchthon's greater concern is to avoid confusing the congregations through a corrective implementation of the public ordination rite, which might cause them to doubt the power and validity of the Evangelical ministry generally or of the Sacraments previously dispensed by the unordained (but called) ministers. Under no circumstance were such opinions, such insecurity, to arise in the congregations. Even if in such exceptional circumstances and emergencies the divine right of the public rite of ordination can be inactive, it still has validity for the organized church structure. Where inspection has been established—that is, where the church finds itself in a normal condition—no one is to be admitted to the office without examination and the public approval

---

[124] CR 8:597: ". . . since those who are now in the ministry are called and also approved by the decision of those issuing the call, even if the public rite of ordination has not been added. . . ."

[125] CR 8:597.

[126] CR 8:597f.

(= public ordination). And in so doing, it is good and proper to use the ancient and innocuous rite of the laying on of hands. In Freder's case in Pomerania, there is an organized church structure, which is why Melanchthon asked that Freder have himself ordained. Melanchthon also had to oppose him theologically since Freder denied the necessity of the liturgical ordination generally, even in organized church bodies. All in all, from the letter to Christoph Fischer, it is clear that Melanchthon viewed Knipstro's position as his own.

However, when the instruction and admonition given to Freder by the Wittenbergers bore no fruit, and Freder carried on further with his denunciation of Knipstro, the duke called a general synod of the Pomeranian clergy at Greifswald on February 6, 1556, which was to conclude the dispute definitively.[127] Knipstro as well as Freder were summoned before the synod. Yet Freder did not appear, but instead traveled to Stralsund and from there advised the synod by letters, in one of which alone two hundred reputed "untruths" of Knipstro were dished up. After the synod examined these accusations in detail, only a few points remained on which it was still found necessary to consult Knipstro particularly. Among these, of interest to our discussion is the question whether Knipstro ascribed to the laying on of hands a particular energy [ἐνέργεια], "as if the Holy Spirit were transmitted through it as through *opus operatum*."[128] Knipstro countered this by saying that "he never spoke of the laying on of hands alone, but of the whole apostolic ordination; this he recommends, has recommended, and will recommend as long as he breathes. . . . It boasts the glorious testimonies of Scripture and the apostolic usage; Paul and Titus used it."[129] Thus Knipstro apparently wished only to deny the bestowal of the Holy Spirit to the isolated gesture of the laying on of hands as *opus operatum*, as an action in itself, but not to that used within the whole apostolic ordination. By this the synod was satisfied on the point.

What tangible results did the synodical proceedings yield? These we must gather from the two documents in which the synodical decision was committed to writing.[130] The first *Sententia* is an *elaborate declaration of the doctrine of ordination*. In the *preamble* are expressed the basic provisions of ordination with equal clarity, their necessity for the maintenance of the office and for the direction of the office, its fundamental distinctness from the bare call, its constituent parts (the examination and the publication of the call through God's Word, the laying on of hands, and the prayer), and its character as a function of the spiritual office, which alone is able to ordain. "Therefore, the synod avows that the ordination of priests, which is done with prayer and the laying on of hands in accordance with our Pomeranian church order, is Christian, good, and salutary and must needs be observed in these lands for the maintenance of the ordered ministry and

---

[127] The synod was composed of twenty city clergymen from Knipstro's diocese and twenty pastors from Rugen, as well as the professors of the Greifswald theological faculty. In the presidium—in addition to the duke's chancellor, Citzevitz, with his legal advisors—sat the general-superintendent of Stettin, Paul von Rhoda, and three other prominent clergymen.

[128] Mohnike II, p. 30.

[129] Ibid.

[130] The text as quoted in Balthasar, pp. 106ff.

for the proper appointment of the church offices. And that, on account of God, the authorities and the church ministers are bound by the duty of their office to keep it faithfully and to curb disorder, and that no man in these Pomeranian churches which possess and employ their certain church order receive or exercise the public church office unless he first be properly ordained according to the apostolic rite, with prayer and the laying on of hands by the priesthood." — "It is also clear that the call or election of the persons, which happens through the Christian authorities or others appointed for the purpose, with the counsel and consent of the other parish pastors, is distinguished from the ordination which is done by the priesthood and includes the examination of doctrine and life and the publishing of the call, which is done in these churches with prayer and the laying on of hands and with the reading of the Commandments and promises of God concerning the preaching office."[131] We may note in this summarizing framework provision how clearly the actual ordination is separated from the call in the narrower sense (the call through the Christian authority cited above), and its execution is referred to the "priesthood," as well as the fact that in the preceding call by the authorities or other persons, "the counsel and consent of the other parish pastors" is assumed. The whole process of the appointment of a person to the spiritual office rests, according to this, in the responsible hands of the spiritual office itself, even though people from the congregation assist in the process.

The synod's purpose in its decree is to clarify that ordination with the laying on of hands, as practiced in Pomerania, "*is Christian, good, profitable, salutary, and necessary* in our Pomeranian church for the following reasons."[132] Four reasons are then provided to this end.

First, appeal is made to the Treptow church order of 1534, composed by Bugenhagen, endorsed by Luther, and recognized universally: "In the same church order, this constitution says brightly and clearly that everyone who wishes to enter into the church office, after a preceding call and examination, is to be ordained by the ordinary superintendent with prayer and laying on of hands."[133] On the justification of this constitution, reference is made to the ancient church order and Luther's Wittenberg ordination: "Now, then, it is irrefutable that this rite was kept and used in the primitive Church, as the church histories and acts of the Council of Nicaea show, and when the ungodly bishops refused to ordain our church ministers, Luther instituted, purified, and used this apostolic rite among us and also advised the Bohemians to use it. Likewise, it is also used in the Wittenberg and Saxon churches and many other churches, with unanimity, without any dispute and needless quarreling. . . . From all of which it is clear that said ordination is not unchristian."[134] On the basis of these facts of the church tradition, the synod comes to the statement "that such a rite and good order cannot be weakened, altered, or made as if free and canceled without injurious disruption and dangerous offense in these churches by anyone, regardless of the person."[135]

---

131 Balthasar, pp. 107f.

132 Balthasar, p. 108.

133 Balthasar, p. 108.

134 Balthasar, pp. 108f.

135 Balthasar, p. 109.

In the *second* point, a closer look is taken at the biblical rationale. First, ordination is defined as "the proper, regular approval and publication of the call, by which the call, if the person is found capable, is confirmed and declared."[136] It is done in the Pomeranian church "according to the use of the apostles and our church order and the example of the universal Church, free from superstition, accompanied by the prayer and laying on of hands, during which the Commandments and comforting promises of God concerning the preaching office, doctrine, life, and the office of ministers are read aloud."[137] Through this ordination, "the ecclesial office is regularly committed to the called man, and both the church and the man thus properly ordained and instituted are assured that God will be efficacious through His voice and office."[138] That this ordination, and the right of calling and ordaining ministers generally, rests on *God's* command and therefore can and must be resorted to by the Lutheran Church as well is biblically supported by Titus 1:5 and 2 Tim. 2:2. In addition to this, the biblical root of the laying on of hands is also emphasized. "The ceremony also has clear testimony in Scripture. The apostles handed down and taught their apostles to use the laying on of hands in the appointment of church ministers, as Paul says to Timothy: 'Lay hands on no man hastily'; that is, ordain no man to the ecclesial office without judgment. . . . Therefore, the rite in itself is Christian, praiseworthy, glorious, profitable, and no 'snare for the conscience,' and makes all godly men mindful of comforting and lofty things."[139] Yet in an elevated state of emergency, the laying on of hands is characterized as dispensable: "Nevertheless, we declare that the ceremony of the laying on of hands in itself, in a true case of necessity, outside of established churches, is free and changeable, such as when one is among ungodly bishops or somewhere else where there is no church order. And even if the laying on of hands in particular had no express and ever-binding command in Scripture, yet because the laying on of hands is attested in Scripture, and has been employed in the church since the beginning of the world in many godly works, above all for the consecration of priests, and is expressly appointed in our Pomeranian church order, it should not be abolished in our Christian Church, nor in others where it is in use, nor should it be left out or disputed according to everyone's personal feeling. We therefore retain it in the ordering of priests without any superstition."[140] The testimony in Scripture and the support in universal church tradition are sufficient grounds for the synod not to view the laying on of hands simply as adiaphoron. Yet here it is stressed that all this discussion about the laying on of hands does not apply to it as an isolated gesture: ". . . and do not give it alone any power of the Holy Spirit *ex opere operato*."[141] It applies to the laying on of hands embedded in the full rite of ordination: "The laying on of hands is not to be viewed naked by itself, but it must be remembered that by it the called man is perfectly appointed

[136] Balthasar, pp. 109f.

[137] Balthasar, p. 110.

[138] Ibid.

[139] Ibid.

[140] Balthasar, p. 111.

[141] Ibid.

and installed in his office."[142] On the basis of these considerations, the synod concluded: "And if a man enters the office without ordination and without laying on of hands and tries to defend the resulting disorder by saying that the laying on of hands is meaningless, powerless, needless, an adiaphoron, and a 'snare for the conscience,' he causes disorder by doing so and by such pretense creates an inroad for the disruption of our church order, from which great injustice and destruction of the ecclesial office will ensue. Wherefore the synod declares that, here in Pomerania, no man shall be permitted by such a contrived pretense to dispute our church order or the ordination of priests which is in use among us."[143]

In the *third* point, the *divine efficacy in ordination with the laying on of hands* is highlighted. "In addition, God is present in our Christian, apostolic ordination and is also effective through the voice of those who are called by our churches and ordained and installed in such a way, and they are able to take comfort in the eternal and temporal promise which God makes known concerning the preaching office,"[144] after which various Scripture passages are cited, including John 20:21ff. and 1 Tim. 4:14. On the latter citation, it reads: "And Paul says that Timothy received a gift through the laying on of the hands of the elders. Here Paul is not speaking of a particular power of the bare" (—note this word!—) "laying on of hands, but is saying that, by a proper ordination, the ecclesial office has been committed to Timothy as a great talent and deposit, with the promise that God will support and assist him with His Spirit."[145] The gift of the Holy Spirit in the laying on of hands is not negated, yet neither is it restricted to the laying on of hands alone, but rather it is related to the *whole* ordination. In the ordination with the laying on of hands, the synod sees the promise given that, through the office of the ordained man, God wills to be efficacious, and thus understands the term "sacrament," which is occasionally applied to ordination, in which ordination must naturally be distinguished from the sacraments which bring the forgiveness of sins.[146] The Holy Spirit is effective through the Word and office of the ordained man even "when the minister is personally ungodly."[147]

The *fourth* and final point asserted for ordination is the motive of *maintaining church discipline and the church's orthodoxy.* Ordination is, for the synod, "the chief means . . . by which church discipline, obedience, good order, and peace are sustained among church ministers, and by examination, all false and foreign doctrine is checked. When it is vitiated, despised, or abolished, savagery, idleness, and disorder invade the preaching office so that infiltrators and rebellious, incompetent, unexamined, presumptuous people usurp the offices for themselves, and great calamity ensues in church and government. In addition, the common flock would thrust out faithful teachers at pleasure and install others after their own desire, who tickle their ears, as Paul says in 1 Tim. 4 [:3]. And, finally, the ministry

---

142 Ibid.

143 Balthasar, pp. 111f.

144 Balthasar, p. 112.

145 Ibid.

146 Balthasar, pp. 112f.

147 Balthasar, p. 113.

among those church ministers would become a wild mass of unruly people, none willing to listen to the other."[148]

Finally, a conclusion is drawn from all these considerations. "For the reasons given . . . it is clear and irrefutable that he who, being unordained, receives the ecclesial office here in Pomerania at the call of the governmental authorities and presumes to administer the church offices without the aforesaid apostolic ordination does so unjustly. . . . Yet much more does he sin and act incautiously if he, being unordained, should exercise his office here and stubbornly insist on defending it with unreasonable, dangerous disputation concerning the laying on of hands, by which the whole ordination of priests is diminished and cast into doubt."[149] The proper point of conflict is expressly referenced again: It may not be said that "he who has been properly issued a call by the authorities is sufficiently ordained when he has only been prayed for from the pulpit: for we have stated above that the call or election of the person must be distinguished from the ordination. The call by the authorities, even if it is carried out under advisement of preachers, is not sufficient for a proper appointment: rather, in accordance with our church order, the presentation and examination [of the called] and publication of the call are also required, which is done in these churches with prayer and the laying on of hands, so that the called man is properly, regularly, and absolutely appointed to and confirmed in his ecclesial office."[150] The synod appeals to the general rule (according to Luther): "In every place where the Church of Christ is, there must also be a true call and ordination to the preaching office."[151] The *Sententia* closes with the exhortation: ". . . and let all kind, honest, Christian hearts preserve, honor, and glorify ordination with great diligence."[152]

On glancing at the formulations of the decree, it becomes clear in several places that Melanchthon's theology was influential here. At very least, it cannot be doubted that Melanchthon was in full agreement with this doctrinal position of the synod. It must be kept in mind that Jacob Runge, who was the leading theologian at the synod, spent a substantial period of time with Melanchthon shortly before and was fully in agreement with him concerning the doctrine of ordination; and further, that Melanchthon (like the Wittenberg faculty generally) had explicitly endorsed Knipstro's book *Von der Vocation und Ordination* in every point, the ideas of which were fairly closely reflected in the doctrinal decree of the synod. There is no reason to question whether the statements of the decree are entirely in keeping with Melanchthon's view.[153]

148 Balthasar, pp. 113f.

149 Balthasar, p. 114.

150 Balthasar, p. 115.

151 Balthasar, p. 114.

152 Balthasar, pp. 115f.

153 Also cf. the letter written by Melanchthon to Jacob Runge after the Greifswald synod, on March 25, 1556 (CR 8:723f.). — Also G. Rietschel (*Luther u. d. Ordination*, p. 94) maintains that the synod formed the basis for the Wittenberg doctrinal reports. Yet we cannot follow Rietschel then when he says that "in the doctrine itself . . . between the Wittenbergers and Freder there was absolutely no distinction" (op. cit., p. 94). This only represents the statement that the laying on of hands as such was not divinely prescribed, but not the total doctrine of ordination. The fault in Rietschel's view lies in his simply taking the *jus divinum* taught by Melanchthon for examination, publication of

The *second Sententia* of the synod contains the specific decision on the dispute between Knipstro and Freder.[154] In it, Knipstro's book *Von der Vocation und Ordination der Kirchendiener* receives explicit approval. The fault in the whole dispute is ascribed to Freder: "And because Freder, being unordained, entered his ecclesial office and twice, without any necessity and when his office did not demand it, presumptuously performed ordination, and wrote two writings in defense of his action, he is responsible for causing this offensive discord."[155] On Knipstro's doctrine, the following is noted: "It is clear . . . that Dr. Knipstro always argues from the whole ordination used in these churches and is plainly speaking of the established church so that it is not a matter of personal discretion. Likewise, he does not argue about the bare laying on of hands alone, nor about its power and efficacy, nor that he might ascribe any power to it or make it a snare of the conscience."[156] Freder's doctrinal deviation is set forth in the following terms: "He argues about the element of the laying on of hands by itself because it has no peremptory command for it—in contrast to the whole apostolic ordination, which is used publicly in these churches—and disputes that it is unnecessary, an adiaphoron, that is, a matter of discretion. Likewise, he contends that he who is properly issued a call by the authorities is sufficiently ordained as long as a prayer is said for him from the pulpit."[157] Incidentally, he is also accused of distorting the true intent of Luther, Bugenhagen, and Melanchthon by citing only those passages in them which speak of the abuse of the laying on of hands but omitting those "which speak expressly of the whole Christian ordination."[158] "For all these reasons, and because he has not appeared after a repeated invitation and request . . . , the synod finds Master Johann Freder at fault and in contempt, but it declares the honorable and most learned Dr. Johann Knipstro a faithful Christian shepherd and minister of the ecclesial office, who in all things has only done his duty and rightly restrained and opposed disorder and, respecting the synod, has satisfactorily answered all that he was asked."[159] —

With this decision of the Greifswald synod in 1556, the case of Freder's dispute in Pomerania was definitively settled, and Knipstro finally obtained a complete victory. According to it, Freder could no longer remain in Greifswald, and in the same year he left Pomerania to take a superintendency in Wismar, where he soon died. —

---

approval, and the prayer in the call process as the *jus divinum* of churchly order while Melanchthon himself intended quite specific individual acts. Freder's deviation did not consist simply of disregarding order but of declaring ordination, as a particular action, unnecessary. — W. Thomas's position on the dispute concerning Freder (op. cit., p. 23 n. 1), unilaterally emphasizing the examination, also remains unsatisfactory.

154 "*Decretum secundum de Controversiis inter Doctorem Knipstrovium et Magistrum Frederum* [Second decree on the controversies between Dr. Knipstro and Master Freder]," Balthasar, pp. 116–27.

155 Balthasar, p. 117.

156 Balthasar, p. 118. Note here that this opinion of Knipstro's is only supposed to apply to the "bare laying on of hands by itself," not to the one rightly used within the total ordination.

157 Balthasar, pp. 119f.

158 Balthasar, p. 120.

159 Mohnike II, p. 33.

From Freder's ordination dispute and Melanchthon's position in it, it is evident that Melanchthon teaches a *jus divinum*—if not of the laying on of hands specifically, yet of the liturgical ordination action (the publication of approval and the prayer). However, he sees it as valid only in relation to the organized church body (*ecclesiae constitutae*) while in exceptional times of ecclesial strife and necessity it is inactive.

An ecclesial state of necessity is also treated by a memorandum: *An Concionator Evang. petere debeat inaugurationem ab Episcopo* [Whether the Evangelical preacher must seek consecration by a bishop], developed by Melanchthon in 1536 for the doctor of theology Jacob Schenk, who was called to the church of Freiberg in a regular manner and exercised the office there but had to defend himself because he lacked an episcopal consecration.[160] Here Melanchthon takes the following position: When bishops become false teachers and demand unjust vows from the ordinands, they do not need to be included. The call being necessary, it is granted to the authorities and the respective congregation in which the preacher is to do his ministry. The ancient Church's ordination practice shows that the bishop brought in from the vicinity must give his voice "in order that the electee may have testimony to his doctrine, as Paul gives charge to Titus."[161] Besides the call, a doctrinal testimony by other ministers is required for the proper call to the preaching office. All this is present in Jacob Schenk: he is properly called by the church of Freiberg and has this doctrinal attestation "through the *gradus* which I publicly received from those who are in the preaching office, and not otherwise than to teach and preach the pure Christian doctrine, according to the understanding of the true and catholic Church of Christ."[162] Dr. Schenk did not receive an actual ordination in liturgical form, but had a testimony to his doctrinal aptitude by other ministers of the Word through his promotion to the doctoral degree. In the situation of necessity where the bishops, as entities of ordination, are unavailable and an Evangelical inspection has not yet been established, the doctoral promotion here counts in some sense as a substitute ordination. "From all this it is clear that I need no further or other consecration by bishops. For I am regularly called and make no dangerous conventicles, but I have good testimonies to my doctrine."[163] It is clear, however, that Melanchthon means by this only to justify an emergency situation.

Now we must look at another statement by Melanchthon from the year 1549 that does not quite fit in the framework which we have set up. The clergy of Hamburg, in connection with the disputes surrounding the Interim, directed an inquiry to Melanchthon concerning adiaphora[164] in which they also included among the true adiaphora "admitting elected and called men to the sacred

---

160 CR 3:182–85.

161 CR 3:184.

162 CR 3:184f.

163 CR 3:185.

164 The query from Hamburg and Melanchthon's response from April 16, 1549, are in CR 7:366–86.

offices by lawful ordination."[165] In his reply, Melanchthon, like them, counts among the true adiaphora "those things also which the most ancient Church instituted and which are conducive both for good order and for teaching or admonishing the simple, the public ordination to the Evangelical ministry," and places these on the same level, e.g., with the "order of feasts and lessons," marriage, and a church funeral, etc.[166] When Melanchthon here calls "public ordination to the Evangelical ministry" an adiaphoron and explicitly traces it back to the institution by the "most ancient Church" (thus the Church of the apostolic era), he does not assume any *jus divinum* for it. It thus belongs for him to the "ancient customs agreeing with the Church of God from that time until the first fathers,"[167] but for him there is no direct *divine* institution.

Now if we wished to make this statement an unambiguous position by which to interpret Melanchthon's other statements on the same subject, particularly those in which Melanchthon speaks of a *jus divinum* for the public approval and prayer, we would have to distinguish in his statements the public approval (or publication of the approval, the attestation before the church) and prayer on the one hand and the liturgical ordination action (public ordination, public rite of ordination) on the other, and we would need to address the former only as actually *de jure divino* in Melanchthon's scheme. Then the phrases appearing elsewhere in Melanchthon to the effect that it is "honest," "most honorable," or "useful to observe and employ the public rite of ordination"[168] could be understood as Melanchthon meaning to say that the public rite of ordination is not mandatory *de jure divino*, but simply good, fitting, salutary, conducive, and beneficial.[169] The great difficulty for this view, however, lies in Melanchthon's position on the ordination dispute concerning Freder. This involved the idea that not just *any* public approval nor *any* prayer (such as one from the pulpit) is sufficient, but rather that *liturgical* ordination (after prior examination), as the true publication of approval and the true ordination prayer, is necessary. Regarding those things which Freder omitted and Knipstro endorsed, Melanchthon taught (e.g., in his *Sententia de ordinatione ecclesiae ministrorum* of 1551 and in his letter to Christoph Fischer in 1555) the *jus divinum* of the public approval (publication of approval) and prayer, and could hardly mean by this something other than the liturgical ordination, which of course accounted for Freder's fault. In the dispute concerning Freder, the precise assertion made was that ordination is *not* an adiaphoron but, in the context of the total ordination, an ordinance of God attested in Scripture. This was also supported by Melanchthon with his doctrine of the *jus divinum* for the publication of approval and of the prayer.

---

[165] CR 7:373.

[166] CR 7:383.

[167] CR 7:384.

[168] CR 5:211 ("most honorable [*honestissimum*]"); CR 7:743 ("honorable [*honestum*]"); CR 15:1335 ("useful [*utile*]").

[169] Yet it is just as possible for the "*publicus ritus ordinationis*" in CR 7:743 and 15:1335 that is to be retained as "honorable" or "useful" to mean the laying on of hands specifically.

It is accordingly difficult to make a unified formula from Melanchthon's opinions on the question of the *jus divinum* of the liturgical ordination action. It is true that his doctrine on this point is found in an indeterminate state, tending in one direction or another. It is also possible that it was the ordination dispute concerning Freder that first inspired Melanchthon to recognize liturgical ordination distinctly as *de jure divino*. Two things, at least, are certain: (1) Melanchthon teaches no *jus divinum* for the specific gesture of the laying on of hands in ordination; and (2) he certainly teaches it for the public approval (or the publication of approval, the attestation before the church) and the prayer in the call process. The factor of insecurity concerns only the question whether this approval and prayer must be undertaken unconditionally and *de jure divino* in a proper, liturgical ordination action.[170] However this question may be decided, it will nevertheless have to be observed that the public rite of ordination is necessary in Melanchthon's view wherever an organized church structure exists (whether *de jure divino* or *de jure humano*).[171]

7. Ordination as Function of the Office

It has already been related above that Melanchthon views the total call process as an act that has to proceed in collaboration between the office and the congregation.[172] As the call in the narrower sense normally falls to the

[170] W. Thomas asserts (op. cit., pp. 24f.): "The attestation or publication, as a rule taking place through the laying on of hands and prayer, appears especially important for him" (i.e., Melanchthon). "He characterizes the whole also as something that must happen *jure divino*. This he did of the individual parts with the exception of the laying on of hands (examination, publication of approval, prayer)." Thomas also relates the *jus divinum* as such—which Melanchthon, in his letter to C. Fischer (CR 8:597f.), teaches as the approval and prayer—to liturgical ordination, but takes the fact that Melanchthon in the same letter does not call for repeating the ordination of those who have entered the office solely by the call in view of an exceptional state of emergency in the church to mean that the concept of *jus divinum* was "generally diminished" for him (op. cit., p. 27). If Melanchthon took the *jus divinum* of ordination in the strict sense, he would have to call for its repetition as well whenever it was omitted. It is possible to see it this way and to perceive in Melanchthon a "diminished *jus divinum*" for the liturgical ordination action inasmuch as he maintains it only with respect to the *ecclesia constituta*, the established church. Even then, it would still hold true that, for Melanchthon, the public rite of ordination has its place in *direct proximity* to the *jus divinum*. This diminution of the *jus divinum* concept in Melanchthon with respect to the liturgical ordination action would, however, be true only for itself, not for the examination, public approval, and prayer.

[171] In the report of the two Culmbach preachers who sought counsel from Luther and Melanchthon on account of ordination in the summer of 1538, in connection to which we have already shared above on p. 202 n. 342, it reads particularly: "And Master Philip tells especially how weddings are a very honorable, needful thing, not for the confirmation but for the revelation of this true marriage which the two have established together. So, too, the ordination following examination and the call to the priesthood is a very honorable and needful thing because these persons have testimony from a whole congregation that they were legitimately and regularly called and appointed to the priesthood . . ." (T. Kolde, "Zur Gesch. d. Ord. u. Kirchenzucht," *Theol. Stud. u Krit.* [1894], p. 222). The *necessity* as such is a firm fact for Melanchthon, even if it may not always be clearly meant in the sense of a *strict jus divinum*.

[172] Cf. above, pp. 294–98.

congregation or its prominent members, so ordination (with examination, public approval, and prayer) falls to the pastors. For this Melanchthon appeals to the *pattern of Scripture and the ancient Church*. In the apostolic era, of which the New Testament informs us, either the apostles themselves or other pastors issued the call to the office and performed ordination with the laying on of hands.[173] Titus 1:5 is scriptural testimony for "pastors being ordained by neighboring pastors."[174] Melanchthon concludes the same thing from 1 Tim. 5:22, from which passage he justifies the statement: "*It is therefore necessary that pastors be ordained by pastors.*"[175] In the ancient Church, the people held an election and the bishop approved it with the laying on of hands in ordination.[176] Augustine bears witness that the "bishops in Africa were ordained by neighboring ones."[177] Ordination was performed only by office-bearers. According to Melanchthon, it would be a contradiction of the *jus divinum* (from Scripture) and the example of the ancient Church if the people were to seize ordination for themselves and the total call process were done without the "judgment and approval of pastors." Melanchthon calls this mob rule [*demokratia*] and categorically rejects it.[178] For him, it is demanded *de jure divino* that the "judgment and approval" be given by pastors in the call, thus in ordination. Apart from the formal rationale in Scripture and the example of the ancient Church, this is contentually justified for him by the fact that the assessment of the ordinand's orthodoxy and aptitude for teaching, which is declared in ordination, can only be imparted by those who themselves occupy the office.[179] On account of the close link between ordination and the doctrinal interview and doctrinal testimony, it is in the hands of the office-bearers and is entirely a function of the office.[180] The authority for ordination is part of the "power of the order of the

[173] CR 7:741.

[174] CR 21:503.

[175] CR 12:490. — W. Thomas does not evaluate this passage for the problem of the entity of ordination according to Melanchthon (cf. op. cit., pp. 20f.). — Vilmar has a keen sense for this Melanchthonian axiom when he sees in the explanation of AC 14 and Ap 14 in Melanchthon "the indubitable adherence to that apostolic and historically fixed order *that shepherds only may be called by shepherds*" (*Lehre v. geistl. Amt*, pp. 70ff.; cf. *Dogmatik* II, pp. 276f.).

[176] CR 12:490; cf. CR 21:503. Cf. above, pp. 294–95, 297–98.

[177] CR 21:503f.

[178] CR 12:490 (passage cited above, pp. 297–98). Cf. esp. the sentence "Mob rule [δημοκρατία], in which the people seize the vote for themselves without the judgment and approval of pastors, militates against divine right and the ancient Church."

[179] Cf. CR 7:742; 15:1333; 12:381: ". . . God wishes those to whom testimonies are given to be seen by the whole Church, that it may be sure about their call, and that their doctrine and character are examined by all the presbytery and those to whom the government of the church has been committed." Cf. Vilmar, *Lehre v. geistl. Amt*, pp. 70f.; T. Kliefoth, *Lit. Abhandlungen* I, pp. 432f.

[180] Cf. F. W. Hopf, *Luth. Kirchenordnung*, p. 27, who characterizes it as a self-evident application of Lutheran doctrine concerning the regular call "that only one personally called to the office, only one personally standing under the command and the promise of the office, has the authority and duty to ordain others."

office."[181] The appointment of the office (at least with respect to ordination) is committed to the office by God.[182] Melanchthon only knows of an ordination through ministers of the Word.

If this universal and continuous Melanchthonian view is kept in mind, we cannot avoid the impression that in Treatise § 72 (*BKS* 492) the formula "when bishops either become heretics or refuse to impart ordination, *by divine right the churches are compelled to ordain pastors and ministers, making use of their own pastors*" is very carefully considered and is plainly meant to express that ordination always remains a function of the office—even when the bishops become heretical and are disqualified as entities of ordination.[183]

> We have already indicated that the phrase "*jure divino*" very probably applies as well to the phrase "making use of their own pastors."[184] Ordination must—when bishops are disqualified—be conducted by pastors according to divine right. That we are adding no authority by explaining the passage this way is first demonstrated by Melanchthon's other statements about *jus divinum* for pastoral ordination which we have highlighted, and then by the whole train of thought of the second part of the Treatise, especially through the passage Tr 65 (*BKS* 490), which speaks of ordination performed by the pastor in his own church. The second part of the Treatise (on the power and jurisdiction of bishops) begins with the fact that for all who preside over churches, the authority of the office is equal *jure divino*, whether they are called bishops or pastors (Tr 60ff., *BKS* 489f.). The distinction of bishop and pastor is only by human right. The bishop *jure divino* has no more authority than the pastor. While the practice developed in the ancient Church

---

181 Cf. above, pp. 264–71 and the passages indicated there.

182 Cf. above, p. 297 n. 82.

183 It should be kept in mind that the Treatise has the purpose—as Vilmar rightly says—"of justifying the emergency right of the Evangelical church at that time (the defection of the bishops which were then hostile to it and the authority to appoint new clergy by means of its own clergy)" (*Dogmatik* II, p. 275). The formula "by means of its own clergy" in Vilmar agrees precisely with what is expressed in Tr 72 by the words "making use of their own pastors." — Cf. H. Busch, op. cit., p. 29; W. O. Münter, *Die Gestalt der Kirche*, etc., p. 46; id., *Begriff u. Wirklichkeit*, p. 31; F. Brunstäd, op. cit., p. 197. — While W. Trillhaas ("Die luth. Lehre de potestate ecclesiastica," *Zw. D. Zten.* [1933], p. 502) says, "These statements are aimed at the ordination right lying exclusively with the clergy"—he disregards Tr 72 ("making use of their own pastors") as well as Tr 65 ("ordination performed by the pastor"). Tr 67 is written not against the ordination right located strictly with the clergy and thus to the ministers of the Word, but against that located strictly with the Roman episcopacy. — P. Brunner opines that Tr 67 provides for the "farthest limit" suggested to the Bohemians (i.e., ordination by the laity) "as a legitimate measure in a state of emergency" ("Vom Amt d. Bischofs," p. 24; also cf. E. Schlink, op. cit., pp. 336 and 341). Yet this supposition does not have a lot of evidence. It must be countered that in 1537, the Reformation churches did not find themselves in the kind of state of emergency that would require ordinations by the laity. The Treatise is explicitly speaking only of ordination by pastors. Cf. Vilmar, *Lehre v. geistl. Amt*, p. 74. (Still it may be permitted, in the actual occurrence of such a state of emergency in which there is no longer any shepherd, to make such an application of Tr 67 that the church then has the right to appoint shepherds itself. Vilmar, too, recognized such a possibility, op. cit., p. 74. But this is not a necessary part of what is proposed in Tr 67.)

184 Cf. above, pp. 297–98.

of bishops alone ordaining,[185] this privilege of the bishops was only by human right and was not a divine ordinance in the Church. Since no grades of office (bishop, pastor) which are distinct with respect to authority have been given *jure divino*, "*it is clear that ordination performed by the pastor in his own church is valid jure divino*."[186] The ordination by a pastor ("ordination done by the pastor") being valid *jure divino* is the target concept, so to speak, of the whole Treatise. In the first part, the pope's exclusive right to ordain is attacked;[187] in the second, the bishops' exclusive right to ordain is attacked. The result is an ordination by pastors which is valid *de jure divino*. Melanchthon is in no way contending here for the validity of ordination by laypeople, but only for the ordination by pastors. Thus the phrase "making use of their own pastors" in Tr 72 is to be taken as entirely programmatic and fundamental. —

But now something further must be said. Certainly there must be pastors *jure divino* who perform ordination. Now then, if pastors do it instead of bishops, this is by no means an ideal or even normal state of affairs for Melanchthon; on the contrary, this is justified *only in necessity*, namely, when the bishops ordinary become enemies of the Gospel. It is never the norm. What is actually proper and given under normal, orderly circumstances is, according to Melanchthon, ordination performed *by the bishops*.

We have shown in our treatment of church polity that Melanchthon has a refined understanding of the significance of superordinate episcopal oversight and that he views the duty of examining and ordaining ministers of the church as given by God to bishops.[188] *Only* when the bishops refuse to do so does this God-given duty revert to the pastors; *primarily*, it is strictly a matter of the bishops and is their proper office. In the ordination certificate for Prince George of Anhalt, who was called and consecrated bishop of Merseburg, Melanchthon writes: "Whereas Paul commanded Titus to appoint ministers in all places, *be it known that this man, being ordained, is commanded by the apostolic voice for this*

[185] Cf. Tr 62ff. (*BKS* 490ff.); Tr 73 (*BKS* 493); CR 8:706; 25:314: "What were presbyters and bishops? They both taught and administered the Sacraments to the people. But this differed: the bishop had the right of administering ordination."

[186] Tr 65 (*BKS* 490). — Note that the whole argument of the Treatise (§§ 60ff.) would be meaningless if it made no difference whether ordination is undertaken by laymen or office-bearers. Why include the proof that the bishop—pastor distinction is only *de jure humano*? Why include any idea of an "ordination performed by the pastor in his own church" or the rationale for the *jure divino* validity of ordination by pastors on the basis of the *jure divino* equality of the grades of the *office*? — Tr 65 is, according to W. O. Münter (*Die göttl. Gestalt*, etc., p. 47), to be seen as a substantiation of the prefixed statement that the power among all office-bearers is equal *de jure divino*. This is very accurate. Also cf. W. O. Münter, *Begriff u. Wirklichkeit*, pp. 75f.; further, P. Brunner, "Vom Amt d. Bischofs," p. 24. — Also recall the passage CR 22:524 (text above, p. 297 n. 82) and the argument with the statemenmt "that the ordination of ministers of the Gospel is just in our churches" contrary to the Articles of the Bavarian Inquisition of 1558 (*Stud. Ausg.*, vol. VI, pp. 301f.). Cf. above, pp. 289–90 n. 30.

[187] Cf. Tr 5 (*BKS* 472): "(the pope) . . . , from whom all bishops and pastors throughout the world must seek ordination and confirmation, who is supposed to have the right of electing, ordaining, confirming, and deposing all bishops."

[188] Cf. above, pp. 280–81.

function, that he should ordain priests to teach and to govern the churches, and that he should inspect their doctrine and way of life, and remember that he, too, is commanded by the Son of God: 'And you, when you are converted, strengthen your brothers.' "[189] The office of bishop, according to Melanchthon, is by divine necessity the office of an examiner, ordainer, and visitor of pastors.

It was a great source of pain for Melanchthon that the bishops ordinary were unable to be admitted as ordainers of Evangelical preachers since they raved against the Gospel and persecuted the confessors of the pure doctrine, at times cruelly. If the bishops for their part were ready to ordain, it was only on condition of unjust oaths.[190] It is only with a heavy heart that Melanchthon teaches that, under such circumstances, it would not be permissible to be ordained by them, but rather necessary—in accordance with Gal. 1:8—to shun them.[191] Yet the fact that it is not possible for ordination to be obtained from the bishops does not leave the Church extinguished[192] since the ordination by pastors also is valid *jure divino*—yet the latter remains an emergency provision, and a restoration of episcopal ordination is to be pursued. This would, however, only be the case if the bishops abstained from all unjust obligations in ordination, abandoned the unjust vows, adopted the Reformation, ceased persecuting our people, and began to disseminate true doctrine.[193] This is the *solitary* way to regain unity with the Roman bishops: "And there is in short no other way to Christian harmony and unity except this, that the bishops disseminate true doctrine and Christian use of the Sacraments, and that we then obey them as prelates of the Church, which we undertake to do."[194]

---

189 CR 5:825f.

190 The ordinands were to swear that they deny the right doctrine and would take a vow of celibacy. Cf. CR 3:185; 7:742; 8:430; 15:1334.

191 CR 3:184f.; 4:995; 5:212: "That we are not allowed to seek the rite of ordination from the bishops . . . has a clear reason: because they ordain no one without ungodly chains"; CR 5:585, 598, 613, 630f.; 8:291: "But since the bishops persecute the true doctrine, it is impossible before eyes" (i.e., to receive ordination from them); CR 8:430: "The rite of ordination cannot be sought from those who, although they rule with the title of bishops and the prerogatives of ordinary succession, as they call it, nevertheless they are plainly enemies of the Gospel and defend idols"; CR 12:519: "And since the ordinations of the Antichrist have ungodly conditions, they are damned even in the psalm, 'I will not receive their drink offerings' "; CR 12:526: "Since the bishops oppose the Gospel, we are compelled by divine command to abandon them"; CR 15:1334; Ap 7.48 (*BKS* 246); cf. *Stud. Ausg.*, vol. VI, pp. 287, 302.

192 CR 5:212; 8:430f.: "nor do true churches have to be without pastors, without forgiveness of sins, simply because the tyranny of the bishops drives away suitable ministers or refuses to appoint them."

193 CR 2:247: "Until now, priests were tormented for marrying wives and such things. Now they will cheerfully submit since the danger has been lifted"; CR 2:745f.; 4:414f., 422, 489, 503, 984; 5:744; 7:175.

194 CR 5:598; cf. CR 5:585; 4:927, 984; 7:179, 262.

Melanchthon fervently wishes that this would become a reality. Yet as long as it failed to become a reality, ordination by pastors, which is also valid *de jure divino*, must remain in place.[195] In summary we can say: Melanchthon teaches ordination as a function proper to bishops, and in emergencies also to pastors, yet certainly of the spiritual office *de jure divino*. —

We have reached the end of our journey through Melanchthon's doctrine of ordination. This can only be conceived of as a portion of his doctrine of the call generally. Ordination in the specific sense is not to be detached from the total process of the call, the organic conclusion of which is formed, in Melanchthon's view, by ordination. Its significance lies in its character which brings the total call process to its conclusion. Thus a legitimate call to the clerical office without cooperation of the same office is for him unthinkable. By this, the peculiarity of the office toward the congregation, resting as it does on the divine institution, is strongly underscored. The accent placed on this is wholly reflective of Melanchthon's determination that obedience to the office is a mark of the Church, or even his designation of ordination to the office as a sacrament. It finds expression in the fact that the effectual reality of the office instituted by God forms a decisive point of Melanchthon's theology. —

[195] It must be judged as a deficiency in Melanchthon that, in face of the disqualification of the Roman bishops, he did not strive more energetically to establish an Evangelical episcopal office but rather allowed development to slide toward the consistorial system.

CHAPTER V

Melanchthon and Luther

Since the doctrine of the office and ordination in Luther as well as in Melanchthon has been the object of our inquiry, a question suggests itself: How do the views of office and ordination in the two theologians relate? Where and to what extent do they agree? In what articles do they differ? In treating this question, it must be acknowledged, first, that Melanchthon in his early period came strongly under the impressive influence of Luther and only gradually grew to realize his theological intentions independently and to accentuate the peculiar character of his doctrinal perspective.[1] We need not commit the error of interpreting Melanchthon's whole doctrine of the office on the basis of certain occasional statements in the *Loci* of 1521 or other early writings. What is characteristic of Melanchthon as a theologian is to be looked for not in his early writings but in his later formulations.

If Melanchthon's doctrine of the office is accordingly examined in its mature stage, it is evident that it is not simply to be equated with Luther's. Clear differences can be identified, even if it will not be possible to say that these differences also imply basic contradictions.

There is in both of them a *large area of fundamental commonality*, which prevents the differing nuances and accents from defining the overall picture of their view of the office to *such* a degree that directly contradictory perspectives emerge. The fundamental positions of an Evangelical doctrine of the office as distinct from the Roman view of the office were set down by Luther and adopted and developed further by Melanchthon. In both theologians, the doctrine of the office is rooted in the doctrine of justification; the office, in its objective necessity, is founded in both on the God-ordained character of the Word and Sacraments as means of grace. The office transmits salvation through the ministry of the means of grace. Thus, for both, the antithesis against the Enthusiasts is just as important as that against the Roman satisfactionary view of the office. The definition of the office as the office of the Word (and Sacraments) has for both this engagement with a double front. Additionally, the emphasis of the functional character of the office is a hallmark of both (although there are stronger accents here in Luther than in Melanchthon). The office is understood not as having intrinsic worth but instrumentally (as ministry of the Word and Sacraments).

[1] Cf. H. Busch, *Melanchthons Kirchenbegriff*, p. 8.

A static view of the office is suspect for both. Corresponding to this is the fact that, in general, the idea of the ministry strongly occupies the foreground, and the danger of holding sway in the office over the faith and life of the congregation is clearly encountered. For both, the essence of the ecclesial office is bound up with its public character and marked off from the private sphere, in which also Word and Absolution are handled (with some restriction). Both regard this public office of the Word not merely as an item of human, sociological necessity but as a divine institution. In this point, no very substantial difference between the two views can be posited. For both it is established from Scripture that God ordained the office in the sense of binding the function of the office to specified officers as a constant institution in the Church and that it is in no way left to the discretion of the Church to administer the ministry of the Word in this way or any other. That the Church has a divine command to appoint persons to the concrete, public office is a firm and indisputable realization in Luther as well as in Melanchthon. That this divinely established office is one and the grades within it are *juris humani* is likewise both men's conviction. Both teach that office-bearers in the office participate in God's authority insofar as they carry out their office in accordance with their commission, and conversely forfeit all authority—indeed, can and must be removed from the office—when they deviate from the commission of their office and no longer offer pure Word and Sacrament. That the congregation in such a case has the right and duty to restrain an unfaithful office-bearer, to avoid him, or, where possible, to remove him is Melanchthon's teaching no less than Luther's. Both agree, however, that the congregation has no final authority over the office.

As in the general doctrine of the office, so in the doctrine of the call and ordination there is a broad basis of commonality. For both men, the absolute necessity of a particular call to the office is firmly fixed; only with a regular call can someone hold the office in good conscience; both judge the exercise of the office in the congregation without the call as objectionable presumption and sin which remains without blessing; both distinguish direct and indirect calling and teach that today only the indirect call still takes place through the Church. The Church is the bearer of the right to call, yet according to both men it exercises it normally through designated persons who stand out because of their official status or personal qualification. According to both theologians, office-bearers, too, must participate in the call; indeed, it may be said that for both the given standard is that the ministers of the Word—that is, primarily the bishops—bear the concern and responsibility for the calling of new ministers, yet in the process the suffrage of the congregation may not be eliminated. For both, the ancient Church's call process has an exemplary significance; both seek to model the call process today on this pattern of the ancient Church. For both, a decisive role is played by the examination, the investigation of doctrine and life prior to the final bestowal of the ministerial commission. And yet for both theologians also, there is no definitive conferral of the office until the specific ordination rite occurs on the basis of the preceding acts. In ordination, according to both men, the call to a specified office is confirmed and the aptitude for the teaching office (with respect to doctrine, gifts, and conduct) is publicly attested by other ministers of the Word, and the ordinand himself is finally installed in the office and blessed for that office. According to both, God acts in a calling, sending, and blessing capacity through ordination. For both, the prayer is an indispensable component of the ordination action in the narrower sense and should normally be tied to the laying on of hands, which is valued by both as a traditional ordination rite. Both, it is true, teach no direct *jus divinum* for the laying on of hands, but they always call for its use. For both of them, it has not only a testifying, signifying meaning in ordination but also a benedictory meaning in connection with the ordination prayer. Luther as well as Melanchthon envisions an office-bearer (bishop or pastor) as a minister of ordination. Thus there is a clear thread of commonality pervading all the individual areas of the doctrine of office and ordination in both theologians. This should not, however, mislead us into overlooking the differences also present between the two men.

The article of doctrine in which Melanchthon's distinctiveness from Luther is most clearly observed is the universal priesthood—or, more particularly, the grounding of the concrete office on the universal priesthood. We have shown that Melanchthon, too, knows of the concept of the universal priesthood of Christians, but that in Melanchthon's doctrine of the office it plays a rather subordinate role while for Luther it has very fundamental significance in the development of the concept of the office (as far as the components thereof are concerned). The interpretation of the concept of the universal priesthood in Melanchthon's approach is also different from that in Luther's. Melanchthon sees the universal priesthood in essence as exclusively an exercise of *those* functions which accrue to every Christian by virtue of his Christian estate, from faith itself, not as the embodiment of the functions of the particular office as well. For Melanchthon, the Christian priesthood means immediacy, the free petitionary access to God, and the ability to offer God-pleasing spiritual sacrifices through faith in Christ. The idea of interceding for others as a content of the priestly concept, which is strongly emphasized in Luther, is wanting in Melanchthon. Of greater significance is the fact that Melanchthon does not take the priesthood as the embodiment of the particular office, the specific administration of the means of grace, as is done in Luther. There are in the periphery occasional expressions by him from which such an idea might possibly be read, yet—if present at all—it plays no constructive role for his concept of the office. The idea of the fundamental equality of all Christians—including the power of the Word and all the Sacraments, which in Luther is directly derived from the universal priesthood and has an important place in the foundation for his doctrine of the office—finds reference in Melanchthon only in the early period and plays no role at all in his later work. When Melanchthon teaches that in an emergency any Christian may administer the Word, Baptism, and the Absolution, he bases this simply on the fact that the Keys are given not to all individual persons (e.g., officers) but to the whole Church, yet in doing so he makes no reference to the concept of the universal priesthood. Luther, on the other hand, grounds this directly in the universal priesthood of all Christians.

A derivation of the particular office from the universal priesthood and from the sociological circumstances of the priestly nation of Christians, as is clearly present in Luther, is out of the question in Melanchthon. The relation which Melanchthon makes between the Christian priesthood and the ministry of the Word is only that the congregation, as God's priestly nation, must have the right to appoint the particular office, to call ministers to the particular office. The character of the congregation as priesthood demands the appointed ministry of the Word within it since the priestly nation cannot live without Word and Sacrament. In no way is the office in Melanchthon a kind of special case of the priesthood while for Luther (in one manner of considering the office in him) it certainly is. Melanchthon sees the concrete office, properly speaking, grounded exclusively in Christ's institution, in the promise in Eph. 4:11ff., and in the command to appoint ministers. The ordination motive is naturally present in Melanchthon too—even with greater emphasis—yet not as one on which the office is grounded, but only as an added illustration of the expediency of the divine institution of the office. The sociological rationale for the concrete office on the basis of the idea of fraternity—in which all have the same rights, but since only one and not all can exercise them, it is committed to him by all—is absent in Melanchthon. There is no trace of a delegatory thinking in Melanchthon's rationale of the office. The idea that the office-bearer stands as a representative of the whole, of the congregation, in the place and name of all, is not encountered in Melanchthon.[2] Melanchthon sees ministers not as representatives of the congregation but only as representatives of the Lord. In Luther we found two layers for the rationale of the office and the view of the office, one built on the universal priesthood and the office derived from it, the other springing from the divine institution of the office. But in looking for these two lines in Melanchthon, we fail to find the first. Melanchthon sees the office exclusively as divine institution and ignores an existential relation of the office back to the universal priesthood.

Possibly connected with this more decisive focus on the divine foundation of the office is the fact that, in the whole body of doctrine about the church, the office receives an even stronger emphasis in Melanchthon than in Luther. In any case, we are speaking here only of a distinction of grade, not of a fundamental, structural one. In Melanchthon, the power of the Church is found even more clearly than the focus on the office. Where Luther, e.g., prefers to identify the congregation per se as the agent of doctrinal assessment, Melanchthon speaks instead of the spiritual office which is duty bound to discern doctrine and reject the doctrine that disagrees with the Gospel. With more clarity than Luther, Melanchthon ascribes to office-bearers the right to establish church orders, and thus to regulate also the external things of the church's life. Generally, in Melanchthon, the positive evaluation of the episcopal arrangement of the Church is more marked than in Luther. Luther, too, desires the maintenance of the traditional episcopal structure of the Church and—as with

[2] Cf. W. Thomas, op. cit., p. 43.

the Bohemians—considers the institution of Evangelical bishoprics, and even performed episcopal consecration himself. Melanchthon's stance, however, is characterized by an even stronger adherence to convention and tradition.[3] For Melanchthon, the office is the refuge of all ecclesial order precisely as a divine institution. Thus he calls it, or the subordination under it, a "mark of the Church," which does not occur in Luther. Objectively, Luther likewise certainly desires obedience toward the office, but he does not include it so fundamentally or with such accentuation in the concept of the church. On the same line is the fact that Melanchthon can endorse a sacramental character for the *ordo*, the ordination to the office—and, indeed, even for the laying on of hands. Luther does not do this, although he, too, occasionally can put the laying on of hands in ordination in parallel with the sacraments. It will probably be justified to say that ordination in Melanchthon holds an even stronger emphasis than it has in Luther, and Melanchthon explicitly refers to the individual parts of the total call process (the call, examination, approval, and prayer) as *juris divini*. While Luther (with the Bohemians) provides for an ordination by the laity in case of necessity, such is not encountered in Melanchthon. In Melanchthon it says, "Pastors must be ordained by pastors" (CR 12:490).

Most of the distinctions mentioned here are disparities either in the periphery or in strength of emphasis. The only radical distinction between Luther and Melanchthon in the doctrine of the office concerns the derivation of the office from the universal priesthood, which is absent in Melanchthon. But since Luther, along with the latter, teaches the basis of the office in the divine institution, there is no actual contradiction in this. Both forms of doctrine in Luther and Melanchthon must be assessed as two branches on one and the same tree. Essentially, both theologians are on the same path.

---

[3] This finds expression, e.g., in the fact that Melanchthon is able to endorse the papacy *de jure humano* while Luther categorically rejects even its *jus humanum*. Cf. SA II 4.7ff. (*BKS* 429ff.) and Melanchthon's subscription to the SA (*BKS* 463ff.).

Concluding Remarks

Our study of the doctrine of the office and ordination in Luther and in Melanchthon has in various ways revealed new aspects which have been given too little or almost no attention in the past. Regarding *Luther*, it has become clear that G. Rietschel's interpretation of Luther's doctrine of the office and ordination, which until now was largely dominant, is in need of supplementation and, in part, correction since despite the pervasive bipolarity of Luther's doctrine of the office, his understanding of the divine character of the institution of the office stands out much more powerfully than was generally expected, especially the fact that the sense of the ordination rite instituted by Luther is not exhausted by a solemn (more or less decorative) confirmation of the prior call. The *unilateral* emphasis on the call in the narrower sense as the decisive process in the appointment of the office, as it is found in Rietschel and also as has come to be practiced fairly generally, gives an insufficient and therefore inaccurate picture. Luther certainly understands ordination as a confirmation of the prior call as well, even primarily so (if perhaps never in the decorative sense!), yet also as the effectual conferral of the office and efficacious installation into the office, and he also knows of the significance of the blessing in ordination. In quite essential points, Luther's view of the office and ordination as we have found it comes closer to the new positions being represented today in Lutheran theology which we discussed in the introduction to this work.[1]

It is the same situation with *Melanchthon*. The representation which W. Thomas gave of Melanchthon's doctrine of the office and ordination, and which (along with the studies by O. Ritschl and H. Busch) constitutes the only specialized study of halfway recent date on this subject, shows variously—we feel—a shift in the direction of a congregational principle, which is for all intents and purposes not present in Melanchthon. The significance which Melanchthon attributes to the divinely instituted ministry of the Church is still substantially greater than estimated by Thomas. The clear demarcation of the office from the Christian priesthood, which exists in Melanchthon, must be highlighted more sharply than has been done previously in scholarship. In this respect, the more recent recognitions of the independence of the office over against the universal priesthood are in complete conformity with Melanchthon's teaching. Also

[1] Cf. the foreword to the German edition not reproduced in this volume. — Yet the difference remains in the derivation of the office from the universal priesthood, which was essential for Luther but has really been abandoned today.

tending in the same direction is Melanchthon's doctrine of the *jus divinum* in the call process, in which more accurate understanding of ordination is being pursued today. Of particular importance in this respect is his position in the ordination conflict concerning Freder.

Concerning the *Confessions'* interpretation of the doctrine of the office and ordination, newer viewpoints are also brought to bear in our study which were variously operative in the confessional theology of the nineteenth century but retreated somewhat into the background since that time. It cannot be ignored that quite substantial aspects of the doctrine of the office in theologians such as Stahl, Vilmar, Löhe, and Kliefoth can really be traced back to the New Testament and to the theology of the Reformation fathers such as Luther and Melanchthon, and especially the doctrine of the Lutheran Confessions. These theologians of the nineteenth century had an eye for much in the theology of Luther and of Melanchthon and in the Confessions that later generations of theologians frequently overlooked or swept aside. In this respect, current Lutheran theology is confronted with the task of sifting through the previous century's great debate about the office once more and evaluating its results for the current questions of our day.[2] —

The present work may be regarded as a small contribution to the resistance of the biased (in a certain respect) and, until now, dominant interpretation of Luther's and Melanchthon's doctrine of the office and ordination and to the furtherance of a comprehensive appreciation of that doctrine. And if the accusation of bias in a different direction can be made against it in one respect or another from another theological position—which individual view of an object would be entirely free of biases!—it may nevertheless, for its modest part, serve the overarching goal of every scholarly effort: the recognition of the objective truth in the sense of the principle "*audiatur et altera pars* [let the other party be heard too]." It consciously adheres to the framework of a purely historical study. But to the extent that new impulses tend to be given precisely from a historiographic work of systematic reflection, it might—to that extent—also be understood as a little contribution to the systematic effort toward the right doctrine of the office and ordination. —

[2] A promising beginning has been made in this regard by the great historiographic study by Holsten Fagerberg, *Bekenntnis, Kirche und Amt in der deutschen konfessionellen Theologie des 19. Jahrhunderts* (Uppsala, 1952). It invites further work in the direction of a systematic analysis of its results.

Bibliography

Achelis, E. Chr. *Lehrbuch der praktischen Theologie*. 3rd ed. Vol. 1. Leipzig: Hinrichs, 1911.

———. "Studien über das 'geistliche Amt.'" *Theologische Studien und Kritiken* 62 (1889): 7–79.

Agende für evangelisch-lutherische Kirchen und Gemeinden. Edited by the church leadership of the VELKD [United Evangelical Lutheran Church of Germany]. Vol. 4. Neuendettelsau: Freimund, 1951; Berlin, 1952.

Aland, Kurt. *Hilfsbuch zum Lutherstudium*. Gütersloh: Bertelsmann, 1956.

Althaus, Paul. *Die christliche Wahrheit*. Vol. 2. Gütersloh: Bertelsmann, 1948.

———. *Communio sanctorum: Die Gemeinde im lutherischen Kirchengedanken*. Vol. 1, *Luther*. Munich: Kaiser, 1929.

Asmussen, Hans. "Das Amt der Bischöfe nach Augustana 28." Pages 209–31 in *Reformation, Schicksal und Auftrag, festgabe für J. Lortz*. Baden-Baden: Grimm, 1958.

———. *Die Kirche und das Amt*. Munich: Kaiser, 1939.

———. *Warum noch lutherische Kirche? Ein Gespräch mit dem Augsburgischen Bekenntnis*. Stuttgart: Evangelische Verlagswerk, 1949.

Balthasar, Jakob Heinrich von. *Erste Sammlung einiger zur Pommerischen Kirchenhistorie gehörigen Schriften*. Greifswald: Buß, 1723.

Behm, Heinrich. *Der Begriff des allgemeinen Priestertums*. Schwerin i. M.: F. Bahn, 1912.

———. "Der character indelebilis des evangelischen Pfarramts." *Pastoralblätter* 70. Edited by E. Stange. (1927–28): 65–72.

Behrens, J. "Geistliches Amt und Laienämter." *Evangelisch-Lutherische Kirchenzeitung* 6, no. 7 (1952): 97–100.

Bekenntnisschriften der evangelisch-lutherischen Kirche, Die. Edited by the Deutscher Evangelischer Kirchenausschuß. Göttingen: Vandenhoeck & Ruprecht, 1930.

Bekenntnisse, Die Fränkischen. Edited by the territorial consistory of the Evangelisch-Lutherische Landeskirche in Bayern rechts des Rheins. Munich: Kaiser, 1930.

Bernau, Heinz. "Die Bedeutung der Ordination nach den lutherischen Bekenntnisschriften." Pages 47–88 in *Kirche und Amt* 1, supplement to vol. 2 of *Evangelische Theologie*. Munich: Lempp, 1940.

Brieger, Theodor. "Die kirchliche Gewalt der Obrigkeit nach der Anschauung Luthers." *Zeitschrift für Theologie und Kirche* 2 (1892): 513–34.

Brunner, Peter. "Vom Amt des Bischofs." Pages 5–77 in *Schriften des Theologischen Konvents Augsburgischen Bekenntnisses* 9. Berlin: Lutherisches Verlagshaus, 1955.

Brunner, Peter. *Nikolaus von Amsdorf als Bischof von Naumburg*. Schriften des Vereins für Reformationsgeschichte 179. Gütersloh: Gütersloher, 1961.

Brunotte, Wilhelm. *Das geistliche Amt bei Luther*. Berlin: Lutherisches Verlagshaus, 1959.

Brunstäd, Friedrich. *Theologie der lutherischen Bekenntnisschriften*. Gütersloh: Bertelsmann, 1951.

Buchwald, Georg. *Ungedruckte Predigten Bugenhagens aus den Jahren 1524 bis 1529*. Leipzig: Heinsius, 1910.

———. "Wann hat Luther die erste Ordination vollzogen?" *Theologische Studien und Kritiken* 69 (1896): 151–57.

Busch, Hugo. *Die Lehre von der Kirche bei Melanchthon* [*Melanchthons Kirchenbegriff*]. Dissertation, Bonn, 1918.

Campenhausen, Hans von. "Die Schlüsselgewalt der Kirche." *Evangelische Theologie* 4 (1937): 143–69.

Corpus Reformatorum: Philippi Melanthonis Opera quae supersunt omnia. Edited by Carolus Gottlieb Bretschneider. Vols. 1–28. Halle, 1834ff.

Credo ecclesiam, festgabe für W. Zoellner. Gütersloh: Bertelsmann, 1930.

Credo ecclesiam: Von der Kirche heute. Edited by Evangelische Michaelsbruderschaft. Kassel: J. Stauda-Verlag, 1955.

Creutzig, Hans-Erich. *Amt und Ämter in der lutherischen Kirche*. Theologie militans 22. Leipzig: Deichert, 1938. *Luthertum* 2 (1938): 114–21.

Dieckhoff, August Wilhelm. *Luthers Lehre von der kirchlichen Gewalt*. Berlin, 1865.

Diehl, W. "Zur Geschichte der Ordination: Halte was du hast." *Zeitschrift für Pastoraltheologie* 23. Edited by E. Sachsse. (1900): 585–95.

Doerne, Martin. *Lutherisches Pfarramt: Rechenschaft und Wegweisung*. Theologia militans 10. Leipzig: A. Deichert, 1937.

———. *See also* Sommerlath, E., "Das Wesen des Amtes nach lutherischer Auffassung."

Drews, Paul. "Einleitung zum Ordinationsformular Luthers." WA 38:401ff.

———. "Die Ordination, Prüfung und Lehrverpflichtung der Ordinanden in Wittenberg 1535." *Deutsche Zeitschrift für Kirchenrecht* 15. Edited by Friedberg and Sehling. (1905): 66–90, 273–321.

Echternach, Helmut. *Segnende Kirche: Eine exegetische Studie*. 2nd ed. Hamburg: Nölke, 1948.

Elert, Werner. *Der christliche Glaube*. Berlin: Furche, 1940. 3rd ed. Berlin: Furche, 1955.

———. *Morphologie des Luthertums*. Vol. 1. Munich: Beck, 1952.

———. "Das Visitationsamt in der kirchlichen Neuordnung." *Jahrbuch des Martin-Luther-Bundes* (1948): 66–78.

Enders, Ernst Ludwig, ed. *Dr. Martin Luthers Briefwechsel*. 19 volumes. Frankfurt a/M, 1884–1932. Continued by Gustav Kawerau.

———. Recension of G. Rietschel, "Luther und die Ordination." *Theologische Literaturzeitung* 25 (1885): cols. 612–14.

Fagerberg, Holsten. *Bekenntnis, Kirche und Amt in der deutschen konfessionellen Theologie des 19. Jahrhunderts*. Uppsala: Almqvist & Wiksell, 1952.

Foerster, Erich. "Fragen zu Luthers Kirchenbegriff aus der Gedankenwelt seines Alters." Pages 87–102 in *Festgabe für J. Kaftan*. Tübingen: Mohr, 1920.

Frank, Karl. *Historische, dogmatische und kritische Beiträge zur Lehre von der protestantischen Ordination*. Dissertation, Greifswald, 1913.

Friedrich, Gerhard. "Geist und Amt." *Wort und Dienst: Jahrbuch der Theologischen Schule Bethel* n.s. 3 (1952): 61–85.

Gottschick, Johannes. *Luthers Theologie*. Supplementary volume to *Zeitschrift für Theologie und Kirche* 1. Tübingen: Mohr (Siebeck), 1914.

Grützmacher, Richard H. "Beiträge zur Geschichte der Ordination in der evangelischen Kirche." *Neue kirchliche Zeitschrift* 23 (1912): 363–79.

Harleß, G. C. A. *Kirche und Amt nach lutherischer Lehre*. Stuttgart: S. G. Liesching, 1853.

Harnack, Theodosius. *Die Kirche, ihr Amt, ihr Regiment: Grundlegende Sätze mit durchgehender Bezugnahme auf die symbolischen Bücher der lutherischen Kirche*. Gütersloh: Bertelsmann, 1947. Unaltered reprint of a work published in Nuremberg, 1862.

———. *Luthers Theologie*. 2 vols. New edition. Munich, 1927.

Heber, J. "Sendung und Segnung." *Evangelisch-lutherische Kirchenzeitung* 9, no. 2 (1955): 26–28.

Hennecke, Edgar. *Zur Gestaltung der Ordination mit besonderer Rücksicht auf die Entwicklung innerhalb der lutherischen Kirche Hannovers*. Forschungen zur Geschichte Niedersachsens 1.1. Hanover: Hahn, 1906.

Heppe, Heinrich. *Dogmatik des deutschen Protestantismus im sechzehnten Jahrhundert*. Vol. 3. Gotha: Perthes, 1857.

Herrlinger, Albert. *Die Theologie Melanchthons*. Gotha: Perthes, 1879.

Heubach, Joachim. *Die Ordination zum Amt der Kirche*. Berlin: Lutherisches Verlagshaus, 1956.

Hilbert, G. "Charisma und Amt." Pages 356–69 in *Das Erbe Martin Luthers und die gegenwärtige theologische Forschung, Festschrift für Ludwig Ihmels*. Edited by Robert Jelke. Leipzig: Dörffling & Franke, 1928.

Hoffmann, Georg. "Die Frage des Lehramts und der Lehrgewalt im Luthertum." *Zeitschrift für Systematische Theologie* 17 (1940): 37–70.

Höfling, J. W. F. *Grundsätze evangelisch-lutherischer Kirchenverfassung*. 3rd ed. Erlangen: T. Bläsing, 1853.

———. *Liturgisches Urkundenbuch*. Edited by Harnack and Thomasius. Leipzig: Teubner, 1854.

Hök, Gösta. "Luthers läran om kyrkans ämbete." Pages 142–79 in *En bok om kyrkans ämbete*. Uppsala: Almqvist & Wiksells, 1951.

Holl, Karl. *Luther*. 6th ed. *Gesammelte Aufsätze zur Kirchengeschichte* 1. Tübingen: Mohr, 1932.

Holstein, Günther. *Die Grundlagen des evangelischen Kirchenrechts*. Tübingen: J. C. B. Mohr (Siebeck), 1928.

Hopf, Friedrich W. *Lutherische Kirchenordnung*. Bekennende Kirche 29. Munich: Kaiser, 1935.

Jacobi, G. "Die Lehre von der Kirche in den lutherischen Bekenntnisschriften und die Kirche in Berlin-Brandenburg." Pages 57–80 in *Die Stunde der Kirche, Festschrift für O. Dibelius*. Berlin: Evangelische Verlagsanstalt, 1950.

Jacobson, H. F. "Über den Begriff der Vokation und Ordination." *Theologische Studien und Kritiken* 40 (1867): 244–93.

Jacoby, Hermann. *Die Liturgik der Reformatoren*. 2 vols. Gotha: Perthes, 1871–76.

Josefson, Ruben. "Das Amt der Kirche." Pages 386–401 in *Ein Buch von der Kirche*. Göttingen, 1951.

Josefson, Ruben. "Det andliga ämbetet i Svenska kyrkans bekännelseskrifter." Pages 180–91 in *En bok om kyrkans ämbete*. Uppsala: Almqvist & Wiksells, 1951.

Kahl, Wilhelm. "Der Rechtsinhalt des Konkordienbuches." Pages 305–53 in *Festgabe der Berliner Juristischen Fakultät für O. Gierke*. Breslau: Marcus, 1910.

Kattenbusch, Ferdinand. *Die Doppelschichtigkeit in Luthers Kirchenbegriff*. Lutherana 5. Theologische Studien und Kritiken: Luther 5. Gotha: Klotz, 1928.

Kawerau, Gustav. *Dr. Martin Luthers Briefwechsel*. 19 vols. Frankfurt a/M, 1884–1932. Begun by Ernst Ludwig Enders.

———v. "Knipstro." *Realenzyklopädie für protestantische Theologie und Kirche*. 3rd ed.

Kimme, August. "Doctrina und ordo ecclesiasticus nach lutherischem Verständnis." Pages 54–75 in *Schriften des Theologischen Konvents Augsburgischen Bekenntnisses* 8. Berlin: Lutherisches Verlagshaus, 1955.

Kinder, Ernst. "Allgemeines Priestertum im Neuen Testament." Pages 5–23 in *Schriften des Theologischen Konvents Augsburgischen Bekenntnisses* 5. Berlin: Lutherisches Verlagshaus, 1953.

———. *Der evangelische Glaube und die Kirche*. Berlin: Lutherisches Verlagshaus, 1958.

———. *Geistliches und weltliches Regiment Gottes nach Luther*. Schriften-Reihe der Luthergesellschaft 12. Weimar: Böhlau, 1940.

Kliefoth, Theodor. *Liturgische Abhandlungen*. Vol. 1. Schwerin/Rostock: Stiller, 1854. Especially part 3: "Von der Ordination und Introduktion," pp. 341ff.

Kolde, Theodor. *Die älteste Redaktion der Augsburger Konfession mit Melanchthons Einleitung*. Gütersloh: Bertelsmann, 1906.

———. *Die Augsburgische Konfession, lateinisch und deutsch*. 2nd ed. Gotha: Perthes, 1911.

———. "Zur Geschichte der Ordination und Kirchenzucht." *Theologische Studien und Kritiken* 67 (1894): 217–44.

Köstlin, Julius. *Luthers Lehre von der Kirche*. Stuttgart: Liesching, [1863].

———. *Luthers Theologie in ihrer geschichtlichen Entwicklung und ihrem inneren Zusammenhang*. 2nd ed. [Stuttgart: Steinkopf,] 1901.

———. Recension of G. Rietschel, "Luther und die Ordination." *Theologische Studien und Kritiken* 57 (1884): 385f.

Kramm, Hans-H. *Bischof, Pastor und Gemeinde*. Luthertum 13. Berlin: Lutherisches Verlagshaus, 1954.

Künneth, Walter. *Politik zwischen Dämon und Gott*. Berlin: Lutherisches Verlagshaus, 1954.

Lezius, Friedrich. "Gleichheit und Ungleichheit: Aphorismen zur Theologie und Staatsanschauung Luthers." Pages 285–325 in *Greifswalder Studien*. Gütersloh: Bertelsmann, 1895.

Liermann, Hans. *Grundlagen des kirchlichen Verfassungsrechts nach lutherischer Auffassung*. Luthertum 11. Berlin: Lutherisches Verlagshaus, 1954.

Lindroth, Hjalmar, ed. *En bok om kyrkans ämbete*. Uppsala: Almqvist & Wiksells, 1951.

Logstrup, K. E. "Die Kategorie und das Amt der Verkündigung im Hinblick auf Luther und Kierkegaard." *Evangelische Theologie* 9 (1949/1950): 249ff.

Löhe, Wilhelm. *Aphorismen über die neutestamentlichen Ämter* (1849) and *Kirche und Amt: Neue Aphorismen* (1851). Gesammelte Werke 5.1. Edited by Klaus Ganzert. Neuendettelsau: Freimund-Verlag, 1954.

Lohse, Eduard. *Die Ordination im Spätjudentum und im Neuen Testament*. Göttingen, 1951.

Luther, Martin. *D. Martin Luthers . . . sämtliche Schriften*. Vol. 19. Edited by Johann G. Walch. Halle: Gebauer, 1746.

———. *D. Martin Luthers Werke: Briefwechsel*. 18 vols. Weimar: H. Böhlau, 1930–.

———. *D. Martin Luthers Werke: Kritische Gesamtausgabe*. 73 vols. in 85. Weimar: H. Böhlau, 1883–.

———. *D. Martin Luthers Werke: Tischreden*. 6 vols. Weimar: H. Böhlau, 1912–21.

———. *Dr. Martin Luther's sämmtliche Werke*. 2nd ed. 26 vols. in 27. Frankfurt and Erlangen: Heyder & Zimmer, 1862–85.

———. *Luthers Werke*. 3rd ed. Edited by Georg Buchwald et al. Berlin: Schwetschke & Son, 1905.

Mahrenholz, Christhard. *Begleitwort zur Agende für evangelisch-lutherische Kirchen und Gemeinden*. Vol. 4. Berlin: Lutherisches Verlagshaus, 1952.

Maurer, Wilhelm. *Gemeindezucht, Gemeindeamt, Konfirmation*. Schriftenreihe, des Pfarrervereins Kurhessen-Waldeck 2. Kassel: Stauda-Verlag, 1940.

———. *Pfarrerrecht und Bekenntnis*. Berlin: Lutherisches Verlagshaus, 1957.

Meinhold, Peter. *Die Genesisvorlesung Luthers und ihre Herausgeber*. Forschungen zur Kirchen- und Geistesgeschichte 8. Stuttgart: Kohlhammer, 1936.

Melanchthon, Philip. *Opera*. Corpus Reformatorum: Philippi Melanthoni Opera, quae supersunt omnia. Vols. 1–28. Edited by Carolus Gottlieb Bretschneider. Halle, 1834ff.

———. *Supplementa Melanchthoniana*. Vol. 1.1: *Dogmatische Schriften*. Edited by O. Clemen. Leipzig: Haupt, 1910. Vol. 6.1: *Melanchthons Briefwechsel 1510–1528*. Edited by O. Clemen. Leipzig: Haupt, 1926.

———. *Werke in Auswahl.* Vol. 1: *Reformatorische Schriften.* Edited by Robert Stupperich. Gütersloh: Bertelsmann, 1951. Vol. 2.1: *Loci communes von 1521. Loci praecipui theologici von 1559* (part 1). Edited by Hans Engelland. Gütersloh: Bertelsmann, 1952. Vol. 2.2: *Loci praecipui theologici von 1559* (part 2) and *Definitiones.* Edited by Hans Engelland. Gütersloh: Bertelsmann, 1953. Vol. 6: *Bekenntnisse und kleine Lehrschriften.* Edited by Hans Engelland and Robert Stupperich. Gütersloh: Bertelsmann, 1955.

Mohnike, Gottlieb. *Des Johannes Frederus Leben und geistliche Gesänge.* Vols. 1–2. Stralsund, 1840.

Müller, Karl. *Kirche, Gemeinde und Obrigkeit nach Luther.* Tübingen: J. C. B. Mohr (Paul Siebeck), 1910.

Münchmeyer, A. F. O. *Das Amt des Neuen Testaments nach Lehre der Schrift und der lutherisdien Bekenntnisse.* Osterode, 1853.

Münter, Wilhelm O. *Begriff und Wirklichkeit des geistlichen Amtes.* Munich: Kaiser, 1955.

———. *Die Gestalt der Kirche 'nach göttlichem Recht.'* Kirche und Amt 2. Beiträge zur Evangelischen Theologie 5. Munich: Lempp, 1941.

Nagel, W. "Besprechung der Agende für evangelisch-lutherischen Kirchen und Gemeinden." *Theologische Literaturzeitung* 78, no. 10 (1953): cols. 627ff.

Niedermeier, Gerhard. "Das allgemeine Priestertum der Gläubigen und das geistliche Amt." *Zeitschrift für systematische Theologie* 7 (1930): 337–62.

Niemeier, G. "Priester—Prediger—Präceptor." *Evangelische Theologie* 9 (1949/1950): 411–22.

Nygren, Anders. "Vom geistlichen Amt." *Zeitschrift für systematische Theologie* 12 (1935): 36–44.

Plitt, Gustav. *Einleitung in die Augustana.* Part 2: *Entstehungsgeschichte des evangelischen Lehrbegriffs bis zum Augsburgischen Bekenntnisse.* Erlangen: A. Deichert, 1868.

Preger, Wilhelm. *Die Geschichte der Lehre vom geistlichen Amt auf Grund der Geschichte der Rechtfertigungslehre.* Nördlingen: Beck, 1857.

Prenter, Regin. "Die göttliche Einsetzung des Predigtamtes und das allgemeine Priestertum bein Luther." *Theologische Literaturzeitung* 86 (1961): 321–52.

———. *Spiritus Creator: Studien zu Luthers Theologie.* Forschungen zur Geschichte und Lehre des Protestantismus 6. Munich: Kaiser, 1954.

Rade, Martin. *Das königliche Priestertum der Gläubigen und seine Forderung an die evangelische Kirche unserer Zeit.* Tübingen: J. C. B. Mohr, 1918.

Rendtorff, Franz. "Luthers 'ungefährliche' Kirchenbräuche." Pages 145–56 in *Studien zur Reformationsgeschichte und zur Praktischen Theologie, Kawerau-Festschrift.* Leipzig: Heinsius, 1917.

Rengstorf, Karl H. *Apostolat und Predigtamt.* 2nd ed. Stuttgart: Kohlhammer, 1954.

———. "Wesen und Bedeutung des geistlichen Amts nach dem Neuen Testament und in der Lehre des Luthertums." Pages 243–68 in *Weltluthertum von heute.* Stockholm: Svenska Kyrkans Diakonistyrelses Bokförlag, 1950.

Richter, Aemilius Ludwig. *Die evangelischen Kirchenordnungen des 16. Jahrhunderts.* 2 vols. Leipzig: Günther, 1871.

———. *Geschichte der evangelischen Kirchenverfassung in Deutschland.* Leipzig, 1851.

———. *Lehrbuch des katholischen und evangelischen Kirchenrechts.* 5th ed. Leipzig: Tauchnitz, 1858.

Rieker, Karl. "Die Entstehung und geschichtliche Bedeutung des Kirchenbegriffs. Pages 1–22 in *Festschrift für R. Sohm.* Munich & Leipzig, 1914.

———. *Die rechtliche Natur des evangelischen Pfarramts.* Leipzig: Hinrichs, 1891.

Rieker, Karl. *Die rechtliche Stellung der evangelischen Kirche Deutschlands.* Leipzig: Hirschfeld, 1893.

Rietschel, Georg. *Lehrbuch der Liturgik.* Vol. 2. Berlin: Reuther & Reichard, 1909.

———g. *Lehrbuch der Liturgik.* 2nd ed. 2 vols. Edited by Paul Graff. Göttingen: Vandenhoeck & Ruprecht, 1951–52.

———. *Luther und die Ordination.* 2nd ed. Wittenberg: R. Herrosé, 1889.

———. "Luthers Ordinationsformular in seiner ursprünglichen Gestalt." *Theologische Studien und Kritiken* 68 (1895): 168–80.

Ritschl, Otto. *Dogmengeschichte des Protestantismus.* Vol. 1. Leipzig: Hinrichs, 1908.

Ritter, Gerhard. *Die Neugestaltung Europas im 16. Jahrhundert.* Berlin: Tempelhof, 1950.

Roth, Erich. *Die Privatbeichte und Schlüsselgewalt in der Theologie der Reformatoren.* Gütersloh: Bertelsmann, 1952.

———. *Sakrament nach Luther.* Berlin: Töpelmann, 1952.

Schian, Martin. "Das 'allgemeine Priestertum' und die kirchliche Praxis." Pages 113–28 in *Studien zur Reformationsgeschichte und zur Praktischen Theologie, Festschrift für Gustav Kawerau.* Leipzig: Heinsius, 1917.

Schirmacher, Horst. "Schlüssel zu Luthers Kirchenglauben und -lehre." Pages 42–69 in *Credo ecclesiam, festgabe für W. Zoellner.* Gütersloh: Bertelsmann, 1930.

Schlink, Edmund. *Theologie der lutherischen Bekenntnisschriften.* 2nd ed. Munich: Kaiser, 1946.

Schlunk, Barbara. *Amt und Gemeinde im theologischen Denken Vilmars.* Beiträge zur Evangelischen Theologie 9. Munich: Kaiser, 1947.

Schmidt, K. D. "Luthers Lehre vom Heiligen Geist." Pages 145–64 in *Schrift und Bekenntnis, Festschrift für J. S. Schöffel.* Edited by Volkmar Herntrich and Theodore Knolle. Hamburg: Furche-Verlag, 1950.

Schöffel, Simon. "Das Predigt- und Hirtenamt." Pages 200–215 in *Credo ecclesiam, festgabe für W. Zoellner.* Gütersloh: Bertelsmann, 1930.

Schreiner, Helmuth. *Vom Recht der Kirche.* Gütersloh: Bertelsmann, 1947.

Schumann, Friedrich Karl. "Amt der Kirche und Berufung zum Amt." Pages 310ff. in *Wort und Gestalt (Gesammelte Aufsätze).* Witten-Ruhr Luther-Verlag, 1956.

Schwindel, K. "Das geistliche Amt." *Luthertum* (1934): 206–20.

Seeberg, Erich. *Luthers Theologie.* Vol. 1: *Die Gottesanschauung.* Göttingen: Vandenhoeck & Ruprecht, 1929. Vol. 2: *Christus: Wirklichkeit und Urbild.* Stuttgart: Kohlhammer, 1937.

———. *Luthers Theologie in ihren Grundzügen.* 2nd ed. Stuttgart: Kohlhammer, 1950.

———. *Studien zu Luthers Genesisvorlesung.* Gütersloh: Evangelischer Verlag, 1932.

Seeberg, Reinhold. *Lehrbuch der Dogmengeschichte*. Vol. 4.1: *Die Lehre Luthers*. 2nd and 3rd ed. Leipzig: Deichert, 1917.

Sehling, Emil. *Die evangelischen Kirchenordnungen des 16. Jahrhunderts*. Vol. 1 (Leipzig, 1902), Vol. 2 (1904), Vol. 3 (1909), Vol. 4 (1911), Vol. 5 (1913). Vol. 6 completed by the Evangelische Kirche in Deutschland's Institut für evangelisches Kirchenrecht in Göttingen.Tübingen: Mohr, 1955.

Sohm, Rudolph. *Kirchenrecht*. 2 vols. Munich & Leipzig: Duncker & Humblot, 1892, 1923.

———. *Weltliches und geistliches Recht*. Munich: Duncker & Humblot, 1914.

Söhngen, Oskar. *Kirchenregiment, Bischofsamt und Predigtamt*. Kirche in dieser Zeit 8. Berlin: Evangelische Verlagsanstalt, 1948.

Sommerlath, Ernst. "Amt und allgemeines Priestertum." *Schriften des Theologischen Konvents Augsburgischen Bekenntnisses* 5 (1953): 40–89.

———. "Das Amt und die Ämter." Pages 292–307 in *Viva vox Evangelii, Eine Festschrift für Landesbischof D. Hans Meiser zum siebzigsten Geburtstag*. Munich: Claudius, 1951.

——— (also M. Doerne and A. D. Müller). "Das Wesen des Amtes nach lutherischer Auffassung." Pages 151–63 in *Die Kirche Jesu Christi und das Wort Gottes*. Edited by W. Zoellner and W. Stählin. Berlin: Furche, 1937.

Stahl, Friedrich J. *Die Kirchenverfassung nach Lehre und Recht der Protestanten*. 2nd ed. Erlangen, 1862.

Storck, Hans. *Das allgemeine Priestertum bei Luther*. Theologische Existenz heute n.s. 37. Munich: Kaiser, 1953.

Stupperich, R., gen. ed. *Melanchthons Werke in Auswahl*. 7 vols. Gütersloh: Bertelsmann (Gerd Mohn), 1951–.

Thieme, Karl. *Die Augsburgische Konfession und Luthers Katechismen auf theologische Gegenwartswerte untersucht*. Gießen: Töpelmann, 1930.

Thimme, H. "Welche Folgerungen ergeben sich aus der Lehre der Kirche für ihre Ordnung." Pages 28–53 in *Schriften des Theologischen Konvents Augsburgischen Bekenntnisses* 8. Berlin: Lutherisches Verlagshaus, 1955.

Thomas, W. *Die Lehre Melanchthons vom geistlichen Amt*. Dissertation, Leipzig, 1901.

Törnvall, Gustaf. *Geistliches und weltliches Regiment bei Luther*. Munich: C. Kaiser, 1947.

Trillhaas, W. "Die lutherische Lehre 'De potestate ecclesiastica.'" *Zwischen den Zeiten* 11 (1933): 497–513.

Troeltsch, Ernst. *Gesammelte Schriften*. Vol. 1: *Die Soziallehren der christlichen Kirchen und Gruppen*. 3rd ed. Tübingen: Mohr, 1923.

Tuchel, Klaus. "Luthers Auffassung vom geistlichen Amt." *Lutherjahrbuch* 25 (1958): 61–98.

Vajta, Vilmos. *Die Theologie des Gottesdienstes bei Luther*. 2nd ed. Göttingen: Vandenhoeck & Ruprecht, 1954.

Vilmar, A. F. C. *Die Augsburgische Confession*. Edited by Dr. K. W. Piderit. Gütersloh: Bertelsmann, 1870.

———. *Dogmatik*. Vol. 2. Edited by K. W. Piderit. Unaltered reprint of the 1st ed. Gütersloh: Bertelsmann, 1937.

———. *Die Lehre vom geistlichen Amt*. Marburg & Leipzig: Elwert, 1870.

Vogelsang, Erich. *Der angefochtene Christus bei Luther*. Berlin: de Gruyter, 1932.

Walch, J. G., ed. *D. Martin Luthers . . . sämmtliche Schriften*. Vol. 19. Halle: Gebauer, 1746.

Walter, Johann von. *Luther und Melanchthon während des Augsburger Reichstages*. Gütersloh: Bertelsmann, 1931.

———. *Die Theologie Luthers*. Gütersloh: Bertelsmann, 1940.

Walther, Wilhelm. *Das Erbe der Reformation*. Vol. 4: *Luthers Kirche*. Leipzig: A. Deichert, 1917.

———. *Luthers Beruf*. Luther im neuesten römischen Gericht 3. Schriften des Reformationsvereins 8.31. Halle, 1890.

Wehrung, G. "Zu Augustana VIII." *Zeitschrift für systematische Theologie* 14 (1937): 3–39.

Wendland, H. D. "Die Kirche nach göttlicher Stiftung." *Theologie militans* 23. Leipzig: Deichert, 1938.

Werner, Gottfried. *Tröstet euch der Ordination*. Bekennende lutherische Kirche 13. Neuendettelsau: Freimund-Verlag, 1954.

Wingren, Gustaf. *Luthers Lehre vom Beruf*. Munich: Kaiser, 1952.

———. *Die Predigt*. Göttingen: Vandenhoeck & Ruprecht, 1955.

Winter, Karl. "Die Lehre von der Kirche in den evangelisch-luthischen Bekenntnisschriften." Pages 3–23 in *Credo ecclesiam, festgabe für W. Zoellner*. Gütersloh: Bertelsmann, 1930.

Wolf, Ernst. "Das kirchliche Amt im Gericht der theologischen Existenz." *Evangelische Theologie* 11 (1951/1952): 517–32.

———. *Peregrinatio: Studien zur reformatorischen Theologie und zum Kirchenproblem*. Vol. 1. Munich: Kaiser, 1954, in which especially "Politia Christi," pages 214–42; "Zur Verwaltung der Sakramente nach Luther und lutherischer Lehre," pages 243–52.

———. "Zur Neuordnung der Ordination." *Evangelische Theologie* 4 (1937): 377f.

Zezschwitz, C. A. G. v. *System der Praktischen Theologie*. 3 vols. Leipzig, 1876, 1878.

Zoellner, Wilhelm. *Das allgemeine Priestertum der Gläubigen und die Bedeutung des Gnadenmittelamtes*. Leipzig: Dörffling & Franke, 1919.

———, and Wilhelm Stählin, eds. *Die Kirche Jesu Christi und das Wort Gottes*. Berlin: Furche, 1937.

Cited Works of Martin Luther

Lieberg Citation	Luther Document	English
WA 1:233–38	Ninety-Five Theses (1517)	AE 31:17–33
WA 1:525–628	Explanations of the Ninety-Five Theses (1518)	AE 31:77–252
WA 2:183–240	Explanation of the Thirteenth Thesis on the Authority of the Pope (1519)	AE 70–71
WA 2:244–49	Sermon Preached in the Castle at Leipzig on the Day of St. Peter and St. Paul (1519)	AE 51:53–60
WA 2:443–618	First Lectures on Galatians (1519)	AE 27
WA 2:658–79	To Emser the Goat (1519)	AE 70–71
WA 2:714–23	Holy Sacrament of Baptism (1519)	AE 35:3–22
WA 3	On the Psalms (1513–16)	AE 10–11
WA 4:1–462	First Lectures on the Psalms (1513–16)	AE 10–11
WA 6:285–324	On the Papacy in Rome (1520)	AE 39:49–104
WA 6:353–78	A Treatise on the New Testament, That Is the Holy Mass (1520)	AE 35:75–111
WA 6:404–69	To the Christian Nobility of the German Nation (1520)	AE 44:115–217
WA 6:497–573	The Babylonian Captivity of the Church (1520)	AE 36:3–126
WA 7:20–38	Freedom of a Christian (German) (1520)	AE 31:327–77
WA 7:42–73	Freedom of a Christian (Latin) (1520)	
WA 7:161–82	Why the Books of the Pope and His Disciples Were Burned (1520)	AE 31:379–95
WA 7:621–88	Answer to Emser (1521)	AE 39:137–224
WA 7:705–78	Response to the Book of Ambrosius Catharinus Defending Sylvester Prierias (1521)	AE 70–71
WA 8:4–35	Psalm 68 (1521)	AE 13:1–37
WA 8:138–204	On Confession (1521)	cf. AE 48:244–47
WA 8:210–40	Psalm 37 [36] (1521)	cf. AE 48:248–53
WA 8:234–40	Afterword to Luther's Exposition of Psalm 37 for the Wittenberg Congregation	AE 74

Lieberg Citation	Luther Document	English
WA 8:247–54	Retraction of the Error Forced by Emser (1521)	AE 39:225–38
WA 8:411–76	Misuse of the Mass (Latin) (1521)	
WA 8:482–563	Misuse of the Mass (German) (1521)	AE 36:127–30
WA 8:676–87	Sincere Admonition against Insurrection (1522)	AE 45:51–74
WA 10/1.2:230–40 WA 10/3:113–24	Vier schöne Sermone durch D. M. Luther zu Borna gepredigt (1522)	
WA 10/2:180–262	Against King Henry of England (1522)	AE 61
WA 10/3:170–75	Ein Sermon vom Predigtamt (John 10) (1522)	Lenker 3:372–82
WA 10/3:176–200	Sermon on Luke 16:19–31 (1522)	AE 78:55–67
WA 10/3:208–16	Ein christlicher Sermon von Gewalt S. Peters (1522)	
WA 10/3:309–12	Von dem Tauben und Stummen (1534)	
WA 10/3:394–99	Sermon on Matthew 9:2 (Pr 246)	
WA 11:94–97	Sermon for the First Sunday after Easter, John 20:19–29 (April 12, 1523)	AE 69:333–39
WA 11:98–101	Ein Sermon von dem guten Hirten (1523)	
WA 11:245–80	Temporal Authority (1523)	AE 45:75–129
WA 11:408–16	That a Christian Assembly or Congregation Has the Right and Power to Judge All Teaching and to Call (1523)	AE 39:301–14
WA 12:11–30	Ordinance of a Common Chest (1523)	AE 45:159–94
WA 12:169–96	Concerning the Ministry (1523)	AE 40:3–44
WA 12:301–41	Sermon on 1 Peter 2 (1523) (Pr 366)	AE 30
WA 12:386–99	Sermon on 1 Peter 5 (1523) (Pr 369)	AE 30
WA 12:517–24	Sermon for the First Sunday after Easter (1523)	
WA 15:391–97	Letter to the Christians at Strassburg (1524)	AE 40:61–71; 49:94–96
WA 15:622–26	Sermon on 1 John 3:13ff. (Pr 474)	
WA 15:717–21	Sermon on John 4:47ff. (1524)	
WA 15:724–34	Sermon on Matthew 18:23ff. (1524)	
WA 16:28–40	Sermon on Exod. 2:3 (1524) (Pr 503)	AE 62–63
WA 16:226–40	Sermon on Exodus 12 (1525) (Pr 519)	AE 62–63
WA 16:394–412	Sermons on Exod. 19:20 and Exod. 19:1:13 (Pr 531)	AE 62–63
WA 17/1:237–45	Sermon on Phil. 2:5–12 (1525) (Po 61)	AE 76:415–23
WA 17/1:325–31	Sermon for July 15, 1525 (Pr 614)	
WA 17/1:354–72	Eine Predigt . . . sich zu hüten vor falschen Propheten (1525)	AE 78:278–306

Lieberg Citation	Luther Document	English
WA 17/1:508–12	Sermon for May 23, 1524 (Pr 470)	
WA 17/2:178–86	Sermon for Lent 1 (Po 51)	AE 76:356–64
WA 17/2:228–43	Sermon on Psalm 26 (1525) (Pr 600)	
WA 17/2:252–63	Sermon for St. Andrew (1519) (Po 116)	cf. Baseley
WA 19:185–251	Lectures on Jonah (German) (1525)	AE 19:33–104
WA 20:348–53	Sermon on Luke 24:36ff. (1526) (Pr 665)	
WA 21:275–89	Church Postil: Sermon for the Sunday after Easter (Po 226)	AE 77:113–25
WA 22:170–87	Church Postil: Sermon for Trinity 10 (Po 271)	AE 78:329–45
WA 25:6–69	Lectures on Titus (1527)	AE 29
WA 26:4–120	Lectures on 1 Timothy (1528)	AE 28
WA 26:144–74	Concerning Rebaptism (1528)	AE 40:225–62
WA 26:195–240	Instructions for the Visitors (1528)	AE 40:263–320
WA 26:261–509	Confession concerning Christ's Supper (1528)	AE 37:151–372
WA 28:464–79	Sermon for Easter Tuesday Morning, on John 20:19–23 (1529)	AE 69:349–73
WA 30/1:125–238	Large Catechism (1529)	
WA 30/1:239–425	Small Catechism (1529)	
WA 30/2:268–356	Exhortation to All Clergy Assembled at Augsburg (1530)	AE 34:3–61
WA 30/2:420–24	Theses against the Whole Synagogue of Satan and All the Gates of Hell (Latin) (1530)	AE 72
WA 30/2:424–27	Theses against the Whole Synagogue of Satan and All the Gates of Hell (German) (1530)	AE 72
WA 30/2:435–507	The Keys (1530)	AE 40:321–77
WA 30/2:517–88	Sermon on Keeping Children in School (1530)	AE 46:207–58
WA 30/2:595–626	Admonition concerning the Sacrament (1530)	AE 38:91–137
WA 30/3:496–509	preface, glosses, and commentary on [Hermann Rab], *Specimen of Papist Theology and Doctrine* (1531)	AE 59:290–312
WA 30/3:518–27	Infiltrating and Clandestine Preachers (1532)	AE 40:379–94
WA 30/3:558–71	Letter to the Christians in Frankfurt am Main (1532)	AE 74
WA 31/1:189–218	Commentary on Psalm 82 (1530)	AE 13:39–72
WA 32:299–544	Sermon on the Mount (1530–32)	AE 21
WA 33:351–68	Sermon on John 7:16–18 (1531) (Pr 1167)	AE 23
WA 33:543–55	Sermon on John 8:16 (1531) (Pr 1179)	AE 23

Lieberg Citation	Luther Document	English
WA 34/1:318–28	Sermon for the First Sunday after Easter (1531) (Pr 1224)	AE 69:377–401
WA 34/1:391–400	Sermon on John 16:24ff. (1531) (Pr 1232)	AE 56:401–7
WA 34/1:430–39	Sermon on John 15:26 (1531) (Pr 1236)	
WA 34/2:222–87	Drei christliche, trostreiche und in Gottest Wort wohlgegründete Predigten von guten und bösen Engeln (1531)	
WA 34/2:287–98	Sermon on Luke 14:1ff. (1531) (Pr 1280)	
WA 36:8–79	Wie das Gesetz und Evangelium recht gründlich zu unterscheiden sind (1532)	cf. AE 57:61–76
WA 37:134–36	House Postil: Sermon for Trinity 12 (Pr 1418)	AE 80–82
WA 37:267–70	Sermon on Acts 9:1ff. (1534) (Pr 1452)	AE 80–82
WA 37:381–85	Zwo Predigten vom Zorn (1534, 1536)	cf. AE 77:216–23
WA 38:195–256	The Private Mass and the Consecration of Priests (1533)	AE 38:139–214
WA 38:423–33	Ordination of Ministers of the Word [*Ordinationsformular*] (1535, 1539)	AE 53:122–26
WA 38:447–667	Annotations on Matthew 1–18 (1534–35)	AE 67
WA 39/1:265–333	Circular Disputation on the Wedding Garment (1537)	AE 72
WA 39/1:345–47	First Set of Theses against the Antinomians (1537)	AE 73:50–53
WA 39/2:146–84	Disputation on the Church (1542)	AE 73:283–322
WA 40/1:33–668; 40/2:1–184	Lectures on Galatians (1531)	AE 26–27
WA 41:79–239	Commentary on Psalm 110 (1539)	AE 13:225–348
WA 41:239–42	Sermon on John 15:26ff. (1535) (Pr 1541)	
WA 41:454–59	Ordination Sermon for Johannes Golhart, Matt. 28:16–20 (1535)	AE 57:190–98
WA 41:541–46	Sermon for the First Sunday after Easter (1536) (Pr 1592)	AE 69:407–17
WA 41:762–63	Ordinationsrede (1535)	
WA 42–44	Lectures on Genesis (1535–45)	AE 1–8
WA 45:265–324	Sermon about Jesus Christ (1537)	cf. AE 57:90–138
WA 45:460–62	Sermon Sketch of Dr. Martin Luther, Written Down for a Friend (1534–36) (Pr 2067)	AE 69:418–23
WA 47:191–96	Sermon on John 3:34 (1539) (Pr 1796)	AE 22
WA 47:208–14	Sermon on John 4:1–3 (1540) (Pr 1799)	AE 22
WA 47:241–51	Sermon on Matthew 18:2ff. (Pr 1804)	AE 67

Lieberg Citation	Luther Document	English
WA 47:297–305	Sermon on Matthew 18:19f. (Pr 1810)	AE 67
WA 47:447–53	Sermon on Matthew 23:8ff. (Pr 1832)	AE 68
WA 49:111–60	Sermons at the Baptism of Bernhard von Anhalt (1540)	AE 58:31–49
WA 49:588–615	Sermon at the Dedication of the Castle Church, Torgau (1544)	AE 51:331–54
WA 49:708–15	Sermon on 1 Peter 2:21ff. (1545) (Pr 1995)	
WA 50:192–254	Smalcald Articles (1537)	
WA 50:468–77	Against the Antinomians (1539)	AE 47:99–119
WA 50:509–653	On the Councils and the Church (1539)	AE 41:3–178
WA 52:563–71	Sermon for St. Andrew's Day (Po 380)	cf. Baseley
WA 53:22–182	Supputatio annorum mundi (1541, 1545)	
WA 53:231–60	Model for the Consecration of a True Christian Bishop (1542)	AE 61
WA 54:425–43	Against the Thirty-Two Articles of the Louvain Theologians (1545)	AE 34:339–60
WA 56	Lectures on Romans (1515–16)	AE 25
WA Br (general)	Luther's correspondence	cf. AE 48–50, 74
WA Br 5:319–20	To Elector John (May 15, 1530)	AE 49:295–99
WA Br 5:435–36	To Melanchthon (July 3, 1530)	AE 49:342–47
WA Br 5:492–95	To Melanchthon (July 21, 1530)	AE 49:378–93
WA Br 6:338–42	To Councils, etc., of Brandenburg-Ansbach and Nürnberg (August 1, 1532)	AE 50:61–67
WA TR	Luther's Table Talk	cf. AE 54